Latin America:
Geographical Perspectives

Edited by HAROLD BLAKEMORE
and CLIFFORD T. SMITH

METHUEN & CO LTD
11 NEW FETTER LANE LONDON EC4

First published 1971
by Methuen & Co Ltd
11 New Fetter Lane, London EC4
© 1971 Methuen & Co Ltd
Printed in Great Britain by
Butler & Tanner Ltd
Frome and London

SBN 416 10820 2

Distributed in the U.S.A.
by Barnes & Noble Inc.

Contents

CONTENTS

Preface

Since the Second World War international attention has been focused most directly on a number of regions and a series of issues closely related to that event. The rise of the super-powers, the United States and the Soviet Union, was itself a product of victory in war, of military might and technological advance derived from a conflict which weakened or shattered other potential rivals. The emergence of Communist China was no less a direct consequence of the worldwide struggle, as was the dissolution of colonial control in Asia and Africa, and the appearance there of a host of new countries led by nationalist leaders. No less compelling in the last two decades, the remarkable resurgence from post-war prostration of western Europe and of Japan has shown the resilience of old civilizations imbued with modern dynamism. Alone among the world's major regions, at least until very recently, Latin America remained a passive rather than an active agent in an era of revolutionary upheaval. In Latin American experience this was nothing new: from the dawn of the colonial era to the very recent past the continent had been accustomed to a degree of remoteness from the mainstream of world events, and to an isolation shaped by historical circumstances, underlined by ignorance of Latin America in the outside world. Today that isolation no longer obtains, and Latin America's peripheral status in the world community diminishes day by day. The revolutions in technology and communications, which are so much a part of the modern world, and the increasing momentum of change in Latin America itself, combine to give the continent long-delayed recognition not only as a significant element in international affairs but also as a distinctive region from which the rest of mankind has much to learn.

The scene of the first large-scale, sea-borne empires of European civilization, Latin America produced in the conflict of cultures and racial fusion which characterized its origins societies which were *sui generis*, and forms of political culture and economic organization which have remained significant to the present day. In their revolutions for independence in the early years of the nineteenth century, the various parts of Spanish America and Portuguese Brazil anticipated the contemporary process of decolonization, and their subsequent search for viable constitutional frameworks, political expression and economic life provides much relevant material for the nations of Asia and Africa today. In the lessons of economic development, in the process of urbanization, which is so much a feature of the modern world, in the search for wider unities transcending national

vii

boundaries, and in countless other ways, the geographical and historical experience of Latin America repays attention, while the current re-shaping of the continent will concern the world as a whole and not only those who live there.

This collection of geographical essays is offered as a contribution to the understanding of Latin America. The authors, all university teachers in the Latin American field, have been selected for their detailed knowledge of, and experience in, the various parts of the continent, but no attempt has been made to impose a uniform treatment, so as to allow each contributor the personal freedom to emphasize in his individual study the aspects and issues which seem to him to deserve particular emphasis. Nor does this book represent any attempt at a comprehensive geography of Latin America if that, indeed, were possible. It is intended above all to present individual analyses of the various countries and regions of Latin America, and provide some guidance, for those who require it, through the complexities of the current Latin American scene.

London, June 1971   H.B. and C.T.S.

1 Introduction

The Editors

By common consent Latin America is a recognizable entity in the modern world. Unity is expressed in ways which need little elaboration: in the existence of the Latin American Free Trade Association; in the relationship of the area as a whole with the U.S.A., as expressed in the Alliance for Progress, the Organization of American States and the Inter-American Development Bank; in such formal organs of the United Nations as the Economic Commission for Latin America, and in a number of other organizations. Participation in formal organizations undoubtedly reflects a feeling of common interest and cultural identity which in turn rests on common cultural traits which are sometimes elusive and intangible, but which certainly exist: the Iberian heritage of language and the emergence of a corpus of peculiarly Latin American literature; the common historical experience of conquest and colonization from Spain and Portugal, and of successive independence movements in the nineteenth century. There are common elements in political and social structures which have been repeatedly stressed in the literature. There is a universal preoccupation with economic development, and yet at the same time a universal preoccupation with the preservation or creation of national and cultural identity in the face of economic change.

There are common economic and social problems, and in almost every chapter of this book certain themes recur with relatively little variation from one region to another. Of all major world regions, Latin America is the one in which population is growing most rapidly. In 1967 the population of Latin America was some 259,000,000 and was increasing at the rate of 2·9 per cent per year, a figure well above the world average of 1·9 per cent and far above the rates of growth experienced by western Europe during its industrial revolution in the nineteenth century or by Japan at its most rapid phase of growth. Death-rates have been falling rapidly and expectation of life is tolerably good throughout almost all of Latin America in comparison with Asia or Africa. Yet infant mortality is unacceptably high in a number of countries and medical services leave much to be desired. Birth-rates are, however, very high and are generally over 40 per 1000. There are exceptions, of course, particularly in Argentina and Uruguay, and to a lesser extent in Chile, where demographic characteristics conform more closely to those of industrialized countries, with a low death-rate and a relatively low birth-rate, resulting in rates of increase substantially lower than those for much of Latin America (see Table 1.1). It has also been suggested that fertility is lower than might be expected among the Indian-speaking populations of Peru and Bolivia. In spite of these exceptions, however, it is hard to resist the conclusion that demographic trends in many Latin American countries do not quite conform to the classic pattern whereby fertility declines with rising incomes. It has been suggested that certain conditions have hindered the spread of family limitation from upper income groups to other strata in society: a relative rigidity in the class structure with a corresponding weakness of social communication among social groups; the high value which continues to attach to relationships within the extended family; the prestige to be derived from evident proof of masculine virility; or the predominance in some areas of loose, casual unions.

The rapidity of population growth poses difficult problems throughout almost the whole of Latin America. The high proportion of young people means that the potential labour force is usually between 30 and 40 per cent of the total population, in contrast to a figure of 40 to 50 per cent in Europe and North America. An excessive burden is laid on the community as a whole in the provision of education, health and other social services. In areas of peasant farming the growth of rural population has often led to underemployment, to the fragmentation of farm holdings, to a search for alternative sources of income from temporary labour, rural industries and crafts, and above all, to migratory movements, sometimes directed to the colonization of new agricultural land, but most frequently to the cities, where populations have often swollen far beyond the capacity of manufacturing industry to employ them.

It is sometimes argued that Latin America is relatively fortunate among the 'developing' regions of the world in that it has large areas of underexploited lands and low average densities of population, and it is true that the population of Latin America is very unevenly distributed and that large areas of the interior lands remain sparsely populated. Over a half of the population of South America lives within 300 km of the coast. The reasons for this distribution are complex and are by no means wholly to be associated with the progress of colonization from a coastal entry by European peoples and a continuing dependence on external trade. In western South America the more advanced Indian cultures, carrying a high density of population, were mainly in the Andean region and thus were frequently within this broad zone near the coast. Yet the main urban foci of Spanish settlement were usually within reach of the coast, though often not directly on it (e.g. Lima, Caracas, Santiago). The interior lands may be sparsely populated, but they are not virgin territory. The backlands of Brazil have been worked over for their minerals and for cattle-ranching, and the forests of Amazonia have been ransacked for their rubber or their cinchona and worked for their valuable hardwoods. But both national governments and the population at large have from time to time been fascinated by the promise of new lands to exploit or to settle, or they have felt the need to integrate their unpopulated and possibly vulnerable frontier regions more firmly into the national economy by the building of communications, by agricultural colonization and by the exploitation of natural resources.

In the nineteenth century there was almost unbounded optimism about the possibilities of these unpopulated regions, thought to need only railways or steamboat navigation to open up for them a glowing future by European settlement. Only in the temperate south and the coffee regions of Brazil was this promise fulfilled. By the late 1920s, however, optimism had come to an end, eroded by the tale of failures in tropical areas, realization of the fragility of tropical soils, and the difficulties of world trade. It is only since the Second World War that pressures of population, the growth of nationalism and the conquest of malaria have rekindled optimistic attitudes. There has been heavy investment in the building of roads; air transport and modest airstrips have put remote settlements within reach, and colonization has been slowly moving forward along the eastern slopes of the Andes from Venezuela to Bolivia, into the remoter, subtropical regions of Argentina, into the Paraguayan Chaco and the interior backlands of Brazil. Brasília is so far the most costly stake which has yet been placed on the future of the empty interior.

The empty lands seem to offer the promise of relief from the overcrowding of rural population on long-cultivated lands, but this has rarely been realized. Organized colonization schemes have often been expensive, sometimes ill-run and occasionally have failed. And even when relatively successful, success is to be gauged by the contribution they make to agricultural output or by the demonstration effect of foreign colonies of skilled farmers on an existing, traditional framework. Colonization schemes have rarely, if ever, successfully relieved a problem of overpopulation, and spontaneous settlement of new land, on the other hand, has often tended to reproduce in a new environment the poverty of the old, or to exchange old problems for new ones.

Indeed, the concentration of population in areas already densely settled, particularly in the neighbourhood of large urban centres, is going on more rapidly than the spread of population into the empty areas. Between 1935 and 1960 those areas with the lowest density of population in Latin America increased their total population by 50 per cent; but those areas with the highest density increased by 80 per cent. The distribution of population is becoming more uneven, not less so. The exuberant growth of the cities is mainly responsible, of course, but in the rural sphere the intensification of agriculture for urban markets or for export has often yielded a greater return on capital invested and a greater return in the form of wages and profits than the colonization of new land, except in areas where new roads have brought access to profitable and growing markets, as in the north-western margins of the Andes in Venezuela or in coastal Ecuador.

The efficient use of land is one of the professed aims, though not often the most important, of the movements for agrarian reform which have spread so rapidly in Latin America during the last decade. It is widely held that existing agrarian structures are unsatisfactory, not only in terms of their social and political consequences, but also because of the obstacles they place in the way of raising agricultural productivity. It is a characteristic feature of many Latin American countries that much land is concentrated in the hands of a very small number of owners and that a very large number of smallholders own or occupy a small percentage of agriculturally useful land. There are few areas with a large proportion of substantial middle-class farmers with enough land, skill and capital to undertake innovations freely. An abundant literature has described the failure of large landowners to use their broad estates efficiently, the anti-social tenures by which they are often worked, the drainage of profits to the towns and the diversion of income from agriculture to other purposes. At the other end of the scale, the small farmers lack the skills and the capital as well as the land to undertake improvements or to accept innovations which involve risk. It was widely argued in the 1960s that land reform, by splitting up large holdings and by creating a substantial peasantry, would create a more equitable distribution of income and provide a market for domestically produced manufactured goods of modest price and quality, and could also lead to a situation in which agricultural productivity might be increased, if only sufficient agricultural extension services, rural credit and technical assistance could also be provided.

In its Latin American context, agrarian reform is usually a term of very wide connotation, implying not only land reform in its strict sense, but also colonization, reform of tenancies, and provision of extension services, credit and technical assistance, together with the provision of roads, irrigation facilities and the like. In short, it has been a term so broad that very many different social and political groups have felt able to give support to a general movement for 'integral' agrarian reform while aiming in fact at very different targets. In the event, relatively little has been achieved. Mexico's agrarian reform occurred over a long period after the revolution of 1910, Cuba's quickly and dramatically after the revolution of 1959, and Bolivia's equally quickly in the revolution of 1952. In these countries there has been substantial change. Elsewhere, legislation has raised hopes or fears, but achievements to date have been relatively small, except perhaps in Venezuela and Chile and now in Peru.

The growth of cities has been one of the most outstanding features of Latin American experience in this generation. In 1930 the twenty-two largest towns in Latin America had a total population of some 10,000,000; in 1967 they contained 40,000,000 people. The percentage of total population in places over 2000 has risen from 39 per cent in 1950 to 46 per cent in 1960. The average rate of growth of the urban population is approximately 4·5 per cent per year. The process of urbanization has been widespread, but the most dramatic increases have been in the capital cities, where rates of growth since 1945 have been over twice the national average in Brazil, Colombia, Peru, Venezuela and Mexico. The cities of many Latin American countries display a markedly primate distribution (the population of the largest city being larger than the sum of the populations of the second and third largest towns, plus one sixth of the population of the fourth largest, following Jefferson's index of primacy). Montevideo, Buenos Aires, Mexico City, Santiago de Chile, Caracas and Lima are the most obvious examples of such primate cities, but the tendency is also apparent in smaller countries. Brazil, Ecuador and Colombia are the major exceptions. The larger cities have everywhere increased their leadership since 1880 and particularly since the 1920s, and it is clear that rapid growth has almost everywhere preceded industrialization on any significant scale.

In some countries, at least, medium-sized cities have also sustained high rates of growth in recent years, notably in Mexico, Argentina, Brazil, Venezuela, Colombia and Peru, a trend which is associated as much with the emergence of new regional capitals as with the growth of industry.

It is, however, the rapid growth of the larger cities which has attracted most attention by the very scale of the problems which growth has created. The flow of migrants into the cities is universal, and their role in relation to urban growth is much debated. Yet it should not be forgotten that natural increase within the cities themselves often contributes a substantial part, and in some cities (e.g. in Mexico, Venezuela and Chile) the greater part, of total growth. The provision of electricity, water supply, sewage, roads and housing has called forth heavy investment and plans which must constantly be revised in the light of new growth. Shanty towns or marginal settlements have grown up in or near most large cities. Again, their significance is debated and, although generalization is hazardous, it seems wrong to dismiss them universally as hopeless slums or semi-rural enclaves in an urban environment. They certainly cannot be identified at all clearly with new immigrants, squatting on the fringes of the city.

Urban growth has usually outpaced the capacity of manufacturing industry to provide employment and in some cases the percentage of urban population employed in industry is declining fairly rapidly. Underemployment and unemployment are often high. In the terms of official statistical returns, a growing proportion of urban populations is classed under the heading of 'services', an umbrella category that includes many of the precarious and marginal trades commonly to be encountered in the streets of any Latin American city.

But in the larger sense, with all its problems the urban explosion is a dominant fact of Latin America. Opinions differ as to its significance and its potential consequences. Many authors have written of over-urbanization or over-centralization in relation to Latin American cities. Epithets such as 'parasitic cities', 'suction pumps' or 'macrocephalism' recall Cobbett's more succinct and forceful description of London as the 'Great Wen'. It is undisputed that the primate cities of Latin America generally receive a more than proportionate share of national income, that they constitute the largest concentrations of demand within their national territories, that they are generally the preferred locations for industrial development, particularly for industries which have been encouraged by policies aimed at the substitution of domestic for imported manufactures. In general, wages are higher than in other parts of the country and levels of provision for health, education and social services are sometimes very much higher.

Processes are certainly at work by which income, revenue and skills are drained from the provinces to the capital or primate cities. The process of migration tends to draw from the provinces young men with levels of education and skill that are higher than the provincial average. Internal migration often involves a 'brain drain' to the capital. Absentee land-owners living in the capital, or firms with headquarters in the capital, draw from the provinces a proportion of the income earned there. Taxation and public expenditure, in very diverse ways, may lead to a diversion of income earned in the provinces to the capital city. The trends may be identified, but balanced quantitative assessments are difficult to make, and even if a drain of resources from the provinces to the primate cities can be shown to be significantly large, does this necessarily imply parasitism or over-urbanization? It may be that the concentration of investment, services and industry within the primate city represents the most economic use of resources in countries poorly endowed with real capital.

Analysts of regional growth have drawn attention to the idea of the city as a 'growth pole' that acts in various ways to stimulate productivity within surrounding regions through the demands they make for labour, foodstuffs, raw materials and manufactured products, and through the demonstration effects they generate. The 'spread' effects that are generated by a focus of growth represent a countervailing force to set against the drain of resources to the primate cities – the 'backwash' effects. The measurement of such 'spread' effects is difficult and it is certain that they do not coincide in spatial terms with the operation of 'backwash' effects. And they are likely to differ in relative strength at different stages of economic growth. Much is uncertain and both empirical and theoretical studies of Latin American situations are badly needed, but it may well be that disparities between the primate cities and the provinces, and ex-uberant urban growth, are at once inevitable concomitants of economic growth and also catalysts of major social change.

The common themes that undoubtedly exist in economic and social problems, literature and politics have called forth a growing volume of literature on Latin American affairs which has itself tended to reinforce the impression of uniformity over the whole of the Latin America field, not least in such matters as agrarian reform, urban growth and colonization. By its very existence this literature contributes to the reality of an intellectual and cultural unity. A feed-back process operates, but it is easy to exaggerate the extent to which uniformities really do exist. There is always a very real danger of generalizing from one or two parts of Latin America to the whole, just as there is sometimes a tendency to see as 'typically Latin American' situations and problems which are discernible in the developing world as a whole, as, for example, the problems of urbanization.

It is, indeed, the diversity within a larger unity that is the main theme of this book, and has suggested the type of regional division that has been adopted. It may be well to review briefly some of the major elements in this diversity. First of all, environmental contrasts are at least as great as in any other major world division (Dorst, 1967, pp. 6–10). Structure and relief are relatively simple at the small scale of the atlas map, though frequently highly complex in detail, but there are, broadly, three major types of terrain in Latin America. Western South America, Mexico and Central America are dominated by the Andean chain and its northern continuations, a region of complex folded and faulted ranges and massifs largely the product of a Cretaceous orogeny and then of later, successive phases of uplift. It is still a region liable to occasional disastrous earthquakes such as that which shook Peru in June 1970, and it is also a zone of volcanic activity. The landscapes of the Andes are infinitely variable, ranging from high glaciated massifs and almost perfect volcanic cones through high-level rolling plains at 3000 to 4000 m above sea-level to deeply cut river gorges, structurally guided troughs and the intricately dissected ranges of hot, humid regions or the stark chaos of arid foothills.

The second major type of region consists of the ancient massifs of the Guiana and Brazilian highlands, the residual massifs of the Pampas and Patagonia. Ancient rocks of the crystalline basement complex are exposed over large areas and are elsewhere overlain by sedimentary or volcanic rocks which are often the major relief-forming features, as for example in southern Brazil. And finally, between the Andes and the eastern massifs are the great lowland basins, filled by debris largely derived from the weathering and erosion of the Andes, and thus reflecting in their general character the nature of the dominant erosional process according to latitude and climate: the thick alluvial spreads of the Orinoco, Amazon and Paraná-Paraguay systems; the loess-covered plains of the Pampas; and the glacial moraines and boulder clays of Patagonia.

The latitudinal extent of Latin America, from 56°S. at Cape Horn to almost 33°N. in Mexico, is greater than that of any other major world division, including mainland Asia. Climatic regimes are correspondingly diverse. Analogues can be found in Latin America for areas as different, for example, as the Congo basin, the Namib desert, the Tibetan plateau, the so-called 'Mediterranean' regions of California or south-west Australia, the Middle West of the U.S.A. or the Norwegian coast, and a few climates can be added for which counterparts cannot be easily found, such as the Patagonian desert or the problem climate of north-east Brazil. In the Andes the effects of altitude, relief and aspect produce a complex variety of local climates and contrasting vegetation patterns: the high altitude tundra vegetation of the *puna* in Bolivia and Peru and its humid equivalent further north in the *páramos* of Colombia and Ecuador; the temperate climates of intermediate altitudes; and the highly varied ecologies of inter-Andean basins at low altitudes, where hot, humid forests often alternate over relatively short distances with hot, dry regions of xerophytic vegetation where rainfall is low and unreliable.

In terms of significance for economic development, however, the diversity of climates, terrain and vegetation or soils over the broad continental canvas is less important than the range of variation within each component state, and it is in this respect that most Latin American countries can display a remarkable complementarity of potential resources within their boundaries. Almost all of the Latin American countries contain environments ranging from arid to humid or from temperate to tropical, some by reason of their latitudinal extent, such as Brazil or Chile, some by reason of altitudinal range, such as Venezuela, Colombia, Ecuador, Peru and Bolivia, and some by reason of both, such as Mexico and Argentina. There are some states to which this generalization does not apply, of course, notably the smallest states such as Paraguay, Uruguay and the Central American countries, but most countries have the capacity to produce a vast range of raw materials and foodstuffs.

There is a similar, though less systematic variety in the mineral wealth and power resources of Latin America. Highly mineralized regions of the Andes, of Mexico and of the ancient massifs of Brazil are less valued now for gold and silver than they were in colonial times, but deposits of ferrous and non-ferrous metal ores, more widely distributed, have generated investment and have created sources of external revenue, increasingly so as lower costs of transport and higher prices have brought new resources such as iron ores and low grade disseminated copper ores within the range of economic exploitation. Venezuela is the giant oil producer of Latin America, but Mexico, Argentina, Colombia, Brazil, Peru, Bolivia and Chile (in that order of production in 1967) all produce significant quantities, and most countries are well endowed with potential sources of hydro-electricity.

The potential complementarity of resources has implications in two major ways: on the one hand for the development of the external sector, and on the other hand for the integration of national economies. It has been suggested (Higgins, 1968, p. 223) that in the assessment of resource endowment for economic development, complementarity is an important element in the growth of the external sector, as well as in internal growth, provided that resources can be brought into play successively as a response to changing marketing structures or technological change, making possible the broadening of an export base and shifts of activity from one region to another as the succession proceeds. Many such shifts can be identified in Latin America: from agricultural development and grain production in central Chile to the mining of nitrates and then copper in the north; from the exploitation of guano in Peru to coastal plantations producing cotton and sugar and to wool and minerals in the Andean sierra; from minerals to coffee in Colombia; from cacao and other tropical products to oil in Venezuela, and thence, possibly, to iron and steel and an industrial base in the east; and in Brazil the shift from sugar in the north-east in the seventeenth century to gold and diamonds in Minas Gerais in the eighteenth century and to coffee in Rio and São Paulo in the nineteenth century. Yet such complementarities, even when fully exploited, have rarely led to progressive regional development and overall growth, sometimes because of the lack of linkages between export production and the rest of the economy, and sometimes because prosperity has been too widely separated in time and place (as, for example, in Brazil), so that impetus has been lost and linkages even further weakened.

The failure, in general, of Latin American countries to achieve high and continuing levels of growth can hardly be attributed, however, to the poverty of resources or to a lack of variety. And it still remains to be seen whether potential complementarity of resource can be fully exploited in the current drive towards industrialization and agrarian change. Argentina, Brazil and Mexico, and to a lesser extent Colombia and Venezuela, have gone some way to realize their potentialities, but almost everywhere progress is hindered by the prevalence of traditional agriculture weakly integrated into the national economy.

The obverse of this potential complementarity of resources is, however, the difficulty and cost of transport facilities to overcome the barriers of distance and relief. Except in a few favoured areas of suitable terrain which enjoyed a booming prosperity in the late nineteenth century (notably the Argentine Pampas and south-eastern Brazil), the railway age failed to integrate regional or national economies, and in general railway-building served simply as a means of connecting the production areas of minerals, raw materials and foodstuffs with the points of export. Heavy investment in road-building, particularly since the Second World War, has laid the foundations for national integration in many areas, opening up new zones for settlement and exploitation, and sometimes linking old-established urban centres into a national network for the first time in their history.

Formerly remote areas of traditional agriculture have been brought within the orbit of the national economy, stimulating social and agricultural change. Emphasis on the improvement of communications must continue, but it is well to recognize that not all the consequences of better communications have been to the good. Traditional activities in craft industries as well as farming have been exposed to the disintegrating forces induced by the competition of national and foreign production. Road-building has often helped to induce currents of out-migration as well as the colonization of new land. And it seems likely that the consequences of better communications have been to increase, rather than diminish, the concentration of wealth and population on the metropolitan regions at the expense of the vigour and vitality of provincial centres and peripheral areas.

If there is diversity in resources and in environmental conditions at both the continental level and the national level, the same is true of economic and social development. It is customary to regard Latin America as one of the 'underdeveloped' regions, or as a part of the Third World, and it is certainly true that incomes and economic development have nowhere reached the levels of North America, north-west Europe or Australasia. Yet it is grossly misleading to view Latin America as a homogeneous unit from this as from other points of view. As Berry (1960, p. 93) has said on the basis of a statistical survey of the regionalization of economic development, 'It is clearly unrealistic to think of any well-defined groups of "underdeveloped" or "developed" countries, given the evidence provided by the fundamental structure. Such allocation of groups can only come from arbitrary segmentation of a continuous array.' On Berry's technological scale, ranking ninety-five countries in terms of their level of development in transport and trade, energy production, national product and urbanization, there is no homogeneity in Latin America. Mexico, Cuba, Venezuela, Brazil, Uruguay, Argentina and Chile all fall into the second quintile of countries below North America, western Europe and Australasia, in a group which also includes Spain, Portugal, Yugoslavia, South Africa and the U.S.S.R. In the third quintile, Peru, Costa Rica and El Salvador may be equated with India, Turkey, Egypt, Rhodesia, Zambia and Tanzania. Bolivia falls into the same group as Indonesia, Persia and South Korea, and only Paraguay and Haiti among Latin American countries fall into the lowest quintile.

A grouping of Latin American countries according to their social structure and characteristics has been attempted by Jacques Lambert (1967, pp. 23–48) in which the major criteria used are income levels, literacy and employment structure. Three major categories are defined. First, a 'developed' group, in which there is a developed national type where the majority of the population has broken its close bonds with the patron, the immediate neighbourhood and the extended family in order to integrate itself into the mainstream of national society. Only Argentina and Uruguay fall into the 'developed' group. Secondly he sees an 'unevenly developed' group, consisting of Brazil, Colombia, Venezuela and Mexico, with Chile as marginal, in many ways more akin to the 'developed' group. These are characterized by a dual social and economic structure in which modernized economies have made deep inroads into traditional society. And, finally, the 'underdeveloped' group includes the Guianas, Ecuador, Peru, Bolivia and Paraguay, where most of the population is shackled by archaic economic and social structures and is but dimly aware of belonging to a national society. Jacques Lambert's classification is, however, indirect, and although awareness of belonging to a national society is included as an important criterion of social development, there seems to have been no serious research into the strength and distribution of national consciousness; some of the criteria adopted in fact are economic rather than social; and Lambert is the first to recognize the frequency of exceptional cases: Costa Rica, Panama and Cuba defy any classification; Chile, Mexico and Paraguay are regarded as exceptional within their groups and, indeed, Chile is so marginal that Lambert classes it with the 'unevenly developed' group on his map and with the 'developed' group in the text! As Berry argues for the world as a whole, so also for Latin America, a ranking order may have more to be said for it than a simple classification.

For selected countries a 'league table' of development in a variety of fields has been drawn up in Tables 1.1 and 1.2 below. A few countries have been omitted because of the lack of available and comparable statistics, leaving twenty-one countries of very different sizes and populations. In Table 1.1 the first four columns give general information of area, population, density and rate of growth of population. The remaining seventeen columns show selected indices of development, which are intended to give some impression of relative performance in general terms (levels of urbanization, gross domestic product per head), and then in agriculture, industry, communications and welfare (education, health and food supply). Where appropriate, figures have been calculated on a *per capita* basis. Ranking orders for each of the columns 5 to 20 were worked out and countries placed in order according to the sum of their ranking positions for the total of 16 indices. It is in this final ranking order that countries are shown both in Tables 1.1 and 1.2, with Uruguay, Puerto Rico and Argentina at the top of the league table and Honduras, Haiti and Bolivia at the bottom. The degree of correlation between each column and the final order was calculated by Spearman's technique of rank correlation, and the correlation coefficients are shown at the foot of each column. All of the results were significant to a level of probability considerably better than 0·01, but there are interesting variations. Among the best indicators of the overall ranking order was the *per capita* production of electrical energy – a conclusion of interest in view of Guyol's advocacy of energy consumption as an index of economic development (Guyol, 1960). Vehicles, telephones in use and newspapers in circulation correlated well and the proportion of total population in cities of 100,000 or more inhabitants proved a slightly better indicator than the value of gross domestic product per head. Gross domestic product per head gave a rank correlation of +0·906 with the overall rank and emerged no better than the seventh closest indicator.

Not unexpectedly, some indices diverged more than others. Health and welfare indices were generally below +0·8, though the ratio of physicians gave a high correlation. Among indices of industrial development it is to be noted that the percentage of non-agricultural population gave an even better correlation than electricity production, energy consumption or cement production. Adequate indices of agricultural performance are difficult to find; yields may be a misleading index, in view of environmental differences and regional specializations, and statistical information on land use and agricultural production is notoriously unreliable. The use of fertilizers and tractors depends not only on agricultural efficiency but also on the nature of soils, terrain and land use (e.g. perennial tree and shrub crops, such as coffee or bananas, make fewer demands on the use of tractors than arable farming). It is not surprising, therefore, to find a slightly weaker relationship between agricultural indices and general patterns of development. Finally, it should be stated that little attention has been paid to the weighting of indices, except that gross domestic product has been given a double weight, but, clearly, the fact that five indices have been used under the general heading of welfare, compared with only two for agriculture, does in itself constitute an important weighting element. The exclusion of welfare from the list altogether, however, would make little difference to the general order except in two interesting respects. Venezuela's rank would be raised from 4 to 2, and Paraguay's rank would be depressed from 15 to 18.

Uruguay, Argentina and Chile are among the leaders. They have high income levels but have suffered slow rates of economic growth and even stagnation in recent years. Their rates of population growth are substantially lower than almost all other Latin American countries, a result of family limitation and relatively low birth-rates rather than high mortality-rates: their average expectation of life is high, except in Chile. They are all highly urbanized, with over a half of their populations in towns of more than 20,000; and they have, correspondingly, well-developed communications and industry. Above all, they are characterized by high rates of literacy, expressed also in the high ratio of newspaper circulation, and their populations are, on the whole, well fed. They are the temperate countries in which nineteenth-century economic expansion was accompanied by European immigration, massive in Argentina, but significant, too, in Uruguay and Chile. In many respects they should surely be classed as 'developed' countries, though average figures certainly conceal great variations in income distribution. They are also the countries in which regional disparities in wealth and commercialization, though important and discussed in detail in later chapters, are not so strikingly obvious as in most other Latin American countries.

Venezuela and Mexico have in common a high rate of economic growth in recent years. Venezuela ranks high in terms of gross domestic product per head and in all of the measures of industrial performance. Mexico has a much larger manufacturing sector, of course, a fact which is obscured by the calculation of indices on a *per capita* basis. Both have very high rates of population growth, and both have substantially higher rates of illiteracy than the three leading countries. Although they are booming in economic terms and are both becoming rapidly more urbanized, they still retain a large and 'backward' sector of impoverished and traditional peasantry, and this is reflected in wide regional disparities of wealth and population, especially in Venezuela. Differences of development among the Central American countries are dealt with in the appropriate chapters, but it is interesting to see the relative status of individual Middle American countries in relation to Latin America as a whole. Puerto Rico, Jamaica, Panama and Costa Rica are fairly clearly in the top half of the league with respect to most criteria; the remainder follow the compact South American bloc of Colombia, Brazil and Peru, which constitutes the median group for the whole continent.

It is, indeed, a heterogeneous group. Colombia takes an intermediate position in most respects, though it has had only a modest rate of growth in income per head since 1950. Incomes are certainly higher in the central zone of Colombia, but problems of regional diversity are perhaps less pressing than in many other Latin American countries. There is a strong regionalist tradition and Bogotá has never achieved overwhelming dominance as a primate city. Regional urban centres such as Medellín, Cali, Barranquilla and Bucaramanga have a prosperity and vitality of their own and are well distributed to serve as growth poles for the regions in which they lie. Since 1945 the improvement of communications, especially by road and by air, has gone far to break down the isolation in which provincial cities and regional identities initially developed. Peru and Brazil have in common the co-existence of relatively advanced and modernized regions on the one hand and large backward and impoverished sectors on the other. Differences of income and development between Peru's coastal region and the sierra are considerable, and the problem is compounded by the predominance in the sierra of an Indian population. In Brazil, the north-east is the region *par excellence* of difficulty and low incomes, combined with instability due to occasional disastrous droughts. South and south-eastern Brazil on the other hand, with an average income per head many times that of the north-east, have a well-developed and flourishing industrial sector, and in many ways would be comparable with the highly

TABLE I.I *Some indicators of levels of development*

Country	General						Agriculture			Industry			Communications				Welfare			
	1*	2	3	4	5	6	7	8	9	10	11	12	13	14	15	16	17	18	19	20
Uruguay	187,926	2,852	15	1.2	40.6	749	59.3	104.0	83	683	788	177.4	71.9	71.9	314	68.6	880	3140	111.7	—
Puerto Rico	8,897	2,754	306	1.5	31.5	1,304	7.7	—	75	2240	2719	553.7	163.8	90.2	102	69.5	1040	2460	63.3	10.1
Argentina	2,776,656	23,983	9	1.5	54.4	600	33.3	14.2	82	747	1411	175.7	75.2	66.7	128	66.6	620	3130	87.6	12.7
Venezuela	912,050	10,035	11	3.5	31.7	977	5.2	20.7	71	1078	2543	242.9	67.7	34.4	62	66.4	1180	2490	65.9	7.0
Chile	756,945	9,566	12	2.4	32.7	518	9.1	45.2	74	723	1151	130.8	26.6	32.6	118	57.1	2320	2720	77.8	7.8
Panama	75,650	1,417	18	3.3	25.3	585	0.6	24.1	57	411	1303	105.9	37.5	41.4	81	59.4	2060	2420	62.3	8.0
Jamaica	10,962	1,959	175	2.4	19.2	466	6.2	35.6	56	545	1010	208.3	39.2	31.1	71	64.6	1490	2430	54.7	3.9
Mexico	1,972,546	48,933	24	3.5	19.8	553	2.3	22.8	48	465	1064	125.2	30.0	24.0	116	59.0	1820	2600	66.8	5.0
Costa Rica	50,700	1,695	33	3.4	20.6	422	6.0	53.7	52	491	346	75.5	30.4	29.6	60	63.4	1860	2610	57.9	8.5
Colombia	1,138,914	20,463	17	3.2	34.2	422	2.6	17.5	53	327	576	115.7	12.9	39.9	53	45.1	2220	2280	53.3	5.5
Brazil	8,511,965	90,840	10	3.0	27.3	291	1.6	13.4	52	420	450	80.2	27.4	17.2	36	42.4	2090	2700	66.5	6.4
Peru	1,285,216	13,172	10	3.1	19.3	268	1.8	13.5	53	370	633	76.4	23.3	12.6	47	54.1	1990	2300	55.4	8.5
Nicaragua	130,000	1,915	14	3.7	13.7	359	1.7	32.6	41	206	349	52.7	12.0	12.3	49	49.0	2570	2350	59.0	4.7
Paraguay	406,752	2,303	5	3.1	13.2	215	1.2	2.4	49	78	141	10.4	5.9	8.3	—	58.0	1660	2520	63.3	8.0
Ecuador	283,561	5,890	20	3.4	17.9	214	0.8	22.7	48	144	261	73.7	9.6	14.9	44	52.3	3030	2020	50.3	6.4
El Salvador	21,393	3,390	153	3.7	13.9	261	0.6	31.1	41	172	200	45.7	13.9	10.9	51	58.4	4340	2000	43.6	5.2
Dominican Rep.	48,734	4,174	83	3.6	12.1	261	0.0	10.9	43	168	205	78.6	9.9	8.6	26	57.8	1940	2000	44.2	3.8
Guatemala	108,889	5,014	45	3.1	11.5	297	0.0	14.5	36	107	240	39.9	10.5	7.2	38	49.1	4140	2220	56.8	2.8
Honduras	112,088	2,495	22	3.4	7.7	248	0.3	15.7	35	93	217	51.7	9.4	4.5	17	49.0	4750	2010	51.0	5.3
Bolivia	1,098,581	4,804	4	2.6	9.9	158	0.4	1.2	35	140	207	14.8	8.2	6.7	23	49.7	3750	2060	51.8	—
Haiti	27,750	4,768	168	2.0	5.0	86	0.1	0.8	20	24	32	7.3	1.5	0.9	5	32.6	13150	—	46.3	1.8

* See page 16 for identity of columns.

TABLE 1.2   Selected indicators of development: ranking orders

	General		Agric.			Industry			Communications				Welfare				Total
	5*	6	7	8	9	10	11	12	13	14	15	16	17	18	19	20	21
Uruguay	2	3	1	1	1	5	8	4	2	2	1	2	2	1	1	(1)	1
Puerto Rico	6	1	4	(2)	3	1	1	1	1	1	5	1	3	8	7	3	2
Argentina	1	4	2	15	2	3	3	5	3	3	2	3	1	2	2	2	3
Venezuela	5	2	7	11	5	2	2	2	4	6	8	4	5	10	6	9	4
Chile	4	7	3	4	4	4	5	6	10	7	3	12	3	3	3	8	5
Panama	8	5	15	8	6	10	4	9	6	4	6	7	12	11	9	6	6
Jamaica	12	8	5	5	7	6	7	3	5	8	7	5	6	9	14	17	7
Mexico	10	6	9	9	13	8	6	7	8	10	4	8	8	6	4	15	8
Costa Rica	9	9	6	3	10	7	13	13	7	9	9	6	9	5	11	4	9
Colombia	3	9	8	12	8	12	10	8	13	5	10	19	14	14	15	12	10
Brazil	7	13	12	17	10	9	11	10	9	11	16	20	13	4	5	10	11
Peru	11	14	10	16	8	11	9	12	11	13	13	13	11	13	13	4	12
Nicaragua	15	11	11	6	16	13	12	15	14	14	12	17	15	12	9	16	13
Paraguay	17	18	13	19	12	20	20	20	20	17	(17)	10	7	7	7	6	14
Ecuador	13	19	14	10	13	16	14	14	17	12	14	14	16	17	18	10	15
El Salvador	14	15	15	7	16	14	19	17	12	15	11	9	19	19	19	14	16
Dominican Rep.	16	15	20	18	15	15	18	11	16	16	18	11	10	19	20	18	17
Guatemala	18	12	20	14	18	18	15	18	15	18	15	16	18	15	12	19	18
Honduras	20	17	18	13	19	19	16	16	18	20	20	17	20	18	17	13	19
Bolivia	19	20	17	20	19	17	17	19	19	19	19	15	17	16	16	(20)	20
Haiti	21	21	19	21	21	21	21	21	21	21	21	21	21	21	21	21	21
r_s	+0·908	0·906	0·899	0·657	0·953	0·931	0·892	0·900	0·923	0·956	0·922	0·780	0·876	0·815	0·782	0·728	

* See page 16 for identity of columns.

NOTES

Column headings are as for the previous Table. Column 21 gives the average ranking position for each country. Column 6 has been given double weight.

Entries for which no data exist are shown in parentheses; an arbitrary rank position has been given according to average rank position.

The final row gives the Spearman rank correlation coefficient (r_s) for each column compared with the average rank of all columns. All results are significant to a level of probability of 0·01 or better. Spearman's rank correlation coefficient yields a result varying from −1·0 for a perfect inverse correlation to 0·0 for no correlation at all and to +1·0 for a perfect positive correlation.

Identity of columns, Tables 1.1 and 1.2

1. Area, km² (ECLA Survey, 1967).
2. Population, 1969, '000s.
3. Density of population per km² (ECLA Survey, 1967).
4. Annual rate of growth of population, 1963–9, percentage.
5. Percentage of population in towns of 100,000 or more, 1966 (U.N. Demographic Yearbook, 1969).
6. Gross domestic product, per head, 1968, U.S. dollars.
7. Tractors in use, per 1000 agricultural population, *c.* 1965 (FAO Production Yearbook, 1969).
8. Fertilizer consumption, tons per 1000 agricultural population, *c.* 1968 (FAO Production Yearbook, 1968).
9. Percentage of economically active population in non-agricultural occupations.
10. Production of electrical power, kWh per head, 1968.
11. Consumption of energy in coal equivalent, kg per head, 1968.
12. Cement production, tons per 1000 population, 1968.
13. Vehicles in circulation, per 1000 population, 1968.
14. Telephones in use, per 1000 population, 1968.
15. Newspapers in circulation, per 1000 population, 1968.
16. Life expectancy at birth, 1960–5 where available.
17. Population per physician (latest data).
18. Food supply, calories per day, *c.* 1963–6 (FAO Production Yearbook, 1969).
19. Food supply, proteins, g per day, *c.* 1963–6 (FAO, 1969).
20. Teachers, per 1000 population.

Where other sources are not quoted, data are from U.N. Statistical Yearbook for 1969.

---

developed temperate regions to the south. But the continental size of Brazil makes comparisons difficult. Ecuador, Bolivia and Paraguay, finally, are fairly uniformly at the bottom of the South American league table, and the very fact of their poverty may, perhaps, lead one to suspect the quality of some of the statistics reported. Except for the contrast between metropolitan areas and the rest of the country, problems of regional disparities of income are less striking in this group than in other South American countries.

Problems of regional development must inevitably lie near the core of a geographical study of Latin America, and receive detailed treatment in many of the chapters which follow. Friedmann (1966) and others have drawn attention to the idea that problems of regional disparities in wealth, and the urgency of development policies, vary according to the overall pattern of development. At a 'pre-industrial' stage, defined as one in which the share of industry in gross national product is less than 10 per cent, development policies are said to be inappropriate. Irregularities in regional growth exist, but the major problem is to create the necessary preconditions for growth (to use a Rostowian phrase), by investment in communications, education, agriculture and construction. At the 'industrial' stage and after, when the share of industry in gross national product exceeds 25 per cent, problems of regional growth are likely to be less severe, though depressed areas may need special attention, as in France or the U.K. It is in the intermediate zone of transition towards an industrial economy, when the share of industry lies between 10 and 25 per cent, that problems of regional development are likely to be at a maximum according to Friedmann. Most of Latin America lies within this critical spectrum. According to the United Nations Yearbook for 1968, the contribution of manufacturing to gross domestic product fell between 22 per cent and 29 per cent in 1963 in the top three countries of the league table, together with Mexico, but in all other Latin American countries for which information is available the percentages fell below 20 per cent. Diversity of regional development is thus yet another of those diversities to be found in Latin America.

REFERENCES

BERRY, B. J. L. (1960) An inductive approach to the regionalization of economic development. In *Essays on Geography and Economic Development*, pp. 78–107. University of Chicago.

DORST, J. (1967) *South America and Central America: A Natural History.* London, Hamish Hamilton.

FRIEDMANN, J. (1966) *Regional Development Policy: A Case Study of Venezuela.* Cambridge, Mass., M.I.T. Press.

GUYOL, N. B. (1960) Energy consumption and economic development. In *Essays on Geography and Economic Development*, pp. 65–77. University of Chicago.

HIGGINS, B. (1968) *Economic Development.* London, Constable.

LAMBERT, J. (1967) *Latin America.* Berkeley, University of California.

2 Mexico

D. J. Fox

Mexico has a greater range of natural conditions and a richer history than any other country in Latin America. The deserts of the north-west, the rain-forests of the south, the volcanoes of the centre, the assortment of fresh foodstuffs in Mexican markets: all are marks of the natural variety of this large country. The many monuments of the Maya, the Aztec, the Zapotec and of other organized societies are a reminder of a long history of civilization; archaeologists now claim that agriculture had been practised for at least 5000 years before the arrival of the Spaniards in 1519 (Mangelsdorf, MacNeish and Willey, 1964, p. 444). The long pre-Columbian past, the colonial era, the nineteenth century and the post-Revolutionary present all contribute to the cultural and material equipment of modern Mexico. The Indian and the European have joined to produce the characteristic Mexican – the mestizo. For some Mexicans life is still cast in the same mould as it was for their ancestors before the Spanish Conquest; for others it is truly cosmopolitan.

With such variety, Mexico has her problems. Many of the phrases that are common currency elsewhere in Latin America are also heard in Mexico. The metropolitan problem, the population problem, the Indian problem, the agrarian problem, the problem of industrialization, all exist and all are discussed. Many of the Mexican attempts to solve these problems have been relatively successful and some have been novel; as a result, she has frequently been held up as an example for the rest of Latin America.

THE PEOPLE OF MEXICO

Mexicans are fond of saying that people are Mexico's most valuable resource. The more thoughtful temper their pride, recognizing the changes and stresses that arise from present population trends. Economic development must not only match the phenomenal growth in population but also satisfy the hopes for an improved standard of living held by an ever-increasing proportion of the population. In recent years for the majority of Mexicans life has improved and continues to improve. The consensus of opinion is that Mexico is making a qualified success of meeting the demands of change – more so, in fact, than are most other Latin American countries.

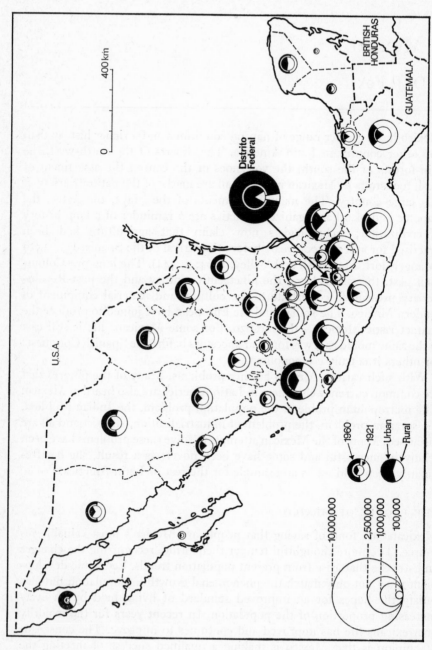

Fig. 2.1 Mexico: urban and rural population 1921–80
(a) Urban and rural population 1921 and 1960

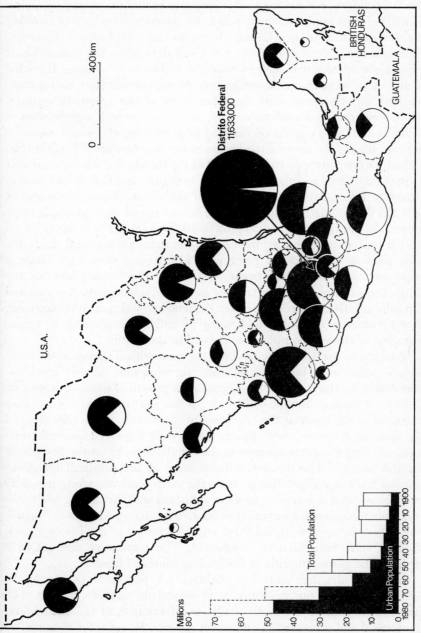

(b) Projected urban and rural population 1980

Mexico is the most populous Spanish-speaking country. It surpassed Spain in mid-1954 and it has now (1970) over 49 million people. It is, after Brazil, the most populous country in Latin America; Mexicans outnumber the combined total of their Central American and West Indian neighbours. Although one is reminded of pre-Conquest days when the population of what is now Mexico may have exceeded 20 million and was larger than that of any other comparable American area of the period, more useful comparisons can be made with the other years of the twentieth century. Mexico entered the Revolutionary decade (1910–20) with a population of about 15 million, a population that had been growing at a yearly rate of 1 per cent during the thirty settled years of the dictatorship of Porfirio Díaz (Duran Ochoa, 1957, p. 197). The toll of the Revolution was so great that in 1921 the census population was actually slightly less than it had been in 1910 (see Fig. 2.1b). With the return of settled conditions, however, not only has the population tripled but the annual rate of increase has become greater; in the 1920s the annual growth-rate was 1·6 per cent, in the 1930s 1·8 per cent, in the 1940s 2·7 per cent, in the 1950s 3·0 per cent, and in the early years of the 1960s 3·3 per cent. These figures show that Mexican population has doubled in twenty-five years. The implications for the future are, perhaps, the most striking aspect of these figures. A recent and carefully calculated forecast (Benítez Zenteno and Cabrera Acevado, 1966, p. 49) postulates a population of nearly 72 million in 1980 and, by extension, one of almost 100 million at the end of the century.

A decline in the death-rate has been the most critical change in the three factors – death-rate, birth-rate and net migration rate – that in combination determine the overall rate of population growth. The 1965 death-rate of 10 per 1000 is under one half of what it was in 1940 (23·2) and less than one third of the figure at the beginning of the century (33·6) (*Statistics on the Mexican Economy*, 1966, pp. 20–1). Greatly improved medical treatment reaching a larger proportion of the population is, of course, one reason for this change. The death-rate from some of the principal infectious diseases has fallen dramatically: from the gastro-enteritic group it is only one fifth of what it was in 1930, from influenza and pneumonia one third, from tuberculosis one quarter (Heredia Duarte, 1966). Malaria and small-pox, which in 1930 occupied third and fifth places in the list of mortal diseases, have been virtually eradicated. The respiratory diseases have replaced the gastro-enteritic as the leading causes of death.

Extremely detailed mortality statistics are published (for example, *Estadísticas*, 1965) but it is unwise to extend the analysis further. The statistics are based upon death certificate information, of variable quality, transcribed and processed in an inexact manner. In 1960, for example, 37 per cent of the death certificates in the Republic were completed without reference to a doctor, the cause of death being determined by the parish registrar on the strength of, if possible, an eye-witness description; in the

Federal District the certificate must be completed by a doctor although he may not have seen the corpse. This undoubtedly is one of the reasons why the infantile mortality from gastro-enteritis and the death-rate from unknown causes are so high. Not unnaturally, post-mortem examination often does not confirm the stated cause of death, but by that time the death certificate is sacrosanct. Although deaths are required to be recorded at the municipal offices in the place of habitual residence, a very useful provision in circumstances where the domestic environment is often the key to the cause of death, this is often not done; in one month of 1966, for example, 12 per cent of those who died in hospital in the sixth *oficialía* or borough of Mexico City had no place of residence on their death certificate, while many others, to qualify for attention, had given a friend's address within the city. Perhaps 20 per cent of the deaths in Mexico City are misallocated (resulting in the paradox that the boroughs with the most extensive hospital facilities have the highest death-rates: Fox, 1972).

The public health services have been transformed over the last thirty years but they are not uniformly available. On the medical side their main success has been in creating an infrastructure of clinics, district nurses and medical aides to reduce calls upon the hard-pressed doctors and hospitals. The capital is much better served than elsewhere and this is true of the more specialized agencies. The Institute of Social Security (IMSS), which in 1950 covered nearly 1 million people for medical and other attention, covered over 6 million in 1965 of whom 5·5 million lived in the towns (*Población*, 1966); the health service covering civil servants (ISSSTE) is the second most important public system and is very heavily weighted in favour of residents of Mexico City (*México*, 1966). Probably one half of the *metropolitanos* but only 5 per cent of the rural population are covered by these two systems.

The Mexicans are very conscious of the role of preventive medicine in reducing the death-rate. One of the most successful campaigns (CNEP) has been fought as part of a larger World Health Organization programme against malaria; repetitive spraying over the last ten years has eradicated it from all parts except the Pacific south. Here, the new cotton-growing areas of Chiapas and adjoining Guatemala have been so thoroughly dosed in chemicals that the drainage canals – the nursery for the larvae of the malarial mosquito – have become dilute solutions of TCP and the larvae have developed a degree of immunity against the insecticide. National campaigns have been mounted against other diseases, for example, smallpox, and immunization against diphtheria, tetanus and polio is becoming more widespread.

Many of the enteric diseases are caused by vectors transmitted in unclean water and food, or by inadequate sewage provision; the respiratory diseases can be linked to poor housing conditions. Some improvements have been made in the supply of public utilities and have doubtless contributed to a lower death-rate. The provision of a safe water supply has probably been the task most energetically tackled in recent years. It is spread between several government agencies and, outside Mexico City and Monterrey, is a federal responsibility. As recently as 1960 only 34 per cent of the non-metropolitan population of Mexico could count on a safe drinking supply; during the past decade, with U.S. aid, it was hoped to ensure supplies to 70 per cent of the urban population living outside Mexico City and to half the population living in villages, but the programme is running behind schedule, particularly in the rural sector. Apart from improved utilities, a more imaginative and effective propaganda programme has been waged, most effectively in the towns, to improve basic standards of hygiene. However, these remain low, even if not as low as previously, and the correlation between mortality-rates and the poorly educated, ill-housed, poorer segments of the population, and especially the infant population, indicates the potential that remains for a further fall in the death-rate.

The birth-rate, unlike the death-rate, has remained little changed since 1929 when reasonably complete registration figures first became available. In the 1930s it was about 43 per 1000 and over the decade 1955–64 was always close to 46 per 1000 (*Statistics*, 1966, pp. 20–1). Small differences are probably of no importance, bearing in mind such factors as late registration and non-registration of births, especially in rural areas; there was a disparity estimated at 913,000 between the population under the age of 5 as given to census enumerators in 1960 and as subsequently calculated from birth certificate returns (Benítez Zenteno and Cabrera Acevado, 1966, p. 26). Such a disparity plays havoc with infantile mortality statistics. Overall figures do hide one fact which may be of some significance: at the time of the census of 1960 the two administrative units with the lowest birth-rates (excluding Chiapas, Quintana Roo and Baja California Sur where under-numeration may be suspected) were the Federal District (Mexico City) and Tamaulipas (including the border towns). More important, the crude reproduction rate, a more significant measure of population change, was 3·16 per cent for the country as a whole but only 2·70 per cent in the Federal District (Benítez Zenteno and Cabrera Acevado, 1966, p. 108). If these figures do indicate a difference between urban and rural behaviour, the implications for the future are important since Mexico is, of course, becoming an increasingly urbanized country. In 1930 only 5·5 million Mexicans, one third of the total, lived in towns (defined, somewhat generously, as administrative units with a population of 2500 or more); by 1960 the figure was 16·7 million or one half (*Statistics*, 1966, p. 19); and by 1980 it is anticipated that 48 million or two-thirds of all Mexicans will live in towns (Benítez Zenteno and Cabrera Acevado, 1966, p. 185). Comment upon the enormous geographical changes implied by these figures will be deferred but it may be noted that the forecast assumes a fall in the net reproduction rate induced by a more urbanized population;

if the distinction apparent today is of no long-term consequence the urban population may be a million more than estimated.

The third factor in the equation yielding population is net migration abroad. One of the interesting contrasts between Mexico and other populous countries of the Americas is that immigration has always been insignificant; the population is almost entirely an indigenous one. This was true in colonial days and remains true today. In 1960 there were only 223,468 foreign-born residents of Mexico, 41,125 more than in 1950, and almost one half of these were born just across the borders in the U.S. or Guatemala (*VIII Censo*, 1960). One half of the remainder were Spanish.[1] Mormon and Mennonite immigrant communities flourish in parts of northern Mexico, especially Chihuahua, and descendants of Chinese indentured labour brought into the north-west in the nineteenth century are recognizable; Negroes are rare.

Immigration, such as it is, is more than balanced by emigration, with, of course, the prosperous United States as the main attraction. The 1960 U.S. census lists 575,875 Mexican-born residents, 124,385 more than in 1950. Since the demand for admission into the U.S.A. is strong, the U.S.-Mexican border is hardly an insurmountable barrier (despite a more rigorous U.S. policy towards illegal immigration since the mid-1960s), and substantial Spanish-speaking populations exist in many parts of the U.S. offering shelter to migrants; the real figures of Mexican emigration are above those given by official statistics. Whatever the exact figures are, however, the net annual emigration rate will not substantially exceed some 20,000, a negligible amount when compared with the figure of over 1 million by which the population is increasing each year through natural growth.

It is, therefore, the balance between a very high birth-rate and an ever-decreasing death-rate that has determined the characteristics of the Mexican population. As a consequence, despite an increase of twenty-five years in life expectancy since 1940, the population is an astonishingly young one. In 1960 over half of the population was under 18 years of age but only 3·43 per cent were 65 or older; by 1970 half the population was either over 65 or under 15. The burden of the provision of economic infrastructure and social services imposed on the gainfully employed sector is severe; in fact, in 1960 the ratio of employed to dependent population was about 100 : 208. By way of comparison the situation in Great Britain in 1965 was totally different with over 12 per cent of the population 65 or more but only 23 per cent under the age of 15 and a dependency ratio of only 100 : 104. On average, the Mexican worker has to support about twice the number of dependents as does his British counterpart.

[1] Including many refugees from the Civil War, warmly welcomed by the Mexican government which still continues to give official recognition to the Republican government in exile and not to that of General Franco.

B

Other stresses are placed upon Mexico by the uneven distribution of population. Central Mexico is the most populous part of the country and in this respect little has changed since Aztec or colonial days. Within central Mexico the valley of Mexico, the basin of interior drainage housing the capital city, remains not only the most heavily urbanized part of the country but also the centre of a large rural population. Today, as in 1930, 1940 and 1950, half the population of the country lives within 300 km of the capital – in an area which is only one sixth of the national total. Over half of the remaining population lives in the border states, more in the north now than in the south (reversing the 1930 situation). The lowest population densities (of under 1 person per km^2) are found in the two peninsulas remote from the seat of affairs – in Baja California and in Yucatán. The Territory of Baja California Sur has never supported anything but a sparse population, but Campeche and Quintana Roo (still a territory and not yet a state) at the foot of the Yucatán peninsula are littered with the ruins of substantial archaeological sites, witnesses to substantial populations in the Mayan past.

Eight million people now live in Mexico City; it is the most populous city between Buenos Aires and New York City (Fox, 1965b). Such a distinction is no new thing to Mexico. Indeed, until the beginning of the last century it was the largest city in the Americas. It did not share in the widespread commercial development nor in the great waves of immigration that characterized temperate America, however, and in 1930, despite a population of slightly more than a million, it only just found a place in the top ten American cities. Recent events rather than a continuation of historic circumstances account for its present outstanding position.

The rate of growth of the city has been startling and has created numerous problems for the authorities. At the turn of the century the city had a population of about half a million. It joined the ranks of the 'millionaire' cities in the late 1920s and by 1950 it exceeded 3 million. Between 1950 and 1960 it increased by 1·8 million, and the 1970 census gives the metropolitan region 8·3 million. It is now growing at the rate of about 600 people a day. Natural increase accounts for most of the current growth, but immigrants from the provinces probably number well over 1000 a week. The Revolution of 1910–17 not only disrupted the existing order of things but also made the Mexican peasantry mobile. The extension of rural bus and lorry services even into parts of the countryside extremely difficult of access, the omnipresence of radio, and the generally more prosperous economy, have made the countryman increasingly aware of the supposed opportunities that await him outside his immediate neighbourhood. Few migrants to the towns are now without friends or relations already there to cushion the shock of a move. Mexico City is not the only magnet but, on the national scale, it is the dominant one. Figure 2.2a makes it clear that the closer migrants live to the capital the more likely they are to move to it rather than elsewhere; it acts as the strongest magnet over three-quarters of the country, drawing migrants from their native state. Figure 2.2b shows that the north-western states, particularly Baja California, and the upper Gulf states in the east and north-east are locally more attractive than the capital.

Figure 2.3 shows in greater detail those *municipios* which have had heavy gains (in black) and losses (in white) from migration in recent years. The national movement to Mexico City is an exaggerated version of what is happening on a lesser scale elsewhere in the country. The provincial towns and cities are powerful draws. Naturally enough, the larger the town the more attractive it is for the migrant. But the relationship is not an exact one. For example, Monterrey, the third city of Mexico, has grown more rapidly than Guadalajara, the second city, since 1950; neither, however, has anything like the same attraction for the immigrant as the capital, over six times as populous as its nearest rival. The old mining states of the centre-north have lost large numbers of people and the zone between 150 and 300 km from Mexico City has suffered substantially. Figure 2.2b suggests that the migrants from Zacatecas disperse themselves most widely over the country.

A powerful suggestion of the overall changes in Mexico is given by contrasting urban and rural growth-rates over the last fifty years (Fig. 2.1). The urban population has been rising at an ever-increasing rate, one which is now about 5 per cent annually; the rural population has increased much more modestly and at a remarkably steady rate of 1·5 per cent per annum. Whatever the precise limitations of using census definitions, the figures show that most of the adjustment to the extraordinary growth of population over the post-Revolutionary period has been made in the towns. The country-side has been able to absorb a limited amount of change, the towns have proved more elastic. These figures emphasize not only the increasingly more urban way of life of the average Mexican, but also the declining importance of rural Mexico in the economic and political life of the country. Such a change in emphasis is common to most Latin American countries and is due, to some extent, to explicit government actions. Today, it is claimed, the interests of the countryside are being deliberately sacrificed to meet the costs of industrialization, the benefits of which largely accrue to the towns; economic advance is being won at the expense of the proletariat. The situation in Mexico is more ironic than elsewhere in Latin America, because Mexico has been governed continuously since the Revolution by a party owing its strength and its origins to the efforts of the rural masses.

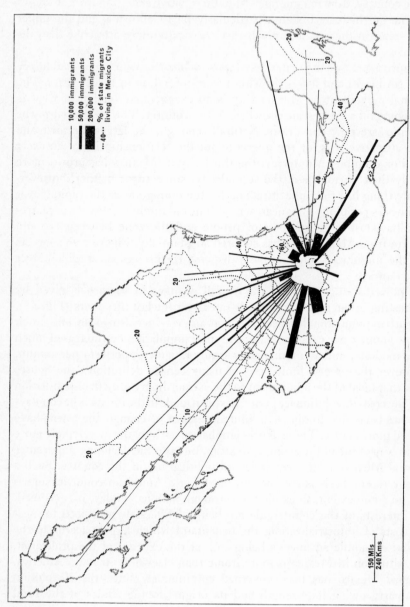

Fig. 2.2 Population migration in Mexico 1950–60
(a) Immigration to Mexico City

10,000 immigrants
50,000 immigrants
200,000 immigrants
...40... % of state migrants living in Mexico City

150 Mls
240 Kms

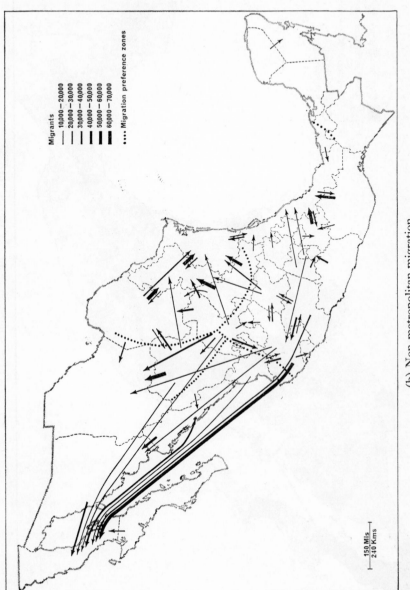

(b) Non-metropolitan migration

Migrants
10,000 – 20,000
20,000 – 30,000
30,000 – 40,000
40,000 – 50,000
50,000 – 60,000
60,000 – 70,000
•••• Migration preference zones

150 Mls
240 Kms

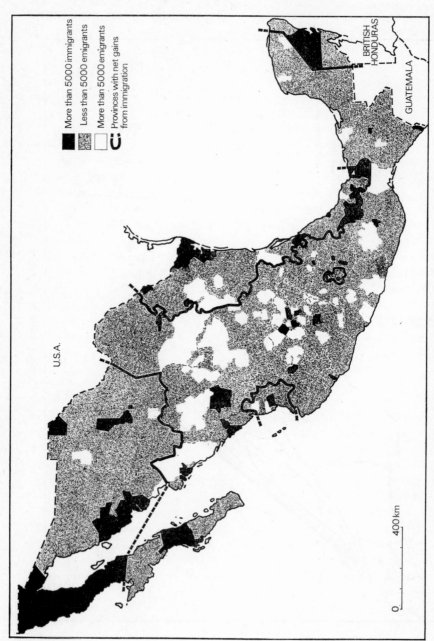

Fig. 2.3 Areas of net migration change in Mexico 1950–60

More than 5000 immigrants

Less than 5000 emigrants

More than 5000 emigrants

Provinces with net gains from immigration

U.S.A.

BRITISH HONDURAS

GUATEMALA

0   400 km

THE QUALITY OF THE LAND

Steep slopes, drought, periodic flooding and low temperatures are some of the natural features that limit the ability of the countryside to absorb more of the rising population; nature has not ideally endowed Mexico for modern agriculture.

Cortés's reputed comparison of Mexico to a crumpled handkerchief exaggerates the prevalence of steep slopes in the country, though it may well strike a responsive chord in the mind of the observant air passenger. More recently Mexican geographers and agronomists by rough-and-ready calculations hold that 26 per cent of the country lies in areas where the dominant relief is in slopes of 25 per cent steepness or more (González Santos, 1957, p. 24). Areas of steep slopes, *par excellence*, include the fretted margins of the central mesa or plateau of northern Mexico – the rugged eastern and western Sierra Madres (West, 1964b). Many of the canyons that score the Sierra Madre Occidental, such as the Barranca del Cobre, are 1500–2000 m deep and, although flattish outliers of the plateau may be preserved on their interfluves, the mass of the Sierra combines very steep slopes and a degree of inaccessibility unmatched elsewhere in the country; it has formed a refuge area for Indian groups like the Yaqui. The relief of the Sierra Madre Oriental is a little less chaotic; it is, in essence, a series of parallel, steep-sided ridges, which rise from the gentle slope of the Gulf plain to heights of 4000 m and are cut through by such spectacular canyons as that of the Moctezuma. Limestone outcrops occur widely and large areas are pitted with steep-walled karstic depressions. The Sierra Madre Oriental is crowned by the highest mountain in Mexico, the beautiful snow-capped cone of Orizaba (5750 m). This New World Fujiyama is at the point where the Sierra intersects the volcanic axis that runs across the country south of the Tropic, and along this axis lie other such splendid volcanic sights as Ixtaccíhuatl (5286 m) and Popocatépetl (5452 m) in the Valley of Mexico, and the Nevadas de Toluca (4392 m) and Colima (4265 m) to the west. They dominate an area in which the repeated pattern is one of enclosed tectonic basins, many of which were once occupied by Pleistocene lakes. Vestiges of some lakes remain to this day, separated one from another by forested uplands of medium-to-steep slope. The Balsas River valley in the south is in reality a series of such basins (for example, the Tepalcatepec) whose slopes have been reduced and whose harsher lineaments have been softened by an infill of volcanic effluent and river alluvium; steep and shallow slopes lie in juxtaposition – easier agricultural land than in the Sierra Madre.

The southern highlands are highly dissected although of moderate elevation. Characteristically, the ridges rise to about 2000 m with the river beds 600 to 800 m below; tracks follow the ridges wherever possible, avoiding the steep and broken slopes of the valleys. Areas of flattish land are sparse and that of the Valley of Oaxaca is the largest. This, like the other, smaller tectonic depressions, such as that of Tehuacán between the Sierra Madre de Oaxaca and the Mesa del Sur, has long been intensively cultivated. The highlands of Chiapas, south of the isthmus of Tehuantepec, present the same, generally unpromising aspect. The Sierra Madre de Chiapas is scoured by deep *barrancas* and rises steeply from the narrow Pacific coastal plain to heights of up to 3100 m; on the lee side the descent is more gentle and small basins, or *llanos*, include areas of shallow slope. The basin of Chiapas is a southern counterpart of the Valley of Oaxaca, and the Grijalva has endowed it more generously with alluvium than the Atoyac has that of Oaxaca. The basin ends abruptly in the north where it is overlooked by the escarpment of the Meseta de Chiapas, an undulating tableland with limestone outcrops pockmarked by small sinkholes and depressions. The foot of the adjoining Yucatán peninsula, although very much lower and nowhere exceeding 200 m, is honeycombed by similar, steep-walled sinks; most are small, but some are several kilometres in diameter and, as in Chiapas, have offered sustenance and seclusion to Indian groups seeking a haven from outside pressures. In contrast, the peninsula of Baja California, at the opposite end of the country, is mountainous and resembles the ranges north of the border. It is a series of tilted blocks with impressive escarpments overlooking the Gulf of California and more gentle westerly slopes. Only small pockets of flat alluvial land are found in the east, whereas these are more abundant in the west and include extensive marine terraces fronting the Pacific.

When we turn to areas of generally gentle slopes, three regions stand out. The largest is the great open sweep of the Mesa Central. In the north this is basin-and-range country familiar throughout the world as the setting of the classical Western film; close to the Sierra Madre Occidental, uplift and recent volcanism have placed greater emphasis on the ranges and the basins tend to be enclosed, but in the east the alluvium of the basins or *bolsones* threatens to bury the ranges entirely and over large areas slopes are barely perceptible. The alluvial fans at the mouths of the canyons where they leave the ranges have proved the most attractive agricultural sites. Further south, the general level rises, the ranges are reinforced by older and more recent volcanic outbursts, the network of river dissection becomes closer, and flat land rarer. In the zone running from the Llanos of San Juan, west of Orizaba, to the basin of Tepic in the west, the flatter basins occupy between only one quarter and one third of the total area. Nevertheless, this is some of the most important agricultural land in the country and includes the Bajío of Guanajuato, a series of linked basins on the Lerma north-west of Mexico City, and the Valley of Mexico itself, basins in which volcanic fall-out and lacustrine sediments supplement the alluvium washed in from the adjoining slopes.

The isthmus of Tehuantepec is a broken area, despite its low elevation, and moderate rather than gentle slopes are most characteristic. In this respect it resembles most parts of the narrow coastal belt that fringes the Pacific. In the north the outwash of the peripatetic rivers of the Sierra Madre has partly buried the irregularities and it is these areas of flatter land along the courses of the Lower Sonora, Yaqui, Mayo, Fuerte and Culiacán that are significant. Elsewhere the coastal plain is either non-existent or, as in the Soconusco of Chiapas, very narrow.

The flat lands bordering the Gulf of Mexico are much more extensive. They are 300 km broad south of the Río Grande and, although they pinch out in the vicinity of Vera Cruz, they widen again southwards and eastwards to form the lowlands of Tabasco and the northern part of the Yucatán peninsula. Very gentle slopes of less than one degree are typical of these lowlands, with rivers slightly entrenched below the general level, breaking the plain into a series of segments. Outliers of hill country, such as the Sierra de Tamaulipas and the Huastec country north of Vera Cruz, and volcanic intrusions occur, introducing areas of medium and steep slopes unsuitable for mechanized agriculture. The amphibious Tabascan lowlands are littered with detritus dropped in the meanderings of the Lower Grijalva and Usumacinta; fossil sand bars, terraces and flood plains produce a local relief full of minor variations. In contrast, northern Yucatán is almost perfectly flat, broken only occasionally by sink-holes, or *cenotes*, and cut by not a single river. Like Florida, its counterpart to the north, the Yucatán peninsula is essentially of limestone composition and is gradually emerging from the sea.

The importance of slope as a limiting agricultural factor depends very substantially upon the farming techniques used and the plants cultivated. The indigenous system practised widely in Mexico is much better suited to exploiting sloping land than is the modern system. In the traditional system seeds or cuttings of plants or trees are planted by hand in holes or mounds and, where desirable, slopes are reduced by various terracing methods; as a consequence of planting a variety of species the soil may retain vegetation throughout the whole year. In this manner slopes are cultivated which are too steep and inaccessible for mechanical working or even for draught animals. By careful selection of plant combinations and the use of only a hoe the soil surface is little disturbed or exposed and the dangers of soil erosion are reduced. The introduction of ploughing and domestic grazing animals in the sixteenth century and the movement towards monoculture brought this relatively conservative system under attack. In spite of a prodigious fall in population in early colonial days soil erosion was aggravated; a rising rural population thereafter has meant that today large areas of Mexico suffer from degraded soils. This is especially true of the southern part of the Mesa Central and in the highlands of Oaxaca and Chiapas. In the basin of Toluca and the Valle de Mezquital even shallow slopes are ravaged and the situation in Tlaxcala is notorious;

in no other state is such a high proportion (over 40 per cent) of land cultivated, in spite of the prevalence of steep slopes, and in no other state is agricultural productivity so low (Yates, 1962, p. 54). In Oaxaca, bald surfaces, corrugated slopes and gashed arroyos are almost as extensive as land that is vegetated and the landscape is a patchwork of green and red or buff. Although there is a strong correlation between steepness of slope and degree of soil erosion, the flat lands of northern Yucatán retain only a very thin and fragmentary soil cover, reminding us that another strong correlation exists between erosion and dense Indian populations and suggesting the way in which the traditional system has broken down.

In the drier north, where the vegetation cover is less complete and where rains falls more violently, soil erosion is more natural. Even so, it has been aggravated by the grazing and browsing of goats and cattle and the Conservation Fund has found that moderate-to-severe erosion (that is, at least 10 per cent of the land surface severely eroded) characterizes half of nontropical Mexico. H. H. Bennett estimated in 1945 that 50 per cent of the arable land of Mexico has been 'ruined for cultivation, nearly ruined, or severely affected' by soil erosion (Stevens, 1964, p. 313). No other Latin American country has suffered so much despoliation.

Another obstacle to successful commercial agriculture may be the moisture regime. Much of Mexico is too dry for field cultivation and some of it is too waterlogged. The Ministry of Water Resources has estimated that over 71 per cent of the country is arid or semi-arid and 1·45 per cent is very humid; the rest is largely classified as sub-humid. Other estimates have been made using somewhat different criteria but all emphasize the climatic deficiencies of Mexico for agriculture.

Although less extensive, the very wet areas and their agricultural problems have attracted considerable attention recently. The heaviest rainfall in the country is on the edges of the Tabascan lowlands where the Sierra de San Cristóbal and the Tuxtla highlands are drenched by mean annual rainfalls in excess of 4000 mm. The lowlands have 2000 to 3000 mm of rain a year; unlike the rest of Mexico they experience no dry season, only a less wet one in February and March. The area is largely under forest, even in places that supported the Olmec and Maya cultures of the past. Drainage control is the principal agricultural problem; vast areas are inundated after the heavy summer rains and the swollen rivers (perhaps 5 km wide when in flood) disrupt communications. The Grijalva–Usumacinta basin has been designated one of the special development areas of the country and has been called 'the last unconquered frontier in Mexico'. More capital has been invested by the Federal Government in the Comisión del Río Grijalva than in any of the other comparable agencies (Sinopsis, 1967). The building of the Netzahualcoyotl (or Malpaso) dam across the Grijalva in Chiapas is one of the tangible results; when it is completed it will be the largest in Mexico and the most ambitious in Latin America. Flood control is the principal objective and it is expected to benefit 350,000 people in the La Chontalpa and El Limón areas, as well as being capable of generating 2500 million kWh of electricity per year. Agronomic studies extending over 370,000 ha of the basin show that 81 per cent of the soils are of first-class quality. The main difficulty in extending agriculture here may be that of persuading Mexican farmers of the opportunities that await them in these uncomfortable lowlands.

The adjoining Papaloapan basin suffers similar problems, although total rainfall is less. The coincidence of the normal wettest season with the occasional September or October hurricane, however, means that the whole of the lower basin, in places 55 km wide, was periodically flooded (Poleman, 1964). A particularly severe flood in 1944 led to the creation of the Comisión del Papaloapan in 1947. Since then the Alemán dam has been built across the Tonto, the main tributary of the Papaloapan, and it is claimed that as a result the whole of the western margin of the Papaloapan as far north as Tlacotalpan enjoys protection. This achievement has been costly; the Papaloapan project has absorbed almost as much capital as has the Grijalva project and one quarter of this has been spent on flood control.

Elsewhere the rainfall map of the country (Vivó Escoto, 1964, pp. 200, 204) shows several patterns. In general, rainfall declines northwards from an average of about 2000 mm on the southern border to one of below 400 mm on the northern; it is less, latitude for latitude, in the west than it is to the east. The map also reveals the pronounced effect of the coastal ranges casting heavy rain shadows inland. The net result is an average rainfall of about 1000 mm and problems of drought are much more familiar to Mexican farmers than the problems of too much water met within the Grijalva and Papaloapan basins. The driest part of Mexico is the north-west – in the interior basins of Chihuahua and Coahuila and, more particularly, in Sonora and Baja California; the Altar and Vizcaino deserts are bone dry and are as hot as anywhere in the Americas. Even in other areas, the coincidence of the rainy season with the longer summer days means that losses through evaporation of such soil moisture as is absorbed are high. Thus about 75 per cent of the rain that falls in the Valley of Mexico, on the semi- and sub-humid boundary, is lost by evaporation and not retained in the soil for possible agricultural use. Nor is the rain that falls in dry Mexico reliable: in most parts of the north the usual year-to-year variation is over 30 per cent of the long-term average rainfall and in the drier parts of Baja California it exceeds 60 per cent. On the arid margins crops may be snatched in wet years but it is the frequency of dry years rather than average rainfall that is significant.

The moisture balance between rainfall and evaporation is partly a question of temperature and temperature is as much a question of altitude as of latitude in Mexico. Most of the tropical lowlands (the *tierra caliente*) have mean annual temperatures of over 23°C and are virtually frost-free.

A killing frost struck southern Tamaulipas in February 1963 (doing much damage to the citrus crops) but this was an extremely unusual event; Yucatán has never registered a temperature below freezing point. The *tierra fría* coincides approximately with the land over 2000 m and, if defined by the 15°C isotherm, includes the volcanic axis of the Mesa Central, the southern part of the Sierra Madre Oriental, extensive parts of the Sierra Madre Occidental and the higher ranges of Chiapas and Oaxaca. The intermediate zone (the *tierra templada*) lying roughly between 1000 and 2000 m is the most densely settled of the altitude zones, with daily temperatures ranging through about 10°C and rarely suffering frosts or very high evaporation rates.

The areas best favoured climatically, not too dry, too wet or too cold, amount to perhaps no more than a quarter of the country. They include almost all the Yucatán peninsula (except, in fact, the only part to carry a heavy agricultural population, that around Mérida), most of the Isthmus of Tehuantepec and the Gulf plains south of the Tropic, the southern part of the Mesa Central including a narrowing zone following the eastern margin of the Sierra Madre Occidental, and the narrow Pacific coastal plain south of Tepic.

AGRICULTURE

The paucity of gentle slopes and a largely unsuitable climate have severely limited agricultural opportunities in Mexico. These limitations are extremely important in a country where half the labour force still works on the land; they perhaps help to explain why agriculture produced only one sixth of the national wealth in 1969. Until recently the pattern of commercial agriculture accurately reflected these conditions, being essentially confined to the well-drained foothills of the Sierra Madre Oriental in Vera Cruz, to the Soconusco strip in Chiapas and, in particular, to the higher and cooler basins of the southern Mesa Central (West and Augelli, 1966, pp. 277–92). Recently, however, the stranglehold imposed by drought upon agriculture in the north has been broken and large capital investments and improved technological methods have permitted the development of the most extensive irrigation programme in Latin America.

The course of development of irrigation is suggested by some figures (*Inventario*, 1964, p. 71). In 1926, before the entry of government effort into this field, there were probably a little under 1 million ha under irrigation; the area irrigated by private enterprise is now approximately double this figure. Far more important, however, are the 2·7 million ha of land irrigated by schemes financed by the government, a figure which includes 1·5 million ha of virgin land never before cultivated. Different sources give different totals for the area under irrigation, varying between 3·6 and 5 million ha (Brand, 1966, p. 101; La economía Mexicana, 1966,

p. 1221); but if a figure of about 4·3 million is accepted as a reasonable compromise, this would represent 30 per cent of the total area cropped in 1965–6. It has been achieved only by the annual expenditure of 10 per cent of the federal budget on irrigation works since 1941 (*Inventario*, 1964, p. 72). Although there has been no drop in proportional expenditure in recent years, the rate of extension of irrigation has been falling, partly because, as the government committed itself to large-scale reclamation schemes, it naturally tackled the easier, cheaper areas first; the amount of land added between 1955 and 1964 was only half of that added in the preceding ten years.

The importance of the irrigated lands does not rest solely upon their size and location (Fig. 2.4). They are also highly productive: average yields are nearly three times as great from irrigated as from non-irrigated land. Bearing in mind that not all the irrigated land is cropped in any one year, it seems probable that half the agricultural production of Mexico now comes from the irrigated areas.

The largest irrigation districts are on the mainland side of the Gulf of California, on the alluvial fans at the foot of the Sierra Madre and on the delta of the depleted Colorado; here, the three driest states of the country produced, in 1967–8, half of the value of all sales from irrigated areas under the control of the Ministry of Water Resources. The single largest district is the Yaqui district in Sonora where about 300,000 ha are under irrigation. Like the nearby Fuerte and Mayo areas irrigation works predate the Revolution and the first large canal dates from the 1890s. Agriculture was delayed by the Yaqui Indian uprising but by 1937, when the government decided upon expropriation, some 66,000 ha were being farmed. Since then the building of the Angostura dam and the opening of the more important Alvaro Obregón dam ten years later, in 1952, have quadrupled the acreage.

Almost as many hectares are irrigated in the Fuerte valley, three times as many as in 1938 when the government assumed control. The Miguel Hidalgo dam (1956) has been the key factor in the Fuerte River Basin Commission's comprehensive development programme. Here, further south, water is more abundant and reliable: with only half the catchment area of the Yaqui the volume of water available is twice as large. A wider range of plants can be grown and even such water-demanding crops as tomatoes flourish. The Mayo district, between the Fuerte and the Yaqui, is only one third as large; it is mainly dependent upon waters stored by the Mocuzari dam (1955). Unfortunately, engineering mistakes have made this one of the problem areas. The Culiacán district (190,000 ha) on the other side of the Fuerte is in better shape and enjoys much the same advantages as does the Fuerte (Sinopsis, 1967; Aspectos, 1967; Dozier, 1963; Henderson, 1965).

The history of irrigation in the Colorado delta began in pre-Spanish days, but the antecedents of the present system include works of mainly

American companies begun in the nineteenth century with the help of Chinese coolie labour. In 1937, when the land was expropriated, about one quarter of the present cultivated area was under crops. Since then the introduction of an elaborate system of control dams and pumping stations, the completion of the Morelos dam (1950) and the tapping of deep well waters to supplement surface flow have increased the total area cultivated to about 180,000 ha and made the delta area the most productive of all the irrigation districts in the country.

The Río Grande basin is a second area of localized irrigation. The Conchos and other upstream tributaries have been dammed to hold back

Fig. 2.4 Major areas of irrigation in Mexico

the drainage of the eastern slopes of the Sierra Madre Occidental; downstream the Río Grande is itself dammed, as are some of the shorter rivers, like the Saltado and the San Juan, which drain the Sierra Madre Oriental. The net result is the cultivation of some 350,000 ha of otherwise barren land, three-quarters of which lies in the 200 km reach of the river valley downstream from the recent (1957) Falcón dam as far as Matamoros. A new dam, La Amistad, has been built across the middle Río Grande above Ciudad Acuña and will create a greater storage capacity than any other dam in northern Mexico. At the present time the lower Río Grande produces about as much as the Fuerte or the Yaqui districts or two-thirds as much as the Colorado delta.

The Lagunera region centred on the town of Torréon in the Mesa

Central was the first large-scale irrigation district to be organized but since the completion of the Cárdenas dam across the Nazas in 1946 there has been no extension of the area cultivated (about 100,000 ha) in spite of recourse to underground water supplies. The region is one of interior drainage and has suffered over-optimistic estimates of the water available to sustain agriculture; at the time of expropriation the area believed capable of irrigation, and distributed, was twice that now productive.

Away from the very dry lands of the north there are large areas of sub-humid land which have been made more productive by irrigation. The colonial granary of Mexico, the Bajío of Guanajuato and Jalisco, is irrigated by the waters of the Middle and Lower Lerma, the Ministry of Water Resources alone controlling about 150,000 ha. A storage dam exerting some control over Lake Yuriria was built as early as 1648 and the shore of Lake Chapala has a long history of irrigation; nevertheless, 100,000 ha of irrigated land have been added since 1926. The Solís dam (1949), serving the area above Irapauto, stores more water than the rest of the works on the Lerma put together. The Tula area, with 45,000 ha under irrigation, has a similar history; since 1900 it has received and, after the initial shock, welcomed the sewage of Mexico City as a rich supplement to the local reservoirs of water. The twenty-year-old Aviles Camacho dam supplies water to irrigate the Valsequillo area south of Puebla in the Atoyac valley. The Atoyac is a headwater of the Balsas and so falls within the jurisdiction of the Balsas Commission, another of the multi-purpose river basin development authorities. Large areas of the Balsas basin are promised water in the future but equally important is the generation of hydro-electric power and the creation of an infrastructure of economic and social services. Other irrigation districts of local importance are found in the drier northern sections of the Gulf of Mexico plain, for example, around Ciudad Mante.

Although the irrigated lands are a visible and very important sign that the problem of drought is not insurmountable, they nevertheless suffer from a number of difficulties and deficiencies. The amount of water available has an economic as well as a physical limit. The economic limit has fluctuated from time to time with changing techniques and priorities but an estimate of 8·2 million ha given in a recent study by the Ministry of Water Resources of long-term planning objectives (*Los recursos*, 1961, p. 210) is probably on the high side. The same qualification seems applicable to the published forecast of 5·9 million irrigated ha by 1975. The cost per hectare irrigated in real terms rises each year (for example, the cost of water stored by the Falcón dam is 0·82 pesos/m³ whereas the estimate for La Amistad dam is 0·95 pesos/m³) and the pace of change must be expected to fall (Sinopsis, 1967).

Forecasts have proved wrong in the past partly because unforeseen difficulties have been experienced in certain of the irrigation districts. More land has been distributed than the water resources have been able to serve: for this reason 12 per cent of the Colorado delta area has had to be withdrawn from cultivation and similar over-extension is reported from the other districts fronting the Gulf of California. In many districts an increasing reliance upon underground sources to make up surface water deficits is proving only a short-term palliative, for more water is being drawn off than is being replenished and reserves are falling. In the Costa de Hermosillo in Sonora, for example, which relies entirely upon underground supplies, the water-table is falling and the future of this district is in jeopardy. Another linked problem has been the accumulation of salts in the soil. This is a condition well known in other irrigated parts of the world and now affects about 15 per cent of the total area under Ministry direction in Mexico. Detailed field studies (de la Peña, 1964, p. 34; Amaya Brondo and Robles Espinoza, 1964; *Programa de Inversiones*, 1964, p. 18) in the late 1950s showed that over one third of the Colorado delta area was seriously affected by salt accumulation and less than one fifth was entirely free of adverse salinity effects; in the Yaqui zone, 15,000 ha on the Gulf side near the limits of the irrigation channels have become too saline to cultivate, and another 25,000 ha are affected. Only the Costa de Hermosillo is unaffected by salinity in the whole of the north-west. 80,000 ha in the Río Grande–San Juan area are affected and production in the Lagunera region has been interrupted. The cure is a threefold one: existing salinized soils are flushed with a liberal application of fresh water to remove existing salts, a satisfactory drainage system is imposed to prevent salinization recurring, and often the area irrigated must be reduced to ensure adequate natural drainage of the soil and to reduce excessive evaporation. These measures are expensive (for example, in 1964 180,000 ha in the Río Grande districts required levelling to improve their drainage) and locally unpopular.

Although Mexico can be justifiably proud of the way in which she has mastered some of the problems of exploiting land naturally too dry for cultivation, the major part of the arable farmland is cultivated without the aid of irrigation and is obliged to suffer the trials of climate and slope that make agriculture difficult in most parts of the Republic.

The distribution of farmed land in Mexico is an accurate reflection of the distribution of population: a statistical comparison by states of their proportion of the national population (excluding the Federal District) in 1960 (*VIII Censo*, 1960) with their proportion of cultivated land in 1959 (Tamayo, 1962, p. 270) gives a 90 per cent correspondence. The areas of most intensive cultivation are, therefore, the central states of Tlaxcala, Puebla and Guanajuato in which more than one third of the land is cropland; in contrast, the average proportion both for Mexico north of the Tropic and for peninsular Mexico east of the isthmus of Tehuantepec is well below one tenth. In practice, only about half the cropland is cultivated in any given year and only about one third yields crops; yet, in spite of these low figures, there are obvious signs that the soil is being overstrained in many places.

The distinction between the traditional type of subsistence farming and modern commercial agriculture is worth stressing. The traditional type is of over 4000 years standing. It relies very heavily on the cultivation of maize, beans and the squashes which, when flavoured by the ubiquitous pepper, still form the staple diet of rural Mexico. In a classic combination the three are planted in the same hole; the maize stalk grows first, later serving as the bean pole, while the large-leafed squashes blanket the ground below, the whole forming a useful and conservative system. The extent to which the traditional system prevails is suggested by the extraordinary importance of these indigenous crops in Mexico. One half of all the cropped land is still devoted to maize and a further one eighth is under beans. Cotton and wheat are the leading commercial crops and lie third and fourth in respect of acreage, but together occupy no more land than do beans alone. Other less well-known plants with a long tradition of cultivation remain important today. One is the agave, the spiky 'century plant' frequently used as a symbol of the country outside Mexico. It is a useful plant partly because it will prosper under conditions too dry for others and it has been successfully turned to commercial uses. The maguey agave yields *pulque*, a widely consumed drink of moderate alcoholic content which, unlike beer, must be drunk fresh and does not travel well; grey-green maguey plantations are a common sight in the northern and eastern reaches of the Basin of Mexico. A spirit, *mescal*, is distilled from another type of agave especially grown in Jalisco (and notably in the vicinity of Tequila). In Yucatán (Fox, 1961) the henequen agave yields a sisal-like fibre and this plant forms the back-bone of the economy of the state; probably one half of the population is dependent upon henequen and it is not surprising that competition from Tamaulipas (Fox, 1965a), from the other hard fibres and perhaps from an artificial substitute are of current concern. Another measure of the extent of traditional elements is the widespread practice of slash-and-burn shifting agriculture. About one fifth of the cropped area is cultivated in this manner. Such cultivation is not restricted to flat lands and the hand tilling that accompanies it has allowed many slopes too steep for the plough to be heavily used. Not uncommonly these steep slopes, often broken by terraces, *trincheras* and other soil-checking devices used since before the Spanish Conquest, overlook flatter alluvial land on which commercial crops of, say, sugar cane or wheat or maize are being grown on the basis of mechanized, fertilized monoculture.

This situation is well seen in Vera Cruz, the most productive agricultural state of the nation with its great variety of agricultural conditions and its proximity to the Central Mexican market. Here agricultural methods range from the most modern to the most traditional. One of the newer commercial crops to gain a foothold in the state is rice, now grown in the swampy lowlands of the Papaloapan and likely to become a more important crop in the other lowland regions of tropical Mexico. Sugar cane is the dominant commercial crop elsewhere in the Papaloapan basin, as it is on the Gulf plain bordering the railway lines running up to Córdoba and Jalapa, along the foot of the Sierra and, beyond the Panuco, in the irrigated districts of southern Tamaulipas. The state of Vera Cruz produces more sugar cane than any other and so suffers from some of the well-known economic and social problems common to cane-growing areas elsewhere in Mexico (notably in Morelos and coastal Sinaloa) and Middle America. Commercial banana plantations are also spreading in the *tierra caliente* of Vera Cruz but it will be a long time before the state recovers from the havoc wrought by Sigatoka disease in the 1930s which led (as elsewhere in Latin America) to a shift of the main banana-producing areas of the country to the west and south-west coasts. In the *tierra templada* of the lower and middle slopes of the Sierra Madre coffee and citrus fruits replace the tropical plants as the major commercial ones. It was on the slopes between Córdoba and Jalapa that these were first established as commercial crops and production continues to rise; today coffee is also grown elsewhere, particularly in Oaxaca and Chiapas, and Nuevo León is a more important citrus-growing area. The Vera Cruz–Mexico City axis has been the heart of many things in Mexico and it is only relatively recently that other parts of Mexico endowed with comparable or alternative advantages for commercial agriculture have become flourishing.

In spite of the importance of commercial crops maize remains the leading crop of Vera Cruz, as of the country, even though relatively less significant than in the past. It is obviously difficult to obtain statistical data for a subsistence crop (and official figures differ considerably) but two points are worth recording. First, Ministry of Agriculture figures show that national maize production changed little during the earlier part of the century but has more than tripled since 1945; whereas until the 1960s Mexico produced no maize surplus to her own requirements, in 1965 maize exports were marginally more valuable than exports of coffee and second only to cotton amongst exports of primary commodities. Secondly, the yields of maize per hectare are still extremely low: for 1964 one published figure (*México*, 1966, pp. 76–7) is about 1·1 metric tons/ha, the highest to date, and compares with 4·4 metric tons/ha in the U.S.A. and 1·5 tons/ha in the Argentine. Thus, although yields of this basic staple have doubled since the mid-1930s (U.N. Food and Agriculture Organization, 1957, p. 17), there is still ample scope for improvement. In fact, yields of other crops have improved at a more rapid rate than maize – for example, yields of wheat have doubled since 1950 (but are still only one third of yields in the U.S.A.) and those of cotton have more than doubled (but are only one half of the yield from the irrigated areas north of the border).

One of the most important mechanisms for creating these improvements has been the introduction of improved seeds. This is obviously easier to do amongst farmers orientated to a cash crop than amongst the more conservative subsistence farmers; nevertheless it is claimed that 20 per cent of the maize crop is now from hybrids. Another factor in improvement has been the more intensive use of fertilizers; consumption has been increasing at an annual rate in excess of 15 per cent since the middle 1950s aided by a booming domestic fertilizer industry incapable of satisfying home demand (*The Puebla Project*, 1970).

An important factor which limits agricultural production is the land tenure system. Mexican agronomists find themselves on the horns of a dilemma. On the one hand, there is clear evidence that land cultivated in larger units is more productive than land cultivated in smallholdings: for example, yields of wheat are one third higher on holdings over 5 ha in size as compared with those of 5 ha or below (Durán, 1966, p. 85). On the other hand, for social and political reasons, the proportion of agricultural land in smallholdings has risen substantially. In 1930, 93 per cent of the agricultural land was in holdings of over 5 ha in size (González Navarro, 1965, p. 217), whereas today the corresponding figure is only 67 per cent and the average size is dropping. The Mexican government in the fifty years following the Revolution has, in rather spasmodic fashion, followed a programme of land reform which, though socially desirable, appears to run counter to the economic demands of modern commercial agriculture. Over 55 million ha (over a quarter of the national territory) has been expropriated and redistributed since 1924. Large private estates (haciendas) still remain, especially in the dry country of the north, but elsewhere they have usually been carved up, the owner (*hacendado*) sometimes being allowed to retain a small part of his estate and to become a so-called *pequeño propietario*. The expropriated land has been redistributed in a variety of ways. Ownership of most has been vested in the nation and the use of it entrusted either to individuals as smallholdings or, rarely now, to a group and farmed collectively. Such lands, called *ejidos*, account for half of the cultivated area today. In recent years the government has actually sold the title of lands whose development it has been anxious to promote (for example, in the irrigation districts of the north and in the pioneer lands of southern Yucatán and the Tabascan lowlands) and moderate-sized *colonias* of 20–50 ha in size have added a further element to the land tenure pattern.

Ejidal lands tend to be less productive than those in private ownership; this is demonstrable on a crop-for-crop basis (Flores, 1967) and is also expressed in the more conservative attitude of *ejidatarios* to the production of industrial and commercial crops. To some extent this distinction is due to the poorer average quality of *ejidal* lands. In Yucatán (Fox, 1961, p. 222) for example, where yields of henequen are lower on the *ejidal* land than on private lands, many of the *hacendados* were permitted to choose the 150 ha they were allowed to retain after expropriation; they naturally chose the better lands of their former estates. In the Fuerte and Mayo valleys and on the Colorado Delta (Henderson, 1965, p. 305) the *ejidos* are on the lower valley lands that had been farmed for decades and have been worst hit by salinization. In general, there is a higher proportion of *ejidal* land in the centre and south of the country than in the more productive north and north-west. Further, the average *ejidal* holding is much smaller than the private holding, the educational standard of the *ejidatario* is poor and he is in a relatively disadvantageous position with respect to access to capital, credit and machinery. However, where all other things are equal (a rare situation one suspects, although it may exist in parts of the north-west) it is claimed (Dozier, 1963, p. 562) that it is impossible to distinguish an *ejidal* plot from a private holding, either in terms of land use or of productivity.

Official information is not always reliable when land tenure matters are in question. Although the reform programme has served its prime objective – control of the countryside has been taken from the hands of the *hacendados* and spread over a much wider spectrum of rural society – anomalies remain or have arisen. Large estates still persist, even in the vicinity of the capital. More widespread, however, has been the fraudulent conversion of *ejidal* land. It is said that many of the *ejidatarios* in the Basin of Mexico lease out their land, or make it over on a share-cropping basis, whilst they take factory jobs; and that between one third and one half of the *ejidatarios* in the Yaqui valley lease their land to others. Another illegal situation which is apparently tolerated by the government relates to the size of holdings, both private and *ejidal*: in the Colorado delta some *ejidal* holdings are twice and others in the Yaqui valley six times the legal maximum; in the Hermosillo region private wheat farms are twice the maximum of 100 ha allowed under the Agrarian Code. In places one person may effectively farm several *ejidal* plots or private farms by controlling the extra holdings through members of his family or other front men: private farms units of this type of 500 and 1000 ha exist in Sonora and Sinaloa. The economic advantages which accrue from these large holdings and receive a degree of tacit official recognition today may be more difficult to maintain in the future as social and political pressures against them become stronger and more insistent.

In 1965 there were about 2,200,000 *ejidatarios* working lands distributed to them or their parents; in addition there were about 2 million landless *campesinos* eligible for *ejidal* dotations and their number rises year by year. Mexico is running out of land available to create new *ejidos*. The programme of land redistribution was expected to be complete by 1970. Altogether about 40 million ha are still available for allocation, but most of this is in the dry north and individual grants will have to be of at least 50 ha to be economically viable: simple arithmetic shows that such redistribution, even if successful, will satisfy the demand of only two-fifths of those currently entitled to *ejidal* land. Thus, despite the social achievements of the land reform programme, it has not removed the landless peasant from the Mexican rural scene and, in fact, one can expect day-labourers, the most lowly members of rural society, to become more and more numerous. A stratified rural society is emerging in which the day-labourer remains in status a solid element below the *ejidatario*; the *ejidatario* is in turn inferior to the colonist; above him, near the top of the ladder is the *particular* or private landowner. The growing awareness of the fate awaiting many rural Mexicans is out of keeping with expectations inculcated at schools and by political leaders; it has already led to some unrest, especially in those areas where alternatives, such as migration to the factories of the cities or to the pioneer lands, are more difficult. It is hard, for example, for a Mayan peasant in Yucatán, used to the peculiar, specialized and limited requirements of work in the henequen plantations, to acquire the radically different skills and outlook required of a pioneer farmer in the south of the peninsula or of an artisan in distant Mexico City; there were mass demonstrations in Mérida in the late 1960s.

The contribution of the pastoral industries (*México*, 1966, pp. 80–5; West and Augelli, 1966, pp. 336–40) to the national economy is relatively slight in spite of the fact that 40 per cent of the country was classified as grazing land in the 1960 census. Animal husbandry accounted for 5·0 per cent of the gross national product in 1969. Three different types of animal husbandry are practised. In most parts of the country goats browse land which would otherwise be unproductive, except perhaps of firewood, and much has been written on the acceleration of soil erosion caused by their omnivorous and voracious appetites. Pigs, sheep, mules and the occasional multipurpose cow are common domestic animals in the ménage of many peasant establishments and supply essentially family or local requirements. These animals, like most domestic animals in Mexico, are, of course, post-Columbian introductions into the traditional agricultural scene.

Elsewhere, and particularly in the northern states of Sonora and Chihuahua, great cattle ranches still exist, a reminder of the days early in this century when Mexico rivalled Argentina as an exporter of meat. The Revolution, the uncertain position of the *hacendados* in the 1920s and 1930s, the loss of the profitable U.S. market, the decimation of the herds by a disastrous epidemic of foot-and-mouth disease between 1947 and 1952, and the expropriation of much of the ranchland, especially since 1958, have all effected notable changes in the industry. For example, a change in government policy in the last ten years has led to the promotion of large co-operative cattle *ejidos* and now almost half the cattle are *ejidal*. Many of the *ejidos* carved from the large estates are themselves large – up to 30,000 or 40,000 ha in semi-desert conditions. The government is also promoting more intensive management by improving the quality of the pasturage, by encouraging the growth and purchase of supplemental feedstuffs where appropriate, and by improving the quality of the stock; it does this by direct action on the *ejidos* and by offering incentives and inducements (including confirmation of ownership of their estates or guaranteeing limited freedom from expropriation) to private ranchers. Some *ejidos* are fortunate in having inherited quality animals: for example the seven *ejidos* created from the former 150,000 ha ranch of the Cananea Copper Company in Sonora are each stocked with 3500 Herefords and breeding stock is maintained. Elsewhere great efforts are being made to switch to more productive beasts, including crossed zebu, and only one in three is now of the traditional *criollo* breed. The proportion of *criollo* is higher on *ejidos* than on private ranches.

Thirdly, there are several areas of intensive cattle-raising. Sale of milk to the burgeoning towns has created dairy zones in the vicinity of the cities and around rural pasteurizing plants. The eastern shore of Lake Texcoco opposite Mexico City is one such area, the Mezquital further north is another. The Huasteca area of northern Vera Cruz and southern Tamaulipas is the most important beef fattening area. Intensive cattle-raising, for meat or milk, is increasingly becoming an adjunct to irrigation farming; this is particularly true of the Bajío and the Lerma valley where more and more alfalfa (lucerne) and other fodder crops are being grown. But there is great room for improvement, despite Mexico's long-standing cattle tradition: the average dairy cow of the *ejidos* yields only 1000 l per year, half that of the private dairy farmer and a quarter of the milk from the best herds in the country.

THE FORESTS AND THE FISHING GROUNDS

The forests and fishing grounds of Mexico (*México*, 1966, pp. 85–96; West and Augelli, 1966, pp. 340–2; Tamayo, 1962, pp. 107–8) are as yet of very little economic importance but both may be potentially valuable resources. The old forests that covered much of Mexico have long been attacked by the agriculturalist, the fuel gatherer and the man searching for constructional timber; in this century the wood pulp miller has joined the exploiters. Few conservation measures have been applied. The pine forests of the highlands of the centre and the western Sierra Madre and the tropical forests of the south-eastern lowlands are now being worked on a more satisfactory basis, but policy decisions are awaiting the completion (perhaps in 1971) of the Forest Inventory of the Food and Agriculture Organization.

Commercial fisheries are limited, partly, like tropical forestry, by the great mixture of species, and partly by the small number of preserving centres, by the distance to the domestic markets of the interior and by the

absence of a fish-eating tradition. The only commercial fishing of significance is on the shrimp grounds of the Gulf of California and the Gulf of
Campeche, encouraged by the demand of the U.S. market and the improved freezing facilities which have developed during the last twenty
years, and on the Pacific tuna and sardine grounds. Shrimps made up over
80 per cent, by both tonnage and value, of the fish exported in 1965. This
last point is of more than incidental interest; the law restricts the fishing of
shellfish to co-operative societies (the maritime equivalent of *ejidos*) and
these supply half of the fishermen and 80 per cent of the value of the
national catch. There are a number of government boards to promote commercial fishing, but although *per capita* consumption of fish is rising, it is
still only a third of that in the United Kingdom.

THE MINES AND THE OILFIELDS

The great days of the Mexican mining industry are doubtless over but
from them much of the geographical structure which affects the pattern
of life in Mexico today has been inherited. The modern economy is not
likely to return to the situation which persisted until this century in which
over one half of the earnings from exports were from the sale of minerals.
Not that the former staples of gold, and particularly silver, have disappeared – Mexico is still the leading world producer of silver – but rather
that other minerals have superseded the precious metals and other sectors
of the economy have expanded more rapidly than the mining sector. By
1900 precious minerals had been overtaken in value by the production of
non-ferrous minerals. Copper was the most valuable until 1930, lead until
1950, and zinc today; Mexico occupies twelfth, fifth and seventh place
respectively amongst world producers of these minerals today. But production of silver and the non-ferrous minerals has changed little in recent
years; on the other hand, production of iron ore and coal has risen and
Mexico is now a leading world producer of sulphur. Most important,
however, has been the development of petroleum. In the mid-1950s the
industry, in value of output, became as important, and in the mid-1960s
twice as important, as the sum total of all other mineral enterprises in the
country.

Changing patterns of mineral production have benefited some areas but
damaged others. A crude division of Mexico into three mineral zones may
help in making the picture clear. A western zone running from north-west
Mexico (Baja California, Sonora and Chihuahua) to Chiapas is the major
source of copper and gold; an eastern zone comprising the Gulf lowlands
produces all the oil, natural gas and sulphur of the country; and a central,
overlapping zone produces silver, lead and zinc. The north has been replaced by the Gulf coast as the focus of mineral activity and shrunken or
ghost towns and mining camps have posed social and economic problems

to the authorities in the dry interior. The population of the famous silver
town of Guanajuato, one of the wealthiest cities of the Americas in the
nineteenth century and briefly capital of the country, is now less than half
the 1880 figure: it has turned to its fine colonial architecture, its nineteenth-
century civic buildings and its picturesque setting for a second life as a
tourist attraction. Taxco in the south, where copper was first mined in
Mexico, has followed a similar path. Other decayed mining centres have
been less fortunate; towns like Zacatecas and Pachuca survive largely
because of their inherited status as administrative centres, but others have
had nothing to replace failing mines. The problem is most serious in the
dry north-western states where local alternatives to mining often do not
exist.

There are, however, some highly flourishing mines in the north-west.
The great open-cast workings of Cananea and the mines of Nacozari in
Sonora produce 40 to 45 per cent of all Mexico's copper; more than 60
per cent of her zinc and lead and one third of her silver come from the
mines of Chihuahua where the ores are commonly mixed and production
of one metal depends partly upon the state of the markets for the other
metals. Durango, Coahuila, Zacatecas, Baja California Sur and San Luis
Potosí are the other leading metallic ore producing states, all vulnerable to
price fluctuations largely outside national control. Until recently many of
the mining companies were owned by foreign interests, perhaps increasing
the vulnerability of the mining areas to external circumstances, but two
changes have reduced the element of risk in recent years. The first has been
the policy of progressive 'Mexicanization' of the mining industry which has
been pursued since 1961 through legislation providing incentives to companies in which Mexican citizens or a trust hold a controlling share of the
stock. Only Mexicanized companies can obtain new mining concessions
and Mexico believes her internal economy is strong enough to make good
any resulting loss of external investment capital. By 1968 90 per cent of
the value of mining and metallurgical production was coming from
Mexicanized companies. The second has been the increasing proportion
of metallic ores absorbed by domestic industry. One fifth of the zinc, one
third of the lead, and five-sixths of the copper was consumed within Mexico
in 1966 as compared with less than one tenth, less than one fifth and less
than one half in 1960. A considerable proportion of the metallic ores,
however, is still smelted or refined outside the country, especially in the
U.S.A.

In contrast to her wealth in precious and non-ferrous minerals Mexico
is not an important producer of the basic minerals, iron ore and coal.
Nevertheless, production of both is rising: over 2·5 million tons of coal
were produced in 1969 (twice the 1950 figure), and 2·0 million tons of iron
ore (three times as much as in 1960). The coal comes from the Sabinas
basin, 100 km north of Monterrey, and is the best coking coal in Latin

America; it is mainly consumed by the iron and steel industry of Monterrey. So is the iron ore mined outside Durango City at Cerro el Mercado, the most important ore field, and this, together with other ore fields in Jalisco and Michoacán, meets half of the domestic steel industry's requirements.

Sulphur (Seawall, 1961) is another newcomer to the mining picture. Since 1954 Mexico has jumped to be second only to the U.S.A. as a world producer. Sulphur domes discovered in the isthmus of Tehuantepec during the course of exploration for oil in 1915 were rediscovered in the 1950s and have yielded a handsome return; their ownership became a political issue and they have now been Mexicanized, partly to ensure the conservative working of a wasting resource.

The peaceful changes in ownership that are now characteristic of the Mexican mining scene are in contrast to the abrupt nationalization of the petroleum industry in 1938. That act was widely regarded within Mexico as a symbol of the coming-of-age of economic independence, but the flight of capital and of technical skills, the loss of export markets and the insecurity of the preceding years were all very damaging. It is only since 1950 (Guzmán, 1964) that the industry has recovered and has moved on to a sounder footing.

Fortunately, although the richest of today's oilfields, the Poza Rica field, had already been discovered in 1930 by the Royal Dutch Shell interests, exploitation had hardly begun at the time of expropriation. This field on the Cazones river is a continuation of the old Faja de Oro or Golden Lane field inland from Tuxpan which produced more than half of Mexico's total production of crude oil prior to 1938 and which had been largely responsible for turning Mexico into the second world producer in the early 1920s. In 1921, the peak year of Mexican oil production, the Golden Lane field alone produced more than did the whole of Mexico in 1966. Today, the Golden Lane field accounts for less than 9 per cent of Mexico's production, whereas the Poza Rica field accounts for 35 per cent of production and contains two-thirds of all Mexico's known oil reserves. The other important early producer was the Panuco–Ebano district inland from Tampico but this, too, is of only minor importance today; the isthmian field of Tehuantepec has never been anything else. Apart from the growth of the Poza Rica field exploration in recent years has been best rewarded at the northern and south-eastern ends of the oil zone. The swampy lowlands of eastern Tabasco doubled output after 1960 and are now producing as much crude oil as the Poza Rica field.

The growth of natural gas production has been remarkable; it has increased eightfold since 1950. The industry is now only slightly less important than is crude oil. Slightly under half of the gas production comes from the Tabascan field, from an area of Mexico which was virtually outside the national economy twenty years ago, and most of the balance comes from the northern Gulf plain in the vicinity of Reynosa on the lower Río Grande

Gas from the north-eastern field passes through an absorption plant in Reynosa; one third of it is exported to the U.S.A. and the rest is sent by pipeline to Monterrey, Monclova, Torreón and Chihuahua (and, in the future, to Mexicali). Ciudad Pemex serves a similar function in Tabasco and there are smaller absorption plants at La Venta and Minatitlán in the isthmus of Tehuantepec; gas lines link Mexico City to both the Tampico–Poza Rica fields and to the Tabascan fields.

Six refineries serve the oil industry; four are in the vicinity of the fields and two are in the interior. The two largest (at Minatitlán and outside Tampico at Madero) convert over half Mexico's crude oil and both are being expanded. The other two refineries on the oilfields at Reynosa and in the Poza Rica field are small. One fifth of the crude oil is refined in Azcapotzalco, a north-western suburb of Mexico City, and the balance is treated in a large refinery in Salamanca, 800 km from the nearest supply and 300 km beyond the main market, Mexico City. Domestic oil production exceeded home demand by about 12 per cent in the 1960s but Mexico is still obliged to import some lubricating oils which cannot be culled from her own crude oil. Reserves of both oil and gas are three-to-four times what they were in 1950. The most successful exploratory drilling programme in the middle 1960s was in the north-east; other wells were being bored in 1967 (Informe, 1967) on the island of Tiberón in the Gulf of California and off shore from Vera Cruz in the Gulf of Mexico.

Some 7 per cent of the combined oil and natural gas production is used to generate electricity (U.N. Economic Commission for Latin America, 1967, pp. 339–50) and such power stations are as important in the supply systems as the better publicized hydro-electric stations. The latter are frequently built as part of the many integral valley development plans, such as those in the Balsas and Grijalva valleys, but their efficiency and economics are not very clear. By 1966 about 15 per cent of Mexico's economic potential had been harnessed and more hydro-electricity was being added to the system at a rapid rate. About half of all electricity produced was consumed in the area within 150 km of Mexico City. Two points about the energy situation in Mexico are worth underlining: firstly, she is self-sufficient and appears likely to be able to continue to meet the rising internal demand for power; secondly, production of energy in all forms is rising at a remarkable rate and it has, in fact, doubled in the last ten years.

MANUFACTURING

A strong manufacturing industry has grown up in Mexico in recent years and it now makes a more substantial contribution to the economy than does agriculture, the forests and fishing grounds, the mines and the oilfields combined. Manufacturing production first became more important than agriculture in 1951 and has remained one of the most dynamic elements of the economy. Between 1955 and 1965 manufacturing production doubled, that of agriculture rose by little more than one third; in 1970 manufacturing was expanding at an annual growth rate of about 10 per cent whereas agriculture and mining were amongst the more sluggish sectors of the economy (Campos Salas, 1967). The impact on the economic geography of Mexico is very important. Whereas the expansion of commercial agriculture to the arid northlands and the tropical wetlands has spread rural wealth more widely over the country, and increasing emphasis on the Gulf lowlands has allowed the benefit accruing from mineral exploitation to be enjoyed more generally, the emerging geographical pattern in the secondary and tertiary sectors of the economy is one of concentration in the cities and especially in the capital. An ambivalent attitude by the Federal government has added to the political and social problems created by this situation.

Certain industries reliant on bulky raw materials – iron and steel and other metal smelting and refining, chemicals, oil-refining, certain of the agricultural processing industries – are, however, well represented outside the capital. Monterrey is the iron and steel centre of the country and has been so since the first works opened in 1903. Together with the nationalized industry at Monclava, this area accounts for one half of Mexico's steel and production is rising. It consumes nearby Sabinas basin coal and iron ore from Durango, and it enjoys a booming local market. Elsewhere scrap forms the basic raw material for the plants including those on the border and in Mexico City. There is a plan to create an iron and steel complex in the lower Balsas valley based upon electric power from the Infiernillo and La Villita dams and the nearby iron ore reserves of Las Truchas. Total production remains small – in 1970 Mexico produced about 3·5 million tons of steel, no more than a single large mill in the United States – although it has tripled in the last decade. Furthermore, costs are high, encouraged, critics claim, by high external tariffs, by inefficient working in the nationalized industry, as well as by the relatively small scale of Mexico's industry. The development of the direct reduction process, in use in the steel mills at Monterrey, may help to lower costs.

The chemical industry is also well represented outside the metropolitan area. It covers a wide range of products and claims to contribute about 6 per cent to the gross national product. Both government and private capital have been attracted to it and investment has been at an annual rate of 12·5 per cent over the last fifteen years. The sulphuric acid plants are offshoots of Mexico's metal refining industries and are found generally in the north of the country. Synthetic fibre plants are found either in conjunction with the petroleum refining industry (if they have a petrochemical base) or in the Mexico City–Guadalajara textile area (if based on cellulose). Chemicals based on natural gas, including ammonium products and fertilizers, are produced as near to the market as possible (for example, at Salamanca in the Bajío) and sulphur-based products are made near the sulphur deposits in the isthmus. The petrochemical industry is largely a subsidiary of the national petroleum board (Pemex) and is linked to the petroleum refineries, especially to those of the Gulf coast and Salamanca. The overall pattern is one in which more emphasis is being given to the Minatitlán–Coatzacoalcos area as a producer of basic chemicals while the Federal District remains the centre of the consumer-orientated chemical industry, retaining (partly because of local saline deposits) what planners believe to be an unduly high proportion of the heavy chemical industry.

Despite important exceptions, however, the manufacturing industry of Mexico is increasingly associated with the capital. Preliminary figures from the 1966 industrial census show that the Federal District and the state of Mexico contained 55·6 per cent of total manufacturing employment and 47·9 per cent of the total value added in manufacturing (Campos Salas, 1967, p. 280). In 1961 and 1956 comparable employment percentages were 43·1 per cent and 29·5 per cent. Other sources give different proportions but all show both the high degree of concentration and the growing concentration of employment and production in the capital. Nowhere else in Mexico is manufacturing such an important element in the local economy, employing as it does 1 in 3 of all employees in the capital; Monterrey offers the closest parallel but elsewhere proportions of 1 in 6 or lower are normal. In 1966 the value of manufacturing output from Mexico City and its suburbs was worth more than the entire crop production of the whole country. The precise industrial structure of the capital is open to different interpretations (Yates, 1962; Bassols Batalla, 1966) depending upon the source used but in the Federal District metal-producing and metal-using industries account for about one quarter and the chemical, food and textile industries about one half of the total. In the outlying districts, beyond the Federal District border, heavy industry, such as paper mills, tyre factories, electrical machinery, basic chemicals and cement works, is important. Among national industries almost exclusively concentrated in or near Mexico City are confectionery, tobacco, pharmaceutical chemicals, soaps and detergents, electrical, tyre and motor car industries.

The attractions of the metropolitan area to manufacturers in general spring not from any abundance of notable raw materials; rather they lie at other stages in the manufacturing process.

In the first place there is no shortage of unskilled labour. In population Mexico City is six times bigger than its nearest neighbour, Guadalajara, and over half of the people living in cities of over 50,000 live in the Federal District (*VIII Censo*, 1960). There is, by Mexican standards, a relatively large supply of skilled labour, for the educational standards of the city are notably higher than those of the other cities of the country, and specially so in the highest levels. For example, the proportion of the labour force with professional qualifications is four times higher in the capital than in Monterrey, which is itself an enlightened industrial city. The actual figures – 216,000 and 7500 respectively – perhaps best emphasize the enormous difference between Mexico City and the rest of the country (*La población*, 1964, vol. 1, pp. 56–7, vol. 2, pp. 156–7).

Mexico City is the outstanding consumer market of the country. In 1960 the average income in the Federal District was 42 per cent above the national average and 25 per cent above that in the other cities over 50,000 in size; *per capita* income outside these cities was only one half of that in the Federal District. In a sample study carried out by the Secretaría de Industria y Comercio in 1962 of the sixteen largest cities of the Republic (*Las 16 ciudades*, 1962, pp. 29, 33, 97) the Federal District with 58 per cent of the families accounted for about two-thirds of family expenditure on food, footwear and clothing, and four-fifths of money spent on such consumer durables as furniture, vehicles and electrical goods; they also accounted for more than nine-tenths of invested money. Two-thirds of the income remaining after meeting the cost of food, housing and clothing was in the Federal District. More than three-quarters of all the urban families with incomes in excess of 3000 pesos a month lived in the Federal District (Monterrey was closest with 6 per cent and Mexicali, on the U.S. border, third with 2 per cent). The spending power of Mexico City has been recognized by government and industrialist alike.

Mexico City is also very central to the national market and has been even closer; the population centre of the country, which in 1930 was only 170 km from the capital, remains only 250 km away (near Salamanca) and the centre of purchasing power only a little further north. This slight demographic shift away from Mexico City has been more than negated by the greatly improved accessibility of the metropolis from all parts of the country. Recent improvements have confirmed the capital as the rail, road and air centre of the country, giving it low distribution costs and an unequalled service. The most important improvements in the last two decades have been in the radical development of the system of paved highways: mileage has quadrupled and since 1958 has exceeded that of the railways. The new road system has reinforced Mexico City's nodal position, one already established by its focal position in the Guadalajara–Vera Cruz railway network. A recent detailed comparison of theoretical minimum distribution costs (using rail, road or a combination of both, whichever was cheapest in 1963) showed that the area tributary to Mexico City was larger than the area tributary to any other transport centre in the country (Togno, 1963). This advantage flows mainly from the superior facilities in and out of the capital. It is augmented by the economies of bulk traffic permitted by the large volume of goods generated by the city. Both underline the attractions of Mexico City as a manufacturing centre for the national as well as the local market.

It is less easy to measure other factors which make the area around Mexico City attractive to the industrialist. Certainly private capital is more readily available in Mexico City than outside, and more people are prepared to invest in local than more distant ventures. For example, only 38 per cent of all new private capital investment in industry during the first half of 1969 was invested in areas outside Mexico City. The cosmopolitan qualities of life in the capital and the mild climate must play a part in attracting and holding Mexican and foreign businessmen and their enterprises. The powers of state governments are relatively weak and Mexico City is the seat of important political decisions.

Political decisions have affected the concentration of industry in the capital in several ways. On the one hand, it is argued that the government has encouraged industry to locate in the capital by providing such facilities as public utilities, loans, etc., not available elsewhere and (by subsidizing certain foodstuffs, notably maize, in the capital) has kept the cost of living down, the wage rates low and the labour market easy. On the other hand, the government has paid lip service in recent years to the social disadvantages of over-centralization and has made some attempt to dissuade industry from settling itself in the Federal District by devices such as new regulations, the strictest enforcement of existing regulations, higher land taxes reinforcing higher land values, and the like. The most notable beneficiary under this latter policy has been the adjoining state of Mexico, however, although some areas distant from the capital have also attracted industry. The northern suburbs of Mexico City now lie in the state, and industrial employment there has increased sevenfold since 1950 (compared with fourfold in the Federal District), and is now equal to the combined total of Monterrey and Guadalajara.

The location of the new automobile industry illustrates the effect of this policy nicely; almost all the new plants have been built near the capital but none in the Federal District (Rettie, 1967). Ford is at Cuantitlán; General Motors, American and Chrysler-Dodge are at Toluca; Volkswagen at Puebla; Datsun at Tejalpa; Renault at Ciudad Sahagún: all of these places are within 80 km of the capital and they account for over 80 per cent of the national productive capacity. The establishment of the car industry is also illustrative of another aspect of Mexican government policy in as far as it affects manufacturing: a decree of 1962 required assembly plants to conform to a national plan which demanded, in effect, the substitution of imported parts by domestically produced parts: a minimum national content of 60 per cent of the total cost is the short-term aim. In return, imports of vehicles were severely restricted, import regulations and duties on parts for companies reaching the desired proportion were eased, and the whole industry benefited from the general exemptions granted under the act for development of new and essential industries.

Import-substitution has, of course, become the classical way of encouraging domestic industrial growth in Latin America, but several factors have recently persuaded the Mexican government to adopt a less rigorous policy.

These include a realization that the higher costs of nationally made products and the loss of import revenue may be too great to be worth sustaining. Further, there are, of course, fewer appropriate industries (labour-intensive serving a large market) left to help in this manner, while the growing strength of the Mexican economy places less of a premium on saving foreign exchange. Acting on these lines in October 1966 the Mexican government reduced the degree of protection granted to new industries and required that selling costs should not be more than 15 per cent above the U.S. equivalent.

Away from the capital there are few manufacturing centres. Monterrey is undoubtedly the most important with substantial brewing, clothing and textile, shoe, glass, paper and electrical industries, as well as iron and steel; it is the second financial centre of the country. Nuevo León (with Monterrey as capital) has about 10 per cent of the manufacturing industry of the country. Jalisco (Guadalajara), Vera Cruz and Coahuila (with Torreón and Monclava) accounted for another 15 per cent. The rest of the country with 60 per cent of the population has only 30 per cent of the employment and 20 per cent of the national total value added in manufacturing. Such states mainly process local raw materials or supply local and limited consumer demand. The National Frontier Programme and State Industrial Estates are attempts to wean industries to new areas, but their impact is small when compared with the overwhelming attraction that the capital area exerts.

COMMERCE AND THE SERVICE TRADES

The pattern of concentration in manufacturing is paralleled in the tertiary sectors of the economy. Although commerce and the service industries have not quite the same relative importance as, for example, in Britain, they employ half as many people again as does manufacturing; commerce alone makes a contribution equal to that of manufacturing to the gross national product. Wholesale and retail trade is of course largely an urban function and in 1960 the Federal District housed one third of all commercial establishments in the country. The five major cities accounted for two-thirds of the total commercial income of the country, though they contained only one third of the country's population. The dominance of the capital in some segments of the service sphere is almost overwhelming (higher civil servants, theatres, medical services, etc.) and the overall pattern that emerges is one of concentration in the larger cities and certain tourist resorts. The dynamic picture is one of very considerable growth in the capital, limited growth elsewhere and very large areas where the impact of modern economic development is slight.

ECONOMIC REGIONS AND GROWTH POINTS

The net result of the developments described above is a very uneven pattern of economic production, with striking contrasts between one part of the country and another, and between cities, towns and the countryside. In 1960 over 43 per cent of the gross national product came from the Mexico City area alone (Denis, 1965) and the proportion today is probably higher. If one divides the rest of the country into three tiers of approximately equal area, the northern tier of the six border states accounted for approximately one half of the remaining production, the middle tier for a further one third and the southern tier, south and south-east of the Guadalajara–Mexico City–Vera Cruz axis, for only one sixth. At a more detailed scale, three-quarters of the national wealth is created in the fifteen small regions, occupying no more than 8 per cent of the national territory, shown in Fig. 2.5

Mexico City has the most varied economic structure and the highest absolute rate of economic growth. The industrial and commercial importance of the capital is being bolstered by the incorporation of adjoining areas into the region. The thrusting industries of Toluca in the west, the more traditional industries of Puebla in the east and the spontaneous and planned industries of the new satellite towns (for example, those of the new railway engineering centre of Ciudad Sahagún in Hidalgo) supplement the industrial income of the area and irrigation helps an intensive agricultural effort. The Monterrey–Saltillo–Monclava triangle is second to the metropolitan region but it is, in spite of its heavy industry and financial importance, only one eighth as significant. It is not very much more important than the Tijuana–Ensenada–Mexicali area in the far north-west. Here sale of irrigated cotton is the main staple, joined by a variety of enterprises loosely covered by the phrase 'the tourist industry'. The National Border Programme of the Mexican government has helped promote the latter, although, recognizing its vulnerability to unilateral changes in United States border regulations, it has also successfully promoted industrial growth. It has aided industries, such as clothing and the electronic assembly industry, aimed at the U.S. market, and allowed U.S. companies through subsidiaries to take advantage of the lower labour costs south of the border. Tijuana is, after all, only about 100 km from Los Angeles, and is over 3000 km from Mexico City. In the Guadalajara regions much of the economic development is based on the processing of local agricultural products or manufacturing goods for the regional market; though a region of significance, the pace of change is slower than in, for example, Monterrey. The economy of the Sinaloan and Sonoran regions is strongly orientated to local agricultural produce – sugar-growing and milling, cotton-growing and ginning and wheat-growing and processing – and has been boosted by sales of fruits, vegetables and shellfish on the U.S. market and by tourism.

In the productive oases on the Mesa Central the mining industry has been replaced as the mainstay of the economy by irrigated agriculture and the growth of a manufacturing industry to meet the needs of the local farmers; natural gas piped in from Reynosa and further hydro-electricity projects will give cheaper power. The lower Río Grande area has the added advantages of local gas resources and proximity to the United States and its economy is expanding at a more rapid rate. There are several growth areas along the Gulf coast with the oil industry of obvious importance. Vera Cruz enjoys some benefit (but perhaps surprisingly little) from her position as the country's major port, and Tampico is also a minor manufacturing centre. The petrochemical plants of Vera Cruz and Tabasco are valuable foci of economic growth though their demand for labour is relatively low. The Yucatecan economy remains in an unhealthy situation dependent largely on a crop, henequen, for which artificial substitutes already exist.

The patterns of economic production are out of harmony with the distribution of population and this naturally has severe repercussions on the well-being of the people. The differences, even at the relatively general level of comparing states, can be great. For example, and admittedly an extreme comparison, one worker in Baja California produces as much wealth as eleven workers in Oaxaca (Yates, 1962, pp. 62–3); his standard of living is about four times as high as is that of his compatriot in Oaxaca (Standards, 1966; Tamayo, 1962, vol. 3, p. 431; *Programa financiero*, 1964). The infant mortality-rate in Oaxaca is twice that in Baja California and overall life expectancies differ by nine years; the illiteracy rate in the north is under one half that in Oaxaca; six times as many houses have running water in the north; the minimum legal salary is four times as high and ten times as many people are covered by social security in the north; over three-quarters of the northerners use electricity compared with only one fifth in the south. Sugar consumption *per capita* in 1963 was three times as great in Baja California as in Oaxaca; three-quarters of the northerners earned over 750 pesos per month, less than one tenth did in Oaxaca; everyone wears shoes in the north, whereas only one in five did in Oaxaca in 1960. Similar, though less extreme, contrasts may be drawn between other more productive and less productive states.

Workers in the Federal District follow those in Baja California and are twice as productive as the natural average. All other states in which *per capita* productivity is above the national average lie along the northern border, as shown on Fig. 2.5. In contrast, workers in the southern Pacific states, the densely settled states of the centre away from the capital, and the old mining states of Zacatecas, Querétaro and Guanajuato, were less than half as productive as the average Mexican. The degree of correlation by states between productivity *per capita* and a combined measure of many criteria of social and material welfare (including those used above) is

c

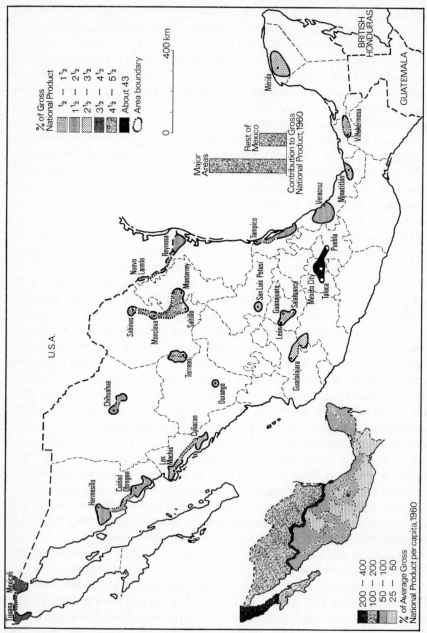

Fig. 2.5 Major productive areas of Mexico 1960

% of Gross
National Product

½ — 1½
1½ — 2½
2½ — 3½
3½ — 4½
4½ — 5½
About 43
Area boundary

0   400 km

U.S.A.

Tijuana
Mexicali

Hermosillo
Cuidad
Obregon

Los
Mochis

Chihuahua

Culiacan

Durango

Sabinas
Monclova
Saltillo

Torreon

Guadalajara

Nuevo
Laredo

Reynosa

Monterrey

San Luis Potosi

Guanajuato

Leon
Salamanca

Mexico City

Toluca

Puebla

Tampico

Veracruz

Minatitlán

Villahermosa

Mérida

BRITISH
HONDURAS

GUATEMALA

Major
Areas

Rest of
Mexico

Contribution to Gross
National Product, 1960

200 — 400
100 — 200
50 — 100
25 — 50

% of Average Gross
National Product per capita, 1960

statistically very exact. A map of one is virtually a map of the other and a clear indication of the way in which economic and social progress go hand in hand. As such it is interesting to note that *per capita* production in Mexico is about the average figure for Latin America and that the range found in the states of Mexico is approximately equal to that in the countries of Latin America: the Mexican living in the well-to-do northern border states contributes as much to the national economy as the average Argentino does to his, whereas the Mexican living in the poorer states of the south finds his closest parallel in Bolivia or Paraguay.

SOME SOCIAL QUESTIONS

The differences in the qualities of life throughout Mexico have led authors to draw comparisons between modern Mexico and remote Mexico, traditional Mexico and cosmopolitan Mexico, peripheral Mexico and nuclear Mexico, Indian Mexico and mestizo Mexico. These phrases are striking and the contrasts are real. They tend, however, to deflect attention away from the large middle ground lying between these extremes and to understress the importance of the transitional areas. Some comments on Indian Mexico are appropriate.

The Indian presence in Mexico is obvious, the Indian heritage a reality, and the Indian myth a not unimportant ideological weapon in the cause – often directed towards the Indian himself – of creating a national identity. Notwithstanding his importance, the position of the Indian today remains unenviable. He is found amongst the poorer, less productive, less literate, more deprived people in Mexico. An Indian problem is discussed as in the Andean countries, but remains largely unresolved, partly because the Indian himself is not easy to identify in a predominantly mestizo country and partly because many of the problems he suffers from are common to other members of the lower stratum of society.

The strictest available measure of the number and distribution of Indians in Mexico is that of language. In 1970 about 870,000 Mexicans over the age of 4 spoke only an Indian language, while a further 2·3 million spoke an Indian language and Spanish: together they made up 8 per cent of the Mexican population (*IX Censo*, 1971; West and Augelli, 1966, pp. 315–17). On the criterion of language (see Fig. 2.6c) the northern half of the Yucatán peninsula (Maya), the interior highlands of Chiapas (Tzeltal, Tzotzil), the southern Tehuantepec lowlands and the Mesa del Sur of Oaxaca (Zapotec and Mazatec), the Sierra Madre del Sur west of Oaxaca City (Mixtec), the refuge areas of the Tuxtlas in Vera Cruz and the southern Sierra Madre Oriental (Nahuatl), the basins around the Valley of Mexico (Nahuatl and Otomi) and the highlands north of Uruapan (Tarasco) are predominantly Indian; only 5 per cent of the Indians, so defined, live outside these areas. The Indians are far from homogeneous: for example,

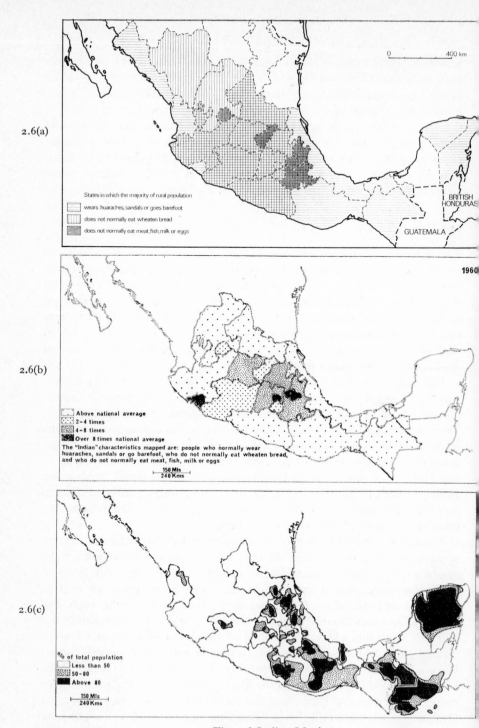

2.6(a)

States in which the majority of rural population

wears huaraches, sandals or goes barefoot

does not normally eat wheaten bread

does not normally eat meat, fish, milk or eggs

BRITISH
HONDURAS

GUATEMALA

1960

2.6(b)

Above national average
2 – 4 times
4 – 8 times
Over 8 times national average

The "Indian" characteristics mapped are: people who normally wear
huaraches, sandals or go barefoot, who do not normally eat wheaten bread,
and who do not normally eat meat, fish, milk or eggs

150 Mls
240 Kms

2.6(c)

% of total population
Less than 50
50 – 80
Above 80

150 Mls
240 Kms

Fig. 2.6 Indian Mexico
(a) Proportion of population with certain 'Indian' characteristics 1960
(b) Density of population with certain 'Indian' characteristics 1960
(c) Proportion of population speaking one Indian language
(After West and Augelli)

forty-five or forty-six different languages are spoken, some, it is claimed, as different from each other as Chinese is from English. This linguistic variety is symptomatic of the great wealth of cultural diversity grouped under the portmanteau label of Indian.

But a linguistic definition is too exclusive to measure satisfactorily the Indian presence in Mexico. Alfonso Caso prefers a social definition and has written that an Indian is one who feels he belongs to and is part of an Indian community, that is, one in which somatic non-European elements are predominant (Rubín de la Borbolla, 1964, p. 123). Census enumerators note certain key features of dress and diet and these may be used to suggest how widespread is the Indian influence in Mexico. In 1960 12·74 million Mexicans over the age of one (37·5 per cent of the population) wore either sandals (*sandalias*, *huaraches*) or went barefoot; 10·62 million Mexicans (32·5 per cent) did not normally eat wheaten bread; 8·15 million (23·3 per cent) did not normally eat meat, fish or eggs or drink milk – that is, their diet was essentially the traditional Indian one. These figures give credence to the visual impression a traveller has in central and southern Mexico (see Fig. 2.6a and b) and to the estimate of Brand that there are some 10 million Indians in Mexico today – more, in fact, than in any other Latin American country. These figures measure the size of the less dynamic, less mobile, portion of Mexican society; they are the people who contribute least to the energy which drives the westernized, partly alien, social and economic system which dominates Mexican life today. So long as the system runs relatively successfully (as it has for the last generation) the significance of the Indian in Mexico will decline; should the system falter this decline will slacken and perhaps even reverse.

Most Indians are poor. It is in this context that some useful work has been done by, for example, the Instituto Nacional Indígenista. Income and production *per capita* in the predominantly Indian-speaking *municipios* are between a third and a half of the national average; federal expenditure per head is only one fifth of the average. In fact, the tenor of much recent sociological work has been to view the limited case of the Indians as part of a wider culture of poverty found not only in the rural backwoods of southern Mexico, but in the slums of the larger cities and in developing countries generally. The Indian problem may thus be seen as part of a larger problem common to many Mexicans: the problem of adjustment to a rapidly changing environment, a problem often magnified for individuals by migration. Many of these problems are seen at their most striking in Mexico City where more than 2 million of the residents were born in the provinces and two-thirds of these probably came from rural localities. The shock of translation to the metropolitan environment can usually be softened by resort to a relative or friends from the same village or even to Indian enclaves speaking the same language. Such relief may be of short duration for housing is scarce, jobs for the poorly skilled are at a premium, old standards have changed and former ties may have been weakened and replaced by new loyalties.

Trustworthy unemployment statistics are not available; even if they were, statistics on occasional, part-time and casual employment would be needed to paint a full picture. Genuine unemployment is probably relatively insignificant. Most people of working age in Mexico City do something and earn something and both the construction industry and the service trades have proved very elastic in their capacity to absorb casual labour. Together with the sweat-shops of the inner city and home industries (perhaps producing goods which compete successfully with the products of their rural cousins), they have taken up much of the slack that might otherwise have developed.

In 1967, however, Eduardo Flores estimated that between 30 and 40 per cent of the statistically employed population of Mexico was in effect underemployed (5 Seminario, 1967, p. 363). This suggests that a figure of about half a million would be a realistic estimate of the number who live in the jungle world of marginal unemployment in the capital city, and agrees with other informed estimates of the situation. The important question arises: will non-marginal employment increase at a sufficient rate to prevent future wholesale unemployment amongst the ever-increasing population of the metropolis? Information does not exist to answer this question satisfactorily, but the indications do not lead one to be optimistic. For example, if one assumes that the demand for labour will rise by 5 per cent per annum and that the population of the city will be between 13 and 14 million in 1980 (Benítez Zenteno and Cabrera Acevado, 1966, pp. 137, 149; Geographical Distribution, 1963), then instead of the present half million or so in marginal employment there will be over 1·5 million. Between 1967 and 1980 about 1·5 million people are expected to move in from the provinces: it is reasonable to suppose that they will have to bear the brunt of an increasing surplus labour problem.

Marginal and irregular employment brings in its wake, for Mexico as for elsewhere, a number of social problems. One is the housing problem. This is particularly obvious in Mexico City where 3 million extra people have found roofs over their heads since 1950, and great numbers of sub-standard houses have risen to meet this need. Fig. 2.7 makes it clear that most parts of the city suffer deficiencies of some nature or degree. Nevertheless, three main types of housing problem deserve specific mention. The crumbling core of the old city is the scene of the worst case of overcrowding. A sample survey (Investigación, 1965) made in 1962–3 of the central 10 km² around the Zócalo, roughly the area of the city in 1850, showed that only 10 per cent of the accommodation was of a satisfactory standard. Most families lived, ate and slept in the same room, a room commonly giving access to a courtyard or inner well shared by dozens of other families. Although five out of six had easy access to running water,

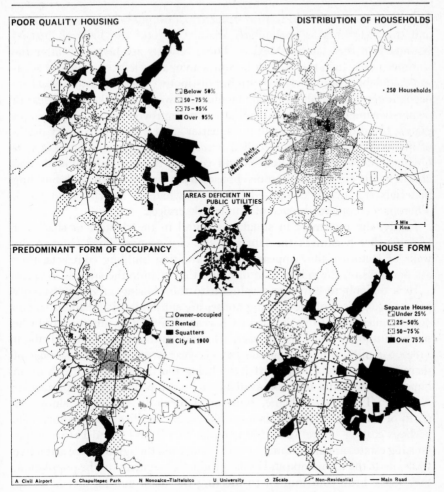

POOR QUALITY HOUSING

Below 50%
50-75%
75-95%
Over 95%

DISTRIBUTION OF HOUSEHOLDS

· 250 Households

AREAS DEFICIENT IN PUBLIC UTILITIES

PREDOMINANT FORM OF OCCUPANCY

Owner-occupied
Rented
Squatters
City in 1900

HOUSE FORM

Separate Houses
Under 25%
25-50%
50-75%
Over 75%

A Civil Airport　C Chapultepec Park　N Nonoalco-Tlatelolco　U University　Zócalo　Non-Residential　Main Road

Fig. 2.7 Housing in Mexico City 1963

fewer than half had any kind of sewage outlet. Oscar Lewis (1964) gives a graphic account of life in one such *vecindad* in his *Children of Sanchez*. The dwellings were once substantial buildings, but now, thanks partly to twenty-five years of frozen rents, they are degenerating beyond redemption into slums.

Squalor is more apparent in the zone of poor quality housing tracts which mar the periphery of the city although the population density is only one eighth of that in the city centre. A distinction must be drawn between the regular estates, subdivisions or *colonias* of detached single-storey, concrete and adobe, one- and two-roomed houses found on land reclaimed from Lake Texcoco to the east of the city, and the littered landscape of semi-finished shacks scattered, for example, on the dry hill slopes beyond

La Villa in the north-east. In the former area most public services are absent and this deficiency is particularly marked beyond the Federal District boundary in the state of Mexico. These *colonias* are best seen after the summer rains; then the ground becomes an opaque jelly of mud and accumulated debris, of uncertain depth but distinctive smell. Improvements are occurring in the supply of public facilities, however, and these are areas of owner-occupiers and private initiative in improvements is apparent in places. Conditions are worse in the squatter areas where the country origin of many of the inhabitants – called *paracaidistas* or parachutists – is very obvious. Most have no kitchens and cook in the open air, animals and children are equally numerous, house floors are of earth and building materials are mixed, composed largely of whatever lay closest at hand. There is a complete absence of municipal services.

Lastly, the uttermost in squalor is found in the clusters of shacks or lean-tos that pockmark the fabric of the city proper. They cling to the walls of factories, they appear on land awaiting building contracts, they are parasites on the rubbish dumps, and they mantle the sides of ravines.

It is difficult to envisage a solution to the housing problem. Seventy per cent (650,000) of the existing houses are substandard and about 50,000 new families have to be housed each year. The British answer would be public authority housing. In fact, Mexican authorities did build about 118,000 family units during the last six-year presidential term, most of them in the capital. But, apart from being too few to make much of an impact, these units are not available to most people. The spectacular Nonoalco-Tlatelolco Scheme, built on a formerly notorious slum site north of Buenavista Station, is for middle-class families able to afford flats perhaps costing several thousand pounds. The ISSSTE and IMSS public housing estates are in the same category and, even though they are attractive additions to the townscape and house productive segments of the population, they make little contribution to meeting the mass housing needs of the city. Even the utilitarian two-roomed houses on the large San Juan de Aragón estates in the north-east cost over £700 each and are only available to those in regular employment capable of carrying a mortgage (Cordova, 1964; Utria, 1966). Ten years residence in the Federal District is a requisite for participation in such schemes. In practice, financial and other demands place housing like this outside the range of perhaps one half of the population needing housing. Studies, such as that made by the Secretaría de Hacienda y Crédito Público in 1964 (*Programa*, 1964), although designed to offer a solution to the problem, instead rather highlight the plight of the urban poor; the striking new public buildings that grace many parts of the city lose something of their appeal when viewed soberly in the context of the greater need. A practical solution, if it exists, will not be a glamorous one: do-it-yourself kits of prefabricated parts, allowing first a one-roomed dwelling to be acquired, and then rooms added as circumstances permit, assembled on a concrete house lot served by basic sanitary facilities, may just fall within the strict financial constraints. This would require efficient organization and would produce a suburban land-scape of regimented ugliness and uniformity. Such an unexciting solution naturally runs counter to the image of Mexico that the Mexicans in power like to project. Similar, though in some respects less severe, housing problems face almost all the smaller cities of the country.

Parallel to the housing problem in Mexico City is the wider one of the provision of public services. The question of an adequate water supply in this semi-arid environment to meet the enormously increased domestic and industrial demand has been a taxing one (Fox, 1965b; Moore, 1968). Until a century ago the water of the springs at Chapultepec were led by open aqueduct to the erstwhile island site. In the first part of this cen-tury wells tapping the aquifers below the city proliferated to supplement this supply. This brought two consequences. Extraction exceeded the natural restoration rate, the water-table fell and supply declined. Secondly, the desiccation of the extremely hydrous clays of the upper subsoil resulted in their contraction and in severe subsidence at the surface: the central axis of the city has sunk by up to 7 m since 1930. The city has had to go outside the Basin of Mexico to slake its thirst and since 1951 the headwaters of the Lerma have been diverted into the metropolitan water system by tunnels through the western ranges. But water remains a perennial problem and more and more distant sources, some 400 km away, are being costed as potential suppliers; pumping water from the wet Gulf plains to the 2500 m altitude of the capital city, using off-peak hydro-electric power generated at the Sierra Madre escarpment, has been a recent suggestion; and more intensive use and re-use of existing supplies is being practised in a limited manner. Distribution within the ever-expanding city is another problem. About one third of the population of the city is without a domestic supply and private and public water tankers supply many of the suburbs. The drainage system of the city is also inadequate, conforming to a plan that is basically geared to the city of 1900. With a twelvefold expansion to date and with subsidence diminishing capacity, the existing sewage system is reduced both in extent and capability and has resulted in unpleasant and insanitary conditions in large areas of the city, especially in the amphibious zone on the eastern edge. Plans are in progress to supplant the Gran Canal, the open sewer that takes the city's effluent northwards through the divide to the Mezquital, by two deep main sewers constructed below the level affected by subsidence; but the system will remain limited.

Poor housing, insanitary conditions, marginal incomes and a largely ill-educated populace make large parts of the city unhealthy places to live. A large number of epidemiological studies and detailed mapping of patterns of morbidity and mortality of individual cases confirm this view. Typhoid (Gonzalez Gutiérrez, Benavides, Kumate and Rangel, 1962) is over three times more prevalent in children living in shacks than it is in those living in the *vecindades* and six times higher than in those living in what are officially regarded as adequate housing conditions. Infantile and premature mortality-rates (Abarca, 1963) and deaths from certain diseases, when checked against place of habitual residence, also mirror patterns of poor housing (Fox, 1972).

But the plight of the urban poor is, in some respects, less severe than that of the rural *campesino*. Social services are more developed in the capital than in the provinces, educational facilities more abundant and, perhaps especially important, the opportunities to improve one's position, both financial and social, are there for the strong in muscle and spirit. Such opportunities may become fewer as the ranks of the poor in the towns continue to be swollen by immigrants from the countryside; a feeling of frustration added to a growing awareness of the political power held by the urban poor could lead to the kind of economic and political debacle from which Mexico has been singularly free since the days of the Revolution.

CONCLUSION

This essay has dwelt on contemporary Mexico. Any conception of a people living purely in the past and dozing today beneath the hot afternoon sun is a caricature; rather, change and activity are the order of the day. Not that Mexicans are unaware of their past. The extraordinary remains of prehistoric civilizations, the relics in the landscape of colonial days, and the anachronisms of modern society, make this an impossibility; to be an archaeologist is to belong to one of the most admired professions. Nor is this awareness of the past of purely academic interest. More than one third of Mexico's foreign exchange now comes from tourists (a proportion comparable to that of Spain) and substantial government expenditure on restoring and preserving ancient monuments is reaping handsome dividends. Furthermore, the long history of the country has been appealed to by politicians anxious to mould a national identity; the vivid murals that adorn so many public buildings carry unequivocally the message that the mainsprings of Mexican culture lie in the pre-Columbian past. Raised high amongst the post-Conquest folk heroes are those with Indian connections – Father Hidalgo who led an Indian army in an abortive insurrection in 1810, Benito Juárez, the Zapotec Indian who was president of the country before Porfirio Díaz, and, more recently, a motley band of revolutionary generals amongst whom Emiliano Zapata and Pancho Villa are perhaps the most widely known. Cynics may claim that such emphasis is merely a sop to comfort the underprivileged and to deflect them from the knowledge that the Revolution has neither reduced the wide disparities in the distribution of wealth nor made a reality of the idea of equality of opportunity. The majority believes, however, that Mexico is in a stronger position today to master existing and future problems than almost any other of her Latin American colleagues and that more than lip-service should be rendered to past events.

One strength of Mexico over the last thirty years has been a stable and generally responsible government. Anti-clerical movements since Independence have removed any question of significant conflict between Church and State, and skilful management of opposition groups has made one-party rule popular and acceptable. Since the exceptional presidential term of Lázaro Cárdenas, which revived the radical aims of the Revolution and made the Revolution itself irreversible, there has been a growing national and, more recently, international confidence in Mexico. Much of this increased confidence can be credited to an expanding economy, some to favourable external circumstances and some to good management. Today the proximity of the United States brings undoubted economic benefits (in refutation of Porfirio Díaz's 'Poor Mexico, so far from God, so near to the United States') and Mexico can claim a gross national product that, in the whole of Latin America, is second only to that of Brazil. The question of wedding economic and social policies still remains an open one.

Confidence at home and abroad is reflected in Mexico's increasing international stature. She is one of the leading members of the Latin American Free Trade Association (although this membership may be more important from the political standpoint than from the economic) and has encouraged the creators of the Central American Common Market. Trade with Europe and Japan rises each year and cultural links are encouraged. She has taken an independent line in the Organization of American States and is less beholden to the United States than most other important Latin American countries. She has increasing influence at the United Nations. She helps focus world attention on herself by playing host to innumerable conferences and to such sporting events as the 1968 Olympics and the 1970 World Football Cup.

The image Mexico presents to the casual visitor is undeniably attractive; below the surface and away from the beaten tourist track the image is more enigmatic. The extent to which indigenous ideas and solutions are being found to meet the changing situation is important for a country whose history has given it good reason to be xenophobic; it is especially difficult for a foreigner to diagnose solutions for a people whose warmth and strangeness, violence and restraint, optimism and cynicism make them easy to like but difficult to understand.

BIBLIOGRAPHY

ABARCA, A. (1963) Morbilidad, mortalidad y letalidad en el servicio de premaduros del hospital infantil de México. *Bol. Med. del Hosp. Inf. de Méx.*, 20, 722–44.

AMAYA BRONDO, A. and ROBLES ESPINOZA, J. (1964) Oficinas de ingeniería de riego y drenaje. *Ing. Hidraulica en Méx.*, 18 (1–2), 122–44.

Aspectos económicos del estado de Sinaloa (1967) *El Mercado de Valores*, 27, 286–8.

BASSOLS BATALLA, A. (1966) *La ciudad de México y su region económica*. Mexico, Prim. Conf. Reg. Latinoamericana, Union Geográfica International, 4, 113–36.

BATAILLON, C. (1968) *Régions géographiques au Mexique*. Paris, Trav. et Mem. de l'Inst. des Hautes Études de l'Amer. Lat.

BENÍTEZ ZENTENO, R. and CABRERA ACEVADO, G. (1966) *Proyecciones de la población de México 1960–1980*. Mexico, Depto. de Investig. Industriales, Banco de Mexico.

BONINI, W., HEDBERG, H. and KALLIOKOSKI, J. (1964) *The Role of National Governments in Exploration for Mineral Resources*. Ocean City, N.J.

BRAND, D. R. (1966) *Mexico: Land of Sunshine and Shadow*. Princeton, N.J.

CAMPOS SALAS, O. (1967) Política Mexicana de desarrollo industrial. *Comercio Exterior*, 17, 279–83.

VIII Censo general de población 1960: resúmen general (1963). Mexico, Dir. Gen. de Estad., Sec. de Industria y Comercio.

IX Censo de población: Datos, 1970 (1971) *El Mercado de Valores*, 31, 88–93.

CÓRDOVA, R. (1964) *Urbanismo y desarrollo de la comunidad*. Mexico, Sección urbanismo, Sec. de la Presidencia de la República.

DE LA PEÑA, L. (1964) Riegos, drenaje y salinidad. *Ing. Hidraulica en Méx.*, 18 (1–2), 34–8.

DENIS, P. Y. (1965) Une dimension nouvelle au Mexique: l'espace économique. *Rev. Géogr. de Montreal*, 19 (1–2), 3–42.

DOZIER, C. L. (1963) Mexico's transformed northwest: the Yaqui, Mayo and Fuerte examples. *Geogr. Rev.*, 53, 548–71.

DURÁN, M. A. (1966) Perspectivas de la producción y del comercio del trigo y del maiz. *Comercio Exterior*, 16, 83–8.

DURAN OCHOA, J. (1957) *Población*. Mexico.

Estadisticas vitales en el Distrito Federal 1960–1962 (1965). Mexico, Dir. Gen. de Bioestad., Sec. de Salubridad y Asistencia.

FLORES, E. (1967) Cómo funciona el sector agropecuario de México. *Comercio Exterior*, 17, 701–5.

FOX, D. J. (1961) Henequen in Yucatan: a Mexican fibre crop. *Trans. and Pap. Inst. of Brit. Geogr.*, 29, 215–29.

FOX, D. J. (1965a) Henequen in Tamaulipas. *J. of Trop. Geog.*, 21, 1–11.

FOX, D. J. (1965b) Man-water relationships in metropolitan Mexico. *Geogr. Rev.*, 55, 523–45.

FOX, D. J. (1972) Patterns of morbidity and mortality in Mexico City. *Geogr. Rev.*, 62, in press.

Geographical distribution of the population of Latin America and regional development priorities (1963) *Econ. Bull. for Lat. Amer.*, 8 (1), 51–63.

GONZÁLEZ GUTIÉRREZ, T. G., BENAVIDES, L., KUMATE, J. and RANGEL, R. (1962) Encuesta inmunológica en la población infantil. *Bol. Med. del Hosp. Inf. de Méx.*, 19, 102–16.

GONZÁLEZ NAVARRO, M. (1965) Mexico: the lop-sided revolution. *In* VÉLIZ, C. (ed.) (1965), pp. 206–29.

GONZÁLEZ SANTOS, A. (1957) *La agricultura.* Mexico.

GUZMÁN, P. (1964) Exploration by Petróleos Mexicanos. *In* BONINI, HEDBERG and KALLIOKOSKI (1964), pp. 125–58.

HENDERSON, D. (1965) Arid lands under agrarian reform in northwest Mexico. *Econ. Geogr.*, 41, 300–12.

HEREDIA DUARTE, A. (1966) Tendencia de la mortalidad por enferme-dades infecciosas en México. *Bol. Med. del Hosp. Inf. de Méx.*, 23, 147–51.

Informe de petróleos Mexicanos (1967) *El Mercado de Valores*, 27, 275–9.

Inventario de la información basica para la programación del desarrollo agricola en la América Latina: Mexico (1964). Washington, D.C., Pan American Union.

Investigación de Vivienda (1965). Mexico, Instituto Mexicano de Seguro Social, vol. 1.

La economía Mexicana (1966) *El Mercado de Valores*, 26, 1212–36.

La población económicamente activa de México en junio de 1964 (1964) Mexico, Dir. Gen. de Muestreo, Sec. de Industría y Comercio, vols 1 and 2.

Las 16 ciudades principales de la república Mexicana: ingresos y egresos familiares 1960 (1962). Mexico, Dir. Gen. de Muestreo, Sec. de Industría y Comercio.

LEWIS, O. (1964) *The Children of Sanchez.* London.

Los recursos hidraulicos de México (1961). Mexico, Sec. de Recursos Hidraulicos.

MANGELSDORF, P. C., MACNEISH, R. S. and WILLEY, G. R. (1964) Origins of agriculture in Middle America. In WEST, R. C. (ed.) (1964a), pp. 427–45.

México 1966: hechos, cifras, tendencias (1966). Mexico, Banco Nacional de Comercio Exterior.

MOORE, W. B. (1968) *Industry and Water for the Valley of Mexico.* Mexico Depto. de Investig. Industriales, Banco de Mexico.

Población amparada al 31 de diciembre de 1964 (1966). Mexico, Depto. de Estad., Subdir. Gen. Tecnica, Instituto Méxicano de Seguro Social.

POLEMAN, T. T. (1964) *The Papaloapan Project.* Stanford, Calif.

Programa de inversiones 1965–1970 (1964). Mexico, Sec. de Recursos Hidraulicos.

Programa financiero de vivienda (1964). Mexico, Sec. de Hacienda y Crédito Público.

RETTIE, J. (1967) Mexico: achievements and problems. *Bank of London and South America Rev.*, 1, 184–91.

RUBÍN DE LA BORBOLLA, D. F. (1964) The Mexican Indian today. In WILGUS, A. C. (ed.) (1964), pp. 121–31.

SEAWALL, F. (1961) Recent developments in Mexican sulphur production. *J. of Trop. Geog.*, 15, 39–45.

5 Seminario nacional de planificación (1967). *Comercio Exterior*, 17, 363.

Sinopsis del informe de labores de la secretaría de recursos hidraulicos (1967). *Ing. Hidraulica en Méx.*, 21, 295–363.

Standards of living in northern Mexico (1966). *Rev. of the Econ. Situation in Mexico*, 42, 485, 15.

Standards of living in the southern region of Mexico (1966). *Rev. of the Econ. Situation in Mexico*, 42, 488, 19.

Statistics on the Mexican Economy (1966). Mexico, Nacional Financiera.

STEVENS, R. C. (1964) The soils of Middle America and their relation to Indian peoples and cultures. In WEST, R. C. (ed.) (1964a), pp. 265–315.

TAMAYO, J. L. (1962) *Geografía general de México.* 4 vols. Mexico.

The Puebla Project 1967–9 (1970) Mexico, Cent. Internat. de Mejoramiento de Maiz y Trigo.

TOGNO, F. M. (1963) Planeación ferroviaria – métodos simplificados para completar la red de México. *Comunicaciones y Transportes*, 5 (27), 16–63.

U.N. ECONOMIC COMMISSION FOR LATIN AMERICA (1967) *Economic Survey of Latin America 1965* (E/CN 12.752/Rev. 1). New York.

U.N. FOOD AND AGRICULTURE ORGANIZATION (1957) *The Selective Expansion of Agricultural Production in Latin America* (E/CN 12.378/Rev. 8). New York.

UTRIA, R. (1966) The housing problem in Latin America in relation to structural development factors. *Econ. Bull. for Lat. Amer.*, 11 (2), 81–110.

VÉLIZ, C. (ed.) (1965) *Obstacles to Change in Latin America*. London.

VIVÓ ESCOTO, J. A. (1964) Weather and climate of Mexico and Central America. In WEST, R. C. (ed.) (1964a), pp. 187–215.

WEST, R. C. (ed.) (1964a) *Natural Environment and Early Cultures*. Austin, Texas, Handbook of Middle American Indians (ed. Wauchope, R.), vol. I.

WEST, R. C. (1964b) Surface configuration and associated geology of Middle America. In WEST, R. C. (ed.) (1964a), pp. 33–83.

WEST, R. C. and AUGELLI, J. P. (1966) *Middle America, its Lands and Peoples*. Englewood Cliffs, N.J.

WILGUS, A. C. (ed.) (1964) *The Caribbean: Mexico Today*. Gainesville, Florida.

YATES, P. L. (1962) *El desarrollo regional de México*. 2nd ed. México, Depto. de Investig. Industriales, Banco de México.

3 The Caribbean

David L. Niddrie

THE PHYSICAL SETTING

The Caribbean Sea, bounded on the west by the Central American isthmus and on the south by the South American mainland, is less easily defined in the north and east, except by a wide arc of islands some forty in number. Within this sea there are several basins separated by ridges and swells whose peaks do not, however, break the surface anywhere, except on the Aves Swell and south of the Yucatán basin (Fig. 3.1). Some of the world's great deeps or oceanic troughs are also found in the northernmost stretches of the basin, suggesting a geotectonic origin for the islands themselves. Such disposition of land and sea is from the outset a serious disadvantage, since there is no centrally located site for a regional centre. A study of the Caribbean islands becomes in effect a description and analysis of peripheries.

Linked tectonically with the eastern flanks of the Yucatán peninsula on the one hand and the west-east folds of Honduras and Nicaragua on the other, the larger islands (the Greater Antilles) stretch some 2400 km as far as Puerto Rico. From this point a string of much smaller islands takes a southward course, while yet another group projects the Venezuelan mountains eastward and northward to complete the arc.

A number of disparate geological episodes is therefore responsible for the creation of the islands themselves, none of which is older than the Jurassic period. Some of the early structural trends suggest a link with large-scale movements involving both the proto-continents of South and North America during the Cretaceous period. Old volcanic cores embedded within successive marine limestones, shales and sandstones intercalated with widespread volcanic detritus, indicate several palaeogeographic outlines differing from those of the present day until the Upper Miocene period, after which eustatic changes fringed many of the islands with coral shores and created widespread coral platforms beyond the boundaries of the Caribbean Sea. A phase of volcanic activity bringing the youngest of the Lesser Antilles into being marks the Holocene period.

So many events crammed into a brief space of geological time created a variety of island land forms, whose polygenetic characteristics make subdivision of the islands possible (Fig. 3.2).

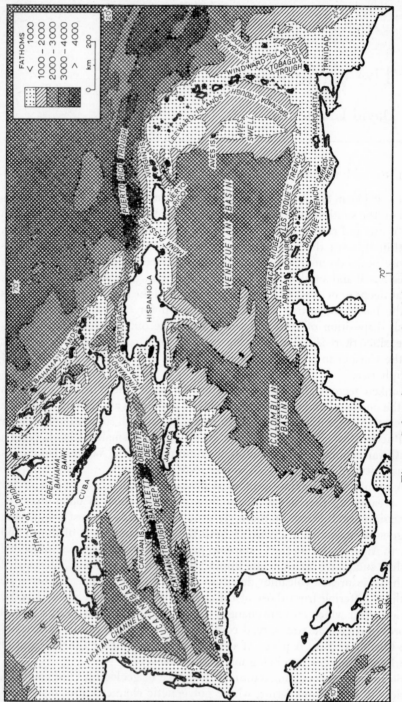

Fig. 3.1 Submarine topography of the Caribbean

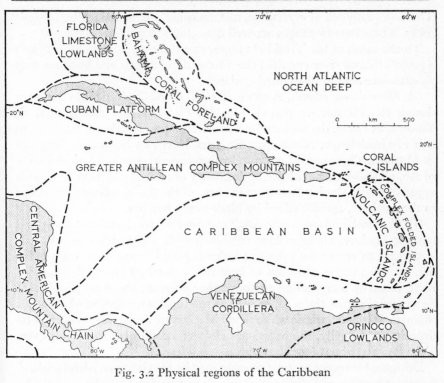

Fig. 3.2 Physical regions of the Caribbean

(a) *The Greater Antillean complex mountains.* This is the oldest core region in the Caribbean. Strongly folded mountain ranges, steeply sloped and strongly dissected, pass from west to east across southern Cuba (Sierra Maestra, Sierra de Nipé and Cuchillas de Toar), Hispañola (Cordilléra Central), Puerto Rico (Cordilléra Central and Sierra de Cayey) and the Virgin Islands.

(b) *The Cuban platform.* The remainder of Cuba is composed of several mountain ranges trending south-west to north-east (Sierra de Trinidad and Sancti Spiritus) in the central area and the Sierras de los Organos in the north, mostly composed of Cretaceous limestones, today strongly affected by karstic erosion.

(c) *Complex folded islands.* Several islets (Barbuda, Marie Galante), Antigua, the eastern half of Guadeloupe and possibly parts of Barbados consist of uplifted, moderately folded sedimentary deposits. These have been eroded subaerially for a long time, yielding a flattish, gently rolling countryside devoid of major heights, an important climatological factor.

(d) *Venezuelan cordillera.* The Netherlands Antilles, Santa Margherita, Trinidad and Tobago and parts of Barbados are an extreme extension of the west–east folded mountains linking the South American mainland.

They are composed of crystalline, metamorphic and, occasionally, volcanic rocks. These narrow ranges are well dissected and moderately sloped.

To the south of the Trinidad ranges, vast thicknesses of sediment from a proto-Orinoco river engulfed the Trinidad mountains and hills, creating an extensive area of ill-drained lowland.

(e) *The volcanic islands.* A chain of small islands, coming into existence during the Pleistocene period, includes Grenada, the Grenadines, St Vincent, St Lucia, the northern half of Martinique, Dominica, the western half of Guadeloupe, Montserrat, St Kitts, Nevis, St Eustasius, Saba and St Maarten. These consist of typical volcanic peaks, some of lava and some of ash, all presenting evidence of dormancy or activity. All have a fringing apron of gently sloping land from the base of the actual volcanic mountain to the seashore, usually edged by black sandy beaches.

(f) *The coral foreland, coral islands and coral fringes.* Local instability and eustatic sea-level changes have combined with a favourable oceanic environment to create the extensive Bahama island group, which are today flat, inconsequential stretches of land to the north of the Caribbean Sea itself, based on a crystalline platform; then there are the coral islands that lie scattered across the area, as well as the broad stretches of shallow sea round most islands, whose white sandy beaches are derived from such coral deposits; and finally, the occasional Holocene coral platform (south-west Tobago) lying about 6 m above present sea-level.

Evidence for recent eustatic changes may be seen on most islands, where wave-cut benches and cliffs well above present sea-level may be traced. The best-known examples are those on Aruba, Curaçao and Bonaire in the south, and along the southern coastlines of the Dominican Republic and Cuba. Attempts to correlate such widely separated phenomena have not met with much success. In fact, very little is known of the cyclic history of the Caribbean, apart from the scattered studies of polycyclic landscapes in western Puerto Rico and the Dominican Republic. Geomorphologists would find much in this area to arouse their curiosity.

ENVIRONMENTAL INFLUENCES AND HAZARDS

Although the Caribbean islands may appear to the casual observer 'full of noises, sounds and sweet airs that give delight and hurt not', there are few elements except a benign temperature regime, considerable sunshine and the trade winds in their favour. There are, built into the landscape, certain other elements the more hazardous because they are uncertain in their time, place and degree.

Earthquakes have always been a natural accompaniment to tectonic events such as shaped the islands (Fig. 3.3). Along the borders of the abyssal trenches north of Puerto Rico and south of Cuba, and following the trend lines of the Greater Antillean complex mountains, there is abundant

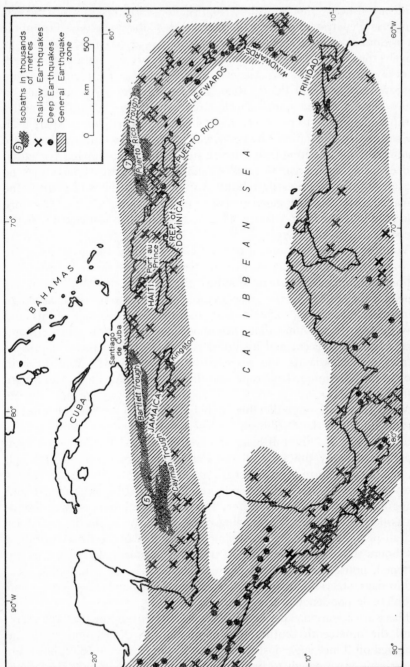

Fig. 3.3 Earthquakes in the Caribbean 1900–60

evidence of heavy shocks, mainly from shallow earthquakes, from the first European penetration of the area. Santiago de Cuba was reduced to rubble on a number of occasions (1678, 1755, 1766, 1932 and 1947), while Port Royal (1692) and Kingston (1907) in Jamaica were virtually destroyed. Shocks are commonly experienced in the passages between Cuba and Hispañola and west of Puerto Rico. The latter island has been shaken on many occasions, and minor shocks are frequent in the Lesser Antilles without giving rise to much comment among the inhabitants. Apart from the severe damage inflicted by occasional large temblors, minor shocks are noteworthy for initiating landslides on steeper slopes, removing vegetation and exposing such areas to rapid erosion. Rural wooden houses may be shaken down, but are easily rebuilt. An unusual Caribbean hazard is the so-called tidal wave or *tsunami* generated by an earthquake whose epicentre is located in the eastern Atlantic. The classic example is associated with the Lisbon earthquake of 1755.

Volcanic activity is confined to the Lesser Antilles, along the inner arc of volcanic islands (Fig. 3.2). Recent chastening experiences of so-called extinct volcanoes elsewhere must induce great caution when Caribbean vulcanism is described. All the present craters are at least dormant, although fumaroles, hot springs, solfataras and other minor phenomena of this kind may be seen in the immediate neighbourhood. There are, furthermore, events from the recent and historical past that confirm the ever-present menace on such islands. The scars left by the eruptions of Mont Pelée in 1902 in the Martinique landscape, and those of Soufrière on St Vincent are still visible today.

More frequent, unpredictable in behaviour, and by far the greatest natural hazard in the Caribbean, are the tropical cyclones known as hurricanes (Fig. 3.4). The full blast of a well-developed hurricane has been experienced many times by all the Caribbean islands except Trinidad, where only one storm of any strength has been recorded in the past thirty-five years (1933). Destructive winds, reaching velocities of 240 km/h and changing direction as the circulatory anticlockwise system passes an island, are associated with heavy damaging rains, which bring floods, landslides and all-pervading mud. All economic activity can be destroyed within a few hours. Cash crops lie broken, trees are uprooted, food gardens are flattened, houses are scattered in fragments across the countryside and, within days, starvation may be followed by infectious plagues, looting and complete despondency in the community.

These are common experiences of the islands during the past 350 years. Until the nineteenth century, the effect, though devastating, could be shrugged off. Once sugar lost its primacy in the Lesser Antilles, however, a hurricane was enough to break the back of a small island's precarious economy. Yet it is remarkable to observe how a community could recover from a violent hurricane within a short period and rehabilitate its cash

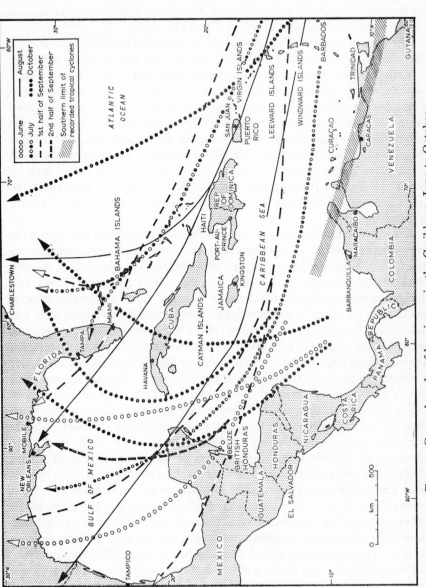

Fig. 3.4 General tracks of hurricanes in the Caribbean, June to October

Legend (map key):

────	August
oooo June	●●●● October
●o●o July	
– – –	1st half of September
●●● ●●●	2nd half of September
/////	Southern limit of recorded tropical cyclones

Map labels:

ATLANTIC OCEAN

BAHAMA ISLANDS

SAN JUAN, VIRGIN ISLANDS, PUERTO RICO

LEEWARD ISLANDS

WINDWARD ISLANDS

BARBADOS

CURAÇAO

TRINIDAD

GUYANA

CHARLESTOWN

MIAMI, TAMPA, FLORIDA, NEW ORLEANS, MOBILE

GULF OF MEXICO

TAMPICO, MEXICO

HAVANA, CUBA, CAYMAN ISLANDS, JAMAICA, KINGSTON

HAITI, PORT-AU-PRINCE, REP. OF DOMINICA

CARIBBEAN SEA

BRITISH HONDURAS, BELIZE, GUATEMALA, EL SALVADOR, HONDURAS, NICARAGUA, COSTA RICA, PANAMA REPUBLIC

DOMINICAN REPUBLIC

COLOMBIA, BARRANQUILLA, MARACAIBO, VENEZUELA, CARACAS

km 0 500

Coordinate labels: 30°N, 90°W, 80°, 70°W, 60°W, 20°, 10°N

crops. The latter are all too often highly vulnerable to high winds, and many changes in agriculture have been effected by substituting another cash crop for those destroyed. By this means the Windward Islands were converted to banana cultivation after Hurricane Janet in 1956.

The normal trade winds that sweep the Caribbean make life bearable for the islanders by providing a cooling breeze and fair sailing conditions. Nonetheless, they produce excessive evaporation and aridity whenever they sweep across the plains and lowlands of Aruba, Antigua, Tobago or Grand Terre in Guadeloupe. Only the presence of high hills and mountains saves the Caribbean from aridity, since these provide the necessary orographic lift to bring high rainfall to the upper slopes, with perennial streams even in the dry season. Even the steady force of a normal trade wind necessitates the building of wind-breaks to protect cash crops such as cocoa and banana from serious physiological damage, and its ability to fan a fire, be it forest, garden or building, is too well known to require comment.

Natural vegetation patterns are also strongly influenced by such wide variations in rainfall and evaporation. On most islands possessing some relief, there would normally occur a series of climax communities ranging from lowland tropical rain-forest, through lower montane forests and deciduous forests adapted to markedly dry seasons, to xerophytic associations. Few of these vegetation types are generally correlated with soil differences. One exception, however, is the limestone landscape, at present in the karstic stage of development. In such areas surface water disappears, leaving a desert-like forest scrub, growing on karstic land forms. The latter are found in northern Cuba, central Jamaica, eastern Hispañola, northern Puerto Rico, Guadeloupe and the Netherlands Leeward Antilles.

For all their manifest physical disadvantages, the Caribbean islands have been inhabited continuously for many centuries. There are today on most islands the remains of once impregnable defences – forts, walls, moats and cannons, all in their heyday appendages of the great empires of Spain, Holland, France and England. Maritime rivalries during the three centuries after Columbus gave them added importance as naval bases safe from enemy fleets. As a result, various islands changed hands at the whim of the treaty-makers, not once but several times, leaving them with a confused succession of cultural, linguistic, religious and imperial influences from Europe. To this must be added the influence of Africa through slavery.

Changing forms and theatres of war have gradually reduced the strategic importance of the Caribbean in the eyes of Europe, but some islands have acquired new status as satellite- or missile-tracking stations, while the Greater Antilles, since the advent of Fidel Castro in Cuba, now represent potential enemy bases to be used not only against the southern flank of the United States, but also against Central and South America.

The types of government that have evolved among the Caribbean islands include cruel despotism, classical Hispanic American oligarchies, the sub-sidized paternalism of a United States protectorate, the well-known British systems of evolutionary colonial governments leading to indepen-dence within a Commonwealth of Nations, and the French and Dutch forms whereby the islands are considered to be part of the metropolitan area, but with a degree of devolution and autonomy. Only the British islands have attempted some form of regional or federal government, and this failed four years after its creation in 1958. Such diverse physical conditions as size and distance, and the varying political institutions that are found today,[1] prohibit any closer association for many years to come. In fact, devolution appears to be the order of the day.

Each of the British islands has in turn sought complete or virtual independence from Britain in favour of free economic association with the Organization of American States or the Central American Common Market; Anguilla, a tiny community, has sought to free itself from its dominant partner, St Kitts and Nevis, while the largest of the group – Cuba – has divorced its economy from that of its closest neighbour, the United States. For the Caribbean islands with their poor resource base, declining soil productivity and rapidly growing populations with few safety valves, independence can only mean individual catastrophe for each community in turn. Although little can be done from the outside to ameliorate such a sorry situation, it is vital to understand the succession of events, influences and geographical factors which brought it about.

PRE-COLUMBIAN OCCUPATION OF THE ISLANDS

Before the arrival of the Europeans there was a considerable aboriginal population of Amerindians, whose numbers, estimated in several hundreds of thousands, were reduced to a tiny fraction within a few years of the ar-rival of the *conquistadores*. Any influence that these communities might have exerted upon European practices was therefore dissipated by genocide and newly introduced diseases (Fig. 3.5). Although much archaeological evidence is now pointing to an earlier pre-Columbian occupation of the islands. Among the first tribes known to have occupied the area were the Ciboney, a group practising a Stone Age culture along the Guaicayarima peninsula in south-western Haiti and throughout the greater part of western Cuba.

The second group of aboriginal peoples, speaking a language known as Arawakan, is thought to have originated in the South American mainland where remnants are found today. These tribes are believed to have migrated from the eastern slopes of the Andes along the Amazon and its

[1] More recently, Caribbean Free Trade Association (CARIFTA) and a Regional bank have been created in order to foster a more flexible Caribbean trading system.

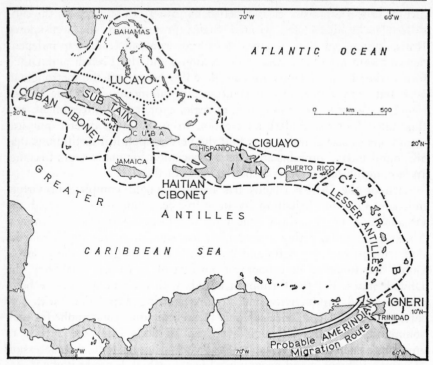

Fig. 3.5 Aboriginal cultures in the Caribbean at contact

tributaries (where they are still fairly numerous), and thereafter along the Orinoco, the coasts of Venezuela, eastern Colombia and Guiana, and finally into the Lesser and Greater Antilles. Some were known to be settling along the Florida Cays during the first stages of Spanish exploration of this area.

The Arawaks were the first people encountered by Columbus and his crew. They possessed a more advanced culture than the Ciboney, with stratified societies and an elaborate religion; they were active farmers and expert fishermen, with some knowledge of metallurgy. Few Arawak-speaking peoples survived the European invasion, although as late as 1900 some 400 Taino were recorded in eastern Cuba.

The third and last of the Caribbean migrations was undertaken by the Cariban-speaking Amerindians, who were moving through the eastern Caribbean arc and into the Greater Antilles contemporaneously with European exploration. The Caribs, some of whom are found today scattered through the Amazon basin, the Guianas, the Caribbean islands of St Lucia, St Vincent and Dominica, and along the eastern lowlands of Central America, also varied very much in racial, ethnic and cultural characteristics, sharing only the Cariban language in common. In the manner of many advancing conquerors, they slew the men among their enemies and carried off the women. In this way the language of the latter (Arawakan) passed to the children, causing seventeenth-century observers to report that the island Caribs spoke only Arawakan with an overlay of Cariban words.

The Caribs were the most mobile of the Amerindian aboriginals. Their long canoes with sails could cover vast distances, so that Puerto Rico, Cuba and Trinidad were never wholly out of reach of these bloodthirsty warriors. Though less agricultural than the Taino, they were skilled in growing and preparing bitter cassava, and could weave and spin the cotton they grew into sails and clothing. Their organization was less formalized, however, than that of the Igneri and Taino. Among early explorers and adventurers the Caribs were notorious for resisting all attempts of the white

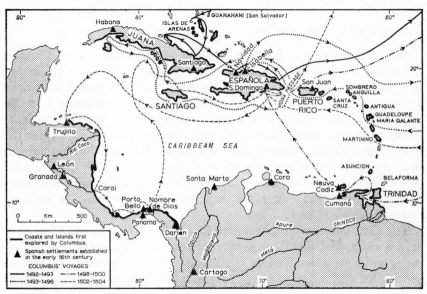

Fig. 3.6 Discovery and early settlement in the Caribbean

man to befriend or enslave them, attacking whenever possible with every intention of destroying all intruders. Many sub-tribes, ruled by 'kings' or chiefs, survived in Trinidad, Tobago and other islands of the Lesser Antilles well into the first half of the eighteenth century, while compact groups in St Lucia, St Vincent and Dominica managed to survive the most vigorous pressures for another seventy-five years. Recent archaeological research in the islands has, however, supported the view that many of the distinguishing characteristics of these Amerindian groups recorded by early chroniclers were unreal and largely a matter of subjective, ethnocentric description.

The voyages undertaken by Christopher Columbus have received considerable attention in the literature of exploration and discovery, and need little elaboration (Fig. 3.6). Between 1492 when he set out on his first voyage, and 1504 when in disgrace and ill health he finally returned to Europe, this hardy sailor had etched the coastlines of the Greater Antilles and the Lesser Antilles. Those who followed him completed the picture by delineating the Gulf of Mexico and filling in the details of the shore of Guiana and Venezuela. These invaders had perforce to man and defend the islands in their rear, not only as naval repair bases, but as reservoirs of manpower for the armies of the *conquistadores*. By so doing they not only founded settlements, but also deliberately evolved a peculiarly Spanish system of colonial administration, land tenure and land usage, in strong contrast to the more casual techniques of the English, French and Dutch who came into the area a century later.

ORGANIZATION OF THE SPANISH ISLANDS

Two objectives were reflected in Spanish forms of settlement. The first lay in the need to defend the windward approaches into the Caribbean Sea. This is demonstrated by the fortress towns that were built at various vital spots – the early landfalls of the sailing ship riding down the trade winds. The great fortress of San Felipé del Morro, together with its associated fortification system enclosing San Juan (Puerto Rico), was the embodiment of the Spanish will to resist all invaders. Furthermore, it protected large forest reserves whose timbers were readily available for ship repairs and shipbuilding, a factor which delayed the full-scale settlement of Puerto Rico for more than 250 years. Havana was similarly fortified as a naval base.

The first Governor of Cuba, Don Diego de Velasquez, was ordered to set up cities, and distribute crown lands to the first colonizers. Seven major cities were founded in the island. Each was granted an area of jurisdiction only vaguely defined at the time and was laid out according to a plan recommended from Spain, with a centre (plaza), a market place, sites for public buildings and building lots for houses. Round the city a strip of land was reserved for common use by all citizens. Beyond this were distributed the larger rural holdings known as *mercedes*. Once established, the councils of each city (*cabildos*) took upon themselves the right to grant these lands from as early as 1536, and only abandoned the privilege when forced to do so by a *cédula* of 23 November 1729.

Apart from necessary food crops, such land was used principally for stock-raising of all kinds, particularly of cattle to supply salt beef for ships and the city, and horses to supply remounts for the armies of the *conquistadores* in Mexico. Consequently, there were few permanent settlers on the island during the next fifty years, and much of Cuba's land remained unoccupied and unalienated, as the island was primarily a staging post for those proceeding to the mainland.

The Cuban system of land tenure during the next two centuries evolved from the Spanish refusal to allow more than a minimal decentralization or delegation of authority. It had clearly been the intention of the Spanish Crown at the beginning of the great westward surge into the Americas to curb the personal ambitions of its captains-general and *conquistadores* who, using the *encomienda* and *repartimiento*, had hoped to enslave the aboriginal peoples and carve out great empires for themselves. The patterns laid upon the landscape of Cuba by the *merced* and its successor, the polygonal holding, persisted for nearly 300 years, until new forms of land utilization drove it from the contemporary scene.

EARLY ENGLISH SETTLEMENTS

The highly sophisticated Spanish systems of colonization and land development were in no wise imitated by the earliest settlers from England, France and Holland who sailed for the Lesser Antilles to take up their forms of colonial life. What particularly distinguishes the English method of colonization is its quite haphazard approach. The Proprietary System, evolving in the royal courts of sixteenth- and seventeenth-century England (120 years after the Spanish had made their first permanent settlements in the western hemisphere), consisted in the granting, by royal favour, of blocks of overseas territory to groups of wealthy, influential persons, intent on making vast fortunes from these lands. In this way Barbados and St Christopher's in 1625 became the sole property of James Hay, the Earl of Carlisle, against strong opposition from the Earl of Pembroke. Jamaica, despite its prior occupation in 1512 by the Spaniards, was similarly exploited under the Proprietary System.

Colonization in these 'English' West Indian islands was thus partly conditioned by earlier experience gained along the eastern Atlantic seaboard of North America and in the Guianas. Clearing the forest, building houses and forts, planting various crops and coming to terms with the aboriginal communities were generally first priorities in these areas. Absence of any form of freehold tenure under such proprietary patents, and even of the most elementary surveys, permitted a chaotic pioneer frontier to move gradually westward into the interior. Tobacco and cotton planted on small cleared patches of virgin soil added further to the disordered nature of the settlement. Accordingly, those who led their parties ashore at St Christopher's in 1624 and Barbados in 1627 were men familiar with such empirical techniques, which they could apply immediately.

In the end, all Caribbean islands with their widely varying forms of settlement and exploitation fell under the domination of the sugar monoculture. Three phases may be discerned:

(*a*) The early period 1638–1763, when St Kitts, Barbados, Jamaica,

Guadeloupe and Martinique received the sugar cane, grew it on small-holdings and began the process of consolidation of holdings essential to greater efficiency of land and slave labour.

(*b*) The middle period 1763–1870, during which the Ceded Islands, Tobago, Grenada, the Grenadines, St Vincent and Dominica, together with Martinique, Guadeloupe, Antigua and St Kitts, grew a major part of Europe's sugar requirements in virgin soils. This was the period of highest slave importation, leading to the protracted struggle for abolition, planto-cracy's period of greatest affluence, followed by technical innovations in

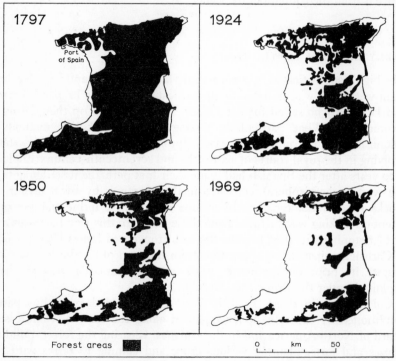

Fig. 3.7 The clearance of forest on Trinidad

sugar manufacture, which placed most absentee landlords in the bank-ruptcy courts.

(*c*) The modern period 1870–1965, during which Cuba, Jamaica, Trinidad, Puerto Rico and the Dominican Republic were subjected to massive capital investment, land purchase and consolidation, centralization of mills and factories and cartelization without the ability yet to mechanize growing and harvesting techniques.

Few remains of the early period are still to be seen in the cultural landscape, except the rare ruins of an old building. It is the middle period that has contributed so much to the relict Caribbean landscape. On every island the successive techniques of sugar manufacture are demonstrated by abandoned windmills, water wheels and steam boilers and the great plantation houses sited on high points to catch the breeze, with the slave barracks below them. Some such houses are encountered in remote areas seldom visited today. On some islands, such as Barbados and Martinique, the fields survive almost in their original shapes of two centuries ago, together with their cane 'banks' discernible still in aerial photographs. It is difficult on the other hand to discern such patterns in many parts of Haiti, Jamaica or Puerto Rico where population has overwhelmed field boundaries. The effects of changing economic circumstances are reflected in the gradual reduction of the forest cover on many of the islands (Fig. 3.7).

By contrast, the modern *central* or factory of Trinidad, Puerto Rico, Cuba or the Dominican Republic, each with its highly organized transport system, its bulk loading warehouse, its *bagasse* and paper mills alongside, represents the only possible way of staving off major competition from the sugar beet. Most of the smaller islands, such as Tobago, St Vincent, St Lucia, Dominica, Montserrat and Nevis, have abandoned sugar plantations during the past fifty years, but their landscapes continue to remind the observer of the crop that made so many wealthy.

The presence of African Negroes is an even stronger reminder that labour for the canefields came not from an indigenous people but from a continent that yielded up to 10 million souls to the western hemisphere. Once Great Britain had in 1807 followed Denmark's example in abolishing the slave trade, the lot of the slave in the West Indies began to improve. He became a valuable commodity not easily replaced except through his progeny. Emancipation in the British colonies in 1834, followed by four years of apprenticeship, was regarded by many as the ideal solution to this problem.

Within the British islands, the Apprenticeship Act, creating in essence a four-year labour contract between ex-slave and master, failed almost without exception. From Jamaica to Trinidad, most freed slaves abandoned their plantations for an independent subsistence life, often as far from their ex-owners as possible. Only in Antigua could it be said that the population passed from slavery to wage-labour without much difficulty.

Although many plantations were inactive by 1834 as a result of bankruptcy, natural disasters or neglect, there was usually a manager or attorney to maintain the owner's authority. His principal task in the years following emancipation was to prevent squatting by ex-slaves on the best plantation lands. Instead, plots were offered for sale on the marginal fringes, usually steeply sloped and useless for sugar cultivation. Where no authority existed to prevent them, ex-slaves set up villages in remote areas, sometimes grouping their houses about a church. In many instances Moravian missionaries were the guiding lights in such settlements, and their names duly reflect this fact. From such villages men went out to grow sugar, corn, roots and tropical vegetables on the steep slopes of the local hillside. An examination of remote villages in West Indian islands shows that people were not forced to seek such isolation. Usually they chose it. The consequences for the West Indies are manifest. In all but a few instances, land title deeds did not exist for such holdings until a few years ago. As a result, the process of inheritance was resolved by customary tenure. Litigation among heirs was, and continues to be, commonplace, exacerbated by the absence, through emigration, of the beneficiaries. Although it was possible in the early years to derive enough food from the soil, lack of conservation, loss of topsoil and many other factors reduced productivity to the minimal level that is encountered today. It is not difficult to visualize the consequences – malnutrition, out-migration to the plantation life again, or to town.

The gap left in plantation life by emancipation was serious enough to reduce many to total bankruptcy. Where it was possible, metayage (share-cropping) was introduced by local managers and owners, and lands, exhausted after a century of exploitation, went further downhill under the system, which persisted on islands such as Tobago into the twentieth century.

Others searched the Caribbean for labour – from Barbados, Grenada and Antigua – with enough success to indicate the likelihood of greater inter-island mobility in the future. Finally in 1838 manual labour was sought in India, from where some 300,000 indentured labourers were obtained, specifically for Trinidad. The consequences of this move, as elsewhere in the world, are only now being felt in demographic and there-fore political terms. Trinidad's Indian population is gradually acquiring parity with its Negro population, and is likely to make its presence felt just as sharply as in Guyana.

POPULATION AND DEMOGRAPHIC CHANGES

There are today probably nearly 20 million people living in the Caribbean islands, which comprise some 250,000 km². The three territories of Cuba, Haiti and the Dominican Republic, with 85 per cent of the total area, contained in 1967 between 12 and 13 million of them. The remaining 7 to 8 million were distributed among the many islands and islets that ring the Caribbean Sea (Table 3.1).

Except for the more obvious cases it would be difficult to break down the total population into categories by race or colour. In the Hispanic and Dutch islands many more white persons are found than Negro. In the British and Francophone islands, Negro populations predominate and probably less than 5 per cent of these populations would be considered white. In all the islands, however, there is abundant evidence of consider-able intermixture, giving rise to so-called mulatto or creole communities of various shades.

TABLE 3.1 *Population characteristics of the Caribbean Islands, 1964*

	Est. pop. mid-1964	Last census total	Rural total	Census year	Land area (km²)	Population density		Av. ann. rate of change %	Crude BR	Crude DR	Crude repro. rate ('61)	Infant deaths per 1,000 live births
						Total	Rural					
Dominican Republic	3,454	3,013	2,104	1960	48,442	62	46	+3·5	41·3	13·7	27·6	79·5 ('62)
Netherlands Antilles	205	189	32	1960	950	199	34	+3·3	29·2	4·8	24·4	15·7 ('64)
Trinidad and Tobago	950	828	511	1960	5,128	161	100	+2·8	34·5	6·3	28·2	42·2 ('63)
Haiti	4,551	3,097	2,755	1950	26,895	115	103	+2·8	44·4	21·6	22·8	N/A
Guadeloupe and dependencies	306	282	176	1961	1,994	141	88	+2·8	34·0	7·6	26·4	36·7 ('64)
Martinique	310	289	162	1961	1,096	264	147	+2·7	33·9	8·1	25·8	38·1 ('64)
Virgin Islands	41	32	12	1960	344	93	35	+2·2	38·1	9·6	28·5	Br. 66·7 U.S. 28·4 ('64)
Bahama Islands	133	85	39	1953	11,405	7	3	+2·1	31·8	7·9	23·9 ('62)	41·8
Cuba	7,336	5,829	2,863	1953	114,524	51	25	+1·9	33·8	7·1	26·7	37·7 ('64)
Windward Islands	336	315	232	1960	2,282	138	102	+1·6	40·7	10·3	30·4	58·1 av.
Jamaica	1,728	1,609	1,093	1960	11,425	141	96	+1·5	40·1	7·7	32·4	36·7
Cayman Islands	9	9	6	1960	282	30	21	+1·4	31·7	6·6	25·1	39·7 ('61)
Barbados	242	232	128	1960	419	555	305	+1·3	26·9	8·8	18·1	39·5
Leeward Islands	145	131	89	1960	1,074	122	83	+1·3	31·6	9·4	22·2	51·6 av.
Puerto Rico	2,572	2,350	1,356	1960	8,862	265	153	+0·6	30·3	7·7	32·4	42·0
Turks and Caicos Islands	6	6	6	1960	430	13	13	-0·5	36·8	11·4	25·4	100·8 ('63)
					235,552							

Differentiation of the islands' populations in terms of race is important only because it serves to distinguish certain marked demographic differences that emerge between one island and another. Experts assert that the 'British' islands owe their generally low growth-rate to the various facets of Negro slavery and what it implied in terms of reproductive capacity. Cuba and Puerto Rico, largely Spanish in origin, showed growth-rates that increased five- or sixfold between 1844 and 1955, whereas the British islands only showed a fourfold increase.

The most pathetic assemblages by race in the modern Caribbean are those who, by rejecting contact with Negro communities, maintained their 'whiteness' in isolation through exclusive inbreeding. Many of these groups have a long lineage and can boast that their remote ancestors were among the first white men in the area. Thus the 'Redlegs' of Barbados, Grenada and St Kitts are still found today in scattered communities, sadly degenerate, living in poverty, degraded in intelligence and wits, without prospect of improvement except where a bolder member breaks away to marry 'outside', often to his and his children's great advantage. There are many such relict communities – the fishing folk of Petit Martinique, the Dutch farmers of Saba and St Maarten, the French on St Thomas, the English of the Grand Caymans, and the German peasants of Seaford, Jamaica.

Marked changes in individual patterns of growth are also noteworthy where there was immigration of alien groups such as the East Indian indentured labourers. These increased their numbers very rapidly because the laws covering their entry to Trinidad insisted that women should be included in the parties of new arrivals. That this was not always possible is reflected in the marked sex-ratio imbalance to be seen on occasion, but for Trinidad it brought about a tenfold expansion in total population between 1844 and 1955. The gap between East Indian and Negro is thus rapidly narrowing.

Immigration on a massive scale from the Mediterranean countries of Europe (particularly Spain) has also been responsible for the continued predominance of white people in Cuba and Puerto Rico. Whereas Cuba in 1841 had some 590,000 Negroes and 420,000 whites, it had 1·4 million whites in 1907, 3·55 million in 1943 and an estimated 6·5 million in 1965 (out of a total of 7·88 million). Similarly Puerto Rico, with only a slight fraction of its present population being of Negro origin, has shown a remarkable capacity for demographic growth.

Generally, the Caribbean island populations have increased according to the conventional demographic processes. They have reacted quickly to health and sanitary measures, which were introduced by the United States into the areas they took over at the end of the nineteenth century, and by the British and French colonial authorities in the twentieth century. Malaria and yellow fever and other diseases were reduced well below danger level, with consequent beneficial effects on infant mortality, death-rates and, in some instances, the birth-rate.

Though food intake is considerably higher than in most underdeveloped countries of the world, malnutrition remains everywhere a barrier to totally healthy Caribbean populations. Furthermore, the ever-present risk of resurgent diseases in such densely populated islands is very great. The pernicious spread of dengue fever in rural Puerto Rico is indeed serious, as are the occasional outbreaks of malaria in islands that disregard preventive programmes. After Hurricane Flora in 1963, Tobago, considered to be free of malaria, suffered a number of fatal casualties as a result of careless mosquito controls. Water-borne schistosomiasis has also been allowed to spread from one island to another.

DISTRIBUTION OF POPULATION

Any map of settlement, however inadequate, shows that most islands have a widely scattered distribution pattern not always easily explained. Such patterns may generally be classified as follows:

(a) Along spurs and ridges in the interior, above the oppressive heat of the deep valleys also associated with malarial infection.

(b) Along the sea coast, strung out in long discontinuous settlements.

(c) In nucleated villages well away from old plantations.

(d) Near or on plantation lands and sugar factories.

(e) In towns, varying considerably in size and function.

URBANIZATION

In the islands as elsewhere in the world, it is the town that has attracted large segments of the population in the twentieth century. No Caribbean island is without is primate city. Usually sited on the leeward coast, safe from the brisk trade winds and the full force of the hurricane, the city nestles snugly along the shores of a deep indented bay, protected on either side by steeply sloping hillsides. In the days of sailing ships these were ideal places for a port or anchorage for unloading cargoes and loading sugar, rum and spices and where men-of-war could lie unseen by enemy squadrons at sea. The commanding hills above were generally occupied by forts and gunsites in case the enemy came too close. Much of the central part of such a town, usually the island's capital, was occupied by government offices.

It is apparent to the observer that such primate cities or capital towns suffer considerable disadvantages in the twentieth century. Growth in the capital automatically means greater concentration on the coastal flats. Expansion of the city core is possible thereafter only by an uphill climb or a series of paternoster satellites along the coast. Industry must find its way to alluvial flats well outside the town and international airports are perforce located at great distances from the city, usually reached only after a long taxi drive across the mountain divide. Thus the capital cities of Tobago (Scarborough), Grenada (St Georges), St Vincent (Kingstown), St Lucia (Castries) and Dominica (Roseau) are today confined by historical circumstances. Even the secondary towns established two centuries ago to provide an outport maintain contact with the capital by sea rather than by time-consuming unreliable roads carved out of steep coastal hillsides. In most of the islands it is quite apparent that new capitals or primate cities should be established in order to meet the requirements of a modern city, including accessibility, the opportunity to expand and the ability to absorb a burgeoning population.

The many towns of the Hispanic Caribbean were deliberately created on the assumption that landscapes were merely an extension of Spain. Because each town is fixed in its position by historical circumstances, many of the natural changes that should have occurred were inhibited. What saved them was the capital design embodied in the original plans, allowing for continuous outward expansion and growth.

Regardless of their origins, all Caribbean towns and cities have suffered the common fate of the world's urban areas – growth, industrial expansion, unrestricted immigration, shanty towns and, ultimately, submergence beneath a flood of humanity. Little is known of the structural changes that occurred in the earlier periods of urban growth in the islands. Most of the coastal port cities remained static after they had been established, wharfside and warehouse giving way to government offices, shops and trading houses. Such towns were not desirable areas for residence, except in the Hispanic islands where most of the original settlers were townsmen from Spain adapting themselves very quickly to tropical conditions.

Largely built of timber, most Caribbean towns suffered periodic fires, which swept through street after street. Until recent years no attempt was made to reduce such risks. Even a destructive earthquake in 1907 was not enough to re-create Kingston, Jamaica, although valiant attempts were made to carry through a commendable 'town plan'. Such plans exist in every island today, but there are few signs that much has been or can be accomplished in the way of modifying the haphazard patterns of historical growth. Castries (St Lucia), seen from above, is divided into two major sections, the old and the new. Only financial aid from the British government following devastating fires in 1948 and 1949 made a rebuilding programme possible.

It would also be difficult to say at what stage urbanization as a demographic process began to make itself felt. The early town life of most Caribbean islands revolved around the slave market, the trading shops and the port. Emancipation brought few changes, because ex-slaves opted for isolation and moved as far away from the town as possible into small

TABLE 3.2 *Growth in population of Cuban cities, 1899–1964*

	Province	*1899*	*1919*	*1943*	*1953*	*1964*
Havana (metropolitan)	Havana	247,000	408,700	868,400	1,139,500	1,517,700
Santiago de Cuba	Oriente	43,000	62,000	118,200	189,200	231,000
Camaguey (Puerto Principe)	Camaguey	25,000	42,000	80,500	129,500	153,100
Guantanamo	Oriente	7,100	14,800	42,400	76,700	122,400
Santa Clara	Las Villas	13,800	21,700	53,900	83,200	120,600
Cienfuegos	Las Villas	30,000	37,300	52,900	62,700	78,700
Manzanillo	Oriente	14,500	22,300	46,300	51,100	78,000
Holguin	Oricate	6,000	13,800	35,900	68,300	77,700
Matanzas	Matanzas	34,400	41,600	54,800	72,900	75,500
Pinar del Río	Pinar del Rio	8,900	13,800	26,200	43,000	66,700
Cardenas	Matanzas	22,000	27,500	37,000	41,200	57,200
Sancti Spiritus	Las Villas	12,700	23,600	28,200	44,900	55,400
Ciego de Avila	Camaguey	3,000	16,400	23,800	40,700	51,000

villages, which in themselves were but nucleations of subsistence farmers. During the nineteenth century there was little in the town to interest most Caribbean peoples, except the port, which offered the chance to emigrate from one island to another, to the United States, South America or Panama. Urbanization is thus a twentieth-century phenomenon, and its motivation is as little documented with certainty as similar movements in the rest of the world.

Disillusionment with 'peasant' farming, rural isolation and sheer poverty on the one hand, combined with the lure of bright lights and the possibilities of some kind of industrial work on the other – the so-called 'push-pull' effects mentioned by Clarke (1964) – all these are sufficient to explain the rapid depopulation that has occurred on every Caribbean island, from the largest to the smallest. Cuba, well endowed with towns and cities, best illustrates the trend (Table 3.2).

Whereas, in 1931, 44 per cent of the island's population was to be found in urban concentrations of 2000 people and more, this had increased in 1953 to 51·4 per cent, and to 58 per cent in 1963. At present, some 60 per cent of the Cuban population is considered to be urban. In 1963 there were twenty-six towns with more than 20,000 inhabitants. Towns of 10,000 to 20,000 in size increased in number from thirteen in 1931 to nineteen in 1953. The primate city, Havana, contains about 23 per cent of the island's population, having grown from 50,000 in 1763 to 247,000 in 1900, and to a little under 2 million today (1968). In terms of water supplies alone, such a flow of humanity conjures up serious difficulties for both national and local governments.

Similar urban patterns may be observed in most of the remaining islands. The population of Kingston, Jamaica, the largest city of the British Caribbean, has increased by at least 90 per cent since 1943. Some 25 per cent of the island's people now live in the capital. All the usual symptoms of rapid growth are present in this city whose present-day layout reflects the half-completed plans for its reconstruction after the 1907 earthquake. Its central business district is sadly cramped and quite inadequate, while at its western end a vast shanty town has mushroomed over many hundreds of square kilometres of valuable industrial-commercial land. Despite a remarkable public and private building programme in new suburbs and residential estates, there seems little prospect of stemming the tide of rural immigrants who take over shacks abandoned by those moving to a new house. Such rural folk account for about 50 per cent of the city's growth, the other 50 per cent being attributable to natural growth.

Since 1943 there has also been an increase in the number of Jamaican settlements with more than 1000 inhabitants, from nineteen to thirty-six, reflecting once more the marked shift of population from rural areas into nucleated communities. In some instances such moves have resulted from deliberate governmental planning or from growth based on industry and mineral extraction. Urban areas in Jamaica are growing at the cost of the rural economy and, in the present state of industrialization in towns such as Kingston, there is little prospect of absorbing more than a small fraction of the immigrants – a feature that characterizes all Latin America.

Despite its remarkable growth, Trinidad does not suffer from over-population. Sugar and petroleum provided an early outlet for surplus labour, while farming land was available for all who sought it. Nonetheless, the island's larger towns, Port of Spain, San Fernando and Arima, have all increased their populations rapidly enough to suggest that incoming rural migrants are responsible for a large proportion of the urban growth. Since Tobago is a ward of Trinidad, there was also for many years a con-siderable flow of Negro families from this island 'paradise' to the oilfields, United States military bases and the factories. As a consequence there are now more Tobagonians in Trinidad than in Tobago itself.

A racial imbalance is also created by the fact that the East Indian section of the community is stabilized in its small towns and villages close to the flat ricefields, sugarlands and horticultural lots, resulting in the virtual exclusion of most Negroes, who fail to meet the high farming standards of the East Indian smallholder. With plantation or estate labour as his only alternative, the Negro Trinidadian prefers the uncertainty of urban poverty to rural helotry, and soon becomes a landless migrant in Port of Spain.

Apart from several persistent patches of shanty town on the outskirts, Port of Spain has not suffered the indignities of overcrowding, mainly because its Hispanic ancestry provided the original, generously laid-out open expanses that exist today. Furthermore, residential and industrial expansion has taken place eastward along the foot of the northern range, creating a coalescing, linear conurbation of smaller towns. San Fernando has found expansion possible along the central ridge of the island. Gen-erally speaking, careful planning, adequate water and energy supplies, together with a fair degree of industrialization, have made Trinidad's problems seem slight compared with those of other Caribbean cities.

Similarly, such towns as Willemstad in Curaçao and Orangestad in Aruba appear to be tropical copies of small seaports in Holland, under complete planning control and developing in an orderly fashion, which belies their phenomenal expansion in recent years.

Few people on the other hand care to define the geographical limits of Bridgetown, Barbados. With an estimated population of 142,000 out of a total island population of 248,000, its widespread network of roads, houses and schools dominates the part of the landscape that is not taken up by sugar cane. The observer can merely reflect upon a contradictory situation by comparing the astonishing degree of overcrowding with the obvious socio-political stability of the island.

Of all Caribbean cities, none is more remarkable for its growth rate than

San Juan, Puerto Rico. Neglected by the Spanish authorities until the late nineteenth century, it retained within its defensive walls a small community of some 35,000 (1900). United States intervention in 1897 brought few changes to the city itself, although along the banks of the rivers and lagoons to the south the first of the shack-dwellers began to congregate. The Puerto Rican sugar industry tied most rural workers to the land during much of the first half of the century, and only with internal, political and social change did rural depopulation begin.

For a variety of reasons, San Juan was by 1950 one of the fastest growing cities in the Caribbean. Its primacy on the island was undisputed. Its boundaries expanded rapidly, absorbing many neighbouring suburbs and small towns (e.g. Bayamon, Río Piedras) until metropolitan San Juan occupied some 445 km² with a population in 1968 of 700,000, representing 38 per cent of the island's inhabitants. It is possible that this conurbation will extend as far as Caguas, some 40 km south, by 1975. An astounding industrial expansion and tourist trade, a steady rise in living standards, and immigration, have all led to a characteristically North American suburban sprawl, which has enveloped large areas of old wooden houses and shanties in the low-lying parts of the city itself. These are occupied by families who earn fair incomes, but seem content to remain with such communities. If vacated and left standing, these shacks are immediately occupied by incoming rural migrants.

There are several other cities in the island, of which Poncé on the southern coast is second in rank. A decision has been made to divert industry and port facilities to this very attractive town in order to remove unhealthy pressures on San Juan. Most other towns, scattered across the island, are today little affected by the rural immigrants who once used them as a temporary staging post on their way to San Juan or New York. Most of these prefer nowadays to make the journey directly, even by-passing the capital. Such towns, with market and transport functions, have been stimulated by 'Operation Bootstrap' factories, but most are in relative decline. Even Mayaguez on the west coast, ranking third in size, has not attracted very many rural people but remains an isolated university town with a small number of industries.

MIGRATION

Total destruction of the Amerindian tribes of the Caribbean islands meant that all succeeding populations were immigrants – from Europe, North America and Asia on the one hand and from Africa on the other. The former came voluntarily while the latter were imported as slaves. From the earliest period of settlement onward, European colonists exercised great mobility. For most sixteenth- and seventeenth-century Spanish immigrants, the three Hispanic islands were but staging points on the way to the Central American mainland, and permanent settlements were sparsely populated until the eighteenth century.

Under the Proprietary Patents of the seventeenth century, British islands such as Barbados and St Kitts attracted freemen and indentured servants from England in large numbers, but, with the growth of the sugar plantation system and consequent consolidation of land, some 30,000 white smallholders left Barbados for North America or other English islands. They moved to any island that was advertising vacant land. Thus St Kitts became the focus of attention in 1714, while the British Ceded Islands attracted so many men away from the large estates in Jamaica and Antigua between 1764 and 1775 that complaints were registered in the British parliament by the plantocracy. Similarly, Frenchmen moved between islands such as St Kitts, Martinique, Guadeloupe and Grenada, though barred from English islands until 1763 if they were Catholics. In an attempt to win over the French Catholic populations of Grenada, St Vincent and Dominica, the English government, by the Treaty of Paris in 1763, adopted a policy of religious toleration in these islands.

European wars occasionally impinged upon this inter-island migration, when whole populations were suddenly transferred by treaty to a rival nation. Evacuation programmes seldom lasted long enough before the onset of another war and in the latter part of the eighteenth century the Lesser Antillean islands switched loyalties on a number of occasions, so that the local communities learned to ignore these external pressures.

European emigration to the Caribbean declined sharply in the early years of the nineteenth century when sugar cane farming ceased to yield quick profits, slaves became expensive and English colonies in other parts of the world were beginning to attract potential settlers. White populations in the British islands, already static, fell away sharply in the nineteenth and twentieth centuries. Those who remain today are traders, shipping agents, bankers, government officials and some retired people, together with a group of plantation-owners fighting a rearguard battle against rising production costs.

The Hispanic islands, in strong contrast, received their major population boost throughout the nineteenth century, principally from the mother country and the Mediterranean fringe. Cuba, the Dominican Republic and Puerto Rico therefore surged ahead of their Negro populations and are today dominantly European. The Dominican Republic has since 1938 encouraged colonization of its western frontier by central European Jewish refugees, Hungarians and Japanese.

Cuba, the largest of the Caribbean islands, presents an excellent example of the variety of influences that affected population growth. In the closing years of the eighteenth century and the beginning of the nineteenth the island was in an excellent position to receive any immigrants who cared to come. Thus, 30,000 persons made their way from Santo Domingo as a result of the instability following the Negro insurrection there. Large numbers of Spanish people also left New Orleans when Louisiana was transferred to France in 1803.

Recognizing the need for increased European immigration, the Spanish government in 1817 issued a decree encouraging foreigners to own land in Cuba. Steps were taken to provide transport costs and a monthly stipend for six months for anyone wishing to settle in newly founded towns in Cuba. Cienfuegos was thus established in 1819 on the basis of a French immigrant group. The towns of Nuevitas, Guantanamo, Nipe Banes and Santo Domingo were all founded about this time. Cuba was also fortunate in its ability to accept a considerable influx of Spanish-speaking peoples from the South American mainland, fleeing from the consequences of the numerous independence movements that were sweeping the continent.

On the other hand, the slave trade, largely concentrated on Cuba in the first half of the nineteenth century, resulted in an influx of some 387,000 Negro slaves between 1800 and 1865, despite the abolition laws introduced by the Spanish government in 1845. These regulations sought also to encourage the migration of a non-Negro population to reduce the effects of so large a Negro influx. Yucatán Indians were deliberately invited to take up residence in Cuba and a campaign to encourage Chinese to enter the island resulted in a total influx between 1847 and 1860 of some 48,000 Chinese immigrants (excluding about 8000 who died en route). This campaign was brought to a halt in 1860 by Governor Francisco Serrano, in view of the rapid local population growth, and only a sporadic trickle of Spaniards was allowed during the next forty years.

The War of Independence and United States intervention changed the Cuban situation once again. Friction between Spain and Cuba was abated, resulting in an increased migration of Spaniards from Spain and the Canary Islands during the following thirty years (Table 3.3). In fact, between 1900 and 1919, 60 per cent of all immigrants were Spanish.

TABLE 3.3   *Immigrations into Cuba, 1902–1919*

Europe		America	
Spain	436,005	Jamaica	50,368
Denmark	6,372	Haiti	39,906
France	3,213	U.S.A.	44,054
Turkey	1,219	Antilles (non-Spanish)	24,976
England	1,013	Mexico	19,621
Germany	636	Puerto Rico	13,631
Italy	760	Central America	4,240
Portugal	108	Panama	4,154
Other countries	838	Other countries	7,420
	450,164		208,370

Chinese immigration was reduced to insignificance. In all, some 1,260,000 immigrants entered Cuba between 1902 and 1931.

In the ten years after the First World War the sugar companies, anxious to find cheap labour for their fields, sought Jamaican, Haitian and Lesser Antillean labourers from islands only too eager to shed surplus population. This trend continued until 1959 specifically among Haitians, some 15,000 of whom were trapped in the island after the Socialist Revolution. In 1933, however, as a result of the world depression, a fall in sugar prices, and the so-called '50 per cent Law' requiring at least half of any pay-roll to be Cuban, the great period of Cuban immigration came to an end. West Indian Negro labourers from neighbouring islands returned home and many Spanish families sailed back to Spain or migrated further afield to Venezuela or the United States.

Movement to and from the United States was a comparatively simple matter throughout the next twenty-five years, but, with the Socialist Revolution of 1959, migrants became refugees who by various means had fled in search of freedom. By 1968 at least 350,000 Cubans had found clandestine or official haven in Miami, from which they have been deliberately dispersed to every corner of the United States in order to avoid too great a concentration of a national group.

No more dramatic instance of the influence of migration upon a socioeconomic situation exists than that of modern Puerto Rico. This island, dominated by sugar cane, was about to receive substantial devolution from Spain in 1897, when it was seized by force of arms and became a United States territory. The only important consequence of this event in the evolution of the Commonwealth of Puerto Rico lies in the fact that the island became part of the domestic United States, permitting free movement of peoples to the mainland. Puerto Rican migrant farm workers who played an important role in the harvesting of various crops in all parts of the United States, were able to move freely about the country, and increasing shortages of labour in the service and textile industries of New York enabled them to take up permanent urban employment there in the late 1930s (Table 3.4). Without this safety valve, Puerto Rico would long since have had to face a population explosion.

Benefiting from United States health services and improvement of local conditions, the island saw its infant mortality-rate fall remarkably, its death-rate decline and its life expectation rise to a value close to that of New York within the brief space of twenty years. 'Operation Bootstrap', a programme designed to industrialize the island, was only able to maintain the unemployment rate at 14 to 18 per cent between 1952 and 1966. Exporting large fractions of its population to New York and other United States cities over the same period prevented a serious socio-economic crisis. Improved education facilities in the island, together with social security pensions provided for workers by the United States, have brought about a

TABLE 3.4   *Net migration from Puerto Rico to United States, 1939–1963*

1939	3,035	1952	59,103
1940	−425	1953	69,124
1941	643	1954	21,531
1942	1,679	1955	45,464
1943	3,204	1956	52,315
1944	11,201	1957	37,704
1945	13,573	1958	27,690
1946	39,311	1959	29,989
1947	24,551	1960	16,298
1948	32,775	1961	−1,754
1949	25,698	1962	11,664
1950	34,703	1963	−5,479
1951	52,899		

Minus sign indicates net outflow from mainland to Puerto Rico.

reverse flow of immigration among both the older generation and the young people, sufficiently large in 1963 to cause a small net immigration into the island. The outward movement of young adults nonetheless goes on, providing valuable technical experience for those who will eventually return. Despite continuous industrial programmes designed to absorb the natural population increase and the incoming rural immigrants, it would appear that accelerated emigration to the United States must continue for many years to come.

In the British islands of the Caribbean the emancipation of slaves in 1838 produced an immediate cry for plantation labour. Before the authorities resorted to East Indian indentured labour there was a widespread attempt to import labour from one island to another. Colonial records contain many references to negotiations between governors bent on importing the 'best' type of labour. This process went on well into the second half of the twentieth century among plantation-owners who sought Grenadians above all others as overseers on their estates. Barbadians, who in the first half of the nineteenth century were regarded as scoundrels and thieves when exported to other islands, have since developed a reputation as the finest engineers, agricultural officers and economic planners throughout the British Caribbean, and the most reliable bus drivers and conductors in the London Transport Authority.

Unwillingness on the part of Negro West Indians to enter plantation life as paid labourers led directly to the introduction of East Indian labourers to the Caribbean. Between 1838 and 1917 many thousands of these indentured men, and their families, came to British Guiana, Trinidad, Jamaica, the Lesser Antilles and the French islands. Their effect was demographically significant in British Guiana and Trinidad only (Table 3.5).

TABLE 3.5 *Introduction of indentured East Indians into the Caribbean islands*
1838–1917

Trinidad	143,900	St Lucia	4,400
Guadeloupe and Martinique	78,600	St Vincent	2,500
Jamaica	36,400	St Croix	351
Grenada	5,900	St Kitts	300

Another source of indentured labour was found among liberated Africans freed from captured slavers in the Atlantic Ocean. These men, unable to return to their homeland, were set ashore in Sierra Leone and St Helena and then dispatched to the West Indies as paid workers for a period of three years followed by a grant of free land (Table 3.6).

The scheme freed the British government from embarrassment, but failed to increase the labour supplies of the West Indian islands to any marked degree. The only probable effect was to revive many African rituals and practices among West Indians who had long since forgotten them after generations of slavery and contact with European cultures. The plea is still heard today from plantation-owners and agricultural officials who yearn to introduce labour from other areas, reflecting the West Indian Negro's complete lack of interest in this sector of tropical economy. It is not unusual today to find temporary immigrants from St Lucia cutting the cane harvest in St Kitts, in spite of this island's abundant and under-employed labour force.

TABLE 3.6 *Released African slaves indentured in the British West Indies*
1849–1853

Jamaica	10,000	St Lucia	730
Trinidad	8,390	Tobago	650
Grenada	1,540	St Kitts	460
St Vincent	1,040		

Although West Indian ex-slaves rejected the indignities of the plantation, they were quick to accept the idea of manual labour in other parts of the Caribbean. During eight years of canal construction in the isthmus of Panama from 1881 to 1888, the French employed 25,000 workers from Jamaica alone, despite high mortality-rates on the site. Most returned home to their island when the French company gave up for lack of funds. A second phase of Jamaican and Barbadian migrations occurred between 1905 and 1913, when the United States took up this abandoned project once more. Some 35,000 Jamaican workers were always present, though individuals constantly replaced themselves with relatives from Jamaica.

The Canal Zone remained a popular work place for many West Indians as late as the Second World War. Consequently there are today in this territory some 65,000 West Indians who keep their British citizenship.

As early as 1887 Latin American countries such as Colombia, Nicaragua, Honduras, Guatemala and Costa Rica used Jamaicans and Barbadians for their vast banana and sugar plantations, until political pressures insisted on their exclusion in favour of local labour. Cuba and Haiti also accepted Jamaican labourers.

The opening of the Venezuelan oilfields in 1916, inaccessible across the shallows of the Gulf of Maracaibo to all but small tankers, resulted in the establishment of off-shore refineries in Curaçao (1916) and later in Aruba (1925). Some 10,000 West Indians from Trinidad, Barbados and Curaçao itself were regularly employed on the Venezuelan oilfields until 1929, when restrictions were once more applied after local objections to foreign workers had been voiced. Both Curaçao and Aruba employed some 10,000 workers who came from as far afield as the Windwards (St Lucia) and the Lee-wards (St Kitts). This figure declined after the Second World War and, with the introduction of increased automation in the past five years, not only has the total labour force on Curaçao and Aruba declined, but West Indians have been required to return to their homes.

The United States, always a favourite haven for Caribbean emigrants, has received large numbers of British West Indians who were able to enter on unfilled British immigration quotas until 1952, and large numbers of these have been absorbed into continental Negro communities. Many have become prominent in the professions and in politics. During the Second World War about 120,000 West Indians were allowed to enter the United States to remedy a manpower shortage in agriculture and industry. Jamaican workers continued to flow in during the 1940s and early 1950s, but have now been severely restricted in numbers. They continue to cut the sugar cane harvest in south Florida. Since the new quota laws, most British West Indians by-pass the United States and take up residence in Canada where their citizenship is not a barrier. Other United States possessions, such as St Thomas and St Croix (where important oil and aluminium plants are being erected), are the target not only of contracted migrant labour from St Kitts and the British Virgin Islands, but of men seeking illegal entry.

Increasing restrictions on permanent movement of people in all islands of the Caribbean has become the norm since the Second World War. Trinidad introduced such legislation as early as 1942, when the island became an important military base, attracting large numbers of migrants from the Lesser Antilles. Permanent entry to any of the islands from Trinidad northwards, in order to seek employment, is virtually impossible today. The British West Indian Federation established in 1958 showed its first disunity over the free movement of peoples.

The remaining outlet for British West Indians was, for those who could endure the climatic transition, the British Isles. The cost of a sea passage was the only barrier to free movement. After the Second World War many West Indians with experience of continuous employment in many areas, sought economic alternatives to poverty at home by migrating to the United Kingdom where many thousands of unskilled jobs were available.

From 1950 onwards, migrants from Jamaica, Trinidad and the Lesser Antilles began to arrive in ever-increasing numbers, carried in Italian and Spanish ships that offered cheap passages to European ports after they had unloaded their cargoes of European emigrants to Hispanic America. Charter flights, particularly from Jamaica, caused this flow to accelerate.

For various reasons accurate statistics of in-and-out migration were not kept in sufficient detail for the United Kingdom authorities to measure this West Indian immigration pattern. Census records in 1951 reveal some 15,301 U.K. residents who were born in the British West Indian islands. The 1961 Census recorded 171,796 in the same category. This was a measure of the rapid increase that took place in ten years, all but a tiny fraction being Negro rather than white. Estimates of the present West Indian population vary considerably. In 1966 one journal, *The Economist*, used the figure 275,093, while another, *The Times*, quoted 430,000 as a likely total.

Political pressures within the United Kingdom brought about the 1962 Commonwealth Immigration Act, severely restricting all in-migration from the British Commonwealth.

TABLE 3.7 *Immigration of British West Indians into the U.K. 1951–61*

Year	Number	Year	Number
1951	1,000 (approx.)	1957	22,473
1952	2,000	1958	16,511
1954	10,000	1959	20,397
1955	24,473	1960	45,706
1956	26,441	1961	66,260

Some immigrants are highly desirable in the eyes of the United Kingdom. Barbados, with its carefully regulated long-standing emigration programme, continues to supply transport workers and nurses to London and other cities.

POPULATION CONTROL

For the islands, the imposition of such immigration restrictions has forced the local governments to re-examine their population problem as one that can no longer be exported but must be solved locally. One solution lies in family planning, and birth control campaigns continue to reduce the birth-rate, which has remained fairly constant throughout the Caribbean, while commendable reductions in death-rates and infant mortality-rates have made even a marked decline in the birth-rate unimportant. Religious attitudes on the one hand, particularly in the Hispanic islands, do not favour such control programmes, while on the other hand *machismo*, a vague male attitude denoting pride in virility through the number of children conceived, acts as a deterrent to such programmes throughout the Caribbean. A further factor is the custom of permissive cohabitation, leading to an illegitimacy rate as high as 40 per cent in some communities.

Puerto Rican authorities, faced with overwhelming population growth, have undertaken during the past ten years, a continuous experimental contraception programme involving chemicals taken orally among its female population, resulting in an undramatic but steady decline of the birth-rate from 39 per cent in 1940 to 27·5 per cent by 1964. Sterilization operations for men and women are also carried out as a matter of routine. The island's population, however, continues to grow alarmingly, despite large-scale emigration to the United States, and cannot lead to any optimistic long-term view of population reduction in this part of the Caribbean.

Barbados introduced a family planning programme in May 1955, following a long soul-searching among its people, religious leaders and legislators. It has been made gradually acceptable throughout the island and appears to all but a few to be at least a modest contribution to the solution of a major problem. It is impossible to visualize a similarly successful campaign and result on an island such as St Lucia where literacy, education and motivation are so far below those of Barbados. A modest programme has been introduced also into Grenada.

Trinidad, with a Roman Catholic nominal majority, and a reputation for being underpopulated, has reversed its policies recently, seeing the high birth-rate as 'a threat to economic and social well-being'. When in full swing, the programme is designed to reduce the birth-rate from 38 to 19 per 1000 in ten years, a decline that can be rivalled by very few countries in the developing world.

PROSPECTS AND PROJECTIONS

No matter what political philosophies or governments prevail in the Caribbean, it is clear that the larger island communities such as Cuba, Haiti, the Dominican Republic, Jamaica and Puerto Rico can offer no unique solution to the problems associated with population growth. Overpopulation as it is understood in some Latin American or Asian countries is absent: i.e. there is land enough (except in Haiti and possibly Jamaica) for those who wish to grow their own food, though without any prospect of rising standards of living. For Haiti, only the most optimistic can envisage anything but a totally Malthusian solution in an island lacking any kind of resource including soil productivity.

The small islands of the Caribbean, with so much of their land consisting of steeply sloping hillsides, or lacking vital water supplies, appear to have reached a point of no return. Unless their inhabitants can miraculously become terrace-agriculturists, such lands cannot support expanding populations. It is possible to advocate a policy of robber-economy during the next generation by making available all forest reserves and unalienated lands for cultivation and encouraging the total destruction of each island landscape, much as Haiti has been reduced to its bare bones. Inevitably this must lead to complete evacuation of the small islands much earlier than is at present anticipated. Given the present technological trends, this is after all the ultimate fate of the smaller islands, which should therefore be granted the opportunity to squeeze every last ounce from their surface.

Yet the trend throughout the Caribbean islands is one of a drift to the town after the abandonment of farms and smallholdings, and therefore of all plantations, which during the next twenty years will face their logical end as subdivided smallholdings. Manufacturing and industrial expansion has already fallen behind in the task of finding jobs for the present generation of immigrants. The alternative – sending people back to their rural plots – has rarely succeeded in any country, and, furthermore, requires a degree of compulsion, which the Caribbean would not tolerate. By 1990 the present total population of these islands will have doubled itself, even under the most optimistic assumptions of slower growth. Unless a dramatic change in attitude towards birth control occurs, there can be little to comfort a student of the Caribbean.

CASH CROPS

Socio-economic patterns in the Caribbean islands, as elsewhere in the Tropics, have always been closely linked with cash crops, produced for the temperate world. Beginning with tobacco in the seventeenth century, eventually cultivated to excess, there followed a succession of plantation crops, whose popularity in Europe waxed and waned in accordance with the potential of other new countries discovered and exploited as colonies.

Tobacco remains a staple crop of Cuba and Puerto Rico in particular, mainly cigar leaf. Other islands have tried repeatedly to grow a cigarette tobacco commercially (where it might have been an import substitute) in order to supply a local factory, but there appears to be little enthusiasm for a crop requiring delicate handling throughout its growing life. A long-range experiment in Tobago among tobacco peasants, who were provided with seedlings, cheap mineral fertilizers and considerable technical assistance, lasted only a few years before it collapsed.

Among the most prominent of the early crops was indigo, which produced a basic cloth dye. A staple for many years on most West Indian
plantations, it gave way to synthetic chemical dyes in the mid-nineteenth
century and exists today only as an historical curiosity among the natural
vegetation of the islands.

In the two centuries before the American South dominated the European
market, Sea Island cotton became an important crop in the Caribbean
islands wherever it would grow. It displaced sugar in Tobago when that
island was invaded by ants in 1766, and remained a vital crop there with
a very high sales value in London as late as 1795. Only a few cotton areas
survive, specifically in Antigua where about 454·5 tonnes are produced
annually from a local ginnery. Other islands such as Barbuda, St Kitts,
Montserrat, St Vincent and Haiti are known to have grown cotton, but
extensive droughts have tilted the balance and caused local growers
to abandon the crop. The destruction by fire of St Vincent's cotton
ginnery in 1959 brought cultivation to an immediate standstill. No attempt
has been made to rebuild the ginnery, so cotton has ceased to be a cash
crop.

A sharp transition to the monoculture of sugar cane in the mid-seventeenth century drove most of the other cash crops out of the islands. Only
in Cuba and Hispañola was it possible to see stock-ranching dominating the
economy. It is not difficult to follow the effects – consolidation of landholdings, slavery, wholly inefficient production and eventually bankruptcy
in the nineteenth century – for most of the sugar planters. Yet a major
resurgence of the industry in Cuba, Puerto Rico, the Dominican Republic,
Guadeloupe, Jamaica and Trinidad in the latter half of the century, and
the persistence of the crop into the present day in Barbados and St Kitts,
are a measure of the power of capital investment in tropical production.
Elsewhere, as in St Lucia, Grenada and Antigua, commercial sugar cane
has disappeared or is in process of disintegrating owing to rising labour
costs (Table 3.8).

Application of socialistic planning programmes in Cuba since 1959 has
made it even more obvious that if sugar cane is to be profitable growers
cannot afford the luxury of experimentation. Field mechanization has not
come quickly to the industry, and as yet only the clumsiest harvesting
machines are available to replace the human cutter with his cutlass.
Despite Cuban optimism and political faith in its systems, the projected
target of 10 million tons of sugar was not attained. Early and late season
cropping, massive 'voluntary' labour from the city and many other devices
have been used in the past three years in an effort to emulate the 1961
harvest total of 6·8 million tons. Serious droughts, institutional changes
such as land reform, factory breakdowns and lack of adequate machinery
have also played an important part in preventing higher production.

Elsewhere in the islands, the sugar cane plantation has been kept solvent

TABLE 3.8   *Production of centrifugal sugar (raw value)*
('ooos metric tons)

	1965–6	1966–7	1967–8
Antigua	8	5	1
Barbados	175	204	162
Cuba	4455	6129	5500
Dominican Republic	691	826	710
Grenada	1	2	2
Guadeloupe	167	137	141
Haiti	59	61	63
Jamaica	40	49	49
Martinique	53	47	50
Puerto Rico	801	742	585
St Kitts–Nevis	39	39	35
Trinidad	214	204	247
Virgin Islands (U.S.A.)	5	2	1

Source: United Nations – FAO

by subsidy, guaranteed price arrangements and an international quota system devised by the United States. Without these aids much of the present-day industry would collapse in the face of sugar beet production. Sugar cane has probably outstayed its usefulness on the Caribbean scene. It is certainly not a smallholder's crop, as many theorists would like it to be. Puerto Rico's experience of land reform has led the government to ignore its anti-cartel policy embodied in the '500 Acre Act', and to restore large-scale exploitation. The vicissitudes of sugar cane cultivation, together with its sensitivity to world prices, rising labour costs, hurricanes, drought and human greed, were well known to the nineteenth-century plantation-owner.

Encouraged by enthusiastic governors he planted various cash crops from one era to another in order to meet world market demands. Sugar cane gave way to coconut groves and copra extraction. Wet hillsides were given over to cacao, long a popular crop in the French and Spanish islands (see Table 3.9 for production figures). Coffee, well established in Cuba, Haiti and Puerto Rico, spread as far south as Trinidad. Dominica became a lime-growing and processing centre. Grenada and others cultivated the nutmeg tree. St Vincent monopolized the world's arrowroot production. Aruba contributed the bitter aloe to the world's pharmacoepia until it was displaced by synthetics. Citrus and pineapple have appeared in Jamaica, Trinidad, Puerto Rico and Martinique in recent years.

News of successes in one or other of these many crops spread from one island to another in colonial dispatches during the nineteenth century, and in the twentieth many agricultural departments and plantation-owners turned from one to another when world markets turned fickle or

TABLE 3.9   *Production of cacao (cocoa) beans (metric tons)*

	1965–6	*1966–7*	*1967–8*
Cuba	1,900	1,500	1,500
Dominica	100	100	100
Dominican Republic	30,500	28,000	29,000
Grenada	2,300	2,700	2,800
Haiti	3,000	3,000	2,700
Jamaica	2,300	1,700	2,300
Martinique	100	—	—
St Lucia	100	100	100
Trinidad and Tobago	5,000	4,200	4,300

Source: United Nations – FAO

plant diseases devastated an optimist's carefully established new crop. It is therefore possible to see on one island visible evidence of the many despairing changes of land use in the relict plant communities – an excellent example being *Hevea Brasiliensis* and *Castilloa elastica* – rubber latex trees that 'escaped' from experimental fields to become part of the landscape in Tobago.

One of the most important innovations in the Caribbean islands was the banana (*Musa Sapientium*). Introduced into Jamaica in the early days of commercial exploitation in the late nineteenth century, it has played a vital role in many island economies, both as plantation and as smallholding crop, and in the Windward Islands could be called the only viable cash crop of consequence. Despite such disasters as Panama Disease, Sigatoka (leaf spot), frequent hurricanes, rains and droughts, the banana has been

TABLE 3.10   *Production of bananas ('000s metric tons)*

	1965–6	*1966–7*	*1967–8*
Cuba	60	55	60
Dominica	50	49	48
Dominican Republic	220	220	200
Grenada	21	21	27
Guadeloupe	162	180	180
Haiti	212	230	220
Jamaica	327	330	300
Martinique	220	229	230
Puerto Rico	118	107	106
St Lucia	82	81	70
St Vincent	48	51	35
Trinidad and Tobago	25	27	27

Source: United Nations – FAO

bred in size and resistance to suit the markets of western Europe and North America. Transportation by sea, rail and road has been superbly organized by several companies, and marketing arrangements are carefully managed from the moment of harvest to purchase in the shop. Here at least is one tropical crop that has succeeded in providing a reasonable living for all who handle it, and will continue to do so until economic depression makes it a luxury once more, and until the ravaged hillsides of the islands can no longer support its roots (see Table 3.10 for production figures).

FOOD CROPS

For those pioneers who landed upon Hispañola and Cuba with Columbus, the Caribbean islands were not a particularly promising source of food. Accustomed to Mediterranean variety, they were discouraged by their inability to transfer wheat, temperate fruit and vegetables to the Tropics. Such native foods as cassava failed to satisfy the colonists, who were forced to import their own requirements. This situation persisted until a time in the Second World War, during the German submarine campaign, when the entire island fringe faced starvation because so many Allied supply ships were sunk – a measure of the increasing dependence on sophisticated European foods.

From the earliest days of slavery, plantation-owners allowed the cultivation of sugar 'banks' for food crops, and the care of livestock near the slave barracks, expecting not only enough for the plantation, but a surplus for sale in the local town market. Such privileges were well guarded and continue today to be part of the payment in kind for workers who commonly receive a plot of land on the less fertile part of the plantation, and have the right to tether and graze cows and goats on the owner's property. The chicken and pig remain an immediately available food source throughout the Caribbean.

Such local husbandry did not suffice, however. Salted cod, imported from Canada and the eastern seaboard of North America, and salt pork, became the basic protein food for slaves (who seldom looked to the sea for their own fresh fish supplies). Salted fish continues to be an important item in the average Caribbean diet, but must still be imported from the temperate north.

With the African slaves came novel foods brought in by sea captains who observed what their human cargo was given to eat while awaiting transfer from West African stockades. Most were starchy tubers such as the many varieties of yam. Others were legumes like the pigeon pea, the black-eyed pea, millets and sorghums. Fruits such as ackee made cod dishes more palatable, while the mango offered an easy alternative to starvation in hard times and continues to do so in modern Haiti. Other vegetables, such as okra, are now a standard item in island diets. Of the exotics introduced into the Caribbean, especially designed to reduce slave food costs, the most important plant proved to be the breadfruit. Although introduced in 1776, it failed to impress the slaves immediately as a possible food and was largely fed to animals. Nonetheless its spread throughout the Caribbean landscape, and the great demand for fruit in local markets, made the tree a vital part of any food garden.

Hence, after emancipation, all ex-slaves were able to take a great variety of food crops (to which could be added the coconut and maize) to their free settlements, and there to subsist quite satisfactorily with the aid of goats, a cow, pigs and chickens. When the time came in the British islands for such people to return to a cash economy, they were reluctant to give up such food security and have continued to devote part of the working week to 'make-garden' on smallholdings often quite far from their home – to the detriment of full-time employment on a plantation, in government, or in private industry. Even those workers who have spent half a lifetime in the Trinidad oil industry, or as cabinet ministers, yearn for their 'piece of land' in the hills. Within the Hispanic islands smallholdings were all too quickly absorbed into large estates, leaving the landless *jibaro* of Puerto Rico a helpless victim to *tiempo muerte* (the dead season following the cane harvest).

Increasing rural depopulation throughout the area has automatically reduced those surpluses which could be sold in the local market place and has led to serious food deficiencies in the Lesser Antilles. Some enterprising islanders have developed a brisk inter-island trade, by transporting breadfruit, plantains, yams and other food crops in schooners from Montserrat and Dominica to Antigua, the Virgin Islands, Trinidad and Barbados. Similarly, Venezuelan farmers bring boatloads of fruit and vegetables to Curaçao and Aruba, both islands being quite incapable of growing their own requirements, despite a remarkable hydroponics garden on Aruba. Food shortages are not, however, a modern phenomenon. There is abundant evidence in the historical records of famine in Jamaica, Antigua, Haiti and Puerto Rico, following serious droughts and hurricanes.

Tourists on holiday in the Caribbean seldom eat the local foods. Every island seeking this trade must therefore allow considerable quantities of frozen, tinned or fresh food and Scotch whisky to be imported. Since these are also displayed in the local retail shop, they become part of an islander's regular purchases. Not all the vast increase in imports of flour and processed foods can be blamed on the increasing tourist trade and a burgeoning population. Tastes are actually changing in all the islands, yet only a few can really afford to neglect local production. Puerto Rico has almost abandoned its 'native' foods in favour of those imported from Miami in ever-increasing quantities. These include fresh meats, dairy products, chicken, pork, fish, fruit and vegetables, all of which could be produced on the island itself. Yet local concerns have succeeded in one area only, that of fresh milk production, and then mainly as a result of powerful help from the United States Department of Agriculture. In other fields, such as chicken and beef production, aggressive competitors from the continent have undercut the local market without any difficulty, especially since the European Common Market placed an embargo on United States broiler chicken imports.

There is in fact no more vexing problem in the modern Caribbean than that of food production. The puritanical dogma of forced self-sufficiency for all communities is no longer held, but every island government since the mid-nineteenth century has entertained schemes for larger food harvests, assuming that peasants, given sufficient encouragement, would remain on their lands. Empty lands were divided into 2 ha and 4 ha holdings and granted to the landless on condition that a certain proportion of all crops should be food. Barbados introduced a strict law requiring 15 per cent of all lands to be devoted to food crops. In the post-Second World War years economic devices such as marketing boards and subsidized or guaranteed minimum prices, accompanied by wide propaganda, have had mixed success. In Jamaica, Barbados and Trinidad they have been firmly administered and have proved themselves within acceptable limits. Elsewhere in the British islands they have floundered amidst incompetence and staff shortages.

SETTLEMENT SCHEMES

Of greater interest to the geographer have been the innumerable settlement schemes initiated mainly by government departments of agriculture in order to overcome agrarian discontent, to raise local food production, or to satisfy political promises. Others on a grander scale have aimed at the total rehabilitation of communities. Some 300 such schemes are known for the British Caribbean alone. Most of these are found in Jamaica, an island suffering intense land hunger and overpopulation. The Yallahs Valley Authority, now in its twentieth year, was designed to restore eroded lands, relocate communities and bring about an economic revival in peasant fortunes. That it has achieved some of its objectives is a tribute to the Authority and the inhabitants of the valley. Few others have succeeded except temporarily in the first flush of enthusiasm. Lack of capital, preparation and education are generally to blame when ultimate failure is analysed.

Settlement projects create many administrative problems. For example, a scheme established in 1966 by the government of Trinidad and Tobago was an excellent planned smallholding project for dairy farming in Trinidad. Unfortunately the soil of the land settlement area ranked among the worst in the island; many of the 'farmers' were selected for their political party loyalties and came straight from a manual labourer's job to a bare few weeks of preliminary dairy training. A similar but more grandiose scheme set up in 1966 for Jamaica nearly collapsed when recruits, after some six months training in dairy practices, found that their farms were not ready for occupation. In Tobago small dairy and pig farms, closely supervised, have been set up on old abandoned estate lands in a desperate effort to produce more food locally and to create a stabilized rural community.

Land reforms followed by planned food production have been the chief preoccupation of the Cuban government since 1959, but it is difficult to pass an opinion on so radical a scheme. A virtually closed society, which has developed as a result of United States embargoes, has been forced to arrange its internal food supplies very carefully. Loss of Chinese rice imports in 1966, and a deliberate reduction in local rice cultivation, have led to severe rationing of a major food item. Beef, milk, sweet potato and maize production have declined steadily as greater emphasis was placed on sugar cane, yet egg production trebled between 1965 and 1966 and it is not unlikely that many vegetables, more nutritious than rice and beans, are being grown on Cuban farms. Since the latter vary from state farms based on the Russian *sovkhozes* to co-operatives and individual small-holdings, it is difficult to discern any patterns or trends that would indicate a greater success on the part of Cubans in handling their food problems than the horticulturist of central Puerto Rico or the East Indian gardener in Trinidad.

FISHING

Since salt cod plays such an important role in all island diets, fresh fish should also be considered as part of the food cycle. Barbados is renowned for its 'flying fish' harvest, but elsewhere until recently the rowing boat, a seine net and co-operative hauls within 450 m of the shore were the only evidence of a fishing industry. Pathetically small catches of under-sized fish and a quick sale to local bystanders remain the current pattern. Training facilities initiated by the FAO and other organizations, together with improved equipment, have done little to increase fish supplies. It has been left to Japanese trawlers to station themselves in Trinidad and Puerto Rico and to set up a tuna-canning industry. Barbados and Trinidad have similarly become shrimping centres for Venezuelan concerns and only in the Dominican Republic is there any sign of an active fishing industry. Cuban attempts to establish large-scale trawling with modern ships have been hampered by local consumer resistance to fish as a substitute for meat, and by a general ignorance, common throughout the whole area, of the ecology of the Caribbean Sea. Otherwise it is the peasant with his handline or his explosives who harvests the greater bulk of sea fish today, and this is but another of the one-day-a-week activities that keep him from being a truly 'economic' man.

LIVESTOCK

Early Hispanic settlement involved a flourishing cattle industry, well adapted to the Caribbean climate and pastures. Until Castro returned it to its rightful place in 1968, this had vanished before the sugar cane field. Cattle were also used extensively as draught animals throughout the sugar era everywhere in the Caribbean, and also became a part of the peasant economy in the nineteenth century. Needless to say, most were scrub cattle and have remained so until recently, but they provided crudely butchered meat and small supplies of milk for local sale. Agricultural administrators have long been aware of the potential value of many of the islands for cattle-rearing. Succeeding generations of veterinarians introduced their favourite breeds from India, Africa and Great Britain, resulting in a wide range of animal breeds and cross-breeds. A deliberate breeding programme carried out in recent years in Jamaica yielded two important types of animal suited to the Caribbean. Jamaica Hope, a dairy cow, and Jamaica Red, a beef stock animal, are represented in all large herds today. At the same time, Friesian dairy animals have been successfully adapted to Puerto Rico, Jamaica, Trinidad and Tobago.

MINERAL RESOURCES

The Spanish *conquistadores* in Hispañola thought for one brief moment in time that they had discovered a sure source of gold. With a few major exceptions, however, the complete lack of minerals of any kind throughout the Caribbean has meant that each community has been thrown back on its only resources – the land and the people.

There are, of course, a few deposits that offer a restricted profit. Pumice on Dominica can be sold in world markets. The white sands of Puerto Rico make excellent bottle glass. Limestone in abundance provides the raw material for cement, while in many islands certain clays offer a good base for a ceramics industry. Trinidad has a rich iron ore lode in its northern range but this resource has not yet created a Caribbean Ruhr, so earnestly desired by local politicians. Significant copper deposits in Puerto Rico, now being worked experimentally, are showing great promise.

Only the Greater Antilles contain minerals of any value to the outside world. Cuba, for example, is undoubtedly rich in minerals. There were some 287 mines in operation in Cuba in 1958: 68 manganese, 9 copper, 12 chrome, 6 iron, 4 pyrites, 2 lead, 1 silver, 1 tungsten, 3 zinc, 2 nickel, 1 cobalt, 4 barytes, 3 gold, 8 gypsum, 6 kaolin and 1 lignite. At that time 98 per cent of the island's production went to the United States, where technical skills made exploitation of some difficult ores possible. It has been estimated that some 3000 million tons of iron ore (consisting of limonite and haematite of varying grades) await exploitation in Cuba.

Similarly manganese, chrome, nickel, tungsten and cobalt, all regarded as strategic minerals in the Free World, are available in that island. Few are exploited at present, however, owing to lack of a suitable market. The well-endowed Soviet Union apparently shows little interest, while the United States, a natural market for these minerals, is hog-tied by political embargoes. The rich iron ores of the Dominican Republic, on the other hand, are exported to West Germany.

The most generously endowed of the Caribbean islands today is Jamaica, whose bauxite resources are the greatest in the world. All the major aluminium companies are engaged not only in exploiting large areas of open-cast deposits, but in establishing concentration plants within the island. In central and northern Jamaica such activities have brought about a considerable but peculiar economic revolution. Since most of the production line has been automated, there is strong competition for jobs in the industry, and only by rationing these have the various corporations been able to preserve some degree of economic stability among local Jamaicans.

The influence of bauxite mining, however, extends far beyond the extraction process. Aluminium companies with mineral rights to extensive landholdings are today part of the island's agricultural developers. They run, for example, some of the island's largest cattle holdings in direct response to local political demands. They also have a vital interest in a variety of settlement schemes in order to make the best use of lands sterilized for future mining operations, or after the completion of open-cast operations. Furthermore, the Jamaican government acquires more than 20 per cent of its fiscal budget from taxation of this industry and is thus able to cope with problems of overpopulation and land starvation on the remainder of the island. By comparison, gypsum mining near Kingston would seem unimportant, but nearly one quarter of a million tons of this mineral are exported annually to the southern ports of the United States.

Petroleum in Trinidad is the only other exploitable mineral of any interest in the Caribbean, though small deposits of it have been exploited in southern Cuba.

The south-western corner of Trinidad was known for its asphalt lake as early as 1572 when Sir Walter Raleigh visited the island. This mineral has been exploited for many years from the same lake. From 1910 onwards a number of oil wells by the lake, as well as a number of later off-shore wells have provided Trinidad with 35 per cent of its national income through three refineries set up to process the crude oil. The strategic value of these refineries has led to plant expansion far beyond local production capacity, resulting in the importation of Venezuelan crude to keep the refineries in full production.

Trinidad's oil industry has not only provided a taxable source, but has enabled many thousands of workers to acquire a variety of mechanical skills invaluable in the island's industrialization programme. Natural and waste gases also provide thermal energy for power production and domestic uses. The only other island with oil pretensions is Barbados, where petroleum has been located at great depths (at present uneconomic). Natural gas has, however, been tapped and provides a valuable source of heating on a fuel-hungry island.

INDUSTRIALIZATION

Economic theorists have commonly postulated that industrialization should absorb the rural migrants and the growing urban populations of the Caribbean. For a variety of reasons such a process is thought capable of bringing about a reduction in population pressure through a lowering of the birth-rate, associated with rising levels of living. It is natural, therefore, to expect island politicians, planners and economists to support industrial programmes and to offer every incentive to manufacturers to establish themselves on a particular island.

Cuba, virtually an appendage to the United States until 1959, is an example of 'natural' economic evolution in capitalistic terms. Its tobacco and sugar provided a major base for additional investment by the United States and local concerns, bringing to the island innumerable consumer industries, ranging from beverages to car tyres, under local tariff protective legislation. In 1958 Cuba was considered to be self-sufficient in about 80 per cent of its consumer commodities. In addition, textiles, leather goods, soap and certain chemicals were able to compete successfully in South and North American markets. Much has changed since 1959 and it is no longer possible to envisage the island's industrial economy in such Free World terms. Having lost its most valuable trading partner, the United States, source of all machinery, spare parts and technical skills, the island has been forced to seek other markets among the Soviet bloc countries.

Industrialization as a panacea for community ills has been best developed in Puerto Rico, a model, too, for many other similar programmes in the Caribbean. Beneath the protective skirt of the United States, the island's administrators were able to pass from vaguely socialistic forms of national industry in the 1940s to an infectious system of free enterprise, which attracted at least 1200 concerns between 1950 and 1967 and provided work for 150,000 Puerto Ricans.

Popularly known as 'Operation Bootstrap', an industrialization programme was devised through a variety of incentives including freedom from taxation for periods of from ten to seventeen years, rented factories, local training of personnel, feasibility studies and massive publicity. Tourism was included in the government's plans and this has yielded large dividends between 1950 and 1970 as the total of American visitors grew with every passing year. Under the pressure of rising costs, increasing anti-*Yanqui* sentiments and deteriorating service, most of the islands 'showpiece' hotels are today financially bankrupt and shut down.

In view of the lack of local resources, it was necessary to concentrate on labour-intensive industries, producing goods that could be processed from imported raw materials and exported to world markets. A wide range of textile manufactures, including men's shirts and women's under-clothing and corsetry, remain among the island's chief exports, but with a general rise in local technical skills, electronic components of all kinds are now being made for delivery to many parts of the United States, mainly by air freight. Apart from fish- and fruit-canning industries, the most important developments in the near future will be in the field of petro-chemicals, based on the by-products of two very large petroleum re-fineries recently erected in the island.

Despite twenty years of frenetic activity, Puerto Rico still suffers from a high rate of unemployment among its labour force, varying between 14 and 18 per cent, a figure that would be higher if migration to the United States were to decline. Attempts to spread industrialization into the re-motest corners of the island do not disguise the fact that San Juan and Poncé are the most attractive areas for capital investment. The former, now so grossly overcrowded, is discouraging further industrial growth through economic disincentives.

Puerto Rico, with ready access to the United States and other countries further afield, is a unique example of industrial development without any natural resources except abundant labour. Unfortunately it is too often considered to be an imitable standard model by other islands in the Caribbean. Without a benign, avuncular overseer such as the United States, Puerto Rico's 'Operation Bootstrap' could not have survived for long after its creation.

The two largest British islands, Jamaica and Trinidad, have adopted most of the fundamental principles underlying the Puerto Rican ex-periment. Although inhibited in the earliest stages by doctrinaire socialism, both governments have gradually come round to long-term tax exemption, tax-free importation of machinery and other incentives in order to attract local manufacturers. Each has given first priority, however, to import-substitution industries employing local labour. Many food products, cigarettes, beer, mattresses, tyres and electronic goods (and, in Trinidad, motor vehicle assembly) are typical of the up-to-date factory in which island labour and management are totally involved. Feasibility studies have been completed for the establishment of an iron and steel industry in Trinidad, but it is difficult to envisage such a project being more than a matter of local prestige.

Most islands have been infected by industrialization fever. Throughout the Lesser Antilles and Virgin Islands, pioneer industrial legislation has been introduced and incentives offered to those who are prepared to manufacture import-substitutes. The smallest islands can thus boast a brewery, a cold drink plant, a cigarette factory, a margarine or coconut oil plant, a mattress factory and a tyre-retreading plant. All have extended their incentives to the hotel and tourist industry, usually in generous terms. Antigua and St Croix are headquarters of petrol refineries and crude oil bunker stores, while the latter island now has an aluminium plant. St Thomas is today the focus of a number of minor industries including watch-assembly lines. The ABC islands of the Netherlands Antilles, now associate members of the European Common Market, are likely under new regulations to become important centres of aluminium processing and certain other industries.

The French Antilles, administered as *départements* of France, have also sought to develop pioneer industries. Major interest is centred on Martinique, the more sophisticated island. Incentive industrial legislation is partly inhibited by metropolitan self-interest and partly by local preference for better-paid white collar jobs. Too many investors also wish to avoid the losses that followed the collapse of French hegemony in south-east Asia, and have in any event found more lucrative openings in francophone west Africa. Thus, a few textile and clothing factories, jewellery and watch-assembly workshops are but appendages of the many sugar and rum refineries, as well as of a variety of fruit-canning plants.

The fourth and fifth Economic Plans of the French government also envisaged a rapid investment in tourism in both islands. Few new hotels, however, have been built, mainly because French hotel companies on the one hand and potential tourists on the other have found little incentive to shift their attention and money away from prosperous Europe to islands whose discontented peoples seem ready for a Cuba-like insurrection.

Following its internal revolution in 1962, the Dominican Republic has been trying to rebuild its economy by encouraging industrial concerns from the United States to take advantage of cheap labour and many incentives offered by the government. Canning and other consumer manufactures have made noteworthy progress in the capital. Glass, cement and textiles are also produced locally. Given continued political stability, the Dominican Republic is likely to become an important manufacturing community.

It is difficult to sum up the value of development programmes involving industrialization. They offer prestige and self-respect to local populations, who begin to feel themselves in the van of progress. They involve relatively few workers compared with the total population, but do cause more money to circulate. On the other hand, Jamaican bauxite companies have adopted a unique practice of rotating jobs at intervals of three months, among the local male population, in order to spread as much of a company's salary budget as widely as possible and among as many people as possible. No factory, however small, could reasonably afford the luxury of a similar turnover of labour. Industrialization, as the culminating stage of an economic cycle to which mineral resources have contributed little or nothing, is at best precarious. For most Caribbean islands it is an act of defiance in the face of overpopulation and poverty. Without massive emigration, a renewed interest in agriculture, and the stimulus provided by jumbo-jet tourism, industrialization has a doubtful future.

BIBLIOGRAPHY

ANDIC, F. M. and MATHEWS, T. G. (eds.) (1965) *The Caribbean in Transition*. Río Piedras, University of Puerto Rico, Inst. of Carib. Stud. Second Caribbean Scholars' Conference, Mona, Jamaica, 14–19 April 1964.

ASPREY, G. F. (1959) Vegetation in the Caribbean area. *Caribbean Q.* 5, 245–63.

BURNS, A. C. (1954) *History of the British West Indies*. London, Allen & Unwin (2nd rev. ed. 1965).

CARIBBEAN ORGANIZATION (1963a) *Caribbean Plan*. Hato Rey, Puerto Rico, Central Secretariat Annual Report.

CARIBBEAN ORGANIZATION (1963b) *Planning for Economic Development in the Caribbean*. Hato Rey, Puerto Rico, Central Secretariat.

CLARKE, C. G. (1964) Population pressure in Kingston, Jamaica: a study of unemployment and overcrowding. *Trans. Inst. of Brit. Geogr.* 38, 165–82.

CUBAN ECONOMIC RESEARCH PROJECT (1965) *A Study on Cuba*. Coral Gables, University of Miami.

DAVISON, R. B. (1962) *West Indian Migrants: social and economic facts of migration from the West Indies*. London, Oxford University Press.

DEERR, N. (1950) *The History of Sugar*. 2 vols. London, Chapman & Hall.

DEMAS, W. G. (1965) *The Economics of Development in Small Countries with Special Reference to the Caribbean*. Montreal, McGill University Press.

EDEL, M. (1962) Land reform in Puerto Rico 1941–1959. *Carib. Stud.* 23, 26–60; 24, 28–50.

ERIKSON, E. G. (1962) *The Caribbean: population and resources*. Washington, D.C., George Washington University.

HARRIS, D. R. (1965) *Plants, animals and man in the Outer Leeward Islands, West Indies: an ecological study of Antigua, Barbuda and Anguilla*. Berkeley, Univ. Calif. Pub. in Geog. 18.

HILLS, T. (1965) Land settlement schemes: lessons from the British Caribbean. *Revta Geogr.*, No. 63, 67–82.

JONES, C. and PICO R. (1955) *Symposium on the Geography of Puerto Rico*. Río Piedras, Puerto Rico.

JOUANDET-BERNADAT, R. (1967) L'économie des Antilles françaises. *Carib. Stud.*, 7, 3–22.

KLASS, M. (1962) *East Indians in Trinidad: a study of cultural persistence*. New York, Columbia University Press.

LASSERRE, G. (1961) *La Guadeloupe: étude géographique*. Bordeaux, Union Française d'Impression.

LOWENTHAL, D. (1967) Race and colour in the West Indies. *Daedalus*, 96, 580–626.

MCFARLANE (1964) *A Comparative Study of Incentive Legislation in the Leeward Islands, Windward Islands and Jamaica*. Mona, Jamaica, Inst. of Soc. and Ec. Research.

MASSIP, S. and PICO, R. (1958) *Antillas*. Geografía Universal, vol. xix. Barcelona, Montaner y Simon.

MATHEWS, T. G. *et al.* (1966) *Politics and Economics in the Caribbean*. Río Piedras, University of Puerto Rico, Inst. of Carib. Stud. special study No. 3.

NIDDRIE, D. L. (1961) *Land Use and Population in Tobago: an environmental study*. Bude, Geographical Publications.

NIDDRIE, D. L. (1963) Hurricanes. *Geog. Mag.*, 27, 228–34.

NIDDRIE, D. L. (1964b) The population problem in Puerto Rico. *Malayan J. of Trop. Geogr.*, 10.

NIDDRIE, D. L. (1965) An attempt at planned settlement in St Kitts in the early eighteenth century. *Carib. Stud.*, 5, 3–11.

NIDDRIE, D. L. (1966) Eighteenth-century settlement in the British Caribbean. *Trans. Inst. Brit. Geogr.*, 40, 67–80.

O'LOUGHLIN, C. (1963) *A survey of economic potential and capital needs of the Leeward Islands, Windward Islands and Barbados*. London, HMSO.

PROUDFOOT, M. J. (1950) *Population Movements in the Caribbean*. Port of Spain, Central Secretariat, Caribbean Commission.

RAGATZ, L. J. (1928) *The Fall of the Planter Class in the British Caribbean 1763–1833* (repr. 1963). New York, Octagon Press.

REVERT, E, (1958) *Entre les deux Amériques: le monde caribe*. Paris, Editions Françaises.

ROBERTS, G. W. (1954) Immigration of Africans into the British Caribbean. *Pop. Stud.*, 7, 235–62.

ROUSE, I. (1949) The West Indies: an introduction: the Arawak, the Carib. *Handbook of South American Indians*, 4, 495–565. Washington, D.C., Bureau of Ethnology.

RUBIN, V. (ed.) (1957) *Caribbean Studies: A Symposium*. Kingston, Jamaica.

SAUER, C. O. (1966) *The Early Spanish Main*. Berkeley, University of California Press.

SMITH, M. G. (1956) The transformation of land rights by transmission in Carriacou. *Soc. and Ec. Studies*, 5, 103–38.

TANNEHILL, D. (1956) *Hurricanes*. 5th ed. Princeton.

WEST, R. C. and AUGELLI, J. P. (1966) *Middle America, its Lands and Peoples*. Englewood Cliffs, N.J., Prentice-Hall.

WILGUS, C. A. (1951–67) *The Caribbean Conference Series*. Vols. 1–18. Gainesville, University of Florida Press.

WOODRING, W. P. (1954) Caribbean land and sea through the ages. *Bull. Geol. Soc. Am.*, 68, 719–32.

ZELINSKY, W. (1966) Population growth in Central America and the West Indies; prospect and problems. *Mineral Industries*, 35, 1–17.

4 Central America, including Panama

D. J. Fox

There are many ways of viewing Central America (Fig. 4.1). An atlas map may suggest the isthmus as a bridge joining the two great Americas – a tenuous link between the land masses to the north and south. A marine chart may draw attention to it as that part of the western hemisphere where the two oceans virtually touch, where the land is almost pinched out, and where man has now pierced the neck of land to make one of the busiest of the world's shipping lanes. A visitor may adopt yet another view: that Central America is, in truth if not in form, a peninsula, the tapering end of North America. This view is likely to be reinforced if the visitor has travelled overland from the north; he may enter by a variety of routes, but, as he continues deeper into the isthmus, his choice is whittled away until he finally reaches the end of the road in the forests and swamps of Darien, on the edge of South America. Beyond that point land travel is as yet unfeasible. Many travellers by sea may share this view. Most ships using the Panama Canal are trading in the northern hemisphere and are forced into latitudes more southerly than direct routing would demand; for them, rounding Central America has taken the place of rounding the Horn. The commercial ties of Central America are largely with the north, and particularly with the U.S.A.; the area has no comparable links with South America.

The viewpoints of the inhabitants of Central America are equally varied. A few have a supranational outlook; they see the isthmus as a unit and political, economic and social integration as a desirable goal. Most, however, view Central America as a chain of independent countries, perhaps geographically contiguous, sharing certain historical associations and producing some of the same products, but with the nation as the real concern, and their neighbours and the isthmus as foreign and hazy concepts. Many Central Americans have an even more restricted view: other parts of their own country may be as remote and unknown as the most distant of countries overseas, and an organized picture of the isthmus is quite outside their comprehension.

The area with which this essay is concerned includes Central America proper – that is, the republics of Guatemala, El Salvador, Honduras,

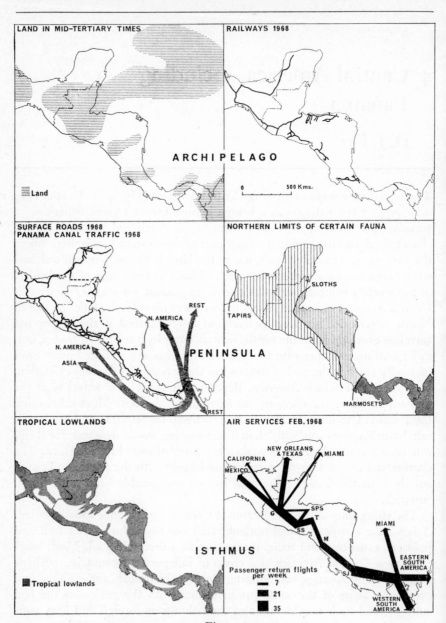

Fig. 4.1

Nicaragua and Costa Rica, and the colony of British Honduras, together with Panama, a country nominally and historically a part of South America. Unless otherwise specified, however, the phrase Central America as used in this chapter includes Panama.

NATURE IN CENTRAL AMERICA

Whatever one's view of Central America today, it is a fact that it has been isthmus, peninsula and even archipelago in the not-so-distant, geological past. It has, therefore, been both a corridor and a barrier to landward movements, and it has been an area in which migrants have flourished, new forms have developed and new ways of life have evolved.

A semblance of the Central America we know today became recognizable early in the known geological history of the area. In Palaeozoic times, it is conjectured that Central America was a peninsula of central Mexico, somewhat wider than it is now, and separated from Andean South America in Darien by a narrow but deepening gulf; it is from this epoch that the folded rocks of central Guatemala, Honduras and northern Nicaragua date. In early Mesozoic time, in contrast, the land connection with North America had become weaker and the isthmus firmly attached to South America as part of a Caribbean land mass, whose north coast ran along the backbone of Cuba and whose south-west coast lay well beyond the modern Pacific coast of Central America. During part of Cretaceous times southern Mexico, northern Central America, Jamaica and Cuba formed a great arcuate land mass. This was separated from North America by a proto Gulf of Mexico, which extended to the Pacific through the Balsas valley, and from South America by straits that submerged southern Nicaragua and all of Costa Rica, but left eastern Panama attached to the mainland. The folds in the rocks exposed in the highlands of northern Honduras and southern Guatemala date from this period; as do the mineralized zones associated with the massive intrusions of igneous rocks that occurred in the four northern republics.

The southern straits remained in Early Tertiary times, but the Caribbean island shrank and became firmly attached to Mexico. Later, in Mid-Tertiary times, the Caribbean island again became detached when the isthmus of Tehuantepec foundered. At the same time three elongated islands arose to the south: one in middle Honduras, another running from the Gulf of Nicoya completely across present-day Costa Rica, and the third lying across central Panama. The straits between these islands proved no barrier to certain plants and animals, and the islands served as stepping stones for the invasion of South America by, for example, the primates. Great volcanic activity in the Mio-Pliocene age and general land uplift resulted in the linking of the islands and the emergence of a true isthmus, narrower in the north-west and wider in the south-east than it is today. The equids (horses) used it to enter South America, the opossums to invade North America. Fossil remains show that the Caribbean side of the isthmus was an easier route for migrants than the Pacific side where volcanic eruptions had started in earnest. Local uplift (especially in Honduras) and depression (particularly in Panama) meant that by about a million years ago (Early Pleistocene times) the isthmus had clearly taken on the shape it has today.

The isthmus has suffered two important changes since that date. In the first place volcanic activity has continued unabated and the beauty of the landscape has been enhanced, not only by the great volcanic cones which now form the high points in most of the countries, but also by the *calderas* and lakes created by volcanic collapse and the blocking of former drainage outlets. There are 109 large volcanoes, some over 4000 m high, and it is the most active volcanic zone in the Americas today. Secondly, the isthmus has been affected by the changing climatic circumstances of the Pleistocene. During the glacial periods of mid-latitudes, the higher reaches of Central America, for example the Cordillera de Talamanca in Costa Rica, carried glaciers, the climate was cooler and the sea-level fell. During interglacial periods the sea-level rose. The presence or absence of Pleistocene straits across the isthmus has been widely debated: the findings of marine biologists suggest that there has been no deep-water connection between the Caribbean and Pacific since the Miocene and that, although a shoal-water link may have persisted into the early Pleistocene, this formed no barrier to the movement of land animals and had certainly ceased to exist well before man arrived on the scene (Hubbs and Roden, 1964, p. 174).

It is in the context of this eventful geological history that the development of the flora and fauna of the area may best be viewed (West, 1964). A tropical situation in combination with a great variety of local relief and climate has not only allowed a large range of species to exist and multiply but has also meant that refuge areas for species endangered by changes in environmental conditions have been widely available. The opportunity Central America has given for insulation of plants and animals – whether by sea or land – has resulted in the evolution of large numbers of endemic species. To these indigenous species must be added the generous infusions since Miocene times of plants and animals from the adjoining continents, creating a biota that in many important respects is richer than that of either North or South America.

The vegetation of the isthmus reflects the various factors that have been at work. There is no barrier to the entry of South American tree species, and the lowland rain-forests of Caribbean and Pacific Central America have, therefore, strong affinities with the *selva* of the South. From the botanical point of view, the Caribbean rain-forests below about 1000 m form a distinctive assemblage of species in which the large number of palms, tree ferns, lianas and epiphytes emphasizes the humidity of the region. It ends in the Maya mountains of British Honduras, north of which the climate is drier. The tropical rain-forest of Panama and eastern Costa Rica gives way on the Pacific side to a dry evergreen forest at lower altitudes; this remains essentially of South American composition. At elevations about 1000 to 1600 m species are fewer and the affinities with North America are stronger. The important trees in the forested highlands of northern Central America are pine and oak as in the highlands of Mexico. The pines do not extend further south than north-central Nicaragua, however, and in the Cordillera de Talamanca of Costa Rica the oaks are joined by conifers of South American provenance (Wagner, 1964, pp. 236-9). Similarly, above the tree line in Guatemala, the bunch-grass assemblage has Mexican and even U.S.A. associations, whereas in Costa Rica, above, say, 3100 m, the shrubby open landscape has closer floristic affinities with the Andean *páramos*. The proportion of indigenous plants increases with height.

The fauna of Central America is essentially a diluted assemblage of nearby South American species, as befits an area on the edge of the Neotropical realm of the zoologists, with a substantial minority of northern creatures, and two highland areas (one western Panama and eastern Costa Rica, the other the Guatemala–Honduras–northern Nicaragua region) that have served as local areas of evolution or endemism (West, 1964; Stuart, 1964). The monkey family, for example, is a southern one. The howler and spider monkeys are the only ones to have reached into Mexico, the long-tailed capuchin reached north-eastern Honduras but the nocturnal douroucouli only as far as eastern Panama; in practice, monkeys are rarely encountered beyond Costa Rica. The opossums, too, are animals with southern affinities. Although the common opossum is found in the U.S.A. and three other varieties reach southern Mexico, the water opossum does not extend beyond Salvador and Honduras, the brown opossum beyond southern Nicaragua or the short-tailed opossum beyond eastern Panama. The jaguar, important in mythology, the ocelot, the jaguarundi and the margay, all members of the cat family, are at home in the South American forests and have spread throughout Central America. In contrast, the puma, like the gray fox and the coyote, is of North American origin; the coyote does not extend into southern Central America. The racoon from the north, which reaches South America, and the kinkajou from the south, which reaches Mexico, are similar, gentle animals that suggest the manner in which different geographical distributions overlap in Central America. The dried armadillos offered for sale in the markets of Central America are representatives of the South American family that includes the anteater and the sloth; the sloth reaches only as far north as eastern Honduras. More familiar to a North American would be the deer, which remain fairly abundant in the lowland forests. There are also surprising gaps in the animal population of the isthmus: for example, although there are bears in Mexico and adjoining South America, there are none in Central America. Perhaps the most distinctive mammal of Central America is the aquatic, herbivorous manatee, which still survives in some of the more isolated lagoons and estuaries of the east, despite persecution for its flesh and blubber; it is larger than its Amazonian cousin.

The various families of land turtles found in Central America have both northern and southern relatives, although there are fewer species here than in either Mexico or in northern South America. The huge fresh water turtle, once distributed throughout Europe, Asia and North America, survives today as a living fossil, only in Central America. The sea turtles are, of course, common to the eastern hemisphere as well. It is the green sea turtle that is most prized for its meat, although, as with other turtles, its eggs are also eaten; although found off both coasts, it is economically most important in the Caribbean. Another reptile, which may also be bought live in Central American markets and which has both northern and southern relatives, is the iguana. These large, leathery lizards may be up to two metres long and can tolerate a great variety of conditions throughout the warm lowlands. There are large numbers of snakes in Central America. Although sculptured rattlesnakes decorate many Mayan bas-reliefs and played a part in the rain cult, in life they hardly penetrate Central America and only one species reaches Costa Rica. In contrast, the bushmaster, the largest of the poisonous snakes of Central America, is a southern reptile and is not met with much beyond the northern frontier of Costa Rica. None of the giant anacondas of South America is found in Central America, but three-metre-long boa constrictors are not uncommon throughout the lowlands; they are even found in southern Mexico.

Central America is extraordinarily rich in bird life, residents being augmented by annual migrants. Parrots are abundant, and the variety of species is very large in the southern lowlands. Humming-birds, too, are numerous and can be seen even in the higher mountains of Guatemala and in the Cordillera de Talamanca. Perhaps the *quetzal*, a trogon, is the best known Central American bird; its brilliant tail feathers were prized by Mayans and Aztecs (and later the Victorians) and have been adopted as a national emblem by Guatemala. At home in the damp cloud-forests from southern Mexico to Panama, it has now become a rarity and is confined to the less accessible parts. The toucan family is essentially from the northern part of South America, but toucans, with their outrageous beaks, do penetrate the isthmus and some even reach central Mexico. Large numbers of North American species winter in Central America, their flight paths converging as the land tapers southwards.

The river fish population of Central America is relatively small and does not show the same variety of types that the bigger rivers show further north and south. Fish with South American affinities naturally become more important in the southern part of the isthmus and the progression has been well established. To the layman perhaps the most interesting fish are the landlocked sharks found in the Nicaraguan lakes and the displaced salt water fish found in Lake Izabal in Guatemala; they have successfully adjusted themselves to relatively recent changes in the physical geography of the isthmus. Very different constraints operate on sea fish. Until late Tertiary times, the Pacific and Caribbean were linked and the species were shared; since then there has been some differentiation, but the similarities are still more notable. The Caribbean banks, particularly those off the Mosquito coast of Honduras and Nicaragua and off Belize are rich fishing grounds and have no counterpart in the Pacific where the shallow water zone is narrow; the Pacific coast has valuable shellfish and the Californian tuna fleet now fishes the waters as far south as Ecuador.

CENTRAL AMERICA IN PREHISTORY

Man was added to the fauna of the Americas relatively late, perhaps about 27,000 years ago. By 9000 years ago, he had spread from the Behring Straits to southern South America, presumably by way of the Central American corridor (Wolf, 1959, pp. 22–3). Unfortunately archaeologists disagree on the identification and associations of the supposedly earliest artefacts so far found in Central America, and, as yet, no date can be usefully offered for the beginning of human occupation of the isthmus. Archaeological sites abound, but many have not been scientifically investigated and serve today solely as convenient quarries for tourist souvenirs. This is a pity because investigations have gone far enough to make it clear that Central America was very close to the centre of the Neolithic revolution, which introduced agriculture to the Americas.

There are two schools of thought on the origins of agriculture in the New World. Sauer's (1952) attractive hypothesis places the agricultural hearth just to the south of Central America in, perhaps, northern Colombia. He believes cultivation began with the planting of roots, such as manioc, by sedentary river folk, and the idea then spread southwards along the Andes and northwards through the isthmus, becoming modified by new techniques and new plants as conditions changed. Given the necessary geographical and botanical environment, security and leisure, the intellectual step required to move from gathering to planting appears seductively slight. It is interesting to note that archaeologists are now placing the American origins of pottery and ceramics in northern South America (Lathrap, 1966, p. 267) and that a planting culture of the type Sauer envisaged was in existence in Venezuela 4000 years ago (Willey, 1960, p. 79). Unfortunately it is in the nature of the evidence that few relics of this period should have survived. It is perhaps partly for this reason that most archaeologists incline to an alternative but more demanding hypothesis, which gives pride of place to the invention of seasonal seed agriculture and regards root-planting as a derivative. The earliest evidence of agriculture is of this type; it comes from northern and central Mexico (Mangelsdorf, MacNeish and Willey, 1964). Amongst the earliest domesticated plants recorded there are various species of *cucurbitaceae* (pumpkins, squashes) and beans, which grow wild in Central America, and it is a noteworthy fact that many of the other plants that became cultigens are indigenous to the isthmus. Recently, prehistoric wild maize was identified for the first time at a site in the valley of Tehuacán (Puebla, Mexico) where agriculture began apparently some 4300 to 5400 years ago; it is not difficult to envisage a similar discovery being made in the future in highland Guatemala. One of the most interesting and suggestive of recent excavations in Middle America was made on the Pacific coast of Guatemala, at Salinas La Blanca, near Ocós, where a kind of non-hybridized maize was grown and a system of agriculture practised, which, it is claimed, were both more advanced than those extant at Tehuacán at the same time (2800 to 3000 years ago). Analysis of the middens shows very clearly that, although vast numbers of shellfish and, especially, crabs from the adjoining estuaries supplemented the agricultural diet, hunting of the locally abundant animals played no part in the economy. Coe and Flannery (1967) believe that it was in an amphibious situation rather than in the dry highlands of Mexico that a properly settled agricultural way of life first became a reality, and that it was made possible by the introduction of highland maize some 3500 years ago. Willey (1960, p. 79) believes that sedentary village life was in existence a thousand years earlier in southern Central America and that the southward spread of maize cultivation (which reached Peru 2700 years ago or earlier) was preceded by a type of forest planting culture akin to that envisaged by Sauer. The most recent work on the archaeology of Panama, however, reveals a pattern of scattered and transitory sites and even suggests that many of the cultural traits that moved to South America from Central America went by sea and avoided Panama altogether (Ladd, 1962).

Whatever early role Central America played in the transformation of man's position in relation to his environment, the archaeological record makes it clear that later developments followed two divergent paths. Northern Central America shared the remarkable culture that blossomed in Yucatán and southern Mexico; in contrast, southern Central America vegetated and attracts archaeological interest today largely because of its curiously negative quality, separating, as it does, the two areas of high civilization, Meso America and the Andes (Lathrap, 1966; Evans and Meggers, 1966). The southern boundary of the high culture area ran southwards approximately from what is now Tela on the Gulf of Honduras, up the Ulua river almost to the border of El Salvador, and then turned south-eastwards some 40 or 50 km inland until it reached the sea by the Gulf of Nicoya in Costa Rica.

The areas in northern Central America shared a number of advanced cultural traits in late prehistoric times. One of the most important, as well as most easily appreciated today, was the development of a monumental stone architecture. Planned ceremonial centres began to appear in a landscape that formerly mustered no more than mud-walled houses loosely grouped together into hamlets and villages. Such centres frequently had an essentially rectilinear plan, which combined stepped and truncated pyramids, platforms and spacious courtyards, perhaps flanked by tiered stands or columnated arcades, in an open and organized design. The earliest of such centres in Central America were in the Guatemalan high-lands; the site of Kaminaljuyu, which is now being engulfed by the suburbs of Guatemala City, is not only one of the most accessible but also one of the oldest. Here, a ceremonial centre was in existence as early as 3000 years ago when agriculture was apparently first practised; at its peak, the centre had at least a hundred major structures and 50,000 people were tributary to it in a type of association that has been compared with sixth-century B.C. Athens. The buildings showed very strong links with central Mexico, but other evidence shows these links weakened in the first millennium A.D. and by its end defensive sites comparable to European hill-forts had replaced the open cities of earlier days. In the centuries immediately before the arrival of the Spaniards, many highland sites took on the character of medieval European castle towns, used as religious, commercial and administrative centres, and as a refuge for outlying peoples. Zaculeu was an example of such a centre that had long been occupied and was able to put up a spirited and damaging resistance to the Spanish when attacked in 1525 (de Borhegyi, 1965, p. 43).

It was in the lowlands of the Yucatán peninsula, however, rather than in the Guatemalan highlands, that the architectural qualities of Meso-American civilization reached their zenith. It was about the time of Christ that Tikál and Uaxactún first rose above the tropical forests of the Petén; 150 years later, the building of Copán in Honduras was in full swing, soon to spawn its daughter settlement at Quiriguá. Such well-known sites are extremely large and impressive and are frequently uncluttered by more recent buildings; some, including Copán, have dramatic settings. Sites are sufficiently numerous for the adventurous to share with such earlier visitors as Stephens and Catherwood the thrill of discovery of major ruins, perhaps all but blanketed by the tropical forest (Stephens, 1963). Tikál, in the north-eastern Petén, is the largest site. Here the central cluster of ceremonial constructions, many linked by causeway, occupy 3 km^2, 'suburban' Tikál occupies another 13 km^2, and there are many detached but associated buildings (Willey and Bullard, 1965, p. 368). In many lowland sites, the underlying, gentle topography was remoulded to fit into the orderly concepts of the planner; in the lower Usumacinta sites (for example, Piedras Negras) the terrain is too accidented and the plans were bent to take advantage of the hills (Pollock, 1965, p. 391). In addition to the major sites, there are innumerable house-mounds and lesser ruins testifying to a substantial population in the first millennium

A.D. The Usumacinta river and its tributary, the Pasión, attracted settlements as did the middle and upper Belize. These, together with the drier north-eastern Petén and the Copán–Quiriguá region, appear to have been the most densely populated parts of the isthmian lowlands at that time. In general, the settlement pattern of the first millennium A.D. appears to have been a dispersed one: the peasants lived in hamlets and periodically visited the ceremonial sites. These sites served not only as centres of religious experience and, presumably, political control, but also as regional and interregional markets; the market as an institution remains one of the lasting traits of northern Central America.

The cause of the collapse of the system, witnessed by the gradual abandonment and neglect of the centres from late classic times (perhaps about 800 A.D.) onwards, remains a matter for speculation. Appeal has been made to such cataclysmic events as earthquakes; epidemics may have scourged the area, but, again, proof is lacking; a critical change in manland relationships, brought about by, perhaps, overpopulation, soil exhaustion and a failing water supply, has also been a popular hypothesis, although difficult to accept as anything more than a local explanation. Internal political changes and pressures from outside seem more likely causes, if difficult to demonstrate conclusively. Mayan civilization proved more tenacious in the highlands (perhaps because it was more urbanized and the centres were not so limited in their functions); it enjoyed a renaissance in the more northerly part of the peninsula under Toltec influence, but even in pre-Columbian days northern Central America had fallen into the role of a buffer zone separating the higher cultural area of Mexico from that of the southern isthmus.

While monumental architecture, mathematics, writing, astronomy and human sacrifices to propitiate the gods were occupying the minds of large numbers in the north, the southern isthmus was a part of a less flamboyant cultural area that included the Caribbean fringes of South America and coastal Ecuador (Lothrop, 1966). There are no signs of large organized communities or of substantial architectural remains; the most interesting archaeological finds relate to pottery and metal-workings. The art of gold-working, derived from South America, was practised in the Azuero peninsula of Panama and in the highlands of Costa Rica for, perhaps, one thousand years before the Spanish Conquest and both these areas were more advanced than the rest of the isthmus. Gold, and cacao from coastal Guatemala, formed items of trade in an area of mainly self-sufficient, thrifty, root crop cultivators; this trade continued into Aztec times.

Between southern Central America and the Maya lands, there lay a fringe area where Maya cultural traits have faded from the archaeological record (Longyear, 1966). El Salvador forms part of this zone and Mayan sites are much more numerous in the intermontane basins of the west than they are in the flatter lands east of the Río Lempa. Oases of high culture existed in the area bordering the Gulf of Fonseca, but links were stronger all through its history with peripheral sites in central Honduras (for example, Comayagua) than with western Salvador. In late prehistoric times, trade in pottery from the Nicoya peninsula of Costa Rica and intervening coastal Nicaragua brought these areas into the Meso-American cultural area.

In summary, the prehistory of the isthmus shows that it was at or near the heart of many of the truly remarkable cultural advances made in the Americas prior to the arrival of the Spaniards. To what extent it owed this to the great variety of opportunities this area offered and to the merging of experience that may have happened as the routes of land migrants converged in the isthmus, it is impossible to know. In broad terms, it is clear that Central America had no distinctive cultural unity in the two millennia preceding Columbus; rather, northern Central America shared many of the attributes of central and southern Mexico, while southern Central America was much more akin to contiguous South America. There was no isthmian unity in 1492.

THE CONQUEST AND COLONIAL INTEGRATION

The divisions in the isthmus before the arrival of the Spaniards continued to some extent during colonial times; they are reflected even in the contemporary situation. The early colonial history of Central America involved two spheres of activity – the one based upon Darien and Castilla de Oro in Panama and the other based upon Mexico City (Sauer, 1966; West and Augelli, 1966, pp. 254–61). It was the lower part of the isthmus that was first brought into European knowledge during the last voyage of Columbus in 1502: he made landfall in the Bay Islands of the Gulf of Honduras and then turned east and south around Cape Gracias a Dios past the Mosquito coast to the gold-bearing areas of Veragua. Had he turned the other way, he might have discovered the high civilization of Yucatán. Loot (especially gold) and slaves drew adventurers to Darien and their numbers were reinforced after Balboa's discovery of the Pacific in 1513. Barbaric treatment and epidemics of diseases carried from Europe soon decimated the native population and antagonized those who survived. Panama City was established in 1519 and became the base for exploration. An expedition under Hernandez de Córdoba led to the founding of both León and Granada in 1524 as centres from which to tap a new source of slaves, some of whom were sent to work the local gold deposits of the Nicaraguan interior while others were shipped south to Peru.

In that same year, 1524, five years after Cortés first entered Mexico City, two expeditions were mounted from Mexico that were to form the springboards for the Spanish empire in northern Central America. On the one hand, Pedro de Alvarado fought his way southwards through the Guatemalan highlands to the lowlands of the Gulf of Fonseca, following established Aztec tribute paths but finding few amenable subjects and little gold; on the other, a sea-borne force was sent by Cortés to the northern Honduran coast where Puerto Caballos (now Puerto Cortés), San Pedro Sula and Trujillo were founded to exploit the placer gold and high-grade cacao of the Ulua and Aguán valleys. Thus the Mexican-based and Panama-based Spaniards met in the same frontier zone that had once served as the major cultural separation in pre-Spanish days.

But, although the early centres of exploration in Central America often survive as political centres today, the major division of early Spanish days was soon reduced. The conquest of Peru by Pizarro in 1532-3 turned Panama into a mere gateway for transients to and from the south; the pacification of Yucatán and the first of the great silver strikes in northern Mexico in the 1540s turned Mexican eyes away from Central America. In 1543, the Captaincy-General of Guatemala, answerable to the Viceroy of New Spain (Mexico), was created with jurisdiction from the Isthmus of Tehuantepec to the empty lands of Costa Rica; Panama, in view of its new function, was incorporated in New Granada and was answerable to the Viceroy of Peru. It was thus in the very early days of the Spanish empire that certain of the prevailing characteristics of the area were established: the political separation of Panama from Central America, the establishment of a core area around the two lakes in Nicaragua, the dualism of the north coast and the interior in Honduras, the emphasis on the Pacific side of the isthmus, the political supremacy of Guatemala, the late emergence of Costa Rica.

In Costa Rica, the core area of today, the cool Meseta Central, was an area unattractive to settlers in the sixteenth century; it proved to have neither gold nor tractable Indians. The small number of white settlers who moved southwards from Nicaragua from the 1560s onwards had to take up subsistence agriculture and to manage on their own. Later, exports of wheat and tobacco placed the colonial economy on a sounder economic basis and encouraged the intensive settlement that characterizes the Meseta Central today. Nicoya and Guanacasti on the Pacific side offered an easy overland route from Nicaragua to Panama and a malleable Indian population and were administered quite separately in colonial times from the rest of present-day Costa Rica. They fell within the Nicaraguan sphere of influence, and the cattle-ranching economy and the more traditional society that arose then persists today. Unlike Costa Rica, the interior of Honduras did contain precious metals, even if the Indians were difficult to subdue, and in the 1570s the silver deposits of Tegucigalpa and Comayagua were discovered. Interior Honduras was to Central America what northern Mexico became to New Spain, and mining and ranching sustained the economy for the next three centuries; the landscape of central

Honduras today, with its red-tiled roofs and white-washed walls, scattered groves of dark-leafed pines, dusty tracks and open views, could easily be mistaken for, say, parts of Guanajuato in Mexico or even parts of Andalusia. The situation in Guatemala was different. Here there was no mineral wealth but there was a sizeable Indian population. Difficult to enslave, the rural Quiché and Cakchiquel were of little interest to any save the Catholic Church and their pacification was left to the Dominican priests. Today, Indians survive in large numbers; the Spaniards never formed a numerically significant proportion of the population and mixed-bloods and *ladinos* (mestizos) represent a much smaller element in Guatemala than they do anywhere else in the isthmus, except for British Honduras and Costa Rica.

After the initial impetus given by the discovery, the Spanish Main lapsed into being a backwater of the empire. The largely unincorporated Caribbean coast provided a safe haven to buccaneers and smugglers, and by the middle of the seventeenth century the English had secured a number of footholds on what was nominally Spanish land. The off-shore islands, such as Providencia, San Andrés and the Bay Islands, the Mosquito coast of eastern Honduras and Nicaragua, and the Yucatán coast of the Bay of Honduras, fell under unofficial English sway. Seventeenth-century pirate strongholds became eighteenth-century shipping points for logwood (from which inferior dyestuffs were extracted) and later mahogany, and English interests extended round the Yucatán peninsula into Campeche. Ephemeral agricultural colonies were started along the Mosquito coast together with more permanent trading centres like Bluefields and Greytown (San Juan del Norte).

The weakness of the Captaincy-General, and the extent to which the Caribbean side of the isthmus was beyond the effective control of the government in Guatemala City in colonial days, is further suggested by the Spanish decision of 1803 to switch nominal jurisdiction over the Mosquito coast to the Viceroyalty of Bogotá (Parker, 1964, p. 234); even today the English-speaking islands of Providencia and San Andrés off the Nicaraguan coast are Colombian territory. Some three centuries of English associations and of neglect by the proper authorities have created a very different cultural milieu on the Caribbean underside of Central America from that on the Pacific side. Amongst the more obvious signs to the contemporary visitor is the English, or an English patois, used as the common language of large areas, the weakness or non-existence of Spanish institutions, and the high proportion of Negroes in the population. In fact, it was not until the middle of the nineteenth century that the political situation of the Caribbean rimland of Central America was regularized: Britain gradually withdrew her protection from the Mosquito coast, but confirmed (although not to Guatemala's satisfaction) British Honduras as a Crown Colony.

The illusion of Central America's colonial unity was weakened in the waning stages of the Spanish empire as interest in, and the ability to maintain, the rigid administrative structure declined. Central America, like the rest of its territories, was viewed from Spain in the light of the contribution it could make to the economy of the mother country. Towards this end trade commodities and routes were restricted, such artificial difficulties compounding those created by nature. Smuggling flourished and the profits and convenience to be won by illicit trading further weakened central authority. Not that Central America offered much to the outside world at this time (Parker, 1964, p. 65); the traditional cacao trade with Mexico persisted, indigo became a speciality crop of San Salvador during the eighteenth century, and the Honduran mines continued to yield silver, but the total trade was small and the interest of Spain correspondingly slight. Within Central America, authority relied on an attenuated set of transport links: coasting vessels were supplemented by trackways, one of which ran the length of the isthmus on the Pacific side between Guatemala City and Panama, another linked the oceans across Panama and two fed the Gulf of Honduras ports.

INDEPENDENCE AND POLITICAL FRAGMENTATION

Independence of Central America from Spain in 1821 came on the coat-tails of Mexico's declaration earlier in the same year. It followed a decade of sporadic insurrections by disaffected regional interests (Parker, 1964, pp. 77–90). After the declaration, effective power lay in the hands of the separate towns of the isthmus, and it took two years for a stable pattern of political alignment to emerge. All except Chiapas eventually rejected union with Mexico, and in 1823 the United Provinces of Central America was proclaimed with its capital in Guatemala City. The five provinces were created through the amalgamation of existing local government districts and approximated very closely to the independent countries of today. They had a total population of about a million and a quarter, with the lion's share in the north (Guatemala around 500,000 and El Salvador around 250,000); the three southern provinces shared the remaining one third (Honduras and Nicaragua about 180,000 and Costa Rica 60,000). The Federation lasted only sixteen years. The liberal ideas that had helped to establish the Federation also helped in its downfall; local quarrels turned into civic unrest and then to civil wars; the three southern provinces seceded first, followed by Guatemala, leaving El Salvador to remain true but only by default. Slowly the provinces declared themselves independent republics and, although the idea of a unified Central America was kept alive, none of the several attempts in the nineteenth and twentieth centuries to resurrect the Federation has succeeded (Castillo, 1966).

Until recently, both internal and external circumstances have been against unification and have worked in favour of the continued Balkanization of the isthmus. Political instability has been one such circumstance. There has never been a sufficiently strong popular mandate to allow unification a chance of success, while the periods of stability have usually coincided with the kind of *caudillismo* for which the isthmus is notorious, and few strong men have had territorial ambitions beyond their national boundaries. Large areas still remain, especially on the Caribbean side, where effective government is still not established; perhaps this task is a necessary alternative or preliminary to extra-national aspirations. It is a situation that reflects the continued small size and uneven distribution of the populations of Central America: the city regions remain and it is only in recent years that transport both within and between the separate countries has been of a nature to encourage the growth of non-local links.

The post-colonial period of political fragmentation has suited outside powers. It suited the British with their *de facto* colonies on the Caribbean shore in the early nineteenth century, and it has suited the United States once the isthmus was brought within its sphere of influence. United States interest stemmed partly from appreciation of the role the isthmus could play in one of the manifest destinies of the United States – the provision of a water route between her east and west coasts. This role first became obvious when the forty-niners retrod the route of the *conquistadores* across Panama and, like them, re-embarked on the Pacific on the way to their El Dorado. The forty-niners also followed the Río San Juan–Lake Nicaragua route. For the next half-century proposals for, and attempts at, canal-building across the isthmus were numerous. It was convenient for foreign negotiators to have alternative governments to bargain with as well as alternative routes to explore. The creation of the Republic of Panama itself is, of course, a striking measure of the manner in which political *minifundismo* was encouraged by United States actions; seen in this light, the creation of the separately administered Canal Zone was a natural corollary.

The manner of the negotiations for the Panama Canal in the early part of this century, the large scale of the enterprise, and the creation of an almost entirely foreign enclave to operate it, all have their counterparts in the other parts of the isthmus. The establishment of the great banana plantations in Costa Rica, Honduras and Guatemala involved similar massive injections of capital, the same abrogation of national rights to United States interests and the immigration of foreign labour, and identified similar poles for recent political agitation. The exploitation of areas so affected involved the building of roads and railways and ports and the creation of other facilities that eventually revert to the local governments; it would have been impossible for the host country to have financed this infrastructure itself. The host countries gained, because areas that had previously been to all intents and purposes outside the national economy were made part of that economy. But the process was a reversible one: the interests of the company became more and more the interests of the country, which frequently had no other significant export to turn to. Institutional changes were made in response to this, sometimes unwilling, identification of interests, while the companies, by spreading their assets over several countries, placed themselves in very strong bargaining positions. These developments did little to improve communications between the republics: in fact, their interests tended to parallel rather than to complement each other. In contrast, links between the individual countries and the United States were strengthened, sometimes to the point of becoming bonds. The strength of these bonds may be judged from the several examples in this century of official American intervention in the internal affairs of the Central American republics – perhaps the presence of U.S. Marines in Nicaragua from 1909 to 1933 is the best example – and the current difficult position in which the United States finds itself in trying to match its officially proclaimed ideals of social justice with the desire of U.S. business interests for political stability in the isthmus.

Not all economic developments in the countries since the middle of the nineteenth century have worked at maintaining separatism. The emergence of coffee as a mainstay of the economies of Guatemala, El Salvador and Costa Rica has introduced a new wealthy class within which there have always been liberals drawn to the political concept of isthmian unity, even though the economic forces in the coffee trade tend to diverge from it. Of more practical importance, however, has been the emergence during the last twenty years of a number of circumstances that have not only made Central American integration more feasible but have also given it a much sounder economic *raison d'être*. An improved road system has helped bring the countries closer; a growing realization that the separate domestic markets are often too small by themselves to support efficient manufacturing industries has helped to promote the idea of a common market; the weakened position of the traditional export staples and the massive increase in population have required a reappraisal of public policy; and the support of the United States and of the United Nations for efforts designed to promote concerted Central American action in tackling some of the economic problems of the isthmus: all these have helped promote a climate in which rebirth of the United Provinces is a political possibility, although the possibility may still be remote. Most of the progress to date has been at the level of economic co-operation where many controversial matters are not solved but sidetracked; the political hurdles to union remain high. The gaps between noble constitutional principles and political reality remain wide in some republics, and the normal, built-in difficulties of reassigning political responsibilities remain very strong in the highly diverse political regimes now in power. Movements towards Central American reunification are well publicized, but a closer look at some of the economic, social and political problems in Central America today may produce a more sober assessment of the weaknesses in these movements.

CONTEMPORARY CENTRAL AMERICA

Fig. 4.2 may serve as an introduction to some of the features of life in Central America today (USAID, 1967). The three cartograms make several facts clear at once. Firstly, Central America is dwarfed in area, population and economic production by Mexico in the north. The isthmus bears the same kind of areal relationship to Mexico that Mexico does to the contiguous United States, each approximately one quarter the size of the other. There are 15 million Central Americans, only one third the number of Mexicans, and the population density of about 180/km² is still very low in comparison with many parts of the world and in particular with the Caribbean islands. In economic terms, Central America produces about one quarter of the volume of goods that Mexico does; this means that, for example, the gross national product of Central America can be equated with that of Northern Ireland or with that of one of the minor states of the United States of America. In the second place, all sets of comparisons between Central America and Colombia are to the advantage of the latter, although the differences are less than those between the isthmus and Mexico. Although less than half the size of Colombia, Central America, if treated as a unit, would rank fifth, immediately after Colombia and before Peru, in any demographic or economic ordering of Latin America.

Fig. 4.2 shows that there are some notable differences within Central America. The disparity between area and population is greatest in the cases of El Salvador, the only Central American country without a Caribbean flank, and British Honduras, the only country without a Pacific backbone. But for large-scale emigration, the population density in El Salvador would be even higher, and illegal settlements in neighbouring countries have been a source of political friction in recent years. Other difficulties, notably those of leading an independent existence in the modern world, face British Honduras, which, with only about 115,000 people, is by far the least populous of any country in the western hemisphere. All the other countries of Central America have a density of population that is above the average for Latin America, although that of Nicaragua is very close to this figure. A more refined measure of man-land relationships is given by the amount of agricultural land available per head of population, especially since the majority of Central Americans still live directly off the land. It is clear that there is relatively less agricultural land available in the three northern countries, albeit for different reasons in each, than there is in the south; the diagram emphasizes the temptation to cross the border offered by the disparity between Honduras and El Salvador. The general relationship between population and economic production is suggested by

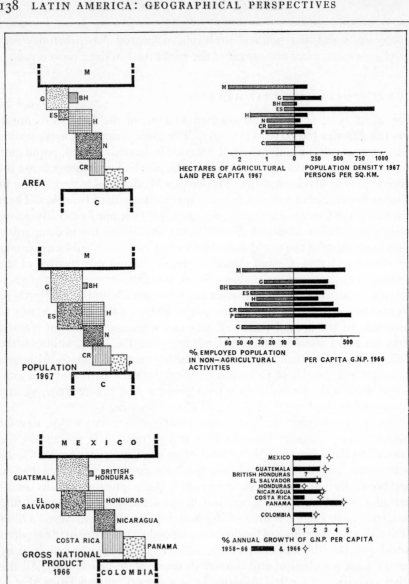

FIG. 4.2 Major characteristics of Central America

the similarities in the two relevant cartograms: Guatemala and El Salvador, although with only one quarter the area, have just over half the population and account for half the production of the isthmus. Nevertheless, a comparison of gross national product on a *per capita* basis shows that the average Panamanian is more than twice as productive as the average Honduran, and that the average Costa Rican is better off than any of his northern neighbours. Such comparisons partially help to explain why Costa Rica was the most reluctant of the countries to join the Central American Common Market, and why Panama, in 1971, still remained outside. The fact that the Costa Rican economy faltered in recent years, whereas that of Panama has continued to boom, may help to explain why Costa Rica eventually joined and Panama, as yet, has not. The weak performance of Costa Rica is exceptional, however, in a pattern of relationships which Fig. 4.2 shows is otherwise consistent: those countries where agriculture plays the smallest role in the overall employment structure enjoy not only the highest *per capita* productivity but also the most rapidly rising overall standard of living. This is a familiar pattern in the developing world. A less universal feature of such developing countries, and certainly not one of some others in Latin America, is the good record of economic growth during recent years. Despite an explosive growth in population, the lot of the average citizen has improved.

Significant though the relative national standings may be at a political level, and important though international boundaries remain in affecting economic developments, many of the features of Central American life today can best be viewed detached from the political map. Some phenomena are common to all the countries, others are regional or local in their impact.

RURAL CONDITIONS

Central America is one of the decreasing number of regions in the world where country people remain in a majority. In 1966 two out of every three Central Americans were classed as rural, compared with only one in two South Americans and one in three North Americans, and many of those classed as urban were farmers living in towns that could perhaps be more properly described as agricultural villages. In 1970, Central America held only a dozen towns with populations over 50,000 and only six of these (all national capitals) exceeded 100,000 people; only one (Guatemala City) passed the half million figure (573,000 in 1964).

Population pressures and land reform

In general, the countryside remains uncrowded. There are a number of areas, however, in which the pressure of population on local resources is becoming difficult, if not impossible, to contain (Fig. 4.3). This is the case in certain of the upland basins of western Guatemala, in the core area of El Salvador, in the Meseta Central of Costa Rica, and perhaps in the area between the two lakes in Nicaragua, in the more densely settled parts of rural Honduras and in western Panama. Rural population densities of over

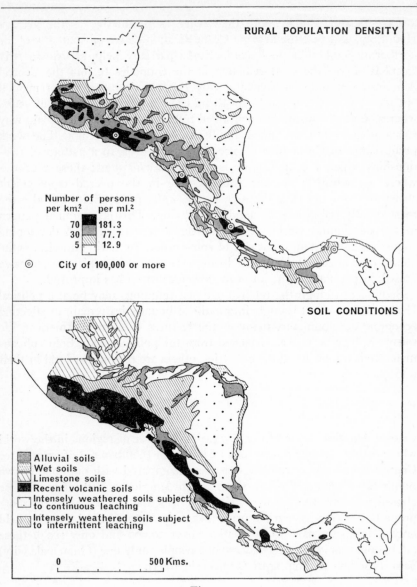

RURAL POPULATION DENSITY

Number of persons
per km.²   per ml.²
70   181.3
30   77.7
5   12.9

⊙   City of 100,000 or more

SOIL CONDITIONS

Alluvial soils
Wet soils
Limestone soils
Recent volcanic soils
Intensely weathered soils subject
to continuous leaching
Intensely weathered soils subject
to intermittent leaching

0   500 Kms.

Fig. 4.3

150/km² exist in places in all the countries except Honduras and British
Honduras, a figure in sharp contrast to the average rural density of below
20/km², and in even more striking contrast with the Caribbean half of the
isthmus where rural densities almost nowhere exceed 5/km² (Nunley,
1967). The effect of this highly uneven distribution of population is being
heightened by the extraordinarily high rate of population growth. No other
country in the world equals Costa Rica's rate of 3·8 per cent per annum;

Guatemala claims a higher birth-rate, but poorer medical facilities give it the lowest overall rate of growth in the isthmus although it is still over 3 per cent annually.

There are several responses open to the hard-pressed country-dweller to counter the economic impact of a population doubling itself in a generation. One is to absorb it by increasing the carrying capacity of the land, already to all intents and purposes completely cultivated, by using improved materials and methods. Another is to supplement local income by working away from home part of the year. A third is to move away altogether, either to another part of the countryside, perhaps as a labourer, perhaps as a pioneer farmer, or to the towns: this may mean moving from one country to another, and perhaps becoming aware of the concept of nationality for the first time. All these reactions are met with in Central America.

The *altiplano* of western Guatemala offers many overt signs of the impact of land pressure (PAU, 1965). It is a landscape in which steep slopes rim such lakes as Atitlán and the western volcanoes, while a blanket of volcanic dust has muted an earlier hill country to the north-east and produced extensive flattish basins crevassed by deep *barrancas*. Substantial villages fringe the lakes and punctuate the basins bearing witness to the heavy population; they may be overlooked by an old Maya temple reminding us of their long history of settlement. The remarkable feature of the region, however, is the almost complete cultivation of the land, no matter how steep the slope; it is particularly notable in a part of the world where, still, most of the land remains uncultivated. Apparently every acre is carefully husbanded, producing a manicured landscape with nothing of the untidiness characteristic of most parts of tropical America. Slopes as steep as 30° are planted by hand and terraces built to minimize the chances of soil erosion. On the flat land the tiny size of the individual plots accurately suggests the minimal size of most holdings and helps explain the intensity of their cultivation; no land is wasted on field boundaries and few fossil structures are permitted to exist in the agrarian scene. This is Indian territory and, unlike most of Guatemala, has been largely protected since the Spanish Conquest from enclosure attempts. Under these circumstances, the overwhelming concentration on food staples becomes readily explicable. In August, the entire agricultural area is under ripening corn – usually maize but with some wheat above 3000 m – usually grown alone, but sometimes in conjunction with beans and squash. The great range of corn grown – early and late, tall and short, hybrid and non-hybrid – ensures that the countryside, far from presenting the geometrical uniformity of monoculture elsewhere, is a polychrome patchwork of greens and browns: a humanized, not a mechanized, landscape.

Perhaps two-thirds of the families own land, but extremely few own more than 2 ha; the population has tripled since the beginning of the century and in many *pueblos* the average land holding is now under 1 ha. Most of the holdings have been inherited, and the land owned by any one family may be scattered as a series of fragments. Land is sold, but only with the greatest of reluctance for it is a form of basic insurance; it is a measure of the dire straits into which many families have fallen that perhaps one quarter of the existing holdings has been acquired by the present owners through purchase. Land that is sold is not normally sold to outsiders, and, since most of the *minifundistas* are Indians, the relatively homogeneous patterns of landownership and rural practices are retained. This introspective attitude unfortunately makes innovations difficult to take root and capital for long-term improvements difficult to obtain. Little money is available for purchase of fertilizers or new seeds, and it is as difficult to persuade subsistence farmers to vary traditional habits here as elsewhere. Continuous monoculture and the ever-increasing incentive to cultivate land which nature places at risk have meant that average yields are probably declining here at a time when most yields elsewhere are rising. Yields of wheat average only about 600 kg/ha, and of maize 800 kg/ha, or approximately half the figure on the Pacific Costa; a moderate application of capital and an effective agricultural advisory service could easily increase these figures. But a *per capita* income, including the value of home-grown food-stuffs, of under 100 U.S. dollars a year, a virtual lack of other funds and an understandably jaundiced view of outside bodies make improvements difficult to achieve. However, the emergence of market gardens in the eastern *altiplano* between Guatemala City and Lake Atitlán (where traditional methods of careful hand tillage on tiny plots are combined with the use of modern fertilizers, insecticides, hybrid seeds, etc., to produce onions, potatoes, flowers and green vegetables) shows that it is possible to overcome these obstacles given appropriate market conditions.

Few, even of the landowning families, can subsist on the products of their plots, nor need their cultivation absorb more than one third of the working year. Forty per cent of the income of the *minifundistas* is now drawn from outside their holdings. The opportunities locally for supplementing income are small: the gathering of fuel and making of charcoal is one, but is becoming more arduous as an increasing demand means that more and more distant supplies are tapped; work in cottage industries is another. Public works programmes are often run only on unpaid local labour. A few families have additional plots in other parts of the country, notably in the Costa, and some men work in the towns or as traders, but it is as migratory agricultural labour that most are able to improve their incomes. Between 200,000 and 250,000 families worked as migrant labour in Guatemala in 1965–6 and most of these were from the *altiplano*, although some came from Baja Verapaz and Jutiapa (Schmid, 1967, p. 1). The coffee harvest of the lower Pacific slopes is the main draw, partly because it begins in November after the corn has been safely harvested at home. The coffee *finqueros* frequently work through contractors (*habilitadores*) who arrange for truckloads of Indians to report at the appropriate time. Sometimes the workers are able to pick over a coffee *finca* on the lower slopes (say about 500 m) in time to move to a higher *finca* in the main coffee zone, but most are away no more than three months. The newer cotton farms and sugar plantations on the Costa itself also absorb some of the migratory labour at harvest time, but, although wages are slightly higher, the harvests fall at less convenient times and working conditions are tougher. The complete lack of any shortage of agricultural labour on these commercial farms on the Pacific slope is a measure of the land hunger in the *altiplano*. Some move from the Costa to temporary employment in the towns or the forests before returning, such is the attachment of the Indian to his *tierra sagrada*.

A number of other escape valves have been opened up in recent years to supplement the temporary relief provided by seasonal work away from the *altiplano*. The improvement in the Inter-American Highway from Guatemala City via Huehuetenango to San Cristóbal de las Casas in Mexico has opened up the limestone soils of the western border to the Indian from the *altiplano* and some have settled in adjoining Chiapas; such a move has changed the cultural milieu in which the Indians live only slightly. Some of the land in Guatemala was supplied from the National Finca, government lands taken from German coffee planters during the Second World War. The improved roads to Cobán and from the capital to Puerto Barrios on the Caribbean have also acted as catalysts to settlement, as will the road to Flores when it is secured. But the most important road to come into commission in recent years has been the Coastal Highway, a surfaced road running along the Pacific coastal plain from the Isthmus of Tehuantepec to the Gulf of Fonseca; it is along this road that the greatest expansion of cultivated land, and of commercial production, has occurred. The largely successful outcome of the campaign begun in the early 1950s to eradicate malaria from these lowlands has also played an important role in opening up this area, as has the world demand for cotton. Although much of the growth has been of large commercial farms raising sugar cane, cotton or cattle, there has been spontaneous and organized settlement by refugees from the *altiplano*, as well as by infiltrators from El Salvador. The best publicized of the organized settlements has been on lands between Tiquisate and Nueva Concepción, which were formerly owned by the United Fruit Company and grew bananas. In 1963, plots of 20 ha each were distributed to needy and favoured individuals and the area now supports a population of about 5000 at a more-than-minimal standard of living. An equal amount of land has been distributed in other parts of the Pacific lowlands, although the land reform programme in general lacks the impetus some would like to see it have.

Many of the characteristics of population pressure extant in the Guatemalan *altiplano* are duplicated in large parts of rural El Salvador and are most obvious in the east and north-east. Forty per cent of the farms in

El Salvador are under 1 ha in area and grow subsistence crops; as in Guatemala, many farmers must supplement their incomes, and it is estimated that about 250,000 move to seek temporary work in the coffee *fincas* and in the cotton and cane fields at harvest time (West and Augelli, 1966, p. 413). But in other respects the situation differs in El Salvador. In the first place, it is a *ladino* population without the cohesion and traditionalism of the Guatemalan Indian. Although maize remains the main staple, sorghum is widely grown in the drier parts (intertilled with maize as an insurance against drier years), and the diet of the rural Salvadorean is more varied than that of his Indian neighbour. It is true that steeper slopes are cultivated by hoe and digging stick, but here the plough may be used on the flatter lands. Another important difference is that most of the smallholders rent their land from the large landowners, paying rent either in cash or kind, and only a minority holds title to the lands. Frequently leases are for a matter of months and security of tenure for more than a year is rare. Such circumstances mean that the Salvadorean does not have the same attachment for the land as his Guatemalan counterpart and has shown himself more prepared to move: nowhere in El Salvador has population pressure built up to the same level as, for example, it has in the vicinity of Quetzaltenango. In the nineteenth century this mobility resulted in the widespread spawning of hamlets and *aldeas*, transforming the colonial landscape of compact villages and towns into one today characterized by a much more dispersed and even scatter of settlement than that found in any other area of comparable size in Central America. Even the poorer land in El Salvador is now in danger of over-exploitation, however, as the pressure mounts, and many Salvadoreans have found it expedient, if not mandatory, to seek a livelihood abroad. Some have taken temporary work in the banana plantations of the north coast of Honduras, and more have squatted on unused land across the Guatemalan and Honduran borders. A detailed map of rural population densities recently prepared shows that there is, in fact, no break as the border is crossed (Nunley, 1967, p. 82). Rather, the level only drops below $75/km^2$ between 15 and 30 km deep into Guatemala, and it is no coincidence that the heaviest rural population density in Honduras, behind Choluteca, is only 30 km from the Salvadorean border. An estimated 200,000 Salvadoreans now live in Guatemala and 300,000 in Honduras, but, since illegal migration is a smouldering issue between El Salvador and her neighbours, which, as recently as 1967 and 1969, has flared into military action, reliable statistics are obviously not available; the figures offered serve to measure the scale of the phenomenon. With the exploitation of the new lands along the Pacific coastal highway settled in the last decade, there is little scope for extension of agriculture to uncultivated areas; the government is concentrating on encouraging the intensification of land use. The Lempa river is already harnessed as a source of power and of irrigation water, and further works are planned.

The only part of Nicaragua with a relatively high density of rural population is the neck of land separating the two lakes near the capital, Managua. The manner in which most people live in the countryside today follows patterns inherited from colonial days. Thus the majority work as labourers on large haciendas or on smaller *fincas*, and some supplement their earnings by working small plots normally rented from the larger landholders; most live in villages sited to serve the convenience of the haciendas. The improvement of the coastal road, to Tanque via Chinandega in one direction, and to Costa Rica in the other, and an anti-malarial campaign have opened up fresh lands and supplied some relief to labourers displaced by mechanization of farm work. The land bounding the Rama road, east of Lake Nicaragua, is potentially the most interesting prospect should the pressure on land in the west increase.

One half of the population of Costa Rica lives, as does that in Nicaragua, within 80 km of the capital, and the populations of the two countries are approximately the same. Nevertheless, the rural population density around San José is four times as high as it is in the lake lowlands of Nicaragua and appears to be reaching saturation point at current levels of management. The difference between the two areas is suggested by the fact that, whereas the proportion of the Nicaraguan population living in the lake lowlands is rising, that in the Meseta Central is dropping: all the municipalities around the Meseta have gained agricultural migrants for whom there is simply no room in the core region of the country. There are other differences. For example, the social structures of the populations are different. The large hacienda is foreign to the traditions of the Meseta Central and, although the average size of farm unit is rising, this is due to the operation of modern cost factors favouring larger enterprises and not to the existence of colonial or post-colonial land grants. The very small holdings are less common also and three-quarters of all farms are owner-occupied. Family labour is more important than hired help. The economic and social ambience produces a more equitable system of rural exploitation, and the fabric of the rural landscape is of a finer, more even texture, reminiscent of certain parts of peasant Europe. Without the focus of the hacienda, the settlement pattern is irregular. Red-tiled and corrugated-roofed houses straggle along the close network of farm roads and, by their pattern and numbers, indicate the way in which pressure on the land has mounted. Some relief has been found by intensifying cultivation of coffee and, west of Alajuela and at lower levels, sugar cane; elsewhere in the higher, more temperate, areas dairying is becoming more important in a mixed farming economy that has been a feature of the Meseta since the end of the nineteenth century. The situation is a far cry from the very limited economy of the Altiplano at similar altitudes in Guatemala.

Emigration from the Meseta Central has taken people in all directions (Sandner, 1962). Some have moved down on to the edge of the Caribbean lowlands and at Siquirres, now accessible by road from the Meseta and long accessible by rail, white and Negro smallholders come face to face, both assisted by their government through various incentives to be success-ful colonists. Former banana lands are being rehabilitated and new villages, with social and other services supplied, have been completed. Other moderately successful colonies have been established on the northern side of the volcanic range. But the most attractive areas of spontaneous settle-ment have been on the Nicoya lowlands on the drier part of the Pacific coast, and on the alluvial soils of the Valle del General in the south. The Inter-American Highway first penetrated the Sierra de Talamanca in the 1930s and San Isidro became the regional centre for the 60,000 people who now live here, 500–700 m above sea-level, within the *tierra caliente*. The dirt highway continues southwards and has attracted settlement, aided by the stimulus of successful banana plantations along the coast. The border between Panama and Costa Rica is now quite densely settled, colonists from Italy as well as the Meseta Central being grafted on to the local population.

Rural population densities are low in Panama, but because shifting agriculture is still important, a figure of $40/km^2$ for the Azuero peninsula creates pressures that other agricultural systems would not; new roads and the possibilities of irrigation should moderate a situation in which demo-graphic growth has only just begun to be matched by economic changes.

Frequently linked to the question of rural population pressures is the question of land reform. It is argued that the traditional pattern of rural life that prevails over most parts of Central America is inimical to the re-lease of those pressures. In most parts lip-service has been paid to the need for rural change, but little has been achieved. Guatemala has its Instituto Nacional de Transformación Agraria, which has redistributed the former German-owned coffee lands and the banana lands formerly owned by the United Fruit Company. Nevertheless, a tiny minority of only 1·6 per cent of the agricultural families own 72 per cent of the land and account for over 56 per cent of the value of agricultural production (Pearse, 1966, p. 62); one thousand large estates occupy over half of the land in cultivation while 27 per cent of the families are without any land to their name. The situation in El Salvador and Panama is not very different. In Nicaragua it is stated that one third of all the privately owned land is divided amongst only 350 estates and probably even fewer families (Crossley, 1962, p. 35). Costa Rica has a different tradition of smallholdings, but even so there are parts (for example, Guanacaste) where the statistics on rural income distribution resemble those of the rest of Central America. Accurate statistics are few and a definitive cadastral survey is only just getting under way, despite active United States encouragement.

Two different social and economic classes characterize most of Central America; they are widely separated by a deep gap, which is apparently widening. It is perhaps fortunate that dense rural populations are the exception rather than the rule. They are exceptions of long standing. A map of the pre-Spanish population of Central America would have shown broadly the same distributional pattern, although without the same degree of concentration in the Meseta Central of Costa Rica. It is notable that this long-standing pattern broadly corresponds with the qualities of soils found in Central America (Fig. 4.3): the highest densities are associated with the young soils of recent volcanic origin subject to only intermittent leaching, while the older, intensely weathered soils carry only light populations; the heavier the rainfall, the more continuous the leaching of the soil and the lower the rural population density. Until a century ago, the correspondence between the volcanic soils and the populous areas of Central America was even stronger than it is today and the growth in importance of coffee as a commercial crop from the 1870s onwards did nothing to weaken the association. The moderate to heavy population densities found on many of the pockets and zones of alluvial soil in Central America are largely a recent phenomenon and their settlement has normally awaited the application of considerable capital resources and technological expertise. Ports, railways and roads have made them accessible and public health campaigns made them habitable. Voluntary migration to these areas has been a much more important demographic fact than the organized land settlement programmes of the various official agrarian reform and colonization agencies that have sprung up in recent years. Nevertheless the large landholder has, in the nature of things, been more important and played a more positive role here than elsewhere in Central America. The incentive for the development of the alluvial lands has been the commercial profits to be won in the export markets and it is the importance of the crops grown for foreign consumption that set these alluvial soils apart from most of the rest of the isthmus.

The export crops

The dependence of the economies of many of the Central American countries upon a small range of certain rural products is notorious. In 1967, over 70 per cent of the total value of goods exported from Central America was contributed by only three items – coffee, bananas and cotton. In the five years from 1962 to 1966, 33 per cent of the total export income was due to coffee, 15 per cent to bananas and another 15 per cent to cotton.

Coffee Coffee was the first of the staples to emerge in Central America: it was first grown there on a commercial scale in the late eighteenth century and had become securely established in Costa Rica in the 1830s. It spread to El Salvador and Nicaragua in the 1840s and to Guatemala in the 1860s; it has attained importance in Honduras only since about 1940. It is a highly profitable crop in Central America and production has risen markedly, not least during the 1960s; annual coffee production in Central America is on a par with that of Colombia.

TABLE 4.1   *Export earnings, 1967*

Country	% of total goods exported			Total value of goods exported (million U.S. dollars)
	Coffee	Bananas	Cotton	
Guatemala	47	6	24	138
British Honduras	—	—	—	12
El Salvador	67	—	18	133
Honduras	14	58	4	125
Nicaragua	16	—	48	116
Costa Rica	48	32	—	113
Panama	—	51	—	110
Total	33	23	16	747

— = nil or insignificant
Source: UNECLA, 1969, pp. 142–5, 179

Several circumstances made coffee successful in Central America. In the first place the region offers excellent natural conditions for the coffee plant, which needs a seasonal, almost monsoonal climate, wet during the early part of the year but followed by several dry months for harvesting the bean. Such a climate is typical of the Pacific slopes of the isthmus. Most commercial coffee is grown at altitudes between 300 and 1700 m, where the narrow annual temperature range falls within the appropriate limits for the plant; the best coffee (that is, mild coffee commanding the highest price on the world market) is grown near the upper altitudinal limits where the bean takes longest to mature.

Coffee grows best in well-drained, fertile soils and the shrubs can be planted safely on steep slopes without necessarily exposing them to erosion since most coffee is grown under shade trees. The soils of the volcanic slopes of the Pacific side of the isthmus are ideal. In some places the shade is from natural woodland, in the lowlands it may be from bananas and elsewhere from trees specially planted for the purpose. In El Salvador, trees whose leaves hang pendant during the night are used, for these generate exactly the right local climatic conditions for the coffee below.

Successful coffee cultivation calls for generous supplies of cheap labour; Central America offers this in abundance. About a million temporary workers help to bring the coffee harvest home each year. In 1967 a family of Guatemalan migrant workers could expect to earn about 90 U.S. cents a day (or 60 U.S. cents after allowing for the cost of food rations) for picking a *caja* (about 45 kg) of beans (Schmid, 1967, pp. 20–9). Total labour costs on a typical El Salvadorean coffee *finca* in the same year could be covered with only one quarter of the f.o.b. price of coffee at the port. Further, reasonable accessibility to shipping points and to the main market, the United States, may be added to the advantages which Central America offers coffee producers.

There are some 150,000 coffee farmers in Central America. This statement in itself might be misleading; 66 per cent of the total area in coffee and between 80 and 90 per cent of coffee production is in the hands of the top 5 per cent of farmers. The concentration of production by a few individuals is more striking in Guatemala and El Salvador, which account for over half the coffee produced, than in the isthmus as a whole. The trend is towards an even higher degree of concentration. Many of the larger coffee plantations in these two northern republics are very well managed and yields may reach 2000 kg/ha. By investing in improved varieties of coffee plant, double-planting the coffee rows, making increasing use of fertilizers and insecticides and making economies, production costs may be kept as low as 30 U.S. cents/kg and the income to the coffee-grower (on which he will, quite legitimately, pay little or no tax) may be in excess of $500/ha. In El Salvador, where the pressure on land is greatest, the average yield is now about 900 kg/ha, compared with a figure of 600 kg/ha for the isthmus as a whole.

Yields are highest in Costa Rica where the natural conditions provided by the Meseta Central for the growth of high quality coffee are almost ideal and where pressure on the land has induced the adoption of the most modern and intensive methods of coffee cultivation. Costa Rica produces as much coffee as do Nicaragua and Honduras combined, and that is from only one third of the area; between 1952 and 1962 production in Costa Rica doubled but the area in coffee remained the same. One feature of Costa Rican modernization has been the amalgamation of many of the traditional small farms to form larger working units. In consequence, even though the structure of land tenure is less unbalanced than elsewhere, one half of the coffee crop is now produced by fewer than 2 per cent of the producers (West and Augelli, 1966, p. 444). The point above which modern intensive production methods begin to lower production costs is measured by a yield of about 1000 kg/ha. It is of interest to note that this would have been the average yield for Costa Rica in 1967 but for the disorganization caused by the recent eruption of the volcano Irazú.

Yields in Honduras and Nicaragua are between only 300 and 400 kg/ha. Natural circumstances are less propitious to coffee cultivation, and cultivation methods, although changing in Nicaragua, remain largely traditional. Nevertheless, coffee is a well-established crop in Nicaragua (Radell, 1964). Its first commercial success was due to the demands created by the forty-niners who followed Vanderbilt's route across the country on their way to California; it remained the most valuable export of the country for almost a century. Half the coffee comes from the volcanic uplands to the south of Managua but here periodic emissions of sulphurous fumes and cinders from the Masaya Caldera are a hazard to the crop and the scarcity of water in the scorching dry season limits the processing of the coffee. Production is on large haciendas, 90 per cent of which are owned by absentee landlords, and a higher proportion of the labour is seasonally employed than is the case elsewhere. Most of the rest of Nicaragua's coffee comes from smaller plantations in the highlands behind Matagalpa where the cultivation methods are extremely poor but the coffee comes from above the 800 m contour line and its better quality commands a higher price than coffee from Masaya. Labour is in relatively short supply and frequently part of the crop remains unharvested.

Coffee has only been recently introduced into Honduras. It is suggestive that this should have occurred only since immigration from El Salvador has reached substantial proportions. It is particularly in the areas adjoining the north-eastern border of El Salvador and the area behind Choluteca that coffee is grown. *Fincas* are small, traditional methods are employed and yields are poor.

One of the interesting aspects of coffee production in Central America has been the stimulus it has provided for the development of improved transport routes (USAID, 1965). The first railway in Guatemala (1877) was built to link the coffee market of Escuintla with the sea at Puerto San José; by 1904 a line ran at the foot of the whole of the coffee zone to the west of Escuintla and a link to Guatemala City had been extended across the country to Puerto Barrios, providing a direct Atlantic outlet for Guatemalan coffee. The Verapaz railway in eastern Guatemala was built in 1884 specifically to serve the coffee interests and it remained open until 1963. In El Salvador the assembly, link by link, of the existing railway system in the late nineteenth century went hand in hand with the reorganization of the land tenure system (which favoured the creation of large estates at the expense of the communal village lands or *ejidos*), and both were spurred on by the profits to be won from large-scale coffee production. In Nicaragua the fragmentary road, railway and river transport systems have always been inadequate. Economic development in general has suffered; even today some of the coffee produced travels by mule train on its way to market (at an approximate cost of ten to twenty times the comparable rates by lorry or rail). The need for a Caribbean outlet for the coffee produced in the Meseta Central was the major factor behind the decision of the Costa Rican government in 1871 to commission the Northern Railway; it was from Minor Keith's association with this enterprise that there sprang the subsequent involvement in the isthmus of the United Fruit Company. Although most coffee now travels by the new roads, there is still no road competing with the Caribbean section of the British-owned Northern Railway, and Puerto Limón, to which the railway leads, still handles a proportion of the coffee exports of the country.

Bananas Good transport routes have been of even more critical importance in the development of the banana economy of the isthmus. This is in part because bananas are a perishable commodity and must be consumed within weeks of being cut, even if they are cut green: unlike most fruits, whose markets have been expanded by modern preserving methods, almost all bananas are eaten fresh. Further, bananas, on a weight-for-weight basis, are far less valuable than coffee and so are far less able to carry anything other than low transport costs. Fast and frequent shipments to market demand large-scale operations and heavy capital investments; were it not for the fact that bananas, unlike coffee, may be harvested throughout the year, such investments would not have been forthcoming. Capital was necessary because in the areas best suited to bananas – the virtually unpopulated alluvial lands of the wet Caribbean coast – not even a rudimentary transport system existed; in contrast the coffee economy flourished in areas already long populated and under circumstances in which production could be expanded fairly easily as markets emerged.

The first commercial banana shipments of any importance were made from the Caribbean lowlands of Costa Rica at the time when the Northern Railway was under construction. The difficult engineering works, disease and other hazards made construction unexpectedly expensive and banana shipments were begun as the Caribbean spur was extended to help recoup some of the high outlay. By the end of the nineteenth century, three districts (the area tributary to Puerto Limón and the Northern Railway, the Bocas del Toro area across the border in Panama and the Bluefields region of Nicaragua) had all been transformed from chaotic tropical rain-forest into geometrical plantations of bananas (West and Augelli, 1966, pp. 384–6). Many of the pioneers in bananas, as in coffee, came from outside Central America. But whereas some of the coffee-growers came to identify themselves (sometimes involuntarily) as Central Americans, the creation of the United Fruit Company in 1899 and then of the Standard Fruit Company in 1924 meant that the banana economy became identified with alien, United States interests and this element of national life became a butt for local politicians.

Between 1900 and the peak year of Central American banana production in 1930, shipments increased fivefold. This was due largely to the taming of the alluvial valleys of the north coast of Honduras and of the lower Montagua valley of Guatemala. In 1930, one third of the world's trade in bananas originated in Honduras. The narrow-gauge railway of the Standard Fruit Company was built to serve the eastern plantations of the northern Honduran coast, and the United Fruit (Tela) and Ferrocarril Nacional de Honduras system was built to serve the west; the restricted purpose of the railway is underlined by the fact that there is still no land link, by road or rail, with adjoining Guatemala. Railway construction, land clearance and drainage, the building of ports, towns and plantation facilities, all required

the importation of labour; as with the building of the Panama Canal, much
of this labour came from the British West Indies, particularly Jamaica,
and many stayed on to man the plantations once installation works had
been completed. Although some of the Negro population of the Caribbean
coast of Central America dates from long-standing British interests in the
area, most of it is a phenomenon of the twentieth century. Today it is
in process of dilution as access from the interior has improved and mestizo
labourers are finding their way to the coast.

During the 1930s, 1940s and 1950s the banana economy suffered a
series of setbacks. Panama disease swept the plantations and the Sigatoka
leaf blight made matters worse. There is no cure for Panama disease and
many plantations were abandoned. There was a wholesale shift of interest
to the wetter parts of the Pacific coast, notably to the Chiriqui area of
western Panama and southern Costa Rica, to the alluvial soils of the
Golfo Dulce and Parrita in Costa Rica, and to the well-drained sandy
soils of the Tiquisate area of Guatemala; but costs were higher. The
economic depression of the 1930s and the disruption of trade during the
Second World War reduced production to the level of 1905, but post-war
recovery was rapid and production in both Costa Rica and Panama soon
reached record levels. There was a shift to new varieties of banana much
more resistant to Panama disease, less vulnerable to high winds and giving
higher yields; they are, however, more fragile and must be shipped in
boxes rather than on the stem. The box is important. On the one hand its
cost represented in 1967 one quarter of the f.o.b. price of boxed bananas,
while on the other hand it has cut handling costs and facilitated direct
retailing in the United States market. It has also created a strong demand
for locally produced cardboard.

Other interesting changes occurred in the banana economies of Central
America in the late 1960s. The position of Central America *vis-à-vis* the
other major American producer of bananas, Ecuador, was improving.
Although Ecuador is free from hurricanes and was developed as Panama
disease swept Caribbean Central America, it, too, is now ravaged by the
plague and is less able to meet the standards of quality now demanded by
the United States market; it is also twice the shipping distance from New
Orleans than is Puerto Limón, and bananas from Ecuador have to bear the
considerable cost of tolls through the Panama Canal. The United Fruit
Company is investing in its Central American holdings in preference to
those in Ecuador. But within Central America not all countries are being
treated equally. Little money is being spent in Guatemala, where floods and
hurricanes are admittedly more of a hazard and where the political situation
in the country is also less settled. In contrast, not only North American but
also European interests have been investing money recently in banana
production in Costa Rica.

Another significant shift has been the withdrawal of the fruit companies from some of their traditional functions. In Costa Rica and in Nicaragua the fruit companies are now acting as marketing agents for independent producers. In Costa Rica the government, as part of its policy to promote new settlements outside the Meseta Central, has helped finance small producers and the fruit companies have assisted with stocking materials and advice. The Standard Fruit Company has guaranteed ten-year contracts. Banana shipments through Puerto Limón greatly expanded in the late 1960s as the construction of new feeder railways brought virgin land into production. In Honduras, the largest producer, the traditional arrangements still persist; the government is not anxious to increase its dependence upon bananas any further and is reluctant to encourage peasant proprietors.

Cotton Large-scale cotton production is a much more recent development in Central America and it is only since the Second World War that cotton has become significant (SIECA, 1967). Production in the middle 1960s was ten times the volume of the early 1950s; in 1965 exports of cotton from the isthmus were marginally more valuable than were exports of bananas. This extraordinary development was a response to the rising world demand for cotton. One of the most important internal circumstances which permitted this reaction was the construction of roads in the Pacific coastal plains of the northern republics which opened up large areas of land highly suited to cotton cultivation (USAID, 1965). The littoral highway in El Salvador was built in the early 1950s and made the alluvial soils east of La Libertad to La Unión easily accessible to the capital; most of El Salvador's cotton comes today from this area. In Guatemala, the newer Pacific coastal road to Mexico has similarly attracted plantations during the last decade. The coastal road from Managua to León was extended to Chinandega and Corinto in the late 1950s and the rich volcanic soils of this new area have become the most important single area of cotton-growing in the isthmus. More recently in Nicaragua the Managua to San Benito section of the improved Inter-American Highway, before it leaves the alluvial soils of the Lake Managua lowlands behind, has become bordered by cotton fields. Land of cotton quality is in shorter supply in Honduras and the Choluteca region is the only area of intensive cultivation, cultivation which awaited the surfacing of the Inter-American Highway in the early 1960s. In Costa Rica and Panama land which might grow cotton is better suited to rice, and rice is the crop preferred.

Nicaragua produces about 40 per cent of Central America's cotton, and the sale of cotton supplies about 40 per cent of her foreign exchange; in no other Central American country are these proportions as high. This situation is in part because coffee and banana cultivation is less advanced than in the other countries, but the major causes are the more favourable conditions for cotton. Average cotton yields were higher, production costs

F

lower and profit margins wider in the 1960s than in any of the other countries of the isthmus. It seems that the risk of adverse weather conditions in Nicaragua is less than in, for example, El Salvador; the cotton areas of El Salvador have suffered more from too dry conditions than have those of Nicaragua where the climate appears to be more reliable. Nicaragua has been freer from insect pests and plagues than the other countries until very recently and has been saved some of the cost of expensive insecticides and spraying. Cotton cultivation is more mechanized and practices are more advanced; it is the only country in Central America where the greater part (60 per cent) of cotton is machine-picked, although at some loss of quality.

Guatemala is second to Nicaragua and accounts for almost one third of the cotton production of the isthmus. Yields have been consistently rising during the 1960s and it is a remarkable fact that, with returns of about 800 kg/ha, Guatemala can claim the highest yields for non-irrigated cotton anywhere in the world. The cotton farms are large and highly mechanized in most phases of their operation, although they also employ large numbers of migrant pickers at harvest time. Ownership is restricted: in 1966–7, there were fewer than 400 cotton farmers in Guatemala as compared with over 3000 in El Salvador and over 4000 in Nicaragua. Prospects for the future expansion of cotton-growing are probably brightest in Guatemala where large areas of the coastal plain seem physically suited to cotton production.

Most of the rest of the cotton produced comes from El Salvador though here circumstances make it a less profitable crop. Yields are lower and have fallen from about 700 kg/ha in 1960 to about 550 kg/ha in 1967 and costs are higher. The fertility of the cotton soils of El Salvador, amongst the first in Central America to be planted in cotton, is dropping and expenditure on fertilizer, which is mounting everywhere in Central America, is highest in El Salvador. The much smaller size of the individual cotton farmer's holding and the fact that most cotton land here is rented encourage a non-conservationist approach to farming. Monoculture, the multiplicity of farms and the longer period during which cotton has been cultivated have all allowed plant plagues to establish themselves and spread more widely. Costs of buying and applying insecticides now represent fully one third of total cotton production costs. For these and other reasons, the area under cotton has contracted sharply and recently many marginal producers have gone bankrupt or have switched to other crops.

Although cotton production is small in Honduras, yields are high and Choluteca resembles many of the other towns of the cotton areas – flushed by the success of the cotton bonanza and alive with advertisements for various brands of fertilizers, insecticides, machinery and seeds, and for the cotton co-operative. Here, as in El Salvador, the smallholder is the typical cotton farmer and in both countries he is backed by strong co-operative processing and marketing organizations.

Marketing Marketing is, of course, one of the crucial aspects of the cotton, coffee and banana economies of Central America. It is worth reiterating that one half or approaching one half of the export earnings of all and each of the Central American republics in recent years has been derived from the sale of one of these three agricultural products. A fall in world commodity prices quite outside the control of Central America may have crippling consequences upon the local economies.

The degree of vulnerability to price changes of the commodities and the countries varies. Banana prices are probably the most stable. Most production and almost all the marketing of Central American bananas is controlled by the United Fruit Company and the Standard Fruit Company: almost all the bananas go to the United States where the two companies control 90 per cent of the market. It is a market which seems almost saturated and production is neatly geared to meet a demand which is only rising slowly. Additional markets, perhaps in West Germany or eastern Europe, are theoretically open for competition but any gain would have only a marginal impact on Central America. The long-term price contracts now available in parts of Central America reflect a fairly stable situation.

Between one half and two-thirds of Central America's cotton is bought by Japan. The resurrection of Japan after 1950 has been one of the key factors behind the cotton boom in Central America: trade between the two areas quadrupled between 1958 and 1965. The Japanese stake in Central American cotton has gone beyond being merely commercial: Japanese expertise, advice and credit have also been made available, while quality standards have established a degree of uniformity in the product which may not be altogether to the advantage of Central America. Although the Japanese market seems secure and western Europe still takes a proportion of the crop, the price obtained is governed by world cotton prices, and these appear likely to continue to fall from their high level in the early 1960s. Most cotton farmers, though, with the notable exception of many in El Salvador, will still obtain a profitable price, and agricultural economists anticipate that production will expand sufficiently to counterbalance any fall in income.

The coffee marketing situation is more critical. At the moment the world situation is one of over-supply. In 1956 the average price of coffee was about 120 cents/kg and exports from the five coffee-producing countries of Central America yielded 61 per cent of their foreign exchange; in 1963, the price had slumped to 70 cents/kg and has not yet recovered. Although exports have risen, there has been no notable increase in the income generated. The drastic fall in prices during the 1960s, which, of course, affected coffee producers everywhere, prompted the producing countries to try to regulate world trade in coffee. In 1962, the first International Coffee Agreement came into force. The effect of this Agreement was to allocate to each producing country within the Agreement a quota of the anticipated market of the major consuming countries, all of whom are signatories to the Agreement, and so maintain prices between agreed levels. Coffee production surplus to the requirements of the signatory consuming countries may find markets elsewhere and at prices arrived at by normal market negotiations. All the Central American republics ratified the Agreement and, to date, less than 20 per cent of their coffee has had to seek markets outside the Agreement (mainly in Japan and the Middle East). There have been times when unusual circumstances have meant that individual Central American countries have been unable to meet their production quotas (and excess coffee from neighbouring countries has been smuggled in to take advantage of this situation). But with more coffee being produced in the world, the strain on the Agreement is becoming greater as an unsold surplus accumulates.

Other economic products   From this review of the three key export commodities of Central America, it may be evident that there is little room for a striking increase in the income to be won in this field in the near future; a modest expansion in production may be anticipated, but a decrease in the real unit price seems to be more likely than an increase. A similar assessment and a reluctance to be so dependent upon such a limited range of products has encouraged Central American governments to promote a number of policies designed to strengthen and diversify their economies.

These policies have taken two directions. One is towards diversification of production for both the domestic and export markets; and the other is towards greater international co-operation leading to certain market advantages of scale not open to the countries of Central America individually. Most attention in the matter of diversification appears to have been devoted to measures designed to encourage the development of manufacturing industries; the success of this endeavour is considered below. It may, however, be argued that diversification of the agricultural sector offers a greater chance of long-term gain. The concentration of agricultural production on coffee, cotton and bananas for the export market and on maize and beans for domestic consumption is paralleled in a geographical sense by the concentrated exploitation of very restricted parts of Central America to the virtual exclusion of other, much more extensive, parts of the isthmus. Diversification policies in the field of agriculture have been aimed, on the one hand, at attempts to reduce the degree of concentration on certain products in areas already settled and well established and, on the other hand, at the exploiting of lands whose resources remain virtually untapped.

Agricultural diversification

It is not easy to find a satisfactory substitute for coffee either in the farming economy or in the national commerce. Much coffee grows on slopes too steep to serve as ploughland, and the profits and privileges to be won from coffee cultivation would be difficult to match in another crop. Further, it appears that, within the coffee-growing regions, returns are governed by the quality of farming enterprise rather than by natural conditions: high yields mean adequate profits and no incentive to diversify; poor yields can normally be equated with a low level of modern farm-management skills, and this is an unpromising situation for any would-be innovator hopeful of commercial success. It has been argued that the taxation on coffee and coffee lands could be increased; this not only might make alternatives to coffee relatively more attractive but might also raise the funds available to help the diversification programme. But, even at the present low levels of taxation, there is widespread evasion of payment in, for example, El Salvador and Guatemala, and it seems politically unrealistic to anticipate the kind of drastic change in this direction which might substantially help a diversifying programme. Locally, alternative crops have replaced coffee. The expanding urban markets for fruit and vegetables have led to some substitution near the capital cities, while tobacco cultivation has received a fillip, notably in Nicaragua, from Cuban refugees. Elsewhere, normal market forces have led to the failure of marginal producers and to a less intensive use of the land. In the context of substitute products for export, it must be remembered that Mexico is in a better position to supply the off-season demands of the United States market, and that her marketing arrangements are often superior.

The situation in the banana and cotton lands is more open; here the policy is not so much one of diversification through substitution as diversification through addition (Stouse, 1967). Cacao, rubber and oil palms are the commercial companions most frequently proposed for bananas. In fact, all have been tried and, for example, Guatemala supplies one third of its own rubber requirements from domestic sources. But many of these and other products have suffered marketing difficulties in recent years, and, because of the absence of a return during the first years of cultivation, they have proved unattractive to the majority of Central American farmers. The proven commercial alternatives to cotton are sugar, maize and rice. Land withdrawn from cotton cultivation in El Salvador is most frequently turned over to commercial crops of maize; in Costa Rica and Panama rice is more favoured, while in Guatemala sugar cane is a more likely contender. All these alternatives are destined mainly for the local consumer market and the prices received by the grower are higher than those obtained on the world market. Sugar is the only one of these products which has an export market, and this is a protected one: the key factor is the United States sugar quota and this may be further increased. Sugar exports still account for less than 3 per cent of the total value of Central American exports and even an increase in income of one third would have less effect on the economy of Central America than a rise of only 2 cents/kg in the f.o.b. price of coffee. Citronella and lemon grass are two other grasses of minor commercial interest: oils for perfumes and vitamin preparations are distilled from them, and their cultivation, which is being extended, is a speciality of the Mazatenango-Tiquisate area in Guatemala.

Pastoralism   Some agricultural economists see the most hopeful future for grass in Central America as the basis of a beef and dairy products industry. Cattle-raising is no novelty in Central America, of course, and many of the traditional features of the colonial cattle ranch still survive, especially in parts of western Panama, Guanacaste, interior Honduras, El Salvador and Pacific Guatemala. Cowboys still solve the problems of a lack of herbage during the dry season by rounding up the cattle and trailing or trucking them up to the high pastures or down to the coast. For several centuries, the Pacific coastal plains of Guatemala, El Salvador and Honduras have fattened cattle brought from the interior prior to slaughter, and today cotton seed, molasses and other crop by-products supplement these superior pastures. A much more intensive form of cattle-raising is evolving on the plains; this is taking advantage both of the considerable work done on developing improved strains of tropical grasses and improved breeds of cattle and of the growing demand, locally and in the United States, for beef. Meat-packing plants have come into existence and chilled and processed beef is shipped by sea and air to the United States; its quality, however, remains so poor that much of it is mixed with low-grade domestic meat and eaten in hamburgers. The Canal Zone itself, and the shipping traffic using the Canal, supplies the main market for beef raised in western Panama. Fresh meat is third to cotton and coffee in the export lists of Nicaragua (more is sent abroad than eaten at home is the rather ambiguous claim), third to coffee and bananas in Costa Rica, and now more valuable to Honduras than silver exports. Central America is free from foot-and-mouth disease, an important attribute from the standpoint of the United States market, and there is still considerable room for applying a wide variety of well-tried improvements to take advantage of the rising demand for meat.

The cattle economy has drawn impetus from two other directions. The banana companies, to meet their own requirements, have introduced quality stock to the Atlantic lowlands and their example has been followed by many smallholders; when such veterinary problems as tick control have been solved, there is no reason why the sloping lands above the plantations should not carry a much larger cattle population. The second impetus has come from the rising demand for fresh dairy products from the Central American towns. Intensive dairy-farming is in its infancy, but Guatemala

City and San Salvador are well supplied, often from herds fed on irrigated feedstuffs, and San José draws on the dairy farms above the coffee *fincas* of the Meseta Central, and urban Panama from the western departments. One interesting recent development is the construction of a dried milk plant near Matagalpa in Nicaragua, drawing its supplies from organized herds in the vicinity; but the generally low fat-content of Central American milk and the relatively abundant alternative sources of cheap dried milk cast doubt upon the economies of this project.

Many Central Americans are aware that large sections of the isthmus at present unexploited could be most profitably used under cattle, but some balk at the cost of making such lands accessible. It has been shown in a part of Guanacaste that the return per hectare from cattle farms is only between one quarter and one third of the return from agricultural farms (Aguilar León, 1966, p. 28). Such disparities in returns give fuel to arguments concerning the best use of the scarce funds available for promoting new developments. Should new lands be opened up or should the money be spent on improving the existing, inadequate infrastructure in these parts of the isthmus, notably those with volcanic or alluvial soils, already occupied and of proven productivity? It may be argued that more attention should be focused on the poorer agriculturalists to help them become more productive so that, by entering the commercial life of the country, they would more fully expand the national economy as consumers not only of primary foodstuffs but also of services and manufactured goods as well. In practice, political issues, the sources and availability of external funds and other relevant factors rarely allow questions of alternatives to be reduced to such simple terms.

Forestry One further topic deserves mention in connection with the diversification of the export economies and wider utilization of the empty lands of Central America. This is the commercial role of the forests. About one half of Central America is forested and, like many other parts of tropical America, the first commercial product of many of its Caribbean shores came directly from the forest. Dyewoods and then mahogany, chicle gum and pine timber formed the backbone of the economy of British Honduras for over two centuries; until about 1960, forest products supplied over half of that country's exports. Mahogany grows best and in purer stands on the drier, limestone soils of the lower Petén peninsula, on the edge of the tropical rain-forest belt; and it was the accessibility that the Belize and Sarstoon rivers gave to these forests, fashionable demand, and the advantages of a stable government, that combined to give the colony its economic *raison d'être* in the nineteenth century. During the first half of the present century, chicle, a gum tapped from the chicle zapote tree and used as the base for chewing gum, became another staple until it was partially superseded by artificial substitutes. Further, with a change in taste, the availability in the United Kingdom of alternative furniture woods, and the removal of most of the accessible mahogany, the timber men switched their attention to cedar and to the stands of Caribbean pine that grow on the leached soils of the interior. Mahogany and cedar drew British timber companies to the Mosquito coast and other parts of Caribbean America during the nineteenth century in much the same way that they were drawn to British Honduras.

It is the pine forests and not the tropical rain-forests that are the more important commercial forests in Central America today. The most extensive coniferous forests are on the heavily, if intermittently, weathered soils (Fig. 4.3) of the interior of Guatemala and Honduras, and on the siliceous soils of the wet lowlands behind Cape Gracias a Dios. It is possible that in neither area is the forest 'natural', but rather a response to long-standing human interference through burning: many areas now under pine are capable of maintaining tropical rain-forest. The number of important commercial species declines from five in Guatemala, through three in Honduras, to two in Nicaragua; only *Pinus oocarpa* and *Pinus caribaea* are common to all areas.

Over half of the coniferous forests are in Honduras, which supplies half of the timber cut in Central America today; timber comes after bananas and coffee in the list of Honduran exports. Most of the timber comes from the interior where haphazard exploitation, frequently in conjunction with shifting agriculture, has given the pinewoods an open and decimated appearance. In the middle 1960s one third of the pine timber of Honduras was destroyed by the spread of the *Dendroctonus* beetle. The best remaining stands and the most hopeful prospects for the future lie in the remote, less populous, national forests of the eastern province of Olancho. A large-scale timber and pulp venture is to be built by a subsidiary of the International Paper Company. Initially, the mature pines will be cut for their timber, and later emphasis will shift to less profitable kraft paper production. This is one of three such projects proposed for Central America. Another is the private Istmo project to produce pulp wood from the pinewoods now being opened up by roads in eastern Guatemala; the third is a Nicaraguan project to use the north-eastern pinewoods tributary to Puerto Cabeza, woods that have been logged-over in the past, to feed a kraft paper mill in the port. All these schemes face difficulties. Large-scale capital outlays are needed to provide the essential infrastructure on which the successful commercial exploitation of these Caribbean backwoods will depend. Private capital will only be forthcoming if timber rights can be convincingly guaranteed for a long period – not an easy thing to do in present circumstances.

Manufacturing industries

It is apparent from any survey of the commercial prospects for the products and regions of rural Central America that possibilities for diversification, extension and improvement of the isthmian economy exist. With positive guidance, these possibilities could be realized. But Central America will still have to rely heavily upon market decisions made abroad and on foreign sources of investment capital for the success of new developments. In order to lessen the vulnerable position that most Central American countries feel themselves to be in, they have resorted to a variety of programmes in recent years to expand domestic manufacturing industry. With few raw materials and only small local markets, governments have been obliged to use all the normal devices of import substitution programmes to encourage growth. High external tariffs have been erected to protect domestic industries and, since 1957, industrial development laws have given new (and some existing) manufacturers certain fiscal exemptions, some extending over periods of up to ten years. In the 1960s, national incentive schemes for promoting industry were supplemented by Central American Common Market legislation, which, by abolishing many tariffs between members (in 1971 only British Honduras and Panama were not members) and by erecting a common external tariff wall, has offered the advantages of a larger market, and sometimes a monopoly of it, to manufacturers of a widening range of products. In addition, the overall growth in gross national products, the widening of the effective markets in the populations of Central America, and the improvements in the transport arrangement of the countries of the isthmus have all made conditions better for the successful development of new manufacturing activity.

There have been certain advances (SIECA, 1965). In the field of import substitution, domestic production supplied a larger proportion (65 per cent) of the internal demand of the CACM countries in 1964 than in 1952 (61 per cent). It is claimed that, perhaps, between one fifth and one quarter of the total expansion in manufacturing activity during the first half of the 1960s was due to CACM legislation. In visible terms, large factories manufacturing detergents, paints, tyres, paper and cardboard articles, certain fertilizers and insecticides exist today where none existed ten years ago; and these supply all or part of a market that itself may not have existed before or, if it did exist, was served from abroad. Such growth is registered statistically in actual and proportional terms: since 1952 the expansion in the manufacturing sectors of the economies of the CACM countries has been at a higher annual rate (of 6 per cent) than the expansion of the economy as a whole (4·5 per cent). In 1950, manufacturing contributed less than 12 per cent of the gross national product of the isthmus; in 1968, it contributed about 15 per cent.

But, in spite of improvements, manufacturing still plays a relatively small part in the economic life of the isthmus and there is little to suggest that industrialization is going to transform the essentially agricultural nature of the Central American economies even in the more remote future; they are underdeveloped countries, far from the 'take-off' stage of self-sustained economic growth. The figures largely speak for themselves. In 1967, the proportion of the gross national product derived from manufacturing ranged from 14 per cent in Nicaragua to 18 per cent in El Salvador, and the proportion from agriculture, forestry and fishing from about 22 per cent (Panama) to 43 per cent (Honduras); in adjoining Mexico, the same source suggests figures of over 26 per cent for manufacturing and under 15 per cent for agriculture, etc. (UNECLA, 1969, pp. 127, 210). The relative insignificance of manufacturing is emphasized by employment data. In 1968, there were only about 450,000 employed in the industries of Central America or perhaps 8 per cent of the economically active population, and no more than 3 per cent of the population at large. Even these low figures were arrived at after taking a generous view of what constitutes 'industry'; if 'cottage industries' are excluded and the phrase 'manufacturing employment' restricted to workers in establishments employing five or more people, only about 250,000 were so employed in the isthmus in 1968. Nor is this figure rising rapidly. Between 1952 and 1962, the annual rate of expansion in cottage and factory industrial employment at 1·7 per cent was below the expansion of the labour force as a whole and the share of manufacturing in the overall employment pattern is continuing to fall.

The scope for the expansion of manufacturing industry in Central America is limited (SRI, 1964). Hydro-electricity is the only domestic source of power; local industrial raw materials are restricted to certain agricultural products, wood and a small output of mineral ores; and the market for manufactured goods is largely restricted to the commercial farmers and the town-dwellers, who together form a minority of a population already small and with a low purchasing power. The existing structure of Central American industry reflects these factors (UNECLA, 1967b). The typical industrial unit is small. In 1962 there were as many people working in cottage industries as in factories (manufacturing establishments employing over four workers) and only one in seven worked in a large factory (one employing 100 or more); in Mexico in 1961, only one sixth of industrial employment was in cottage industries and over half the industrial work force was employed in large factories. Larger factories are usually more efficient and Central America is no exception: 70 per cent of the value added in manufacturing in 1962 came from factories, and in all the countries factories were more productive than were the cottage industries, even though it was only in Costa Rica that cottage workers were outnumbered by factory workers. The preponderance of small enterprises is reflected in the great importance of traditional industries: over 80 per cent (85 per cent in 1962) of industrial production in the isthmus is of this type. The food, drink and tobacco industries alone account for over half the total value added in manufacturing, employ about 40 per cent of the industrial labour force, and occupy about one third of all factories employing more than four workers. A further 20 per cent of production in 1962 came from textile, clothes and shoe manufacturers giving employment to 28 per cent of the industrial working population. Very little capital is required to reach a relatively efficient level of production in these fields. The wood-working industries, including furniture-making, and the leather and printing industries make up the rest of the traditional industries. The participation of cottage workers and the smaller factories in the newer industries is much smaller. Typical of such industries and accounting for over one third of this type of activity is the chemical industry, perhaps the most dynamic element during the 1960s and stimulated by the rising demand for fertilizers and insecticides. Oil-refining is of major importance in Panama and of lesser importance in the other republics; it is a novelty and makes little direct impact on the employment structure of the isthmus. Metal-working, including the assembly of motor cars, is another growth sector of the economy, but employment statistics are inflated by the inclusion of essentially repair establishments. Even if, as anticipated, the newer industries expand production at twice the rate of the traditional ones, the latter are going to dominate the industrial scene for a long time to come.

The location of industrial activity in Central America follows a fairly simple pattern. In the first place, there are industries such as sugar mills, coffee *beneficios*, cotton gins, lumber mills, fish-processing plants and cement works, which are located close to their raw materials, frequently in the nearest small town. Secondly, those based on imported raw materials may be in or near the ports: the oil refineries or fertilizer plants of, for example, the new national port of Matias de Gálvez near Puerto Barrios in Guatemala, Acajutla in El Salvador, Puntarenas and Puerto Limón in Costa Rica, and Colón and Panama City, are representative of this category. Finally, the great majority of industrial employment is in the large towns and particularly the capital cities. Two-thirds of all factory employment in Central America, in 1962–3, was in the ten most populous towns, and the larger the town the greater its share of industry. Guatemala City could claim one fifth of all industrial establishments and employment in the isthmus, followed (in order but at a distance) by San José, San Salvador, Managua and Panama City. The inflated commercial role of Panama City helps to account for its disproportionately low rank amongst industrial towns of the isthmus. The dominance exercised by these cities over the national industrial structure is often very strong: three-quarters of Costa Rica's industry is in the San José metropolitan area, two-thirds of Guatemala's industry is in Guatemala City, Managua accounts for half of Nicaragua's industry, and even in El Salvador and Honduras, where the capital cities are least dominant, they each accommodate one third of the national total. Only in Guatemala has there been any deliberate governmental attempt to disperse industry more widely in the country (for

example, to Amatitlán) but with little apparent effect: the market advantages, the better public utilities and facilities and the easier access to sources
of finance and influence are powerful centralizing factors.

The distribution of industry within the towns is not remarkable.
Detailed mapping substantiates casual observation that smaller workshops
and factories are scattered through the fabric of the towns, although they
are less frequently met in the better class housing areas (SRI, 1964, p. 58;
López Toledo, 1965, p. 9). Larger factories are frequently related to
transport facilities: such is the case in the older industrial areas around the
railway terminals in San Salvador, Guatemala City and San José, and the
newer factories along the exit roads to Escuintla and the west in Guatemala
City. The roads leading to the airports from the other capitals have special
attractions; they are invariably the best quality roads, and conditions
suitable for airport construction are similar to those required for modern
industrial sites.

Between one country and another there are differences in the degree and
pace of industrialization. It is interesting to view these in the light of one of
the stated aims, variously interpreted, of the Central American Common
Market countries to promote a balanced industrial development in the
isthmus. In absolute terms Guatemala accounts for just over 30 per cent,
and with El Salvador, 50 per cent of the industrial production of Central
America; Panama, Costa Rica, Nicaragua and Honduras follow in that
order, with British Honduras of negligible importance. In relative terms,
industrial production is of greatest importance in the economy of El
Salvador, followed by Panama, Guatemala, Costa Rica, Honduras and
Nicaragua. The greater significance of industry in El Salvador is in part a
reaction to the more limited opportunities offered by agriculture and in
part a reflection of the settled political climate of recent years. It is notable
that El Salvador has harnessed a larger proportion of her hydro-electric
potential than any other Latin American country, with the exception of
Uruguay; Costa Rica has, however, a larger installed capacity and each of
the other Central American countries (except British Honduras) has a
larger potential (UNECLA, 1967a, p. 62). Doubtless El Salvador does reap,
in the form of reduced distributional costs, some industrial advantage from
her small size and relatively good transport system. Honduras, on the other
hand, one of the least industrialized countries of the Americas, suffers
from a poverty of roads, has few raw materials and has a smaller and more
dispersed national market. San Pedro Sula is almost as important as
Tegucigalpa, but both offer a market comparable to Santa Ana, the second
city of El Salvador, rather than to the capital, San Salvador. Industrial
capacity in Nicaragua, stimulated by the interests of President Somoza and
the continuing cotton bonanza, is increasing more rapidly than in Honduras.
Panamanian industry is less protected from external competition but does
have easier access to investment capital, and has some stimulus from the

passing needs of canal traffic; these factors help explain the presence there of the only steel mill, even if it is a small one, and the largest oil refinery of the isthmus.

Panama is not alone in possessing an oil refinery. It is an interesting reflection on the industrial policy of the Common Market countries that four of the five now possess a domestic refinery (Guatemala has two, Honduras plans to build one), and all were built in the 1960s. One refinery, or at most two larger ones to meet the needs of the Common Market would have been more economical. In this way, oil-refining would have been treated as an integration industry under the terms of the 1958 industrial regulations of the Common Market Treaty. These regulations, which have since been strengthened, were designed to encourage the establishment of industries of a scale to serve the whole Central American market; their products were to be given free entry to the national markets and protection from outside competition. Up to 1968, however, only three integration industries had been designated: tyre plants in Guatemala and Costa Rica (making different sizes of tyres) and a caustic soda and insecticide plant in Nicaragua (BOLSA, 1968). This poor response arises in part from the success of another aim of Common Market policy – the reduction and abolition of industrial tariffs between the countries of the Common Market – and in part from the fact that better terms, apart from those incentives specific to Common Market regulations, may often be obtained from individual countries. In the particular case of the oil refineries, no doubt the symbolic status of a national oil refinery played a part in countering the generally stated objective of industrial development.

A stronger impact of Common Market legislation is visible in the increase in trade, in particular trade in locally produced, manufactured goods, between the Central American countries. In general, the Common Market countries shelter behind a higher common commodity tariff than did the separate countries before the treaty became effective, and this helps to explain why intra-regional trade now accounts for over 20 per cent of the total as compared with 6 per cent as recently as 1960 (UNECLA, 1969, p. 22). There are other reasons, of course, and amongst these the greatly improved physical accessibility of neighbouring countries is important. In 1971, paved roads linked all the capitals of the Central American Common Market and Belize is connected to the Mexican road system; a tortuous section of the road leading to Panama in southern Costa Rica remains unpaved. Trailer trucks and scheduled buses run almost the length of the isthmus, despite anachronistic customs arrangements, and the practical possibilities of pan-isthmian co-operation and exchange have been transformed in recent years. The industrial element in Panama's economy differs substantially from that element in the other republics, and the peculiar circumstances of the Canal Zone and different industrial forces at play make it difficult to envisage an easy adjustment should Panama enter the Common Market. British Honduras is apart, too, for such industry as she has is largely directed to processing primary products for the protected United Kingdom or United States markets.

SOME POLITICAL QUESTIONS

(1) *British Honduras and Independence*

British Honduras is an anomaly in Latin Central America (Fox, 1962). It is the only remaining colony in an isthmus where all other formal colonies disappeared a century and a half ago; it has nominal self-government, but, as yet (in 1971), no firm date for independence. It is by far the least populous of the Central American countries; its population of about 100,000 is less than one tenth of the population of any of the republics. The majority of the citizens are Negro and English is the common language. The three staple export crops of Central America – coffee, bananas and cotton – play almost no part in the economy of the country. In people, outlook, history and past connections, British Honduras is closer to the British West Indian islands than to the other Central American countries. Peripheral to Central America and on the rim of the Caribbean, British Honduras seems to experience only the disadvantages of such a position. The problems of accommodating British Honduras to modern life may not be insoluble; they are certainly very difficult. The country is, at the moment, too small, too empty and too poor to stand completely alone on her own feet as an independent country, yet she rejected association with the abortive West Indian Federation and is too divergent in sympathies to relish political attachment to, or absorption into, her Latin American neighbours.

History has given British Honduras, as it has given Panama, an outlook at variance with that of the other countries in the isthmus (Waddell, 1961). Overseas contacts have been of great importance here. British Honduras may be viewed as a beach-head set up by buccaneers and smugglers, loggers and slaves; the Belize river was a main route inland to the forests of the interior, and Belize town grew up on the mangrove swamps at its mouth. It is significant that Belize is the only capital in Central America proper that is at the same time a port. Successful lumber operations demanded freedom to scour the forests for marketable species; they did not allow the rigid master-slave relationships of, for example, the British West Indian sugar islands. There was initially no real clash of interest between the logger and the indigenous Mayan Indian. The Indian practised shifting agriculture and valued the trees only for the land they occupied; the logger had a completely opposite attitude. The Negro logger based himself on Belize or on one of the logging camps from which he worked the forests seasonally; the Indians accepted the incursions of the loggers and were left almost unbothered by the British colonial administration. The urbanized Negro lumberjack regarded agriculture as effeminate; even the gathering of chicle was left to the Indians. It is possibly for this reason that only about 5 per cent of the country is farmed and an even smaller proportion is actually under cultivation at any given time (Weight, 1959).

In an easy social milieu and with no lack of unexploited agricultural land, the indigenous Indians have retained their traditional manners and a large number of immigrant groups have come to the country. This has given a remarkable variety to the small population. It has also added to the present-day problems of incipient independence. The largest single element is the English-speaking Negro or Creole; his main focus is Belize, a town of 30,000 to 40,000 inhabitants. Another Negro group is centred on Stann Creek, the second largest town of the country, but with a population of only slightly over 5000 in 1960. This group is Carib-speaking. They are descendants of those escaped Negro slaves who had absorbed the culture of the Carib Indians in St Vincent and, after deportation to Ruatán island, spread to the shores of the Gulf of Honduras in the early nineteenth century. A third group is Latin American. The Indian Wars of Yucatán in the 1850s led some Mexicans to move south and settle in northern British Honduras, and about one quarter of the country's population today is Spanish-speaking. Other white refugees came from the Confederate States after the American Civil War and settled on the south coast around Toledo. Since 1957, some 3500 German-speaking Mennonites have established several thriving agricultural colonies in the Cayo and Orange Walk areas where they have been promised a greater degree of autonomy than they found in Mexico, Canada or the United States (Sawatsky, 1969). Sprinklings of British administrators and expatriates, Lebanese entrepreneurs and Chinese businessmen add further spice to the immigrant mixture. Even the indigenous Indians are not homogeneous. In the northern interior they are Mayan-speaking and many are of mixed, and some are of very mixed, blood; in the south, away from the main mahogany stands and less exposed to outside influences, many live on the Kekchi reservation and speak no Spanish or English. The net result is a 'colony of colonies', a potpourri of peoples speaking several different languages, in which the task of creating a unified national outlook seems near-impossible (Furley, 1968).

The portents for true, economic independence seem no more cheerful. In 1965, British Honduras had a balance of trade deficit of over £4 million. This was about £40 per head in a country where *per capita* annual income was only £140. British Honduras has been an apparent drain on the United Kingdom economy for many years and the subsidy rose sharply in the 1960s. This coincided with a marked diversification of the economy with the old and ruthlessly exploited staple, timber, in decline, and with sugar from the Corozal area, tinned citrus fruits from Stann Creek and fresh and frozen lobster and crayfish now on the upgrade. Without the protected British market, it is probable that only the luxury seafood trade to the United States would remain.

The present population of British Honduras is too small to provide a market for large-scale domestic industrial development, let alone to support the administrative superstructure of an independent country. There is agricultural land available in British Honduras and surplus labour in the English-speaking Caribbean islands. But it is difficult to harmonize these two elements. Few West Indian emigrants seem to relish the role of a pioneer farmer in Central America as an alternative to life in an English city; and even the limitations of the Commonwealth Immigrants Act have produced no increase in migration to British Honduras – a country after all almost as remote for West Indians and as expensive to reach as is the United Kingdom. Nor has British Honduras paid much more than lip-service to the need to encourage immigrants.

Her land neighbours are no great help to the concept of independence. Guatemala has reiterated the claim that 'Belice es nuestro' and, for a time, political factions in British Honduras played on this claim. The claim rests upon Guatemala's assumption that she inherited from Spain the lands of the Captaincy-General of Guatemala and that these included all British Honduras. This is disputed by Mexico, who has a dormant claim to the northern part of the colony, which may have been part of the Captaincy-General of Yucatán. Both claims ignore the fact that the United Kingdom has had *de facto* possession of British Honduras since before the disintegration of the Spanish empire. Whatever the merits or demerits of these claims, it is difficult to imagine British Honduras deriving any long-term benefit from becoming, in fact, the department of Belice, for so long claimed on the maps of the Guatemalans. A marriage – willing or unwilling – with Guatemala would run into difficulties. The political instability of Caribbean Guatemala might spread northwards; the majority of British Hondurans would find themselves a coloured minority speaking an alien language, governed from a capital at present inaccessible by land and within an economic system isolating them from their traditional markets. Belize might reap some economic advantage as an entrepôt in the event of the Petén being developed. A union of British Honduras with Mexico, not attractive in itself, might be less unattractive than union with Guatemala.

Within British Honduras, the declared aim at the moment of the leading political party is independence and close ties with Central America; the hope is for a more varied economy shored up by financial aid from Britain and the United States.

(2) *Panama, the Canal Zone and the Panama Canal*

Panama is a corridor as British Honduras is a beach-head, and just as the imprint of Britain is clearly visible in the landscape of that part of northern Central America, so that of the United States is unmistakable in the Canal Zone. As Britain is preparing to relinquish its sovereign rights in British Honduras, so the United States is revising its attitude towards its undeclared colony in Panama. Implicit in any discussion of Panama and the future of the Canal Zone is a discussion of the prospects for the Panama Canal; it is the growing inadequacy of the Canal as much as any change in world political climate that is prompting a reappraisal of the situation in Panama (Fox, 1964).

The United States first became officially involved in Panama in 1846, when it guaranteed the neutrality of the isthmus in return for freedom of movement across it for American citizens (Howarth, 1966). The American West was just beginning to be opened up. In 1849 the Panama Railroad Company of New York acquired a concession from the government of New Granada (Colombia) to build a railway or canal across the isthmus. A Committee of the U.S. House of Representatives supported the project but recommended a canal as a better long-term proposition. No financial aid was forthcoming, however, and had it not been for the sudden influx of the forty-niners and their successors en route for California, no railway would have been built. That railway was in use well before its completion in 1855; although expensive to build, it had a virtual monopoly of traffic over the isthmus and was highly profitable. In 1866, the U.S. Senate ordered a survey of all feasible routes for a ship canal through the isthmus; nineteen were considered and a route through Darien favoured. The authoritative First United States Interoceanic Canal Commission in 1876 favoured a route through Nicaragua, a decision which coloured United States opinion until the beginning of this century. Meanwhile, a French company headed by Ferdinand de Lesseps, builder of the Suez Canal (and President of the Geographical Society of Paris), actually began the first serious attempt to join the oceans by a sea-level canal across Panama. Two-fifths of the work had been completed when, in spite of a late switch to a lock canal design, the De Lesseps Company collapsed in 1889. By 1903, the United States government was ready to build a canal. An official investigation reported that there was little to choose between a route through Nicaragua or one through Panama and the former was authorized. It was only then that the French company holding the concession rights through Panama came to heel. This was followed by the unilateral declaration of independence from Colombia by the Panama Republic. The situation changed in favour of the Panamanian route; the extraordinarily generous treaty terms offered by the fledgeling republic clinched the choice of the new route. A very narrow majority decision in the U.S. Senate favoured a cheaper lock canal over a sea-level cut, and the construction of the present canal began. The route chosen closely followed the railway and the railway in its turn closely followed the sixteenth-century Camino Real, over which much of the gold of Peru and silver of Bolivia had made its way to Europe; all these routes recognized the fortunate coincidence of the lowest point in the Continental Divide with the narrowest portion of the isthmus. In so doing, the importance of Panama City as the fulcrum of the country was reinforced.

The good fortunes of the Republic have strongly reflected, directly or indirectly, the success of the Canal since it opened in 1914. In 1967, some U.S. $115 million reached the Panamanian economy annually through Canal operations and from the activities of other official U.S. governmental agencies; this figure alone represents about one sixth of the gross national product, or half the export earnings of Panama, and does not cover many other direct and less tangible economic benefits brought by the Canal. The future of the Canal is, therefore, of crucial economic importance to the Republic.

The Canal, planned over sixty years ago and little modified since, is still capable of meeting most of the demands placed upon it today. Almost each year has brought record traffic and the rise from about 30 million tons of cargo carried in the early 1950s to about 100 million tons in the late 1960s was dramatic. But, when the Canal was built, it could accommodate all ships then afloat; today a growing number of ships (400 in 1968) are too big to use the Canal. The size of the lock chambers closes the Canal in effect to fully laden ships of over 80,000 tons and to many below this size. Meanwhile, the world trend to larger ships continues, with vessels of over 300,000 tons currently on order. The effect of this limitation on the use of the Canal is being increasingly felt and longer shipping routes, avoiding the Canal, are becoming genuine alternatives. In 1967, it was cheaper to send bulk cargo from the east coast of the U.S.A. to Japan around the Cape of Good Hope (24,500 km, taking 38 days) in a 100,000 ton ship than to use a 50,000 ton vessel on the more direct route (16,000 km, taking 25 days) through the Canal.

The time element in passing through the triple-stepped Gatun locks at the Caribbean end of the Canal imposes restrictions on the flow of vessels. There is a limit to the supply of water available to replenish the canal after each lockage. The demand for lockages through the canal is naturally uneven; sailing schedules can rarely be governed solely by considerations of Canal convenience. In 1952 there were about 7200 ship transits through the Canal and the number has been rising steadily; in 1968 it was over 15,000. Changes in patterns of trade and in ship design have to be considered before any reasoned estimate of the numbers of vessels demanding transit at a future date can be estimated. All past estimates have proved too conservative and these precedents give added weight to the statement of the new Atlantic-Pacific Interoceanic Canal Study Commission in 1967 that the saturation rate of 20,000 annual transits will be reached by 1980.

This new Commission is one reflection of the concern that the potential plight of the Canal has raised in all circles. Suggestions for relieving future pressure have followed four lines. The first is to increase the capacity of the present canal. If the bottleneck at Gatun were broken by the construction of an additional, third, flight of locks, more vessels could use the Canal; in fact, this was begun and $75 million were spent until work was suspended in 1942. To permit larger vessels to use the Canal would require sets of larger lock chambers on both sides of the divide and the widening and deepening of the existing canal in many places. New water storage capacity would be needed.

A second alternative approach demands the construction of an entirely new canal as a replacement or a supplement to the existing canal. All the traditional choices of routes have been reconsidered and the earlier controversy over the relative merits and costs of a lock canal and a sea-level channel has been revived. The advantages of a sea-level channel, recognized in 1905, remain valid today: it would be cheaper to operate and passage time would be shorter. It has been proposed that nuclear explosions be used in the excavations. A variety of estimates suggests that a canal so built would be considerably cheaper and quicker in construction and wider, deeper and easier to maintain than one built by conventional engineering methods. The U.S. Atomic Energy Commission expected to have mastered the new techniques by 1970, and was fully confident that radio-active fallout could be limited to acceptable levels and areas; land- and air-borne shock waves proved more of a problem. It appeared that the question whether or not to use nuclear devices revolved not so much around engineering problems but around political considerations: to allow such explosions to take place, the International Test Ban Treaty of 1963 would have to be amended and – possibly most important – the sentiments of the host country assuaged.

In early 1970 the most likely site for a new seaway constructed by nuclear engineering was approximately 160 km east of the present canal; that is, from Caledonia Bay to the Gulf of San Miguel (Route 17, or the Sasardi–Morti route); the route is 80 km long and cuts through the divide at a point 370 m above sea-level. It would require 300 megatons of nuclear energy to construct and the largest single explosion would be about 10 megatons. Should it appear, however, that such explosions would generate seismic or acoustic shocks structurally damaging to, say, Panama City, the most attractive alternative route would probably be across the foot of the isthmus in Colombia, the Atrato–Truando route, or Route 25. This is longer (150 km), but runs through virtually uninhabited country and could be built by a combination of conventional dredging and nuclear engineering. In 1964, the possible construction costs of the two routes were put at $747 million and $1440 million respectively. If, however, nuclear engineering is not to be permitted, then a sea-level canal through or near to the present Canal Zone would be the most economical to build. It is, in fact, this solution that the Canal Commission recommended in its final report to President Nixon in December 1970; the inability of the Atomic Energy Commission to guarantee 'clean' atomic devices led to this conclusion. Such a Panama Seaway would cost at least $2880 million to construct and this figure will doubtless defer speedy adoption of the plan. If it were impossible to reach agreement with Panama, a Colombian canal, built by conventional methods, would be the next most economical alternative. The consideration given to a Nicaraguan route appears to be for diplomatic reasons only. Whichever the route and whatever the construction method, and assuming the most expeditious conclusion of any political problems, the earliest date an isthmian seaway could be in operation is 1985.

The third and fourth approaches to the plight of the Canal are aimed at deflecting traffic; it seems that whatever other decisions are taken some such steps will be required by the 1980s. The bulkiest cargo using the Canal is petroleum (over 16 million tons in 1970): the creation on either side of the isthmus of deep-water terminals linked by oil pipeline might remove some of the pressure on the Canal. The other approach is a fiscal one (CTRS, 1967); it would manipulate the toll structure to make it more expensive to use the Canal and other routes more attractive. An investigation in progress in 1969 suggested that, allowing for differences already existing in the impact of tolls on the costs of transporting different commodities, differences in anticipated sources of supply and demand, and consequently differences in the sensitivity of traffic to toll changes, a canal tonnage in 1990, now anticipated at about 140 million tons, could be reduced to 124 million tons by a 25 per cent toll increase and to 101 million tons by a 50 per cent increase; a maximum income would be generated with a flow of 85 million tons in 1990. The terms of reference for the Panama Canal Company have so far required it only to cover running costs. The use of increased tolls is obviously a cheap and easy way to ensure that the existing canal does not become choked with traffic but such a measure would raise shipping costs and so be to the disadvantage of current users. It is to be noted that in the 1960s, two-thirds of all cargo using the Canal originated in, was destined for or was part of the intercoastal trade of the United States. The whole concept of deliberately killing growing traffic is alien to United States philosophy, and would probably accentuate the demand for a new canal.

A decision must be made soon on the future of the Canal. If that decision were against Panama and if a new Colombian seaway were built, the consequences for Panama would be serious. The only political importance that the Republic has in the world and in relation to the United States arises from the presence of the Canal. Economically she would lose seriously in the supply of goods and services to United States agencies in Panama and the Canal Zone, to Canal users and to passengers in transit. Even if a new seaway was built through Panama, such a seaway would make fewer demands on and give fewer benefits to Panama. The present Panama Canal Company employs 14,000, of whom three-quarters are Panamanians enjoying a higher standard of wages than might otherwise prevail in Central America; it would need only about 1000 to run a seaway. If the seaway were to follow an alternative route, Panama City and

Colón would lose their present valuable tourist trade and the successful Colón Free Zone, which has an annual turnover worth $200 million, might become less attractive. The impact of the abandonment of the present canal would be serious; it is no accident that over 80 per cent of Panama's economic production originates within 20 km of the Canal.

In the meanwhile, Panama is fortunate in possessing the most attractive geographical route for a new seaway. In the political background, the United States no doubt will take into consideration that problems of ownership, sovereignty and employment (all of which arise with any canal across the isthmus) are, perhaps, more easily soluble if the Canal runs through a smaller political unit. Recent negotiations to change the status of the Canal Zone have shown that Panama has a fairly strong hand. Under the terms of the original treaty, Panama gave the United States perpetual jurisdiction over the 16 km wide Canal Zone; to all intents and purposes the United States was given sovereign right over the territory and has treated it since as an extension of itself. A new treaty, not yet ratified, would explicitly state the Republic's sovereignty in the Zone, would turn the Canal over to Panama in the year 2000 (or sooner if a seaway came into existence), and would increase the annual payments made to the Republic tenfold (to $22 million) within five years. These concessions came after anti-American rioting in 1964 and reflect concern that the atmosphere should be clearer before fresh negotiations over a possible seaway begin, perhaps in 1971. At one time it was thought that the United States might wish to remove a possible political embarrassment by persuading other maritime nations to join her in the construction of a new channel; this belief that other nations might help to provide what the United States must have has no serious basis.

Any canal through the isthmus cannot avoid being a political animal; a simple shift to a new site in Panama or elsewhere is likely to carry continuing political problems for the U.S.A.

CONCLUDING REMARKS

British Honduras and Panama have their peculiar characteristics and problems but share with the rest of Central America many others common to developing countries elsewhere. For example, the towns are growing rapidly and strains are being placed on municipal resources and abilities. So far modern architecture is little in evidence away from the capital cities and the townscapes of Central America retain their traditional lines. But the population pressures are already present and substantial changes in urban functions and form can be anticipated. In the countryside new roads have transformed life in certain limited areas but large regions still remain completely isolated. Ambitious plans exist for the development of the Caribbean lowlands and of the Gulf of Fonseca area through the aegis of

SIECA (the economic arm of the Central American integration organization) but these appear premature. For these plans to be successful the political strength of the integrating policy of SIECA would have to overcome the traditional centripetal policies of national governments. Political instability and authoritarian rule in the countries of the isthmus make it difficult both to mesh policies and to anticipate a sustained and deliberate move towards integration: political wheels are turning more slowly in the direction of a united Central America than are those of industry and commerce.

BIBLIOGRAPHY

AGUILAR LEÓN, L. A. (1966) *Ensayo metodológico: estudio para el desarrollo agropecuario de una región.* Turrialba, Instituto Interamericano de Ciencias Agrícolas.

BENNETT, C. F. (1967) A review of ecological research in Middle America. *Lat. Amer. Res. Rev.*, 2 (3), 3–27.

DE BORHEGYI, S. F. (1965a) Archaeological synthesis of the Guatemalan Highlands. In WILLEY, G. R. (ed.) (1965), pp. 3–58.

DE BORHEGYI, S. F. (1965b) Settlement patterns of the Guatemalan Highlands. In WILLEY, G. R. (ed.) (1965), pp. 59–75.

BOLSA (Bank of London and South America) (1968) Central America: the progress of integration. *BOLSA Review*, 2, 323–32.

CTRS (1967) *Canal Tolls and Route Studies.* Hearings before the Subcommittee on Panama Canal of the Committee on Merchant Marine and Fisheries, House of Representatives, 90th Cong., 1st Sess. HR 6791, 9 and 18 May 1967.

CASTILLO, C. M. (1966) *Growth and Integration in Central America.* New York.

COE, M. D. and FLANNERY, K. V. (1967) *Early Cultures and Human Ecology in South Coastal Guatemala.* Washington, D.C., Smithsonian Contributions to Anthropology, vol. 3.

CROSSLEY, C. (1963) Agrarian reform in Latin America. *The Year Book of World Affairs*, 17, 123–49. London, Institute of World Affairs.

ECKHOLM, C. F. and WILLEY G. R. (eds.) (1966) *Archaeological Frontiers and External Connections.* Austin, Texas, Handbook of Middle American Indians, vol. 4.

EVANS, C. and MEGGERS, B. J. (1966) Mesoamerica and Ecuador. In ECKHOLM, G. F. and WILLEY, G. R. (eds.) (1966), pp. 243–64.

FOX, D. J. (1962) Recent work on British Honduras. *Geog. Rev.*, 52, 112–17.

FOX, D. J. (1964) Prospects for the Panama Canal. *Tijds. Econ. Soc. Geografie*, 55, 86–101.

FURLEY, P. (1968) The University of Edinburgh British Honduras–Yucatán Expedition. *Geog. J.*, 134, 38–54.

HOWARTH, D. (1966) *The Golden Isthmus*. London.

HUBBS, C. L. and RODEN, G. I. (1964) Oceanography and marine life along the Pacific coast of Middle America. In WEST, R. C. (ed.) (1964), pp. 143–86.

IUCISE (Instituto Universitario Centroamericano de Investigaciones Sociales y Económicas) (1964) *Encuestas socio-económicas en zonas agrícolas seleccionadas de los paises centroamericanos – resultados y analisis.* San José.

IUCISE (1965) *Algunas consideraciones sobre tenencia de la tierra en relación con el desarrollo agropecuario de los paises centro-americanos.* San José.

LADD, J. (1962) *Archaeological Investigations in the Parita and Santa Maria zones of Panama.* Smithsonian Institution, Bureau of American Ethnology, Bull. 193. Reviewed in *Science*, 150 (1965), 1017.

LATHRAP, D. W. (1966) Relationships between Mesoamerica and the Andean areas. In ECKHOLM, G. F. and WILLEY, G. R. (eds.) (1966), pp. 265–76.

LONGYEAR, J. M. (1966) Archaeological survey of El Salvador. In ECKHOLM, G. F. and WILLEY, G. R. (eds.) (1966), pp. 132–55.

LÓPEZ TOLEDO, J. (1965) *Informe sobre la colonia San Diego.* Guatemala City, Estudios Geográficos, Dir. Gen. de Obras Publicas.

LOTHROP, S. K. (1966) Archaeology of lower Central America. In ECKHOLM, G. F. and WILLEY, G. R. (eds.) (1966), pp. 180–208.

MALDONADO-KOERDELL, M. (1964) Geohistory and paleogeography of Middle America. In WEST, R. C. (ed.) (1964), pp. 3–32.

MANGELSDORF, P. C., MACNEISH, R. S. and WILLEY, G. R. (1964) Origins of agriculture in Middle America. In WEST, R. C. (ed.) (1964), pp. 427–45.

NUNLEY, R. E. (1967) Population densities using a new approach. *Revista Geográfica*, No. 66, 55–93 (Rio de Janeiro).

PAU (Pan American Union) (1965) *Tenencia de la tierra y desarrollo socio-económico del sector agricola: Guatemala.* Washington, D.C.

PAU (1967) *Inventory of Information Basic to the Planning of Agricultural Development in Latin America: Central America.* Washington, D.C.

PARKER, F. D. (1964) *The Central American Republics.* London.

PEARSE, A. (1966) Agrarian change trends in Latin America. *Lat. Am. Res. Rev.*, 1 (3), 45–77.

POLLOCK, H. E. D. (1965) Architecture of the Maya lowlands. In WILLEY, G. R. (ed.) (1965), pp. 378–440.

RADELL, D. R. (1964) *Coffee and Transportation in Nicaragua*. Berkeley, University of California, Dept. of Geography.

SANDNER, G. (1962) *Colonización agrícola de Costa Rica*. 2 vols. San José, Instituto Geográfico de Costa Rica.

SAUER, C. O. (1952) *Agricultural Origins and Dispersals*. New York.

SAUER, C. O. (1966) *The Early Spanish Main*. London.

SAWATSKY, H. L. (1969) *Mennonite Settlements in British Honduras*. Berkeley, University of California, Dept. of Geography.

SCHMID, L. (1967) *The Role of Migratory Labor in the Economic Development of Guatemala*. Madison, University of Wisconsin, Land Tenure Center.

SIECA (Secretaría Permanente del Tratado General de Integración Económica Centroamericana) (1965) *Bases para un programa Centroamericano de desarrollo industrial*. Guatemala City.

SIECA (1966) *Situación de algunos productos agrícolas centroamericanos de exportación*. Guatemala City.

SIECA (1967) *El algodón en Centroamérica*. Guatemala City.

SRI (Stanford Research Institute) (1964) *An Industrial Park Development Program for Central America*. Tegucigalpa, Central American Bank for Economic Integration.

STEPHENS, J. L. (1963) *Incidents of Travel in Yucatán*. 2 vols. New York.

STOUSE, P. A. D. (1967) *Cambios en el uso de la tierra en regiones exbananeras de Costa Rica*. San José, Instituto Geográfico de Costa Rica.

STUART, L. C. (1964) Fauna of Middle America. In WEST, R. C. (ed.) (1964), pp. 316–62.

SUAREZ DE CASTRO, F. (1965) *Estructuras agrarias en la América Latina*. San José.

UNECLA (1964) *Possibilities of Integrated Industrial Development in Central America*. New York.

UNECLA (1966) *Evaluación de la Integración Económica en Centroamérica*. New York.

UNECLA (1967) Latin America's hydroelectric potential. *Econ. Bull. for Lat. America*, 12 (1), 55–62.

UNECLA (1967b) Small-scale industry in the development of Latin America *Econ. Bull. for Lat. America*, 12 (1), 63–101.

UNECLA (1969) *Economic Survey of Latin America 1967*. New York.

UN/FAO (1967–) *Uso potencial de la tierra*. 6 parts. Rome.

USAID (U.S. Agency for International Development) (1965) *Central American Transport Study Summary Report*. Guatemala City, Regional Office, Central America and Panama Affairs.

USAID (1967) *A.I.D. Economic Data Book: Latin America*. Washington, D.C.

WADDELL, D. A. G. (1961) *British Honduras*. London.

WAGNER, P. L. (1964) Natural vegetation of Middle America. In WEST, R. C. (ed.) (1964), pp. 216–64.

WEIGHT, A. C. S. *et al.* (1959) *Land in British Honduras*. London, Colonial Office research pub. 24.

WEST, R. C. (1964) The natural regions of Middle America. In WEST, R. C. (ed.) (1964), pp. 363–83.

WEST, R. C. (ed.) (1964) *Natural Environment and Early Cultures*. Austin, Texas, Handbook of Middle American Indians, vol. 1.

WEST, R. C. and AUGELLI, J. P. (1966) *Middle America, its Lands and Peoples*. Englewood Cliffs, N.J.

WHETTEN, N. (1961) *Guatemala: the Land and the People*. London.

WILLEY, G. R. (1960) New World prehistory. *Science*, 131, 73–86.

WILLEY, G. R. (ed.) (1965) Archaeology of Southern Mesoamerica. Austin, Texas, Handbook of Middle American Indians, vols. 2 and 3.

WILLEY, G. R. and BULLARD, W. R. (1965) Prehistoric settlements patterns in the Maya lowlands. In WILLEY, G. R. (ed.) (1965), pp. 360–377.

WILLEY, G. R., ECKHOLM, G. F. and MILLON, R. F. (1964) The patterns of farming life and civilisation. In WEST, R. C. (ed.) (1964), pp. 446–98.

WOLF, E. (1959) *Sons of the Shaking Earth*. Chicago.

5 Venezuela and Colombia

D. J. Robinson

COMPLEXITY IN DIVERSITY

Few areas in Latin America provide so great a challenge as the territories of Venezuela and Colombia to those who seek to describe, understand or explain the dynamic relationship between man and nature, culture and landscape. All writers on these countries stress the diversity and complexity of both natural and human phenomena. Viewed together, Venezuela and Colombia stand, as they have stood for so long, at a strategic location in the Americas, apart from but part of both Caribbean and Andean regions and intimately linked by both natural and cultural history to Meso-America as well as to South America. Though northwards, from approximately Pasto in southern Colombia, the Andean mountain system diverges into separate ranges that decline in altitude northwards and eastwards, it was south- wards, across a late-glacial Central American isthmus, that man spread into southern America. Across Colombia and Venezuela historic migrations took place, migrations not only of man, but of plants and animals. Though much more needs to be learnt of earlier habitats, it is now well established that by the fifteenth century A.D. the area of present-day Venezuela and Colombia was inhabited by a diverse mixture of agriculturalists, fishermen, hunters and gatherers, none of whom had attained that higher cultural status that distinguished the Central Andean region or Meso-America. With the exception perhaps of Chibcha territory, Venezuela and Colombia formed part of an intermediate zone.

Within the pre-Hispanic period, however, one can still identify a wide range of adaptation of cultures to ecology and examples of the interaction of the two. The distinction between bitter manioc vegeculturalists and maize horticulturalists may have been as significant as that between swidden farmers of the forest and hunters of the grassland plains, though much more needs to be known of the rhythms of life, of agricultural imple- ments, of social structures and of the range of domesticated plants and animals before it will be possible to attempt to distinguish meaningful regions within the northern part of South America before the arrival of the Europeans.

Their coming, however, marked a turning point in the historical geo- graphy of the area, yet, despite the ubiquitous activity of Spanish authority, diversity, from a cultural viewpoint, was increased rather than diminished. By complex processes of assimilation, adaptation and introduction, people, products, plants, animals and a new technological age were spread through the area. The maritime margins became colonial contact zones, Hispanic modes of urban and rural settlement spread first inland and thence overland to and through all parts of Venezuela and Colombia. The objectives of the Spanish colonists demanded a reappraisal of indigenous cultures and peoples, ranging from their potential as suppliers of precious minerals, or as a labour force, or as new citizens of Spain, to their role as enemies of civilization and obstacles to the colonial experiment.

Upon the indigenous patterns, then, were imprinted Hispanic frameworks: road networks, trading organization, rhythms of activity, value systems, agricultural practices, urban living. The processes of contact, diffusion and acculturation were themselves differentiated throughout Venezuela and Colombia, no less dependent upon routes of penetration and personal ambitions and decisions as upon the distribution of aboriginal population and mineral and agricultural resources. New settlements were founded, older ones deserted; in some areas forest was cleared, while elsewhere grassy savannas became more woody; turf-covered flat land was ploughed whilst terraced hill slopes were abandoned. Here, dispersed native population was in part congregated, elsewhere driven further towards the forested margins of colonial control. Where densely settled Indians died of introduced diseases, they were sometimes replaced by imported African Negro labourers. Skin colour added to the distinction between highland and lowland, forest and grassland, coast and interior. The development of the colonial economic system engendered the growth of isolated, independent city regions. Their numbers, size and interrelationships resulted from many factors. Within the latitudinal ecological grain of Venezuela a small but increasingly significant core of activity developed, centred on the coastal and highland zone of the north. In Colombia, on the other hand, the more complicated longitudinal and altitudinal ecological components enhanced a process of even more distinctive regionalism, economic activity in Colombia's case being not only more dispersed but also more varied.

Once more Venezuela and Colombia found themselves in an intermediate position. Venezuela, administered first from Santo Domingo, later fell within the jurisdiction of Santa Fé de Bogotá, a colonial centre that never attained the status of Mexico or Lima. As far as population, agriculture and mining were concerned, the area was of secondary significance to the Spanish crown. Venezuela and Colombia were subcentres of colonial activities, whose margins were some of the most peripheral parts of the empire.

It is interesting to note that when a political challenge to Spanish rule did appear within northern South America in the early nineteenth century, the

foothold established in just such a forgotten corner of the empire, Venezuelan Guayana, was of critical importance. From this base, with links to
allies in Caribbean islands, the independence movement spread territorially
across the *llanos*, to take the colonial administrative centre of Caracas from
the rear. Progress thence lay in moving from one former colonial centre to
another. Politically independent, the new nations, whose adolescent
attempt at political integration had failed miserably, faced the task of
adjusting to new conditions. They had to come to terms with industrializing
north-western Europe and with the economic forces that this process was
unleashing throughout the world. New crops or products were developed
to satisfy the demands of new markets. In Venezuela gold, then oil,
replaced agricultural products as major contributors to the national
exchequer. In Colombia, upon a more diversified base, coffee cultivation
eventually assumed paramount importance. New landscapes were created;
regular plantations of coffee trees and lines of oil derricks spoke of management and capital investment. New settlements were founded as communal
necessities. Elsewhere older agricultural areas declined, settlements were
deserted, population migrated to the nearest town in search of the urban
El Dorado. Success bred success. Depending upon the number of growth
points and their spacing, so the population distribution clustered into
either one large area, such as that in northern central Venezuela, or into a
scatter of competing regional centres, as in Colombia.

As subsistence farmers became increasingly involved in commercial
markets, so the communication links underwent important modifications.
New crops and mineral resources meant new roads or new waterway
utilization, depending upon the location of these in relation to previous
economic activity. Where the resources coincided with previous development there was a conflict of interest and an intensification of use; where
they lay at the margins of settlement some had to await the funds or demand
necessary for their development. In more recent years planning has been
the catchword to success. Developments are viewed in terms of a new
regional science, complete with its own language, in which cities become
'urban nodes', communications 'linkages', and the future is conceived in
terms of 'corridors' or 'poles of growth'. Yet the fact remains that, as
Venezuelans and Colombians realize, it is necessary to question continually
the means and ends of development or directed change, whether the change
be political, economic or social. The past and the present must be carefully
considered before North American or European 'models' are utilized, and
before this region of Latin America accepts another colonial offering that
might in the future be regretted. Those who would pass on their methods
of work, their style of living and their cultural goals need to assess carefully
their qualities and suitability before doing so. It is particularly important
to remember in the new age of planning that an inherent danger is the
alienation of the planners from the planned. Venezuelans and Colombians

have to ask themselves whether they live and work for tomorrow or the next generation, whether they are prepared to make sacrifices now for the promise of better days.

The most important characteristic of the cultures, landscapes and peoples of contemporary Venezuela and Colombia is the number and degree of visible or discernible contrasts. Whilst one can rarely escape the influence of nature, neither can one find many areas that do not bear the imprint of man. Though, in places, one can travel long distances without noting change, in others kilometres are compressed into metres and the observer is confused by the kaleidoscopic interaction of culture and nature. Faced with tropical forest and Andean snow, sprawling metropolitan centres and aboriginal longhouses, microwave radio links and dirt roads, blast furnaces and wooden ploughs, the visitor cannot fail to become curious as to why and where such contrasts exist, or for how long they have existed and may continue to exist. In Venezuela and Colombia, within an area endowed by nature with a remarkable richness of variety, it is possible to trace, albeit still in a qualitative and fragmentary manner, the process of cultural development that helps one to understand the juxtaposition of landscapes, societies and economies of the twentieth century alongside those of the eighteenth or sixteenth, close by others nearer to the millennia before Christ.

THE PHYSICAL FRAMEWORK

Altitude above sea-level is of great importance for these two tropical countries. The third dimension induces variations within the physical geography of the area that have been of significance to man since the remote past. Entering the south-west corner of Colombian territory, the high Andes, less than 200 km wide and comprising two parallel ranges separated by a high plateau, diverge as they pass northwards into three main ranges separated by block-faulting and known as the Cordillera Occidental, Cordillera Central and Cordillera Oriental (Fig. 5.1). The central range, a massive crystalline block topped by volcanic peaks over 5500 m, is divided from its eastern and western counterparts by the Magdalena and Cauca rivers respectively. The Serranía de Baudó, adjacent to the Pacific coast north of Buenaventura, forms a structural outlier of the Cordillera Occidental and is noted for the roughness of its surface caused by intense differential erosion of uptilted strata. The Cordillera Occidental is separated from this coastal upland by a lowland strip picked out by the courses of the rivers Atrato and San Juan. Eastwards the land rises steeply up the flanks of the Cordillera Central, whose northern extremity fans out before plunging beneath the sediments of the Caribbean coast, dissected by the rivers Sinú, San Juan, Porce and Cauca, the latter stream having traversed northwards through spectacular gorge sections from its upper structural trench section south of Cartago. Like the Cauca, but in a different mode, the Magdalena valley reflects its origin in orogenic faulting and folding; its valley is deep as far south as Girardot, with rapids at Honda and south of Neiva. The geomorphic history of this part of Colombia is witnessed by the relationship of drainage to structures and surfaces, though it still remains to be written.

From around Pasto the Cordillera Oriental trends north-eastwards, towards the Venezuelan border, its physique characterized by discontinuous high mountain crests that stand above the series of intermontane

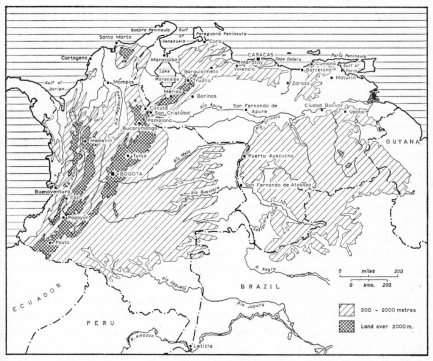

Fig. 5.1 Relief and drainage

basins in which are situated Bogotá, Tunja and Sogamoso, and the rugged relief features of its periphery, particularly on the south-eastern margin. Crossing into Venezuela the Cordillera de Mérida still attains altitudes of 4900 m, but the width of the range decreases consistently as it trends ever more parallel to the southern Caribbean shore, providing little space for the intermontane basins such as those around Mérida, Valera and Trujillo. This elongated arm of the Andes continues eastwards through the central highland zone of northern Venezuela, in which are found small depressions, occupied by Lake Valencia and the river Tuy, until east of Cumaná they leave Venezuela along the Paria peninsula for Trinidad.

North of the Andean ranges are found several important upland areas. In Colombia, west of the Gulf of Urabá, rise mountains that continue into Panama; east of the Caribbean lowlands around Barranquilla the abrupt crystalline slopes of the Sierra Nevada de Santa Marta reach high enough to justify their name. In Venezuela the rocky headlands of the peninsulas of Guajira and Paraguaná stand out from the lowlands; east of Lake Maracaibo a tract of plateau country is dissected on its eastern edge by the waters of the Yaracuy and Tocuyo.

Whilst in the densely populated regions of northern Venezuela and north-western Colombia relatively level land is in short supply, in the southern and south-eastern portions of the two countries the opposite is true. On the *llanos* one moves within a horizontal rather than vertical world, where the only relief is between low tabular interfluves and shallow meandering, braided river courses. Although the terrain may vary markedly from one area to another, the overriding feature of this area that extends from the Amazonian tributaries to the Orinoco delta is its similarities. If, in the north and west orogeny and erosion are keys to understanding the land forms, in the south and east it is deposition. To the east and south the sedimentary trough abuts against the old structures of the Guiana Shield that in Venezuela form the distinctive region of Guayana. The planation surface steps rise from the Orinocan fluviatile terraces around Ciudad Bolívar, across the lateritic inclusions of the lower Caroní to reach their maximum altitude in the Gran Sabana's southern margin, the plateau of Roraima.

Within and between such major relief components as have been briefly described in Venezuela and Colombia there exists a complexity of variation that defies brief description. Rivers are found shallow with deltas, or deep with estuaries; coasts high and rocky, elsewhere flat and sandy. Ruggedness is influenced not only by rock type and dip but also by past and present erosional or depositional activity. Whereas in one area the economic benefits of geology accrue from deposition, in another they derive from erosion and exposure (Vila, 1960).

Such degrees of diversity of altitude and relief are reflected through the climatic patterns of Venezuela and Colombia. A distinction can be made between sharp altitudinal variation and the general seasonal climatic rhythm. To the Spanish colonists, as in their Mediterranean homeland, time and weather were synonymous, and the seasonal droughts and rains formed the basis for their division of the year. In the plainlands of the *llanos* the seasonal change of precipitation total and type, of cloud cover and thickness, of direction of winds and rates of evapotranspiration, affects both the ecology and the economy. In the mountains, on the other hand, altitude induces great variety in local climate, in spite of low seasonal ranges of temperature. Sharp differences of rainfall between small areas are common and a vertical zonation of average annual temperatures is commonly recognized, extending from the 'hot land' below 1000 m to the 'cold land' above 2000 m (Fig. 5.9). Such approximate divisions based on altitude are better set aside in favour of the more subtle indices of vegetation and crops and the rhythms of economic activities. Climate has always meant more than mere rainfall and sunshine in Venezuela and Colombia; it has continuously and variously affected the pattern of vegetation, both before and during its alteration by man and it has promoted, permitted or prevented the spread of diseases, crops and human population. It may be said that in certain places man himself, on both the localized scale of urban building and the more general scale associated with forest clearance and reservoir construction, is affecting the micro- and macro-climatic patterns of the area. In the past the southern Caribbean shore's longitudinal succession of arid and humid conditions was of more than local significance, as was the altitudinal seasonality of Colombia. Today man's impact on the balance of nature, his reduction of natural variety by cultural demands, has affected both the short- and long-term importance of climate. The critical thresholds that initiate soil erosion or that prevent plant regeneration have in many areas been crossed.

It is impossible to describe the patterns of soil and vegetation without reference to the seasonality of the climate, climatic change, the variation of parent material and the rates and types of erosional and depositional processes at work. It was not without good reason that aboriginal Indians shifted their *conucos*, that the colonial plantation-owner put a premium on the flat coastal, lacustrine or riverine zones. It is relevant to note that within the vegetational sequences of Venezuela and Colombia one can find problems that still challenge the biogeographer: the status of the so-called virgin tropical rain-forest; the significance of riparian vegetation; the origin of the tropical grass and woodland savannas; the introduction and spread of alien plants. The variation and richness of the flora of this part of South America has caused comment since the early colonial accounts of Gumilla and Castellanos, long before Linnaeus sent Löfling to collect and classify the plants of eastern Venezuela and Guayana, and comment concontinued through the work of Humboldt and Depons, Codazzi, Ernst, Hettner and Pittier in the eighteenth and nineteenth centuries.

If the patterns of contrasts and variety were the corner stones of early work in the physical geography of Venezuela and Colombia, in the more recent period greater, and justifiable, emphasis has been placed upon processes of change. Just as in a spatial context certain patterns and processes may alter, so, too, in the temporal context such elements as duration of activity, intensity of effort and impact and frequency of action are of great importance. On all sides in northern South America one can find evidence for change in the physical framework. Rivers appear to be 'misfits' in their valleys, and anastomosing channels speak eloquently of climatic change. From the Caroní to the Sinú evidence is available in the shape of

G

depositional and erosional features: river fall-lines, *ciénegas*, ox-bow lakes, raised marine and fluviatile terraces. Geological processes of volcanic activity have produced ash-filled valleys or fault belts have briefly added a new dimension to natural instability. As relief and drainage have changed, so have vegetation, soils and climate, all five in some complicated relationship. New techniques make it possible to reconstruct the vegetational succession of the past, to date deposits and the surfaces upon which they rest.

The physical framework of Venezuela and Colombia should be regarded not only in terms of an evolving physical milieu, but also as a milieu for man in his many guises and activities. Soils and vegetation have to be viewed in terms of economic potential and cultural preference. The grassy savannas may now appear infertile and of little potential, but, as the archaeological remains and literary sources demonstrate, they once were the home of other specialized peoples; peoples to whom the seasonal flow of the rivers, the flooding of the banks, the acidity of the water, the migration of fish, turtles and birds, were of critical and well-comprehended significance. Only through the medium of cultural relativism can one comprehend such terms as irrigability, erodability, navigability and fertility; flat land and steep slopes, like hot and cold climes, are not merely quantifiable phenomena but remain relative to their cultural context.

PRE-HISPANIC CULTURES

Developments to A.D. 1500

At least as long ago as 12,000 B.C. man was to be found in Venezuela, and probably also in Colombia (Rouse and Cruxent, 1963, p. 27). Both countries endured different climatic conditions from those of today. Average temperatures were lower and precipitation totals were higher, both caused, like the lower level of the sea, by the presence of glacial ice sheets within North America. At that time the present complexity of lagoons, inlets, promontories and islands of the southern Caribbean shore was probably non-existent, replaced by a wide coastal margin that extended westwards to a wider central American isthmus. Relatively large ice masses were present on the highlands of the Sierra Nevada de Santa Marta, around Caracas and Mérida, and over considerable portions of the three Colombian ranges. The pattern of rivers was different, too – in Venezuela, for example, the Orinoco entered the Atlantic by the extreme southern edge of its present delta; a wider Caroní entered the Orinoco further east than its present junction, and Lake Valencia's level stood higher and had an outlet southwards to the Orinoco. Although little is known of the late Pleistocene and Holocene landscape of Colombia, recent palynological studies have shown that in the Andes the tree-line fluctuated by some 1600 m from its present position, and that during the fluctuation of pluvial and interpluvial periods the margin between woodland and grassland varied considerably (Reichel-Dolmatoff, 1965, p. 41). During the so-called Palaeo-Indian epoch (15,000 – 5000 B.C.) man had moved into and through northern South America by a variety of possible routes. They included the southern Caribbean coastal zone; the lowland valleys of Magdalena and Cauca that led south to the Andean ranges and in turn gave way to the Orinoco and Amazonian river networks; and the Pacific coastal route south from the isthmus of Darien to the latitude of Buenaventura or Tumaco, whose short rivers led east to the highland core. In Venezuela south from the Caribbean it would have been relatively easy to cross the narrow coastal ranges or avoid them by passing through the former exit of the Orinoco to the Caribbean, around the mouth of the modern river Unare (Fig. 5.1).

In the area during that time roamed large mammals, including mastodon and horse, and it was as hunters that men lived, besides collecting fruits of the forest. At Canaima in Venezuelan Guayana and Tolima in Colombia remains have been located of hunting kill sites or stone spear-making localities. Settlements were widely dispersed and temporary in character, and population densities were exceedingly low.

By about 5000 B.C. the climate had improved and conditions were quite similar to those of the present. The large mammals had become extinct, possibly because of shortage of forage in the Boreal and pre-Boreal drier periods, or else through the increasing success of specialized hunting. Whatever the cause of the disappearance of the mammals, the beginning of the Holocene presented man in this area with a major problem of ecological adaptation. With smaller game unable to provide his dietary requirements, man began slowly to adapt to coastal fishing and forest agriculture. A series of coastal shell middens, stretching from the Paria peninsula to Barranquilla, are eloquent expressions of such adaptation. Other Meso-Indians who did not turn to fishing and sailing found it possible to obtain sufficient nourishment from fruits and seeds they collected from the forests and grasslands. Yet others, who in Colombia had moved south up-valley from the coast, and in Venezuela inhabited the forested mountains and basins of the north, began the process of plant domestication. At Rancho Peludo in Venezuela and Malambo in Colombia non-ceramic artefacts suggest bitter manioc (*Manihot esculenta*) cultivation as early as 1000 B.C. The striking similarity of associated pottery from this Colombian site to that of a Venezuelan series near Barrancas formerly supported the postulated origin of manioc cultivation in eastern Venezuela and its spread westwards into Colombia, though even this hypothesis is now being challenged. In Colombia especially, sedentary village life still had a riparian orientation. Rich resources of fish, amphibians and bird life never made agriculture so necessary as elsewhere in the Americas.

Nevertheless, agriculture was adopted as a means of subsistence, not only manioc cultivation but also the domesticated grain, maize. At Rancho

Peludo near Maracaibo and at Momil on the lower Sinú (Fig. 5.2) evidence suggests that at some time around 1000 B.C. a change was made from a root crop staple to the new seed crop. Though evidence is tentative, based upon the identification of manioc griddles and maize grinders, it seems clear that the use of maize was being spread into Colombia and western Venezuela from its domestication centre in Meso-America. Its arrival involved the learning of new agricultural techniques and the reappraisal and utilization of formerly under-used land; it included the possibility of larger and more durable surpluses. The distinction between the maize cultivation to the west and the manioc cultivation to the east of northern South America was to be of enduring significance. Hunting, fishing and gathering gradually became secondary to agriculture as a means of subsistence, except probably in the isolated interior areas of Guayana, the southern *llanos* and parts of the highland basins of Colombia. For Venezuela it is possible to distinguish three geographical regions during the time of the Neo-Indians (1000 B.C. to A.D. 1500), but in Colombia the cultural diversity makes such generalized divisions worthless. Western Venezuela (Fig. 5.2) was culturally closely affiliated with Colombia. Its maize and, in the highland, potato cultivation, its pottery styles, its modes of burial and its earthworks distinguished the west from the east. If a nuclear area had to be chosen for western Venezuela, it would probably be the basin of Maracaibo. In the eastern region the lower Orinoco basin was its counterpart. From about 700 B.C. a series of Indian migrations down the valley of the Orinoco forced other groups east and northwards, driving them to the northern coast where they either migrated west or out into the Antilles, or else east and southwards into the delta of the Orinoco. This movement resulted in a displacement of pre-existing groups out of the lower Orinoco area, either north to the coast and thence along it westwards, or out into the Antilles, or alternatively east into the delta zone and south-east along the Atlantic coastal margin.

Between east and west there was a zone of transition (Fig. 5.2), characterized by flows of peoples and crops and probably agricultural techniques and other cultural traits. Within this transitional region at least two centres were of more than local significance. One such centre was the locality around present-day Puerto Cabello. Here a number of routes converged: the coastal Caribbean passage; the Maracaibo–Yaracuy valley route; the Andean highland route out of modern Colombia to the Caribbean coast; and the Valencia–Tuy valley and upper *llanos* routes from the east. Further south the junction of the rivers Apure and Portuguesa represented a convergence of routes from the lower Orinoco basin, the Amazonian–Orinoco headwater region, the Andean ranges of Mérida and the central highlands of northern Venezuela.

In Colombia it is more difficult to identify meaningful large cultural regions in the period between 1000 B.C. and the eve of Spanish Conquest.

With their new crop, maize, lowland horticulturalists gradually spread southwards into the valleys and on to the flanks of the Andean ranges, heralding a period of regional diversification – of agriculture, settlement forms and social and religious structures. The spread of settlement also involved isolation and localization of groups of Indians: river valleys, mountain flanks, upland plateaux – each saw the gradual development of their particular group. The influence of Meso-American culture, felt

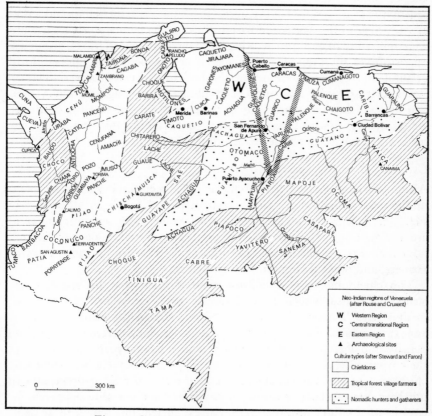

Fig. 5.2 Cultural regions on the eve of conquest

significantly around 1000 B.C. with the introduction of maize, was felt again around 500 B.C. with the landings of aboriginal colonists along the Colombian Pacific shore around Tumaco. From these footholds their influence spread eastwards into the Andean core area and thence downstream along the major river valleys. Gradually, at centres such as San Agustín, Tierradentro, Calima and Quimbaya intensive maize agriculture, metallurgy and a form of social stratification appear to have developed. Elsewhere, on the northern lowlands the earlier patterns and rhythms of land and life continued as before, influenced by coastal contacts from

Panama at Cupica, and north-western Venezuela. Cultural variation was superimposed upon, and reflected, physical diversity. Access and contact were enhanced by the relatively dense network of waterways navigable by canoe. As in Venezuela, historic centres of contact can be identified, as exemplified by Zambrano where links existed between coast, Sierra Nevada, the Sinú valley and lands to the south. From the first century A.D. until the arrival of the Spanish, aboriginal developments in Venezuela and Colombia were probably characterized by an increasing density of sedentary agriculturalists in the northern and western highlands and fringe areas, whilst to the south and east and along the coastal margins Indians were migrating to and fro, adapting and being influenced by the ecological opportunities of savanna, forest, marsh and lagoon. The interaction of cultural and ecological evolution resulted in the complex variations in styles of dress, food habits, form of dwellings, types of agricultural systems and range of implements, and in the differentiation of social institutions, which was the first feature to attract the attention of the Spanish as they made contact with this zone (Sauer, 1965).

Cultural patterns around A.D. 1500

A simplified and generalized subdivision of the cultural types to be found in the area around the Spanish contact period has been attempted in Fig. 5.2. Necessarily, boundaries between cultures are as approximate as are the locations of many of the aboriginal groups. The key feature, however, is the tripartite division into chiefdoms, tropical forest village farmers, and nomadic hunters and gatherers.

The chiefdoms were a cultural type characterized by small, class-structured states, which have variously been designated 'federations', 'realms' and 'kingdoms'. They have been viewed (Steward and Faron, 1959) as products of surplus agricultural production, increasing population density and intensification of military and religious practices. Whatever their origins, a useful distinction may be made between the militaristic chiefdoms of the Colombian area and their theocratic counterparts in northern Venezuela. For the former, warfare was not only necessary for co-operative efforts towards territorial expansion, but remained of paramount importance in the provision of human victims for temple rites. In the theocratic chiefdoms, however, warfare was far less important than religion as a means of community integration. It is of interest to note that the chiefdoms were by no means restricted to the highland areas, but extended downslope to include large areas of lowland savanna. Indeed, it might be said that general characteristics of the chiefdom zone included the absence of extremely large areas of tropical forest and, in several areas, the need to irrigate agricultural land. In most chiefdom groups intensive farming provided the basis of economic life, so that hunting, fishing and gathering never attained the significance they held for the tropical forest farmers. In several areas the land available for agriculture was extended by means of terracing and, in the case of the Chibcha of Colombia, and the Timoto-Cuica of Venezuela, irrigation systems were established (Eidt, 1959). Crop diversity was another characteristic of the chiefdom zone and provided not only more abundant food, but, equally important, a well-balanced diet. Millennia of plant introductions and experimentation had produced a long list of domesticates: maize, sweet potatoes, sweet and bitter manioc, beans, peanuts, pineapples and avocado in the lowlands; at higher altitudes *quinoa, achira (Canna edulis)*, potatoes and *ullucos (Ullucus tuberosus)*. The variety of domesticated plants contrasts sharply with the paucity of domesticated animals. In the absence of large mammals, guinea pigs, muskovy ducks, mute dogs and bees provided alternatives to the vegetable harvests. Evidence also suggests that in most chiefdoms a very important protein source was that provided by riverine or coastal fishing, or, in the special case of the Gorrón in Colombia, by means of fish-breeding. A wide range of fibres, especially cotton, had engendered an interest and proficiency in weaving textiles, many of which in the highland areas were clearly related to central Andean practices. Pearls, gold and emeralds were but three of the highly valued commodities that entered into the trading economies of the chiefdom peoples. Their settlements were of two basic types; much of northern Venezuela and Colombia were characterized by relatively large wood-palisaded townships, with populations of over 1000 inhabitants; elsewhere in the highland zones defensively sited villages were common. The peoples of these chiefdoms, the Cumana-gotos, Caquetíos and Cuevans were some of the first peoples of Tierra Firme to come into contact with European man (Sauer, 1965). It was only later that their more culturally advanced counterparts, the Timotos and Chibchan peoples, were encountered.

The second major cultural division of Venezuelan and Colombian territory was the region occupied by tropical forest farming communities, some of whose Indian groups, such as the Motilones west of Lake Maracaibo, still resist contact and assimilation. For decades the oral histories and linguistic affiliations of many of the Indian groups of these areas have posed problems of interpretation. Hypotheses relating to migrations, plant domestication and relationships between the forest groups and non-forest groups abound. Swidden appears to have formed the basis of the subsistence agriculture of at least a part of the tropical forest zone, though in south-eastern areas the staples of bitter and sweet manioc, beans and peanuts, which replace the maize-beans-squash complex more typical of north-western Colombia, are known to have been cultivated on fixed plots. The *montones*, or mound plots of the vegecultural *conuco* system of Venezuela could be contrasted with the seed-based farming systems of the more complex Colombian areas. In all of the forest areas fish and small game provided vital sources of protein to balance the dietary qualities of the starch-rich crop foodstuffs. Though of the forest, the Indian settlements were dominantly riparian in location, the river networks providing excellent channels of intercommunication. Canoe construction, together with basket manufacture and heddle-loom weaving, characterized the diversified economic base of many of these Indians. The extensive range of forest products utilized included *anatto* (*Bixa orellana*) and *genipa* dyes, *barbasco* fish stupefiers, and calabash utensils. Though their political organization was rudimentary compared with those of the chiefdom peoples, the tropical forest Indians were structured upon a kinship base, and sex-differentiated occupational structures and shamanism were common elements. In certain groups that came within the knowledge of the Spanish, cannibalistic practices were evidently of long standing. Perhaps the most significant features of this major region were the low densities of population, usually between a tenth or twentieth of the chiefdom area, and the lack of well-developed social structures and economic specialization.

The area of hunters and gatherers constituted the third major division of pre-Hispanic northern South America. In this zone small bands of nomadic Indians, within a more limited environmental setting, gathered fruits or hunted small game, peccaries, deer and armadillos in the riparian forests or extensive grassland savanna. Fire was an essential tool in their delicate relationship with the savanna grasslands, the marshes and swamps, and the narrow bands of woodland. The absence of agriculture as a mainstay of the economy was as fundamental a feature in setting them apart from their neighbours as was their relatively simple social organization. Although field evidence is continually being discovered of earlier, more intensive use of many of the areas of savanna grassland, the Orinoco plains, away from regular air routes, may yet provide more such data; the fact is that by the time of the arrival of the Spanish this zone was occupied by dispersed and exceedingly low densities of population.

This, then, was the general situation in Colombia and Venezuela on the eve of the Spanish Conquest: the impact of the intrusive Spanish culture on the diverse and distinctive cultures of the area was to be affected by the choice, or chance, of penetration routes, the types of contact made, and the extent to which the Indians were incorporated within first colonial and later national economies and social systems. The fact that in the present century neither Colombia nor Venezuela have significant Indian elements in their population is as much related to the situation at contact as it is to later developments in acculturation and assimilation.

COLONIAL CONTRASTS AND SIMILARITIES

That both Colombia and Venezuela were peripheral and second-rank Spanish colonies there can be little doubt. The Viceroyalty of New

Granada, an administrative design to accommodate the northern portion of South America, never achieved the status of its northern and southern counterparts of Lima and Mexico. Nevertheless the differentiation of colonial developments within the region of modern Venezuela and Colombia, and their combined strategic location at the junction of Caribbean, Central and South America, provide an instructive basis for interpreting the processes of change after the removal of colonial political controls. In mineral and agricultural development, rural and urban settlement patterns, demographic change, the establishment and development of trade and communication networks, and the evolution of administrative frameworks, the region emphasized more than anything else the complex nature of the adaptations, extension and effectiveness of colonial institutions, practices and modes of life.

Fundamental to any understanding of Hispanic colonialism is the role of the urban foundation as the symbol and instrument of colonization. In northern South America, as elsewhere, towns became the foci of authority, the centres from which economic enterprise extended, the cores of cultural contact, the stepping stones in the effective control of territory (Morse, 1962). In Colombia and Venezuela during the sixteenth century colonization was characterized by its ephemeral nature. From early coastal bases such as Cumaná and Coro colonization proceeded slowly and haltingly, hampered continually by hostile Indians, unsuccessful land settlement and disorganized administration. With the flow of gold objects along the Coquibacao–Curiana route interrupted by Spanish activities in northern Colombia, the mineral potential of Venezuela was soon seen to be extremely limited, and it was only after the middle of the sixteenth century that the number of urban settlements increased in harmony with agricultural development (Fig. 5.3). By 1600 there had been laid down a network of settlements, which lay predominantly on or near to the Caribbean coast and its mountain hinterland. Only Santo Tomé on the Orinoco lay outside this zone. In Colombia likewise primary coastal centres at Santa Marta, Cartagena and on the Urabá gulf preceded a penetrative phase of foundations that included the settlements of Cali, Popayán, Santa Fé de Bogotá and Tunja. Naturally enough, the chronology and location of such settlements reflected the various enterprises of Spanish *conquistadores*: in the Colombian area Federmann moving south-west from Coro; Quesada and Vadillo penetrating south from Santa Marta and Cartagena; Belalcázar moving north from Quito to Popayán and Cali. In Venezuela Berrío and Ordáz led exploration parties into the Orinoco basin, while Ehinger and others colonized the lands of the western region (Morón, 1954). Despite the popular preoccupation of many authors with the niceties of the exact dates of foundation of colonial urban centres, of far greater significance was the ubiquity of settlement shifts. A great variety of factors led to settlements being moved. Some, like Venezuelan

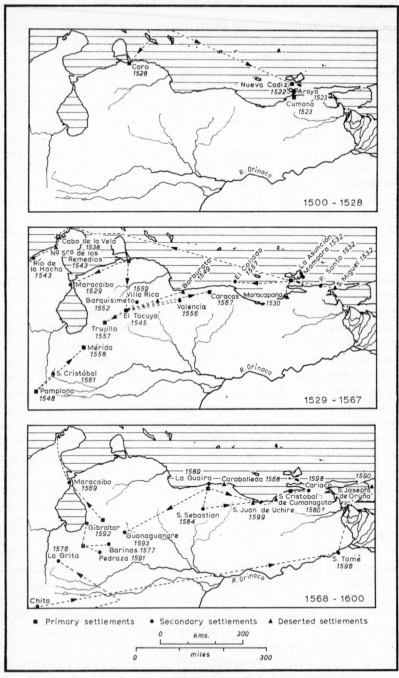

Fig. 5.3 The spread of settlement in sixteenth-century Venezuela
(after Vila, 1965)

Angostura (previously Santo Tomé), were moved for strategic reasons; others, such as Remedios in Colombia, were moved owing to the exhaustion of the local resource base. Fires, insect plagues, health hazards and Indian attacks were common factors. The process was by no means restricted to the early phase of colonial rule. As the settlement frontier expanded and new situations arose, so there were many settlement casualties (Vila, 1966; Houston, 1968). Even in the seventeenth and eighteenth centuries,

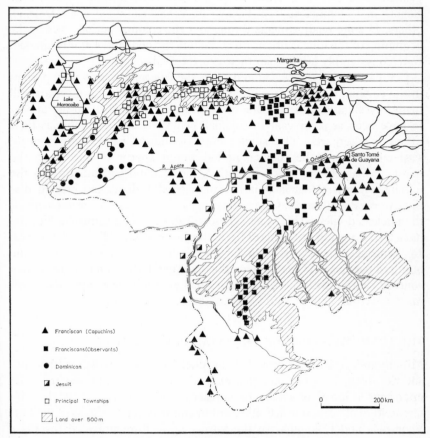

Fig. 5.4 Catholic mission foundations in colonial Venezuela

through the amalgamation of dispersed small settlements, abandonment and removal were commonplace (Martínez, 1967).

Perhaps the commonest denominator of the urban settlements was their form. The basis of their plan was a rectilinear grid of streets dividing the built-up area into blocks. The *plaza mayor* and the location of church, *cabildo* and other functionally specialized buildings gave most of the settlements a formal, planned aspect. In many cases, of course, local conditions of site and circumstances necessitated modification to this simplified model (for plans see Martínez, 1967, and Ricardo, 1967). Even the term 'urban', when applied to such settlements, needs careful definition, and barbarism was probably never very far from the central square, even in the largest towns.

Another hallmark of Hispanic urbanism was the hierarchical nature of the settlements. As early as 1600 there could be identified one or two primate settlements in northern South America; in size Santa Fé de Bogotá in Colombia and El Tocuyo in Venezuela stood apart from all others. Despite readjustments throughout the colonial period, even at the beginning of the nineteenth century, Bogotá (25,000) and Caracas (48,000) were considerably larger than their nearest rivals.

Compared with the *ciudad* and *villa*, the *campaña* was as unimportant in the colonial period as it is often regarded today. Though there are still many investigations to be made on rural settlements, they do not appear to have been as significant in colonial Venezuela and Colombia as their urban counterparts. The single most significant rural component of settlement during the colonial period would appear to have been the mission village (Vila, 1965). In both Venezuela and Colombia it was the missionary orders that colonized, congregated Indians and created distinctive rural landscapes. Over wide areas a new settlement form emerged, the nucleated village (Fig. 5.4). These villages can be contrasted with the nucleated form and functions of the arable haciendas and livestock ranches. In Venezuela these agricultural settlements often contained over one hundred persons. In Colombia, on the other hand, the larger urban centres contrast sharply with the widespread small gold mining camps, *minas* and *ranchos* (Armas Chitty, 1961; West, 1952).

THE ECONOMIC BASIS OF COLONIAL DEVELOPMENT

Mining and agriculture provided the dual base upon which settlements and the colonial population either expanded or declined. One of the most important colonial processes in northern South America was the differentiation of economic activities within and between the areas of modern Venezuela and Colombia. In the former agriculture provided the most significant stimulus to development; in the latter it was mineral resources – although neither mining nor agriculture was ever exclusive to each area. Local variations within this generalization have yet to be fully assessed.

Venezuela

Although it was the pearl beds of eastern Venezuela that first attracted the attention of the Spanish to Tierra Firme (Ojer, 1967; Morón, 1954), mineral wealth was soon found to be singularly lacking in the explored areas of northern Venezuela. Though the Welsers in the west and the

Spaniards in the east searched diligently for vein and placer deposits, only small amounts of gold, and later copper, were found. Small amounts of gold were extracted during the second half of the sixteenth century in valleys to the west of Caracas, but during the seventeenth century the only significant mineral extracted was copper in the Cocorote mines (Brito-Figueroa, 1963, p. 82). Such mining necessitated the importation of Negro slaves to replace indigenous labour. Though colonial records mention eighteenth-century mining in places as far apart as Guayana (iron ore) and the Andean areas of the west, it never became an important element in the economic progress of the region. This paucity of mineral wealth undoubtedly had several fundamental effects on the development of the region. It meant first that it was to be largely by-passed during the sixteenth and seventeenth centuries as colonists were drawn to the riches of New Spain and Peru. It also involved the development of an agricultural colony that, compared with other areas, was to prove highly successful – at least from the point of view of the Spanish crown and the entrepreneurs involved. This agricultural base meant that for the most part the distribution of population and its changing structure, associated forms of settlement and concentration of wealth were controlled by the interaction of ecological and economic factors.

The basic feature of agricultural development in colonial Venezuela was the regionalization of activities and the establishment of dual systems of enterprise. The first was subsistence production based on small-scale units and related to aboriginal methods of cultivation; the second was commercial production on large, extensively used holdings. The extension of private ownership of land in the hands of a small but important group of families, and the concentration of the wealth derived from commercial agriculture in restricted zones, principally in the north-centre of the regions, were also significant processes (Brito-Figueroa, 1960; Arcila Farías, 1946).

As previously mentioned, the initiation of colonial agriculture was centred upon early urban foundations. In most parts of Venezuela the establishment of a township involved not only the distribution of urban *solares* between members of the community, but also the allotment of Indians, who were initially viewed as the means of cultivating the land or tending livestock. If one maps the location of *encomiendas* and the principal residences of their *encomenderos* (Fig. 5.5), one can see the overwhelming significance of the north and western zones of upland Venezuela (Arcila Farías, 1946). As a result of recent researches, it is now possible to trace the evolution of both arable and livestock farming in central Venezuela from the late sixteenth century through to the nineteenth century (Brito-Figueroa, 1961, 1963; Vila, 1965).

In the province of Caracas private agricultural land was acquired principally through *mercedes de tierras*, grants of land given to persons

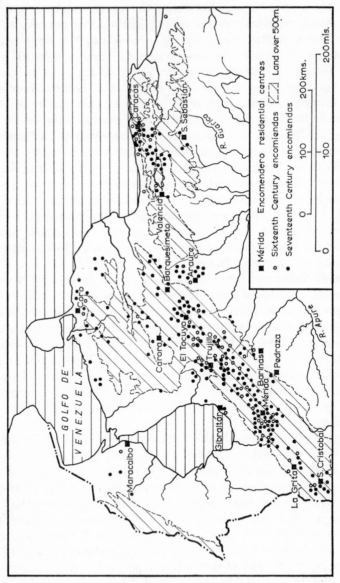

Fig. 5.5 Distribution of *encomiendas* in north-west Venezuela

intimately connected with the foundation of the principal civil settlements. By 1600 almost 13,000 ha of land had been alienated from Indian groups in the northern valleys of Tuy, Caracas, Aragua and Barlovento. Of this land, some 50 per cent was controlled by twelve owners. The formation of large estates proceeded at an ever-quickening pace throughout the next two centuries. During the seventeenth century almost 1 million ha of agricultural land were included within private estates, almost 45 per cent of the total area of these valleys (Brito-Figueroa, 1963; p. 157). In the decade 1736–46 alone, a further 500,000 ha were incorporated within 190 estates. Holdings of over 2500 ha were relatively common. By the end of the eighteenth century, an estimated 18 per cent of the total area of the province of Caracas was in private ownership. Two associated features of estate formation were the control of most of agricultural production by a diminishing number of owners, and the low intensity of land use within the estates. By 1750, for example, some fifty owners controlled approximately 73 per cent of the agricultural land of the province of Caracas. As little as 4 per cent of the total land in estates was actually cultivated. The absorption of Indians into the labour pool of these estates, and the usurpation of their land by private owners, account for the widespread desertion of Indian settlements during the period 1600–1800. Caracas province alone lost at least sixty such settlements. Not only were large estates being created, but another significant trend during the colonial period was the reduction in the total number of commercial agricultural holdings, principally by purchase or inheritance. The number of cacao plantations, for example, was reduced from around 440 in 1746 to a mere 160 by 1800. Wealth was being concentrated in fewer hands, and in a decreasing number of centres.

Of all the arable crops cacao was the most important during this period. It provided the basis for plantation agriculture in many parts of northern Venezuela. By 1750 over 5 million cacao trees were under cultivation in the province of Caracas. The fifteen plantations of a single family, the Pontes, accounted for over 250,000 trees at that date. Cacao cultivation was located in the fertile soils of the valleys of northern Venezuela, extending from Cumaná in the east to Trujillo in the west. The two most important centres of production were the northern part of the province of Caracas, and around the margins of the Maracaibo basin, especially to the east of the lake. By 1800 almost 1000 plantations were in operation, involving some 13 million trees and 29,000 ha of land. During the whole of the colonial period Venezuelan agricultural production was dominated by cacao. Considering the inadequacy of the indigenous labour force (numbers were relatively small at contact and decreased through disease), it was not surprising that, as elsewhere in the Americas, the plantation-owners imported large numbers of Negro slaves (Brito-Figueroa, 1963, pp. 93–112). A high correlation is to be noted between areas of commercial plantation agriculture and negroid elements in the population. However, the Venezuelan total of 120,000 slaves legally imported during the colonial period accounts for a mere 12 per cent of the total entering Spanish American colonies.

Besides cacao, other commercial crops such as tobacco, indigo, cotton, coffee, wheat and sugar cane were cultivated within Venezuela. Tobacco, cultivated by the Indians of the Tocuyo district on the arrival of the Spanish, suffered from serious setbacks during the entire colonial period through the interference of the metropolitan monopolists. Though it was an important crop in the Valencia, Barquisimeto and Barinas regions, it never became an important item of export. Wheat was another crop widely cultivated during the sixteenth and seventeenth centuries, but it lost ground to the increasingly profitable cacao in the eighteenth. In the late colonial period, the focus of wheat cultivation was in the Andean zone centred on Mérida. Sugar cane was another ubiquitous crop, which was provided principally for the Venezuelan market. Indigo, elsewhere in the colonies an important agricultural product, was left to grow wild in the northern central valleys until the 1760s when price increases made its laborious cultivation economically viable. In the Aragua valleys, west of Caracas, it attained great local significance during the last two decades of the eighteenth century. Cotton was also grown widely in Venezuela. From the middle Yuruari basin to Tocuyo it provided the basis for local textile industries.

It must be remembered, however, that these crops, accounting for less than 10 per cent of the area of private agricultural holdings, took the form of oases of intensive agriculture amidst a general scene of continuing aboriginal practices. Beyond, and probably within, the boundaries of private land lay large areas in which the aboriginal staples of manioc, maize, beans and plantains were cultivated by various methods of swidden. Though the newly introduced ploughs, water-wheels, stone aqueducts and the like affected great changes in certain localities, their innovative effects on agriculture were limited. Over large areas mestizos and Negroes appreciated the suitability of indigenous agricultural techniques. What colonial crop agriculture did was to create a new, highly contrasted, agricultural economy and landscape.

The impact of arable plantation agriculture within the northern areas of Venezuela can have been no greater than that of colonial livestock ranching in the vast plains of the Orinoco basin. It is now known that, prior to the development of extensive ranching over the *llanos*, livestock farming was intimately associated with arable cultivation in the northern valleys. In the latter part of the sixteenth century, indeed, cattle were the most significant elements in agriculture from the basin of Valencia to Tocuyo. Only through the competition afforded by cacao and other crops was ranching displaced and extended southwards, downslope towards the river Orinoco. Gradually, during the seventeenth and eighteenth centuries, cattle ranches (*hatos*) were established in the *llanos*. Penetration of ranching practices into the plainlands came from three principal directions: from the Andean area south-east into Barinas and Apure; from the central northern valleys south via San Sebastián into Guárico; and from the eastern coastal lowlands around Barcelona-Cumaná, south to Zaraza and the Orinoco. The complicated chronology of advance cannot be discussed here. Suffice to say that, as in the arable areas, large estates (*latifundios*) emerged as the dominant unit of organization and production. By 1740, for example, there were more than seventy *hatos* in the valleys of Guárico and Apure and more than 500,000 ha of open range had been alienated within the preceeding fifty years. Some 300,000 head of cattle were grazed on the forty largest *hatos*, providing employment for almost 4000 persons, Negro slaves accounting for 10 per cent of the total. Some of the largest *hatos* had herds of over 50,000 head (Brito-Figueroa, 1963, p. 217). The extent of the ranching area can be seen in Fig. 5.6. Within the *llanos* zone two distinct subregions can be identified. The first, the core area of ranching, extended around the southern fringe of the uplands, where free range grazing was possible throughout the year. The second area was one of seasonal transhumance on the northern bank of the lower Orinoco, cattle being moved north and southwards, as seasonal variations in precipitation presented problems of flooding and drought. It was in the upper *llanos* area that the introduced cattle multiplied rapidly. With no fences, the ranching economy and landscape was influenced by river lines, waterholes and scattered patches of woodland. Outside these two zones many secondary centres of livestock agriculture persisted until the end of the colonial period. The development of cattle-ranching under the syndicate system of the Capuchins in the Caroní–Yuruari area, the specialization of the Mérida district in sheep-rearing, and the north-east in goat-herding, provide good examples of localized developments during the eighteenth century.

Though Fig. 5.6 attempts to summarize the salient features of Venezuelan colonial agriculture, what it cannot do is to highlight some of the most important aspects and repercussions of the pattern. Space precludes any analysis of the local variation that was so prevalent. Individual valleys differed in their crop combinations; agricultural practices and tools were localized; production, productivity and efficiency were related to ecological circumstances, economic pressures and personal whims (Quijada, 1968). In widespread localities fishing provided a valuable addition to food supplies. In some areas aboriginal terraced land was abandoned, elsewhere irrigation systems were introduced and extended. To the *conuquero* were added the *hacendado* and the *llanero*, new Venezuelan folk figures (Mendoza, 1947).

Although the colonial period had witnessed an expansion and diversification of agriculture, in Venezuela the principal benefactors had concentrated with their wealth and families primarily in and around Caracas, or at least within the central northern zone, close to the coast. Though earlier the towns had spread economic activities into rural areas, as the colony flourished wealth and influence gravitated towards those same towns. Cattle estates and arable plantations were controlled by absentee landlords residing in the Caracas area. The mode of agricultural development had reinforced, rather than modified, the distribution of population.

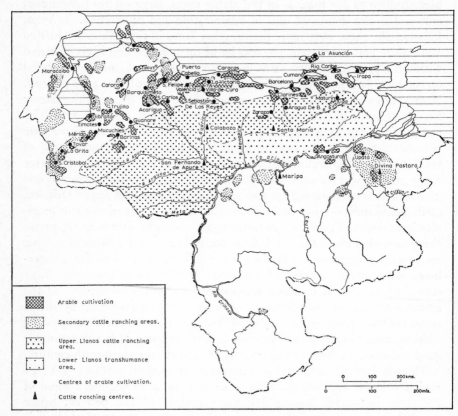

Fig. 5.6 Colonial agriculture in Venezuela

Colonial Venezuela had become differentiated: the northern regions contrasted with those of the south, the countryside had become equated with work, the town with wealth.

Colombia

It has been said that 'gold was for New Granada, up to a point, what hides, cacao and indigo were for Venezuela' (Bushnell, 1954, p. 3). This generalization has much to commend it. Colombia's most important economic resource during the colonial period was its mineral deposits, the exploitation of which brought about a pattern of settlement, a demographic history and a location of wealth and power quite different from those of Venezuela. Within the limits of modern Colombia diversity was a recurrent theme between A.D. 1500 and 1800, as it was before and has been since. Though mining was of paramount importance, agriculture also developed along lines similar to those in Venezuela, but to a lesser degree.

The three principal areas of gold-mining (both placer and vein) were within the Cauca valley, the upper and middle reaches of the Magdalena, and along the Pacific coast (Fig. 5.7). Perhaps fortunately for Colombia, no one area completely dominated production or development at any one period. The Spanish entry into modern Colombian territory was at least in part a result of reports of gold deposits that had been heard of from the beginning of the sixteenth century. By the 1530s parties from the Caribbean coast and Quito had entered the area to find abundant evidence in both graves and functioning mines of the presence of gold and emeralds. The complexities of exploration and early settlement history have been traced in some detail by Henao (West, 1952). Gold-mining expanded rapidly in many localities. In the middle Cauca valley around Anserma and Cartago vein-mining was especially important, though the depletion of ore bodies necessitated the repeated removal of settlements. In the upper Cauca valley, around Popayán, placer deposits included within dissected Tertiary gravel trains provided rich but decreasing amounts of gold from the late sixteenth century.

Similar in morphology but of Plio-Pleistocene age were the flights of auriferous gravel terraces on the western flanks of the Cordillera Occidental. Between Buenaventura and Barbacoas, practically every river basin provided ample returns. North along the littoral the Chocó district was rich not only in gold deposits but also in hostile Indians (West, 1957). Of special importance during the colonial period was the mining that went on around and within the Antioquia batholith at the northern end of the Cordillera Central. At Buritica, the Spaniards had simply to persuade the Indian miners to continue their work, so productive were their methods. Although the constant shifts of the mining camps (*minas*) makes it exceedingly difficult to reconstruct the exact sequence of mining in the area, it appears that during the colonial period a gradual shift was in progress from Buritica northwards. This included the establishment of settlements at Cáceres and Zaragoza (Fig. 5.7). Only with decline of gold production in these northern areas in the second half of the seventeenth century was attention turned to the dissected high altitude gravel spreads (*cerros*) within the Antioquia region north of Medellín (West, 1952, p. 27).

Another important mining district was that on the west bank of the Magdalena, centred on Ibagüe. Activity spread northwards from this area to include the new and *ambulante* settlement of Remedios. In sharp contrast to the abundance of deposits in the central and western Cordillera

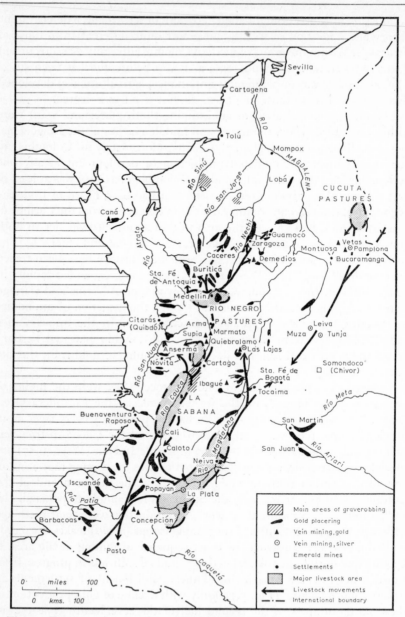

Fig. 5.7 Patterns of economic activity in colonial Colombia (after West, 1952)

was the low mineralization of the Cordillera Oriental. With the exception of the introduction of iron for tipping tools and water-powered stamp-mills, there were few technical innovations in colonial gold-mining in Colombia. Aboriginal methods of stream and pit placering, and panning, were extended over a much wider area. Far more important were the effects that mining had on agriculture and the demographic and settlement history of north-west Colombia.

Two processes characterized colonial agricultural change: first the development in and adjacent to the mining areas of subsistence arable cultivation, and secondly the establishment and expansion of much larger scale commercial farming units, predominantly engaged in livestock-ranching, in the higher altitudes of the main mountain ranges, especially in the level *altiplanos* of the Cordillera Oriental (West, 1952; Marciales, 1948). Within each of the forested lowland mining districts were to be found plots in which first Indians and later Negroes cultivated maize, beans and sweet manioc. As the supply of maize previously provided by tribute *encomienda* Indians gradually diminished, its role, especially along the Pacific littoral, was taken over by the introduced plantain. In some areas the agriculturally unfavourable location of the gold camps made it necessary to utilize more distant fertile soils. Sugar cane was also widely grown within the lowland zone, providing a variety of strong liquors that did something to mitigate the hard labour. The most significant protein source available for the slave gangs and others employed in the goldfields, far outweighing local sources such as fish and *manatí*, was meat, produced on pastures as close to the populated areas as ecology and economy allowed. The flat, unforested floors of Andean river valleys and montane basins were ideal sites. In the middle and upper Cauca and the upper Magdalena (Fig. 5.7) extensive areas were allotted to cattle farms (*estancias de ganado*). In the savannas around and to the north-east of Bogotá abandoned aboriginal agricultural mounds had been grassed over and provided pastures for large herds of unfenced stock (Broadbent, 1968). In Cauca, Boyacá, Cúcuta and Medellín alike colonial documents record the establishment of the cattle industry (Crist, 1952, p. 83; Fals Borda, 1957, p. 143; Parsons, 1949). Unsuccessful attempts were made to clear forest-land for cattle (West, 1957, p. 147). Meat, either fresh, dried or salted, became a permanent feature of the weekly food rations given to the workers. To be added to the complex pattern of arable and pastoral agriculture was the altitudinal differentiation of grain varieties. Dibbled maize plots of the northern humid lowlands gave way southwards to ploughed wheat fields that provided flour for the expanding mining communities. Compared with Venezuela, therefore, the colonial economic geography of Colombia was considerably more complex. A combination of mineral and agricultural exploitation, influenced by the variety of topographic and climatic conditions, produced a differentiation that was not to be found in agricultural Venezuela.

DEMOGRAPHIC PROCESSES AND PATTERNS

To date few scholars have concerned themselves with the demographic character of colonial Venezuela and Colombia. Compared with the statistical analyses that have been made for Mexico and Peru, relatively little is known of this marginal area. If Eidt's (1959, p. 380) figure of 600,000 is accepted as the Chibchan population around A.D. 1500, then Colombian territory may well have contained as many as 1 million Indians on the arrival of the Spanish. For Venezuela it is unlikely that the more densely populated northern highlands held more than 250,000 Indians, which, added to an estimated figure for the remainder of the territory, means that Venezuela may have contained between 350,000 and 450,000 Indians by 1500. By the end of the eighteenth century Colombia's population was estimated at 1·5 million, that of Venezuela 900,000. Such totals, however, say little of the intervening years of demographic change, change that included not only periodic fluctuations in total population, but also major structural modifications to the ethnic and social character, and spatial distribution of the inhabitants of the area.

One of the most significant processes that affected and characterized the colonial period was the steady reduction of the Indian component in the population and its replacement by either Iberian colonists or their African Negro slaves. While miscegenation between all these three groups gradually blurred the ethnic qualities of individuals, social status became all the more important. The aboriginal inhabitants of the area suffered grievously during the sixteenth century. After the psychological shock of the Spanish Conquest, which itself produced many instances of mass suicides, alien European diseases such as smallpox, tuberculosis, measles, typhoid and influenza began to take their toll. Of equal, if not greater, importance for the increased severity of these diseases was the continual intermixture and concentration of Indians. Whether by the practices of *mita* labour in the Venezuelan Andes, or the use of Indians in the placer mines of Colombia, decimation rapidly ensued. Some of the epidemics, such as the smallpox one in 1588, appear to have affected almost the entire area of Spanish contact. Within specific areas, however, the incidence and impact of disease was probably not unrelated to the general conditions of work endured by the Indians. From West's researches on the mining communities of Colombia, it can be seen that in many cases disease merely completed a task that arduous work and poor diets had begun. In Venezuela, too, the occupations of pearl-diving, mining and *encomienda* agricultural labour were often fatal for Indians. Not that attempts were not made to prevent these processes. Much more positive than the Utopian ideas of Las Casas in Cumaná were the many reservation tracts (*resguardos*) set aside in Colombia from the late sixteenth century for Indian communities (Parsons, 1949; Fals Borda, 1969). However, by that date much of the damage had already been done, and throughout the seventeenth century and in widely separated areas the migration of Indian groups out of reach of the Spanish can be noted. Only toponymic traces remained of many Indian groups by the year 1700. Elsewhere Indians were less harshly treated by the newcomers. In the widely dispersed mission villages hard work was only the price of spiritual salvation. In these communities Indians lived long enough to accept short-cropped hair and the clothes, language and music of their 'civilizers'. The Indians, for their part, demonstrated their native skills and adaptability. Other Indian groups remained, throughout the entire colonial period, outside either the knowledge or control of the new authorities. Their contact with other cultures had to await the nineteenth and twentieth centuries.

The demographic counterbalance to Indian decline was secured by the importation of Negro African slaves. Though the influential white population gradually increased in numbers, it was this forced mass migration of labour that allowed the colonial system to function (Escalante, 1964). Very quickly it was perceived that what Indians could not, or would not, do, slaves could be forced to do. In Colombia the distribution of negroid elements soon reflected the patterns of gold-mining (West, 1952). In Venezuela their counterparts were to be found within the cacao plantations of the north. Although Negroes appeared less affected by hard labour in the tropical lowlands and less susceptible to European diseases, the combination of unbalanced and inadequate diet with their own imported diseases (especially yaws) resulted in high mortality-rates (Vila, 1965; West, 1952). Intense economic activity, high mortality-rates and population replacement went hand in hand. Naturally, Negroes were not exclusively to be found in the agricultural plantations and mining camps. Every township had its negroid population, engaged in household service and other menial tasks. Wherever work had to be done, there Negroes were to be found, be it on the river boats, in cattle ranches, sugar mills or cathedral choirs. Exceptionally Negroes escaped their allotted role by fleeing to the more remote areas. More significant, especially during the eighteenth century, was the legal attainment of their freedom. Some 50,000 such free Negroes formed a most important element in the agricultural economy of northern central Venezuela during the 1780s (Brito-Figueroa, 1963). In Colombia such Negroes spread outside the mining zones to settle pioneer lowland and highland areas during the same period (Parsons, 1949). The integration process that Negroes underwent, which so effectively adapted them to the habitat, economy and society of the colonies, is still little researched, let alone understood. Locally, where numbers or special circumstances permitted, they made many significant contributions to the cultural milieu, not least in music and agriculture (Fals Borda, 1969; West, 1957).

In Colombia and Venezuela Indians and Negroes were instructed, ruled and manipulated by the third ethnic element, the whites/mestizos. Ethnic origin and social class, if not caste, were closely related. The whites' employment, income, residence, status and influence set them apart from all others. They stood at the top of the social scale as an aristocratic élite, an urban power group whose wealth and importance flowed from their hold over the organization of economic enterprise, and their manipulation of prices, interest rates and markets. Below them, and ever mindful of their relative position, came the group of mestizo artisans whose role in the functioning colonial economy is still little understood. One step further down stood the poor whites and mestizos, scorned by non-whites for being white and by other whites for being poor. The social stability of three centuries of colonial rule hinged on the acceptance by the majority of their social station.

The following figures reflect the numerical significance of each of the ethnic groups in Venezuela and Colombia at the end of the eighteenth century: Indians 18 per cent; Negroes 60 per cent; whites/mestizos 22 per cent (Brito-Figueroa, 1961; Parsons, 1949; Vila, 1965). Of perhaps greater geographical significance was the spatial distribution of the influential white/mestizo class. Their locale was the urban settlement, not as the site of factories, but as the node of administrative and trading networks and symbol of culture. In Colombia this meant primarily the group of highland towns centred on Santa Fé de Bogotá. What the viceregal capital boasted could be found, albeit on a smaller scale, in many of the regional urban centres such as Cali, Popayán, Cartagena and Medellín. Only of necessity, and then often temporarily, did whites live in what were considered the unhealthy tropical northern lowlands (Parsons, 1949; Scott, 1968). In Venezuela likewise population was concentrated within the northern highland zone, and even though in the 1780s only 37 per cent of the population of the province of Caracas was urban, that sector contained the most notable entrepreneurs. The dominance of urban settlement in Venezuela is reflected in the fact that by 1810 out of a total of some 500 settlements, fifty towns accounted for one third of the total population. Not only was a significant proportion of the population urban, but the most important towns were clustered within a narrow northern region, unlike Colombia's more widely dispersed pattern. Moreover, the continuing primacy of a select group of Venezuelan towns can be demonstrated (Table 5.1).

As a result of agricultural development (principally the cacao export crop) during the seventeenth and eighteenth centuries, the foci of commercial and administrative activities had been stabilized. Caracas dominated the central northern region, while to the west Barquisimeto and Maracaibo, and to the east Cumaná, Barcelona and, to a lesser extent, Angostura, each had their own distinctive hinterlands (Gormsen, 1966). The Caracas region contained within it by far the greatest concentration of

TABLE 5.1   *Rank order of Venezuelan urban settlements 1772–1810*[1]

	1772		1784		1810	
Rank	*Town*	*Population*	*Town*	*Population*	*Town*	*Population*
I	Caracas	18,986	Caracas	18,669	Caracas	37,937
2	Barquisimeto	8,756	Cumaná	10,470	Maracaibo	24,000
3	San Carlos	8,617	Maracaibo	10,312	Cumaná	19,000
4	Cumaná	7,010	Barquisimeto	8,776	Barcelona	14,000
5	Turmero	6,894	San Carlos	7,346	Guanare	12,300
6	El Tocuyo	6,799	Valencia	7,237	Mérida	11,500
7	Valencia	6,894	Barcelona	7,000	Barquisimeto	11,300
8	Maracaibo	6,200	Turmero	6,918	San Carlos	10,885
9	La Victoria	5,742	Coro	5,823	Barinas	10,000
10	San Felipe	5,623	Maracay	5,558	Quibor	9,970

[1] Based on table on pp. 270–1 in Brito-Figueroa (1963).

financial capital in the whole of colonial Venezuela. In both Colombia and Venezuela the steady accumulation of secular wealth had been accepted and reinforced by the attitude and activities of the Catholic Church, whose increasing revenues from tithes and estates made it one of the most influential owners of land and financial resources (Brito-Figueroa, 1961; Fals Borda, 1969). The key feature of the late colonial period was the agglomeration of wealth in and around the principal urban settlements; in Venezuela this meant almost entirely the Caracas region, in Colombia, though perhaps less dominant, the Bogotá district. The benefits and profits from colonial economic enterprise were slowly but surely siphoned from cattle ranch, plantation and gold mine to the urban centres. The consequences of an urban-based colonization process had begun to appear; centripetal forces had replaced the centrifugal.

PATTERNS OF TRADE AND COMMUNICATIONS

The significance of the various settlements and zones of economic activity during the colonial period can best be judged by the type and state of the communications that linked them to the oceanic routes. For Colombia and Venezuela the critical interface between hinterland and foreland was the southern Caribbean shore, dominated by the ports of Cartagena and La Guaira. The scattering of smaller ports stretching from the Orinoco delta to the river Patía in south-western Colombia merely served as foci for restricted trading areas. Second only to the ports were the communication nodes formed by the administrative centres. It was between these and to the coastal settlements that the relatively rare main highways (*caminos reales*) ran. In northern South America the most important of the *caminos reales* entered Colombia from the south, passing by way of Pasto, Popayán and Bogatá and thence into Venezuela via the Andean aboriginal route from Mérida and Trujillo on to Caracas. This was the northernmost extension of the Lima-Caribbean route. From and to this unpaved trail ran numerous less important tracks, often known as *caminos de herradura* (pack trails), reflecting the significance of that ubiquitous colonial animal, the mule. In certain sections of Colombia the terrain was seasonally too difficult even for this sure-footed beast and Indians carried heavy burdens over precipitous slopes (West, 1952). Traffic between settlements in such physically isolated areas as central Colombia put a premium on the availability of low passes. Even without a carting network present elsewhere in the New World, altitude often became a critical factor in determining the type of produce and the regularity of trade within colonial Venezuela and Colombia. In south-eastern Colombia and the major portion of Venezuela the overland trails were of critical importance. In Venezuela they connected La Guaira to Caracas, and Caracas to the agricultural valleys along and between the southern flanks of the coastal ranges. Along such tracks cacao, tobacco, cotton and hides moved out to the ports for export. Inwards in return came brandy and textiles and the necessary manufactured goods from across the Atlantic (Arcila Farías, 1946). In Colombia nature had bestowed upon the area a ready-made pattern of communications. Between the grazed mountain ranges ran slow-moving and navigable rivers. In no other Spanish colony were water transport links so important as in Colombia. Goods trans-shipped at Cartagena could penetrate far inland to the mining areas before the need for time-consuming and expensive mule trains or human porterage. In Venezuela, on the other hand, except for localized traffic, the colony turned its back to one of the continent's most extensive river networks. The Orinoco and its north bank tributaries remained on the margin of the unknown, rather than providing lifelines of commerce. The *piraguas* of the Orinoco could never match the *champanes* of the Cauca and Magdalena in the amount of produce carried; but then Venezuela did not suffer the inconveniences of what were reputed to be the worst trails in the Spanish Indies. As the heavy cedar dug-out canoes gave way southwards to lighter rafts, so the seasonal regime of the longitudinal rivers affected the economic rhythms. In the wet seasons, when water was superabundant for sluicing out gold in the mountains, the rivers raced so fast as to make it impossible to pole upstream to collect or deliver products. Only in the dry season could trade be continued, and the building of river boats was a local industry in northern Colombia. While the Pacific rivers also had their own trading hinterlands they were never large enough to compete with those of central and northern Colombia (Parsons, 1949). Implicit in the use of mules, and in special cases ox-drawn carts, was the provision of pasturage along the main overland trails. When extensive trade in livestock on the hoof was concerned, this became of even greater significance. Some of the routes of livestock movements are shown in Fig. 5.7.

Although the outline of the pattern of communications is known for both Venezuela and Colombia during the colonial period, relatively little is understood of the trading system used within those areas. West's (1952, 1957) researches in Colombia were the first to identify the activities of the itinerant merchant who appears to have been a key figure in the operation of the gold-mining industry. These merchants, who travelled on regular circuits within the goldfields, not only sold large amounts of imported produce, which were later delivered to the purchasers from warehouses in the port of Cartagena or the larger settlements of the interior, but they also carried gold dust back to the regional smelting centres on behalf of mining camp operators. Illegal practices were rife in this trading system, as was often the case in the Indies, since the merchants could equally well perform the function of smugglers – either bringing illicit goods into the mining zone to sell direct to the Negroes or Indians, or taking gold out to the eager hands of French or English traders. The itinerant merchant was thus a middleman operating between the rich entrepreneurs who traded produce in the principal settlements and the dispersed population that characterized the northern region of Colombia. In Venezuela such a system does not appear to have operated so widely, though the significance of the trader class in both Caracas and Barquisimeto during the colonial period has been noted (Gormsen, 1966). Rather than itinerant merchants, there appear to have been periodic markets in most of the larger urban settlements. Thus the annual tobacco fair at Barinas attracted traders from over a wide area; cattle could likewise be purchased from the upper *llanos* settlements of Calabozo and San Fernando de Apure. In the north Caracas, Maracaibo and Cumaná each had its market for the sale and purchase of produce. Only in peripheral areas such as the south-east did merchants wander amongst the mission villages bartering hides, tobacco and cacao in exchange for metal wares and other imported products.

The pattern of trade routes reflected the geography of economic development in both Colombia and Venezuela. In the former they were orientated north–south (except the overland route to Venezuela), providing links between the urban centres of the interior and the Caribbean ports. Transverse links across the grain of the topography were less important and acted as mere feeders to the main routes. In Venezuela, with the topographic controls trending east–west parallel to the Caribbean shore, trade routes likewise shifted their direction. In Venezuela, however, distance between the principal agricultural centres of production and the Caribbean ports was never as great as in Colombia. Such proximity may well have made Venezuela more outward-looking during the colonial period. News soon reached Caracas from the Caribbean islands. Another distinguishing feature of Venezuelan trading was the use by Philip V of the monopolistic trading company to attempt to increase the productivity of the province of Venezuela during the eighteenth century. From 1728 until 1781 the Royal Guipúzcoa Company was ensured of monopolistic control over all production and trade (Hussey, 1934). Although some of the plans of the Company, such as the extension of wheat acreages in the Andean area, came to fruition, much resentment was caused amongst the influential merchants and landowners of Caracas. Eventually the monopoly was rescinded in favour of previous practices. The Barcelona Company, concentrating its efforts on the stimulation of agriculture in north-eastern Venezuela, appears to have been modelled along lines similar to those of the Guipúzcoa. After a brief spell of success, it also ceased to have any effective power.

THE END OF AN ERA

It might be argued that by the end of the eighteenth century the economic forces that had initiated and modified the process of Spanish colonial rule in northern South America had been practically spent. The reforms of the late eighteenth century created the *audiencia* of Caracas and therefore retained the Maracaibo basin for what was later to become Venezuela. They freed commerce from some of the more exasperating controls that had prevented the development of intercolonial trade, and they reorganized the administrative hierarchy. But there had been few economic changes. Agricultural production was still based upon serving the demands of Spain. Absentee landlords cared little about soil erosion or over-use, or about declining productivity. They were not permitted, let alone encouraged, to plan for new products or markets. All enterprise and initiative had to be set aside in favour of royal edicts. And all this while news was continually entering Venezuelan and Colombian territory from Dutch, French and English sources of the events that were gradually transforming western Europe. So much of what had been done in colonial Venezuela and Colombia might only have been possible by means of the strict and initially adaptive regulations of the Spanish authorities. After three centuries, however, their adaptability was becoming ever more suspect, and restrictive measures had reached almost the stage of economic self-strangulation. What was needed was a reappraisal of the situation by the men who had formed the colonial tradition, Spanish Americans.

THE BEGINNING OF TRANSITION

In the same way as the conquest of northern South America by the Spanish in the sixteenth century initiated the establishment of a traditional order, or, as Fals Borda would prefer, a 'seignorial order', which evolved slowly during some three hundred years of Spanish colonial rule, so the early nineteenth century marked the beginning of yet another formative period in the history of Colombia and Venezuela. Political independence from Spain heralded the beginning of a transitional phase in the development of the area. Whereas in the sixteenth century the complex regional variation of aboriginal patterns of economy and society provided the backcloth to Spanish endeavours, in the nineteenth it was the colonial system and patterns that were to be selectively retained, modified or elsewhere completely replaced by new elements. It was essentially a process related to the developments in northern industrializing Europe. The pace and direction of change from the colonial models of Colombia and Venezuela were controlled by the interaction between capital, techniques, personnel and ideas of non-Latins, and the newly established economic, social and political power groups within those territories. Again, as during the colonial period, a characteristic feature of the transitional period has been the divergent evolution of Colombia and Venezuela. Patterns, distributions, proportions, forms and functions within the cultural landscape have reflected as much the opinions of individuals, the preferences of strata of society in Caracas and Bogotá, and a host of other lesser centres, as they have the geographic differentials of the two areas. Both countries have experienced a number of common changes. Each country has had, however, its own distinctive response. The search for profitable and exportable resources, the attempts at extending the frontier of agricultural exploitation, the increasing concentration of population in larger settlements, the conquest over disease and the subsequent increase in human numbers – these were but a few of the changes common to both countries. In part they reflect a more widespread transformation, which was to affect much of the tropical world.

THE INITIAL IMPACT OF POLITICAL INDEPENDENCE

Perhaps the most significant feature of the political independence gained by Colombia and Venezuela in the early nineteenth century was its insignificant effect upon the social structure and order within the old colonies. The former overseas centres of control were replaced with indigenous counterparts; in the main the individuals, families and strata within the society of the late eighteenth century took over the task of ruling the new republics (Picon-Salas, 1962). For the majority of the inhabitants of the two countries, independence meant new masters rather than new power or influence, although there were exceptions to this generalization. The progress through the nineteenth century of insurrection, war and economic change naturally produced new members for the élite. Charismatic warlords and enterprising businessmen added their names to the roll of the strong.

That the initial impact of the independence movement was demographically, socially and economically disruptive, in certain regions almost of catastrophic proportions, there can be little doubt. Perhaps, like the comparable impact in the sixteenth century, it was a small price to pay for 'progress'. Though statistics of population in the early nineteenth century are notoriously unreliable, it is clear that a significant loss of population was experienced during the first two decades of that century. Population reduction was, of course, selective. Those settlements that lay on or near to what became historic routes of the independence army marches were severely affected by the conscription of their male population for service in the liberating armies. At least one fifth of the Venezuelan population is estimated to have been lost in the cause of freedom, through death on the battlefields, or through disease or hunger. More difficult to estimate, but undoubtedly of great significance, was the economic effect of the reduction in the males able to work the land on the farms of Venezuela, or in the mines in Colombia. In the labour-intensive systems then operative population and production were in delicate balance, and the sudden reductions caused grave hardship in certain regions (Bushnell, 1954). In Venezuela south of the Orinoco, in the bridgehead area of the Caroní plains, the impact of war, disease and economic disruption was exceptionally severe and the majority of the villages lost more than 80 per cent of their population. Westwards, in the *llanos* and foothills of the mountains villages had been deserted, the population fleeing to the forest or savannas to escape the notice of those organizing their freedom and seeking their services (Carrera Damas, 1964). In addition to the hunger and disease and the relentless cost in human lives of the wars themselves, natural disasters occasionally added to the toll, as in the 1812 earthquake, which cost a further 10,000 lives in Caracas. The demographic history of the period is still to be written. In the same way economic disaster followed hard on the heels of death and destruction; farms were deserted and crops were destroyed by plundering troops or invading weeds. Colonial irrigation systems were allowed to fall into disrepair, as had their aboriginal counterparts in the sixteenth century. The vast herds of cattle and horses in the savannas provided the perfect mobile, highly desired export products that could pay for the arms, ammunition and all the paraphernalia of armies that had to be imported and paid for by the liberators. As in Africa in the twentieth century, European mercenaries were an expensive item in the budget of the new republics. Of equal but longer term significance was the drawing off of the scarce operating capital of the business communities in both Caracas and Bogotá to repay the debts incurred during the war period. By 1820 the economic balance sheet in both countries looked little short of disastrous, but to the idealistic heroes of the period it was a small price to pay for political freedom and the right to make one's own mistakes.

RECONSTRUCTION, RENOVATION AND INNOVATIONS

Given the essentially political nature of the independence movement in Venezuela and Colombia, it was to be expected that the first of the many tasks facing the new authorities was that of reorganizing the system of government and administration. Inspired by Bolívar, the notion of a single unit based upon the three former colonial units of Quito, Nueva Granada and Venezuela was accepted at Angostura in 1819. The new territory was to be called the 'Republic of Colombia', known better by the title given it by historians, 'Gran Colombia'. That such a large unit could have emerged by 1820 says much for the enthusiasm and personal qualities of leadership found in Simon Bolívar, all the more so since the period between 1810 and 1816 had been fraught with intercity and interprovincial rivalries and petty jurisdictional squabbles. However, even with a Great Colombia in name, there remained the question as to whether it should be a federation of independent states or a centralized union. The federalists' strongest support came from within the heartland of old Nueva Granada, with Caracas favouring the idea of union. The most significant defect of the grand design lay in the geographical variation that was to be found within its borders, a diversity of interests and uneven distribution of power and wealth, and economic advantages that were not adequately reflected in the administrative units proposed. Even in the stable days of the colonial period, the three colonies had enjoyed little more than peripheral contact with each other; given the heady days of almost continual change and adaptation, it was highly unlikely that they could be welded together. Even within all three colonies inter-regional disputes and rivalries over representation at the federal level continued after 1820. It was also decided that the three former colonies would be divided into departments, provinces and cantons, each approximately the same size, both to rationalize the democratic representation of the population, and also, by the necessary division and amalgamation of former units, to destroy some of the outmoded loyalties and traditions of the colonial past. The fact of the matter was that with population, and thus power and influence, so unevenly distributed, areal size of the administrative units was one of the least equitable factors to be taken into account. Why, it was argued by Caracas, should the newly created department of Apure have equal rights with Caracas, when it was so relatively insignificant? There were many cogent arguments put to the federal authorities. Great Colombia was just too great, and what purpose was served by paper symmetry of representation when the decentralization of power was hardly ever discussed (Bushnell, 1954)? Like so many of the republican proposals, the administrative hierarchy of *cabildos*, provincial governors and departmental intendants beneath the federal authorities was an excellent intention, but proved quite impractical in operation.

The product of personal inspiration and a common enemy, Great Colombia could not survive the secession of Venezuela. Perhaps the greatest enemy to success was sheer distance, or rather the cost and time of travel. With communications still affected by an almost total standstill in certain seasons, the movement of people, products and opinions could not take place from one area to another quickly enough to make so large a unit practicable. Other factors mitigated against success. In spite of the small-scale trade between the departments of Venezuela and Cundinamarca, and the family connections that tied the western Andean population of Venezuela closer to Colombian settlements than to others in Venezuela, the territories were too alike in their agricultural self-sufficiency and their range of imports and exports to make trade a possible catalyst of interdependence. But of still more significance was the deep-seated rivalry between Caracas and Bogotá. Caracas, the 'cradle of liberty', thought itself far more important than the 'Athens of South America'. There was a distinct reluctance in Caracas, as the centre of revolution, to accept the departmental status of some of its own former satellite regions, and to relinquish ultimate authority to a remote federal centre allegedly dominated by 'backward mountaineers' (Bushnell, 1954, p. 289). Maracaibo remained quite favourable to the idea of the large federal unit, but regional problems made the whole notion of Great Colombia meaningless east of Caracas and to the south on the bandit-infested *llanos*. Support for the idea decreased in proportion to distance from Bogotá. Perhaps the war with Spain had ended too quickly, and technological changes had not made sufficient advances. It is difficult to explain the dissolution of the first major post-colonial administrative framework. After 1830 the independent nations, with minor adjustments to their boundaries, were left to pursue their separate destinies.

Just as in the sixteenth century the primary zone of cultural change had been along the southern shore of the Caribbean sea, so, too, in the early nineteenth century the Caribbean islands and the northern ports of Venezuela and Colombia were critical staging posts in the transference of ideas, products and personnel. From Trinidad, Jamaica and Barbados, and from other islands, came the foreigners who were to organize the early phase of economic renovation in Venezuela and Colombia. It was to the ports and later to the inland cities of Colombia and Venezuela that they brought their capital, influence and skills. Angostura, formerly a stagnating landing place on the south bank of the Orinoco, was completely transformed by the arrival of immigrant merchants, sailors and entrepreneurs. Very rapidly the tonnage of shipping using the port had increased by more than 200 per cent (Nichols, 1954). From overseas came a range of goods that could not be manufactured under Spanish colonial rule: textiles, ironware and machinery. Even more important were the imported foodstuffs, which were cheap enough to dominate domestic markets. Through the expanded ports were exported the products in demand in Europe and

North America: hides, beans, coffee, gold, timber and the like. Gradually, spheres of influence were extended inland from these ports, tapping the resources of Venezuela and Colombia, as they still do. The relative size of the traffic through the ports may be taken as a reflection of the changing and relative prosperity of its hinterland. In Venezuela the national trading hinterland was dominated by the centrally located port of La Guaira during the nineteenth century (Fig. 5.8 (b)). Of equal importance during the nineteenth century was the role of customs revenue in funding governmental projects. In part at least, the reliable revenue from this source prevented any government from prejudicing its potential progress by erecting tariffs, or developing competitive production within its national territories. Port dues were almost too easy to collect, even if illegal practices reduced their true value by as much as 50 per cent.

If, however, trade was to prosper within either Colombia or Venezuela, then it was clearly vital that foreign traders should be able to obtain the agricultural or mineral resources they required. This involved both an extension of existing resources and an improvement in the system of communications within each of the countries. This, it was hoped, would mean more and cheaper products for the ports to export, and a better method of distributing imports internally.

During the nineteenth century very little improvement or extension was made to the network of roads in Venezuela and Colombia. For the most part they remained dirt tracks, seasonally impassable, and providing the minimal conditions for wheeled traffic. The horse and mule remained the principal mode of passenger transport until the arrival of the train and the motor car, and the inadequacy of the road system was felt most in terms of commercial developments. The basic pattern of roads remained as it had been at the end of the colonial period; the only extensions to it in either country were prolongations from the existing network to new areas of economic activity or to new entrepôts of trade on coast or river. In Colombia the mining industrial developments of the 1830s, but more especially the expansion of settlement in and around Antioquia, involved an elaborate process of network extension (Parsons, 1949). Especially significant was the development of improved linkages between Antioquia and Cartago (Fig. 5.7). Counter to the principal direction of Antioqueño colonization, efforts were made, most unsuccessfully, during the 1840s to open a route to the sea via the Urabá panhandle. A complex history of concessions, fruitless schemes and much endeavour has recently been revealed by Parsons (1967). In Venezuela the most important roads are shown on a map of postal routes in the 1880s (Fig. 5.8 (a)). As can be seen, by far the greatest concentration was in the northern third of the country, reflecting the intensity of economic activity in that area. The two penetration roads leading southwards to San Fernando de Apure and Angostura demonstrate the increasing significance of those two areas after 1850 – the

H

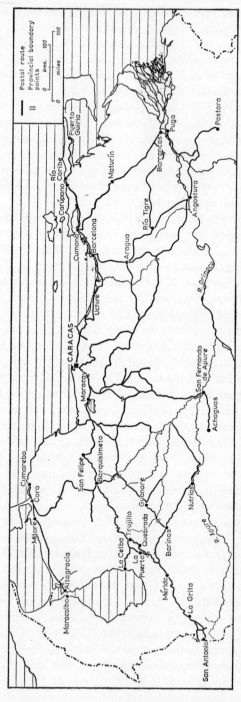

Fig. 5.8 (a) The network of postal routes in Venezuela during the 1880s

Postal route

Provincial boundary points

0   kms.   100
0   miles   100

CARACAS

Maracay

Puerto Guiria
Río Caribe
Carúpano
Cumaná
Barcelona
Uchire
Maturín
Barcelonas
Puga
Pastora
Río Tigre
Aragua
Angostura
R. Orinoco
San Fernando de Apure
Achaguas
Cumarebo
Coro
San Felipe
Barquisimeto
Guanare
Nutrias
R. Apure
Mitaré
La Ceiba
Trujillo
La Puerta
Quebrada
Barinas
Mérida
La Grita
Maracaibo
Altagracia
San Antonio

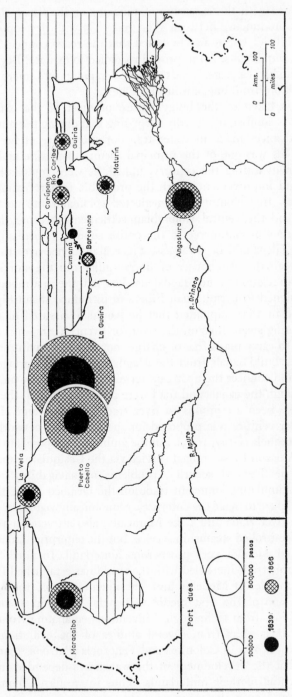

Fig. 5.8 (b) Developments in port traffic in nineteenth-century Venezuela

former concerned with the extension of ranching on the *llanos*, the latter reaching great prominence between 1860 and 1885 with developments in the Caratal goldfield. It can also be noted that the roads connect riverine or coastal port settlements. All improved roads led to exports. Beyond the limits of profitable carriage, roads decayed rapidly into mere tracks, difficult to pick out from one season to the next.

If account is taken of the bulky nature of most of the exports of Venezuela and Colombia, it is hardly surprising that during the nineteenth century the advances made in water transportation were of far greater significance. This was one of the principal sectors of private and public capital investment during the century, linked, as were comparable port installations and improvements, with the profitable import–export trade (Parsons, 1949). In Colombia, the neglected colonial route northwards from Bogotá and the central Colombian settlements became the most important channel of commerce in the entire country (Harrison, 1952). The river Magdalena now began to assert its real influence over the traffic in goods between the warehouses of Barranquilla and the stores of the capital. It was in relation to the Magdalena river that the first monopolistic contract was signed to permit Juan Elbers to introduce steamships. The contract signed in 1823 stipulated that he would be assured of the sole rights of operating steamships on the river for twenty years, in return for which he had to carry mails free of charge, not exceed certain maximum freight charges, build canals from the Magdalena to both Cartagena and Santa Marta, and connect the upstream terminus to Bogotá by means of a new road. Though the canals and road were never completed, the project appears to have been a stimulus to river trade (Gilmore and Harrison, 1948). A similar venture was proposed for the vast water network of the Orinoco in Venezuela (Gray, 1945), but the ambitious proposals to link the Orinoco and Amazon by steamboat service via the Casiquiare canal failed through lack of financial security, problems of navigability and the difficulties of stimulating sufficient trade on the Orinoco above the confluence of the Apure to make the enterprise economically viable. In western Venezuela the river Zulia and Lake Maracaibo also attracted a proposal for a German-controlled steamship service, but the enterprise failed owing to the restricted and not very prosperous hinterland. In north-western Colombia riverine trade increased with the road links established from the thriving communities of Medellín and Antioquia (Parsons, 1967). Water transport was one of the first media to benefit, albeit in a somewhat haphazard fashion, from technological inventions emanating from north-west Europe. It is clear from several studies of the evolution of the transportation networks in Colombia and Venezuela (Parsons, 1949, 1967; West, 1957) that the development of the waterways depended upon the economic potential of their hinterlands. Thus in western Colombia the Chocó rivers, and even the short navigable streams west of the Cauca valley, never developed to the same extent as the Magdalena. Not only was investment capital in short supply, but other links proved more attractive to the entrepreneurs involved. There is also much evidence to suggest that the improvements in navigation on the principal rivers of Colombia were economically worthwhile only because the principal staple for trade, coffee, was sufficiently highly priced to withstand the transport costs, and make investments profitable (Harrison, 1952).

Urrutía (1969) has noted that through the steady reduction in transportation costs on the Magdalena during the nineteenth century, British textiles could threaten the artisan trade in the Colombian textile centres. Until the advent of steamships, distance and topography had protected the home industry more efficiently than any tariffs. Reliable bulk shipping, unaffected by seasonal regime or shifts of wind, had brought north and south closer together. Coastal shipping and the river trade were certainly profitable and helped to spread wealth by way of the ports and landing stages involved in the traffic.

In a similar manner the initiation and extension of railways in Colombia, and less so in Venezuela, also hinged on economic incentives (Rippy, 1943). Whereas in the difficult terrain of Colombia coffee paid for the reduction in grades, in the vast open plainlands of the Venezuelan *llanos* not a single line was ever laid. Only in the Yuruari savanna zone of the extreme southeast of Venezuela was a line proposed, and that, dependent upon the gold boom of the 1870s, never got further than a pile of rusting metal on the wharf at Ciudad Bolívar.

DEVELOPMENTS IN AGRICULTURE

Although little detailed research has been carried out into the overall evolution of agriculture in nineteenth-century Colombia and Venezuela, it is clear that for the most part stagnation, rather than rapid development, was its chief characteristic. Codazzi's surveys of the 1830s had shown that in Venezuela only 0·5 per cent of the national territory was under cultivation, approximately the area of the island of Margarita. In both countries the incessant troubles of the domestic political scene made agriculture a precarious enterprise. Uprisings had periodically removed the labour supply, damaged farm property and cropland, and devastated livestock herds. It is true that some of the earliest legislation ratified by the federal authorities of Great Colombia had involved measures to prevent the entailment of estates, to reduce clerical mortmain and *ejido* land areas, and to subdivide the communal lands of the Indians (henceforth to be known as *indígenas*) to permit them the dubious pleasure of private ownership. But most proposals were little more than paper plans. It has also to be remembered that relatively large proportions of the agricultural land remained effectively outside the national market until late in the century. Included in this category was church land (approximately a third of the cultivated land in Colombia), Indian commune land, *resguardos*, and town *ejidos* (Urrutía, 1969). When, in 1850, Colombia lifted the restrictions on the scale of *resguardo* land, the rapid enclosure movement that was precipitated benefited local capitalists; Indians fell into the grips of usurers. With new large estates (*latifundios*) being created, the Indians left the land, either to seek their fortunes in mining or to work as labourers in the expanding coffee zones; others remained as tenants. Cheap labour was just what was needed in the new boom areas. So it happened that the 'proletarianization of the workers benefited plantation agriculture rather than industry' (Urrutía, 1969, p. 28).

If it proved almost impossible to reform radically the existing agricultural systems of tenure and cultivation (Carrera Damas, 1964), this did not mean that it was not possible to look forward to new agricultural ventures. Indeed ambitious colonization schemes have a long history in northern South America. On paper they had much to commend them: they usually proposed the occupation of land previously under-utilized; they often involved foreign capital, labour supply and technological expertise; and they needed little but the blessing of the respective national governments. Unfortunately, another common characteristic was their almost total failure. In Venezuela, from the Orinoco to the Andean mountains, various colonies were attempted, but, except for the German 'Colonia Tovar' west of Caracas (which still provides for the tourist an interesting example of physiological regression stemming from intermarriage), all were to fail (Rasmussen, 1947). In Colombia, too, colonization schemes were never short of official support, whether they were in the tropical forests of the north (Parsons, 1967, p. 34) or the cooler uplands of the central area.

The only exception to the general rule of economic stagnation in Colombia was the southward spread of Antioqueño settlement, and the growth of coffee cultivation. From the heartland around Antioquia a steady stream of pioneer farmers spread upslope along the margins of the Cauca valley. A happy combination of circumstances – remoteness, regional incentives to colonize, plentiful supply of fecund population, a crop complex that rapidly adjusted to the new lands, a technology that permitted radical changes in the ecological controls – all these and more stimulated one of the few true agricultural frontiers of nineteenth-century Latin America (Parsons, 1949). The upslope movement of population meant an escape from the unhealthy malarial conditions of the *tierra caliente*. Gradually from the dispersed rural settlements of the '*raza antioqueña*' clearings were made in the lower forested slopes for coffee trees. New species of grasses were introduced and planted at differing altitudes. By the twentieth century the 'Africanization' of the Colombian tropical savannas was well under way. From the 1880s new breeds of cattle from Europe were introduced to graze the *pará* pastures of the lower Cauca: Friesians,

Durhams, Holsteins and Ayrshires. With barbed wire fences and alien grasses and livestock, absentee farmers made a healthy profit from rotational grazing along the lower Cauca. Slowly but surely in Colombia and Venezuela the introduction of agricultural experimentation began to affect the landscape radically. Soils previously gullied were anchored with a thick sward of *yaraguá* and *micay*; slopes formerly covered with forest, which had provided resources for swidden cultivation for centuries, were cleared and cultivated, and then deceptively afforested with coffee shade trees. The forests of Colombia provided a much richer store of exploitable products than those of Venezuela, being nearer to the potential supply of labour. In Colombia hardwoods were extracted and *tagua* palm nuts (*Phytelephus* spp.) were exported to Europe to be manufactured into buttons. Rubber trees were injudiciously felled in the haste to obtain the highly priced latex, and cinchona bark figured prominently in export lists. The steel axe and the iron hoe had put new power into the hands of potential settlers. Within the altitudinal zonation of Colombia, diversity took on a new and more pervading dimension and ecological variation was at once extended and exploited (Fig. 5.9).

Coffee cultivation spread into Colombia during the latter half of the eighteenth century from Andean Venezuela, but its significance in the

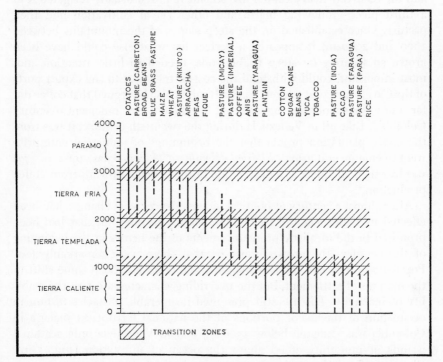

Fig. 5.9 Altitudinal variation of selected crops in Colombia

Colombian economy was not attained until over a century later. In 1818 it was being grown on a commercial scale in the Cúcuta valley, and gradually spread south-eastwards along the Cordillera Oriental to Cundinamarca. It was in this locality that the experimentation in cultivation took place in the 1850s, and, of equal importance, it was in that district that prosperous landlords could afford the time, energy and capital to stimulate its spread by means of practical demonstration and, above all, propagandist literature. But it would have been a fruitless exercise had coffee not been promoted in Europe and the United States as the perfect accompaniment to intelligent discussion and pleasant company. Like tobacco, drinking chocolate and tea before it, coffee production had to await a stimulated demand. But, as the coffee habit began to be accepted, Colombia appeared a paradise for cultivation. Under the expert advice of Mariano Ospina, who had recently arrived from Guatemalan coffee plantation areas and was able to suggest the most suitable soils and climatic conditions, the crop area was rapidly extended. The extension of the railways brought more zones into the economic catchment area. Prizes were offered for production, and during the last two decades of the century mechanized processing equipment began to be imported. Coffee was not, however, the primary crop in the Colombian agricultural frontier complex. Its five-year maturity period, and the relatively heavy capital investment required usually relegated it to a third place – following maize and other cereal cultivation and then pasture. Once established on the steep slopes of the mountains between 1000 and 2000 m, it appeared a perfect fit; what else could have been grown so securely on steep friable soils, needed so little attention and, most important, could withstand the cost of transport to the export ports of the Caribbean coast (Beyer, 1948)? It might also be argued that coffee did far more than increase agricultural production in nineteenth-century Colombia. Like oil in Venezuela during the twentieth century, it was from the coffee plantation profits that the beginnings of industrial enterprise were to emerge and grow. 'El árbol del milagro' (Picon-Salas, 1962, p. 373) was less than adequate as a description of the benefits flowing from coffee production.

After almost a century of political independence, what changes had been effected in Venezuela and Colombia? Bearing in mind all that had been promised in the idealistic pronouncements of the heroes at the beginning of the century, the answer must be that there were remarkably few. Population totals had increased slightly and there had been some shift in the margins of settlement, but the overriding characteristic was the stability of inactivity. Disease still presented insuperable obstacles to human occupation of the major portions of the national territories; malaria in Colombia was endemic below 1500 m, and in Venezuela only scattered islands of immunity stood above the ocean of infestation (Fig. 5.10). Elsewhere hookworm, dysentery, typhoid and yellow fever took their annual toll. In the coffee *fincas* intestinal parasitism thrived in the damp soils trodden by shoeless labourers. For the most part settlements established during the colonial period slumbered on, unaffected by the industrial revolution in northern Europe and the United States. In Venezuelan Guayana it is true that the gold strike had brought in Hamburg lager by the crate, elaborate mining machinery, Negro labourers from the Antilles, British, German and French capital, and all the necessities of a latter-day

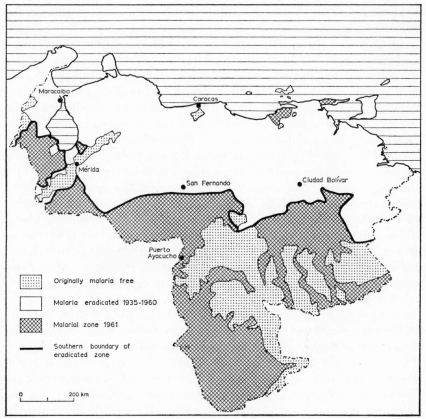

Fig. 5.10 The eradication of malaria in Venezuela 1935–61 (after Marrero, 1964)

California. But the dance halls were soon empty and the population dispersed, and the forest closed back in on this temporary economic heartland of Venezuela.

The huge *llanos* zone, though still occupied by very large cattle ranches, suffered from permanent rustling. Here, as elsewhere in the country, farming remained a way of life rather than a business. The *mayordomo* cared for the estate while the owner and his family sojourned in one of the more 'modern' urban settlements of the north. Indeed, it was in the north that change was taking place. It was to Caracas and La Guaira that the telegraph came in 1856, and, in 1883, the telephone. Here in the north were to be seen the first attempts to put the new technology to work: tramways and steam trains; plans for elaborate copper works at Aroa; and, equally abortive and ingenious, Cochrane's mechanized pearl-fishing using a diving-bell. For the majority of the population, however, a livelihood was only to be gained through hard work in agriculture, cultivating crops that had been cultivated for generations. The further away one was from the capital, or the ports, and thus the influence of the exterior, the closer one was to the colonial tradition.

In Colombia the areas affected by the influences from abroad were undeniably more widely distributed. The distribution of population called for better communications and this in turn meant a wider spread of knowledge, products and ideas. From the Cornish stamp mills in the resuscitated goldfields of Antioquia, to the incipient labour unions among Bogotá textile workers in the south-east, the transformational process had been at work. In Colombia's case coffee had provided the need for, and to a large extent dictated the pace of, the introductions. But the Colombian situation did not yet permit the steady progress from a developing agricultural to a thriving industrial nation, which was seen by some as a logical progression. Like Venezuela, Colombia's history had been punctuated by a succession of civil wars and armed insurrections. Conservative 'centralists' and liberal 'federalists' spared the country no economic harm to win their way to power. In Venezuela, too, militarism became a sure means to an end, and the country repeatedly succumbed to civil strife (Gilmore, 1964). Petty municipal regulations maintained the façade of decentralized control, but when anything significant had to be decided it was to the capital that everybody turned. It was in the capital and the larger cities that the majority of the immigrants were to be found in 1900, traders who recognized the advantages of being close to the centre of political power and influence. Even though the custom of shaking hands had become commonplace in Bogotá and Caracas, it was clear that the impersonal business methods of Europe had not replaced any of the Latin preferences for personalism, nepotism and, to no small extent, corruption. The commercial entrepreneurs soon adapted themselves to the economic environment in which they found themselves.

The most significant feature of the transitional phase throughout the nineteenth century was the replacement of the Spanish colonial system based on political control, by an economic system geared to producing raw materials for overseas markets in return for manufactured products.

However, the practice of securing maximum returns for minimal effort by foreign capital clearly benefited only a minority – the politically and economically powerful – while the masses, fatalistic or realistic enough to accept stagnation, found the struggle to survive no less pressing than their forbears had in previous centuries. Their prospects remained dim, and a better life was as remote as the very centres from which came the products of progress.

PROBLEMS OF THE TWENTIETH CENTURY

If the principal struggle in Colombia and Venezuela during the nineteenth century was concerned with political independence and the search for national identity, its counterpart in the twentieth has been the dilemma of establishing a satisfactory equilibrium between rapid population growth and economic development, which would improve the living standards of the majority of the inhabitants of the two countries. On the credit side there have been the technological innovations that have made so many more things possible than was the case before 1900: advances in communication systems; progress in disease control; the manufacture of chemical fertilizers and pesticides; rapid and accurate survey by aerial photography; pre-fabricated building techniques; large-scale earthmoving equipment; mechanized (and latterly computerized) factory systems; new power generation methods – the list is extensive. On the debit side there stand equally significant facts: more people to feed, with a longer life-expectancy than ever before; higher proportions of the population either too young or too old to form part of the national labour force; increasing demands for a higher standard of living; the conflicts between polarized sectors of society wishing to maintain customary procedures and ideals, and others wishing to restructure society radically, to make it better adapted to the changing economic environment.

Population problems

Lopez (1963) has suggested that the demographic history of Venezuela should be divided into two distinct phases, before and after the year 1920, and this argument also holds for Colombia. This date separates the characteristic features of the nineteenth century from those of the modern period. Before 1920 population grew slowly or not at all and was principally rural and immobile. Since 1920 population has grown rapidly, has become extremely mobile and has congregated in larger and larger settlements. The key to the initiation of this transition is to be found in the impact of the medical revolution, which affected much of Latin America, but especi-ally the northern tropical countries, after 1910. Of great importance was the experience gained, often at high cost, in the building of the Panama Canal. During this enterprise North American technicians could only be protected from the ravages of tropical diseases with the aid of research into methods of combating them and reducing their effect. In this way malario-logy was pioneered and yellow fever studies proliferated. For the adjacent countries of Colombia and Venezuela this meant that in the 1920s and 1930s, with the aid of the Rockefeller Foundation and other agencies, a start could be made, profiting from previous experiences, to reduce the long-standing obstacles to tropical settlement and development. In Venezuela twenty years saw the eradication of *Anopheles darlingi* and *A. albimanus* from over 400,000 km². The disease frontier was pushed south from the Caribbean coast to the latitude of the Orinoco–Apure rivers. The malaria-free area has increased remarkably since 1935 (Fig. 5.10). In Colombia, too, the low altitude tropical zones of the north were being cleared by spraying the forest with DDT. It might be argued that the benefits from improved methods of sanitation and medical aid accruing to the majority of Colombian settlements after 1920 far outweighed the possible gains for Colombia if she had retained control of the Panama route. Perhaps at that point in time only the U.S.A. could have done so much in so short a time to make the Canal project feasible, and at least there were compensations (Miner, 1940). Again, the improvements made in standards of hygiene, in diet, in housing conditions and particularly in the use of footware, all began to have an effect on the mortality-rate of the population. Tuberculosis, typhoid, bronchitis and dysentery and many other ailments have increasingly been attacked with the weapons of anti-biotics and trained technicians. Though one may well argue that measures already taken are quite insufficient, what is clear is the fact that the death-rate was greatly reduced during the 1920s. Before 1920 in both countries mortality-rates had stood at over 30 per 1000; by 1945 they were reduced to less than 20, and in the 1960s had fallen below 10 per 1000. While this process continued the birth-rate remained high at between 30 and 40 per 1000. The result was a rapid natural increase in population. Whereas it took sixty years for the Venezuelan population to double before 1945, from that date it took a mere twenty. Colombia's total population rose from 2 million in 1841 to 8 million in 1938 and almost 20 million in 1970. By 1980 it is estimated that the two countries should contain at least 42 million people, only just short of the total Latin American population of the 1880s. Some, viewing with alarm the threat of burgeoning numbers, might wish that the desire to procreate had been reduced in harmony with the extension of longevity, but this was not to be. With life-expectancy increasing from 46 years in 1940 to 63 in 1970 in both Venezuela and Colombia, the large family is still the rule for the majority of cohabiting couples. Church and state have done little as yet to make contraceptive devices more widely available.

The strains imposed upon the economies of the countries by the total increase in population have been great. Whereas in western Europe the rapid increase in population went hand in hand with industrialization and the provision of cheap housing units for the urbanizing population, in Colombia and Venezuela, as elsewhere in the developing world, the population increase took place initially in rural areas. It was here, often remote from the facilities of twentieth-century living, that the balance had been tipped against nature. Gradually it became clear that if the next generation was to improve its opportunities it would have to search out new avenues of self-betterment: one method that was cheap and involved little risk was migration, usually to the nearest town.

The distribution of population in Colombia and Venezuela during the present century has been remarkably stable, in spite of the migration of population to urban settlements. In Venezuela, as Friedmann (1966) has demonstrated, the majority of the population was distributed throughout the period 1920-60 in a relatively restricted zone of northern Venezuela. Of paramount importance from the 1930s was the dominance of the Caracas area as a major focus. In Colombia, on the other hand, a wider spread of settlement centres may be noted. The majority of the foci of urban population are to be seen in Fig. 5.11. Though restricted to the north-western area of the country, the south-eastern plains being practically empty, the pattern was one of dispersed regional centres, Bogotá accounting for no more than its regional share of the national total. The location of the nodes within a roughly triangular area, seen in Fig. 5.11, has earlier been noted by Cole (1965, Fig. 13.2).

Changes in these basic patterns of distribution have been slight during the past forty years. In Venezuela the oil boom in the Maracaibo basin during the 1930s and 1940s attracted some population from the Andean highlands, as did the similar developments in the Tigre area during the 1950s. Elsewhere population concentrated in developing agricultural and transportation centres such as Barquisimeto (Gormsen, 1966), San Cristóbal and Barcelona. The basic flows in population were latitudinal, all of them to the benefit of the centre and to the detriment of the peripheral regions (Robinson, 1969, p. 31). In Colombia migration was more complex. Almost every regional centre became a magnet whose attractive field was proportional to the size of the centre. Industrial developments in Cali, Medellín and Bogotá, and growing transportation, port and agricultural centres at Barranquilla, Cartagena, Buenaventura and Manizales, all attracted population.

The migration of large numbers of people to the towns had a marked effect on both social structures and urban morphology. Marchand (1966) has shown that the evolution of the *ranchos* (shanty towns) of metropolitan Caracas was a complex and little-understood process, bearing little relation to the oft-quoted rush from rural primitivism to urban squalor. With their numerical increase fluctuating in relation to political controls, and their spatial expansion determined as much by job opportunities and journeys to work as the availability of occupied land, they represent a special case of self-help suburbanization. In a whole range of other communities in both countries similar processes were at work. While in Caracas colonial patios

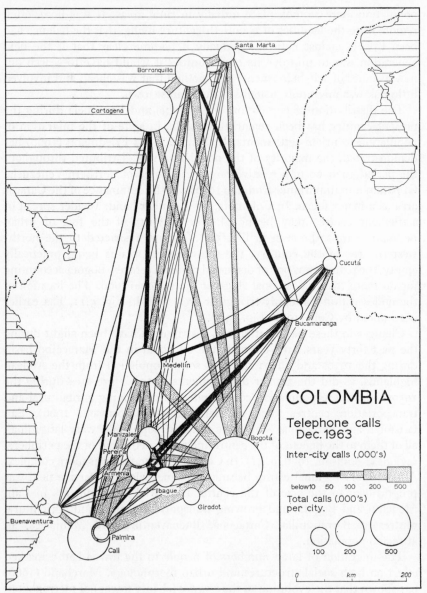

Fig. 5.11 The volume of intercity telephone calls in Colombia

made way for skyscraper blocks of offices and flats, in Bogotá the élite residential areas were changing in form, location and function. Colonial Spanish-style houses gave way progressively to English suburban and California ranch houses (Amato, 1968). The whole urban system, be it housing, transportation, social networks, sewage disposal or relation of city to region, was rapidly changing. While differences in defining 'urban' settlements in both countries makes it difficult to obtain comparative data, it is clear that the pace of urbanization has been increasing. In Colombia the proportion of urban to total population more than doubled between 1918 and 1960. In Venezuela since 1926, although total population has risen very quickly, the phenomenal growth has been in the urban component, which now includes some 70 per cent of the total population and is predicted to rise at an ever-quickening pace during the next twenty years.

The reasons behind this move to the cities are as different as the peoples involved. For most migrants it is looked upon as a means of improving one's chance, or at least that of the next generation, to benefit from a better paid job and better education. It often involves suffering the rigours of unemployment, shortage of money and poor housing facilities, but migrants are usually well prepared by age, outlook or experience to discount such trifles in the hope of future possibilities. For the governments the problem is one of fulfilling the hopes of so many. Simple statistics speak eloquently of the magnitude of the problems: in Colombia 200,000 persons a year enter the labour market, while the entire manufacturing industry employs no more than 300,000; when an estimated 4000 teachers are required each year, this involves a tenfold increase in the number of trained teachers; in 1964 an estimated 290,000 living units were required in towns of over 10,000 inhabitants (Galbraith, 1966, p. 26), yet the government agency in charge of the housing programme is delighted to reach an annual target of 30,000 units. Similar statistics could be provided for Venezuela. Such data give rise to the suggestion that perhaps it would have been better to have prevented the population from having migrated from the rural areas – until one examines the effects of transition there.

AGRARIAN ADJUSTMENTS TO TRANSITION

Before details are given of the respective experiences of agricultural development in Colombia and Venezuela, it must be stressed that for each country the agricultural sector of the economy has played quite distinctive roles. Whereas in Venezuela the exploitation of the oilfield resources during the last thirty years permitted agricultural production to fade into relative insignificance, in Colombia agriculture remained the most important contributor to the gross national product (IBRD, 1956). Even though agriculture in Venezuela contributes a mere 5·7 per cent of gross national product, it still provides the largest single source of employment, 32 per cent in 1963. Besides these fundamental differences between the two countries, it must also be remembered that regional variations within them are essential features of agricultural methods, motives, production and potential. Generalizations inevitably exclude the unique regional qualities that characterize many areas within Venezuela and Colombia.

Colombia entered the twentieth century on a wave of agricultural expansion, which had followed the commercial plantings of coffee in Cundinamarca. By the end of the nineteenth century exports had begun that were to increase steadily in significance for the national economy. The spread of the mild *arabica* coffee bush reflected not only suitable climatic and edaphic conditions, but also the availability of farming capital and expertise. Elsewhere in the country colonial and nineteenth-century patterns of land use were maintained unchanged into the modern period. When the Currie Mission (IBRD, 1950) examined the state of agriculture it was noted for the first time on a national scale the extent to which flat, apparently rich, bottomlands were occupied by low-intensity livestock-ranching estates, while slopes steep enough to make cultivation a hazard to life were occupied for crop farming. It was a state of affairs that would not have surprised Humboldt. Equally significant was the demonstration that the Magdalena, only a quarter the length of the Mississippi–Missouri, annually flushed out to sea as much sediment as that river (Galbraith, 1966, p. 93). Such erosion of an undeniably valuable resource also demonstrated the primitive nature of agricultural methods. There are an estimated 200,000 farmers who merely subsist on their land, living in continual fear of upsetting the natural balance, of taking one crop too many from the friable soil, of opening too large a swidden plot, of being unable to stop the spread of their chief agricultural tool, fire. For the agriculturalists who obtain enough from the land to keep their families alive by means of cultivating plantains, beans, maize or sugar cane, developments in twentieth-century agriculture have meant little. The key sector in agriculture that has developed most in recent years has been that concerned with commercialization, with agriculture not only as a way of life or a means of occupying otherwise idle hands or feeding otherwise hungry children, but as an integral part of the process of economic development. Given the new expectations of the majority of the rural population, what chance was there, or is there in the future, of agriculture providing sufficient reward to keep people on the land?

A prominent feature of Colombian agriculture, as in Venezuela, was, and still is, the uneven distribution of land amongst the farming community (Smith, 1967). In the early 1960s an estimated 4 per cent of land in farm units was held by 60 per cent of the total number of farmers, each unit averaging 3 ha, while 60 per cent of the land was held by less than 3 per cent of the total number of farmers in units of over 100 ha. Such average figures in fact hide the huge range of size variation best summarized in two words – *minifundios* and *latifundios*. Not that variation in size of units alone is necessarily harmful for agriculture – many instances could be cited to show ecological or economic requirements for this. But in the Colombian situation it is a result of neither of these two factors that the land is so apportioned. It reflected, and still reflects, the colonial legacy of large estates held not only for agricultural use but also as a symbol of status and, since political and financial stability had apparently vanished for ever, as a security against inflation. Many of the larger properties were, economically speaking, under-utilized and could be contrasted to the densely populated hill slope plots of the majority of farmers. Under these circumstances, land reform ought to have made sound economic sense, but it met stiff opposition from the wealthy and politically influential estate-owners.

Two other factors complicated the agrarian scene. Since 1900 many squatters had occupied land, often without the owner's knowledge and usually illegally; elsewhere share-croppers and tenants had wrangled interminably with landowners over their rights to grow commercial crops, a practice that threatened the owner's monopoly of profit. Three possible solutions were identified during the 1940s and 1950s: first, it was proposed that modifications should be made to alter the essentially colonial agricultural system, by means of rationalization through subdivision or amalgamation, whichever was needed; second, it was suggested that new agricultural communities could be settled in apparently virgin regions, leaving the existing situation to be ameliorated gradually by the reduction in population pressure on the land; third, there emerged a school of opinion, voiced most strongly by Laughlin Currie, that suggested that the best method of increasing the efficiency of Colombian agriculture would be to allow fewer, more technically sophisticated farmers, using all the technological aids available, to farm land vacated by the majority of what can only be considered as inefficient agriculturalists. These would be permitted, or should be persuaded, to migrate to the towns. The Colombian government, whether through political realism, economic argument or philosophical idealism, opted for a combination of the first two methods. By 1959, under the pressure of urban unemployment, a start had been made with colonization projects on the bank of the Ariari river in Meta department (Fig. 5.12). 1961 saw the establishment of INCORA (Colombian National Agrarian Reform Institute) and the first agrarian reform scheme was initiated in the department of Tolima, west of Bogotá. Here, in place of the more usual dispersed family farms, were established nucleated villages whose economy depended on common pasturage of livestock (Holt, 1964, p. 91).

Colombian domestic politics during the decade after 1948 had reached a nadir of inefficiency, even for a country that had known much violence and bloodshed since independence (Fluharty, 1957). The power struggles of the Conservative and Liberal parties had degenerated into a bloodbath of rural guerrilla activities, civil disorder and generalized brutalization of the rural peasantry in parts of the north-west of the country. The phenomenon, which probably accounted for at least 200,000 lives and employed at its peak perhaps 20,000 guerrilla fighters, is known as 'La Violencia'

(Fals Borda, 1965; Gúzman, Borda and Luna, 1962). It was in the centre of the area affected by *La Violencia* (Fig. 5.12) that the government began agrarian reform. By 1967 some 50,000 families had been settled on 1·6 million ha of expropriated land in the densely populated north-west, and the programme was gaining momentum. Key problems have been the determination of the optimum size of farm holdings, the provision of credit facilities, the establishment in rural districts of facilities such as schools,

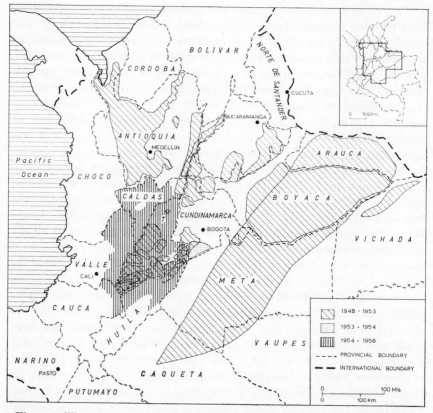

Fig. 5.12 The extent of *Violencia* in Colombia 1948–58 (after Gúzman, 1962–4)

roads and hospitals, and last, but by no means least, the delays and cost of expropriating land through an elaborate, legalistic eighteen-step process, as well as the problems of allotting compensation.

Agricultural colonization has, for the most part, taken place in areas formerly unoccupied or under-utilized (Eidt, 1968; Hegen, 1966). Problems abound, including the task of constructing costly penetration roads to link the production zones to regional markets, as well as the wide range of problems associated with agronomic experiments in difficult environments. Irrigation, flood control and resource management have proved highly successful in certain areas (CARC, 1956; IBRD, 1955).

In Venezuela agrarian reform and land colonization have also constituted the two-edged sword of agricultural transformation. Statistics reveal that only a very small proportion of the land area of the country (91 million ha) is even included within farms (22 million ha), and of that only 7 per cent is cultivated (IBRD, 1961). The neglect of agriculture in the early years of oil production had been partly overcome, but the fact is that Venezuela can afford the luxury of importing a large proportion of its food requirements. Wheat imports rose between 1950 and 1961 from 2000 to 345,000 tons. Nevertheless, by 1965 an estimated 115,000 families had received land (though perhaps half have since deserted it) over an area in excess of 2·7 million ha. A partial explanation to the pace of Venezuelan reform may be found in the excellent organization of the farming community (Federación Campesina de Venezuela) and the continued support of the programme by the Acción Democrática party, which had long promised help and which held power from 1958 to 1969 (Warriner, 1969, pp. 347–71). As in Colombia, colonization of new land has had a somewhat chequered history. Since the costly Guárico irrigation scheme of the 1950s, settlements have been established in the south-west Maracaibo basin at various sites along the upper *llanos* piedmont, in the Orinoco delta zone and Venezuelan Guayana (Crist and Leahy, 1969; Marrero, 1964, p. 316).

In both countries agrarian adjustments have proved difficult, and there are many explanations that might be offered. Perhaps of paramount importance is the fact that agriculture is, in the middle of the twentieth century, no longer regarded in either country as the best method of material improvement. Except for the few who make large profits from it, it is viewed as a little old-fashioned (Hill, 1962). Besides that, it is also an occupation that demands residence in the countryside, precisely where it is most difficult to obtain, and expensive to provide, social facilities. Without the facilities and opportunities, therefore, the young dynamic population migrates to the city to leave the rural areas with even worse problems. Farming may have been an essential feature of traditional Colombia and Venezuela, but, in the face of twentieth-century commercialization and competition, it is all too clear that the transition to more productive methods will take time, and may be painful.

INDUSTRIALIZATION AND REGIONAL DEVELOPMENT

The colonial predominance of agriculture in Venezuela and mineral exploitation in Colombia have been almost entirely transposed since independence. What coffee has done for Colombia, oil has done for Venezuela. Since the beginnings of the commercial production of oil in

Venezuela, a transformation, perhaps unequalled elsewhere in the whole of Latin America, has taken place. Oil revenues have lubricated the path towards economic development. In Colombia, on the other hand, oil resources lay inland, inaccessible and unprofitable until recently. Nature could hardly have selected a better location for the principal oil-bearing strata in Venezuela than the Maracaibo basin. Here, following the strike of Royal Dutch-Shell with well Mene Grande I (now a much-photographed relic of modern industrial archaeology), exploration, extraction and exportation rapidly ensued. On the crest of the boom in oil, Venezuela for thirty years has enjoyed one of the highest, sustained rates of economic growth of any nation in modern history. The figures speak for themselves: an annual *per capita* growth-rate in excess of 7 per cent; gross domestic product rising each year by over 3 per cent; crude oil production rising from 1·1 million barrels per day in 1946 to 3·5 million in 1965. While the excellent historical study of Liewen (1954) details the early developments in the industry, it is important to stress the recent changes in the industry, particularly the problems that have affected it since the early 1960s. Oil is a capital-intensive industry; while it provides 19 per cent of the gross domestic product it employs less than 1·1 per cent of the total labour force; although average *per capita* income levels are quoted at U.S. $800 for Venezuela as a whole, more than 80 per cent of Venezuelans receive less than $200 per annum. Through a colonial legal legacy that gives the state the ownership of all subsurface deposits, including oil, a delicate balance has to be maintained between successive Venezuelan governments and oil producers, all of whom attempted to obtain the maximum benefits to the nation while still keeping exploitation a profitable economic proposition for the foreign companies involved. The original 50-50 share of profits from oil has, in recent years, swung in favour of the government to reach 70-30 proportions, but an enduring feature until recently has been the significance of foreign enterprise in the industry. Further exploration within Venezuela opened the eastern fields centred on El Tigre, though the western basin maintains a 75 per cent share of total production. In the last two years intensive investigations have discovered major oilsands within the Orinoco basin.

The wealth from oil has undoubtedly produced or emphasized regional and sectoral inequalities in Venezuela. Wage-rates in the industry have remained far in excess of all others; the value of output of one worker in the industry is estimated to be over one hundred times greater than that of a farm labourer. Much of the money that entered the national exchequer before 1960 has been either misappropriated or misspent on non-essential building projects. Furthermore, those in charge of 'sowing the seeds of oil' have hesitated to broadcast them outside the central northern region of the country. While government and private investment may have been heavy in Venezuela during the 1950s, spatially it has been concentrated within the north-central region, as is exemplified by the distribution of government loans (Fig. 5.13).

Not only within Venezuela has the oil industry faced, or produced, problems during the last decade. As a commodity of world trade, and of international political and strategic significance, it has had to meet stiff competition from the new or reinvigorated production areas of Africa and the Middle East. The flood of cheap oil has made Venezuela ever more

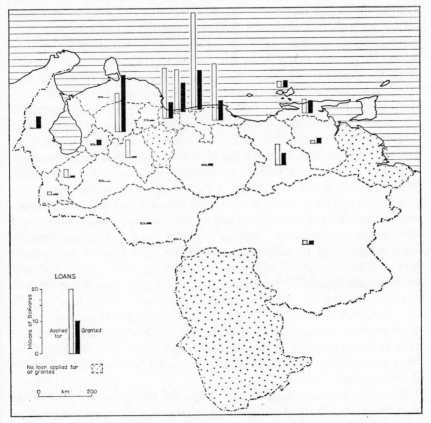

Fig. 5.13 Distribution of central government loans in Venezuela 1965

cost-conscious: Venezuelan wells are five times the depth of their north African competitors, and daily flow per well is a mere tenth. With super-tankers of more than 250,000 tons reducing transportation costs to negligible proportions, Venezuela is in danger of losing the advantage endowed by location within the western hemisphere (Crist, 1969, p. 70). Demands in North America for a reduction in atmospheric pollution caused by automobile exhaust fumes poses yet another threat to sulphur-rich Venezuelan petroleum. The effect of legislated improvements in the environmental standards of the developed world on Venezuela's future as a major exporter of oil and petrochemical products is difficult to estimate. The hope may be that gradually Venezuela will be 'developed' enough to pollute her own or her South American neighbours' environments.

Colombia has likewise to tread the tightrope of international demand. When the balance of payments, industrial investment and activity and stock market prices fluctuate with the price quoted for coffee in New York, it is clear that this means far more to Colombia than market fluctuations in any other agricultural crop. This one product accounted for 69 per cent of Colombia's foreign exchange earnings in 1963; a 10 per cent fall in the price in New York can instantly reduce the national income by almost 2 per cent, or, put another way, a variation of 2 cents per kg in the export quota can make the country richer or poorer by U.S. $8 million – enough to build two modern ports on the Urubá gulf.

In spite of the problems that oil and coffee exports have brought to Venezuela and Colombia, they have also been the precursors of industrial development. In Colombia coffee cultivation produced a demand for consumer goods that stimulated the growth of industry in Antioquia from the turn of the present century (Urrutía, 1969). A series of interrelated factors, including the availability of the liquid assets of the Antioqueño mine operators, the existing small textile industry and artisan craftsmanship of the zone and the need to supply the coffee-processing plants with small pieces of machinery, combine to explain why Colombia progressed more rapidly than its neighbour during the early part of the century. However, by the 1930s Venezuelan entrepreneurs were establishing small manufacturing plants in Maracay and Valencia and, with the profit from oil far outstripping that from coffee, Venezuela could have rapidly advanced. But it did not. It was too easy to purchase from overseas the necessary manufactured articles. While the opportunity existed to plough back revenue into the development of agriculture and manufacturing industry, economic progress had to be sacrificed for the political stability of dictatorship.

Not until the beginning of the 1960s did the government of either country pay much attention to the problems of economic diversification, decentralization and planned growth. But since such items entered the vocabularies of politicians, newspapers, electoral campaign speeches and journals spoke of little else. The empty interiors, the strategic margins and the decaying neglected national peripheries became the focus of comment. Resource management, integrated development and conservation have more recently been added to the symbolic language of purposeful development. For Venezuela John Friedmann's (1966) penetratingly simple model of development highlighted the lopsided geography of its development. Plans were made for the promotion on the southern bank of the Orinoco of a new counterbalance to the metropolitan industrial and population core region of Caracas. There within a radius of 200 km a government-controlled integrated development area, rich in power resources and minerals, has been successfully included within the national economic planning framework. Centred on Ciudad Guayana, the city region's growth during the past seven years has begun to have, and will continue to have, a marked effect on the patterns of population migration, on employment opportunities and on educational facilities (Rodwin, 1969; McGinn and Davis, 1969). For the major portion of northern Venezuela the national planning agency (CORDIPLAN) and other specialized teams have reviewed the future demands for transportation systems, power generation and distribution, industrial location, agricultural development and urban growth (Soberman, 1967). Gradually there are emerging the 'planned landscapes' that represent the twentieth century's contribution to the process of transition. Plans for a chain of highly flexible new cities, due to make Ciudad Guayana appear an overstructured obsolescence, are ready for implementation; national parks, forest reserves and nature trails counterbalance the effects of new industrial plant; prominent progress has been made in the development of the electric power grid, new roads, bridges and housing stock. While the capital gains a subterranean railway system, the international airport of Maiquetía already prepares to accommodate the largest and fastest jet aircraft.

In Colombia the overconcentration of population and investment has never been of the same magnitude. Evidence provided in the form of the volume of telephone calls made in Colombia (Fig. 5.11) demonstrates the joint importance of more than seven centres.[1] The northern and southern clusters of urban population have long enjoyed relatively close interconnection. In Colombia as in Venezuela the past ten years have seen the establishment of planning agencies and development authorities: Venezuela's CVG (Guayana), CORPOANDES (Andes), FUDECO (northwest) and CONZUPLAN (Zulia) find their equivalents in the Colombian Cauca Development Corporation (CVC). Industrial development still suffers from the costs of difficult transportation, but this has not prevented the growth of an iron and steel plant at Paz del Río, north-east of Bogotá, well placed to serve the national market (Unión Panamericana, 1956). The output from manufacturing industry, which is estimated to employ 300,000 workers, was said to account for some 17·5 per cent of the gross national product in 1963, and had risen by 1967 to over 20 per cent. Regional specialization in production is marked: Cartagena forms the centre of a growing petrochemical complex (cf. El Tablazo and Santo Tomé in Venezuela), Manizales has metals and Bucamaranga has foundary products. In both countries industrialization is gaining momentum. Industrial expansion, sectoral diversification and the geographical location of investment

[1] I have to thank Dr Alan Gilbert for making available the data upon which Fig. 5.11 is based.

in plant, labour and marketing systems are all items that are likely to achieve increasing significance in the future.

TOWARDS THE TWENTY-FIRST CENTURY

Given inadequate statistical bases and the rapid technological changes that are affecting Venezuela and Colombia, prediction of future developments is necessarily a hazardous task. Fig. 5.14 represents no more than the overall pattern of developments that may have been accomplished by the end of the present century. Perhaps the most striking feature of the map is the division of the whole area into two portions, slightly unequal in area. The southern region, when viewed from the national metropolitan centres forming the 'interior' or periphery of the economic centres of the two states, represents the northern portion of the empty heartland of South America. This region is characterized by extremely low densities of population, small settlements being widely dispersed and with only regional functions. Of paramount importance for changes in the economic structure of the region is the possibility of major resource developments, witnessed in the exclusion of northern Guayana from the region. Mineral deposits, power resources and major civil engineering projects, such as barrage dams and lake construction, as well as massive agricultural colonization schemes based on drainage or irrigation, could all affect this region. More probable during the next thirty years is the development of a significant tourist industry utilizing the 'wilderness' of the Orinoco–Amazon to attract increasingly wealthy European and North American visitors. Modern technology puts the 'lost world' of the Venezuelan *tepui* no more than an hour's air-conditioned flying time from Ciudad Guayana; the immodest speed of the hovercraft will make practically nowhere safe for the few remaining groups of forest and plains Indians, cultural relics of the pre-Hispanic past. The eastern end of this major region would be greatly enlarged if Venezuela were to be successful in her claim to a substantial portion of Guyana, though the dispute seems likely to be shelved in lieu of other more pressing claims to time and money.

The approximate path of the projected South American Marginal Highway, which roughly borders the northern margin of this region, is also shown in Fig. 5.14. This represents the northern segment of a major penetration route that may yet provide some integrative force to the scattered development on and below the eastern slopes of the Andes. Depending on developments in the Guianas, it might be extended southeastwards to serve their hinterlands as well.

The second major region represents a portion of the developed periphery of the continent. Here are located the majority of the inhabitants of each country, of whom three out of every four may reside in or close to one of the major metropolitan centres. These nodes of high density population are linked both by paved roads and a complex telecommunications network, each nation having access for external communications to a space satellite. The corridors of development that embrace the majority of major urban centres are well served with infrastructures capable of supporting either industrial or agricultural production, and contrast sharply with the scattering of 'problem areas', such as the Chocó in Colombia and the

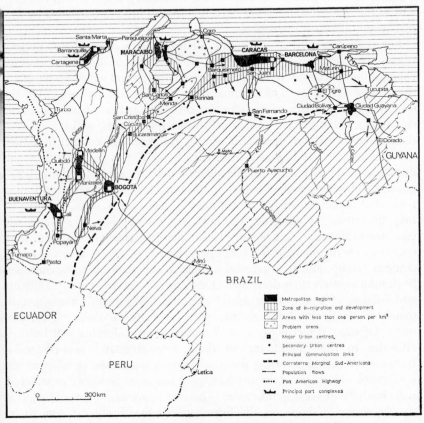

Fig. 5.14 Developments in Venezuela and Colombia towards A.D. 2000 (after Friedmann, 1966)

Lara-Falcón plateau in Venezuela. Here, for a variety of physical and economic reasons, communications are difficult and population densities low. The areas remain to be integrated fully into the national space economy. In this northern region the continental international road link is provided for in the Pan American Highway, and its extension via Bogotá to Ciudad Guayana. On the coastal rim of the Caribbean, but less so on the Pacific side, are located major port complexes. The continental shelf, besides posing problems over territorial jurisdiction, is providing useful supplies of oil, natural gas and fish. Coastal resorts for the tourist industry are to be found from Margarita in the east to the Colombian Caribbean island outposts of San Andrés and Providencia. Depending on the choice of route for the proposed new interoceanic isthmian canal (Parsons, 1967, p. 94) the Gulf of Urabá may yet become one of the most significant settlement growth zones at the western end of the proposed Caribbean Transverse Road (*Carretera Transversal del Caribe*), the northern counterpart of the Marginal Highway, extending from Turbo to Barcelona by way of Barranquilla and Maracaibo.

For such a pattern of economic organization to come about, present trends have necessarily to continue. If, for example, the magnitude of changes that occurred in Venezuela between 1910 and 1960 are repeated, then there is little hope of the prediction proving at all accurate. On the other hand, if population trends are not curbed by massive family planning campaigns, if the present rate of urbanization continues, and if industrial developments remain successful against international competition then the outline may not be too unreal. Clearly, as in the past, the pace and direction of development will be determined ultimately by the national governments acting individually or in unison. This pace and the continuing success of twentieth-century transition for the majority of the population may be critical in deciding whether the present political systems can continue to function, or whether revolutionary changes are required. Both countries are members of the Latin American Free Trade Area and of the Andean Group, and international economic and political co-operation is beginning to affect their decisions. Questions of financial stability, inflation and balance of payments problems are, and will probably remain, intimately involved with developments in the international economic environment. Of more direct concern to Venezuela and Colombia will be their attitudes to the exploitation of their renewable and non-renewable resources. Whether planning for contingencies continues, or whether the long-range objectives of the national good are more seriously considered, will clearly be of great significance. Whatever happens most would support the expression of hope for the future voiced by President Leoni in his 'View from Caracas' in 1965 (Crist, 1969, p. 72) that 'though we may have made a late entrance into the twentieth century, we now live in the serene conviction that we will arrive on time at the threshold of the twenty-first.'

REFERENCES AND SELECT BIBLIOGRAPHY

AMATO, P. W. (1968) *Analysis of the Changing Pattern of Elite Residential Areas in Bogotá, Colombia.* New Haven, Conn.

ARCILA FARÍAS (1946) *Economía colonial de Venezuela.* Mexico.

ARMAS CHITTY, J. A. (1961) *Tucupido, formación de un pueblo llanero.* Caracas.

BEYER, R. C. (1948) Transportation and the coffee industry in Colombia. *Hisp. Am. Hist. Rev.*, 2, 17–30.

BOCKH, A. (1956) *El desecamiento del Lago de Valencia.* Caracas.

BRITO-FIGUEROA, F. (1960) *Ensayos de historia social venezolana.* Caracas.

BRITO-FIGUEROA, F. (1961) *La estructura social y demografica de Venezuela colonial.* Caracas.

BRITO-FIGUEROA, F. (1963) *La estructura económica de Venezuela colonial.* Caracas.

BROADBENT, S. (1968) A prehistoric field system in Chibcha territory. *Ñawa Pacha*, 6, 135–47.

BUSHNELL, D. (1954) *The Santander Regime in Gran Colombia.* Newark.

CARRERA DAMAS, G. (1964) *Materiales para el estudio de la cuestión agraria en Venezuela 1800–1830,* I, *Estudio Preliminar.* Caracas.

CARC (Corporación Autonoma Regional del Cauca) (1956) *The Unified Development of Power and Water Resources in the Cauca Valley.* Bogotá.

COLE, J. P. (1965) *Latin America: an economic and social geography.* London.

CRIST, R. C. (1952) *The Cauca Valley, Colombia.* Baltimore.

CRIST, R. C. and LEAHY, E. P. (1969) *Venezuela: Search for a Middle Ground.* New York.

EIDT, R. C. (1959) Aboriginal Chibcha settlement in Colombia. *Annals Assoc. Am. Geog.*, 49, 374–92.

EIDT, R. C. (1968) Pioneer settlement in Colombia. *Geog. Rev.*, 58, 298–300.

ESCALANTE, A. (1964) *El Negro en Colombia.* Bogotá.

FALS BORDA, O. (1957) *El hombre y la tierra en Boyacá.* Bogotá.

FALS BORDA, O. (1965) Violence and the break-up of tradition in Colombia. In VÉLIZ, C. (ed.) *Obstacles to Change in Latin America.* London. 188–205.

FALS BORDA, O. (1969) *Subversion and Social Change in Colombia.* New York.

FLUHARTY, V. L. (1957) *Dance of the Millions: military rule and the social revolution in Colombia 1930–1955.* Pittsburgh.

FRIEDMANN, J. (1966) *Regional Development Policy: a case study of Venezuela.* Cambridge, Mass.

GALBRAITH, W. O. (1966) *Colombia: a general survey.* London.

GILMORE, R. L. (1964) *Caudillism and Militarism in Venezuela 1810–1910.* Athens, Ohio.

GILMORE, R. L. and HARRISON, J. P. (1948) Juan Bernardo Elbers and the introduction of steam navigation on the Magdalena River. *Hisp. Am. Hist. Rev.*, 28, 335–59.

GORMSEN, E. (1966) *Barquisimeto: eine Handelstadt in Venezuela.* Heidelberg.

GRAY, W. H. (1945) Steamboat transportation on the Orinoco. *Hisp. Am. Hist. Rev.*, 25, 455–69.

GÚZMAN, G., BORDA, O. F. and LUNA, E. U. (1962–4) *La Violencia en Colombia.* 2 vols. Bogotá.

HARRISON, J. P. (1952) The evolution of the Colombian tobacco trade to 1875. *Hisp. Am. Hist. Rev.*, 32, 163–74.

HEGEN, E. E. (1966) *Highways into the Upper Amazon Basin: pioneer lands in southern Colombia, Ecuador and northern Peru.* Gainsville.

HILL, G. (1962) *La vida rural en Venezuela.* Caracas.

HOLT, P. M. (1964) *Colombia Today – and Tomorrow.* London.

HOUSTON, J. M. (1968) The foundation of colonial towns in Hispanic America. In BECKINSALE, R. P. and HOUSTON, J. M. (eds.) *Urbanisation and its Problems.* Oxford. 352–90.

HUSSEY, R. D. (1934) *The Caracas Company 1728–1784.* Cambridge, Mass.

IBRD (International Bank for Reconstruction and Development) (1950) *The Basis of a Development Program for Colombia: report of a mission headed by Lauchlin Currie.* Washington, D.C.

IBRD (1955) *The Autonomous Regional Corporation of the Cauca and the Development of the Upper Cauca Valley.* Washington, D.C.

IBRD (1956) *The Agricultural Development of Colombia.* Washington, D.C.

IBRD (1961) *The Economic Development of Venezuela.* Baltimore.

LIEWEN, E. (1954) *Petroleum in Venezuela: a history.* Berkeley.

LÓPEZ, J. E. (1963) *La expansion demográfica de Venezuela.* Mérida.

MARCHAND, B. (1966) Les ranchos de Caracas, contribution a l'étude des bidonvilles, *Cahiers d'Outre-Mer*, 19, 105–43.

MARCIALES, M. (ed.) (1948) *Geografía histórica y económica del norte de Santander.* Vol. I. Bogotá.

MARRERO, L. (1964) *Venezuela y sus recursos.* Caracas.

MARTÍNEZ, C. (1967) *Apuntes sobre el urbanismo en el Nuevo Reino de Granada.* Bogotá.

MCGINN, N. F. and DAVIS, R. G. (1969) *Build a Mill, Build a City, Build a School.* Cambridge, Mass.

MENDOZA, D. (1947) *El Llanero: ensayo de sociología Venezolana.* Buenos Aires.

MINER, D. C. (1940) *The Fight for the Panama Route.* Columbia.

MORÓN, G. (1954) *Los orígenes históricos de Venezuela.* Madrid.

MORSE, R. M. (1962) Some characteristics of Latin American urban history. *Am. Hist. Rev.,* 317–38.

NICHOLS, T. E. (1954) The rise of Barranquilla. *Hisp. Am. Hist. Rev.,* 34, 158–74.

OJER, P. (1967) *La Formación del Oriente Venezolano.* Vol. I: *creación de las gobernaciones.* Caracas.

PARSONS, J. J. (1949) *Antioqueño Colonisation in Western Colombia.* Berkeley.

PARSONS, J. J. (1967) *Antioquia's Corridor to the Sea.* Berkeley.

PARSONS, J. J. and BOWEN, W. A. (1966) Ancient ridged fields of the San Jorge River floodplain, Colombia. *Geog. Rev.,* 56, 317–43.

PICON-SALAS (1962) *Venezuela independiente 1810–1960.* Caracas.

QUIJADA, J. L. (1968) Panaquire, pueblo de latifundio. *Boletín Histórico* (Caracas), 16, 11–37.

RASMUSSEN, W. D. (1947) Agricultural colonisation and immigration in Venezuela 1810–1860. *Agric. Hist.,* 21, 152–62.

REICHEL-DOLMATOFF, G. (1956) *Colombia.* London.

RICARDO, I. (1967) *Atlas de Caracas.* Caracas.

RIPPY, J. F. (1931) *The Capitalists and Colombia.* New York.

RIPPY, J. F. (1943) Dawn of the railway era in Colombia. *Hisp. Am. Hist. Rev.,* 23, 650–63.

ROBINSON, D. J. (1969) The city as centre of change in modern Venezuela. In *Cities in a Changing Latin America.* London.

RODWIN, L. and associates (1969) *Planning Urban Growth and Regional Development: the experience of the Guayana program of Venezuela.* Cambridge, Mass.

ROUSE, I. and CRUXENT, J. M. (1963) *Venezuelan Archaeology.* New Haven, Conn.

SAUER, C. O. (1965) *The Early Spanish Main.* Berkeley.

SCOTT, I. (1968) Colonial urban development in Hispanic America: the case of Santa Fé de Bogotá. *Bull. Soc. Latin Am. Studies,* 10, 20–6.

SOBERMAN, R. M. (1967) *Transport Technology for Developing Regions: a study of road transportation in Venezuela.* Cambridge, Mass.

SMITH, T. L. (1967) *Colombia: social structure and the process of development.* Gainsville.

STEWARD, J. H. and FARON, L. (1959) *Native Peoples of South America*. New York.

UNION PANAMERICANA. (1956) *Proyecto Sogamoso-Paz del Río*. Bogotá.

URRUTÍA, M. (1969) *The Development of the Colombian Labour Movement*. New Haven, Conn.

VILA, P. (1960–5) *Geografía de Venezuela*. 2 vols. Caracas.

VILA, P. (1966) Consideraciones sobre poblaciones errantes en el periodo colonial. *Revista de Historia* (Caracas), 12, 11–24.

WARRINER, D. (1969) *Land Reform in Principle and Practice*. London.

WEST, R. C. (1952) *Colonial Placer Mining in Colombia*. Baton Rouge.

WEST, R. C. (1957) *The Pacific Lowlands of Colombia*. Baton Rouge.

6 The Guianas

D. J. Robinson

CONTRASTS IN THE 'LAND OF MANY WATERS'

Few who look at the political or cultural patterns within South America can fail to puzzle over the anomalous group of territories known as the 'Guianas'.[1] Their origins and continued existence within a subcontinent dominated by Iberian culture invite analysis. Yet there have been few detailed studies that consider the Guianas as an entity. The elementary textbook coverage usually does little more than describe each of the political units in turn, and only Lowenthal's (1960) study of differential population distributions, and Devèze's (1968) introductory survey pay more than lip-service to the analysis of these contiguous colonial cultural enclaves. The majority of recent publications keep strictly within the political boundaries of individual territories, thereby avoiding the problems posed by source materials in five or more languages (Cummings, 1969; Sanderson, 1969; Kruijer, 1960). Yet it is only when the Guianas are placed within the wider context of the settlement of the Guiana region that their full significance can be appreciated.

The Guianas clearly provide excellent case studies in the neglected field of colonial geography (Lowenthal, 1950). The key questions are: how did non-Iberian Europeans manage to occupy a coastal margin of South America exceedingly close to Europe? Why and when did the Dutch, French and British effect their occupation, and what significance can be attached to the different modes of settlement and development? What have been, and continue to be, the implications of these varied colonial experiences for each of the territories in terms of problems of growth, change and development during the present century?

The process of cultural differentiation, whether concerned with economy, society or features in the human landscape, has taken place within a physical

[1] It should be noted that here the term 'Guianas' is used to describe collectively the three political units of Guyana (formerly British Guiana), French Guiana and Dutch Guiana (Surinam). Complexities arise when one meets French and Spanish terms. In French the 'Guianas' are Les Guyanes, and French Guiana is La Guyane Française (occasionally Cayenne); in Spanish 'La Guayana' refers to the Venezuelan portion of the Guiana shield, Las Guayanas to the 'Guianas'. The most recent addition to the regional terminology is Guayana Essequiba – namely, that portion of Guyana presently claimed by Venezuela.

setting of striking homogeneity. In general terms, the whole of the Guiana region, as its aboriginal name implies (Cummings, 1964) is surrounded and characterized by an abundance of water courses (Fig. 6.1). The incredible Casiquiare canal closes the water circle that includes stretches of the Atlantic Ocean and the rivers Orinoco, Negro and Amazon. Topographically the core of Guiana is centred on Mount Roraima (2810 m) from which point the altitude of the land surface falls away in a series of step-like surfaces whose identity becomes increasingly indeterminate with distance from the core (McConnell, 1968). East of the depression containing the rivers Essequibo and Courantyne, the land surface rises in a series of hilly ranges, which forms the Atlantic–Amazon watershed. The location of the core of high land in the north and west of the Guiana region has resulted in the uneven distribution of rivers and areas of broken topography. The Guianas, for example, occupy only the northern edge of the larger region, being provided with a restricted area of coastal plain in comparison with the extensive plainland periphery of the south-western edge of the Guiana region. While the Venezuelan and Brazilian territories include the long penetrating river valley systems, the Guianas are characterized by relatively short, north–south orientated water courses. Only in Guyana do two east–west links attain any significance: those of the Cuyuní and Rupununi. The precipitous progress of the majority of rivers towards the Atlantic coast is marked by well-developed series of waterfalls and rapids. The edge of the crystalline complex has long impeded riverine navigation. The coastal margin of Guiana sweeps in an arc between the mouths of the Orinoco and Amazon, broadening here and narrowing there in response to the orientation of the coast, which either hinders or assists the spread of Amazonian silt westwards. While French Guiana can boast of surf and sand beaches, in Surinam and Guyana, as in Venezuelan Guayana, marshy vegetation anchors accretionary sediment moving westwards. The rivers disgorging from the south make their way with difficulty to the sea through lagoons and across or around coastal bars. The progressive extension of the coastal plain seawards is perhaps most noticeable in Surinam where hundreds of ridges mark former shorelines (Eijk, 1954).

Climate and vegetation also differentiate the coastal margin from the interior of the Guianas. With the heat equator running parallel to the Atlantic coast as far east as 5°N. before crossing the Atlantic towards Africa, high annual average temperatures are the rule. Diurnal temperature differences exceed those between coldest and warmest months. Except on the highest slopes of the sandstone mountain core, altitude does little to reduce the heat. Rainfall and humidity are also monotonously high. The short drier season from August to November brings with it less cloudy skies and, therefore, higher temperatures. The 80 per cent humidity levels of the coast are made bearable only by the constant on-shore breezes.

The dominant vegetation type is dense rain-forest, which extends throughout all the Guianas. The southern margin of Guyana includes a wide area of dry savanna, which links with the Río Branco savannas of Brazil. The seasonally inundated grassy plains of southern Guyana are known by their aboriginal name, Rupununi (Eden, 1964).

The subtle natural contrasts contained within the Guiana region have been emphasized, but more particularly eclipsed, by the effect of European man. Whereas natural divisions are difficult to distinguish and merge

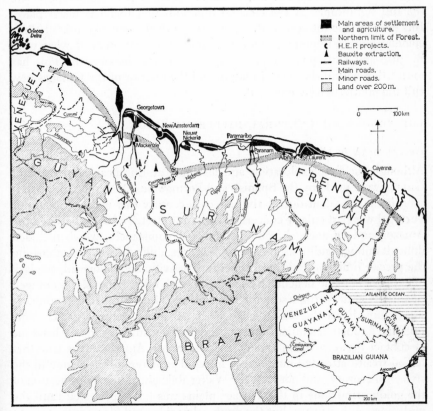

Fig. 6.1 The Guianas

imperceptibly one into another, the hand of man has increasingly heightened the pre-existing contrasts and, by occupying the land and exploiting its resources, has created new contrasts. The significance of contrast or differentiation within Guiana has a long history. While the prehistoric patterns are still being investigated, it is clear that since European man's arrival the coastal-interior division has been fundamental. The peripheral settlement nodes along the Orinoco, the Atlantic and the Amazon and its tributaries provided points of departure for inland exploration. Where

I

facts were few myths could multiply. Guiana has been, and continues to be, a land of many El Dorados (Lowenthal, 1960; Swan, 1958).

The coast of Guiana has been the focus of human activity, at least since the early seventeenth century. It was in the margin and not the interior that settlements were created and population expanded, and it was there that the primitive landscape was affected. It must be remembered, therefore, that the history of developments in the Guianas has to be compared with that of the Venezuelan and Brazilian segments if we are to appreciate the full significance of the cultural differentiation that has taken place. Indeed, the true interest in the Guianas lies in the effective role of three colonial powers impinging upon the spheres of influences of what were Spanish and Portuguese empires, as Quelle (1951) has shown. This has meant that within the coastal margin and the interior of the Guianas new cultural contrasts have emerged.

THE PROCESS OF CULTURAL DIFFERENTIATION

Developments to 1800

Although the first exploration and attempts at European settlement of Guiana were made by the Spanish and Portuguese (Ojer, 1966, p. 202), it soon became evident during the sixteenth century that neither Spain nor Portugal was particularly concerned about the stretch of coast between the Amazon and Orinoco. A combination of circumstances, which included difficult sailing conditions, inhospitable shores, difficulties over establishing the precise limits of their legal spheres of activity, and, above all, the lack of easily obtainable benefits in comparison with other regions, discouraged Spaniards and Portuguese alike from giving Guiana much attention. It was assumed that the region could be left as an unoccupied buffer zone, fulfilling a function similar to that of the Chaco wilderness in another zone of contact between Spain and Portugal in South America. It is true that fabled wealth attracted numbers of intrepid explorers to the region in the sixteenth century, and not least Sir Walter Raleigh, whose identification of the goldbearing zone in the Yuruari plains was not appreciated until the mid-nineteenth century, but the mythical peoples and places were soon to be rationalized away in terms of Indian legend or natural seasonal phenomena. Exploration had been, by the close of the sixteenth century, essentially peripheral, utilizing the major navigable waterways of the Orinoco and Amazon. The Atlantic coast had been surveyed. But for the most part few expeditions had penetrated deep inland into the Guiana region from the main rivers. From the Atlantic coast, on the other hand, it was possible to make relatively easy journeys southwards up the Essequibo, Corentyne, Suriname and Oyapock, at least to the first major fall-line that demarcated the northern edge of the highland zone.

With Spain and Portugal occupied elsewhere, it was possible for English,

Dutch and French adventurers, representatives of what were minor colonial powers in the Caribbean and Latin American context, to make the most of the possibilities in Guiana. Not unnaturally, the central portion of the Atlantic coastal margin was the prime target area; it was as far as possible from both Spanish and Portuguese enterprises, and it could be supplied and serviced if necessary by sea. From the beginning of the seventeenth century, Dutch, English and French settlers established a series of settlements at the mouths of the major rivers of the Guianas. The precise chronology and locations of the early centres of activity are extremely complicated. Different colonial powers founded settlements, were dislodged, refounded them and spread out from them in intricate stages. The principal phases and characteristics may be best understood if each of the colonial ventures is considered briefly in turn, remembering that interaction between them was one of the salient characteristics.

Early Dutch interest centred on the lower Essequibo where, after being dislodged by the Spanish from Pomeroon in 1581, a small settlement had been established by 1615. Desultory colonization, however, was replaced by purposeful planned action following the incorporation of the Dutch West India Company in 1621. The key settlement was a new fortified township called Kyk-over-al sited at the junction of the rivers Mazaruni, Cuyuní and Essequibo. During the first century of colonial activity the Dutch were as interested in trading with the Indian peoples of Guiana as in cultivating the land to produce subsistence or export crops. A wide network of trading posts was established during the remainder of the century. Trade links were established between the Atlantic coast and Indian groups living deep within what was indisputably Spanish and Portuguese territory in the middle Orinoco and Río Negro basins. Gradually, along the Essequibo and, after 1627, along the Berbice, small plantations of tobacco, cotton, coffee, cocoa and sugar were established. In 1667 a Dutch fleet took from the English the settled zone of land at the mouth of the river Suriname, and by the Treaty of Breda of the same year Surinam, as the area was known, was ceded to the Netherlands. In exchange Britain received what is now New York State (Newman, 1964, p. 18).

During the seventeenth century, a significant feature of the economic developments in the Dutch controlled areas was the introduction in increasing numbers of west African slaves. Without this supply of labour the colonies could never have developed. During the eighteenth century major modifications to the pattern of settlement and economic activities were brought about. Of singular importance was the role of a newly appointed *Commandeur* of Essequibo, Laurens Storm van Gravesande (1742–72). Gravesande was undoubtedly an able administrator; during his period of office new settlers, the majority in fact English, were attracted to free land in the Demerara region, particularly after 1746. Indeed, the process of coastal colonization, often at the expense of the up-river estates, was a fundamental feature of the eighteenth century (Swan, 1958, p. 34). After the Treaty of Utrecht (1713) the coast had become a somewhat safer place to live. There was also some evidence to suggest that the more easily settled land on higher reaches of the rivers was losing its fertility and, faced with the difficulty of clearing forestland, settlers were only too willing to benefit from company-planned drainage schemes in the coastal plain and the resourcefulness of Dutch agricultural colonists, guided by the West India Company, was to be seen in Essequibo, Demerara, Berbice and Surinam alike (Lier, 1949).

Yet the abandonment of the river lands and the cost in cash and human labour of empoldering the fertile clay soils of the coast was only made economically feasible by the increasing significance of one of the crops – sugar. A sugar plantocracy was rapidly emerging after 1750. Disease, harsh treatment and the aftermath of numerous slave rebellions may have caused the death of hundreds of thousands of black slaves; for the plantation economy the principal preoccupation was profit. Despite Dutch political control over the coastal region during the eighteenth century, the English were always a significant element amongst private estate owners. Amidst a diked and drained polder landscape were to be found estate names that reflected the cosmopolitan nature of the colonial venture: Vryheid's Lust, Better Success, La Bonne Mère, Hampton Court, Bergen op Zoom and Gage d'Amour (Lowenthal, 1960b, p. 43). Considering the extent of British involvement in the Caribbean area during the late eighteenth century, it is not surprising that Dutch control in Guiana should have been challenged. When war broke out between England and Holland in 1781, Demerara, Berbice and Essequibo were taken by the English, but some months later were occupied by the French who were then at war with England. The only significant feature of the two year period of French rule of the 'Three Rivers' was their initiation of a new town at the mouth of the Demerara, to be called Longchamps. The restoration of the colonies to the Dutch in 1783 saw their adoption of the Longchamps site as a new colonial capital – Stabroek. The troubled years that followed Dutch reoccupation in 1783 were in part the result of resentment among the planters who were only too delighted to see the end of the West India Company in 1792, when its charter expired. Neither the savage repression of rebellions nor the improvements in public utilities could stem the tide of liberal ideology, and when, in 1796, Holland and England found themselves at war, once again the colonies were taken from the Dutch. Final control of the colonies was ceded to the British in 1814, but from 1796 British control and development was of paramount importance. By the early nineteenth century, therefore, Britain had taken possession of a sugar colony on the South American mainland, which had been created by the efforts of Dutch commercial companies. Surinam, too underdeveloped to attract attention, slumbered on.

In what was to become French Guiana the history of economic development had been quite distinctive. Following the unsuccessful activities of seventeenth-century commercial companies supported by the French government, what restricted land occupation had taken place centred on the small township of Cayenne. To the south lay a scattering of small, isolated farming and gold-prospecting communities, out of the reach of authority and malarial mosquitoes alike. During the second half of the eighteenth century efforts were made to develop agriculture along Dutch lines but, for a variety of reasons, the attempts were abortive (Lowenthal, 1952). Whereas in their Caribbean islands the French were engaged in profitable sugar cultivation, in 'Cayenne', as the mainland colony was often called, the enormity of the task of empoldering the coastlands deterred all but the very brave (Papy, 1955). 'Cayenne' was a place in which to live, not work.

Nineteenth-century changes

Significant changes in the social and economic geography of the Guianas took place during the nineteenth century. Since the colonial models had differed up to that date, so the changes that occurred affected French Guiana, Surinam and British Guiana differently. The most significant single change was the abolition of slavery, a process that was to alter fundamentally the ethnic structure of populations in all three colonies, but especially in the most economically advanced, British Guiana. At the beginning of the century, the large-scale, heavily capitalized sugar estates of the coastal plain put sugar on to the world market at a time when Jamaican production was in decline. British Guiana was part of a West Indian 'frontier' of productive agriculture (Ragatz, 1928, p. 332). Yet with costly modern milling equipment being utilized, many kilometres of canals needing continual repair, and the perpetual need for hands in the cane fields, it was vital to the estate owners to be able to obtain cheap labour. Fox's Bill of 1807, forbidding British subjects to trade in slaves, threatened not only labour supplies but also the very existence of the sugar colony itself. When to labour scarcity were added the difficulties of selling sugar, following the abolition of Imperial preferences between 1846 and 1854, the situation became even worse (Newman, 1964, p. 21). Falling prices, rising wages and a shortage of capital among the planters meant the closure or consolidation of many estates. From a total of 380 coastal estates in 1800 the number fell sharply to 230 by 1829, to 180 in 1849 and to 64 in 1896. It was by means of purchasing cheap estates during the nineteenth century that Bookers, the present giant sugar enterprise in British Guiana, were able to enter the economic arena.

Besides reducing the labour force engaged in sugar cultivation, emancipation also involved a redistribution of the negroid element in the population of the colony. Instead of choosing to move deep into the interior, most

Negroes settled in the coastal zone close to Georgetown and the other large centres, on abandoned or collectively purchased estates. Without any suitable cash crop to cultivate, they remained willing to serve as part-time labourers for the estate operators. It was soon clear, however, that without a more secure and larger labour force, sugar would soon become an un-economic industry. The search began for new labour. After small numbers of West Indians, Portuguese from Madeira, Chinese and other groups had been brought into the colony, massive introductions of indentured Indian labourers characterized the population changes during the nineteenth century. Between 1846 and 1917 some 239,000 entered British Guiana in comparison with the 35,000 entering Surinam (Lier, 1949).

Such importations of new ethnic elements into the social geography of British Guiana were bound to affect pre-existing patterns. One notable feature was the migration of the Chinese and Portuguese immigrants from the agricultural lands to take up residence and employment in the urban centres. With the Negroes already in large numbers in or near the urban areas, the distribution of the later East Indians in the rural areas produced a marked differential ethnic distribution. Not only had the social pyramid been reshaped following emancipation but the geographical location of class and status groups had also been dramatically altered.

In Surinam the nineteenth century saw relatively little in the way of fundamental changes in the economy of the colony. Since the previous hundred years had seen little agricultural development, except in the lower reaches of the Suriname, Commewijne and Cottica rivers, where defence was possible against attacks from Negroes who had escaped into the interior, the disruption of agriculture following the abolition of slavery in 1863 was not as great as that felt elsewhere in the Guianas. Paramaribo certainly expanded rapidly with the migration of freed Negroes from the plantations (Kool, 1956), and the indentured Hindustani labourers did add a new constituent to the social fabric of the colony (Oudschans Dentz, 1943). Surinam continued to consist of relatively small isolated clusters of agricultural communities each dependent on confined polder schemes, with a marked tendency towards separatism.

In French Guiana the only significant innovation was the establishment of the penal colony in 1852, an attempt to alleviate the shortage of labour created by the abolition of slavery in 1848. The aim was simple enough: convicts would work towards their freedom on the plantations (Gritzner, 1964). But yellow fever, malaria and the misappropriation of funds jeopardized the scheme. The notoriety of conditions in the camp at St Laurent (popularly, but misleadingly, called Devil's Island) was to tarnish the image of French Guiana for more than a century (Lowenthal, 1960a, p. 530).

During the whole of the nineteenth century little change affected the interior of any of the Guianas. Though numerous scientific expeditions penetrated deep into the upland zone, the only significant economic events were the numerous small-scale gold strikes in French and British Guiana after 1840. Of more than local importance was the gold 'boom' in the Yuruari basin in Venezuelan Guayana, which attracted large numbers of prospectors from the Guiana coastal region (Robinson, 1967, pp. 572–630). For the remainder of the century, the interior regions of the Guianas were little more than pleasurable retreats for collecting plants, hunting animals and observing Amerindian cultures.

PROBLEMS OF THE TWENTIETH CENTURY

As a result of their colonial status, the Guianas have each continued to develop separate identities during the present century. While all three areas, even independent Guyana, still demonstrate the characteristic features of an externally orientated economy, coastal 'peripheral' population distributions in terms of their territories, metropolitan linkages in financial, administrative and other aspects of political control, each of the Guianas has continued to increase the contrasts between it and its neighbours. The precise differentiation of economic and social changes is best presented by brief views of their individual progress during the present century.

French Guiana

With an area one third the size of France and a population in the mid-1960s of less than 40,000, French Guiana may be considered somewhat under-developed though the region has great development potential. However, for a variety of reasons, few attempts have been made, and few appear likely to be made, to modify the present condition of one of France's more peripheral *départements*, at least in the near future. Having acquired the status of a *département* in 1946, and having enjoyed billions of francs annually poured in by the metropolitan exchequer to provide the luxuries of public health services, free care of mothers, infants and the elderly, free education and other social services, French Guiana's residents may well view with scepticism the desire for massive development projects, whether based on agriculture or on mineral exploitation. The suggestion of massive immigration into the territory, bringing with it problems of cultural assimilation, invites the comment that to date French Guiana has avoided the conflict that has characterized other nearby political units; better, perhaps to be happily undeveloped than suffer the inevitable pains of economic and social 'progress'. So long as France continues to subsidize its piece of Guiana, that may be a justifiable argument. Certainly very little development has taken place in the area in the last twenty years. The distribution of population, 50 per cent of the total living in Cayenne and its environs, and only some 10 per cent living in the interior, reflects the unchanging nature and location of activities since the early nineteenth century (Hauger, 1957). In 1965 a start was made on the construction of a space station at Kourou, allegedly sited to make full use of the equatorial rotation boost in proposed rocket launches, but before the $100 million spent on clearing the site could be saved, the European Launcher Development programme collapsed (*Economist*, 22 August 1970). Recent attempts to diversify the economic base of French Guiana have included rice cultivation schemes and livestock-ranching on the southern savannas. For the most part, however, the area remains *terra incognita* as far as resource development is concerned. Numerous surveys have demonstrated the existence of minerals, timber stands and fertile soils. What is quite clear is the fact that since past activities have generated such low, almost non-existent, levels of infrastructural capital investments, any developments in the future will be all the more expensive.

Surinam

As an autonomous member of the Kingdom of the Netherlands and an associate member of the European Economic Community, Surinam is in a good position to receive funds for development projects and, indeed, since the 1920s Surinam has had a relatively large number of schemes implemented. Initially, agricultural colonization and rationalization of land-holdings were the foci of interest (Verkade-Cartier, 1937), and recently plans have been prepared for an extension of arable cultivation, using modern techniques of cultivation and processing (Wit, 1960). What is clear from the studies of planners is the need not only to develop the transport network, but also to find the optimal diversification programme for the economy (Stichting Planbureau, 1963; IBRD, 1952). With family farms producing rice, sugar cane and bananas, there can be little hope of economic progress, and thus since 1954 a central aim of the government has been the initiation of a process of slow but steady industrialization. Several hydro-electric schemes have been completed, notably at Broko-pondo and Afobaka on the Suriname river. In 1965 an aluminium smelter was opened at Paranam, some 80 km south of Paramaribo (Geijkes, Leentvar and van Donselaar, 1965; Sanderson, 1969, p. 22). At least two companies are at present exploiting bauxite deposits, and extensive studies have been made of the timber resources of the south. Far more than in French Guiana, Surinam has witnessed the spread of economic activity along the coastal plain and more recently southwards. Yet for a country five times the size of Holland its population of some 350,000 is still very small (Hawath, 1956).

The population of Surinam is far more divided ethnically than that of French Guiana. The occupational and locational differentiation of individual ethnic groups is also quite distinct from that of Guyana. Such differences reflect the particular historical process in Surinam since the abolition of slavery. Hindustani immigrants (i.e. from India as opposed to the East Indies) arrived relatively late in the nineteenth century and they, together with Javanese from Indonesia, have found acculturation a slow and difficult process. Political parties find their support in particular ethnic communities, which, together with the racially homogeneous village groupings, has tended to promote cultural contrasts. It is to be hoped that contrasts do not lead to conflict as happened in Guyana; one ominous sign is the differential population increase between Creoles and Hindustanis. As a colony in all but name, Surinam's main difficulty in the future will be to find markets capable of absorbing her potential industrial output. Economies of scale dictate limits to many potential plans, but then, at least, Surinam rid itself of the shadow of sugar in good time to be able now to consider further sectoral shifts in the economy.

Guyana (British Guiana)

The economic history of British Guiana, as the Republic of Guyana was called before May 1966, provides a perfect target for those who wish to denigrate the activities of European capitalist entrepreneurs. As has already been seen, the colonial period produced a sugar monoculture, which was export orientated, controlled by a plantocracy, and served by an enslaved labour force. The profitability of the plantation system before the abolition of slavery and the fall in cane sugar prices, brought about by the rapid expansion of beet in the last quarter of the nineteenth century, meant that imports of all the necessary manufactured products could be afforded. There was no foreseeable motive for agricultural diversification. Given the physical conditions of the coastal plain, it was argued that only large-scale, heavily capitalized operators could make sugar pay. Gradually sugar came to dominate the entire economic productivity of the colony – that is to say, productivity measured in terms of return on capital investment, or purchasing power, rather than in terms of workers' satisfaction with their standard of living. By a series of preferential tariffs and latterly a Commonwealth Sugar Agreement (1951), the price of, and demand for, the product on the world market has been regulated to ensure disposal of the major portion of the Guyana crop. Since only two companies now control the entire sugar industry in Guyana, further fuel is added to the Marxist fire.

Several studies have suggested that, even with the most sophisticated techniques of cultivation and processing, sugar may have already reached its optimal level of production, and the future can hold out little hope for further expansion (Kundu, 1963, p. 373). Since, however, few analytical studies of the changing economic organization of the industry have yet been carried out (an exception is Auty, 1968) such a forecast may be somewhat suspect. What appears clear from all governmental and other analyses is the desire in social, political and economic terms to reduce the relative role of sugar in the economy, not by cutting back on sugar production but by stimulating the growth of other industries (IBRD, 1953, p. 23; British Guiana, 1965).

One of the earliest moves to diversify agriculture came in the 1940s, with schemes to expand the area devoted to rice production. More than nine major schemes have been successfully completed; between 1955 and 1965 rice cultivation increased from 68,000 to 108,000 ha (Singh, 1967, p. 73). Since Guyana consumes only one third of its rice production, a valuable commodity has been made available for export, but competition is fierce. As well as increasing the acreage of rice, active developments are taking place to extend the planting of coconuts, the country's third most important crop, and to improve both stock and pastures available for livestock-ranching in the Rupununi savanna region. Although many natural deficiencies have to be accepted, the spread of *pangola* grass and the eradication of foot-and-mouth disease should produce welcome advances (Hills, 1961).

Since George B. MacKenzie acquired bauxite-bearing land on the Demerara river in 1914, that mineral has provided a major proportion of the total value of exports of the territory. Guyana is now the world's fourth largest producer (after the U.S.S.R., Jamaica and Surinam). Although, since 1961, an alumina plant has been operating in Guyana, these mineral-based capital-intensive enterprises provide few jobs for an unemployment pool that in 1964 had reached the high level of 18 per cent of the total labour force (Newman, 1964, p. 63). Prospecting has revealed copper deposits at Aranka on the Cuyuní, the possibility of rare minerals in several localities in the interior, and off-shore oil resources.

In spite of the apparent ease with which the economy of Guyana may be, and has been, diversified, it should be noted that long, and at times acrimonious, debates continue over the best means of producing economic growth with fuller employment in the shortest possible time. In Guyana the contending schools of opinion have supported an industrialization programme and an agricultural programme. Equally important as the facts of development are the needs for it, the constraints placed on the varied proposals, and the results of any development. British Guiana had witnessed no more rapid change in its constitutional developments before the 1920s than it had in its stagnating economy. When, therefore, universal suffrage was extended to voters in the 1953 election, a new radical group of voices was heard. The new party was the People's Progressive Party (PPP), its leaders Cheddi Jagan and Forbes Burnham. Progress towards independence, highlighted as it was by riots, repressive Whitehall measures and the spread of racial tension and nationalistic fervour, certainly accelerated after 1953. Details of the complicated manœuvres have been admirably set out by Smith (1962). The result of all these political problems has been the increasing significance of ethnic groups as elements to be considered in planning policies. The rural rice development project may thus be con-

THE GUIANAS 259

sidered a pro-Indian measure, while support for developments centred on expatriate enterprises such as sugar or mining, may be considered neo-colonialist. What may be noted is the slow progress in British Guiana, in comparison with Surinam, in developing such resources as hydro-electricity. Yet, again, it is all too easy to recognize the fact that any major project will need financing either by very large companies, which might become dominant forces internally, or by foreign governments, which, in turn, raises problems of nationalism and sovereignty. Little support is likely to be forthcoming from international agencies for a country only the size of Britain, with a labour force of a mere 220,000, a gross national product of not more than £50 million and acute political problems. Independent Guyana can now no longer turn automatically to Britain for assistance. Problems, like unexploited resources, appear to abound. Yet, within a wider South American context, the Guyanese may find solace in the relative status of some of their Latin neighbours who achieved their political independence a century and a half ago.

THE GUIANAS IN PERSPECTIVE

An almost inevitable suggestion to solve the common problems of the three political units considered above is some form of economic or political union. But geographical proximity has to be set against historical ties. It is evident that, generally speaking, the Guianas display similar features: empty, exotic interiors (Hanif and Poonai, 1968); fascinating Amerindian cultural relics (Hurault, 1963); rapidly expanding population; overgrown urban concentrations peripherally located with respect to their potential hinterlands. Yet many of these similarities disappear if a stronger lens is placed before the eye. Differences in attitudes and ideals may be discerned, and contrasts in landscapes, dress, language, diet and religious belief can be identified. The old Amerindian regional term no longer serves a useful purpose: the 'land of many waters' has given way to a land of many peoples.

REFERENCES AND SELECT BIBLIOGRAPHY

AUTY, R. M. (1968) *The Demerara Sugar Industry, 1930–1965: A Geographical Study of Rural Change.* Unpub. M.A. Thesis, University of Toronto.

BRITISH GUIANA-GUYANA (1965) *Development Plan, 1966–1972.* Georgetown.

CUMMINGS, L. P. (1964) The name Guiana: its origins and meaning. *Journal of British Guiana Museum*, 38, 51–3.

CUMMINGS, L. P. (1969) *Geography of Guyana.* London.

DEVÈZE, M. (1968) *Les Guyanes.* Paris.

EDEN, M. J. (1964) *The Savanna Ecosystem – North Rupununi, British Guiana*. Montreal.

EIJK, J. J. VAN (1954) *De landschappen van noord Suriname*. Paramaribo.

GEIJKES, D. C., LEENTVAR, P. and VAN DONSELAAR, J. (1965) *Biological Brokopondo Research Project, Surinam. Progress Reports*. Utrecht.

GRITZNER, C. F. (1964) French Guiana penal colony: its role in colonial development. *Journal of Geography*, 63, 314–19.

HANIF, M. and POONAI, N. O. (1968) *Wildlife and Conservation in Guyana*. Gainsville.

HAUGER, J. (1957) La population de la Guyane française. *Annales de Géographie*, 66, 509–18.

HAWATH, J. J. (1956) The economic-geographical structure of Surinam. *Tijdschrift voor Economische en Sociale Geografie*, 47, 165–6.

HURAULT, J. (1963) *Les Indiens de Guyane française*. The Hague.

HILLS, T. (1961) The interior of British Guiana and the myth of El Dorado. *Canadian Geographer*, 2, 30–43.

IBRD (International Bank for Reconstruction and Development) (1952) *Surinam: Recommendations for a Ten Year Development Plan*. Baltimore.

IBRD (1953) *The Economic Development of British Guiana*. Baltimore.

KOOL, R. (1956) Paramaribo: het economische leven van een stad in tropische land. *Tijdschrift voor Economische en Sociale Geografie*, 47, 276–88.

KRUIJER, G. J. (1960) *Suriname: en zijn buurlanden*. Meppel.

KUNDU, A. (1963) The economy of British Guiana, 1960–1972. *Social and Economic Studies*, 12, 307–80.

LIER, R. A. J. VAN (1949) *Samenleving in een grensgebied: een sociaal-historische studie van de maatschappij in Suriname*. The Hague.

LOWENTHAL, D. (1950) *An Historical Geography of the Guianas*. Unpub. M.A. Thesis, University of California.

LOWENTHAL, D. (1952) Colonial experiments in French Guiana, 1760–1800. *Hispanic American Historical Review*, 32, 22–43.

LOWENTHAL, D. (1960a) French Guiana: myths and realities. *Transactions of the New York Academy of Sciences*, 523–40.

LOWENTHAL, D. (1960b) Population contrasts in the Guianas. *Geographical Review*, 50, 41–58.

MCCONNELL, R. B. (1968) Planation surfaces in Guyana. *Geographical Journal*, 134, 506–20.

NEWMAN, P. (1964) *British Guiana: Problems of Cohesion in an Immigrant Society*. London.

OJER, P. (1966) *La formación del Oriente Venezolano*. Caracas.

OUDSCHANS DENTZ, F. (1943) *De Kolonisatie van Guyana*. The Hague.

PAPY, L. (1955) La Guyane française. *Cahiers d'Outre Mer*, 8, 209–32.

QUELLE, O. (1951) Die Bevölkerungsentwicklung von Europäisch-Guyana: eine antropogeographische Untersuchung. *Die Erde*, 3, 366–78.

RAGATZ, L. J. (1928) *The Fall of the Planter Class in the British Caribbean, 1763–1833*. London.

ROBINSON, D. J. (1967) *Geographical Change in Venezuelan Guayana, 1600–1880*. Unpub. Ph.D. Thesis, London.

SANDERSON, I. T. (1969) *Surinam*. New York.

SINGH, J. L. R. (1967) *A Geographical Study of Rice in Guyana*. Unpub. M.Sc. Essay, London.

SMITH, R. T. (1962) *British Guiana*. London.

SWAN, M. (1957) *British Guiana: the Land of Six Peoples*. London.

SWAN, M. (1958) *The Marches of El Dorado*. London.

STICHTING PLANBUREAU (1963) *Integraal opbouwplan Suriname, 1963–1972*. Paramaribo.

VERKADE-CARTIER VAN DISSEL, E. F. (1937) *De mogelijkheid van landbouwkolonisatie voor blanken in Suriname*. Amsterdam.

WIT, T. P. DE (1960) *The Wageningen Rice Project in Surinam*. The Hague.

7 The Central Andes

Clifford T. Smith

In common with other Latin American countries, Ecuador, Bolivia and Peru share an overwhelming concern with the problems of poverty and underdevelopment. The central Andes as a whole is the poorest major region of South America, at least in terms of average income per head. National averages are low, but they conceal great regional differences within each of the countries concerned. As in other Latin American countries, the sharpest gradients in living standards are those between certain sectors of the major cities, but nowhere else, perhaps, is there so brutal a contrast between one region and another. In Ecuador the commercially orientated and expanding agriculture of the coast can be set against the poverty and subsistence farming of the sierra and the emptiness of the *oriente*; in Peru the contrast between the coast and the sierra in terms of urbanization, living standards and productivity is even more emphatic; and even in Bolivia the grinding poverty of the *altiplano* has to be measured against the modest prosperity of the *valles* and the opportunities of the *oriente*.

Harsh and abrupt contrasts in regional income and economic development are, in part, related to the existence of large Indian populations in the intermontane basins of the Andes. The problem of integrating the Indian into the economic, social and political life of the nation has been a recurrent theme in the history of all three Andean countries, and nowhere can it yet be said that these problems have been resolved. The presence of so large and compact a block of Indian population is a distinctive characteristic of the central Andean countries. As in other parts of Latin America agrarian reform is at present a dominant issue, but the problems posed by the maldistribution of ownership, anti-social land tenures and the need to raise agricultural productivity are rendered more acute by the harsh difficulties of the Andean environment and the Indian problem.

Finally, all three of the central Andean countries contain within their boundaries some share of the undeveloped interior lowlands of South America and, for Peru and Bolivia at least, the colonization and settlement of new land in the east has become an important issue since 1950, all the

The editors and publishers wish to thank *Geography* for their kind permission to reproduce Figs. 7.5, 7.7, 7.8, 7.9, 7.10 and 7.11, which were originally published in 'Problems of regional development in Peru' by Clifford T. Smith, *Geography*, 53, July 1968, 260–81.

more so since the opening up of new land seems to present opportunities for relieving local overcrowding in the sierra while diverting attention from pressures aimed at the breaking up of the *latifundios*. But within each country the role of the eastern lowlands is quite different: Ecuador has a similar but more accessible environment in its coastal zone; for Bolivia, with no Pacific coast, the east is the only part of the national territory that can produce tropical foods and raw materials; and in Peru the role of the *selva* is more complex and more controversial.

ENVIRONMENTAL CONTRASTS

The coast

The coastal zones of Peru and Ecuador are the most important economic regions of their respective countries, by reason of their accessibility as much as by their inherent resources. Yet coastal Peru is one of the most arid regions in the world. Lima, for example, has an average annual rainfall of only 41 mm, much of it falling as light drizzle (*garúa*) during the winter months when low stratus cloud and fog normally envelop much of the coastal region. Aridity is the product of circumstances similar to those found in other tropical west coast countries, such as south-west Africa, southern California or Western Australia, and is closely associated with the existence of cold water off shore and location with respect to tropical high pressure cells. Off Peru, two cold currents are distinguished: the outer or oceanic current, varying in temperature from 14° to 18°C from northern Chile to northern Peru; and the inner or Peruvian coastal current, which is colder, moves north or north-west at a faster rate, and is a product of the upwelling of deep, cold bottom-water to the surface. Subsiding air from the south Pacific high pressure cell, already cool and stable, is further cooled as it passes across cold coastal waters, producing a deep inversion layer of cool and humid air that laps up against the barrier of the Andes. Temperatures in the coastal region are anomalously low for the latitude (Lima at 12°S. has a mean annual temperature of 19°C compared with 25°C at Bahia, 13°S.); relative humidities are high (averaging 87 per cent at Lima) and, during the southern winter, overcast skies are common in the coastal region, though there are important regional variations, winter cloudiness decreasing away from the coast itself and northwards towards the Equator. During the southern summer insolation is sufficient to disperse clouds in shore and weather is warmer, though still humid. But even during the summer, convectional development over warm land is inhibited by the permanence of the temperature inversion, thus preventing heavy rainfall in all but those most exceptional years when cold upwellings off shore are weak, warmer water off shore permits the development of unstable air, convectional rainfall occurs and disaster comes to the coastal region, adjusted as it is to arid conditions.

One other aspect of the coastal ecology has been of fundamental importance to Peru in historical and modern times. Cold, upwelling bottom-water is rich in mineral nutrients and supports a dense population of plankton, which in turn supports a fish population of enormous quantity and variety. Under the off-shore cloud blanket, diatoms thrive better nearer the surface than under sunlight so that there is an abundant food supply for pelagic species of fish, which in turn support abundant bird life: cormorants, guanay, pelicans, gannets and many other species follow the shoals of fish, but the most important from the point of view of Peru's development have been the species that nest in great communities reaching densities of 130,000/ha on the twenty or more off-shore islands and the isolated peninsulas of the coast. Vast thicknesses of bird droppings, rich in nitrogen (14 to 17 per cent) and phosphates (c. 11 per cent), have accumulated to form workable deposits of guano, highly valued from early times as a fertilizer. Just as the fishing industry has been a major activity and source of external revenue in recent years, so the guano deposits were the resource that drew Peru into the mainstream of international commerce in the nineteenth century.

The possibilities of the Peruvian coast for agriculture clearly depend on irrigation and therefore on available water supply in relation to the extent of suitable soils and gently sloping terrain. The supply of land suitable for irrigation varies in each of three morphological regions. In north-western Peru relief is low and tabular with much faulting; much of the area is covered by sands of recent origin; and fairly level land suitable for irrigation exists if water can be brought to it. In the central coast as far south as Ica the sierra penetrates to the coast in many places. Valleys are separated by the lower spurs of the Andes, which often end in a magnificent cliffed coast. Narrow, steep-sided Andean valleys debouch in a series of alluvial aprons containing thick infill brought down during fluvial/glacial episodes in the high Andes. Modern streams are slightly incised into this infill, and in some areas alluvial aprons coalesce to form more or less continuous gently sloping land near the coast. But in general potentially irrigable land is limited. Surplus water from one valley can sometimes be transported by canal to a neighbouring area of deficiency, as, for example, the water from the Pativilca river is carried over to the Fortaleza valley. In southern Peru the character of the coastal region changes. A coastal range of igneous rocks is exposed in the Ica region and continues southwards into Chile. The trough between the coastal massif and the main Andean range is filled with sediments and volcanic rocks. Streams break through the coastal massif in narrow gorges, but upstream have incised themselves deeply into the softer rocks, carving flat-floored and irrigable valleys. In the south, then, irrigable land is scarce, and in contrast to the northern and central regions it is also, for the most part, remote from the coast itself and was fairly inaccessible until the building of the Pan American Highway in 1940.

Water supply is the other major limiting factor in coastal agriculture and is governed by the regime of Pacific-flowing drainage deriving from the high Andes. In central and northern Peru the high sierra above 3000 m is moderately well watered, but rainfall decreases southwards and the western flanks of the Andean ranges are increasingly arid. Arequipa, for example, receives only 115 mm of rain annually. Precipitation is also seasonal, with a wet season from October to March and a marked dry season in June, July and August. River regimes faithfully reflect this pattern, and streams fed solely by rainfall frequently dry up completely during the southern winter. In general it is only the streams nourished by snow-melt, glacier ice or natural lakes that have a substantial winter flow. Of these the Rimac and the Santa rivers are the most important, the latter the only river to break through the western cordillera to drain an important interior basin.

In the neighbourhood of the boundary between Peru and Ecuador the coastal zone changes with striking abruptness from the aridity of northern Peru to the hot, wet equatorial climate characteristic of much of coastal Ecuador. The cold Peruvian current turns westwards and the coastal waters off Ecuador are relatively warm. The south-western part of Ecuador receives a seasonal rainfall from January to April of about 200 mm and average temperatures are higher than in coastal Peru. But towards the Andes and the north rainfall increases to 1700 mm a year and the rainy season extends from January to June. Temperatures are generally higher, and at Guayaquil, for example, mean temperatures range from 24°C and 27°C between the coldest and warmest month.

The Andes

The scale, majesty and complexity of the Andean ranges, overwhelming when seen from the air, are no more than dimly suggested by the contours of an atlas map. Some 120 km wide in Ecuador, the Andean region spreads out southwards to a zone some 800 km across in Bolivia; its highest peaks, rising to over 6000 m, have fired the imagination of travellers and have attracted mountaineers since the time of Whymper's exploits in the volcanic peaks of Ecuador in the nineteenth century.

The Andean countries are built around the axis of the great Cretaceous batholith of acidic igneous rocks, which forms a large part of the western cordillera of Ecuador, Peru and Bolivia, though it is frequently obscured in southern Peru, western Bolivia and in Ecuador by overlying sedimentary and volcanic rocks. To the east of the Cretaceous batholith, sedimentary rocks ranging in age from Palaeozoic upwards have been folded, faulted and metamorphosed, and culminate in the high ranges that form the eastern cordillera of Ecuador and the central and eastern cordilleras of Peru and Bolivia. In general the more recent rocks form the most easterly of the folded and faulted ranges that subside into the sediments of the Amazon basin, themselves largely composed of the debris produced by the weathering and erosion of the uplifted Andes.

Structural troughs and basins of tectonic origin reach their maximum extent in the central plateau of Bolivia, are continued into southern Peru in the basin of Lake Titicaca, and represented further north by the central trough of Ecuador. Similar but smaller and less continuous troughs form zones at less than 3500 m in other parts of Peru and these are of the greatest importance for settlement and agriculture. Most of these tectonic basins, and especially the *altiplano* of Bolivia and southern Peru, are partially filled with relatively undisturbed sediments, lavas and volcanic ash of fairly recent origin; some have formerly supported lakes, which are now represented by areas of lacustrine sediments. The *altiplano* of southern Peru and Bolivia is still, indeed, a region of internal drainage to the basin of Lake Titicaca, Lake Poopo and the saline flats of south-western Bolivia. Varied in size, accessibility and the quality of their soils, the tectonic basins are the agricultural oases of the Andean regions in all but the most arid and saline plains of the south-west, for there are few other zones, except for the steeply sloping sides and narrow floors of deeply incised river gorges, that fall below the altitudinal limits for productive arable farming.

The landscapes of the Andes consist only in part of the high, glaciated massifs rising to over 5000 m or the tectonic basins and troughs. There are, too, spectacular volcanic features such as the impressive cones that flank the central trough of Ecuador, including the famous peaks of Cotopaxi and Chimborazo, or the volcanoes of southern Peru and western Bolivia, and volcanic landscapes also extend over much wider areas in the form of lava-capped plateaux and thick deposits of highly erodible volcanic ash and tuff.

Over much of central and southern Peru and in parts of Bolivia there are, however, large areas of rolling relief and occasionally monotonous high plains at approximately 4200–4400 m. In Bolivia and Peru this has been named the *puna* surface after the predominant vegetation of high altitude tundra, and is probably an erosion surface of sub-aerial origin formed near sea-level before the major uplift of the Andes to their present position. In southern Peru it is flexed downwards towards the coast, declining to *c.* 1000 m; in northern Peru it can be traced at an altitude of about 3600 m, but is much more strongly dissected than further south. But whatever the origin of the *puna* surface, it is certainly one of the great misfortunes of Peru and Bolivia that its altitude is too high for cultivation and too high even for the grazing of sheep on a large scale. The barren, tundra-like pastures of the *puna* are useful only for the grazing of llama and alpaca.

Terrace features and erosion surfaces of more limited extent have been traced at lower levels in Bolivia and Peru, perhaps marking phases in the irregular uplift of the Andes, and these are of local importance in providing moderately level surfaces for arable cultivation, e.g. in the basins of eastern Bolivia. The other major features of Andean landscapes are the river gorges dug deeply into the Andean surfaces, particularly in the eastern and central parts of the area where precipitation and therefore headward erosion from the Amazon basin have been much greater than in the more arid west and south-west. They sometimes offer narrow strips of potentially cultivable land, but more often they present difficult barriers to communication, especially from east to west across the region, for the major drainage trends are parallel with the major strike of Andean faulting and folding. Pacific-flowing rivers rarely penetrate beyond the crest-line of the western cordillera, partly because of the continuity and relative resistance to erosion of the predominantly igneous rocks, but also because of the relative aridity of the western cordillera. The watershed between Pacific- and Atlantic-flowing streams lies as near as 150 km to the Pacific coast in some places, and except in northern Peru presents a continuously high barrier to communications.

Yet in a number of ways communications have been easier and less costly between the coast and the high Andes than between the Andes and the eastern plains: the absence or sparsity of vegetation on the Pacific slopes has facilitated easier movement by men on foot, by llama herds or by mule traffic, whereas dense vegetation to the east has always presented a difficult barrier to movement. The short Pacific-flowing streams cut a direct passage from highland to coast, but, in the lower eastern Andes, the intricate dissection of softer rocks under hot and humid conditions makes for steep slopes and circuitous routes of access, quite apart from higher costs of clearing, construction and maintenance.

It is as difficult to generalize about the climates and vegetation of the Andes as it is about the landforms and terrain. Differences over small distances often overshadow the general tendencies. In Ecuador there is a drier season between June and September and a maximum from November to May. There is a general tendency for precipitation to decrease southwards: Quito has a rainfall of 1000 mm, Cuenca 925 mm and Loja 768 mm. This tendency is continued in Peru where wet and dry seasons are more strongly accentuated, and the wet season lasts from October to March. Isohyets are roughly parallel with the coast in central and northern Peru, swinging inland in southern Peru and across Bolivia in a generally north-west to south-east direction. South-west Bolivia is truly arid country. But even in central and northern Peru deep Andean valleys are often surprisingly arid, and precipitation is highly variable from year to year in most of the highland basins to the south of Ecuador. Drought is one of the major agricultural hazards. But in the eastern zone of the Andes there is very often a sharp transition from a landscape of semi-arid aspect with worn pastures and xerophytic vegetation to luxurious jungle. In Peru this is the *ceja de la montaña* (the brow of the mountain) a zone of 'cloud-forest', in which precipitation increases sharply and a dense growth of small trees, epiphytes, ferns and grasses may appear up to 3300 m, giving way eastwards to true tropical forest at lower altitudes. In Bolivia it is represented by the sharp transition to the *yungas*, as for example to the north-east of La Paz.

In terms of farming and land use, the effect of altitude on temperature regime is of major importance throughout the region. Mean annual temperatures show the effect of altitude directly and mean annual range of temperature tends simply to reflect latitude, with very low ranges of 1° or 2°C near the equator, increasing southwards to 4·4°C at La Paz. But what is much more important is the diurnal range of temperature. At Huancayo, in central Peru at 3300 m, the diurnal range may be as much as 13°C in the wet season, rising to 19°C in the dry season. Night frosts are regular from May to August and may occur in any month except at the height of the wet season in January to March. Further south in Peru and on the Bolivian *altiplano* the frequency of night frosts is even higher. High diurnal ranges limit the period during which temperatures are above the minimum required for plant growth. The growing season needed by plants, measured in terms of days, is longer than at lower altitudes, and the growing season available is limited by the occurrence of night frosts. The short growing season needed by barley, for example, is a major reason why it is suitable for cultivation at high altitudes. Barley, potatoes and indigenous root crops and grains such as *cañahua* and *quinoa* will thrive up to 4000 m and potatoes even above this; the effective limit for wheat is usually about 3500 m and for maize 300 m lower. In addition to drought, frost at unexpected times is a major hazard to farming, particularly in November and December during the growing season; hail is the third major hazard.

In the Peruvian Andes, grasslands of varied composition are the major form of vegetation and woodland is rare except for the survival of *quinual* in sheltered places up to 4500 m and the occurrence of planted eucalyptus, usually below 3600 m. At high altitudes there is a transition to tundra conditions with mosses, lichens and grasses of poor nutritive value, among which tussocky grasses such as the *ichu* are dominant. In the drier regions of the south the low, tough, xerophytic *tola* shrub is widespread. In Ecuador the high level grasslands are more humid and support a richer flora, including many cacti, and are described usually as the *páramos*.

The eastern regions

Although there is sometimes a sharp and definitive transition from the Andean front to the plains of the Amazon basin, the outer ripples of the Andean storm have left traces in the form of low ranges well to the east of the main Andean front. The plains themselves are by no means uniformly level. In Peru a distinction is made between the *selva alta* and the *selva baja*. The *selva alta* (400–1000 m) has a substantial range of relief and there are

broad open valleys with good agricultural possibilities on relatively im-
mature soils. Below 400 m the *selva baja* consists for the most part of three
terrace-like regions: a marginal zone of well-dissected terrain; the high
terraces, in general some 60 m above the lower terraces, slightly dissected,
and frequently capped by leached, mature and agriculturally poor soils;
and, thirdly, the low terraces (*restingas*), fairly level and undissected, but
with considerable micro-relief reflecting the course of former meander
scars, and in part liable to flood (Pulgar Vidal, n.d.).

Climate and vegetation show significant variations through the region.
In eastern Ecuador rainfall is high and well distributed through the year;
further south totals are greatest near the eastern flanks of the Andes,
reaching as much as 4000 mm, but there is a rainfall maximum from
November to May and a minimum from June to October. The tendency to
a wet-and-dry regime is accentuated southwards into south-eastern Bolivia,
where total amounts are less, and there is a transition towards the extreme
seasonal variations of the Gran Chaco. Forest is the natural vegetation of
most of the area, with a broad variation from scrub and thorny woodland
south of Santa Cruz to semi-deciduous forest and palm savanna to the true
rain-forests of north-east Bolivia, eastern Peru and Ecuador. But even
within the rain-forest areas there are often fairly large spreads of savanna
grasslands and even thorn scrub, which are only now becoming fully
known as a consequence of systematic aerial photography of these empty
regions.

HISTORICAL ANTECEDENTS

The physical environments of the central Andean countries are highly
contrasted and in many ways difficult for human occupation, apparently
destined to consist of very many nuclei of population widely separated
by distance and by barriers of high relief, desert wastes or thick forests.
Yet political and cultural unity has been repeatedly imposed over large
parts of the region, not least in pre-Columbian times during the Inca
empire and also during the earlier Tiahuanaco period (*c.* A.D. 900–1100)
and. even before this, if only in a cultural sense, during the Chavín period
(*c.* 1000–500 B.C.) The continuing strength and vigour of the Indian population owes a great deal not only to the isolation of scattered communities,
but also to the legacy of high Indian cultures and the sheer weight of
their numbers in comparison with those of their Spanish conquerors. More
than anywhere else in Latin America the social and economic problems
of integrating the Indian population into national life have proved difficult and intractable. Some have thought to restore the dignity of the
Indian by an appeal to the great traditions of the Indian past, and have
considered the Incaic tradition as an important'element of distinctive
nationality; *indigenismo* is a common theme in the literature of the central

Andean countries. But the dominant theme has, of course, been the hispanicization of Indian groups – by the 'formal' processes of conquest, conversion to Christianity, and education, or by 'informal' processes such as racial mixture, conscription, migration to the cities and the penetration of commercialization to remoter regions.

The Indian heritage

When the Spaniards arrived in Peru they found an empire that extended from northern Ecuador through the central Andes into north-west Argentina and central Chile. Coastal and Andean cultures alike had been welded into a highly centralized and despotic empire administered from Cuzco, the capital city and cradle of the Incas. The administration may have been less uniform than was once thought and regional variations considerable, but a remarkable unity had been created in less than a hundred years. An excellent system of communications by road was as important to the Incas as it had been to the Romans in western Europe as an instrument for administrative and military efficiency. Roads were carefully engineered, often with surfaces of stone and rubble, sometimes tunnelled into precipitous slopes or paved and stepped to facilitate the rapid movement on foot of messengers and armies, since there was no knowledge of the wheel. Suspension bridges crossed rivers and deep gorges, and pontoon bridges were supported by bundles of reeds over broader, shallower rivers such as the Desaguadero at the foot of Lake Titicaca. On the coast Inca roads replaced or supplemented previous systems, and often consisted of walled highways in irrigated areas and of cleared tracks marked with stones in the open desert.

Other mechanisms had helped to create a unity of the Inca empire, notably the system of massive forced labour migration by which young men of 17 to 30 were liable for military and labour service in any part of the empire; whole populations were resettled or exchanged to ensure the subjugation of recently conquered or potentially rebellious territory. If possible such movements were organized between areas of similar climates and agricultural possibilities: peoples from Ecuador were moved into the Cajamarca region and there was some settlement in the Quito area by people from the Titicaca basin; loyal subjects from central Peru were moved to southern Bolivia. The means by which a fairly homogeneous empire was created and by which Quechua was spread to regions as far apart as north-western Argentina and Ecuador were often ruthless, but they were effective enough to create among the Spaniards the impression of a monolithic structure, and to make it possible for Spanish rule to replace that of the Incas with remarkable rapidity.

The Inca empire was, however, but the culminating phase of a long cultural development in the central Andes in which intensive use had been made of potential resources on the coast and in the sierra. It is an area of major world importance as a hearth of domesticated plants and animals, though some cultivated plants were undoubtedly introduced from Central America and there is still room for doubt as to the precise location of domestication of others. Squash and beans, with chili peppers, cotton and various indigenous fruits, were the basis of the earliest agriculture in the coastal region. The introduction of maize, probably from Central America *c.* 1400 B.C., ushered in a great expansion of cultivation and was also associated with the cultivation of other new crops such as peanuts, avocado pears and, later, manioc or *yuca*. In the highland regions *quinoa* and *cañahua*, grain crops still of considerable importance in the region, were first cultivated between about 300 B.C. and A.D. 200. The earliest evidence for the cultivation of potatoes in the Lake Titicaca region is dated at 400 B.C. and the potato must have opened a new range of opportunities for cultivation throughout the high Andes, just as it was to do later in western Europe in the seventeenth and eighteenth centuries. Another wave of domestication took place during the period of cultural and demographic expansion approximately dated from the first century A.D. to 600-900. Sweet potato, *papaya*, the pineapple and other crops were added to the agricultural repertoire in coastal and warmer regions, and root crops such as *mashua*, *oca* and *olluco* appeared in the highlands. Finally, the domestication of the llama and the alpaca was probably an accomplished fact by 1000 B.C., probably originating in the Lake Titicaca region where there is the greatest variety of wild and domesticated types. Grazing of llama and alpaca gave value to high natural pastures, which were useless in other parts of pre-Columbian Latin America.

The rural landscapes of the central Andes still bear the imprint of the painstaking effort of pre-Columbian Indian peoples to make the maximum use of resources in a difficult land. Water control was carried to a high pitch of efficiency, particularly in the desert coast. Archaeological studies of coastal Peru, notably in the Virú valley, have traced the elaboration of water control systems and their close association with developing socio-economic patterns of settlement and regional control. Wittfogel (1957, chapters 2-4) classified the Andean cultures among the so-called hydraulic civilizations in which water control demanded large-scale public works and thus implied the coercion of labour and the emergence of a despotic élite. Early settlement was scattered, sparse and uncontrolled, depending on shallow water-tables for the cultivation of beans and squash, but controlled irrigation made its appearance with the cultivation of maize, initially on a small scale and near river courses or the highland margins (Willey, 1953). Water control on a much larger scale came later, involving the improvement of water distribution to cultivation plots, the building of stone-faced terraces, and large-scale canal-building, which involved the territorial organization of whole valleys as single units. Settlement patterns took on a more organized form with a substantial increase in the number of sites, and the creation of large, compact villages, often on terraced ground above the irrigated valley floor.

The elaboration of irrigation systems continued to about A.D. 900 when the maximum population may have been reached in some of the coastal valleys and when the cultivated area of individual valleys may have reached limits not yet surpassed, or exceeded only since the mid-twentieth century. In the Chicama valley the pre-Columbian canal of La Cumbre, some 120 km long, is still used to irrigate part of the valley. Regional political units emerged, which transcended the boundaries of individual valleys (e.g. the Mochica culture of northern Peru or the Nazca culture of the south). The pre-Columbian range of cultivated crops was completed, guano was used as a fertilizer, and the extension of terrace systems on hill slopes seems to imply not only an enduring concern for the conservation of soil and water, but also a pressure of population on resources which made necessary a heavy expenditure of labour and effort to secure a relatively small increment of land for cultivation. Limits may have been reached, for some of the coastal valleys seem subsequently to have suffered a decline in the efficiency of irrigation and the extent of cultivation, particularly in those valleys that had been reduced to a marginal position at the fringe of coastal empires.

Less is known of the extension of the cultivated area in the sierra in regions where rainfall is adequate for farming. Massive and elaborately constructed terraces are found in close association with some of the most important Inca sites, faced with worked stone, equipped with staircases and stone canals for the distribution of water, and with level 'treads' even on steep slopes. Such terraces are to be found at Pisac or Machu Picchu, for example, and they seem to be associated with Inca garrisons and fortresses. But terraces of a more informal and irregular character are widely spread in many other areas around the margins of Lake Titicaca on terrain of moderate to steep slopes; in the Bolivian *altiplano*, and in many of the upper sections of the coastal valleys of Peru. Murra (1960) has tentatively expressed the view that terracing may be associated with the introduction of maize into the highlands, the cultivation of which was bound up with ceremonial and religious practice, but much of the higher terracing around Lake Titicaca is above the altitudinal limit for maize cultivation. Much is uncertain, but, in the sierra no less than on the coast, the existence of terracing points to a carefully controlled attempt to maximize the area under cultivation, to conserve water and soil, and to secure successful harvests at the highest limits of the altitudinal range for particular crops.

Similar preoccupations are also to be seen in the practice of ridged cultivation on flat, badly drained land in the neighbourhood of Lake Titicaca, where flat-topped ridges were artificially raised above flood-level for cultivation. In all, some 82,000 ha of land organized in various patterns of ridged cultivation can still be traced in the area, again pointing to a substantial pressure of population on the arable resources of the region in pre-Inca times (Smith, Denevan and Hamilton, 1968). Elsewhere in the central Andean region similar features occur near Guayaquil and in the Mojos region of north-east Bolivia, which were both areas outside or marginal to the Inca empire, possessing dense population and well-developed cultures before the arrival of the Spaniards. Both are regions liable to seasonal flooding (Parsons and Denevan, 1967).

The organization of agriculture and of rural society was much more varied in the Inca empire than is suggested by the simplifications of some of the post-Conquest witnesses. The conventional view is that land was divided among the community, the Inca and the Sun, but local chiefs (*curacas*) sometimes held land on their own account and many chiefs retained land even after their conquest by the Incas. Peasant communities were organized into *ayllus*, which had a territorial connotation and within which the extended patrilineal family was the most important kinship group. It is, however, difficult to say how far land was collectively operated. The periodic redistribution of land within the *ayllu*, often noted by chroniclers, may not have been widespread. Individual ownership of at least the usufruct was normal near Lake Titicaca in the 1560s, annual redistribution was not practised, and peasant holdings were inherited by surviving children, and only redivided among the *ayllu* if there were no surviving issue. Grazing of llama and alpaca was also organized in *ayllus*, but in addition to communally owned flocks there were others individually owned by chiefs and peasant households. But all grazed freely on land held for common use. Finally, the *ayllus* were also units within which systems of mutual labour aid were operated, and although this is a custom that has survived to the present, it is constantly threatened by increasing commercialization and growing economic differentiation within peasant groups.

In an indirect way the *ayllu* still has a role to play. Modern *comunidades* are numerous in all of the central Andean countries. In Bolivia there are about 4150, in Ecuador *c.* 1200, and in Peru some 1600. They have a corporate legal entity and most have common grazing lands, the defence of which against encroachment is often a major *raison d'être* of the *comunidad*. Some, but by no means all, have common property, including arable land, and a few, such as Muquiyauyo in central Peru, have made considerable economic progress. Some authors have seen the *comunidad* as a lineal descendant of the *ayllu*, and also as a hope for the development of co-operation in farming and thus as a potential institution making for economic growth. Both of these views are debatable, for many *comunidades* can trace their existence no further than the beginning of the twentieth century, but the *idea* of a lineal descent is important in so far as it encourages a spirit of local cohesion and collective aspiration.

The indigenous heritage thus persists in the rural landscape and in rural tradition, but one of the most important achievements of the central Andean cultures, the development of an urban society, has left few comparable traces except at Cuzco and in the ruins of ancient cities. Urban evolution has been traced from the grouping of rural settlements in a fairly clear relationship to ceremonial and pyramidal mounds to the more complex proto-urban structures of Tiahuanaco times, which were much more than gathering places for defence or religious celebrations, since they had acquired administrative functions and were centres for the collection of tribute in kind and probably in labour from surrounding rural areas. They were centres, too, for specialized craftsmen, water control and perhaps the control of trade (Schaedel, 1966). They were often large and segmented into sections. Defensive walls and embankments, street systems and the distribution of water were all carefully planned.

In the coastal regions the great phase of the city-builders which followed early expansion occurred about 250 years before the Inca conquest when the coastal empires were ruled by urban élites, who created for themselves elaborately planned cities, generally rectangular in basic conception with symmetrically arranged streets and canals. These, too, were often segmented into large walled compartments containing gardens, pyramids, reservoirs, storage bins, palaces and houses. Chanchan, the largest of the coastal cities and capital of the Chimú empire of the northern coast covered an area of some 15 km². But it was, of course, Cuzco, heart of the Inca empire, that was the greatest city of them all, perhaps containing a population of 50,000 at the time of the Spanish Conquest, and built of stone with that meticulous attention to craftsmanship and finish that can still impress the modern visitor. Temples, palaces and fortresses were the main foci around which were grouped craftsmen, warriors and priests, as well as the massive drafts of forced labour brought in from the provinces to serve in construction, military service, domestic tasks and the like.

When the Spaniards arrived, therefore, they were confronted by a numerous population, highly skilled in the agricultural arts as well as in the production and working of precious metals, and, above all, highly urbanized and socially stratified, ruled and exploited by an urban élite. And it was the urban élite, the religious and administrative structure, that was the main target of the Spanish Conquest; the indigenous urban tradition was replaced by the Mediterranean urban culture of the Spaniards.

Conquest and the colonial regime

The conquest of Peru by Pizarro and his men in 1532 ushered in a new phase in the developing geography of the central Andes. The Spaniards approached the Andean environment with a different perception of its resources, new attitudes to the exploitation and control of labour and new techniques in farming, industry and trade; above all, they brought contacts with a wider world and new, devastating diseases. A new regional balance emerged in which neither coastal Peru, as in the time of the city-builders, nor the Cuzco region, as in the time of the Incas, but the capital city of Lima and the mineral deposits of Peru and especially Potosí were the major foci around which development took place.

It may well be that diseases of European origin had preceded the Spaniards in the Inca empire and that smallpox, arriving between 1524 and 1526, had already been responsible for great losses of population (Dobyns, 1963). High mortality among the Indians continued at least until the 1560s, most probably as a result of influenza, measles and smallpox as well as of the disturbances due to conquest and civil war. In 1571, when 311,257 Indians paid tribute from an area corresponding roughly to the coast and sierra of Ecuador, Peru and Bolivia, the total population was perhaps 1·5 million. Guesses at the pre-Conquest population range from some 6 million to between 30 and 35 million, but an estimate of the order of 9 to 12 million is probably nearer the truth (Smith, 1970), a figure not again reached until the present century. Depopulation was probably most drastic in the coastal region, in which there were very few Indians to be found even when Cieza de León travelled in the area c. 1540, and in which decline from c. 1520 to 1570 may have been of the order of 95 per cent or more. In the sierra numbers declined less catastrophically by c. 75 per cent from 4·6 million to 1·35 million in 1571. The coastal regions, formerly the site of powerful empires and flourishing cities, had less than 10 per cent of the Indian population by 1571, and chroniclers remarked again and again of the shortage of Indians, the ruined buildings and the abandoned fields.

As elsewhere in Latin America, conquest was followed immediately by the foundation of towns. They were symbols of imperium, centres of administration, foci for the work of the church, centres from which *encomenderos* commanded the labour of Indians under their control, and centres to which flowed the produce of the countryside and the labour of its inhabitants. As regional centres they had a reciprocal relationship of sorts with the countryside, though the flow of goods and services was heavily unbalanced in favour of the Spaniards in the towns, with little tangible flow in the reverse direction. From the beginning the towns were the instrument by which the *conquistadores* and their successors were able to establish themselves as citizens (*vecinos*) and thus to lay claim not only to urban property for houses and gardens, but also to substantial agricultural holdings and common rights of grazing in the land that was allotted to the newly founded township. Given that good arable land was so scarce in the central Andes, a careful choice of town site may frequently have allowed the annexation of a significant proportion of available arable in many districts.

In the central Andes poor initial choice of town sites was often easily corrected in the sixteenth century when buildings were still makeshift and little investment had yet gone into the embellishment of churches and public buildings. In some cases the initial site was unhealthy, in others movement was from cold, high-altitude sites down to warmer climates and more abundant agricultural land. Huánuco el Viejo, for example, was founded in 1539 near an Inca city, but was soon abandoned because of the civil wars, the cold climate and the lack of wood. It was refounded in 1543 in the attractive and fertile valley of the Huallaga several thousand metres below. Huamanga (Ayacucho), Ica and Arequipa were other major settlements that were shifted for various reasons. The capital of the Viceroyalty was initially to have been at Jauja at c. 3000 m in the rich and densely peopled Mantaro basin but accessibility to the sea was regarded as more important, and in 1534 the capital was shifted to Lima on the river Rimac in the midst of fertile irrigated land equipped with a supply of Indian labour nearby – a decision of the utmost importance for the subsequent development of the central Peruvian Andes.

Few important colonial towns in Peru were founded directly on Indian centres of importance (Cuzco, Cajamarca and Quito were the major ones), though the proximity of Indian labour supplies was essential, and many towns were founded near to former Indian cities: Trujillo near Chanchan, Lima near Cajamarquilla, Ica near Tambo Colorado.

Most of the Spaniards in the central Andean regions in the late sixteenth century were urban dwellers. A rough census of 1571 puts the total of Spaniards at no more than 6720 (Morales Figueroa, 1866, pp. 41–64). Of these, 4580 or 68 per cent lived in the fifteen towns that had more than 100 Spaniards each, and the remainder in smaller towns or 'among the Indians'. In respect of its Spanish population, Lima had already established its primate position, with 2500 Spaniards, or some 37 per cent of the total. Potosí already had 800 Spaniards and Cuzco, Quito and Arequipa were the only other cities with over 400; La Paz followed with 300. Total populations were much larger, of course, for among the Spaniards dependent households were usually large and there were always substantial numbers of Indians, mestizos and Negro slaves engaged in service, trade, construction, crafts and industries. Even by 1571 the Negro population of Lima, some 12,000 to 15,000, far outnumbered the Spanish.

By the end of the sixteenth century an urban pattern had been established, which has remained remarkably constant. Very few towns of modern importance were founded after the end of the sixteenth century, and, although all of them were tiny by modern standards, there has been relatively little change in the *ranking* of important places, except for the changing fortunes of mining centres and the growth of La Paz, Guayaquil, Iquitos and Huancayo.

Agrarian life was fundamentally changed by the Conquest, most radically in the coastal region, much more slowly in the sierra. New crops, domesticated animals and agricultural techniques were introduced and assimilated to Indian systems of farming. There was some specialization of production for the market. And there were basic changes in the structure of land-holding and the patterns of rural settlement.

In the coastal zone of Peru a new agriculture was created. Land was available for the creation of Spanish estates, partly through the disposal of municipal land in the neighbourhood of Spanish town foundations, and partly because the extent of Indian depopulation must have meant that much irrigable land had gone out of cultivation. The coastal valleys were accessible to markets for agricultural produce not only in Lima and Guayaquil, but also further afield in other parts of the west coast of Latin America. Spanish farming enterprise was attracted and by the 1620s there were at least a few Spaniards with farms in almost all of the coastal valleys, though very few of them possessed *encomiendas*. Indian labour was brought down from the sierra, but Negro slaves played an important role on coastal plantations, serving to change significantly the racial composition of the region. Of the Pisco region it was said in 1628: 'On every farm they have a Negro village for the exploitation of the vineyards . . . and there will be 10,000 Negroes in this valley' (Vasquez de Espinosa, 1628, pp. 479–80). Even allowing for exaggeration this must have represented many more than the 700 or so native Indians reported there about the same time.

Maize was quickly adopted as a staple grain by the Spaniards, but wheat was grown, and, although the high humidities of the coastal climate must have made wheat liable to wilt and rust, flour and biscuit were exported to Lima and Guayaquil. Alfalfa was widely introduced as a fodder crop, nourishing the mule trains used for coastal transport from Paita to Lima, and for transport into the sierra. But the major specialities of the coast were sugar and vines, both introduced into Peru before 1550. Sugar did well in the upper parts of coastal valleys where water supply was good and insolation higher than in lower zones, but by the end of the sixteenth century the northern coast near Trujillo and in the Chicama valley had acquired the reputation for sugar production that it still enjoys. The regions around Ica and Pisco were already well known for their vineyards and for their wines, which are still a speciality of the area. Wine was exported along the west coast and to the sierra mining regions as far afield as Potosí. In Ica, particularly, there was substantial Spanish rural settlement in order to supervise the cultivation of the vine, an art alien to the Indian cultivator. Of the Ingenio valley in southern Peru it was said in 1628: 'All the vineyards are in a tract three leagues up the valley. The owners live beside them, each in his own personal establishment' (Vasquez de Espinosa, 1628, p. 480). Olives, too, supplied a modest export trade and were cultivated near Lima itself.

Change was, perhaps, less radical in the coastal regions of Ecuador, but cacao plantations were set up by the residents of Guayaquil for trade along the west coast, though they were less carefully tended than those of Central America, and the major industry was the extraction of timber for export to

Lima and for the local shipyards, for this was the last point southwards at which timber was available until central Chile was reached. Henequen was cultivated for the manufacture of cordage and the area was already known for bananas and avocado pears.

In the sierra, Spanish settlement was much more limited to the towns, except for some rural settlement in the Mantaro valley and in the Callejón de Huaylas. Most agriculture outside the towns remained the responsibility of the Indians, who served their Spanish masters either by the provision of service labour in *encomienda* or as *mita* (the institution of forced labour taken over from Inca practice), or by the payment of tribute in kind or in cash. Under such circumstances, agricultural change and the introduction of European crops and stock were highly selective. European crops had to find their niche, for example, in the careful altitudinal zoning of traditional Indian farming. Thus, barley could fit into the high altitude crop range as a supplement to potatoes, *cañahua* and *quinoa*, chiefly because of its short growing season, and it was slowly assimilated into Indian farming up to altitudes of 4000 m. Wheat was a bread grain in demand by Spanish settlers and fitted well into the system between 3000 m and 3500 m where it yielded at least as well as maize. By the early seventeenth century wheat had spread fairly widely in the inter-Andean basins of Ecuador, in northern and central Peru, and in the *valle* region of Bolivia near Cochabamba and Sucre.

Some European crops could be assimilated into Indian systems of farming with the minimum of disturbance: grain crops in general could be fitted into the Indian agricultural calendar and cultivated with traditional equipment; most fruits could be grown side by side with their indigenous counterparts, though the vine required specialized treatment and was rarely grown without Spanish supervision. Custom and consumer preference also affected the acceptability of European crops: tobacco made little headway (except around Moyobamba and Jaén) against the Indian preference for coca; flax was little grown when cotton provided an alternative textile fibre. Sugar, on the other hand, was so highly valued for its flavour and its capacity to produce alcohol that it was fairly rapidly adopted in the deeper inter-Andean valleys, even though its cultivation required new techniques. But in general the Indians remained faithful to their ancient practices and, even where Spanish demand for European crops induced change through higher prices or through the exaction of tribute, there often developed a dual agriculture by which Indian crops were grown for subsistence and European crops for exchange.

Sheep were widely and rapidly accepted by the Indians and even in the 1560s were increasing in numbers in areas such as southern Peru, where there was little Spanish settlement. Sheep could graze at altitudes almost as high as the llama and were easy to rear and more productive of wool. Their unit cost was low, and they supplied raw material not only for domestic cloth production along traditional lines, but also for the woollen mills of northern Peru or Pasto and Riobamba in Ecuador. The rearing of cattle and horses remained much more the prerogative of Spanish-controlled estates. The plough, too, was only slowly accepted by Indian farmers, and its use is even now by no means universal. It was regarded very much as a concomitant of hacienda agriculture and of mestizo rather than Indian farming. The plough was unsuitable for the cultivation of very steep slopes, and its use also implied investment in stock and an attendant revolution in the rhythm of traditional farming, which Indian communities were unable or unwilling to undertake.

The evolution of the hacienda was one of the most important features of the colonial regime to have an enduring effect on the life of the central Andes. In early colonial times it was control over labour rather than the possession of land that mattered and this was achieved by the system of *encomienda*, by which Spaniards were granted the right to labour services in various forms from the Indians of specified areas or villages. In the central Andes most *encomiendas* were relatively small, and there were no less than 538 by 1570. Initially a right to labour, the *encomienda* soon became a right to tribute and then to a money payment, so that there was, in principle, no transition from *encomienda* to landownership as such. The annexation of land to newly founded townships formed the nuclei of some Spanish estates, and the crown also had the right to dispose as it wished of the lands formerly belonging to the Inca, the lands of the Sun and waste land or abandoned lands. The decline of population must have been accompanied by abandonment of cultivated land, and the operation of the *mita*, the forced labour system by which a proportion of Indians were liable to be drafted from their native villages for labour in the mines, in construction work, in factories and in the towns, often resulted in further abandonment of cultivated land by Indians who never returned to their native villages (Rowe, 1957). And it may well be that much land was granted, or simply occupied, which was properly the unenclosed grazing land used, or formerly used, by Indian communities. And some may have been fallow for long periods under the Andean system of shifting cultivation. At all events, the hacienda was firmly established as the dominant form of landownership in many parts of the central Andes by the end of the colonial regime, though important stages in the further concentration of holdings were yet to take place in the nineteenth century.

It was chiefly as a storehouse of precious metals that Spain and the rest of the world regarded the Viceroyalty of Peru. Once the riches of the Inca empire had been looted, the central Andes were ransacked for gold and silver ores. Widely scattered mining centres attracted Spanish and, later, Portuguese miners and supported urban settlements, local agricultural specialization and route networks to serve as supply lines. All was based, of course, on Indian labour. Quito had its sources of precious metals and provincial centres such as Cuenca and Zaruma exploited gold and silver. Rich sources of alluvial gold stimulated settlement in north-eastern Peru near Moyobamba and Chachapoyas; in central and southern Peru the Callejón de Huaylas, Castrovirreyna and Carabaya to the north of Lake Titicaca were centres of mining for silver or gold. In Bolivia, Oruro was founded in 1607 shortly after the discovery of silver there and a few years later had more than a thousand Spaniards.

But it was Potosí that stood out like a giant among the producers of precious metal. Silver ores were discovered in 1545 in the ridge of Potosí at an altitude of over 5000 m. By 1570 it had a population of about 120,000 and was by far the largest settlement in the whole of the Americas, though its Spanish population was not much greater than 4000 at the height of its prosperity. The silver ores were rich, but at such an altitude that the environment presented difficulties for mining, which were only overcome by incurring heavy costs in life, labour and capital. Lack of wood meant that grass was used as fuel and the area was devastated for many kilometres around. The short rainy season meant that a complex series of reservoirs was needed to supply water power for crushing mills. *Mita* labour was drawn from as far afield as Cuzco. From 1553 a mercury amalgam was used in Mexico to extract silver more efficiently, and ten years later cinnabar ores were discovered in central Peru at Huancavelica. The mercury ores of Huancavelica rapidly assumed such strategic importance in relation to Potosí that the mine was taken over by the crown. Potosí and Huancavelica became 'the poles on which this kingdom is supported'.

The impact of Potosí on the economic geography of the central Andes and, indeed, on the whole of Spanish America, was considerable. Lima was the greatest single beneficiary as the centre of administration, because the official routes for the transport of silver and for the supply of imported European goods passed through Lima and then by sea to the isthmus of Panama. The route from Potosí to the coast by way of Arequipa or Arica stimulated the production of foodstuffs and of fodder for the mule trains. Wines and sugar were imported from the Peruvian coast. Cattle trails linked Potosí with Chile and north-western Argentina; and the illegal 'backdoor route' through Buenos Aires, of increasing importance through the seventeenth century, foreshadowed the reorientation of the area towards the Atlantic. But within the central Andes it was Potosí (and Oruro), through its demands for foodstuffs and manufactures, which stimulated the growth of agriculture, population and trade in the basins of central Bolivia at altitudes low enough to produce wheat, fruits, meat, sugar and the like. Cochabamba and Tarija grew, but it was Chuquisaca (Sucre) that reaped the greatest benefit, since it was the most important basin near to the wealth of Potosí. The colonial architecture of Sucre still hints at the former wealth it enjoyed. But the initial wealth and the richest ores were skimmed off by the end of the seventeenth century, and poor techniques, inefficiency and

K

corruption led to decline in the production of precious metals. There existed as yet neither the demand nor the transport facilities to justify the exploitation of the wider spectrum of non-ferrous mineral ores.

Within a hundred years of the Conquest, major changes had been wrought in the geography of the central Andes. The sierra was still largely Indian with a small, largely urban minority of Spaniards and mestizos; the coast had experienced a major structural change as a result of the cata- strophic decline of its Indian population and the growth of Spanish, Negro and mestizo groups. A hierarchy of new towns had been created, dominating the countryside and linked by networks of trade and com- munications, which had little in common with the former patterns of the Inca empire. The impact of colonial society on land use systems and agrarian structures was by no means fully worked out, but the foundations had been laid. Not until the second half of the nineteenth century were new changes of equivalent magnitude to be brought about, and only then as a result of the impact of modern industrial demands from western Europe and North America for raw materials and foodstuffs, and it is to the implications of this later movement that we must now turn.

EXPORT ECONOMIES AND MODERN DEVELOPMENT

After the achievement of independence in the early nineteenth century, each of the three central Andean states that emerged was confronted with similar problems. Each was drawn into the international commercial world after a period of revolution, war and political upheaval following declara- tions of independence. Export economies were superimposed on an ex- colonial society that was singularly lacking in its capacity for entrepreneur- ship, capital formation or financial or industrial expertise, particularly since the movement for independence had removed the initiative and experience provided by the *peninsulares* from Spain itself. Success in the production of foodstuffs, minerals and raw materials for export made it possible to finance investment in railways, roads, urban construction and port facilities, but in general terms material progress resulting from the expansion of export economies was restricted to limited geographical sectors of each country. Precise geographical limits can rarely be assigned to the 'modernized' and 'traditional' sectors of dual economies resulting from the growth of metropolitan regions and the expansion of export sectors, nor can the 'spread effects' associated with them be worked out in the detail that one would like. But the concept is a useful one, particularly since regional inequalities in the distribution of income have been all the more acute because of the relatively sharp social and geographical cleavage be- tween predominantly white and mixed or Indian groups.

Industrialization, stimulated by events during and immediately after the Second World War, and since then by deliberate policy, has made some progress, especially in Peru, but the prospects for industrial growth, notably in Bolivia and Ecuador, have been severely limited by the size of the *effective* internal market, much lower than total populations seem to imply because of the persistence of poverty and of large sectors of predominantly subsistence farming. On the whole, industrialization has also served to accentuate regional imbalance, primarily because of the concentration of industry in the capital cities or large towns.

In common with other Latin American countries the central Andean republics face the consequences of a rapid growth of population, which has inevitably meant an increasing pressure on the land, particularly among small farmers, and the fragmentation of land into *minifundios*. There has been an increase in rural underemployment and a search for alternative sources of income, often involving seasonal employment elsewhere or permanent migration to regions of greater economic opportunity. Lima, La Paz, Quito and Guayaquil are the great magnets for population. Urban populations have swollen beyond the capacity of new industry to employ the thousands who are attracted by the amenities of the city and the chance rather than the promise of employment. Distress and poverty are to be seen in the makeshift settlements on the fringes of the cities in the *barriadas* (euphemistically the *pueblos jovenes*) of Lima, in the regularly flooded slums of Guayaquil or in the upper quarters of La Paz, but it may be argued that the urban migration is, nevertheless, a positive force making for change both in the towns and in the countryside.

The growth of numbers and the spread of commercialized farming have also served to sharpen the contrast between the large estates on the one hand and the fragmentation of smallholdings at the opposite end of the agrarian spectrum. Land reform is widely felt to be a possible solution to the social inequities in the distribution of land, but only in Bolivia, and more recently in Peru, have events forced rapid progress in this direction. Agrarian reform is seen not only in political and social terms as a means of raising the status of underprivileged and dependent peasantry, but also in economic terms. To many in Latin America, agrarian reform implies the raising of agricultural productivity at least as much as a thorough-going land redistribution. And it is therefore argued that if the agricultural productivity of peasant farms can be substantially raised, imports of foodstuffs will be reduced and an internal market will be created for cheap industrial goods that can be produced by a domestic manufacturing industry. But agrarian reform is rarely seen in geographical terms in relation to the spatial and regional implications of land reform and agrarian improvement.

Finally, one other issue of importance to all three countries is the question of colonization. All three have large, undeveloped territories in the eastern regions, which are potentially sources of tropical crops ranging from rice and manioc to rubber and coffee, and which may have great potential for cattle-raising. Planned colonization is expensive and heavy investment is needed in transport in order to open up new land and provide access to markets. For Peru and Bolivia the east has greater importance than it has for Ecuador, where the accessible coastal region has similar environmental potential. But for all three countries the question of whether or not scarce capital should be invested in eastern settlement poses a number of fundamental problems. Is there a political necessity to settle the national territory effectively? Where can markets be found for tropical crops once internal domestic markets have been satisfied – and, if so, for what crops? Is the return on capital and effort in eastern settlement likely to be greater than the return on similar expenditure incurred in programmes of agricultural intensification in older settled regions? And, finally, is the existence of available land for peasant settlement in the east an adequate alternative to and substitute for a programme of land reform in older settled areas?

Ecuador

The central Andean republics are thus faced with common problems, but to see them in their national and geographical context it is now necessary to consider separately each of the component countries. The territorial framework of Ecuador has its roots in the status accorded to Quito as a royal *audiencia* from 1563, at first within the Viceroyalty of New Castile, and later as a *presidencia* within the orbit of New Granada. This northerly orientation was confirmed in the immediate years after independence in 1822 when for eight years the area was included within the Federation of Gran Colombia with Colombia and Venezuela. But since 1830 Ecuador has remained an independent state, jealously preserving its separate identity against the territorial inroads made by its neighbours. At its independence from Gran Colombia, Ecuador had an area of 706,000 km^2 and its boundaries extended eastwards along the navigable Amazon to a point well below Iquitos. But the eastern territories have been eroded: by Brazil in 1904; by the cession of a zone to the south of the river Putumayo to Colombia in 1916; and as a result of the annexation by Peru, after a short and disastrous war in 1941–2, of much of the territory then remaining to Ecuador in the eastern lowlands of the Amazon basin.

The active participation of Ecuador in world commerce was delayed until the 1870s. In colonial times Quito had maintained a modest but varied commerce based in part on products of the sierra: woollen cloth from Quito and Otavalo; gold, hides and leather, and even flour and biscuit, from the Quito district. The sparsely inhabited coastal region exported sugar, cacao, tobacco, timber and straw hats. When expansion took place, however, it was almost entirely based on the export of tropical crops from the hot, humid coastal region. Various products have enjoyed a period of boom conditions, but the economy has been all the more vulnerable to fluctuations in world prices because of an excessive dependence on only

one or two products at any one period. The distinction emerged even
before the end of the nineteenth century between the commercially orientated coastal region and the traditional agrarian structure of the sierra, and
between the ancient colonial capital of Quito and the thriving commerce
and business activity of Guayaquil. It was a regional distinction, which
found political expression in the conflict between traditional, Catholic and

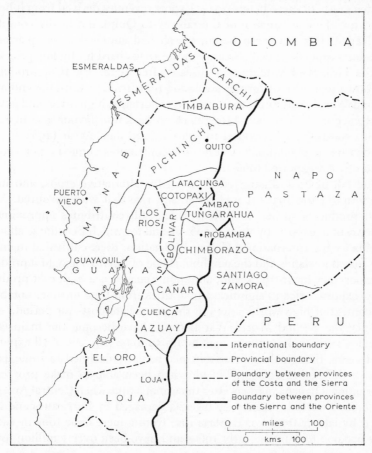

Fig. 7.1 Ecuador: provincial and regional boundaries

conservative groups associated with Quito and the sierra, and the progressive and commercially dominated liberal groups who achieved power in
1896, in turn associated with Guayaquil and the coast.

Cacao was the first of the boom crops, dominating exports from the end
of the nineteenth century until 1924. Exports increased from 5540 tons in
1838–40 to 11,194 tons in 1871–80 and reached a maximum level of
c. 40,000 tons a year between 1910 and 1924. Most of the plantations were
located in the neighbourhood of Guayaquil in two main zones: to the north,

above the regularly flooded plain of the river Guayas (the *cacao de arriba*), and on the eastern margins of the Gulf of Guayaquil (the *cacao de abajo*). All but a few thousand tons were channelled through the port of Guayaquil, the boom town of the period. In 1910, with a population of 60,000, it had already surpassed Quito in size, and by 1920 the population had topped 100,000. Almost the entire economy of Ecuador was built on the 'golden grain' of cacao before 1914. Export revenues derived from it helped to finance the construction of the railway to Quito, not finally completed until 1908. But the cacao boom, which had supplied three-quarters of Ecuador's exports, ended abruptly in the 1920s hard hit by low prices and by the ravages of witchbroom disease after 1922. By 1924 production was down to a third of former levels and remained low until the end of the Second World War. Since then post-war shortages, high prices and government encouragement have brought cacao back into favour and in recent years exports have recovered to some 44,000 tons a year (1963–6) from 130,000 ha of plantations. Cacao now contributes some 15 per cent by value of total exports (1966–9).

The fall of cacao instigated a search for alternative crops, and in the lean years of the 1930s it was coffee and rice that were favoured. Many small producers turned to coffee, which still contributes approximately 20 per cent of exports by value (1966–9), and for which Ecuador is allocated a quota by the International Coffee Association. Rice, cultivated mainly in the Guayas lowlands and the neighbourhood of Puerto Viejo, first produced an export surplus in 1928, and, although Ecuador is a high cost producer, it has exported rice in significant quantities from time to time, notably in the context of high world prices in the immediate post-war period.

Since the Second World War bananas have become the mainstay of Ecuador's external economy, making up 50 to 60 per cent of all exports in most years, though their predominance recently declined to some 44 per cent in the period 1966–9. Ecuador had been able to make progress in international banana markets after the war at a time when Central American plantations were threatened by disease, damaged by hurricanes and hampered by labour troubles. Exports rose from a mere 9000 tons in 1925 to over 600,000 tons in the early 1960s and have been over 1 million tons in recent years.

Although Ecuador is still the world's largest exporter of bananas, expansion seems now to have come to an end. Central American and Caribbean producers have always been more favourably placed in relation to markets in U.S.A. and Europe, not only because of distance, but also because shipment to the Atlantic must face charges on passage through the Panama Canal. In recent years expansion of banana production in Central America has been undertaken with the aid of new strains of high-yielding and disease-resistant Cavendish types, and with a switch from the traditional method of exporting bananas in stems to careful packing in cartons or boxes. Ecuador has therefore been losing ground in U.S.A. markets and in western Europe, and has sought alternative outlets in Japan, eastern Europe and other South American countries, to which there has been a substantial increase in exports (Preston, 1965a).

Central American production is still dominated by the United Fruit Company and the Standard Fruit Company, and large plantations are normal. In contrast, Ecuador's production is not, for the most part, in the hands of foreign-owned companies, and although the average size of the producing unit (47 ha) is substantially larger than the average farm in Ecuador, it is fairly small by other standards and smallholders make a considerable contribution, especially in the newer zones of production. The Dirección Nacional del Banano, established by government, is active in the support of the industry as the country's main earner of foreign currency.

In view of the uncertain outlook for bananas and the intensely competitive international market, encouragement has been given in a variety of ways. Panama leaf disease remains a problem, but Sigatoka, the other major threat, has been fairly successfully controlled since 1950 by spraying from the air. Most Ecuadorean plantations have been of the Gros Michel variety, but a campaign is under way to convert plantations to the higher-yielding and disease-resistant Cavendish types. In 1967 less than 10 per cent of Ecuador's plantations were of this latter type, and in 1968 some 15 per cent. Change is taking place fairly rapidly and it was hoped that a third of the area planted would be of the Cavendish type by 1970. Other recent trends have been towards improvements in quality, particularly through changes in transport and grading, and the export of bananas in boxes rather than in stems, a change which was virtually complete in 1968. A major problem is presented by the enormous wastage of fruit. Of total production, only a third is actually exported. Some is used for domestic consumption, but about 45 per cent is lost or rejected. There is a constant search for more efficient usage for the part of the crop that is not up to the exacting standards required for export. Plants have been established for the production of dehydrated bananas, banana flour and banana wine, but nearly a half of the wastage, or about 20 per cent of total production, is fed to livestock, the rearing of which has consequently become a significant coastal occupation (Preston, 1965a). But over a longer period, it may be necessary to reduce substantially the area under bananas. The Junta Nacional de Planificación y Coordinación estimates that a reduction of up to 75 per cent may be necessary and efforts are accordingly to be made to encourage conversion of marginal plantations to oil seeds, oil palm, manioc, rice or livestock.

About 60 per cent of banana production is in the Guayas lowlands, near Guayaquil, and the northern zone is relatively less important now than it was in the 1940s. Expansion of the area under bananas has followed the building of new roads – along the road from Quito to Santo Domingo in 1947, along the road to Quevedo, completed in 1961, and near the roads from Santo Domingo to Esmeraldas and Chone. Indeed, cultivators have frequently anticipated the building of new roads in their haste to take advantage of new opportunities. The southern coastal area is also an expanding area, for, although irrigation must be used, lower humidities reduce the incidence of disease.

The coastal region as a whole contributes about 90 per cent of Ecuador's total exports. Agricultural productivity per hectare and per man is higher than in the sierra. In 1963 agricultural productivity per man was calculated as £120 in the sierra and £310 in the coastal region (Bottomley, 1966). Large estates exist, but there are opportunities for the medium- or small-scale farmer, and the elaboration of the road network linking coastal towns with each other and the sierra has opened up new possibilities of settlement on virgin land, of which the most notable examples are to be found in the neighbourhood of Santo Domingo, a flourishing, bustling 'frontier' town. There is experiment and development in the production of new crops for domestic consumption or for export: sugar, cotton, citrus fruits and pineapples, for example; cattle-ranching is important in Guayas and has considerable potential. Mineral resources are less striking, but the oil of the Santa Elena peninsula has been exploited since 1910 and prospecting is going forward for off-shore deposits; natural gas has been found in the Gulf of Guayaquil; silicon-bearing sands and ferrous black sands are seen as possible industrial raw materials. In general, therefore, the coastal region may be seen as the 'leading geographical sector' of the country, more commercially orientated than the sierra, more opportunistic, agriculturally more productive and certainly much less disease-ridden than it was before the scourge of malaria was conquered.

The contrast is striking between the coastal region and the intermontane basins of the Andes, and not only in terms of the environmental differences between hot, humid, equatorial lowlands and the temperate climates of the intermontane basins or the cool, damp grasslands of the high páramos. The coast is a region of mixed population in which a negroid element reflects the former predominance of slavery; the sierra is mainly Indian and mestizo and has much more in common with the Peruvian sierra to the south. Sierra farming is devoted much more completely than coastal farming to subsistence or to the supply of local urban markets (Preston 1965b). Maize and potatoes are the major crops, together with wheat and barley and indigenous crops. The high páramos above 3000 m are grazed by sheep and cattle, though much has yet to be done in the improvement of breeds. The intermontane basins are areas of dense rural population and excessive pressure on arable land, especially where soils based on weekly consolidated ash have been badly eroded. There are examples of efficiently run estates, e.g. between Cayumbe and Latacunga, well-organized dairy farming near Quito, experimental production of pyrethrum, and intensive fodder crop production with irrigation in the drier basins. But these are exceptions, and the dominant scene is one of under-used *latifundios*, small-scale farmers with inadequate holdings, and the survival, at least until recently, of oppressive forms of tenure, which for generations have stifled the initiative of the Indian peasantry.

According to the census of 1962 the total population of Ecuador was then

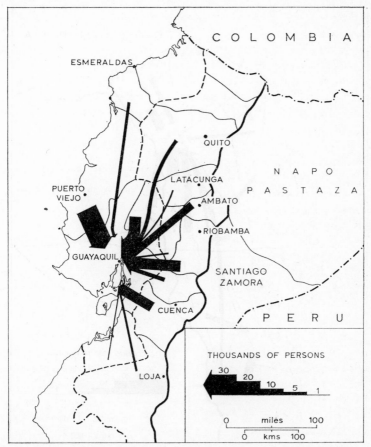

Fig. 7.2 Ecuador: net interprovincial migration to Guayaquil

4,476,007, of whom 2,127,358 lived in the provinces that can be classified as coastal, 2,271,345 in the sierra, and only 74,913 in the *oriente*. Mid-year estimates for 1968 put the population at 5,700,000: the rate of population growth is high, even for Latin America, at 3·4 per cent per year, but the population of the coastal region has grown much faster than the average. Between 1950 and 1962 the population of the coastal region increased by 68 per cent and the coast's share of total population increased from 41 to

48 per cent; the sierra population grew by only 22 per cent over the same period, and two provinces actually declined in numbers (Cotopaxi and Tungurahua). But in all Ecuador it is the towns, and especially Quito and Guayaquil, that have grown most rapidly: Quito from 210,000 in 1950 to 354,746 in 1962; Guayaquil from 259,000 to 510,804. No other town approaches 100,000. On a scale much smaller than in most Latin American countries, Ecuador is experiencing a marked drift to the cities, and it is

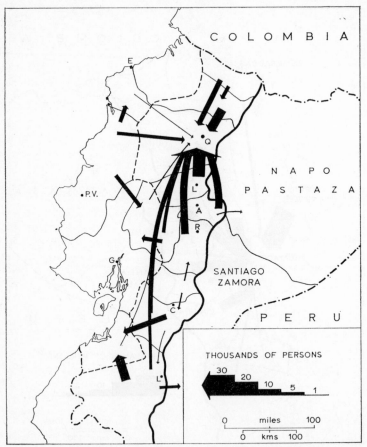

Fig. 7.3 Ecuador: net interprovincial migration excluding Guayaquil

perhaps to her advantage that both the coastal region and the sierra have their own urban pole of attraction as a regional stimulus for agrarian and industrial change. The currents of net interprovincial migration show, above all, the importance of Quito and Guayaquil, particularly the latter (see Figs. 7.2 and 7.3) (DEC, 1962). In comparison, other interprovincial movements are relatively small, though they do hint at a movement down from the sierra to the coastal region.

The relative status of individual provinces with respect to a number of criteria of social and economic development is shown in Table 7.1 (DEC, 1962) (see also Fig. 7.1 for the location of provinces). It is not, unfortunately possible to distinguish Quito and Guayaquil from the provinces in which they lie (i.e. Pichincha and Guayas, respectively). But it is clear that these

TABLE 7.1   *Ecuador: indices of development, by province and major region*

1	2	3	4	5	6	7	8	9	10	11
Ecuador	4,476,000	+40	38·2	44·5	1290	29·0	3·3	20·6	37·5	65·2
Coast										
Esmeraldas	124,881	+65	33·6	32·9	670	4·0	2·7	13·0	12·2	55·3
Manabi	612,542	+53	16·8	26·0	810	9·4	2·1	13·4	11·7	58·1
Los Ríos	250,062	+67	21·3	22·6	1060	3·3	1·9	16·7	17·9	55·7
Guayas	979,223	+68	72·0	64·7	1620	67·5	4·2	58·5	61·0	76·0
El Oro	160,650	+79	43·2	37·2	1130	44·0	2·3	30·3	49·2	79·0
Sierra										
Carchi	94,648	+24	28·8	39·0	585	1·2	3·0	32·4	38·4	74·0
Imbabura	174,039	+18	27·3	50·0	890	17·2	2·8	28·1	37·8	53·0
Pichincha	587,835	+52	65·8	72·1	1130	46·0	5·9	61·8	75·9	75·1
Cotopaxi	154,971	−7	13·4	33·5	873	6·4	2·1	17·6	27·2	52·0
Tungurahua	178,709	−5	36·1	44·3	850	12·6	3·1	32·9	32·9	67·5
Bolívar	131,651	+20	11·9	17·0	830	0·1	2·0	9·9	16·1	57·5
Chimborazo	276,668	+27	27·2	28·8	1001	4·5	2·1	15·5	39·7	45·0
Cañar	112,733	+15	11·5	27·3	—	—	1·8	12·7	15·5	55·1
Azuay	274,642	+9	23·9	40·5	840	14·1	2·8	21·2	23·6	65·0
Loja	285,448	+31	17·0	26·3	760	4·8	2·2	12·8	17·9	68·6
Oriente										
Napo Pastaza	37,946	+49	6·0	31·0	554	0·6	3·8	18·5	13·6	52·5
S'tiago Zamora	36,967	+76	—	20·5	—	—	3·7	8·9	11·0	63·8
Coast	2,127,358	+68	44·0	44·9	1230	37·7	3·1	36·0	37·8	67·2
Sierra	2,271,345	+22	33·1	42·8	920	16·8	3·4	30·6	40·5	63·1
Oriente	75,913	+65	3·4	25·9	554	0·6	3·8	13·7	12·3	58·1
Coast, excluding Guayas	1,148,135	+60	25·6	27·2	890	11·3	2·1	15·9	17·3	59·3
Sierra, excluding Pichincha	1,683,545	+14	21·7	32·5	850	5·8	2·5	19·5	27·9	59·2

Columns: 1, Provinces and regions. 2, Population, 1962. 3, Percentage change in population, 1950–62. 4, Percentage of total population in towns of over 2000. 5, Percentage of active population in non-agricultural occupations. 6, Average wages in industry (*sucres*). 7, kW h used in industry, per head. 8, Percentage of professional and technical workers to total employment. 9, Percentage of houses with electric light. 10, Percentage of houses with piped water. 11, Percentage of population aged over 6 and literate.

two provinces lead the field in almost all respects. Together they have 77 per cent of all industrial establishments in the country (Pichincha 42 per cent, Guayas 35 per cent). They have 76 per cent of the personnel employed in industry, and the wages paid are higher than in other provinces. They also have over a half of all professional and technical workers in the country, and, of course, the highest proportion of houses with piped water or electric light.

Industrial expansion, given considerable encouragement by the state since 1955, has contributed substantially to the growth of Quito and Guayaquil. Until recently Ecuador had few industries. Its staple exports have led to relatively little processing industry. From the mid-nineteenth century the country was renowned for its so-called Panama hats made from the straw of the toquilla palm. Originally concentrated in the coastal region, manufacture was encouraged in the 1860s in the Andean provinces of Azuay and Cañar and especially at Cuenca which is still the major centre. Since the inter-war years production has declined with changing fashions, but as a small workshop industry it has created an important source of employment and supplementary income. A modest textile industry has existed since colonial times among the Otavalo Indians and has been industrialized, chiefly in Quito and Ambato, and the industry provides much of Ecuador's needs. Oil-refining, cement (from 1934 at Guayaquil, from 1956 at Riobamba and with new plans for expansion), brewing (at Quito and Guayaquil), flour-milling, pharmaceutical industries, plywood, paper and printing have all had modest success in the protected internal market.

Since 1955 tax incentives, high allowances for depreciation, credit facilities and favourable import regulations have encouraged industrial growth and the National Institute of Planning and the Centre of Industrial Development have made detailed inventories of resources and feasibility studies of industrial possibilities, proposing a variety of possible enterprises such as the manufacture of furniture, banana wine and fishmeal. Power supplies are to be supplemented by four new generating stations by 1976 with a capacity of 500,000 kW h, which would more than double present capacity.

In the 1960s industrial output has increased by 6 per cent per year, but the internal market is necessarily limited, not only by the size of the population, but also by the poverty of the great majority of the population, of which only a quarter has incomes of over £50 per head, and of which a third hardly enters into the money economy at all. Those factories that do exist often tend to be uneconomically small and to run below installed capacity. Textile factories, for example, average 1400 to 2500 spindles, though the minimum economic number is estimated as 10,000 and many of these factories, in any case, operate at only half their capacity (Bottomley, 1965).

The improvement of communications has also received priority in development policy. The road network has been extended from 5350 km in 1935 to 10,750 km in 1958 and 16,700 km in 1966. The basic pattern of communications is simple, and an adequate basis for detailed elaboration: a longitudinal Andean road (the Pan American Highway) from Colombia to Peru, a more or less longitudinal road in the coastal region from Esmeraldas to the Peruvian frontier, together with a radial spread from Guayaquil, and no less than eight transverse links from the intermontane basin to the coastal zone (including the railway from Quito and Otavalo to San Lorenzo completed in 1957). Three spur roads provide, or are planned to provide, access to the *oriente* and the navigable tributaries of the Amazon. The immediate effect of road construction has been to encourage the spontaneous settlement of new land in areas where urban markets or export opportunities have suddenly become accessible, but they must also serve, in the long run, to integrate a national market to a greater extent than was ever possible in the past.

It is evident that agricultural productivity must be raised if Ecuador's standard of living is to rise, or if industrialization is to succeed, and in common with other Latin American countries, Ecuador pins great hopes on its programme for agrarian reform, instituted in 1964 as IERAC (the Ecuadorian Institute for Agrarian Reform and Colonization). Achievements to date have been mainly concerned with regulating and directing spontaneous colonization and the planning of settlement projects in the developing zone between the coast and the highlands, and to a lesser extent in the *oriente*. Something has been achieved in the sierra in the way of resettlement of peasant families on properties that have come into the hands of the state, and efforts have been made to rid Ecuador of semi-feudal tenancies, but powerful interests and a lack of finance have meant that little progress has been made so far in the radical reorganization of agrarian structures either in the sierra or on the coast. In the four years from 1964 to 1968 IERAC is reported as having granted land title to only 7517 families for the possession of 274,000 ha, though the Junta de Planificación has recently recommended the full implementation of the current reform programme in the period 1970-5 and envisages further progress towards an integrated agrarian reform in the sierra in the following quinquennium, coupled with an effective land settlement programme in the *oriente*.

For Ecuador, however, the settlement of the *oriente* seems much less important, except in strategic terms, than the settlement of equivalent regions is for Bolivia and Peru. The enumerated population of the eastern provinces was no more than 46,471 in 1950 and 74,913 in 1962. Settlement projects under the aegis of IERAC are planned in the Upano river to the south, where gold is already exploited and this is to be linked with Cuenca by road. A military colonization project was begun in 1962 in the Putumayo region near the Colombian frontier, and this is an area certainly likely to develop rapidly, but in association primarily with oil exploitation.

Indeed, optimism for future settlement in the *oriente*, and perhaps for the future well-being of the external economy of Ecuador, centres on the prospects for oil, which promises to be the new bonanza. Following the discovery of rich oil deposits in south-west Colombia, in the basin of the river Putumayo, just across the Ecuadorean border, Texaco–Gulf secured from Ecuador concessionary rights on 1,430,000 ha in the *oriente*. In early 1967 oil was struck at Lago Agrio near the river San Miguel and some 200 km east-north-east of Quito. Out of twenty-three wells drilled by early 1970 in the region only one was dry and two others commercially unprofitable. Potential output from the twenty successful wells would be of the order of 4000 m³ per day, together with supplies of natural gas. Other oil companies have rushed to share in the apparently rosy prospects of Ecuadorean oil since 1969 when Texaco–Gulf were made to rescind all their concession over and above the 500,000 ha maximum decreed by Ecuadorean law. A pipeline is to be built by 1973 from Lago Agrio to Esmeraldas on the coast in Ecuadorean territory, and there is to be a small spur line from Lago Agrio to Orito, the Colombian centre of oil activity across the border. The major expansion of Ecuador's production and export of oil must clearly await the completion of this pipeline, but meanwhile negotiations are under way for the supply of oil to Brazil by way of the Amazonian river system.

The real impact of oil on Ecuador and its *oriente* has yet to be felt. It seems likely that settlement, improved communications and the oil and gas resources may stimulate a modest amount of new agricultural colonization, as they have done in the Santa Cruz area of Bolivia, and may do in the region across the border in Colombia. But results are likely to be slow, and the long-term agricultural importance of the *oriente* to the economy of Ecuador must surely be viewed in the light of the fact that abundant land is still available in the coastal region which is endowed with a fundamentally similar natural environment as far as most tropical crops are concerned, and is much better placed in relation to external and internal markets.

Peru

For twenty years after Peru achieved its independence from Spain in 1824 the country was ravaged by war and its economy stagnated. Mining had declined and Lima had lost much of the brilliance that its population of *peninsulares* (about a third of the population in 1776) had formerly helped to give it. Agriculture served mainly domestic needs and local trade. But from 1840 Peru was jerked into the mainstream of international commerce. Its coastal guano resources suddenly gained value at a time when the age of high farming in England and the beginnings of agricultural chemistry in Germany were creating a demand for fertilizers that could easily be satisfied by the simple quarrying and loading of guano from the off-shore islands. Guano production increased from 7000 tons in 1830 to about 400,000 tons in 1860, when guano was the largest single export from any Latin American country. Directly and indirectly, revenue from guano exports or loans secured on export revenue served ultimately to finance public works (Levin, 1960, chapter 2). *Criollo* entrepreneurship was stimulated and new immigrants, particularly to Lima and other coastal towns, brought a new range of occupations and new attitudes to trade and commerce.

Railways were of undoubted importance in opening up the sierra and the coast to new commercial currents. The Southern Railway was opened in 1870 from Mollendo to Arequipa and to Puno in 1874, thus linking the *altiplano* of northern Bolivia to the coast by way of steam navigation on Lake Titicaca, and making possible the further extension to Cuzco. In central Peru the dramatic and ingenious engineering of Henry Meiggs created the line from Lima to Oroya over a pass at 4780 m, later extended to Huancayo and northwards to Cerro de Pasco. The optimistic hopes that accompanied the planning and execution of the railways into the Andes were never fully realized, but the railways brought new life to old sierra mines, such as Cerro de Pasco, and made possible the exploitation of lead, zinc, copper and other non-ferrous metals in addition to the traditional mainstays of silver and gold. A new commercial interest began to infuse haciendas in the sierra when the profitability of merino and alpaca wool was realized. Indeed, one of the major consequences of the impact of a commercial economy in the sierra, in conjunction with the legal encouragement given to the individualization of land tenure, was to give a monetary value to extensive natural grazings, which had formerly been regarded as waste or common land. Large areas of natural pasture were incorporated into haciendas and a new impetus was given to the purchase of Indian lands and the disintegration of traditional *comunidades*.

Unwarranted optimism about the possibilities of the forested east led to desultory attempts to encourage European immigration and to set up agricultural colonies in the *montaña*, e.g. the German settlement at Pozuzo, but very little of permanent importance was achieved in the face of difficulties presented by isolation, ignorance, disease and official neglect. In the east, high profits from the collection of wild rubber and cinchona produced a wave of ruthless exploitation both of labour and resources. But this brief boom in activity ended with the successful introduction of cultivated rubber and cinchona (as a source of quinine) in the East Indies, and it was, in any case, part of an economy focused on the navigable rivers and the boom town of Iquitos, which had more connection with Manaos and Brazil than it had with the coastal and Andean economy of Peru.

The major impact of new commercial enterprise was in the coastal region. Sugar had been a staple from early colonial times, but production increased rapidly in the late nineteenth century with the introduction of steam power, largely by foreign immigrants. The industry now became strongly localized on the northern coast, retreating from the upper coastal valleys elsewhere. At first the ownership of sugar *centrals* was independent of sugar plantations, but with the increasing concentration of landowner- ship in the late nineteenth century both cultivation and processing fell into the hands of a few large enterprises, some of which continued to be foreign- owned. In the Chicama valley, for example, sixty-five haciendas had been amalgamated to seven by 1918 and to four by 1950. Cotton cultivation began on a larger scale at the time of the American Civil War when the cotton famine in Europe initiated a search for alternative sources. Peru was fortunate not only because of the accessibility of its coastal valleys for export, but also because of its possession of highly valued long-staple varieties: Piura cotton in the north, and the very fine high grade Tangüis type. Output expanded with the Lancashire boom of 1900-10, and even before 1914 a small cotton textile industry was established in Lima.

By the end of the century the guano resources, grossly over-exploited, had ceased to have importance in Peru's foreign trade, and the boom in nitrates from Tarapacá was of no further significance to Peru after the annexation of the province to Chile at the end of the War of the Pacific (1879-84). But Peru's external economy had become firmly based on a healthy variety of exports, which continued to predominate until the 1950s: sugar, cotton, minerals and wool. But there have been important changes in the last fifteen years. In the decade 1956-66 the real value of exports more than doubled and their composition changed as a result of the dramatic growth of fishmeal exports and a new surge in mineral production. The fishing industry, like the guano boom of a century earlier, exploits the remarkable ecology of coastal waters, and the growth of mineral exports rests on the large-scale exploitation of low grade copper ores and high grade iron ores easily accessible from the coast. The varied composition of Peruvian exports has certainly helped to reduce the vulnerability of external trade to price fluctuations in individual commodities, yet it still remains true of Peru that her exports are almost exclusively of basic raw materials and foodstuffs (98·6 per cent in 1968), with only a minimal contribution from semi-manufactures and manufactured goods (0·5 per cent and 0·9 per cent respectively in 1968). The export of a Peruvian-built ship, of equipment for a fishmeal plant, or of furniture, is hailed as a major achievement.

From 1950 to 1967 the economy as a whole maintained a high and fairly steady rate of growth at 5·5 per cent per year (see Fig. 7.4). Agriculture and stock-rearing grew slowly at 3·3 per cent per year, but this average conceals two phases: from 1950 to 1963 exports were increasing rapidly at 6·3 per cent per year and production for the domestic market stagnated; from 1963 to 1967 the value of agricultural exports declined, but production for the domestic market showed more substantial growth, though it sadly failed to keep pace with consumption, and imports of foodstuffs have continued to rise to the point at which they represent 23 per cent of the total import bill. The explosive growth of the fishing industry from 1955 to 1964 has levelled off, and, although the mining sector has grown by 7·7 per cent per year, expansion has fallen off in recent years. Manufacturing continued to increase fairly steadily at 7·8 per cent per year, and there has been expansion

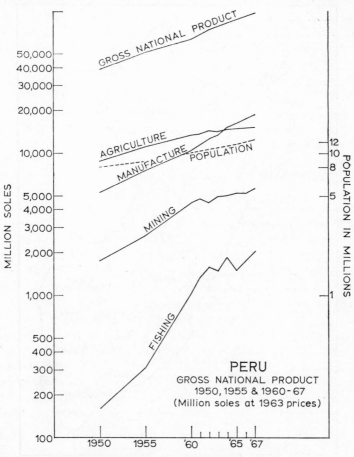

Fig. 7.4 Peru: economic growth 1950–67

in a wide variety of consumer goods industries and also in fishmeal, chemicals, shipbuilding and vehicle assembly.

Until very recently, then, the Peruvian economy flourished, and, given the wealth and variety of natural resources, there is no reason to suppose that such rates of growth may not recur in the future, but there was a setback in 1968 and 1969. Gross national product rose by only 1·4 per cent in 1968 and 1·7 per cent in 1969; industrial output increased by only 1·9 per cent in 1969, mining by 2·7 per cent and agriculture by 2·4 per cent. There was a decline in income from fishing and from construction.

Nevertheless, in spite of setbacks, gross national product has, on average, risen faster than population since 1950, and population is growing with a rapidity characteristic of tropical Latin America. In the years between the censuses of 1940 and 1961 population rose from 6,208,000 to 9,906,746 at

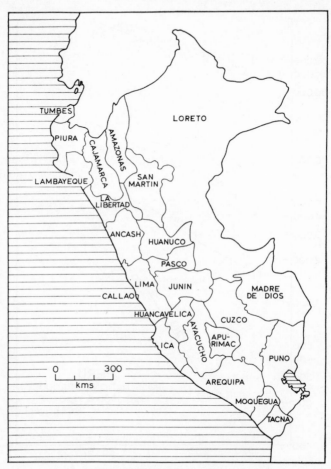

Fig. 7.5 Peru: departments

an average rate of 2·5 per cent per year, and there is evidence that the rate of growth is still rising. Between 1950 and 1967 the average rate of growth was 2·5 per cent and the annual mid-year estimate for 1969, which put the total population at 13,171,800, indicated an even faster rate of growth at 3·15 per cent. Birth-rates are very high (42·9 per 1000 in 1968) and death-rates have fallen to a level (11·4 per 1000) comparable with those of much more advanced industrial countries. No less than 43·3 per cent of the total population were less than 15 years of age in 1961, implying a relatively low proportion of 'economically active' people (55·5 per cent), a high degree of potential mobility in geographical terms, and also a potentially high burden to the economy in terms of education, social welfare and consumption. Yet, in spite of the pressure of an increasing population,

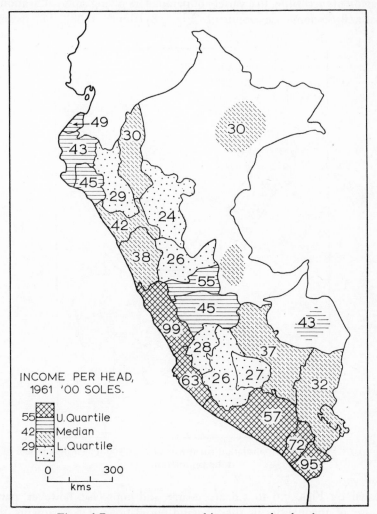

INCOME PER HEAD, 1961 '00 SOLES.

55   U.Quartile
42   Median
29   L.Quartile

0   300
kms

Fig. 7.6 Peru: average annual income per head 1961

gross national product per head has risen from £64 in 1950 (calculated at 1963 prices) to £104 in 1967.

Growth has been very uneven from one region to another, tending in general to accentuate existing regional differences. In terms of income per head, for example, the departments of Lima and Callao had an average of £132 in 1961, which was nearly twice the national average of £69 (Banco Central de Reserva, 1968), but at the other end of the scale, several departments of the northern and southern sierra averaged little more than half the national figure (see Fig. 7.6). Similar regional disparities are evident in the extent of urbanization (Fig. 7.7), and in the ranking of departments according to a variety of parameters giving some indication of social and economic development (Fig. 7.8) (Smith, 1968). The patterns

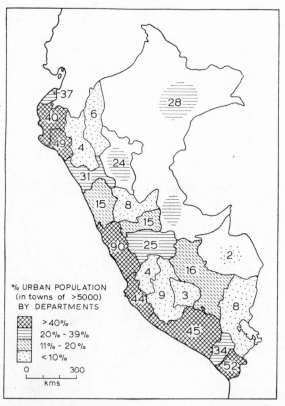

Fig. 7.7 Peru: urban population (in towns of over 5000) as a percentage of total population

revealed by Figs. 7.6 to 7.8 are coarse and imprecise, however, partly because of inequalities in the size and populations of departments, and partly because a number of departments include widely different ecological and cultural regions within their boundaries.

The major regional inequalities are best seen, perhaps, in two ways: the contrast between Lima, with Callao, and the rest of the country; and the contrasts between the coast, the sierra and the *selva*. In terms of its size and wealth, and of the range of economic and social activity, Lima is so clearly differentiated from other urban centres in Peru that the contrast between metropolitan Peru and the rest of the country seems more worthy of emphasis than the more usual categories of 'town' and 'country'. Its growth continues at an astonishing rate: in 1940 the provinces of Lima and Callao had 645,172 people; by 1961 numbers had almost tripled to

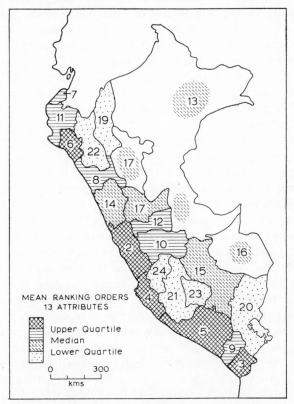

Fig. 7.8 Peru: development and living standards, average ranking order of thirteen attributes, by departments. Parameters included are: percentage of population in towns of over 5000; number of industrial establishments per head; value added by manufacture per head; percentages of households provided with electric light, means of cooking with fuels other than grass and wood, sewing machines, radios, refrigerators, piped water; percentage of houses with concrete, timber or tiled roofs; percentage of literate population over 17 years of age; percentage of children over 4 at school; percentage of farm units given fertilizer

1,845,910; and estimates for 1966 put the population at 2,447,084, or 20 per cent of the total population. The primacy of Lima in the urban structure of Peru is nothing new, of course, and may be traced from the early colonial regime, but the proportion of the total population living in the metropolitan area has increased substantially, rising slowly at first from

3·75 per cent in 1876 to about 4 per cent in 1908, and then fairly rapidly in the inter-war years to 10 per cent by 1940.

According to the industrial census of 1963, Lima and Callao held a clear industrial leadership over the rest of the country. Together, they then had two-thirds of all industrial establishments in the country and two-thirds of the personnel engaged in manufacture. Average wages were 30 per cent higher than the average for the rest of Peru. Much of the industrial production in other parts of Peru is geared to the processing of raw materials for export, so that the leadership of the metropolitan area in terms of industrial production for the national market is even more striking. According to Cesar Levano (1969, pp. 176–7) Lima-Callao produces no less than 82 per cent of the consumer goods made in Peru for the national market and 92 per cent of a much smaller output of durable consumer goods and capital goods.

As a market for industrial goods, Lima-Callao is much more dominant than population figures would suggest. Together they receive 42·5 per cent of the national income and contain over a half of the Peruvian population with incomes above the subsistence level. It is not surprising therefore, that new industries orientated towards the substitution of imports should be located near to the largest single market and the major importing port. Much of recent industrial expansion has been of this character: the manufacture, preparation and packaging of chemicals and pharmaceuticals, plastics industries, furniture, clothing and the planning of a new acrylic fibre plant to supplement the cotton textile industry of older origin. Recent expansion in the number of motor vehicle assembly plants has been dramatic and perhaps excessive, giving rise to considerable duplication. Attempts are, therefore, now being made to rationalize production, to increase national participation and also to increase substantially in the near future the proportion of domestically produced components.

Industrial growth is giving new shape to the urban pattern. Small workshops and domestic crafts are scattered throughout the built-up area, but larger scale industries are thrusting out towards and even beyond the margins of the city. Much of the older industrial growth was in Callao, along the roads linking Lima with Callao, and in transpontine Lima across the river Rimac, and there was also early growth along the Central Highway and the Central Railway towards the north-east to Chaclacayo. These continue to be preferred locations, but recent growth has pushed far out towards the north-west along the Pan-American Highway and towards the south-east.

There are many other reasons, besides the existence of a large and expanding market, why industry should be located in Lima rather than elsewhere in Peru. There are external economies to be gained from the presence of a fairly wide industrial base and the presence of associated industries, marketing structures, banking expertise, a pool of labour with varied skills and an adequate professional and managerial class. International middle-class standards of housing, shopping facilities, professional services and recreation make it attractive (for many the *only* attractive location) for entrepreneurs, executives and businessmen. Proximity to the

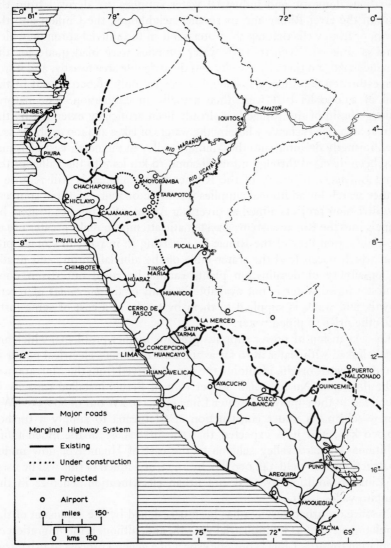

Fig. 7.9 Peru: major roads and the Marginal Highway project

seat of government and the highly centralized bureaucracy is also important. And the traditional preference of absentee landlords for urban living, which has always drained revenue from the countryside to the towns, has undoubtedly focused purchasing power to an even greater extent on Lima since the 1930s with the growth of easy communications by air and by road.

Growth has put continuing pressure on the urban infrastructure and particularly on the provision of adequate supplies of water and power. Irrigation, domestic and industrial water supplies are derived from the basin of the river Rimac and its smaller neighbours, the Chillón and the Lurin, or from wells that tap the water-table in the alluvial apron on which Lima is situated. Even in 1956 water supplies were inadequate for the demands made on them by the city and the irrigable area nearby, and it was then estimated that there was enough water for only 16,000 ha out of the total of 24,000 ha that were then actually in cultivation. The natural drainage basin of the Rimac has already been artificially extended by the Marcapomacocha scheme whereby the waters of lakes at 4400 m above sea-level, formerly draining into the Mantaro valley to the north-east of Lima, have been diverted through a tunnel some 10 km long to the valley of the Santa Eulalía, a tributary of the Rimac. Future demands will require a further search for additional supplies from one or more of three sources: new diversion projects aimed at diverting Atlantic-flowing headwaters by tunnels into the Rimac system; a systematic attempt to make greater use of the high season flow of the Rimac by diverting it, in part, to storage pits from which it can feed the water-table of the alluvial apron; and finally the possibility of desalination plants cannot be ruled out. Even now, domestic piped water is not available in many of the *barriadas* of recent growth, and water is supplied to them by trucks at a cost of some forty times the price of piped water.

The expansion of power supplies presents further problems, which are closely linked with water in so far as the bulk of Lima's electrical power is of hydro-electric origin, including the power derived from the Marcapomacocha diversion. No less than 80 per cent of Peru's installed capacity is orientated to the supply of Greater Lima (485,150 kW out of 600,550 kW). A new scheme is under construction at Matucana to supply a further 120,000 kW, and it is expected that the first stage of the much more ambitious Mantaro valley scheme to the east of Huancayo, now under construction, will yield 342,000 kW by 1973, and much of this will be used for Lima in addition to rural and urban electrification schemes in the Mantaro valley itself.

Pressure on urban services has been occasioned by the explosion of the population as well as by industrial growth, and, although the migration of population towards Lima is but one aspect of a general process of urbanization in Peru as a whole, it is by far the most important population movement in the country. Net movement to Lima is much more important than any other interdepartmental flow (see Figs. 7.10 and 7.11) and, in 1967 alone, 75,000 immigrants were reputed to have moved into the city and its environs. The characteristics of the migrants and the reasons why they move are the subject of continuing investigation, in part to confirm or refute the view that they are typically of illiterate peasant origin, constituting a rural or semi-rural enclave in the city, difficult to assimilate, and threatening the very fabric of urban life by their numbers and because of the difficulties of finding adequate housing or employment. A greater proportion of the migrants to Lima come from the sierra than from the coast, reversing a former pattern of coastal predominance. But a fairly high proportion of migrants come from provincial towns rather than directly from

Fig. 7.10 Peru: net migration to Lima 1961

the countryside. Migrants tend to be young and the pioneers from a particular area tend to be more ambitious and receptive of change than their stay-at-home neighbours. In common with migrants in Chile and Guatemala, those going to Lima tend to be among the better educated and of relatively high social status in their region of origin. Unemployment rates for migrants in Lima tend to be lower than those for non-migrants, and those who come from the larger towns to Lima seem to have the greatest chance of success in their search for jobs. In short, the evidence does not, in general, suggest that migrants are at a particular disadvantage in comparison with natives of Lima, nor does it suggest that the migrants are unusually resistant to assimilation into an urban way of life, though they do keep strong associations with their home towns or provinces.

Yet it remains true that the growth of population is outstripping the capacity for employment provided by manufacturing industry. In spite of substantial industrial growth, manufacturing industry is employing a

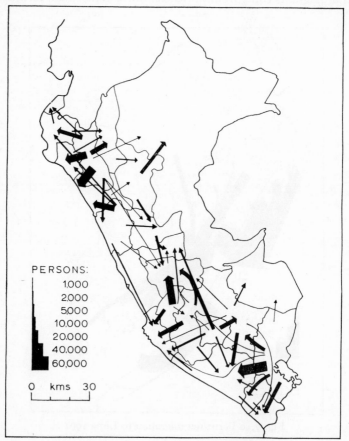

PERSONS:
1,000
2,000
5,000
10,000
20,000
40,000
60,000

0   kms   30

Fig. 7.11 Peru: net migration 1961, excluding movement to Lima

steadily decreasing proportion of the labour force (from 20 per cent between 1955 and 1960 to an average of 14 per cent between 1960 and 1965). Between 1940 and 1961 no less than 60 per cent of the increase in the labour force went into the general and amorphous census category labelled 'services'. Underemployment is widespread, and, although very difficult to calculate, the estimate has been made that 19 per cent of those employed in commerce in Lima are underemployed, 25 per cent of those in industry and as many as 49 per cent in services. Whatever the implications, the expansion of the services sector (so often involving tasks which contribute little to economic growth and much to the comfort of the middle classes) and the failure of employment in manufacturing industry (as opposed to small-scale domestic or workshop industry) to keep pace with the growth of the population are dominant factors in the Peruvian economy and the urban structure of Lima.

The physical expansion of the urban area to accommodate the swollen urban population of Greater Lima has been dramatic. Shanty towns, squatter settlements or *barriadas* have grown up, sometimes literally over-night, on the fringes of the built-up areas. They are not all new, the first being traced to 1924, but they are mostly of recent origin (142 out of 182 such settlements were started between 1955 and 1966) and they contain perhaps 20 per cent of Lima's population. Such squatter settlements are, of course, common in Latin America and in the developing world as a whole, but they have spread very widely in Lima, not only because of explosive population growth, but also because the arid environment of the coast makes their proliferation a relatively simple matter. Poor initial construction of reed matting, similar to those commonly found in rural settlements along the coast, and often later replaced in the *barriadas* by more solid brick and adobe constructions, are by no means intolerable in the arid climate of Lima. Bare and arid hill slopes, quebradas and alluvial plains, devoid of vegetation and agriculturally useless, have been occupied without let or hindrance from outraged owners. Living conditions are certainly bad, housing is poor, and piped water, sewerage and electric power are often not available, but it may well be that conditions are at least as good as they are in many parts of the sierra. Opinions differ greatly as to whether the *barriadas* represent semi-rural, chaotic slums of despair and delinquency (Mangin, 1967), or whether they represent a potential suburban, family-based stability in which that spirit of self-help, so highly commended by Samuel Smiles, is a continuing motif from the moment of their creation.

The coast, the sierra and the *selva*, so obviously distinctive in ecological terms, are also divisions traditionally recognized in Peruvian regional consciousness; each has its own cultural tradition expressed in literature and music; and each has a popular image, not always accurate or compli-mentary, for the inhabitants of the other two. There are, of course, impor-tant differences within each of these zones, particularly among northern, central and southern sections, which are in part related to environmental and historical circumstances, and which are also related to the strength or weakness of Lima's pervasive influence. But one general characteristic of location seems common to almost all Peru. Nuclei of population and econo-mic activity are small and discontinuous. Locally dense populations exist, as for example around Lake Titicaca, in the Huancayo basin or in irrigated coastal valleys, but they are usually separated by large areas of virtually unpopulated country: the oases of the coast are separated by barren stretches of desert; in the sierra zones of settlement are separated by deep gorges or high, barren *puna*; and in the *selva*, settlements and cultivated land are but islands in a sea of forest. To overcome the problem of distance must always be a major preoccupation of policy, therefore, quite apart from the inherent difficulties and cost of building and maintaining communications in terrain such as that of the sierra or the *selva*.

The coastal region is the richest and most productive area of Peru (see Fig. 7.6 and Table 7.2). The table provides a comparison of coast, sierra and *selva* in terms of several indices (calculated from CONESTCAR, 1968). The coastal region still contains a smaller proportion of the total population

TABLE 7.2   *Peru: coast, sierra and selva: population and agriculture*

	Coast	Sierra	Selva	Total/ average
	%	%	%	%
Contribution to exports, by value, 1964	74·5	6·6	18·9	100
Total population, 1940	25·1	61·7	13·2	100
Total population, 1965	39·7	51·0	9·3	100
Rural population, 1965	16·3	71·2	12·5	100
Area under crops, 1965	31.9	52·8	15·3	100
Area under crops, *per capita* (ha)	0·14	0·18	0·28	0·17
Area under crops/rural inhabitant (ha)	0·66	0·25	0·26	0·34
Value crop production/ha in crops	£153	£68·5	£97	£101
Value crop production/rural inhabitant	£95	£17·3	£26·6	£33.8
Value stock products/rural inhabitant	£6·9	£2·8	£0·3	£3·2
Value agricultural production/rural inhabitant	£101·9	£20·1	£26·9	£37·0
(Prices at 1963 values)				

of Peru than the sierra, but is growing at a faster rate, partly because of a higher natural rate of increase, but also through net immigration (particularly to Lima, of course). In Peru as a whole there is only 0·17 ha of cultivated land per person, though this figure rises to 0·28 in the *selva*. But in terms of *rural* population there is much more land per head on the coast than in the sierra or the *selva*, though these figures may be misleading because the narrow definition of rural population in the census excludes many nucleated settlements that are primarily agricultural. Finally, the leadership of the coast in terms of its contribution to exports, and in terms of agricultural productivity per head and per hectare is evident: five times that of the sierra and nearly four times that of the *selva*.

Except in the extreme north, near Tumbes, irrigation is a necessity for crop production in the coastal region. Since the late nineteenth century the area under irrigation has doubled; between 1906 and 1965, 120,293 ha have been newly irrigated and water supply has been improved on a further 178,000 ha. Much was done by traditional methods to increase the area under sugar and cotton by the construction of simple take-off canals from uncontrolled rivers, then later by the sinking of tube wells, the number of which increased very rapidly after 1945. In the Ica valley there were only 49 in 1938, 80 in 1944 and 476 by 1956. Where underground water is sufficient at suitable depths, tube well irrigation has had the advantage of liberating farmers from irksome rules and traditional usages, but it has favoured entrepreneurs with capital and in some areas water-tables have been lowered significantly as a result of over-exploitation (Smith, 1960). Since 1950 attention has turned to more ambitious projects involving the building of dams to regularize flow, the construction of longer canals to distribute water to areas of deficiency, or the diversion of Atlantic-flowing drainage across the watershed to the Pacific slope. Some of these schemes (e.g. at Marcapomacocha above the Rimac valley, or the Choclococha scheme above the Ica valley) have involved the diversion of high level lakes to new outlets across the relatively level country of the *puna* surface at over 4000 m. Relatively short tunnels and diversion channels have been needed, but construction work is often costly because of the inaccessibility of the sites. Some of the more recent projects to be undertaken, such as that at Olmos in the north, involve much longer and more expensive tunnelling operations. The cost of irrigation of new land in the coastal area is therefore high, and new projects tackling more difficult engineering problems are even more expensive. The average costs of providing water in fifteen projects now completed has been £295/ha of newly irrigated land and £87/ha of improved water supply (at 1963 prices) (Chungsuk Cha, 1969). In five new projects that are planned or in construction the average estimated cost is £582/ha, and in the two largest, planned to irrigate 59,000 ha from the Rio Majes in southern Peru, and 87,000 in the Olmos region of northern Peru, costs are estimated as £865/ha and £656/ha.

There is local specialization in a number of the coastal valleys, some of it already established in colonial times, such as the concentration on viticulture in the Ica valley. Rice cultivation is strongly localized on the clay-loam soils of the Lambayeque valley and neighbouring areas in northern Peru; market-gardening, fruit and vegetables are concentrated in the Lima region, as one would expect. But it has been sugar and cotton that have dominated coastal agriculture since the late nineteenth century. Sugar occupies only 86,000 ha on the coast, but by value represents about 16 per cent of coastal output, and yields are about three times the world average. The industry is efficient, using modern techniques and high-yielding varieties of cane. Controlled irrigation coupled with moderately high temperatures and good insolation throughout the year make possible a rotation of harvests such that a controlled and continuous supply of cane can keep the mills in full operation throughout the year. Linkages with other industries have been strong since bagasse is the raw material for the manufacture of paper and a small chemical industry has been created to supply raw materials for sugar-processing. By-products provide fodder for cattle fattening. Indeed, it has been observed that, although the sugar industry contributes substantially to exports, about a third of the output is retained for internal consumption. But the considerable expansion of post-war years in yields and area under cultivation has come to an end. Prices are low and future prospects depend almost completely on the U.S. quota for Peruvian sugar. And the large sugar haciendas have been the first target for the new agrarian reform announced in June 1969.

Cotton occupies no less than a third of the area under crops in the coastal region and annual output is also about a third of the total coastal production. But, like sugar, it is now less profitable than it once was, and both output and area under cultivation have declined in recent years. Between 1950 and 1963 output increased from 1·6 million quintals to 3·2, but has since fallen back to 1·9 in 1967.

The growth of the fishing industry from insignificant proportions in 1950 to its present status as the world's largest in terms of tonnage of fish landed has made a considerable contribution to the national income and to the export sector. Output declined after a record catch of over 9 million tons in 1964, and fears of overfishing led to the establishment of a close season during June, July and August. Levels have recovered in the last few years, with another record catch in 1968 of 10,262,000 tons. Some 2400 fishing vessels are employed, operating from no less than forty-seven ports, many of which are tiny settlements landing no more than a few hundred tons. The major centres are Chimbote (with a catch of 3,674,000 tons in 1968), Tambo de Mora (1,109,000 tons), Pisco (1,078,000 tons), Callao (986,000), Supe (685,000) and Ilo (589,000). Chimbote superseded Callao as major producer in 1963 and now lands about a third of the total catch; and in recent years the productivity of northern fisheries has tended to increase faster than those of the centre or south. Some 98 per cent of total output is the small sardine-like anchoveta used for the manufacture of fishmeal, a product which has found a rapidly expanding market in recent years as a fertilizer and as an animal feeding stuff with high protein content. The expansion of fishing has thus been closely associated with the building of fishmeal-processing plants, particularly at the major ports. Both the fishing industry and fishmeal manufacture have created important backward linkages to other activities, quite apart from their intrinsic importance in creating employment, providing exports and contributing to national income. A modest shipbuilding and repair industry, consisting of some ninety-six yards, has sprung up chiefly in Callao. Firms specializing in the construction and manufacture of fishmeal plants have been created and in minor ways demands of fishing have stimulated national industry in the manufacture of nets, pumps, centrifuges, rope and carpentry (*Actividades productivas del Perú*, 1966, pp. 199–207). In a regional sense, fishing has helped to spread new activity and non-agricultural employment in a number of places such as Casma, Ilo, Supe and, above all, Chimbote, a boom town which has become an important focus for immigration from the sierra. Future prospects depend in part on the size of the annual harvest, but also on the possibility of expanding the production of white fish for human consumption, perhaps from fishing grounds further afield. And it has been the undoubted importance of the fishing industry to Peru's economy which underlies recent claims to a 300 km limit for territorial waters.

Mining, too, has made its contribution to the economic growth of the coastal region. Growth in mineral exports during the early 1960s has been derived largely from two sources: the open-cast exploitation of low grade copper ores on the Pacific slope of the southern Andes at Toquepala, opened up in 1961; and the mining of high grade iron ores near Nazca from 1953. Both have been accompanied by investment in infrastructure: the creation of a new port and heavy duty roads at San Juan for the export of iron ore and the building of a new railway to the coast in the south. Plans exist for the exploitation of other nearby deposits: of iron ore from Acarí, and of copper from Cerro Verde near Arequipa. In northern Peru oil has been exploited since the late nineteenth century, and, although production from wells at Talara has been relatively stable in recent years, off-shore drilling has been fairly successful. Finally, other plans are being put into operation for the investment of $100 million in the phosphate deposits of the Sechura desert. Mineral exports, formerly the main contribution of the sierra to the external economy, are now derived to a much greater extent than formerly from the coastal region.

The coastal region as a whole possessed 86 per cent of all industrial establishments employing more than five people in 1963 (industry being very broadly defined), but, even if Lima and Callao are excluded since they alone contain 68 per cent, the remainder of the coast has 19 per cent of industrial establishments compared with 9 per cent in the sierra and 4·5 per cent in the *selva*. Much of the coastal industry is concerned with the processing of raw materials and foodstuffs: sugar-refining, fishmeal production, cotton-processing and dairying industries in Arequipa and Chiclayo, but there are also chemicals (Paramonga), textiles, cement and light engineering, as well as a small and high cost steel industry at Chimbote.

Coastal Peru is the 'leading geographical sector' of the country in economic terms and has been so from at least the mid-nineteenth century. It is also distinctive in social and cultural terms. Even in colonial times the sparsity of Indian population and the use of Negro slaves in coastal plantations meant that the area rapidly acquired a different racial character from the sierra. In the nineteenth century the immigration of Chinese, either as traders or shopkeepers or as coolie labour for the exploitation of the guano quarries and the building of the railways, added a new strain to the racial character of the coastal zone. There was a revival of immigration from Europe, but it has always been the Indian immigrants from the sierra who have predominated in numerical terms to accentuate the generally mestizo character of the area. There are still occasional enclaves of traditionally mestizo culture, relatively static in economy, mobility and society, and such groups have been described at Moche and Santiago de Cao and can be traced in the Ica valley, but the norms of coastal Peru are more nearly those of an urbanized society. Levels of literacy are higher than in the sierra, and the labour force is more articulate and more highly organized. But the relative prosperity and higher income levels of the coast are constantly undermined by the immigration of cheap, unskilled labour from the reservoir of poverty and population in the sierra.

The poverty of the sierra is evident from Fig. 7.6 and Table 7.2. In those departments that lie wholly within this zone, average *per capita* incomes in 1961 were as follows (1963 values): Huancavelica £38, Apurimac £36, Cajamarca £38. In terms of urbanization, possession of durable consumer goods, provision of services and education, non-agricultural employment, agricultural productivity and literacy, the sierra falls far below the standards achieved on the coast. Rural incomes among the peasantry are frequently quite inadequate to support farm families at a satisfactory level of living.

There is no doubt that the sierra presents very difficult conditions for efficient, modern methods of farming. Reasonably flat land is scarce at altitudes suitable for crop farming; in many regions rainfall is deficient or, more seriously, highly variable from year to year, and the extension of irrigation is much to be desired. Above 3500 m late or early frosts and hail are difficult hazards; many mountain soils are severely eroded or highly erodable, and the introduction of temperate crops and animals, or of temperate agricultural techniques, is complicated by the occasional failure to understand the important differences between apparently temperate climates at high altitudes and temperate climates of the middle latitudes. But the possibilities of the sierra environment should not be too readily dismissed. There are important areas in which progress has been achieved, particularly in central Peru where the accessibility of the Lima market or the proximity of markets in the mining areas and in Huancayo have served to stimulate commercial peasant farming. In the Tarma valley, for example, a careful and intensive system of farming is orientated to the production of vegetables and flowers for the Lima market. The Mantaro valley is also a zone of relatively intensive farming, where incomes and the material standard of living are noticeably higher than in most of the sierra. There are some very efficient pastoral haciendas in central Peru and in the south, and small-scale cattle-fattening enterprises around Lake Titicaca are efficient at a low level of technology. Possibilities certainly exist for the intensification of farming in the sierra of northern Peru on reasonably good, well-watered land in the Cajamarca region, and near Chachapoyas. Much of the sierra is necessarily committed to pastoral activity and wool has always been a mainstay of the sierra economy, but productivity is in general low and the future market for wool uncertain. Yet there are considerable possibilities: the improvement of natural pasture by controlled grazing or reseeding, the cultivation of fodder crops and the extension of irrigation, the introduction of hardy beef stock to improve poor *criollo* cattle, the replacement of deteriorating merino or Corriedale wool sheep by mutton-producing breeds such as the Cheviot, and the scientific improvement of alpaca and llama.

Agricultural progress has been slow and hesitant in the sierra as a whole, in spite of the provision of some technical assistance and agricultural extension work. General levels of farming are miserably low, whether on haciendas or on peasant farms, so that yields of wheat average 950 kg/ha, maize 1065 kg/ha, barley 1010 kg/ha, and potatoes 5990 kg/ha. Lack of capital, poor technical assistance, uneven facilities for rural credit and a difficult environment are only some of the elements in the situation. Even where costs of transport would permit commercial farming, on-farm price levels often provide little stimulus to change from subsistence farming and are not likely to do so as long as imports of food are freely admitted or as long as prices are fixed at low levels for the benefit of Lima consumers. Levels of rural education are generally inadequate and agricultural education at the intermediate level has been sadly neglected. The rural infrastructure is usually poor, and although the programme of Cooperación Popular was well founded as a means whereby government would provide help and materials for constructional work, the labour being provided by local communities, political and financial difficulties have meant limited progress.

Apathetic attitudes towards the possibility of change and progress and reluctance to accept innovation have frequently been noted among Indian peasantry, and to some extent such attitudes seem inevitable where farmers live so close to the margin of subsistence that any innovation involving real or imaginary risk is likely to be rejected, or where farmers rarely realize benefits from innovation because of an increase in effective rent. The cultivation of attitudes more receptive of change and new ideas has proved moderately successful in the Vicos experiment conducted by Cornell University, and there is growing evidence that some at least of the Indian communities are responsive to changing situations under favourable circumstances, e.g. in Huaylas or Muquiyauyo. Education, experience away from the village region as a result of military service, temporary migration, information and help from expatriate communities in Lima, and the dissemination of news and ideas by radio, are all factors making for change and the acceptance of change.

L

Given the social structure and the social and economic attitudes of the sierra, the major obstacle to change is perhaps the pattern of land tenure. The concentration of landownership in the hands of *latifundistas* is more marked than on the coast and many of the haciendas are grossly under-capitalized. Practices whereby hacienda owners grant the use of a small plot of land to Indian farmers in return for labour services and perhaps an exiguous wage have been normal; on pastoral estates *colonos* are similarly allowed to graze their animals on the hacienda in return for services in caring for the hacienda flock; indebtedness to the hacienda store retains peasants on the estate, sometimes under harsh conditions. In remoter regions, landownership is sometimes valued as much for the personal power it conveys as for the income it generates; there is often little effort to maximize income or to raise productivity, partly because revenue from the estates may be more profitably invested in urban land (especially near Lima), in other enterprises or even abroad, and partly because income is spent on consumption. Very little revenue is, in general, ploughed back as capital investment to improve productivity and yields. Hence, in many areas, extensive forms of exploitation prevail on large estates while peasant farmers in neighbouring districts coax a subsistence crop from a couple of hectares or less of poor and over-exploited land. Absentee ownership is common and much of the income generated on large holdings is siphoned away to Lima and thus fails to nourish regional activity in the sierra itself. On the other hand, on *minifundios* and in the *comunidades*, farms are nor-mally too small to produce adequate subsistence, let alone the accumula-tion of capital. The growth of population has led and continues to lead to the fragmentation of holdings, so that urgent pressures exist to supplement farm incomes by other employment, either in local towns and in craft industries or by migration to the coast, to Lima, or to the *selva*.

Within the sierra, however, there is relatively little non-agricultural employment and few prospects for any immediate increase. Industrial possibilities are limited, and although there are modest enterprises in Huancayo, Cuzco, Puno and Juliaca, chiefly concerned with food, drink, textiles and construction, they rest for the most part on the special needs and tastes of the sierra Indians and are thus dependent in the last resort on agricultural productivity in the region itself. Mining is locally important, particularly in the central sierra along the Central Railway to Cerro de Pasco, and also in many scattered sites throughout the region, but employ-ment offered by mining is relatively little and the impact of mining on regional agricultural economies has not been great (except perhaps in the central zone). Small-scale craft industries exist in many parts of the sierra, and whole villages often concentrate on the production of a range of goods for which they are well fitted by resource or traditional skills. But possi-bilities of expansion are clearly limited, again, by peasant income levels and by the growth of the potential tourist market.

In spite of the fact that the sierra still contains over half the population of all Peru it has received less attention in government policy and very much less public investment in the improvement of its basic infrastructure than either the coast or the eastern regions. Price policies favour the urban consumer in Lima. It could be argued that in some quarters distrust and social prejudice militate against investment in predominantly Indian areas. Nevertheless, the departments of Puno, Cuzco, Pasco and Junín were designated as priority areas for the application of the Agrarian Reform Law of 1964, though little had been achieved by 1969 when it was superseded by the more drastic proposals of a new decree (June 1969). It is in the sierra that agrarian reform may be expected to have the most positive results, but only if the expropriation of haciendas is accompanied by intensive and effective programmes of technical assistance, rural credit, marketing and agricultural extension work.

To promote the settlement and colonization of the empty, forested regions of eastern Peru has seemed at times a possible solution to some of the country's pressing problems. From the 1940s road construction into the *montaña* has been followed by, and sometimes anticipated by an extension of settlement, especially in the central zone (along the road from Cerro de Pasco to Tingo María and thence to Pucallpa, and in the zone of Satipo, Oxapampa and Chanchamayo) and to a smaller extent in the area north of Cuzco in La Convención. Coffee, tea, bananas and other tropical fruits have supplemented coca as major profitable crops, though rice has been successful, especially in the far north, near Bagua. During the Belaunde regime of 1963–8 settlement of the *selva* was a major target of government policy. It was argued that eastern colonization would increase national production, create new sources of external revenue, substitute domestic sources for imported foodstuffs and raw materials, relieve over-population in the sierra, and help to divert the current of migrant population away from Lima and the coast. It could also be argued that a colonization programme would remove some of the pressure for land reform in other regions of Peru. Detailed resource studies, an ambitious roadbuilding programme and a number of colonization projects were undertaken. The Grand Design of Belaunde's *Carretera Marginal* (the Marginal Highway) was to link the eastern regions of Andean countries from Venezuela to Paraguay, and more specifically to link up existing settlements in eastern Peru by a longitudinal highway (see Fig. 7.9). The economic function of such a route has repeatedly been questioned and the heavy investment involved could scarcely be justified, though individual links of the *Carretera Marginal* have value in so far as they provide road access to isolated settlements from the coastal region by way of existing trans-Andean links. At the present time, construction of the *Carretera Marginal* has virtually ceased, at first because of financial difficulties and more recently as a result of policy changes. The cost of roadbuilding is high (£50,000 to £60,000 per km for the *Carretera Marginal*) and maintenance likely to be expensive. Costs of penetration roads are lower, but even so it has been estimated that assuming an effective zone of influence of 5 km on each side of a new road, the cost of road frontage alone would be £40 to £50 per hectare of land opened up, and this cost would rise proportionally, of course, with the amount of unusable land through which such a penetration road would pass.

A number of colonization projects were established during the Belaunde regime on the basis of resource and feasibility studies. A brief summary is given below:

Zone	Area to be settled (ha)	Families to be settled	Cost	Cost/ hectare	Cost/ family
Tingo María–Tocache	26,080	5,250	£2,000,000	£77	£380
Right bank Apurimac	7,000	338	250,000	£35	£760
Perené–Satipo–Ene	15,000	500	485,000	£32	£970
Alto Marañon	9,275	(900)	230,000	£25	£250
(1965 values)					

These are official estimates based on project budgets and do not, of course, include the general administrative costs of the colonization programme, nor do they include the costs of roadbuilding. They are almost certainly underestimates of the true costs, perhaps grossly so. Costs such as these could only be justified on the grounds that the secondary and multiplier effects of new roads or new projects will provide axes or nuclei for much more intensive settlement at a later date, and this must, in turn, depend on the economic prospects for the agricultural production of the *selva*.

Of the major crops produced in the *selva*, coffee has proved its worth on international markets and exports have increased significantly in the last decade. But international agreements, poor prices and high transport costs limit possibilities of much further growth. Tropical fruits such as pineapple, citrus, passion fruit and papaya have limited possibilities for supporting an export trade as fruit juices or canned, but are unlikely to be highly important. Bananas are an important *selva* crop, but they face coastal competition and cannot compete in international markets with, for example, Ecuador. Rice is a good prospect for the home market, especially from the northern area around Bagua where it is already well established, and beef may have good prospects as a future industry if domestic prices are maintained at a higher level than at present or if imports of foreign beef are restricted. Many other crops are grown, of course, some on no more than an experimental scale, but in general the difficulties and expense of transport to the coast, or by navigable water to Iquitos, greatly restrict competitiveness. Some products must compete with coastal production more favourably located: sugar, cotton, rice and fruits, for example. Beef faces competition from the sierra as well as the coast. The nearest, most obvious and accessible market is, of course, the sierra itself, but as long as the sierra market is limited by the poverty of its inhabitants, there is little hope in this direction, except for the small-scale marketing of coca, coffee, citrus fruits and the like.

Environmental contrasts in Peru are as abrupt and varied as anywhere in Latin America; processes of economic and social development have, in general, served to heighten regional differences between the coast and the sierra, corresponding very approximately to the 'modernized' and 'backward' sectors of a dualistic economy. Such a division may, in truth, be too simple, ignoring as it does the extent to which the sierra has progressed towards a modernized economy, not only in the enclaves associated with the mining industry, but also in areas of prosperous and relatively efficient farming, and in its larger cities. The metropolitan dominance of Greater Lima has exerted its influence on regional economies in the central zone of the sierra and the central *selva* no less than on the coast. Little attention has so far been paid to regional planning in Peru, though industrial estates have been established in provincial centres such as Arequipa and Chiclayo in the hope of stimulating 'growth poles'. Regional studies have been made, notably the intensive survey of southern Peru as a part of the abortive Plan del Sur, and smaller regional surveys have been made in connection with plans for eastern colonization. Nevertheless, economic and social policies have had important implications for regional development. Until recently a relatively free economy has encouraged investment in the external economy by domestic and foreign capital, and this has certainly stimulated the exploitation of coastal resources and economic growth in fishing, mining, irrigation and sugar production. The emphasis placed by the Belaunde regime on roadbuilding, especially in relation to the colonization of the *selva*, may have been an important factor in the vast increase in public debt and in the creation of balance of payments problems, but the Velasco military regime from 1968 has not so far pursued the same kind of active policy in relation to the *selva* regions.

Since its inception the Velasco government has followed a nationalistic policy, aiming at the modernization of archaic social and economic structures, greater national participation in industry and commerce, and the rationalization of government bureaucracy. One of its first acts was to take over the International Petroleum Company's holdings (though not the remainder of the oil industry). It has insisted that Peruvian nationals must own 51 per cent or more of the shares in motor vehicle assembly plants, 75 per cent or more of the ownership of shipping companies established in Peru and over 75 per cent of the share capital in national banks, and it has also insisted on total Peruvian ownership and editorial control of national newspapers. Greater government participation or public ownership is envisaged in communications and power, and in the control of water resources. Emphasis is being given to further industrialization; and important import restrictions have been established. In terms of regional and social change, however, the new Agrarian Reform Law of 24 June 1969 is likely to have the most far-reaching consequences, symbolically issued on the '*día del indio*', which has itself no less symbolically been renamed as the '*día del campesino*'.

The new agrarian reform law supersedes that of 1964, under which relatively little had been achieved in terms of the redistribution of holdings. Its provisions, if and when they are implemented, are intended to bring about great social change, particularly in the sierra, where agrarian reform is seen as a basic tool in the integration into a national society of the predominantly Indian rural population. Large estates are to be redistributed. Those which consist of abandoned, idle or deficiently worked land may be expropriated in their entirety and so also may estates which are leased out for rent, operated by share-croppers, or worked by *feudatorios* paying labour services for their right to cultivate a plot of land or to graze stock. Sugar haciendas, too, are liable to total expropriation, and coastal Peru has already been profoundly affected by the application of the new law. Directly and efficiently operated estates may normally retain 150 ha of irrigated land on the coast, 15–55 ha of irrigated land in the sierra and the *selva* or 30–110 ha of dry-farmed land in the sierra and the *selva*, or, on pastoral estates, that amount of land which will graze 5000 sheep units or their equivalent. The areas exempt from expropriation may be increased under certain circumstances, so that it would be possible, for example, for a well-run pastoral estate of up to 20,000 ha to survive. Even these areas may be expropriated, however, if the lands are needed in order to provide minimum peasant holdings for sitting tenants and *feudatorios* on the estate itself, or in neighbouring communities. Compensation is in cash and in bonds of various classes, but cash payments are never to be more than 100,000 *soles* (c. £1000) for land, or more than 1 million *soles* for improvements.

In principle, beneficiaries of the reform are to receive not less than 3 ha. Preference is given to co-operatives, societies of 'social interest' and existing *comunidades*, and it is clearly envisaged by the state that co-operative forms of farming, assisted by agents of the agrarian reform organization, will normally succeed to the large estates. This is indeed what has already happened on some of the estates in the sierra which have been reformed. Individual small-scale peasant proprietorship will be the basis of the reform, with various degrees of co-operation in production and marketing, not only to gain some advantage of scale economies, but also to facilitate direction, guidance and advice from officials of the agrarian reform organization and agricultural extension services. Procedures for the valuation, expropriation and allocation of the estates have been made much more simple and rapid than they were under the reform law of 1964, when they were so cumbersome that two years was regarded as the minimum time in which a land reform could be achieved on any single estate.

Immediately after the promulgation of the law, government intervened to begin the process of reform on the largest sugar haciendas of the coastal region. In the sierra, priority was given to the application of the new law in the central region and in Puno and Cuzco, following the regional priorities of the previous regime. By the end of 1970, 3·3 million ha of land had been expropriated and 1·3 million ha had been handed over to some 65,000 families, though it is clear that some of the essential preparation for the expropriation of land in the sierra had been taken by the previous reform organization.

There are clearly many problems, not least in the apparent shortage of trained personnel to carry out the reform quickly and efficiently, to organize co-operatives and to provide the agricultural extension work and advice which will be needed if productivity is to be sustained or improved. It is estimated that 1·4 million ha of cultivable land will be made available for redistribution by the reform law, but there are thought to be some 650,000 families of landless rural labourers and 612,000 rural families with less than the minimum 3 ha. There is evidently not enough land to go round. A large proportion of landless labour will continue to exist as such, and many of those who have less than one hectare will probably lose that which they now possess or will not receive additional land to make a viable holding. But this kind of arithmetic on a national scale is very misleading, for local disparities in the pattern of large estates and small peasant holdings will make it even more difficult, if not impossible, to ensure equitable holdings for all. Finally, the costs of agrarian reform are always high and, even though cash payments for compensation are reduced to a minimum and the disposal of land to peasant farmers is to be paid for, continuing progress is bound to depend on annual budget decisions and the provision of public funds.

It is still too early to reach any kind of verdict, of course, and it is the application of the law, rather than the consideration of its provisions, that matters. The Peruvian agrarian reform is likely to have a profound effect, and in the long term its impact is likely to be greater in the sierra than on the coast even though it is the sugar estates that have been affected earliest. A greater degree of rural stability and security in the sierra, a more equitable distribution of income in favour of the small peasant and the elimination of the absentee *latifundista* may well help to reduce the drain of income to Lima and to create a modest effective demand within the sierra itself for foodstuffs and manufactured goods, which will, in turn, stimulate national industrial production and even, perhaps, accelerate spontaneous movements towards the colonization of the *selva*.

Bolivia

Of all South American countries it is Bolivia that faces the most intractable geographical and economic problems, not only because of its poverty and its excessive dependence on exports of tin and associated minerals, but also because of its position as a landlocked state and its lack of internal cohesion. In spite of their regional contrasts, Peru and Ecuador have identifiable 'leading geographical sectors', which focus on the nodal regions created round Lima, Guayaquil and even Quito. But neither the export economy nor metropolitan dominance have succeeded in creating for Bolivia a strongly established nodal region that might serve to counteract the centrifugal tendencies of its peripheral regions. And until very recently it has also demonstrated in extreme form that dichotomy between traditional subsistence economy and export-orientated activities which may be taken as a hallmark of the 'dual economy'.

Its poverty within South America is evident from those indices that are often taken as a general measure of economic and social development. Of the ten countries of South America (excluding the Guianas), Bolivia shares with Paraguay the distinction of being at the bottom of the league table of development, with a gross domestic product per head of £50 in 1964, an urban population (in settlements of more than 2000), of 30 per cent, a low energy consumption and a weakly developed manufacturing sector. An illiteracy rate of 70 per cent and an average of 3700 people per physician, higher than anywhere else in South America, are symptomatic of inadequate provision for health and education. Landlocked and with a small population of only 3·7 million in 1966, yet faced with the problem of integrating a large and sparsely populated territory of extremely diverse and difficult terrain, Bolivia is clearly one of the weakest states of Latin America.

Political and economic weakness have been evident from the time when Bolivia achieved its independence in 1825, carved from the Viceroyalty of La Plata and consisting essentially of what had formerly been the *audiencia* of Charcas. At its creation, Bolivia contained approximately 2·3 million km², stretching from the Pacific to a rather indefinite northern boundary in the Amazon basin and across the Gran Chaco to an equally indefinite boundary in the south-east. Now, with an area of some 1·1 million km², it covers less than half of its former extent as a result of the loss of territory to all its neighbours. Brazil and Peru appropriated unexplored and sparsely populated rain-forest, swamp and savanna in the north and north-east during the nineteenth century when the search for cinchona and wild rubber gave sudden but temporary economic value to these remote forested areas. To Paraguay, Bolivia lost much of its claim to the thorn and scrubland wastes of the Chaco as a result of its humiliating and crushing defeat in the disastrous War of the Chaco as recently as 1935. But the most important loss, to which Bolivia has never been entirely reconciled, was the loss of its window on the Pacific to Chile as a consequence of the War of the Pacific (1879–83). Bolivia thus became the landlocked state it now is, and the creation or the maintenance of external links by the building of railways and roads or by the improvement of river navigation has continued to pre-occupy Bolivian policy.

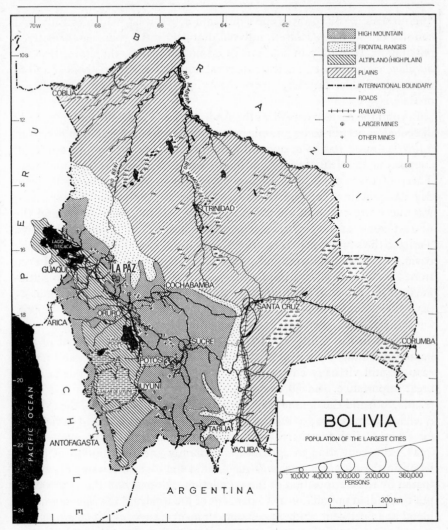

Fig. 7.12 Bolivia

No less important than the vulnerability of a landlocked state is the internal lack of cohesion within the existing boundaries. Regionalism is a force that has, at times, threatened the unity of the state, particularly in the eastern regions: 'a citizen of La Paz or Santa Cruz is apt to speak of himself and think of himself as a *Paceño* or a *Cruceño* rather than a *Boliviano*' (Edelmann, 1967). In part this lack of cohesion is associated with the harsh realities of terrain and climate and the possibilities of settlement. The *altiplano*, enclosed between the western cordillera, which forms the boundary with Chile, and the eastern cordillera, which contains the major zone of mineralization, is itself divided by climatic boundaries, for rainfall

322 LATIN AMERICA: GEOGRAPHICAL PERSPECTIVES

diminishes rapidly towards the south and south-west, which is truly arid country of salt-pans (*salares*), internal drainage and a sparse and scattered population. It is only in the north-east of the region, therefore, that the *altiplano* can support a fairly dense rural population, especially near and to the south of Lake Titicaca, core of the Aymara-speaking Indian population of Bolivia.

Beyond the eastern cordillera the Andean massif is deeply and intricately dissected, a barrier to communications and barren of population except in a few favoured basins at approximately 2700 to 3200 m above sea-level, supporting an adequate range of food crops and a dense rural population. Three of these *valle* regions have played an important role in Bolivian development since colonial times, when the area around Sucre (Chuquisaca) was the nearest area of supply for the city and mines of Potosí and the nearest zone of comfortable temperate climate for Spanish residents. Tarija to the south was never so intensively developed, but the Cochabamba basin, largest of the three, and accessible from the Oruro mines and even from La Paz, has always been a major zone of Indian and mestizo settlement. Taken together the *altiplano* and the *valle* region contain about 85 per cent of the total population with about half the total area of Bolivia. Of the rest, the greater part is concentrated in the expanding zone of settlement in the south-east around Santa Cruz, the department of that name containing 9 per cent of the total population. The north and north-east are still virtually empty, except for a few riverine settlements of no great importance. Indeed, except for the urban agglomeration of La Paz (*c.* 400,000) and the dense rural population near Lake Titicaca, the existing nuclei of population are relatively small, widely scattered and difficult or expensive to link together by reason of terrain as well as distance.

The differentiation in agricultural economy and distribution of population in the *altiplano*, the *valle* region and the eastern lowlands is accentuated by the composition of the population. Estimates of the 1950 census put the Indian population at 50 per cent of the total and the *cholos* of mixed blood at 35 per cent, with 15 per cent white or near white. The *altiplano* is overwhelmingly Indian, except in La Paz, with an important distinction between the Aymara country near Lake Titicaca and to the south, and Quechua-speaking populations elsewhere in the sierra, especially in the *valle* region, where mestizos are more numerous, especially in the towns. Whites and mestizos, with a greater proportion of Guaraní blood, are more frequent in the eastern regions. The Aymara in particular retain a sense of community, and prevailing attitudes of whites and mestizos to the Indians, or of the Indians to the mestizos, have at times encouraged the regionalism inherent in Bolivian geography.

Centrifugal tendencies of the eastern lowlands and the *valle* region have also been encouraged in the past by the extent to which the pattern of communications has tended until recently to link nuclei of settlement more strongly to the outside world than to each other. Railway-building policy was primarily orientated from the beginning to the creation of external links by which Bolivia's mineral wealth could be tapped. Completion of the Southern Peruvian Railway to Puno in 1874 and the introduction of steam navigation on Lake Titicaca provided the first link to La Paz, though the railway link from Guaqui to La Paz was only finished in 1903. The Antofagasta–Bolivian Railway to Oruro was built by 1892, and reached La Paz in 1911; the Arica line was completed in 1913; and the railway across the *altiplano* from Uyuni to Villazon and thus to Argentina was finished only in 1925. This western system, however, remains unconnected with the two eastern lines of later construction linking Santa Cruz with Corumba and Brazil on the one hand (completed in 1955) and Yacuiba and Argentina on the other (finished in the early 1960s), both built in the wave of optimism for eastern settlement and oil exploration. Emphasis on eastern development is recently reflected in new plans (1970) for a railway to be built in conjunction with Argentina from Santa Cruz to the Mamoré river, and new Bolivian hopes have been aroused by plans for an integrated development of the drainage basin of the Paraná–Paraguay–Uruguay and Plate, involving co-operation of Argentina, Uruguay, Paraguay, Brazil and Bolivia. Resolutions of 1968 imply joint regional planning for power projects, navigation and roadbuilding. In 1969, examination began on the feasibility of establishing a new Bolivian riverport (Puerto Busch) on the river Paraguay.

It is still, however, the Pacific outlets that remain by far the most important for Bolivian trade. The Antofagasta line carried a third of all freight on Bolivian lines in 1957–61 and the three Pacific lines carried a half of all freight traffic – more than was carried by all the internal lines put together (see Table 7.3).

The western railway systems, built to a large extent for the export sector and stressing external links rather than internal integration, are now in poor condition and badly maintained and are, of course, losing traffic to road and air transport. The creation of a network of communications that will tend to integrate the disparate nuclei of population and settlement into a truly national system is largely of recent origin, and it was only in 1953 that the most important link was completed between Cochabamba and Santa Cruz, a good road that has had a profound effect in linking the zone of eastern settlement with the *valle* region and thus with La Paz. Recent emphasis has been on the improvement of road systems linking the *altiplano* with the *valle* region and on the provision of penetration roads into the north-eastern and eastern lowlands to assist in the colonization and settlement of new areas, and with the hope of making connections to the navigable waters of the Amazon system. Caranavi (north of La Paz), the Cochabamba Highway and Santa Cruz are the springboards for new roads of this type.

TABLE 7.3   *Bolivia: railway traffic, average annual totals 1957-60*

	Passengers carried	%	Tonnage (metric)	%
Western system				
a) *Externally orientated lines*				
Oruro–Antofagasta	412,678	18	426,820	33
La Paz–Guaqui	52,588	2	126,000	10
La Paz–Arica	84,161	4	88,330	7
Atocha–Villazon–Argentina	138,716	6	76,320	6
	688,143	30	641,310	50
b) *Internal lines*				
Bolivian Railway (La Paz–Atocha)	647,574	28	407,960	31
Others	689,312	32	87,030	7
	1,336,886	60	494,990	38
Eastern system				
Santa Cruz–Corumba	78,535	3	27,350	2
Santa Cruz–Yacuiba	160,793	7	53,270	4
	239,328	10	80,620	6
Total	2,264,357	100	1,293,240	100

The weakness of internal integration in Bolivia may be associated with the failure of the export economy to generate spread effects in the economy as a whole. Until the 1950s at least Bolivia could be regarded as a classic example of a dual economy in which a traditional and largely subsistence economy had not been greatly modified by the superimposition of a modernized sector associated with mineral production. Tin ores, often found together with bismuth and silver or tungsten, antimony and gold, are located in a mineralized zone in the eastern cordillera from the Peruvian frontier into Argentina (see Fig. 7.12). Tin mining began seriously c. 1895, rapidly replacing silver as a major product with the increase in prices following the growth of the tin plate industry in South Wales before 1914. Oruro is the major centre and over a half of Bolivia's production comes from within 100 km of it, though there are other important mining centres near La Paz and Potosí and further south. The growth of production and exports rising from less than 10,000 tons in 1900 to 40,000 in 1930, was closely bound up with the fortunes of the tin empires of the Patiño, Hochschild and Aramayo families. The Patiño empire, for example, became an international enterprise involving the finance of tin-smelting and processing in Britain and the U.S.A., but in Bolivia itself the Patiño empire alone provided 50 per cent of the public finance of the country and over 80 per cent of Bolivia's foreign currency (Klein, 1965). Patiño capital was invested in electric power, banking, railways and agricultural industry.

The Bolivian economy rested almost exclusively on tin and associated

minerals, which make up 95 per cent of Bolivia's exports. 'Whatever
infrastructure was present in Bolivia prior to the 1952 revolution was almost
entirely produced, either directly or indirectly by the mining industry'
(Zondag, 1966, p. 21). Labour for the mines was certainly drawn from
subsistence farmers in the *altiplano*, but low wages and therefore low
purchasing power induced few secondary changes in the farming of surrounding areas and most of the food requirements for the mining population
were in fact satisfied by foreign imports. 'One might say that two civilizations gradually came into existence in Bolivia. One was highly mechanized
and highly capitalized, employing large numbers of foreign technicians who
tended to build their own world with modern comforts, while the other
civilization was based completely on the old way of life, which had not
changed for hundreds of years. Mining camps constituted practically the
only link between the two' (Zondag, 1966, p. 21).

Since the revolution of 1952 by which the Movimiento Nacional
Revolucionario (MNR) was swept to power and instituted a series of
profound changes, the movement towards the integration of the national
economy and towards diversification has been greatly accelerated, though
not without important setbacks. Even before 1952 a development corporation had begun to encourage the establishment of sugar, cement and dairy
industries; there had been efforts to colonize the eastern lowlands; road and
railway building had been undertaken to promote new settlement and to
create the all-important link, planned from 1945, between Cochabamba
and La Paz.

In 1952 the greater part of the mining industry was nationalized, most of
the railways were brought under state control and agrarian reform, already
sweeping the country, was recognized and extended. New efforts have been
made with the help of foreign capital to improve communications, to
develop sources of power, to provide new stimuli to industrialization and
to promote the colonization of the east. Until relatively recently highly
unrealistic rate structures, imposed by government, made it unprofitable
for private foreign capital, formerly dominant in the provision of electrical power, to extend investment. Bolivia has suffered, therefore,
from a shortage of power, which is only now being removed. In 1966 a
publicly owned hydro-electric plant with a capacity of 50,000 kW came
into operation on the river Corani some 60 km north-west of Cochabamba,
supplying the city and nearby mining areas. A further loan has been raised
to build another dam on the Corani (the Sta Isabel project) to supplement
power supplies for Cochabamba and Oruro. The installed capacity serving
La Paz was increased in 1966 by 50 per cent by a new, privately owned
hydro-electric plant, and loans have been raised to expand the power
supplies of Sucre and Potosí. Santa Cruz is to be served by a thermal electric
plant using local natural gas.

Since the 1920s exploration for oil in south-east Bolivia has been attended by great hopes for the future development of the region, though hope has waxed and waned according to the success of exploratory drilling, the condition of the world market for oil (since costs of transport are always likely to make Bolivia a marginal producer) and, above all, political circumstances. Oil companies operating in Bolivia were expropriated in 1937 after the War of the Chaco, and little new work was done until after the revolution of 1952 when greater investment in oil exploration yielded good results in the Camiri region. From 1953 to 1955 output increased sufficiently to provide for Bolivia's internal needs together with a small surplus for export to neighbouring countries. A natural gas field near Santa Cruz supplies local power and raw materials, and exports are envisaged to Argentina by a new pipeline shortly to be completed to Yacuiba. Initially, oil development was wholly in the hands of the YPFB (Yacimientos Petrolíferos Fiscales Bolivianos), but in 1956 Bolivia was again opened up to foreign oil companies because of the lack of internal resources to handle the expansion of the industry. By 1959 twenty companies had been allocated exploration rights in more than 10 million ha. Between 1953 and 1959 production rose from 79,000 metric tons a year to 413,000 and stabilized more or less at that level until 1965. Pipelines were built linking Camiri and Santa Cruz with Sucre, Cochabamba, Oruro and La Paz. Gulf Oil led the expansion, and the completion, with Gulf capital, of the pipeline to Arica in 1966 allowed Gulf to begin exporting Bolivian oil to its refineries on the west coast of the U.S.A. In 1966 Bolivian oil production rose to 779,000 tons and in 1968 to 1,970,000 tons, of which 80 per cent were produced by Gulf Oil, most of it exported to the U.S.A. Oil exports were beginning, therefore, to lead a much-needed diversification of Bolivian external trade away from the dominance of tin. Immediate prospects were, however, jeopardized by the expropriation of Gulf Oil's Bolivian properties in 1969, immediately following the military *coup* by General Ovando and the initiation of a nationalistic policy similar to that being pursued by Peru.

Industry is still weakly developed and chiefly limited to food-processing and the production of textiles and a few consumer goods. Such industry as there is is located almost entirely at La Paz, Cochabamba, Oruro and Santa Cruz. But in general 'industrial' enterprises are small, employing few workers and operating well below capacity. Productivity is low and many of the 120,000 employed in industry are small craftsmen in handicrafts and workshops rather than in factories. The internal market is small by reason of low incomes and the predominance of subsistence farming as well as the low total population. Encouragement to the establishment of industry is given through the Instituto Promotor de Inversiones en Bolivia (INPIBOL) created in 1965. Plans exist for the expansion of the dairy industry in La Paz and for the establishment of a glass industry. At Santa Cruz there are more ambitious plans for the production of paper, petrochemicals, fertilizers and explosives. Cochabamba has recently begun the production of cement and the canning of oils and lubricants in addition to its existing preoccupation with food-processing. The major industrial possibilities for further industrialization seem, in general, to be associated with the exploitation of natural resources: sulphur, salt and natural gas near Santa Cruz, phosphates near Sucre, or asbestos near Cochabamba.

The mining industry suffered a setback after nationalization of the three-quarters of the industry in the hands of the Patiño, Hochschild and Aramayo interests. There was an emigration of technicians and managers, many of them foreign, labour was high-cost and an excessively large labour force was employed in spite of the fall in output. The industry had to meet increasing costs because of high taxation levied to meet the costs of social legislation. Mines deteriorated and production fell (Fox, 1967). From 1960, however, attempts have been made to revive the mining industry with the Triangular Operation by the U.S.A., West Germany and the Inter-American Development Bank to make capital available for modernization and for more intensive exploration to discover new mineral deposits. Bolivia remains a high-cost producer of tin in spite of its position as the second largest producer in the Free World after Malaysia, and the only major source of tin in the western hemisphere. In part, high costs have been due to poor management, labour problems and poor organization, but they are also a result of the declining grades of ore exploited (from 3 per cent in 1938 to 0·82 per cent in 1964) (Fox, 1967). In general, too, shallower ores have been richer than the deeper ores, which are mined under more difficult conditions. Concentrates of c. 33 per cent tin content have in the past been exported chiefly to Britain, the U.S.A. and West Germany for smelting, but in 1966 an agreement was reached with a West German firm to establish a tin-smelting plant at Oruro, and this was nearing completion in early 1970. But Bolivia is still heavily dependent on its mineral exports, which made up 88 per cent of total exports in 1966. Tin alone made up 62·2 per cent of all exports, the remaining minerals consisting of silver, lead, copper, antimony, wolfram and zinc, in that order, by value, with smaller amounts of bismuth, sulphur and gold. Recent efforts have been directed to the establishment of domestic smelting industries for zinc, antimony and bismuth as well as tin; and investment in mineral exploration, neglected for many years, has recently been resumed on a larger scale. Exploratory studies are being made, for example, for alluvial tin in the north-east in Pando and Beni. The occurrence of rich uranium ores, with some silver and copper, has been reported to the south-east of La Paz. Deposits of silver, lead, zinc and cadmium at Matilde to the north of La Paz are to be developed with U.S.A. capital, and attempts are being made to develop the large, high quality iron ore deposits at Mutun in eastern Bolivia. There are possibilities for some diversification within the mining industry, therefore, but in the foreseeable future it seems likely that the external economy must lean heavily on mineral exports, and must therefore remain highly vulnerable to changes in world prices, which have fortunately been high in recent years.

As in Peru and Ecuador, growth of the internal economy must rest on improvement of agricultural productivity and output. Great hopes are entertained for the settlement of new lands in the east, more important to Bolivia than to either of her northern neighbours as the only zone with a substantial potential for lowland tropical crops. As in the more northerly countries, colonization of the empty lands is seen as at least a partial solution to several problems: as a means of redistributing the overcrowded rural population of the northern *altiplano*; as a means of reducing the imbalance of population density between the *altiplano* and the rest of the country; and as a means of increasing domestic food supplies, thus reducing imports and releasing foreign exchange reserves for other, more important imports of capital goods. But in Bolivia the settlement and colonization of the east would also serve to strengthen national unity, creating an integrated state in which the link between Santa Cruz, Cochabamba and La Paz would form a strong and interdependent economic axis. Santa Cruz is the major nucleus around which new settlement has been encouraged in recent years, though successful settlement has also been achieved in two other important areas: to the north-east of La Paz in the Alto Bení region, and in the Chaparé region near Cochabamba.

Foreign colonies of Mennonites, Italians and Japanese have been encouraged, particularly to the area of Santa Cruz. Between 1953 and 1962, for example, some 2430 immigrants from the Ryukyu Islands were settled in three colonies to the east and north-east of Santa Cruz, cultivating some 7000 ha of land, and, although beset by early problems, have now achieved reasonable economic success, particularly in the production of timber, rice and sugar. A relatively small-scale capitalistic agriculture has been inserted into an area of *latifundios* and squatting settlement (Tigner, 1963). However successful such foreign colonies may be in raising agricultural production and in acting as demonstration models for Bolivian farmers, it is with the latter that the future must rest and for whom there is the greatest concern. In the Chaparé region to the east of Cochabamba colonization by migrant squatters, chiefly of Quechua-speaking origin, has received relatively little attention by the state until recently (Edelmann, 1967). Before 1952 squatters or *tolerados* settled and cleared land on the big estates and were often allowed to stay until the landowner felt the need to take over the land they had cleared. Since the revolution of 1952 and the land reform that assured migrants into the *yungas* of their right to land, the stream of colonists has grown, some 2400 families migrating between 1954 and 1962. Viable settlements have been created (notably near Todos Santos) and road networks and schools have been built with the minimum of government assistance. Locally organized unions (*sindicatos*) have set up their own self-government in the area and have organized the allocation of land to new settlers in plots of *c*. 10 ha per family. Government help has increased in recent years, but the Chaparé settlement has certainly proved much cheaper than more ambitiously organized projects.

Similar spontaneous settlement north-east of La Paz took place after the building of the road to Caranavi in 1958. In four years about 3000 families moved into the area, quite apart from the planned settlement of the Alto Bení. The Alto Bení project near Caranavi, at 450–1000 m above sea-level and 240 km by road from La Paz, has been financed by a USAID programme and the Bolivian Development Corporation since its inception in 1959 (CBF, 1965). Preliminary assessments of soil quality, agricultural possibilities, health and educational needs were made; roads were built; selected colonists were provided with 10–12 ha of land (1 ha of which is previously cleared and planted in rice, maize, bananas and *yuca*); and they were given temporary housing, tools, clothing and seed. Schools and clinics have been built and allocations of land made in conjunction with a planned settlement pattern that reflects the preference of the Aymara Indians for a fairly nucleated structure. Rice, maize and *yuca* are the main subsistence crops, bananas provide a quick yielding cash crop, and coffee of good quality has found a market in La Paz with limited possibilities of export; coca, cacao and citrus are also exported from the region. By 1965 some 554 families had been settled, costs were not too high (estimated at $2000 per family) and the failure rate of colonists was estimated to be as low as 6 per cent (Edelmann, 1967), much lower than in the early stages of other schemes.

The major area of settlement, however, has been in the region of Santa Cruz, particularly important since the completion of the road to Cochabamba in 1953. An army colony was established two years later for soldier-colonists, in part from the *altiplano*, whereby they received 20 ha of cleared land and a house after completion of national service. A United Nations colony at Cotoca was established in the same year and by 1958 had received 227 colonists at the very high cost of nearly £2000 per family (Crossley, 1961). More ambitious and less expensive schemes have been planned by the Bolivian Development Corporation by which some 15,000 families have been settled (Fifer, 1967).

In Bolivia, colonization of the empty eastern lands has been fairly successful so far. The population of Santa Cruz is reputed to be growing at a rapid rate and it enjoys the atmosphere and optimism of a boom town. Agricultural production has increased and the country has been made self-sufficient in sugar and rice in a short space of time. Cattle-raising has reasonably good prospects in many parts of the northern and eastern regions, particularly if native stock can be improved and natural grazings controlled or supplemented by more nutritious introduced varieties. Cotton cultivation is increasing and can also substitute for imports.

Vegetable oils and fibres have similar possibilities. But the long-term prospects must be inhibited to some extent by the continuing problem of the small size of the internal market and the high costs of transport both to the *altiplano* and to external markets, and this in turn makes it difficult to compete satisfactorily on international markets.

Notwithstanding the substantial progress made in the eastern regions of Bolivia, future prosperity is bound to be dependent on the mining industry and on the fortunes of the old-settled regions of the *altiplano* and the *valles*. And it is in these areas that land reform has had a profound effect since 1953. The concentration of landholding and the persistence of the traditional hacienda economy and of servile tenures were formerly at least as oppressive in the Bolivian *altiplano* as anywhere in Latin America. There was the same contrast between the large estates and the inadequate holdings of the Indians in *minifundios* and in *comunidades indigenas* as in Peru and Ecuador. According to the census of 1950, 90 per cent of the private agrarian property was held by 4·5 per cent of the total number of landholders, yet 70 per cent of the farm units together comprised only 0·41 per cent of the area exploited. In the *altiplano* the familiar pattern of the central Andes was normal whereby *colonos* were allowed a plot of land in return for their labour and the labour of their families on the hacienda lands. Sharecropping systems existed by which peasants often provided seed, manure, transport and labour and the owner provided only the land in return for a half share of the crop. In the *valle* region both forms of tenure existed, together with cash renting, and the fragmentation of holdings occasionally reached extremes, as in the Cochabamba valley.

Land reform was undertaken as a part of the revolutionary policy of the MNR in 1953, though it is difficult to establish how far the agrarian reform law was initiated from above or was simply a result of pressure from the indigenous population and a recognition of the fact that land invasions were taking place already on a large scale, especially in the Cochabamba region and near La Paz (Heath, Erasmus and Buechler, 1969, pp. 37, 372). Expropriation of the haciendas took place rapidly, often achieved by hastily formed peasant unions and inspired by middle-class urban dwellers, miners or local peasant leaders, but legal recognition and the issuing of titles were often long delayed. By August 1967, 7·9 million ha had been allocated to 191,500 families under the Agrarian Reform Law, but it was only after 1960 that the issue of titles reached a fairly substantial annual rate. Perhaps a third of the agricultural population of the country has benefited from the reform, more widely in the *altiplano* and the Cochabamba region than in the eastern regions, which were less affected (and in which the land problem was in any case less severe). Areas redistributed per family were sometimes small, too small indeed to provide an adequate family farm: e.g. over 8000 families in the Cochabamba area received less than 1 ha.

The effects of reform have been very considerable, but mainly in social and psychological terms rather than in terms of agricultural production. Reports suggest a fall of 15 per cent in agricultural output between 1951 and 1960, though statistics are unreliable and it has been pointed out that, whereas 1951 was a year of optimum weather conditions, 1960 was a year of drought and difficulty in the *altiplano*. Since 1960 agricultural production has revived and there has been a general tendency for stock production to fall relative to grain and root production as old pastures are ploughed up. And it seems certain that many peasants have eaten better than ever before.

Marketing structures were profoundly altered. Under the former system the *hacendados* often received their rents in kind at the door of their town houses for disposal to buyers. They thus performed a middleman function which some developed further when their estates were lost, buying produce from their former dependents instead of merely receiving it as rent. But the peasants themselves have also organized their own new outlets for the sale of surpluses through markets and fairs which have sprung up in new locations more conveniently placed in the *altiplano* at closer intervals than the old centres (Preston, 1969). New towns have begun to emerge in the *altiplano*, and these reflect the existence of greater surpluses and greater purchasing power in the hands of the peasants. Changes in urban pattern are seen to be a result of changing social structure.

Other changes have been of equal if not of greater importance. The traditional leadership of peasant communities has been challenged through the existence of peasant unions, which have often persisted as a result of the continuing need for negotiations with authority because of the long legal processes whereby titles are finally secured. And the participation of active and younger men makes for greater receptivity to other innovations. The possibilities of social and geographical mobility have increased. Those *hacendados* who did not fall to the ranks of the peasantry, working the rump of a former estate, have of necessity had to find a new outlet for enterprise in trade and commerce or occasionally in industry and handicraft. Material welfare of the *campesinos* seems to have improved, and observers have remarked on the increase of *calamina* roofs, bicycles, transistor radios and the use of western styles of dress, though these signs of material progress may not necessarily be attributable, of course, to agrarian reform alone. The pejorative or at best negative term '*indio*' has been replaced by '*campesino*', a change symbolic of the rise in status of the peasantry, and of a recognition of personal dignity and worth. 'One of the most striking features of Bolivia's land reform and social revolution is the degree to which *campesinos* have begun to assume the roles of citizens and to participate in social systems that were not only closed but virtually unknown to them a decade ago' (Heath *et al.*, 1969, p. 387). It is also evident that much remains to be done, particularly in education and in raising agricultural productivity, improving methods of production and providing rural credit, but the changes in social structures, attitudes and values associated with land reform may have created a fertile soil in which such innovations may take root and spread, if and when the market opportunities exist.

REFERENCES AND BIBLIOGRAPHY

Actividades Productivas del Perú (1966), Vol. 5, *La industria pesquera.* Lima.

BANCO CENTRAL DE RESERVA (1968) *Cuentas nacionales 1950–67.* Lima.

BENNETT, W. C. and BIRD, J. (1949) *Andean Cultural History.* Hale.

BOTTOMLEY, A. (1965) Imperfect competition and the industrialisation of Ecuador. *Inter-American Economic Affairs,* 19 (1), 83–94.

BOTTOMLEY, A. (1966) Planning in an under-utilization economy: the case of Ecuador. *Social and Economic Studies,* 15 (4), 305–13.

CHUNGSUK CHA (1969) *El rol de la selva en el desarrollo agrícola del Perú.* Lima.

CONESTCAR (1966) *Perú: estadística agraria 1965.* Lima.

CBF (Corporación Boliviana de Fomento) (1965) *Reseña histórica del Proyecto Alto Bení.* La Paz.

CROSSLEY, J. C. (1961) Santa Cruz at the cross-roads. *Tijdschrift voor Economische en Sociale Geografie,* 1–21.

DEC (División de Estadísticas y Censos, República del Ecuador) (1962) *Segundo censo de población y primer censo de vivienda.* 4 vols.

DENEVAN, W. M. (1966) The aboriginal cultural geography of the *llanos de Mojos* in Bolivia. *Ibero-Americana* (California), 48, 160.

DENEVAN, W. M. and PARSONS, J. J. (1967) Pre-Columbian ridged fields. *Scientific American,* 217 (1), 93–100.

DENEVAN, W. M., SMITH, C. T. and HAMILTON, P. (1968) Ancient ridged fields in the region of Lake Titicaca. *Geographical Journal,* 134 (3), 354–67.

DOBYNS, H. F. (1963) An outline of Andean epidemic history to 1720. *Bulletin of the History of Medicine,* 37 (6), 493–515.

DOBYNS, H. F. (1966) Estimating aboriginal American population. *Current Anthropology,* 7, 395–449.

EDELMANN, A. T. (1967) Colonization in Bolivia: progress and prospects. *Inter-American Economic Affairs,* 20 (4), 39–54.

EIDT, R. C. (1962) Pioneer settlement in eastern Peru. *Annals of the Assn of American Geographers,* 52, 255–78.

FIFER, J. V. (1967) Bolivia's pioneer fringe. *The Geographical Review,* 57 (1), 1–23.

FOX, D. J. (1967) *The Bolivian Tin-mining Industry: some geographical and economic problems.* International Tin Council.

HEATH, D. B., ERASMUS, C. J. and BUECHLER, H. C. (1969) *Land Reform and Social Revolution in Bolivia.* New York.

KLEIN, H. S. (1965) The creation of the Patiño tin empire. *Inter-American Economic Affairs,* 19, 3–24.

LEVANO, C. and ROMERO, E. (1969) *Regionalismo y Centralismo.* Lima.

LEVIN, J. V. (1960) *The Export Economies.* Cambridge, Mass.

LINKE, L. (1960) *Ecuador.* R.I.I.A.

MANGIN, W. (1967) Latin American squatter settlements: a problem and a solution. *Latin American Research Review,* 2 (3), 65–97.

MARKHAM, C. (1894) *A History of Peru.* London.

MORALES FIGUEROA, L. de (1866) *Colección de documentos inéditos relativos al descubrimiento . . . de las Indias.* Vol. 6. Madrid.

MURRA, J. V. (1960) Rite and crop in the Inca state. In DIAMOND, S. (ed.) *Culture in History.*

OSBORNE, H. (1964) *Bolivia.* London, R.I.I.A.

OWENS, R. J. (1963) *Peru.* London, R.I.I.A.

PRESTON, D. A. (1965a) Changes in the economic geography of banana production in Ecuador. *Trans. Inst. Brit. Geographers,* 37, 77–90.

PRESTON, D. A. (1965b) Negro, mestizo and Indian in an Andean environment. *Geographical Journal,* 313 (2), 220–34.

PRESTON, D. A. (1969) The revolutionary landscape of highland Bolivia. *Geographical Journal,* 135 (1), 1–16.

PULGAR VIDAL, J. (n.d.) *Geografía del Peru.* Lima.

ROWE, J. H. (1957) The Incas under Spanish colonial institutions. *Hispanic American Historical Review,* 37, 155–99.

SCHAEDEL, R. P. (1966) Urban growth and ekistics on the Peruvian coast. *XXXVI Congreso de Americanistas,* 1, 531–9.

SMITH, C. T. (1960) Aspects of agriculture and settlement in Peru. *Geographical Journal,* 126, 397–412.

SMITH, C. T. (1968) Problems of regional development in Peru. *Geography,* 53 (3), 260–87.

SMITH, C. T. (1970) Depopulation of the central Andes in the 16th century. *Current Anthropology,* 11, 1–12.

TIGNER, J. L. (1963) The Ryukyuans in Bolivia. *Hispanic American Historical Review,* 43, 206–29.

VASQUEZ DE ESPINOSA, A. (1628) *Compendium and Description of the West Indies.* In *Smithsonian Miscellaneous Collections,* 102 (1942).

VELLARD, J. A. (1963) *Civilisations des Andes*. Paris.

WILLEY, G. R. (1953) *Prehistoric Settlement Patterns in the Virú Valley*. Bureau of American Ethnology, Bulletin 155.

WITTFOGEL, K. A. (1957) *Oriental Despotism*. New Haven, Conn.

ZONDAG, C. G. (1966) *The Bolivian Economy 1952-65*. New York.

8 Brazil

J. H. Galloway

Brazil has emerged as a country of great diversity and regional contrast, and some outlines of the diversity are easily recognized. The distribution of population divides Brazil into settled and virtually unsettled areas. Two-thirds of the country still have a population of less than ten per km². For the most part Brazilians have hugged the coast, and this coastal distribution of population has been one of the constants of the historical geography of the country (Fig. 8.14). A second broad division is that between traditional and modern Brazil. This division began to emerge during the nineteenth century, and today the line separating these two Brazils is not easily drawn. Traditional Brazil is rural and agricultural. The population is largely of Indian and African origin; people of European origin are but a small infusion at the top levels of society. Society is strongly hierarchical, there is a high degree of illiteracy and the standard of living is low. Modern Brazil is, by comparison, more urbanized, more industrialized, its agriculture more productive. A large part of the population is of European stock, and is generally more literate and more prosperous. Interior Brazil is traditional, with an economy based on pastoralism, hunting, collecting and shifting cultivation, enlivened only by an occasional flash of sudden and ephemeral wealth. The coastlands at least as far south as Rio are also part of traditional Brazil with their plantation agriculture and long colonial past. The boundary between the traditional and the modern is blurred. Belo Horizonte is not part of traditional Brazil, nor is Brasília, but most of rural Minas Gerais, the old gold towns and the state of Goiás are. The Paraíba valley, inland from Rio, has suffered from the exploitative agriculture associated with traditional Brazil, but is being drawn into part of modern Brazil, mainly through the establishment of industry. The most modern parts of Brazil are the industrial south-east and the south.

Regional disparities in standards of living and rates of population growth are very strongly marked (Table 8.5). The extremes in 1960 were the states of Guanabara[1] and Piauí in the north-east with *per capita* incomes of 291 per cent and 29 per cent of the national average respectively. An

[1] The former Federal District of Rio de Janeiro. When the capital was moved to Brasília, the Federal District became the State of Guanabara. It in fact includes little more than the city of Rio de Janeiro. There is also a state of Rio de Janeiro.

obvious concern of the Brazilian government is to try to prevent these regional disparities in income from increasing. To reduce the gap between rich and poor will require massive investment and extraordinary economic growth in the most deprived regions, but it is probably unrealistic to expect a marked change in their relative economic positions. A region's economy must grow more rapidly than the national average if it is to increase its share of the national income. During the 1950s, a period of rapid economic growth for Brazil as a whole, there was in fact little change in the share each region received (Table 8.6). Understandably, discrepancies in regional

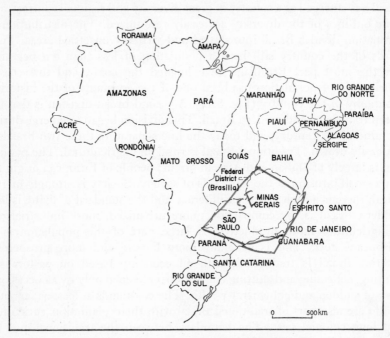

Fig. 8.1 The states and territories of Brazil

income have influenced internal migration in Brazil. People move to those regions that offer greater opportunity, notably the agricultural frontier in the central west and the industrializing south (Table 8.5).

The regional diversity of Brazil is found not only in statistical analyses of incomes and growth-rates and in descriptions of land use, but also in the minds of the people. Brazilians are very conscious of the distinctiveness of the different parts of their country and associate themselves with a particular region, whether it be a state or collection of states. The words used to identify people from different parts of the country such as *Paulista*, *Mineiro*, *Pernambucano*, *Nordestino* or *Sertanejo* tell a Brazilian more than just the place of origin of a person; they tell him also of his background, of a regional style of living, of inherited historical attitudes. Regionalism and regional consciousness are very much present in Brazil. It is indeed one of the achievements of Brazil that, despite the disparity between regional economies and the diversity of regional loyalties, the country remains united.

The unfolding of the Brazilian experience is taking place on an enormous stage. Brazil covers an area of 8·5 million km², which amounts to almost one half of South America and makes it the fifth largest country in the world. Much of Brazil is composed of two extensive plateaux, the Guiana highlands and the Brazilian highlands (Fig. 8.2). These highlands are

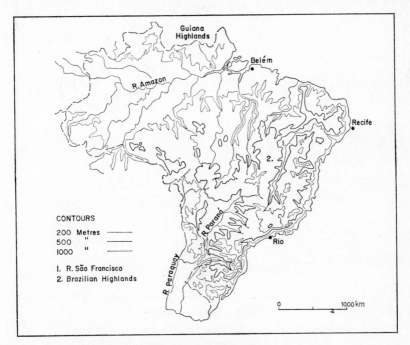

Fig. 8.2 Brazil: relief

composed of pre-Cambrian rocks, in places overlain by a mantle of sedimentaries, particularly sandstones and limestone. Along the east coast there is a steep escarpment fronting the Atlantic called the Serra do Mar. In the north-east of the country this escarpment is known as the Borborema escarpment and the plateau behind it as the Borborema plateau. On these highlands, where the crystalline bedrock is exposed, the relief is gently undulating; more resistant crystalline rocks form ranges of hills or *serras* while the remnants of the sedimentary mantle stand out as tabular uplands. In the southern states, the land rises in a series of escarpments, separating plateaux or *planaltos*. The Amazon basin is the most extensive area of lowland in Brazil. Only a small part of the Paraná–Paraguay lowlands comes within Brazil, nothing more than a narrow fringe along the south-western frontier and the seasonally flooded region known as the Pantanal in Mato Grosso. Elsewhere in Brazil lowland is restricted to the narrow plain between the Serra do Mar and the sea, and to a few river valleys.

Brazil is in large part a tropical country with a range of tropical climates (Fig. 8.3). All of Amazonia has a humid tropical climate, but there are variations in the amount and seasonal intensity of rainfall from one part

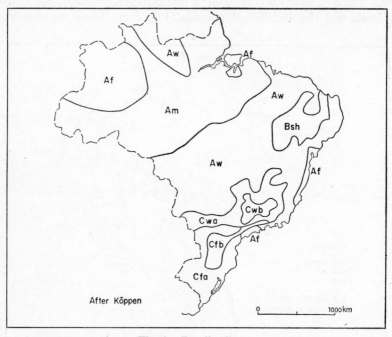

Fig. 8.3 Brazil: climate

Af, Am	Wet, with no cool season and no really dry season
Aw	Wet, with no cool season and distinct dry seasons
Bsh	Hot, semi-arid
Cwa	Wet, with mild, dry winters and hot rainy summers
Cwb	Wet, with mild, dry winters and cool, rainy summers
Cfa	Wet, with mild winters, hot summers and no dry season
Cfb	Wet, with mild winters, cool summers and no dry season

of the basin to another. Humid tropical climate is found along the Atlantic coast to about the latitude of Rio de Janeiro, where seasonality becomes more marked and the annual range of temperature greater. South of Rio the climate grades rapidly through subtropical to temperate. The climate of the Brazilian highlands is moderated by altitude and over much of the highlands there is a marked drier season of the year. An anomalous climate in Brazil is that in the interior of the north-east, reaching from northern Minas Gerais to the coast of Ceara and Rio Grande do Norte. Here, where

a more humid climate might have been expected, the climate is semi-arid.
Not only is rainfall sparse, but it is extremely variable from year to year.
This region is often referred to in Brazil as the *polygono das sêcas*, the
'polygon of drought'. Only the southern states of Brazil have a temperate

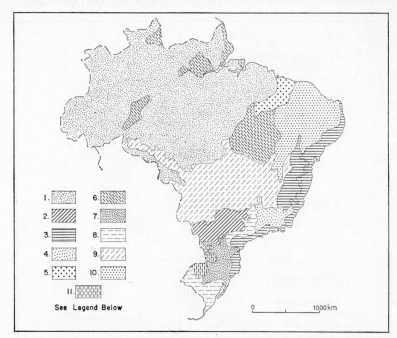

Fig. 8.4 Brazil: vegetation (after *The Physical Geographic Atlas of the World*
(Moscow, Academy of Sciences, 1964), pp. 170–1)

1. Constantly humid and variably humid evergreen equatorial Amazon forest
2. Brazilian variably humid evergreen tropical forest
3. East Brazilian variably humid evergreen tropical forest
4. South Brazilian moderately humid evergreen tropical mountain forest
5. Brazilian palm forest
6. Brazilian tropical tall-grass savanna (Campos Limpos)
7. Araucanian forest
8. Brazilian tropical treeless savanna
9. Brazilian savanna with xerophytic trees and shrubs (Campos Cerrados)
10. East Brazilian spiny shrub and cactus tropical woodland (caatinga)
11. Humid evergreen subtropical forest

climate. In northern Paraná frosts occur and further south they become
more frequent, which causes a distinct change in agriculture.

The vegetation of Brazil is shown in generalized outline in Fig. 8.4. The
natural vegetation of large regions of Brazil is forest. As is to be expected
from the size of the country and range of climate, the type of forest varies
greatly, from the rain-forest of the Amazon basin to the Araucanian or

Paraná pine forests of the temperate south. The vegetation of the 'drought polygon' is xerophytic forest, a dry scrub woodland referred to often as *caatinga*. Over much of the Brazilian highlands and in parts of the Amazon basin and of the south, the forest cover is not continuous; various gradations of vegetation cover are found between forest and open grassland. The

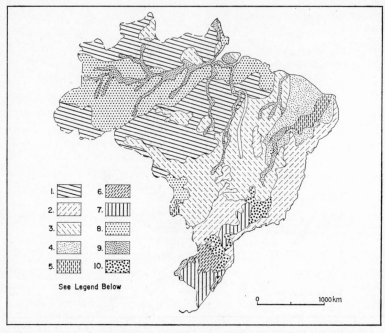

Fig. 8.5 Brazil: soils (after *The Physical Geographic Atlas of the World* (Moscow, Academy of Sciences, 1964))

1. Red-yellow lateritic (mainly ferrallitic) soils of constantly humid tropical forest
2. Red lateritic (ferrallitic and ferritic) soils of seasonally humid tropical forest
3. Red lateritic (ferrallitic and ferritic) soils of tall-grass savanna
4. Brownish-red laterized (ferrallitized and ferritized) soils of xerophytic tropical forest
5. Red-brown soils of dry savanna and reddish-brown soils of desert-like savanna
6. Yellow soils and red soils of humid subtropical forest
7. Reddish-black soils of subtropical prairie
8. Tropical bog soils
9. Alluvial soils
10. Yellow and red mountain soils

origins of these savannas or grasslands are still disputed. At least three explanations have been offered attributing the grasslands to climate, to edaphic and geomorphological conditions, and to the activities of man. Whatever the origin, man has certainly been responsible for extending the area of grassland during recent centuries through cultivation and grazing cattle.

The fact that the country is largely tropical has underlain much writing and thinking about Brazil. The tropical climate has permitted the argument of climatic determinism to explain the lack of development and, even if the crude application of this doctrine is seldom now made, aspects of the tropical environment appear to have been handicaps to economic progress. The climate does favour the spread of disease. Tropical soils are often fragile and their fertility easily exhausted. Western man has not mastered these soils as he has the soils of temperate regions. The physical geography has in other ways hindered the development of the country. The Serra do Mar is a barrier to movement inland, the rivers of the Brazilian highlands drain to the Paraná–Paraguay system and do not provide direct routes towards the Atlantic stream of commerce; the usefulness of the São Francisco river as a route is severely impaired by the falls at Paulo Afonso, which block navigation from the sea. The fact that Brazil has no west coast, a goal to draw people into and across the interior, may be of some psychological significance, and also the sheer size of the country may be a drawback to development.

THE COLONIAL PERIOD 1500–1800: THE LAND USE OF A TROPICAL COLONY

Cabral, in 1500, was the first European known to have visited Brazil; he named this new land Vera Cruz – land of the True Cross – and claimed it for Portugal. After cruising briefly along the coast he continued his voyage to India. Cabral was followed to Brazil by Dutch, English and French as well as by other Portuguese; all came to explore and to log the tropical forest for valuable timbers. The name of Vera Cruz was forgotten and the land became known from the most sought-after of these woods – Brazil wood. The active Portuguese settlement of Brazil began in the 1530s, the aim in part being to reinforce Portugal's claim to the country by effective settlement and to forestall claims by rival European powers.

Portugal was hardly well equipped to undertake such a gigantic task as the settlement of Brazil. Portugal's population was small and, despite the eastern trading empire, it was relatively poor. The colonization of Brazil proceeded slowly. The crown tried to divest itself of the burden of colonization by dividing the coast between the Amazon and southern Brazil into *donatarias*, each containing a limited stretch of coast and reaching back into the interior, and awarding them to wealthy nobles and adventurers. The resulting subdivision of Brazil is shown in Fig. 8.6. It was the responsibility of the grantee or *donatario* to organize, finance and adminster his domain, and he was permitted to recoup his expenses through taxes, duties and the distribution of land, though some sources of revenue were reserved for the crown. The scheme failed. In several of the *donatarias* settlements were not even established and some settlements were destroyed

by Indians. Only three – São Vincente, Bahia and Pernambuco – survived
as agricultural colonies, in part through luck, in part because the *donatarios*
were able men and commanded substantial financial resources. In 1549,
the crown assumed responsibility for administering Brazil. All that survives
of the *donatarios* in modern Brazil are the place names and, possibly, some
influence on state boundaries, especially in the north-east. On the plateau
of southern Brazil, however, at São Paulo, there arose a settlement that,
in the early years of colonization of Brazil, was really beyond government

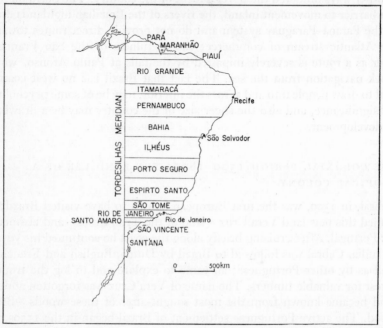

Fig. 8.6 The *donatarias* (Holanda, 1960)

control. São Paulo was a community of Indians and Portuguese, which
became the home base of the *bandeirantes*,[1] men who roamed in large
groups over the interior of Brazil, exploring, and enslaving Indians.

The sugar coast

When the Portuguese began to colonize Brazil, they had long been familiar
with sugar cultivation. Sugar had been introduced to the Mediterranean
lands possibly as early as the eighth century by the Arabs and it had become
an integral part of medieval Mediterranean agriculture. In the west, it was
grown in Sicily, southern Spain and Portugal itself, in the Algarve and
even as far north as Coimbra. Sugar, too, was associated with the earliest

[1] The word probably derives from *bandeira* (flag). The *bandeirantes* marched
with a flag at the head of the column.

phase of Portuguese expansion overseas: it was grown on Madeira and by the mid-fifteenth century was being exported from there to Europe. In Madeira, the cultivation of sugar was still on European lines. It had to be irrigated and much of it was grown on small estates or farms. In the second sugar colony established by the Portuguese, São Tomé, off the west coast of Africa, the humid tropical climate made irrigation unnecessary and the crop was grown entirely on large estates, worked by African slaves. It was the type of sugar plantation evolved in São Tomé that the Portuguese carried with them to Brazil. The plantation of Brazil represented, therefore, not an experiment in tropical land use, but the transfer across the Atlantic of an already tested and successful institution of the Portuguese commercial empire.

The narrow plain that fronts the Atlantic along the east coast of Brazil has a climate suitable for sugar cultivation from Natal to Florianópolis, but differing circumstances determined the location of sugar colonies. The Indians of what is now Espírito Santo were warlike and able to prevent colonization until after the end of the colonial period. To the south, distance from Europe was a major handicap. São Vincente and Rio de Janeiro were secondary producers of sugar during the colonial period, and proximity to Europe, as well as a sparse Indian population, helped to make the coastal plain in the north the most favoured location. From Pernambuco and São Salvador sugar cultivation spread north and south until by 1800 sugar was grown from Rio Grande do Norte to southern Bahia. Here, for two centuries, was the heart of colonial Brazil.

The sugar plantations were called *engenhos*, a word that literally means mill but was applied to the entire complex of caneland, the mill for crushing the cane and the factory in which the sugar was manufactured. Land-holdings were large, to be measured in square miles rather than in acres, and had their origin in grants of land or *sesmarias* awarded to individuals by the crown or colonial governors as rewards for services rendered, and in the hope that the new landowners would encourage settlement. The plantation itself occupied only a part of these vast estates. Plantations, therefore, were often widely separated and even at the end of the colonial period much of the coastal plain was still in forest. Three factors limited the effective exploitation of a *sesmaria*: accessibility, the size of the labour force and the capacity of the mill. The prevailing level of technological knowledge of the planters, together with the choice of power for the mills – wind, water or animal – severely limited the size of mills. Moreover, since transporting cane was costly, it was more economical to build a new mill some distance from the old, rather than extend the plantation around the old mill. Thus, new plantations were created, which frequently kept the name of the parent plantation, but added a distinguishing suffix or prefix such as *novo* (new), *cima* (above) or *baixo* (below).

By building a new plantation a wealthy landowner could increase his acreage of cane; through the lease of land, landowners without ready capital could pass to others the burden and expense of clearing land and founding new plantations. Two forms of lease came into common use. In one, land was leased on a share-cropping basis, the tenant undertaking to grow cane as his main crop, to send it to be crushed in his landlord's mill and to surrender the molasses and one half of the sugar as rent. In the second form of lease, the tenant had the use of the land for eight to twelve years, rent free; but, in return, he had to clear the land and build a plantation complete with mansion, mill and slave quarters, which at the end of the lease became the property of the landlord. Both types of tenants were known as *lavradores* – literally, cultivators – and obviously they were people of some means with movable goods such as slaves and oxen. *Lavradores* commonly owned between six and ten slaves and the importance of this class is suggested by the fact that in Pernambuco at the end of the colonial period there were two or three of them attached to each estate. There was another poorer group of tenants known as *moradores*. Usually they were settled at remote points on an estate to keep an eye on the landlord's property and were permitted to build a cabin and cultivate a few provision crops. *Moradores* were retainers in a society that measured a man's importance by the breadth of his land and by the number of people he kept about him. Towards the end of the colonial period and in the nineteenth century the nature of this tenancy changed. As slaves became more difficult to obtain and more expensive, *moradores* were increasingly drawn into the running of the plantation, being required to work in the fields and mills a given number of days a week.

But throughout the colonial period, slaves worked the plantations. In the early years of settlement attempts were made to coerce the Indians into the labour force. However, they could not be obtained in large enough numbers: the Indian population was small, could easily retreat into the interior and there was no indigenous market, as there was in Africa, for slaves and dealers from whom slaves could be bought. Expeditions had to be mounted to capture the Indians. Slaves were more easily obtained from Africa than in Brazil, though the impressment of Indians continued until the eighteenth century. Slaves were brought from the west coast of Africa between Guinea and Angola, and even from Mozambique. The slave trade and the close ties between Brazil and Africa continued until the mid-nineteenth century.

The size of the slave labour force varied greatly from plantation to plantation, but on the larger plantations there were gangs of about 150. Whatever the size of the plantation and whether or not it was operated by a *senhor dê engenho* (owner of a plantation) or *lavrador*, the pattern of land use was the same. The cleared land was divided into canefields, pasture and provision grounds. The cane was grown from cuttings planted in trenches or in rows of holes dug across the fields. Shoots appeared within twelve to fourteen days and the cane was harvested a year or more later, depending on the type of soil and the weather. Following a harvest, the roots of the cane were left in the ground to produce further crops, a custom known as ratooning. Over the years, ratoon crops gave progressively poorer yields, the better soils producing five to six profitable crops, the poorer soils three at the most. Only in fields on the most fertile alluvial soils in river valleys were the old roots dug up and new ones planted; elsewhere, the fields were abandoned to rough pasture and the forest. No deliberate attempt was made to preserve soil fertility. The manure of plantation livestock was not used, and cattle pens, such as those moved across the fields of West Indian plantations, were unknown. The only fertilizer the soil received was ash from the burning of the debris of clearing and of harvesting. Land was plentiful, and so seldom could a landowner, even with the help of his tenants, cultivate all his land that there was no incentive to preserve the fertility of the soil. It was easier and cheaper to clear new fields and let the old revert to forest as soon as ratoon crops no longer gave a worthwhile return. New clearings and patches of second growth forest soon became characteristic features of the landscape of the sugar coast.

On each plantation there were pasturelands and fields of provision crops. The staple provision crops were maize, manioc and beans, all borrowed from the Indians, and yams, which were the most significant African contribution. The pasture was required for the plantation livestock. No attempt was made on the plantation to breed livestock, which were raised in the interior of the country and sold to planters at fairs that developed along the margins of the sugar-growing region. In some districts of the coast a second cash crop was grown. Tobacco was cultivated in Bahia for export either to Europe or to Africa, where it was exchanged for slaves, while towards the end of the eighteenth century some plantations on the drier margins of the coastal plain began to grow cotton in response to the demands created by England's Industrial Revolution. Both tobacco and cotton were also grown by smallholders as well as by planters, and cotton in particular, because it gave better yields in a dry climate, led to the extension of cultivation westwards on to the Borborema plateau.

The productivity of the agriculture in the north-east of Brazil during the colonial period was almost certainly low. Perhaps because of the apparent abundance of land, a wasteful and exploitative approach to resources developed early. Soils were not fertilized, shifting cultivation was adopted and timber was used for fuel (for boiling the cane juice) rather than burning *bagasse* (the crushed cane-stalks). The Portuguese also abandoned the plough for the digging stick used by the Indian and African labourers. Throughout the colonial period there was no important change in agricultural technology: cultivators unthinkingly followed the methods of their forefathers and a society was moulded from which the idea of progress was absent. During the seventeenth century knowledge of the cultivation and manufacture of

M

sugar had flowed from Brazil to the West Indies, but, by the end of the eighteenth century, the plantations of the West Indies were far more productive.

This was an economy that even in the early years attracted few immigrants. Sugar colonies are not lands of opportunity except for those few individuals with influence and capital to acquire land, build mills and obtain labour. The migration from Portugal to the sugar-growing regions of Brazil was a small one, in which men were predominant, and they mingled easily with the Indians and Africans. The blending of races from three continents in the north-east began the cherished Brazilian tradition of racial tolerance. The population was almost entirely rural. The only towns of any size were the administrative centres and sugar-exporting ports of Salvador and Recife. The sugar industry of the north-east of Brazil enjoyed a period of prosperity during the sixteenth and early seventeenth centuries when the Portuguese still maintained a near monopoly of supplying sugar to Europe. This was followed by a prolonged decline and lapse into poverty. The Dutch invasion of the north-east, beginning in the 1620s, led to thirty years of guerrilla warfare during which extensive damage was done to the sugar plantations. While in Brazil, the Dutch learnt the techniques of sugar production, and carried this knowledge to the West Indies. From the mid-seventeenth century onwards, the plantations of the north-east found it difficult to compete with the West Indian plantations, which were closer to Europe. The first 'boom' in the development of Brazil was over.

Gold

The discovery of gold in the last years of the seventeenth century began the second 'boom' in the history of Brazil, leading to a major gold rush and to the opening up of a large part of the country's interior. Since the beginning of colonial times the hope had existed that precious metals and gems would be discovered, but for two centuries the exploring and slaving expeditions of the *bandeirantes* had wandered over the rich mineral zones of the Brazilian shield without coming across or recognizing gold or gems in paying quantities. This failure can be attributed partly to bad luck and partly to ignorance, for most *bandeirantes* had little or no idea of what precious metals looked like in their natural unsmelted state, nor did they know of the most likely places to find them. The exact date of the first discovery of rich deposits of gold is uncertain, but by the early 1690s gold in large amounts was known to exist in the valleys of the Serra do Espinhaço in the present state of Minas Gerais (literally the General Mines). This was the first of many discoveries of gold and diamond fields during the eighteenth century in Goiás and Bahia, in Minas Gerais and in the Mato Grosso. The richest strikes of all were those around the Serra do Espinhaço and on the northern margins of the Pantanal in the Mato Grosso. Gold mining became the mainstay of the Brazilian economy in the eighteenth century, and these two regions in particular were the centres of activity.

Most of the gold obtained in Minas and elsewhere in Brazil during this century was alluvial or placer gold recovered in the simplest manner. Wealthy miners employed slaves to pan for them and there were instances of entrepreneurs damming and diverting streams to permit a thorough search of the stream bed. Actual gold mines – shafts following veins of gold into the rock – were few and small. The mining technology of the Portuguese was extremely limited and there were no mines in colonial Brazil that could be compared with those of Potosí or Zacatecas in Spanish America.

The discovery of gold made Brazil a mining colony in addition to being a sugar colony and turned it into a land of opportunity for the first time. To become a planter required capital; to become a miner required very little capital and little or no skill: a poor man could hope that with luck he might become rich. This chance of a short cut to wealth brought a rush of people to the gold workings – from São Paulo and the north-east as well as from Portugal. The densely populated provinces of Minho and Douro in northern Portugal, the Azores and Madeira provided most of the Portuguese emigrants. So large did this exodus of agricultural workers become that the government of Portugal became alarmed and endeavoured to restrict it. Possibly as many as 800,000 Portuguese came to Brazil in the hundred years following the first discovery of gold. Not all went to Minas; many made their way to mining camps further in the interior while others stayed in the coastal towns.

The first people to the mines were *Paulistas* – people from São Paulo – who were gradually outnumbered by the arriving Portuguese. Male emigrants from Portugal by far outnumbered the female and this imbalance was made even worse by the practice common among the well-to-do Portuguese of putting daughters into convents, either in Salvador or in the home country. An outcry against this practice resulted, in 1732, in legislation to prevent women from leaving Brazil without official government sanction. This legislation was relaxed a year later to permit wives to leave with their husbands without first having to obtain official permission! Nevertheless, there were few Portuguese women in Minas Gerais and the miners, therefore, found wives and mistresses among the Indians and Africans, with the result that the mining camps were just as much racial 'melting pots' as were the plantations of the north-east.

By the mid-eighteenth century, the population of Minas Gerais was over 300,000, widely distributed through the valleys of the south-central part of the state, particularly in ephemeral mining camps. Camps near exceptionally rich deposits of gold, on important routes, or selected as administrative centres, evolved into permanent settlements and even into sizeable towns. The towns had a distinctive appearance. They grew up

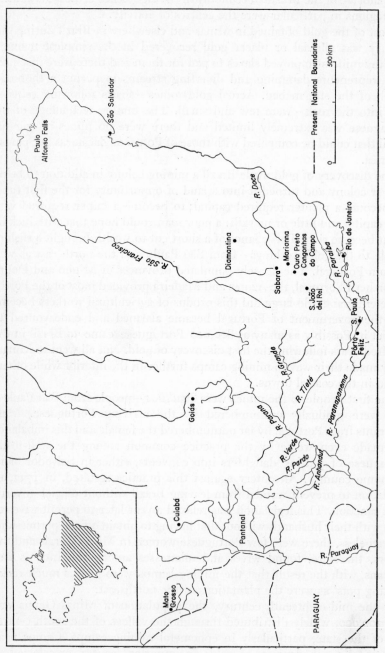

Fig. 8.7 Brazil: the gold country

Present National Boundaries

0   500 km

São Salvador

Paulo
Alfonso Falls

R. Doce

R. São Francisco

Diamantina

Sabara
Marianna
Ouro Preto
Congonhas
do Campo

S. João
del Rei

R. Paraíba

Rio de Janeiro

S. Paulo

Porto
Feliz

R. Grande

R. Paraná

R. Tietê

R. Paranapanema

Goiás

R. Verde

R. Pardo

R. Anhandui

Cuiabá

Pantanal

R. Paraguay

PARAGUAY

Mato
Grosso

haphazardly, in deep valleys and along steep hillsides; the streets were narrow, cobbled and often stepped; the houses of the rich stood flush with the street and were large and solidly built, two or three storeys high, with heavy wooden balconies, and many were decorated with the traditional Lusitanian tiles. The faithful and the fortunate endowed many churches, ornately decorated with gold leaf and sculptured soapstone. Here, in the wilds of Minas in the eighteenth century was produced some of the best baroque architecture in Brazil. Such were the towns of São João del Rey, Congonhas do Campo, Sabara, Mariana and, above all, Vila Rica do Ouro Preto – Rich Town of Black Gold – the capital of Minas Gerais, which was the largest town in Brazil at the height of the gold rush with a population of about 60,000.

The fact that these towns, and indeed the entire gold rush area, lay in the interior of the country and in a formerly sparsely populated part of it created special difficulties: the provision of the population with food, the export of gold and import of consumer goods and the enormous demands for beasts of burden to transport the goods raised new problems. Travel to and from the mines was never easy and always slow. There were several possible routes to the coast – all were long and all had their drawbacks (Fig. 8.7). The São Francisco valley provided a route between the Minas and the *sertão*[1] of the north-east. So many cattle in fact were driven along this valley to the Minas that a shortage of cattle was experienced on the sugar plantations. However, as a route to the coast the São Francisco had the great handicap of the Paulo Afonso Falls, which blocked access to the sea. Travellers left the river well above the falls and reached Salvador by a long trek across hot and difficult terrain. The route from the mines to the coast via São Paulo was circuitous, but drove roads crossed the Captaincy of São Paulo to the plains of southern Brazil, another source of cattle and of mules for Minas. The shortest route to the coast was down the valley of the Rio Doce, but it was made unusable by the warlike Indians of Espírito Santo. The comparatively short route leading to Rio de Janeiro meant crossing two mountain ranges – the Serra da Mantiqueira and the Serra do Mar – but it was this last route that was selected as the official route between the coast and the gold mines, and along it the government attempted to direct the gold and imports from Europe to facilitate the collecting of crown revenues. With Minas as its hinterland, the small port of Rio de Janeiro grew rapidly in size and importance and in 1763 replaced Salvador as the capital of Brazil.

The demands of the miners for beasts of burden and beef encouraged the growth of ranching in the backlands of much of eastern Brazil, but other foodstuffs were expensive to transport and had to be produced locally. Food in the mining areas was always expensive and never plentiful. The

[1] A word frequently used in Brazil, which may be roughly translated as 'backlands'. One who lives there is a *sertanejo*.

Indian crops of maize and manioc were grown in the traditional slash-and-burn manner. Agriculture and the need for timber and charcoal led to a concerted assault on the forests with the result that during the course of the gold rush the hills of central Minas were stripped bare.

The economy of Minas Gerais during the eighteenth century was an exploitative one: the mining did not generate lasting industrial or agricultural development. Gold production reached its peak probably during the 1750s with annual output valued at £2·5 million. Thereafter, there was a decline as the richer washings were worked out and no further bonanzas were found. By 1780, the annual production of gold had dropped to less than £1 million in value. Less gold meant that fewer people could be supported, and, during the second half of the century, there was a slackening in trade and a decline in population. A drift of people to the coast or back to São Paulo set in, though some miners, buoyed up by the hope of finding new El Dorados, ventured further into the interior. Towns were depopulated and became villages: Ouro Preto by 1800 had only 8000 to 10,000 inhabitants. Those people who did remain in Minas eked out a living by prospecting, by washing and rewashing the gravel in the streams of the Serra do Espinhaço for a small return, by subsistence agriculture and by ranching. The forests had gone, the hills were bare, the beautiful baroque towns stagnated, marking time, unchanged by new activities, and in the minds of the people there arose a nostalgia for the past – the source of a distinctive regional consciousness.

The course of the gold rush to Mato Grosso and Goiás has many similarities to that of Minas Gerais. There was a rapid assembling of a racially heterogeneous population, the more successful mining camps grew into towns such as Cuiabá and Mato Grosso, forest was felled for timber for fuel and to make way for the cultivation of food crops and cattle-ranching began. With the exhaustion of the placer gold, there was a similar story of decline, of stagnating towns and dwindling population, of the decay of commerical agriculture into subsistence shifting cultivation and largely subsistence pastoralism. After the gold rush a sparse population survived in a land scarred by traces of hasty and exploitative settlement.

Like Minas Gerais, the mines of Goiás and Mato Grosso were discovered by the *bandeirantes* – those of Goiás in the late seventeenth century and those of Mato Grosso in 1718 and in following years. The Goiás discoveries were eclipsed by those of Minas Gerais and attracted comparatively small numbers of people; far more went to Mato Grosso, for news of gold here came after the novelty of Minas Gerais had worn off and, even more important, after some of the richest washings in Minas had been worked out. Cuiabá, the main gold camp in Mato Grosso, grew so rapidly that by the mid-1720s it had a population of 7000, of whom 2600 were slaves, and it had been awarded the legal status of a town (*vila*). The gold rush to Mato

Grosso led to a marked decline during the 1720s in the population of São Paulo.

Transport to these distant mines was even more of a problem than to those of Minas Gerais (see Fig. 8.7). The route from São Paulo to Goiás was long and tedious, leading northwards through the present towns of Campinas and Uberaba, a trip of many weeks. From Goiás one could continue westward to Cuiabá. However, the usual route to Cuiabá was via a network of rivers. Starting at Pôrto Feliz, near the town of São Paulo, the route descended the Tiête to the Paraná, down the Paraná to its confluence with the Pardo, up the Pardo to its headwaters, then a portage to the basin of the Paraguay and so up the Paraguay and its tributaries to the gold camps. The trip was made by canoe, usually dugouts hollowed from a single trunk. These were stronger and more durable than the bark canoes sometimes used by the *bandeirantes* on their explorations. The river route passed through lands held by warlike Indians, whom for long the Portuguese were unable to subdue. For the sake of defence, therefore, the canoes set out in convoys for Cuiabá, with as many as several dozen canoes to a convoy. The convoy that accompanied the first governor of Mato Grosso to Cuiabá in 1726 comprised 108 canoes and 3000 people. There was only one convoy a year in each direction. This usually left Pôrto Feliz sometime between March and mid-June, taking five to seven months to reach Cuiabá. The return journey took only two months: the loads were lighter – gold instead of imported goods – and there were fewer passengers. These annual journeys were known as 'monsoons' (*monções*), an apt borrowing of a term to suggest clearly a seasonal event and an annual arrival of the utmost importance. 'Monsoons' continued with little change until the first decades of the nineteenth century, when they became smaller and increasingly irregular. The last convoy for Cuiabá set out about 1838, the year of a severe epidemic of typhoid along the banks of the Tiête, which carried off many boatmen and river pilots. But by this date, also, the alluvial gold of Mato Grosso had been largely washed out.

The gold rushes of the eighteenth century were short lived, but they had a lasting impact on the development of Brazil. The discovery of gold, in addition to its repercussions on the finances of Brazil and Europe, attracted immigrants, led to the growth of Rio de Janeiro and extended Portuguese influence and settlement into the interior of the country. The gold camps of the Serra do Espinhaço, Goiás and Cuiabá formed the nuclei of the present states of Minas Gerais, Goiás and Mato Grosso. These camps were springboards for further explorations. By the 1730s, expeditions from Cuiabá had reached into the Amazon basin. The search for gold and the wanderings of the *bandeirantes* permitted Portugal to stake a firm claim to the vast area that is now the interior of Brazil.

Cattle

In the first phase of its development Brazil was a sugar colony; in its second phase a gold mining colony; both sugar and gold mining created a demand for beasts of burden and the population required food – beef – so that on the margins of the sugar and gold country and, indeed, everywhere the Portuguese and the *mameluco* wandered they raised cattle. For the sparsely populated frontier lands of Brazil, ranching was an almost ideal form of land use. It required only a small labour force, it was tolerant of a wide range of climatic conditions and variations in quality of pasture, the animals could be driven to market and the hides provided a valuable export. Finally, ranching was a stand-by form of livelihood that the population could turn to when other means of earning a living failed. Ranching incorporated both Brazilian and European traits. Ranching was of Iberian origin, and the cowboy, the lasso, branding and the round-up were brought across the Atlantic. Abundance of land in Brazil made for vast ranches; the cowboys were of Indian or of mixed Indian and Portuguese descent, and the cowboys of southern Brazil borrowed the Indian bolas instead of using the lasso. In two regions of Brazil during colonial times ranching became the predominant economic activity and lent powerful support to the economy of the country: the *sertão* or backlands of the north-east and the plains to the south of São Paulo, between the Paraná and Uruguay rivers and the sea, a region which became known variously as São Pedro do Rio Grande do Sul, the Banda Oriental (the east bank of the Uruguay) or the Vacarias do Mar (the Cattle Ranges of The Sea).

In the north-east, ranching began as an offshoot of the sugar economy of the coast to satisfy the need of the plantations for oxen. At the very beginning of the colonial period, cattle were raised on the coastal plain, but, with the extension of sugar cultivation, ranching retreated inland to the Borborema plateau and eventually to the dry plains of the interior. With few predators and little competition for the pasture the number of cattle increased rapidly. By the early eighteenth century an estimated 800,000 head roamed the *caatinga* to the north of the São Francisco, while in Bahia and the valley of the São Francisco a further 500,000 were reported. These cattle were descended from Portuguese stock, but in the harsh environment of the *sertão* they evolved into relatively small animals, hardy, and almost feral.

As with the sugar plantations, the ranches were established on large land grants or *sesmarias*. The headquarters of a ranch or *fazenda* were located where possible by a river, and scattered over the land grant at sites where water was available were subsidiary centres known as *ranchos* or *currais*. At each *rancho* there was a herd of between 200 and 2000 head with a cowboy or *vaqueiro* in charge. It was his responsibility to tend to the herd and protect it from wild animals and even from Indian attack. On some *fazendas* there were twenty or more *ranchos*. *Vaqueiros* were not usually paid during the first few years of their employment, but then received one of every five calves born in the herds under their charge. A *vaqueiro* could then accumulate a herd of his own and, given the abundance of land on the ill-defined and unpoliced Luzo-Brazilian frontier, could aspire to become a landholder and rancher in his own right.

Drove roads led from the cattle lands to fairs along the margins of the sugar-growing region. These fairs marked the boundary between the predominantly pastoral districts of the north-east and the predominantly crop-growing districts. With the extension of the cultivated area, the fairs were forced further into the interior. The drove road from the *sertão* of Paraíba and Ceara once penetrated to Iguaraçu, only a few kilometres from Recife, but the fair was removed first to Goiana, and eventually, in the nineteenth century, to Campina Grande, in Paraíba. During the colonial period, cattle from the interior of Pernambuco were sold at Vitória de Santo Antão at the foot of the Borborema escarpment where this escarpment juts eastwards towards Recife, while in Bahia, Feira de Santana became the main cattle fair. Many of these fairs led to the growth of small towns and thus have had a lasting effect on the settlement pattern.

Cattle-ranching in the north-east provided a means of settling and realizing some wealth from a harsh environment. From an economic point of view, ranching was essentially a support of the sugar industry but it did also produce a valuable by-product in hides. At the end of the colonial period, when the sugar industry was in relative decline, hides were the third most important export of Recife, after cotton and sugar, and counted for 10 per cent of the value of all exports.

By contrast, cattle-ranching in the Vacarias do Mar did not develop as an appendage of another agricultural economy. This vast region between São Paulo and the river Plate remained throughout the colonial period a sparsely populated borderland between the Spanish and Portuguese empires, with neither gold nor precious stones nor a cash crop to attract population and official attention. During the sixteenth and early seventeenth centuries the Jesuits founded missions on the borders of this region, in southern Paraguay and in what is now the Misiones Province of Argentina, missions that were pillaged from time to time by armed bands from São Paulo searching for slaves. The herds of the Vacarias do Mar descended from cattle that had escaped from these missions. With nearly empty fertile humid lands to roam over, the cattle rapidly increased in number to the extent that by the end of the seventeenth century there were estimated to be 4 million. Cattle were hunted by a sparse population of mixed Spanish, Portuguese and Indian origin; the hides were exported, and the carcasses left to rot upon the ground.

The eighteenth century brought a significant change to the cattle economy of the Vacarias do Mar, occasioned in part at least by the gold rush in

Minas Gerais, which created a market, thereby giving a greater value to land and livestock. Instead of merely hunting feral cattle, the people of the region now laid claim to ownership of lands and herds. The ranch or *fazenda*, the round-up, branding, the cowboy – here known as the *gaucho* – in fact the paraphernalia of Iberian cattle culture long familiar in the *sertão* of north-east Brazil, now appeared in the south. Hides continued to be exported in large numbers, but cattle were also driven north. The breeding of mules on a large scale began, the mules being employed in transporting goods between the mines and the coast.

An appreciation of the growing importance and potential wealth of the territory led Portugal to reinforce its claim of possession. A fortified settlement, the Colonia do Sacramento, was founded on the river Plate across from Buenos Aires, while a government-sponsored immigration from the Azores resulted in the establishment of several villages along the coast of Santa Catarina. This attempt at the integration of the Vacarias do Mar into Brazil was only partly successful: dispute of possession continued into the nineteenth century with, finally, Brazil retaining the larger share of the region, and the southern fringe becoming the independent state of Uruguay. At the end of the colonial period, the Vacarias do Mar was still very sparsely populated; there were no towns or ports. Possibly the greatest change in the landscape to have taken place was the extension in the area of grassland.

The end of the colonial period provides a convenient point at which to attempt an assessment of what had been accomplished in Brazil by the Portuguese over three centuries. The work of exploring the country was over in the sense that the lie of the land and the course of the rivers were known in major outline. This had been accomplished in large measure by the *bandeirantes*. But in effect the Portuguese colony occupied only about half of the territory of what is now Brazil, for over the Amazon basin and other remote regions of the interior Portugal's control was nominal even though its claim was recognized. In the far south, its claim to possession was still in dispute. There was a multi-racial population of approximately 2·5 million, exclusive of Indians still unassimilated into Luzo-Brazilian society. This society was already distinctive, formed out of Indian, African and Portuguese contributions, yet with a sufficient sense of identity to maintain Brazil as a unit following Independence. It was, however, far from being a technological society, and in its agriculture it was conservative, backward and wasteful. Already by 1800, the landscape of Brazil was scarred by traces of the destructive use of resources.

Economic activity and population were very unevenly distributed. In only two regions of the colony, the forest zone of the north-east and the goldfields of Minas, had there been any approach to intensive exploitation and it was in these two regions that large numbers of people had been assembled (Fig. 8.8). The north-east contained about 40 per cent of the population of Brazil, nearly all on the coast, and 28 per cent of the population (about 400,000 people) still remained in Minas Gerais. In the cattle-ranching regions the population was very sparsely distributed and in the far north of the country the Luzo-Brazilian population numbered only a few thousand. In Maranhão, a small number of planters and traders lived in and around São Luiz; in the Amazon there were some missions and garrison posts, such as Belém and Manaus (both of comparatively recent foundation – 1609 and 1721 respectively). The population of Brazil in 1800 was overwhelmingly rural. The largest towns were on the coast, ports and administrative centres: Rio de Janeiro with an estimated population of

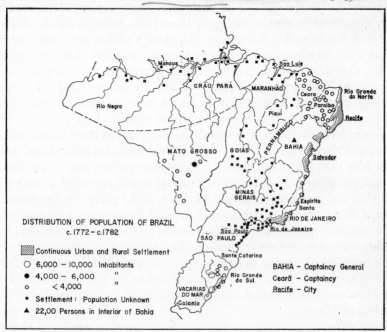

Fig. 8.8 The population of Brazil towards the end of the eighteenth century
(Alden, 1963)

100,000, São Salvador with about 50,000 and Recife with about 25,000. All three of these towns were growing, Rio the most rapidly. The gold-mining towns were in decline, some by now all but deserted. Elsewhere there were a number of small centres which had the legal status of a *vila* or *cidade* because of some official function performed there, but these were little more than a collection of a few huts, a church or two, perhaps a garrison, with little or no commercial function being carried on. The town of São Paulo, as distinct from the captaincy of the same name, even though it was 260 years old, was in reality still only a village with few inhabitants.

The outlook for Brazil at the end of the colonial period was not good. Its sugar economy was depressed: the richest deposits of gold had been washed out and, though cattle-ranching provided a livelihood, it did not provide a very good one or much revenue for Portugal. There was, moreover, no readily discernible source of wealth. Yet the nineteenth century was to bring more speculative 'booms', a new flow of immigrants and a departure, in parts of Brazil, from the pattern of development established during the colonial period.

THE NINETEENTH CENTURY: THE EMERGENCE OF TWO BRAZILS

Brazil passed from colony to independence gradually and comparatively peacefully during the early years of the nineteenth century. In November 1807, the Prince Regent of Portugal, Dom João, with his family, government and retainers fled Lisbon, as Napoleon's armies neared it, for Rio de Janeiro, which became in 1808 the temporary capital of the Portuguese empire. One of the first acts of the exiled government was to throw open the ports of Brazil[1] to the shipping of friendly nations, and other long-standing, restrictive mercantilist measures were relaxed. In 1815, João, now king, raised Brazil to formal and legal equality with Portugal. João appears to have liked Brazil; certainly he was loath to leave it and did not do so until 1821. His eldest son, Dom Pedro, remained behind and it was under him that Brazil was proclaimed an independent empire in 1822, a fact not recognized by Portugal until 1825. Brazil remained a monarchy until 1889 and then became a republic. Perhaps the greatest achievement of imperial Brazil was that it managed to weld Portuguese America into a single nation. Opposition to independence by Portuguese garrisons was speedily overcome, and the regional rebellions of the first half of the century, which usually had a secessionist tinge to them, all failed. In 1828 the long-standing dispute over possession of the lands to the north and east of the river Plate was finally settled, with the creation of the independent buffer Republic of Uruguay.

Brazil was now in charge of its own destiny and this political change, therefore, did have some effect on the historical geography of the country. Perhaps this can be seen most clearly in immigration policy. Attempts were made to attract immigrants not only from Portugal but from all Europe and to settle them in the south. Portugal had prevented the establishment of industries in Brazil; now industries could be founded. The nineteenth century saw a quickening of the economic life of the country: railways were built, small ports grew into large commercial cities, the population increased from about 2·5 million in the late 1700s to over 17 million in 1900. But the approach to land use, ingrained during the colonial period, also persisted as economic booms were followed by slumps, and resources were wastefully used. In fact, what can be seen emerging during this century are two Brazils, one conservative, technologically backward and with a low standard of living, the other progressive, technologically more

[1] The Amazon remained closed to foreign shipping until 1867.

advanced and reaching towards a higher standard of living. The contrast between these two Brazils was to produce political and economic problems in the country.

The north-east: a deepening crisis

The north-east has come to form part of traditional Brazil. The social and cultural characteristics of the *Nordestinos*, which made them so unresponsive to the need for change and helped to make their agriculture so wasteful ✓ and unproductive, persisted throughout the nineteenth century. Few attempts were made to revive the economy of the region and it is probable that the standard of living, never high for the mass of the population, suffered a decline. The relative decline, therefore, of the economy of the north-east *vis-à-vis* the rest of Brazil, already noticeable before the end of the colonial period, continued; the political power of the region underwent eclipse and by the twentieth century the north-east had sunk to the level of a depressed region. There has been a tendency until recently to regard these years between the end of prosperity in the eighteenth century and the present era of development plans as a period in which little or nothing of importance happened in the north-east. It is true that sugar, cotton and livestock continued to be the dominant constituents of the regional economy, but the agriculture of the region did, in fact, undergo some modifications, which brought with them changes in population distribution and settlement patterns.

Developments in the sugar industry governed the changes that took place in the coastal region. Even in 1800 this part of the north-east was still comparatively sparsely populated and much land remained in forest, making possible a large expansion in the acreage of sugar. Despite the poor economic climate, the number of plantations continued to increase, by both the traditional method of subdividing large estates through inheritance and the carving out of new plantations along the agricultural frontier. About mid-century, plantations were being built along the foot of the Borborema escarpment, a fact which suggests that by then all land in the coastal region had passed into private ownership. In Pernambuco alone the number of plantations increased from about 300 in the late eighteenth century to about 1000 in 1830. The wasteful methods of the sugar industry together with the low level of productivity at the beginning of the century left plenty of scope for improvement. The first advance was the introduction in 1810 of the Bourbon variety of cane to replace the Creole variety that had been cultivated since the beginning of colonial times. The Bourbon cane provided higher yields per hectare while its juice contained a higher sucrose content. Indeed, the advantages of Bourbon cane were so readily apparent that within a decade of 1810 it had replaced the Creole. The use of ploughs became more widespread; by mid-century they were to be found on the better managed plantations. Manuring, too, became more common, producing higher yields and probably allowing fields to be cultivated for a greater length of time than before. The capacity and efficiency of some mills was improved by the replacement of the old-style vertical rollers by heavy horizontal presses. A few planters even installed steam engines, but their cost, the great demands they made on fuel, and the difficulty of finding mechanics to make repairs, persuaded most planters to stick to animal or water power. The collective result of these improvements, and of the extension in the acreage of sugar, was a large increase in exports. During the first half of the century, exports of sugar from Recife rose from 10,000 to 50,000 tons annually.

Clearly, there was still a market for Brazilian sugar abroad. The experience of the industry during the first half of the nineteenth century does suggest a revival from a nadir reached some time at the end of the colonial period. However, it appears probable, judging by complaints planters made of their financial position, that a very low level of profit was accepted. Part of the expansion can perhaps be attributed not to economic forces but to the innate conservatism of a society that could bring itself to accept no other form of livelihood, even though capital might have produced higher returns if invested in enterprises other than sugar, outside the region. Indeed, the founding of some plantations required not so much liquid capital as labour. Though, admittedly, slaves cost money, the existence of the *morador* class meant that work was to be obtained in return for the use of land, which planters had in plenty. This continuing demand for Brazilian sugar may also be attributed in part to the difficulties competitors were experiencing, difficulties that the north-east was to encounter only in the second half of the century.

In the nineteenth century, producers of cane sugar not only had to contend with competition from beet for the first time but also had to meet two further basic problems that were to transform the industry: a labour crisis brought on by the end of slavery and a massive reorganization of sugar production occasioned by advances in the technology of milling and manufacturing sugar, which rendered the old style plantations obsolete. The labour problem was the first encountered. The successful slave revolt in St Domingue, now Haiti, in the late eighteenth century brought about the destruction of what was the most productive sugar industry in the Caribbean, while abolition in the British West Indian islands led to a movement of ex-slaves away from the plantations and so to a decline in production, particularly in Jamaica. In Brazil, slavery continued until 1888. During the sixty or so years preceding abolition, slaves came to form a smaller and smaller proportion of the labour force in the sugar industry. Slaves were expensive, particularly with British attempts to suppress the Atlantic slave trade, and planters had turned to the *moradores* for labour, who outnumbered slaves on most plantations well before abolition. Abolition in the forest zone of the north-east was merely the final act of a long period of transition, and it was followed by a movement of ex-slaves leaving one plantation to become *moradores* on another, or going to the towns or to the interior to try to better their lot. The decline in sugar production was slight and temporary, but abolition did have an important effect on the settlement pattern. Slaves lived in quarters adjacent to the plantation houses, *moradores* at scattered points on the estates. The decline of slavery and its eventual abolition led to a dispersal of the population from the plantation nuclei. The plantations ceased to be important elements in the pattern of population distribution; with the reorganization of the sugar industry, they also ceased to be the basic units of production.

By the mid-nineteenth century, technological advances had culminated in the building of factories for the processing of sugar, and these could mill far more cane per day and extract more juice from the cane than the old mills. Moreover, new refining techniques permitted the factories to improve on the *muscovado* and *clayed* grades of sugar that the old mills produced. But the factories were expensive to build, and to operate at capacity they required far more cane than the usual plantation grew. They were, therefore, normally built by companies rather than by individuals and, to ensure supply of cane, the companies bought up the plantations or contracted with planters for their crops. In Brazil the first factories (referred to as *usinas*) were built in the last quarter of the century. Difficulties of financing in the north-east slowed the introduction of the system, and well over half a century elapsed before the bulk of the sugar of the north-east was milled and manufactured in *usinas*.

Where it was adopted, the new system brought changes in agricultural practices, in the class structure and in the settlement pattern. Large companies could afford new equipment and could conduct research more easily than individual planters. By 1920, tractors and ploughs were far more common in the districts where the central factory system held sway than where it did not. The purchase of land by *usinas* and agreements to buy cane from planters meant that more and more of the traditional mills went out of use. Many planters withdrew from the countryside to Recife or Salvador or even to Rio. Their crumbling plantation houses and abandoned mills are nostalgic reminders in the landscape of today of the passing of a system of sugar production and of a way of life that by the end of the nineteenth century was already more than three hundred years old. The planters who did remain to grow cane for the *usinas* became known as *fornecedores* (suppliers of cane) and their former position at the peak of the class pyramid was assumed by the owners of the *usinas*, the *usineiros*. *Moradores* were not immediately affected, though hired labour did become more common. But the *lavradores* as a class did suffer. No longer did they have a role in establishing new plantations, and the *usinas* preferred, where possible, to cultivate their own cane rather than to rely on share-cropping arrangements. Around the *usinas* there grew up new nuclei of population in small company towns and villages with regularly laid out streets, churches and company stores, and inhabited by a wage-earning proletariat.

During this period of transition the amount of sugar grown and manufactured in the north-east continued to increase and markets continued to be found. In the middle years of the nineteenth century, competition from other producers of cane sugar as well as from beet weakened the north-east's hold on its traditional markets in Europe and North America, but the rapid growth of population in southern Brazil and Argentina was creating an alternative market. This change in the pattern of exports was accelerated by the introduction of the central factory system. The qualities of sugar it produced were not well received in the traditional markets, but were readily accepted in the new markets to the south. Ironically, the modernization of the sugar industry of the north-east did not lead to the retention of its traditional markets but contributed to their loss.

This large increase in the amount of sugar produced and the reorganization of the industry did not bring a return of prosperity to the forest zone. Compared with many other sugar-producing regions, sugar production in the forest zone was still costly and inefficient. Even in the domestic Brazilian market, competition from sugar plantations in the states of Rio de Janeiro and São Paulo was beginning. No alternative form of land use to sugar was in the offing, yet the monoculture of sugar was more widely practised than ever before. During the nineteenth century, the commitment of the forest zone to sugar had been strengthened, making change even more difficult. From a social point of view the abolition of slavery was probably the only favourable development. Landownership and wealth had become even further concentrated, the ranks of the landless peasantry had greatly swelled, food shortages associated with the monoculture of a cash crop had not been eased, and it appears probable that, despite the rise in sugar production, the increase in population meant a decline in *per capita* income. Of the forest zone's problems at the end of the colonial period, only that of slavery had been solved: the others had increased.

In the *sertão* of the north-east, the nineteenth century was a period of very rapid change. There was an intensification of settlement, a great extension of the cultivated area and a depletion of some of the resources, but also there were first attempts to tackle the basic problem of the *sertão*: drought. The *sertão* was still sparsely settled at the opening of the century, but the population grew rapidly both by natural increase and by the arrival of runaway slaves and freemen. The *sertão*'s share of the total population of the north-east during the nineteenth century rose from about 10 per cent to about 50 per cent. One of the *sertão*'s products, cotton, came for a time to rival sugar as an export, and became permanently established as an important cash crop. It was during this century that the *sertão* came to occupy a more significant place in the economy and society of the north-east than it had before.

The attraction of the *sertão* lay in its open spaces; cultivable land was still available and was more easily come by than near the coast. The agricultural frontier in the north-east, which at the end of the eighteenth century had lapped along the foot of the escarpment of the Borborema plateau, was pushed westwards across the plateau until by the end of the century it had reached the margins of the driest districts of the north-east. Further inland, the lack of rainfall was to limit cultivation to the dry beds of seasonally flowing streams, to valleys of the Cariri in southern Ceara watered by artesian wells, and to ranges of hills that caught orographic rainfall. The relatively humid eastern portion of the *sertão* acquired its own local name – the *Agreste*. Manioc, beans and maize, the typical food crops of the north-east, were grown in the *Agreste*, some to be sent to the forest zone, and cotton became the main cash crop. The strong demand for Brazilian cotton, which began in the second half of the eighteenth century, continued through the early years of the nineteenth. In the *Agreste* some cotton plantations were established, but much of the cotton appears to have been grown by smallholders, employing only family labour. In the mid-years of the century, however, the *Agreste* suffered from the competition of the southern United States and it is probable that the acreage of cotton declined. The *Agreste* produced poor quality cotton, and the primitive method of ginning often broke the fibres. The American Civil War led to a revival of cotton cultivation and during the last decades of the century the place of cotton in the economy of the *Agreste* was firmly established as demand became more stable with the creation of a domestic textile industry.

This extension of cultivation inland to an area in which cattle-raising had previously been the predominant form of land use led to the familiar conflict between rancher and farmer. Ranching on the *Agreste* continued to be an integral part of the local economy, but the landscape became criss-crossed with fences to separate animals from crops. The spread of cultivation also led to the removal of the cattle fairs from the borders of the forest zone to the *Agreste* and even further inland on the margins of the dry *sertão*. Ranching itself underwent a change. Formerly cattle had been the most numerous livestock, with some raising of horses and mules, but by the early 1900s sheep and goats had come to outnumber cattle, in the backlands of Pernambuco at least. Sheep and goats can make do with poorer feed than cattle, and their appearance, therefore, in such large numbers during the century is indicative of a deterioration in the quality of the grazing. Overgrazing may have resulted from the cycle of wet and dry years, the herds increasing in size in the wet years and grazing the land bare in the dry. Soil impoverishment and soil erosion caused by shifting agriculture and deforestation may have produced in some districts a vegetation cover in which only sheep and goats could find fodder.

The growth of population in the interior of the north-east meant that the droughts which from time to time afflicted the region now caused great suffering and loss of life. The drought of 1877–9 took a terrible toll. Of the one million inhabitants of Ceara, it is believed that one half died. Many *sertanejos* fled to the coast, though, once there, thousands died from exhaustion and disease. Some refugees emigrated to the Amazon. Yet after the droughts many of those who had fled returned to their homes. In fact, the threat of drought has not been a deterrent to the settlement of the *sertão*. The disaster of 1877–9 did force the government of Brazil to start thinking of ways of mitigating the effects of drought, but little was accomplished. Some dams to create reservoirs were proposed, though it was not until 1906 that the first one was completed, and only in 1909 was a government agency formed to prepare for drought. Drought and what to do about it has been since 1877 a persistent theme in the politics of the north-east.

A further aspect of change in the north-east during this century was the growth of towns. This was not only a result of more trade and more people but also of the beginnings of a rural–urban migration, which has greatly accelerated in the present century. By 1900, Salvador and Recife both had a little over 100,000 inhabitants; these cities continued to be as they were in the colonial period, the principal ports, and during the last decades of the nineteenth century they were linked to their immediate hinterlands by railways. These were typical 'colonial' lines in that the primary purpose was to facilitate the export of a cash crop by linking areas of production with the ports. Fortaleza, Natal, Maceio, Aracaju, only minor garrisons or villages at the beginning of the nineteenth century, became sizeable towns, provincial capitals and ports. Away from the coast, however, even as late as 1900, there were no large towns, only many small ones, which were dependent on a cattle fair or a railhead, or on the trade generated by the local agriculture, or which were, in the forest zone, attached to a *usina*. These towns consisted of little more than a sparse network of unpaved streets, a square and church.

By the end of the nineteenth century none of the problems the north-east had inherited from the colonial period had been solved and new ones, such as the need to deal with droughts in the interior, had been added. The rapidly increasing population, then reaching 6 million (one third of the country's total), made the task of raising the standard of living all the more difficult. In 1900, the north-east was already, compared with other parts of the country, 'depressed' and backward.

Coffee: the development of São Paulo

As the production of sugar and gold had dominated the economy of Brazil during the colonial period, so coffee became the mainstay of the economy in the nineteenth century. Coffee was brought to the Americas at least as early as the beginning of the eighteenth century. It became an important export crop in the French colony of St Domingue, but elsewhere was grown only in small quantities: in Jamaica and Central America and in Brazil on the hillsides around Rio de Janeiro. Throughout the eighteenth century there was never a strong demand for coffee, and it was only during the nineteenth century that it became a popular drink in Europe and North America. In the United States alone, between the years 1821 and 1844, the *per capita* consumption of Brazilian coffee rose from 28·35 g to 2·27 kg. This suddenly acquired but lasting taste for coffee led in Brazil to the spread of coffee cultivation across the south-eastern part of the country from the state of Rio de Janeiro to Paraná, to a large inflow of settlers, many of them from Europe, and to an accumulation of wealth, which was used to build the city of São Paulo as well as to finance the beginnings of the industrial development of Brazil.

From the early nineteenth century to about the 1880s the Paraíba valley, across the Serra do Mar from Rio de Janeiro, was the principal region of coffee production in Brazil. The beginnings of Luzo-Brazilian settlement here really only date from the previous century and the decline of the gold rush when a backwash of *mineiros* abandoned the exhausted diggings and moved into the valley to raise cattle. Few of these settlers had a good legal claim to the land they used, and boundaries to properties were at best only vaguely known. There was plenty of land and, so long as the agriculture was predominantly subsistent rather than commercial, little value was attached to land. With the onset of the coffee 'boom' and with the realization that the Paraíba valley, so close to the port of Rio, was suited to coffee cultivation, a scramble for land took place. The wealthy and the powerful soon claimed large holdings, dispossessing squatters and smallholders alike to make room for plantations. These first appeared on the south side of the valley, in the state of Rio de Janeiro, and gradually coffee cultivation was extended up the valley towards São Paulo and into the hills on the north side, in Minas Gerais.

At first, the quality of the coffee produced was poor, for the planters had no previous experience of coffee cultivation and had to learn the business more or less through trial and error. Only gradually were improvements made, but by mid-century the pioneer period was over. There was by then a dense rural population and an active business and social life in the prosperous small towns of the valley, while planters could afford to build themselves elegant mansions and play prominent roles in the political affairs of the country. This prosperity, however, was not to endure. There were two serious flaws in the economy: the exploitative agricultural methods employed and, as the plantations were worked by slaves, the labour crisis that the impending abolition of slavery would bring. At the time, slavery was the issue most talked about and its abolition generally considered the most serious threat, but the real, though ignored, problem and the one that brought lasting damage was soil erosion. The forests were gradually cut down to make way for coffee, the trees being planted in rows aligned downhill. After three years the first harvest was collected, but it took six years for the trees to mature. During these early years, food crops were grown between the rows of trees. As the groves of trees began to age and their yields decreased, further stretches of forest were cleared and new groves planted. Whenever the hillsides were left without an adequate cover of vegetation, the topsoil was washed away, and the practice of planting the coffee trees in rows downhill helped channel the waters of the subtropical downpours into rivulets, which rapidly deepened into gullies. These eroded lands were invaded by weeds, coarse grass and ants, and so made uncultivable. When no more forest remained to be cleared in the valley and no new coffee plantings could be made, coffee production began to decline. Sir Richard Burton, who travelled across the valley in 1862 commented on the extent of erosion (Burton, 1869, I, p. 42); by 1888, the year of abolition of slavery, many plantations were well on the way to being ruined by the mismanagement of land. Rather than spend their profits on belated attempts to repair and conserve, the planters founded new plantations, opening a frontier of coffee cultivation further west, and left behind them a ravished valley, with a depressed and declining population, which turned to making a living from that traditional Brazilian stand-by in times of economic collapse – cattle-ranching.

The new frontier opened up during the second half of the nineteenth century lay to the north and west of the city of São Paulo, as shown in Fig. 8.9. In this region of varied geological structure, relief, soil and vegetation, planters learnt to be selective in siting their coffee groves. It was soon realized that coffee grew better on the wooded hillsides than on the open savanna, and that the so-called *terra-roxa* soils gave the best yields. These soils have developed on flows of diabase and are reddish-purple in colour, porous, deep, and rich in humus. The abundance of *terra-roxa* in the neighbourhood of Ribeirão Preto and São Claro made these towns centres of coffee production. For a time, Campinas, at the focus of routes leading from these two districts of the frontier to the coast, gained population more rapidly than the city of São Paulo itself. In the last two decades of the century, another region of *terra-roxa* soils around Botucatu was planted to coffee. On these new plantations, the methods of preparing and grading coffee beans greatly improved, but the exploitative methods of cultivation that had characterized the plantations of the Paraíba valley were continued, with the same results of soil erosion and soil exhaustion. The productive life of a plantation appears to have been of the order of thirty to fifty years. The coffee frontier, therefore, continued to move and, during the twentieth century, pushed northwards into Minas Gerais and Goiás, as well as westwards along the *terra-roxa* soils into the state of Paraná.

The expansion of this frontier was only made possible by the building of

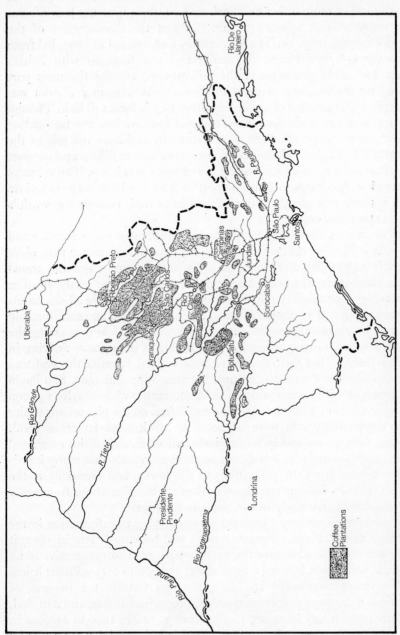

Fig. 8.9 Distribution of coffee in São Paulo at the beginning of the twentieth century (after Monbeig, 1952)

railways, for distances from the coast were now becoming too great to make the use of mule trains practical. Indeed, for a time the lack of adequate transportation appears to have slowed the development of the frontier around Campinas. The first railway line, opened in 1867, led from Santos through São Paulo to Jundiaí and was financed with British capital. The rapid extension of the rail network was for the most part financed by the *Paulista* planters themselves. As soon as a district was producing a fair amount of coffee, agitation began for a rail link. Though the companies had ambitious plans to build railways into the far interior of the country – some of which were eventually realized – the role of the railway in São Paulo in the nineteenth century was to follow and support the coffee frontier, rarely to precede it and open new lands. The railways converged on São Paulo city and its port of Santos, which in the last years of the century was greatly extended and improved, became the world's largest exporter of coffee.

A major contrast between the plantations on the new coffee frontier and those of the Paraíba valley was the employment of free rather than slave labour. The new frontier, after all, was 'opened up' when the transatlantic slave trade was over. The regions into which the coffee frontier was moving were sparsely populated and could not provide all the hands that were needed. The planters looked to Europe for immigrants, forming their own immigration companies to subsidize passages or persuading the state of São Paulo to pay subsidies. The trickle of immigrants arriving in the mid-years of the century turned into a flood towards the end and continued into the twentieth century. Between 1887 and 1900, São Paulo state received more than a million immigrants, with nearly 140,000 arriving in the peak year of 1895. The conditions on the plantations under which these immigrants were expected to work were far from good. Tenancy, poor wages and lack of schools and medical facilities combined to make opportunities for advancement seem so remote that many immigrants retreated from the plantations to the towns, and especially to the city of São Paulo. Labour was also recruited for the plantations from other parts of Brazil, particularly in the states to the north.

The nineteenth century witnessed an astonishing transformation in the geography of São Paulo. A poor, remote and backward state in 1800, it was by the end of the century the most prosperous and progressive in all Brazil. Its population increased from about 150,000 to 2·25 million; it had a rail network unequalled in Latin America outside the pampas of Argentina; there were numerous sizeable, prosperous towns, and a capital, São Paulo, which had increased in size from 30,000 in 1870 to 239,000 in 1900. The profits from coffee were invested in industrial development; by the end of the nineteenth century, the city of São Paulo had become the financial and industrial centre of Brazil. There were, nevertheless, problems. The economy of the state and, indeed, of Brazil as a whole had come to rely very heavily on the export of coffee, which was soon to be overproduced and difficult to market. Coffee also led to the phenomenon of the 'hollow frontier', a frontier in which the population is denser and economic activity greater along or near the frontier than in the older settled regions behind it. The frontier moves not by pressure of population behind it, but by the exhaustion of resources along it, as well as by the promise of greater rewards to be earned in the new lands beyond it. How often and how closely the actual conditions in São Paulo approached this description of the ideal 'hollow frontier' is difficult to say. The Paraíba valley may provide the best example. Certainly, in the old plantation tracts of São Paulo there was a period of readjustment, and a running down of economic activity. In the Paraíba valley, if not also in other districts, there was a decline in population. People turned to cattle-ranching and to the cultivation of sugar, cotton and food crops. Small-holdings, owned and operated by immigrants, became much more numerous.

The south

For the three southern states of Paraná, Santa Catarina and Rio Grande do Sul, the nineteenth century was a period of transition from traditional to modern Brazil. In 1800 these southern states were remote and sparsely inhabited, with an economy based on cattle-ranching; by the end of the century, they had acquired a substantial population, much of it through immigration from Europe; there was an active agricultural frontier, and one of the most productive agricultural economies in Brazil was in the making. Compared with the nineteenth-century migration to North America or even to São Paulo, the numbers of immigrants reaching southern Brazil were comparatively small. This immigration was sponsored in the first instance by the government of Brazil and later by the state governments[1] as well as by private colonization companies. Immigrants in the first half of the century were mostly German, and in the 1870s and 1880s Italian, while in the last years of the century the national origins were much more diverse. These immigrants settled in the forested lands, avoiding the grasslands, for the forest soils were considered, generally correctly, to be the more fertile.

The government of Brazil in 1824 founded the first of its European colonies at São Leopoldo in Rio Grande, to strengthen Brazil's hold on these southern reaches of its territory. São Leopoldo lies in fertile forested land between the Jacuí river and the escarpment of the *planalto*. Two more German colonies were founded in 1829, at Rio Negro on the borders of Paraná and Santa Catarina, and at São Pedro de Alcantara, near Florianópolis. These two colonies, much more isolated than São Leopoldo,

---

[1] The Republic, established in 1889, turned over the responsibility of promoting immigration to the states.

remained small while São Leopoldo by 1830 had 5000 colonists and became the nucleus of an expanding region of German settlement. Progress was hindered by the civil war in Rio Grande of 1835–45, but in the late 1840s settlement spread westwards through the forestlands on the north side of the Jacui valley. The colony of Santa Cruz was founded in 1849. German immigration to Rio Grande was checked in 1859 by the so-called Heydt rescript. By this order, the Prussian government, shocked by the treatment accorded Germans in Brazil, especially on the coffee plantations of São Paulo, stopped further Prussian emigration to Brazil, and this example was followed by other German states.[1]

The nucleus of Italian settlement in Rio Grande was to the north of São Leopoldo, on the *planalto*. Such colonies as Caxias, Garibaldi and Veranópolis founded in the 1870s and 1880s quickly attracted a population of over 20,000. During the later years of the century colonizers of German, Italian and Luzo-Brazilian descent were moving into the valleys of the upper Jacui and Ijui rivers and their tributaries. A German colony, Santo Angelo, was founded in the Ijui valley as early as 1855. This frontier was supported by the building of a railway from Porto Alegre, which reached Passo Fundo in 1895 and Erechim in 1910. By the beginning of the twentieth century, the only large stretch of forest in Rio Grande still unpenetrated by colonists lay along the Uruguay river in the northern part of the state.

In Santa Catarina, a second nucleus of German colonization, privately sponsored, was established in a region of small valleys and dissected escarpment near the coast to the north of Florianópolis. In 1849, the Kolonisationsverein von Hamburg bought land from the Prince of Joinville, a connection of the Brazilian royal family, and founded the Dona Francisca colony with headquarters at the town of Joinville. The colony prospered, its population increased and settlement began to spread inland. By 1910 a railway linked Joinville with São Bento. In the Itajai valley, Dr Herman Blumenau in 1850 founded the town which bears his name. This colony, too, was successful and by 1882 contained a population of 16,000, of which 70 per cent were German. From Blumenau settlers began to move inland. In 1897 an affiliate of the Hamburg Company acquired land on the upper Itajai where it founded Hamônia (now Ibirama), linked to Blumenau by rail in 1909. From Ibirama, settlement spread into the valleys of the tributaries of the Itajai.

European immigration to Paraná began late. The state has only had a separate existence since 1853 and the active promotion of colonization did not begin until the 1860s. Small groups of Germans, Italians and Poles were settled on the lower *planalto*, a region of grassland and forest, many in the vicinity of Curitiba, the capital. Towards the end of the century,

[1] This rescript was not withdrawn until 1896 and then only for the southern states.

Ukrainians began to arrive in large numbers, founding a large colony in 1896 at Prudentopolis on the second *planalto*, across which a railway was then being built from São Paulo.

By the end of the nineteenth century the only forested districts beyond the agricultural frontier in southern Brazil were in western Paraná and Santa Catarina, as well as the Uruguay river country of Rio Grande. The clearing and cultivation of these districts was to be the work of the twentieth century, when a second frontier was also opened in an attempt to cultivate the grasslands.

In all three states colonists cultivated small properties. In Rio Grande, during the course of the century, there was a reduction in the size of property awarded to the arriving colonist. The original settlers at São Leopoldo had been given about 77 ha (160,000 *braços* square); after 1851, colonists were awarded 48 ha and, in 1890, 25 ha became the standard grant in both government and private colonization schemes in that state. The colonists raised large families and inevitably, through inheritance, the properties rapidly became subdivided. Indeed, excessive subdivision of land resulted in the creation of *minifundia* – properties too small to provide the owner with an adequate living – and was to become a major problem in the twentieth century. Sons who could not hope to inherit an adequate parcel of land in the home colony moved to the frontier, thus helping to provide the manpower for the settlement of new regions. In contrast to the frontier in São Paulo, the frontier in these states was not 'hollow'.

The standard of agriculture in these regions of nineteenth-century settlement was at first disappointingly low. In the strange environment and in the midst of the work of clearing the land, the colonists were unable to use European agricultural practices; they copied instead the techniques and crops of the Luzo-Brazilian, growing the traditional crops of maize, manioc and beans under a system of shifting cultivation. This subsistence agriculture supported only a very meagre standard of living. Along the far frontiers of settlement and in isolated areas, where colonists were few in number, this acculturation to a Luzo-Brazilian way of life was hardest to resist and most complete and it persisted longest. Wherever there was access to a market, improvements in agriculture could be made and colonists began to cultivate potatoes, rye, upland rice and even wheat, to keep a cow or two and to raise hogs. With livestock on the farms, it became possible to manure the soil and evolve from rotation of land to rotation of crops. A further stage in the improvement of agriculture, but one reached by only a small percentage of colonists before 1900, was well-developed mixed farming, based on crop rotation and stock-raising, supplying city markets as well as local creameries and cheese factories. On some farms, tobacco was a cash crop and the Italians of Rio Grande began to specialize in viticulture. The keys to success for this European colonization

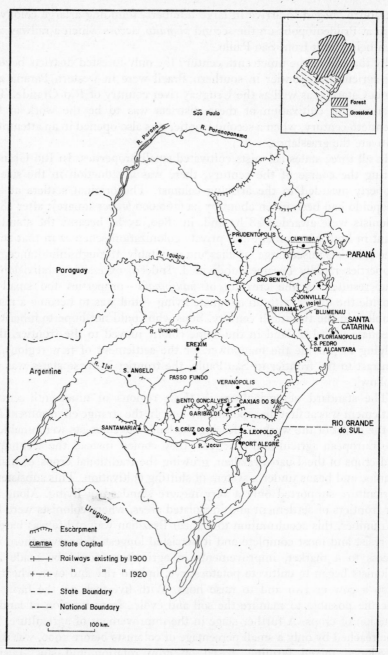

Fig. 8.10 Nineteenth-century colonization of southern Brazil (after L. Waibel, *Capitulos de Geografia Tropical e do Brasil* (Rio de Janeiro, Serviço Gráfico do Instituto Brasileiro de Geografia e Estatística, 1958), facing p. 208)

appear to have been fertile forest soils, access to a market and settlement in large compact groups. Success was achieved most markedly in three areas: around Curitiba, in the older German and Italian districts of Rio Grande, and in the vicinities of Blumenau and Joinville. Here there existed, by the end of the nineteenth century, small towns and villages built in a distinctive European as opposed to Luzo-Brazilian style, and a population speaking German, Polish or Italian in preference to Portuguese, living from the cultivation of small properties and enjoying a standard of living far above that to be found anywhere else in rural Brazil.

While the colonizing of the forestlands of southern Brazil was taking place, there was little change on the grasslands. They were still sparsely populated and were the domain of large estates, of traditional cattle-raising, and of the gaucho. To the south, in Uruguay and on the pampas of Argentina, there had been a revolution in livestock-ranching during the second half of the nineteenth century (see Chapter 9), but in Rio Grande, for reasons not yet clear, this revolution had scarcely begun by 1900. Despite the introduction of some pedigree livestock from Uruguay in the 1880s, the Brazilian register of pedigree livestock was not opened until 1906, and by 1915 only 301 animals had been registered in Rio Grande.

The transformation of the southern states of Brazil from a sparsely populated and scarcely exploited outpost of a colonial empire into the 'bread basket' of modern Brazil had begun by 1900: the agricultural potential of the forestlands was being realized and a start had been made on turning the lower Jacui valley and the land around the Lagoa dos Patos into irrigated rice fields. Although the agricultural revolution on the grasslands had still to begin, by 1900 traditional Brazil was yielding to modern in these southern states.

The Amazon

For much of the interior of Brazil, the nineteenth century brought few changes. Across the hills and plains from Minas to Mato Grosso, a scant population drowsed through a life of cattle-ranching, shifting cultivation and half-hearted searching for gold and diamonds. The old towns continued to decay from their eighteenth-century baroque magnificence. In Minas there were only rare and isolated sparks of new activity, such as the smelting of iron ore, the beginnings of a cotton textile industry at Juiz da Fora and, at the very end of the century, the building of the new capital Belo Horizonte. In one large region of the Brazilian hinterland, the valley of the Amazon, there was a dramatic, even frenzied, burst of activity.

The Amazon was the last large region of Brazil to be drawn into the national economy. This came late in the second half of the nineteenth century and provides yet another example of the cycle of 'boom and burst', which has characterized the development of Brazil. Until this time, little serious attempt had been made to exploit the region. Some garrisons had been established at a few strategic locations, and here and there along the main stream and its tributaries missionaries had attempted to assemble the local Indians into villages. There was some export of tropical woods and of what were sometimes called 'backland drugs' such as cinnamon, cloves and sarsaparilla. Around Belém, small quantities of sugar, rice and, in the eighteenth century, coffee were grown. There was some cattle-ranching, especially on Marajo Island. The commerce of the Amazon had been discouraged by the ban on foreign shipping, which was not lifted until 1867. The population was small, consisting of some Christianized Indians, a few slaves, some missionaries, soldiers and traders, and, deep in the forest, Indian societies still survived. In fact, the major result of European contact with the Amazon had so far been to disrupt and reduce the indigenous population through disease and slavery rather than to bring prosperity and progress.

The 'boom' in the Amazon was based on rubber. *Hevea Brasiliensis*, the species of tree that is by far the major source of natural rubber, is native to the Amazon basin and is widely distributed there. Until the discovery of the process known as vulcanization in 1839, rubber was of limited value, for it was difficult to use, melting easily when warm and becoming brittle in cold weather. Vulcanization corrected these deficiences, thereby greatly increasing rubber's usefulness, and this improved product found an enormous, expanding market in an industrializing world. Exports of rubber from the Amazon increased from a few thousand kilogrammes a year before vulcanization to 42,000 tons in 1912.

The demand for labour created by this 'boom' could not be met by the local population, but it attracted the poverty-stricken peasantry of the north-east, labouring under the desperate conditions of life in the *sertão*. Accurate statistics of this migration are hard to obtain, but it seems probable that, between 1870 and 1910, 200,000 people left the north-east for the Amazon. Few of these *Nordestinos* 'made good'. Rubber-collecting was arduous, dangerous work, the land was already in private ownership, and the landowners and exporters controlled the trade, reaping the profits. The rubber-collector or *seringueiro* was advanced money for food and equipment and assigned a stretch of forest. He tapped the rubber trees and, at his base camp on some creek or tributary, moulded the latex into large balls, which were then collected and taken to a port of export. The latex the *seringueiro* collected was somehow never enough to pay off his debt to his employer.

Belém and Manaus became the centres of the rubber trade. Both grew rapidly. In 1865, Manaus had a population of 5000; by the end of the century, its population was 50,000 and that of Belém about 80,000. Nearly a third of the export trade of Brazil, by value, was made up of rubber passing through these two ports. They were cosmopolitan cities, with large numbers of English, French, Germans, Syrians and Lebanese involved in the rubber trade. The enormous profits were spent on luxuries and ostentatious buildings, private mansions and government palaces, theatres and elaborate public squares. Little thought was given to the future. No money was invested in improving the rubber industry or in other resources in an attempt to diversify the economy. Even agriculture was neglected so that food had to be imported from other parts of Brazil or even from abroad at great expense.

The end of the 'boom' came rapidly, in the early years of the twentieth century. Seeds of *Hevea Brasiliensis* had been taken to Kew Gardens, London, in 1876 and there successfully planted. These plantings provided the stock to establish rubber plantations in south-east Asia during the 1890s. Plantation rubber was found to be cheaper to produce and of a higher and more uniform quality than the wild rubber of the Amazon. On plantations it was relatively easy to introduce quality control, the trees could be cared for and made to yield a greater quantity of rubber per year than trees in the Amazon, and labour costs could be reduced, one man being able to tap far more trees per day on a plantation in Malaysia than was possible in the forests of the Amazon. As the acreage of plantation rubber increased in south-east Asia, Amazonian rubber lost its hold on the world market. In 1905, less than 1 per cent of the world's rubber came from plantations; by 1910, this share had risen to 10 per cent and to 93 per cent by 1922. In the Amazon, trade slid almost to a halt. In Manaus and Belém the theatres closed, palaces began to crumble and grass grew in the streets. Once more in the history of Brazil, a population assembled by a 'boom' turned to ranching and cultivation when the 'boom' was over. Only a trickle of exports now came from the Amazon: nuts, hardwoods and a little rubber.

BRAZIL IN THE TWENTIETH CENTURY

Physical geography still presents Brazil with problems of size and distance, and the varied environments offer different opportunities. The past has left a strong tradition of primitive, wasteful cultivation and the need for an enormous amount of repair work. Political decisions have been made with far-reaching consequences about the use of mineral resources, encouragement of industry and exploitation of frontier areas. Brazil, too, has more than shared in the world population growth: the annual average rate of population increase between 1900 and 1950 was about 2 per cent, and between 1950 and 1960 it was 2·4 per cent, rates above the world average, with the result that the population of Brazil has increased from some 17 million at the beginning of the century to about 95 million at the present. There is a movement of people from countryside to towns to the extent that some regions are now more urban than rural. The human geography of Brazil is very much in a state of transition.

Agriculture

Modern Brazil is still a predominantly agricultural country. Agriculture is the major employer[1] and in the 1960s agricultural products accounted for nearly 90 per cent of the value of the country's exports. But as is usually the case in developing countries, agriculture forms a very conservative section of the economy. Agricultural techniques remain backward and yields are low. In much of the country little attention is given to manuring, seed selection or rotation of crops. Shifting cultivation is the rule, the hoe and machete the usual tools. It is in agriculture that the Indian element in the cultural amalgam of Brazil is most pronounced. Agriculture really forms part of traditional Brazil, except in some districts of São Paulo and the southern states where the most productive and the most mechanized agriculture in the country is to be found. According to the 1960 census, more than 80 per cent of all tractors and ploughs in Brazil were in São Paulo and the south. During the present century there has been a sharp increase in the quantity of agricultural goods produced, but this increase has come not from improving yields per hectare, but from an extension in the area of cultivated land, which has increased from 6·6 million ha in 1920 to 30 million ha in 1960. Much of the farmland is either in large estates or in very small holdings. In 1960, 45 per cent of the farms in Brazil were less than 10 ha in size and comprised only 2 per cent of the agricultural land, while farms of over 100 ha, only 11 per cent of the total number of farms, accounted for 80 per cent of the farmland. The smallholdings are usually too small to provide an adequate living, the large estates only partially exploited. If rural Brazil is to become part of modern Brazil there will have to be a far-reaching agricultural reform in the very broadest sense of the phrase. There must be a rationalization of the land tenure pattern to consolidate smallholdings into viable economic units and to detach unused land from the large estates to make it available to people who will use it. Education of the rural worker, diffusion of better agricultural techniques, improved transportation and storage and packaging facilities for agricultural products must all be part of the reform.

Nowhere in Brazil is the need for reform more desperate than in the north-east, where 70 per cent of the gainfully employed work in agriculture, the levels of productivity are low and the standard of living for the vast majority of the population is abysmal. Part of the low productivity can be blamed on the climate, for in much of the region the scant and unreliable rainfall severely limits the agricultural possibilities. But the manner in which the land has been settled and exploited is also to blame. Deforestation and overgrazing have diminished the resource base, man has relied on wasteful and backward agricultural techniques, and patterns of land tenure and the types of agriculture have severely contributed to the present crisis.

[1] In 1960, 52 per cent of the gainfully employed worked in agriculture.

Land tenure in the north-east is characterized by large landholdings, some dating from colonial *sesmarias* and by smallholdings with origins in squatters' plots. The large landholdings, or *latifundia*, when defined as holdings providing employment for twelve or more people, occupy 53 per cent of the land. Only 6 per cent of the land in *latifundia* is actually cultivated.[1] This figure is a regional average and obscures the fact that in the *sertão* there is much uncultivable land just as in the coastal region far more than 6 per cent of the land is in crops. Land is also used for forest and pasture. It is evident that the *latifundia* withhold land from cultivation. In medieval Portugal, the *sesmaria* was designed to ensure cultivation of land; in Brazil it has led to a system of land tenure that has the opposite effect. There has evolved a tradition of prestige in landownership in which status derives from the extent of land owned as well as from the income gained, and this tradition helps to maintain large, partially used estates. Furthermore, the tendency in Brazil to favour squatters' rights, permitting a person who has cultivated a plot for some time to claim ownership or at least immunity from eviction, discourages renting of land and particularly the granting of long leases. Smallholdings or *minifundia* also limit agricultural production. Agricultural techniques on the *minifundia* are more backward than those on the *latifundia* and yields are lower. Indeed, *minifundia* at best only marginally enter the commercial economy and many are subsistence holdings. *Minifundia*, when defined as plots of land too small to provide full-time employment for two men, occupy only 7 per cent of the area of the north-east, yet account for 72 per cent of all farms. The pattern of land tenure is a major obstacle to increased agricultural production.

Agriculture is geared to the cultivation of commercial cash crops. The production of food crops on large estates is a sideline; they are usually grown by the smaller farmers and the *minifundistas*. Hence food is in short supply and, given the local wage level, expensive. The north-east is still an agricultural region in which the people are ill fed. In the coastal region, sugar survives as a monoculture and is still the major source of income for the north-east, but by world standards production is inefficient. Yields are low (35 tons/ha, compared with 60 in São Paulo, 120 in Cuba and 200 in Hawaii) and the industry is unmechanized and labour-intensive, employing 3·6 man-days per ton produced, compared with 1·3 in Cuba, 1·2 in São Paulo and 0·3 in Hawaii.[2] With cheap and abundant labour

[1] From the preliminary results of the 1960 census. The results of this census have not yet been fully published and data from the 1970 census are not yet available.

[2] These figures were given in a special report on the north-east in the newspaper *O Estado de São Paulo*, published in São Paulo, Sunday 28 April 1963. The FAO provides the following figures for 1968–9 in metric tons/ha: Brazil 45·4, Argentina 50·0, Cuba 39, Mauritius 64·5, Jamaica 69·1, Barbados 90, Hawaii 230 (1965–6), U.S.A. (including Hawaii) 93·1. From the *Production Yearbook*, Food and Agricultural Organization of the United Nations (Rome, 1969), pp. 91–5.

there has been little incentive to invest in machinery. The region is responsible for a declining share of Brazil's sugar production. In 1945, the north-east produced 53 per cent of Brazil's sugar and São Paulo 21 per cent, but in 1960 these figures were 38 per cent and 43 per cent respectively. The industry is subsidized by the federal government, most of the sugar is used within Brazil, and only a little is exported. The economy of the interior of the north-east revolves around cotton, sisal and livestock. The cotton supplies the Brazilian textile industry. Sisal was introduced from Mexico and began to be an important crop during the Second World War. It is well suited to the climate, finds a good market and has in some areas displaced cotton. The livestock industry is only gradually being improved. Zebu cattle have been interbred with the original stock and the feed has been improved since the 1930s with the planting of *palma*, a South African forage crop, which, mixed with cotton seed cake, is used during the dry season. None of these commercial forms of agriculture provides a high income or permits the paying of good wages.

Since the end of the last century attempts have been made to mitigate the problems of the north-east. In 1900 the government of Brazil established the National Department of Works Against Droughts, responsible for stockpiling food against severe shortages during droughts and for building small reservoirs in the *sertão*. But it has functioned only fitfully, and has made no attempt to improve the quality of cultivation or tackle the issue of land tenure. All too frequently the reservoirs, though built at public expense, have benefited only the already wealthy landlords who own the surrounding property. In 1948, the government founded the São Francisco Valley Commission and the São Francisco Hydroelectric Company to develop the resources of the São Francisco valley. Hydroelectric power is now generated on the São Francisco and an extensive programme of rural electrification has been nearly completed, one of the few concrete achievements to the Commission's credit. The most promising attempt yet to tackle the problems of the north-east began in 1959 with the founding of The Superintendency for the Development of the North-East (SUDENE), which was charged with the planning of all aspects of the regional development of the north-east. The main features of the agricultural section of the regional plan drawn up by SUDENE are the rationalization of land tenure, and an agricultural extension programme aimed at raising the educational level of cultivators as well as introducing new varieties of crops and improved techniques. It is hoped to increase the yield of sugar per hectare so that land can be released from sugar cultivation without causing a decline in total sugar crop, and this land is then to be used for food crops. There is a programme to attract industry with the aid of tax concessions. However, reformed agriculture and industrial development will not provide sufficient employment for the increasing population; migration to São Paulo and other points in central and southern Brazil has been going on for many years and can be expected to continue. People from rural areas are also flooding into the cities of the north-east. A small number of people have been encouraged to settle in the still sparsely populated state of Maranhão. SUDENE has achieved some success, but the amount of work to be done and the social, political and economic problems to be overcome in raising the standard of living of the north-easterners are still formidable.

The problems bequeathed by past land use in São Paulo are of a different order and scale than those in the north-east. To simplify, it is possible to see the agricultural development of São Paulo in the twentieth century as revolving around two themes: stabilizing the coffee frontier and solving the problem of the excess production of coffee and, secondly, the creation of new forms of land use in the old plantation tracts.

During the early years of this century, the coffee frontier continued to advance south-westwards along the course of the tributaries of the Paraná, keeping to the *terra-roxa* soils (Fig. 8.10). In the 1920s and 1930s, coffee cultivation crossed from São Paulo into the state of Paraná. This was the last southward advance of the coffee frontier. In northern Paraná climate varies with altitude from subtropical to temperate, winters are cooler than in São Paulo, radiation frosts are common, and occasional cold spells do occur. There is in northern Paraná risk of damage to coffee trees from frost, but further to the south the incidence of frost is so frequent that coffee cannot be cultivated with any realistic hope of success. The development of this region has been guided by a colonization company, originally English-financed, known as Paraná Plantations Ltd. The company was organized in 1925 and had by 1927 acquired over 10,000 km² of land. Two subsidiary companies were established: one, the Companhia de Terras Norte do Paraná, to subdivide and administer the lands; the second, the Companhia Ferroviária São Paulo-Paraná, to build a railway to link the region with São Paulo and the Port of Santos. The English management of this settlement scheme ended with the Second World War. In 1939, the Brazilian government acquired the railway, and in 1944 a group of *Paulista* capitalists bought the land company, renaming it the Companhia de Melhoramentos do Norte do Paraná.

The region the company controlled consists of a deeply dissected plateau. The soils are mostly *terra-roxa*, but there are areas of sand. Roads were laid out along the interfluves, converging on selected points where towns or villages were planned. The grid of road and service centre was such that no part of the company land was more than 15 km from a centre. The land was divided into long and narrow allotments, laid out parallel to each other between roads on the interfluves and rivers in the valley bottoms. This subdivision of land gave each settler access to transport, to water and to a range of soils, vegetation types and micro-climates. It was a pattern of land subdivision subsequently copied on government colonization schemes

N

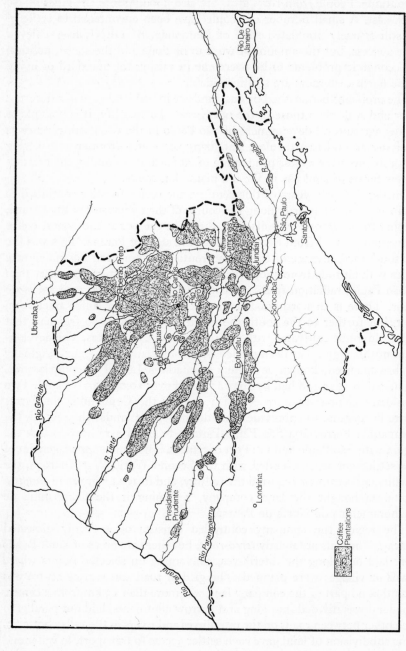

Fig. 8.11 Distribution of coffee in São Paulo, later 1920s (after Monbeig, 1952)

elsewhere in southern Brazil. The company also took the precaution when originally acquiring its land to buy out all claimants to a given property, even if this meant, as it often did, paying for land several times over, to ensure that the company's settlers would have clear titles to their plots and so be spared the legal wrangles over ownership and threats of dispossession that have marred many settlement schemes in Brazil. Land was sold to colonists, and, following the change in the ownership of the company in 1944, large holdings have been allowed for the cultivation of coffee.

It had been the original intention of the English planners to cultivate cotton, but coffee soon became the predominant crop. Cotton, however, quick to mature, served the useful purpose of providing farmers with a cash income while the coffee trees were growing. Coffee was planted on the valley sides, particularly on the slopes facing the north. More care has been taken with these groves than of those in the old plantation tracts. The soils have been manured, the trees planted along the contour rather than aligned downhill, and attention given to new varieties, with the result that yields are high and less damage has been done to the soil. Other crops are grown according to the local climate: oranges and cotton in the warmest districts, wheat, maize and other mid-latitude crops in the cooler districts. Land is also used for grazing cattle. This diversified agriculture, with its variety of cash crops, the security of tenure possessed by the farmers and good transport has been the key to the successful planning of northern Paraná. There is here now a dense and prosperous rural population, and several rapidly growing towns such as Londrina. The coffee used to be exported via São Paulo and Santos but is now sent from the Paraná port of Paranagua. The revenues from coffee have been invested in promoting the economic development of Paraná, helping to make it one of the richest states of Brazil, and transforming the capital, Curitiba, from a dull provincial town into a bustling modern city.

Coffee has also spread into the southern Mato Grosso, into Goiás, and there has been some revival of coffee cultivation in the state of São Paulo. Coffee is also grown in Minas Gerais and Espírito Santo and in several other states. During the 1960s, in terms of value of production, coffee was the most important crop. Brazil in the 1960s was growing nearly half the world's coffee crop and coffee accounted for nearly 50 per cent of Brazil's export earnings, but the government is now trying to reduce the country's dependence on coffee and to diversify agriculture in predominantly coffee-growing districts. Substantial financial inducements are offered to reduce the number of trees, and during the 1960s the area planted to coffee decreased greatly.

In São Paulo diversification of agriculture began with the passing of the coffee frontier. There was a search for alternative crops and sugar, cotton, citrus fruits, manioc, maize and rice have all become important. The quality of pasture has been improved, new breeds of cattle have been introduced, and now dairy farming and the raising of beef cattle are major activities. The huge urban population of south-central Brazil provides an accessible market for the produce. The worn-out soils of the old plantation tracts have gradually been made productive with the aid of fertilizers, and some of the steep slopes have been terraced. There has also been a change in landownership. When the coffee plantations became run down, land values declined and immigrants or their descendants were able to buy land and so became farmers in their own right. Japan has been a second source of farmers. The Japanese have been emigrating to Brazil in comparatively small numbers during this century, and most have gone to São Paulo, where they have set themselves up as market gardeners. The agriculture of São Paulo is now more advanced and productive than that of any other state in Brazil.

In southern Paraná, Santa Catarina and Rio Grande do Sul the course of agricultural development has continued along the lines laid down during the last years of the nineteenth century. The long-established European colonies are now prosperous regions of mixed farming with an important production of wine and tobacco in Rio Grande do Sul. The distinctive cultural landscape survives and the ancestral languages are still spoken. The birth-rate in these colonies has been high. One result of this has been the subdivision of landholdings to produce *minifundia*; a second has been a movement of population to frontier regions. Today, in the half of Rio Grande north of the Jacui river, 65 per cent of all landholdings measure less than 100 ha and in some districts 95 per cent of all landholdings measure less than 100 ha. This is an excessive subdivision of land, which retards the development of really efficient agriculture and contributes to soil exhaustion and soil erosion. In the more recently settled districts, where rotation of land is still practised, some holdings are so small that land must be re-cleared and cultivated before the soil has been able to regain its fertility. The settlement frontier is now along the upper Uruguay river in northern Rio Grande, in western Santa Catarina and southwestern Paraná. On the frontier the national origins of settlers are still discernible from language and landscape, but the amalgamation with Luzo-Brazilian culture has proceeded much further than in the old colonies. Settlers on the frontier work in lumbering, in collecting the leaves of *Ilex Paraguayensis* for yerba maté or Paraguayan tea, which is a popular drink in southern Brazil as well as in Paraguay and Argentina, and in cultivating small properties. Kidney beans, soya beans, manioc and maize are the main crops and this frontier region has also become noted for pig-rearing. An attempt has been made to cultivate wheat on the forest-grassland borders. For several years following 1945 the harvests were promising, but yields have since often been disappointing. A succession of bad summers is partly to blame, but the incidence of disease in the wheat has been high, a reflection of the generally poor methods of cultivation. The southern states account for nearly all the wheat grown in Brazil, but this amounts to only 10 per cent of Brazil's annual consumption.

In the Jacui valley, immediately to the south of the German colonies, people of Luzo–Brazilian descent were starting to cultivate rice by the beginning of the nineteenth century. Rice cultivation now extends through the river valleys of central Rio Grande and also around the coastal Lagoa dos Patos. The rice fields are irrigated, but cultivation is not very intensive, for the land is periodically left fallow to be used as pasture for cattle. Rice is an increasingly important food in Brazil and rice from Rio Grande is sent to the urban populations of the south centre of the country.

The grasslands of the south and especially those of the *Companhia* along the borders of Uruguay are still the domain of the large estate and of livestock ranching. The quality of the livestock has been greatly improved, especially since the 1930s, through importing pedigree European livestock for cross-breeding. There is still room for further improvement in the stock itself, in the pasture and in methods of packaging and processing the meat. Some of the meat is now frozen and exported, but many carcasses are still turned into *charque* (dried meat).

The two-thirds of Brazil that includes the Mato Grosso, Goiás, the interior of Minas and the Amazon basin contributes as yet only a small portion of the total agricultural production of Brazil. This vast interior of Brazil can be regarded as one immense frontier region: not a frontier where Luzo-Brazilian settlement is taking place for the first time, for these territories have been roamed over by cattle-ranchers, shifting cultivators and others for two centuries or more, but a frontier of improvement. Frontier work today consists of improving transport, transforming subsistence shifting cultivation into stable commercial agriculture, and raising the quality of ranching. In fact, the aim is to exploit these lands more effectively, and to mesh them firmly into the Brazilian economy, thereby also realizing a long-standing Brazilian ambition of a '*marcha para oeste*' – a march to the west.

Improvements in transport began in the first decades of the century with the building of railways westwards from São Paulo across the southern Mato Grosso to Corumba and Ponta Pora and northwards into Goiás. These lines opened up a small part of the interior to the markets of south-central Brazil. Railway towns such as Campo Grande and Anápolis became important regional commercial centres while the areas served by the lines became the foci of economic activity in the states of Mato Grosso and Goiás. The state of Goiás went so far as to transfer its capital from the remote, gold mining town of Goiás to a new capital, Goiânia, built during the 1930s near the railway. In recent years the building of Brasília and the linking of this capital through a network of roads to the other major cities of the country has given a further boost to the agricultural development of the interior. Brasília itself is a market for food crops, albeit a limited one, and the roads permit cheap transport of goods to the coastal centres of population. The Belém–Brasília highway has made the eastern margins of the Amazon basin relatively accessible for the first time, and the highway now under construction from São Paulo and Brasília to Peru should do the same for the southern and western margins of Amazonia. In the Araguaia river valley in northern Goiás, capital has already been invested in cattle-ranching. The scheme is financed from São Paulo, managed by people with long experience in the cattle industry and employs northeasterners who have filtered through to the new settlements on the Belém–Brasília highway. However, despite increased accessibility and some improvements in agriculture, much of the agriculture of Mato Grosso and Goiás is still primitive, unproductive shifting cultivation. The agricultural development of the Amazon lags behind that of Mato Grosso and Goiás. There are only pockets of commercial cultivation. The most notable area is around Belém where rice and other food crops, as well as jute, are grown. Japanese colonists have settled near Belém quite successfully. Elsewhere in Amazonia, agriculture is limited to ranching and shifting cultivation. The attempts to establish rubber plantations have so far failed.

The intensive agricultural exploitation of the interior and its incorporation into the economic life of the country lie many years in the future. The reform of agriculture is also going to take many years to effect. From a strictly economic point of view, it might be questioned if it is wise for the two to go forward together, since possibly the capital and personnel for agricultural development would be better invested in improving agriculture in the accessible coastal regions with large urban populations than in spreading or trying to improve cultivation in the distant reaches of Mato Grosso or Amazonia. But the political arguments against ignoring distant regions of a country are probably the more compelling.

Industry: the resource base

The resources for the industrial development of Brazil are not as abundant or as varied as the sheer size of the country might lead one to expect. As yet, however, the country has been imperfectly explored, and in all probability more discoveries of natural wealth will be made. The shield is the source of a wide range of minerals and precious stones. *Garimpeiros* (prospectors) are still to be found in the backlands, panning for gold and diamonds. Gold is mined today, as at the Morro Velho mine at São João del Rey, but the main mineral wealth of the shield now is high grade iron ore. The iron ore reserves of Brazil are among the richest in the world; ore bodies are known in Piauí, Ceara, southern Mato Grosso and in the so-called Iron Quadrangle, south and east of Belo Horizonte in Minas Gerais. It is the ores of the Quadrangle that are being exploited for they have a high iron content, are easily mined and are near to the centres of industry. These ores have been mined on a small scale since the beginning of the nineteenth century, but large-scale mining dates only from the Second World War, with the growth of a domestic iron and steel industry and the decision to encourage the export of ore, a reversal of the traditional Brazilian policy of preserving resources for future domestic needs. The export of ore from Minas is largely controlled by the Companhia Vale do Rio Doce, a government-owned company. A railway connects the Iron Quadrangle, via the valley of the Rio Doce, with the coast of Espírito Santo. Exports of ore via this route began in 1942 with a total of 34,000 long tons; 1·5 million tons were exported in 1951 and 11·5 in 1967. The new port of Tubarão, near Vitória, the capital of Espírito Santo, was open in 1966 and exports reached 21·7 million tons by 1969.

The demands of the iron and steel industry, domestic and foreign, have led to a great increase in the mining of manganese. Approximately one half of the annual production is now exported. The largest mines are those of the Serra do Navio in the territory of Amapá to the north of the Amazon. The Bethlehem Steel Company of Baltimore has an important interest in these mines. The United States Steel Company, through a subsidiary, has begun to mine the manganese ores at Mount Urucum near Corumbá, and manganese is also mined in Minas Gerais. Lead is produced in Bahia, phosphorus at Olinda, near Recife, and, along the arid coastland of Rio Grande do Norte and Ceara, most of Brazil's salt is made by evaporation from the sea. Brazil also produces small quantities of a wide variety of minerals such as zinc, tungsten, nickel and bauxite. Minas Gerais remains the most important mining state, not only because of the ore bodies there, but because of its better communications and proximity to industrial centres. Distance and expense of transport as well as lack of demand mean that the exploitation of many Brazilian ore bodies is still uneconomic.

The forests of Brazil have been and still are a valuable resource. Tropical woods were a staple export in colonial times and today Araucanian pine is possibly the most important commercial tree. It has given rise to a wood-working industry in the southern states, manufacturing such commodities as boxes, furniture and plywood. Wood is the traditional fuel of Brazil. It was used in the sugar mills and to power the railways. Even today, wood is still the fuel of the countryside, and many of the blast furnaces of Minas Gerais depend on charcoal. The demand for wood for a fuel has led to extensive deforestation.

Coal has played a very modest part in the industrial development of Brazil. Known coal reserves are small, the quality of the coal is poor and unsuitable for coking, and there is little likelihood of new coalfields being discovered. Coal is mined in each of the three southern states and during the late 1960s annual production was of the order of 4·5 million (metric) tons, more than half of which came from Santa Catarina. The coal is used for power and gas and, to a limited extent, in the iron and steel industry. Brazil imports coal, particularly from the United States and Germany.

The oil industry in Brazil is controlled by a government corporation, Petroleo Brasileiro S.A., known as Petrobras. Petrobras has the monopoly of exploration for oil, has built and operates refineries, and has recently acquired privately owned refineries. The most significant oilfield in Brazil is in the *Recôncavo*, the lowland area around Salvador. Production began in 1939 and has increased thirty-five times since the mid-1950s, but still amounts to only some 40 million barrels a year at present. Oil, therefore, is also imported. The search for oil in Brazil has been disappointing. Small quantities are now pumped at Carmópolis, in Sergipe and in Alagoas, but traces only have been found in the Tocatins valley and near Manaus in the Amazon basin, in Maranhão as well as in the Paraíba valley. The exploration of the Lagoa dos Patos region of Rio Grande do Sul is still in progress without success so far.

With coal and oil in such short supply, Brazil has come to rely on hydro-electric power. The hydro-electric potential of Brazil is among the highest of any country in the world, and, as yet, only a small portion of it has been developed. Use of hydro-electric power began in Brazil at the very end of the nineteenth century to light the cities of São Paulo and Rio, to power their tramways and to supply the nascent industries. In 1901 a plant was built on the Tieté river, 32 km downstream from São Paulo; by 1912 the capacity of this plant had been increased sixteen times, and work began in 1913 on realizing the hydro-electric potential of the Sorocaba River. Power plants were also built in the mountains around Rio, and in the 1920s a major project was undertaken on the Serra do Mar, near Santos. The westerly flowing Rio Grande river was dammed, diverted and dropped 700 m over the Serra to generating stations at Cubatão. There has, however, often been a gap between the increasing demands for electricity and the building of new facilities. Before and after the Second World War power failures were a familiar feature of Brazilian life. The production and distribution of hydro-electricity is coming increasingly under government control, and for the past several years the government has been putting into effect an extensive programme for building new hydro-electric stations. This programme has been aided by the continuing improvement in the methods of transmitting power, permitting the harnessing of rivers at greater and greater distances from the consuming centres. Several large projects have already been completed. On the São Francisco river, power generated at Paulo Afonso, where the river drops over the lip of the Brazilian plateau, is used for new industry in the north-east and for rural electrification; the Tres Marias plant provides power for Minas Gerais. Present projects include the development of the power potential of the Parnaíba river on the border of Maranhão and Piauí and of the Paraná basin. However, most of Brazil's electricity is still generated in the south-east. The installed hydro-electric capacity of Brazil in the late 1960s was about 8 million kW with another 9 million kW under construction. It is certain that hydro-electricity will become an increasingly important form of power in Brazil in the foreseeable future.

A final major resource to be considered is manpower. There is no shortage of labour in Brazil – quite the reverse – but the general level of education and technological competence is low. In the early days of Brazil's industrial development, technicians and even skilled labourers were brought in from abroad; now in the established industrial centres a skilled labour force has been built up. However, the lack of training and even the wrong frame of mind for industrial employment handicaps migrants from the countryside in the search for jobs.

There are some weaknesses in Brazil's industrial resource base. The failure to find oil in large quantities has been the keenest disappointment. The shortage and low quality of coal, a major drawback in terms of nineteenth-century industrialization, is less and less serious as world industry turns to other fuels.

Industrial Development

The mercantilist policies pursued by Portugal successfully stifled any attempt at manufacturing in Brazil during the colonial period. In the early nineteenth century iron-working based on local ores and using charcoal for smelting was begun on a limited scale in Minas Gerais and a cotton textile industry was established later. During the twentieth century Brazil has provided an example of industrialization aimed at import substitution. Gradually Brazil has been changing from a country exporting agricultural products and importing manufactured goods to one capable of manufacturing many of its own industrial requirements, though still dependent on agricultural exports. Whenever foreign exchange difficulties or war made importing expensive or difficult an impetus was given to the development of domestic industries. During the First World War, the number of factories in Brazil doubled. The largest sectors of Brazilian industry, which in 1920 employed 30,000, were textiles and food-processing. The Depression and the Second World War led to further industrial expansion, adding chemical and pharmaceutical industries, the manufacture of tools and machinery and an integrated iron and steel industry. Since the Second World War, industrial development has proceeded at a rapid rate and, in terms of industrial output, Brazil now ranks first in Latin America.

Not all parts of the country have shared in this industrial growth. Certain industries, such as the processing of foodstuffs, brewing and the manufacture of textiles, can be found in most of the larger cities, but heavy industry is much more localized and is concentrated in the south-eastern and southern parts of the country. The state of São Paulo alone accounts for 55 per cent of Brazil's industrial production. In fact there is emerging in Brazil one large industrial region, often referred to as the *Triangulo* as it is roughly delimited by the cities of São Paulo, Rio de Janeiro and Belo Horizonte (Fig. 8.12), as well as several smaller nodes of industrial activity in other parts of the country.

The reasons for this concentration of industry in the *Triangulo* are partly historical. Towards the end of the nineteenth century it was in São Paulo, and to a lesser extent in Rio de Janeiro, that the capital existed for investment in industry as a result of the 'boom' in coffee. For the types of

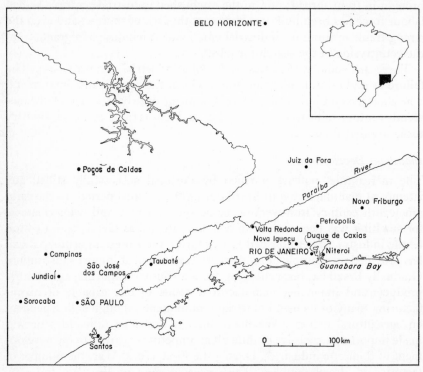

Fig. 8.12 The industrial 'Triangle' of Brazil

industry first established – the manufacture of consumer goods – ease of access to the market was an important locational factor, and in the above two cities there was a concentration of buying power without rival in the rest of the country. The lack of coal in the *Triangulo* has become much less of a handicap to industry with the development of hydro-electric power, and the region does contain such basic raw materials as iron ore. The *Triangulo* has been the first part of Brazil to develop an adequate transportation system, a result of the coffee era and of the need to link the two most important cities of Brazil. Continuing improvements in transportation and the fact that during the course of this century proximity to the market has become an increasingly important factor in the location of industry have confirmed the *Triangulo* as the most attractive region in Brazil in which to establish new industries.

The industry of the *Triangulo* is centred upon the cities of Rio de Janeiro and São Paulo and the iron mines of Minas Gerais. Rio, which was the capital of Brazil and still contains a large part of the government bureaucracy, is a major commercial and financial centre, port and resort as well as an industrial city. The first industries to be established in Rio during the second half of the nineteenth century were food-processing, the manufacture of light consumer goods and textiles. Since the First World War, heavy industry such as metal-working, foundries and ship-building has been gradually added, and the new oil refinery at Duque de Caxias, on the northern margins of the city, has encouraged the growth of a petrochemical industry. The rate of industrial growth in Rio, however, is now beginning to slow down. The city occupies a constricted site between mountains, Guanabara Bay and the sea. Flat land is scarce and expensive and, moreover, the city has suffered from chronic shortages of electricity and water. New industry has increasingly begun to locate itself immediately to the north of the city in the state of Rio de Janeiro and in towns even further inland. Niteroi, the capital of the state of Rio de Janeiro; Petropolis, the old imperial summer capital; Novo Friburgo, once a Swiss agricultural colony – these are but a few of the towns in the state of Rio now being industrialized. Volta Redonda in the Paraíba valley has been turned into an iron and steel town.

In the city of São Paulo there has been a similar progression from light consumer goods industries and the manufacture of textiles to the establishment of heavy industry. The city of São Paulo now contains the largest single concentration of industry in all Brazil. As around Rio, there has been a decentralization of industry to smaller towns, particularly in the eastern part of the state. Campinas and Sorocaba are now industrial centres. Jundiaí, once a railhead, now has railway workshops as well as textiles and electrical industries; São José dos Campos is a centre for chemical and pharmaceutical industries, and there is an automobile factory of Willys-Overland do Brasil in Taubaté, a town of colonial origin in the Paraíba valley.

The history of Minas Gerais has revolved around mining: gold, diamonds and iron. Industry here began with iron-working and this remains a fundamental sector. Recently the decision was taken to build an aluminium smelter at Poços de Caldas. Production is expected to satisfy the Brazilian demand. There is also a long tradition of textile-working in Minas; some of the earliest mills in Brazil were built at Juiz da Fora. The industry of Minas is now becoming more diversified with general manufacturing.

This trend towards the dispersal of industry from the three original centres and the resulting industrialization of the small towns in the

Triangulo has been greatly helped by improvements in transportation. Railways and good roads now connect these towns with the major consuming centres and with the ports. In addition, the intensification of agriculture within the *Triangulo* to supply the huge urban populations has led to the establishment of numerous food-processing factories. This dissemination of industry through the region can be expected to continue.

Possibly the most striking developments in the industrialization of Brazil since the Second World War have been the establishment of an integrated iron and steel industry and an automobile industry. Both these industries are located in the *Triangulo*. Brazil now produces more iron and steel than any other country in Latin America and its automobile industry is the largest on the continent and ranks eleventh in the world. In the 1930s,

TABLE 8.1   *Production of iron and steel 1955–65*

	1955	1960	1963	1965	1969
			Quantity (1000 m.t.)		
Pig iron	1069	1750	2477	2355	3718
Steel ingots	1162	1843	2737	2896	4919
Finished rolled products	982	1358	2030	2022	3899
Ferro-alloys	18	34	38	45	—
			Index Numbers (1955 = 100)		
Pig iron	100	164	232	220	348
Steel ingots	100	159	236	249	423
Finished rolled products	100	138	207	206	397
Ferro-alloys	100	189	211	250	—

Source: Brazil Today, Instituto Brasileiro de Estatística, Rio de Janeiro, 1968; and *Atualidade estatística do Brasil*, Instituto Brasileiro de Estatística, 1970.

Brazil was manufacturing about 60,000 tons of iron and steel a year, in small foundries and mills, using charcoal for smelting. This amount fell far short of the country's requirements. The difficulties of importing iron and steel during the Second World War, coupled with a desire to expand the national industrial base, led to the establishment of a fully integrated iron and steel works. The site selected was the small town of Volta Redonda in the Paraíba valley some 80 km from Rio de Janeiro. This inland location reflects in part the strategic considerations of a now distant war. There are advantages to the site: ease of communications with the largest markets in Brazil – São Paulo and Rio de Janeiro – as well as proximity to the sources of iron ore, limestone and manganese in Minas Gerais. Coal is brought in through Rio de Janeiro, from Santa Catarina and abroad. Construction of the plant began in 1942 and in 1946 the first steel was produced. By the mid-1960s, annual production was of the order of 1·5 million tons and it is planned to double this amount by the 1970s. This increase in the capacity of the Volta Redonda plant is but one aspect of a continuing expansion of the Brazilian iron and steel industry. The decision taken in 1956 by Juscelino Kubitschek (President, 1956–61) to establish an automobile industry in Brazil meant that much more iron and steel would be required. The government directly encouraged the iron and steel industry by investing in the companies and by permitting them to import equipment at favourable foreign exchange rates. In Minas Gerais, the capacity of a number of small integrated steel works was expanded and new plants built. In 1956, a German company began to manufacture steel tubes in the *Cidade Industrial* of Belo Horizonte. This plant uses local iron and smelts with electricity. During subsequent expansion another blast furnace was added, which uses coking coal brought from Germany in return for iron ore, which is 'backloaded' along the Rio Doce railway. At Ipatinga, to the east of Belo Horizonte, an integrated iron and steel works has been built, designed to produce 2 million tons a year. Ipatinga also relies on Minas ores and uses imported coal for smelting. There are also a large number of charcoal-fired blast furnaces each producing less than 30,000 tons of pig iron a year. Most of these iron works are in small towns to the west of Belo Horizonte, but there are also some at Governador Valadares, in the Rio Doce valley of Espírito Santo. There is a new integrated iron and steel mill at Cubatão at the foot of the Serra do Mar, near Santos, and, like the one at Ipatinga, it is designed to produce 2 million tons a year. The raw materials can be assembled by sea and the finished products distributed by sea to the large coastal cities of Brazil as well as by rail to São Paulo. Steel works are now planned for the south of Brazil and for the north-east. Brazilian steel consumption has been growing at a rate of 10 per cent a year since the Second World War; by the mid-1960s it had reached 3·5 million ingot tons, and is expected to climb to 8 million tons by the 1970s. Domestic production is still inadequate to satisfy this demand and steel has to be imported, particularly specialized steels.

The automobile industry is the showpiece of the industrialization of Brazil. Before 1956 only a few cars were assembled in Brazil and there was one government-owned factory manufacturing trucks. Foreign companies were invited by the Kubitschek government to establish branch plants in Brazil and pressed to manufacture more and more of the parts for their vehicles in Brazil. Almost all parts are now made in Brazil and one company, Willys-Overland do Brasil, an offshoot of the Kaiser interests of the United States, is still the only company actually to design cars in Brazil. The automobile industry now manufactures about 350,000 vehicles a year, directly employs 50,000 workers, the élite of the Brazilian labour force, and through a network of companies manufacturing parts helps generate employment for a further 400,000. Difficulties of the industry are the smallness of the market, a reflection of the generally low standard of living in Brazil, and the high costs of production, which can partly be attributed to the small size of the market. Economies of scale are difficult to achieve. Within the industry, there are several competing companies each producing relatively few vehicles, which means that the administrative and advertising costs per unit produced are high. The costs of supplying parts to what is still quite a small industry when compared with the world's leading automobile industries are also high. For instance, in 1966, a ton of steel for auto bodies cost $210 (U.S.) in Brazil as compared to $130 (U.S.) in Japan. The industry is situated in and around the city of São Paulo, and especially in the suburb of São Bernardino. Ease of assembly

TABLE 8.2   *Production of motor vehicles 1957–69*

	Production (No. of Units)	Index Numbers (1957 = 100)
1957	30,700	100
1960	133,078	433
1963	174,126	567
1965	185,173	603
1966	224,575	732
1967	225,000	
1968	278,936	
1969	352,192	
Projected		
1973	450,000–500,000	

Sources: Brazil Today, Instituto Brasileiro de Estatística, Rio de Janeiro, 1967. *Visão*, São Paulo, 22 November 1968, p. 64; and *Atualidade estatistica*, 1970.

of raw materials, local capital and entrepreneurial skill, as well as the fact that São Paulo, the most prosperous state of Brazil, is the main market, account for this location. In 1966, the first automobile factory outside the state of São Paulo opened at Jaboatão, near Recife. Here, Willys-Overland do Brasil manufactures about 500 jeeps and pick-up trucks a month (Table 8.2).

The advantages of locating in the *Triangulo* are so great that it is difficult to persuade industry to select sites in other parts of the country and especially in the north-east and north. In the north-east it is not the lack of people – there are about 30 million – but the scarcity of natural resources and the great poverty that hinders industrial development. The total purchasing power in the north-east is small, no more than that of the city of São Paulo. In the north there is not only poverty but a sparse population. Until recently, industry in the north-east was limited to textile mills, many of them dating from the nineteenth century, as well as some food-processing and manufacturing of a limited range of consumer goods. SUDENE has attempted to attract industry to the north-east by offering substantial tax concessions to companies, whether foreign or Brazilian, willing to invest in approved projects. By the end of 1968, nearly 600 industrial projects had been approved, of which over 100 had been put into effect. There have been failures, most notably, perhaps, that of the synthetic rubber factory at Cabo, just to the south of Recife, as well as some notable successes, of which the jeep factory at Jaboatão is an example. The *Recôncavo* oilfield has helped promote industry in Salvador, and recently the state government of Bahia, with the aid of SUDENE, has established an industrial park at Aratu on the outskirts of Salvador. To encourage the economic development of the north, the government has copied the SUDENE model and has set up SUDAM, the Superintendency for the Development of the Amazon. In an effort to industrialize Manaus, the city has been declared a free port. Industries set up in the free port area are able to import raw materials and export manufactured goods without paying import and export duties.

The industry of the three southern states of Brazil is based on the manufacture of consumer goods for a relatively prosperous population, on the processing of agricultural products, and on the exploitation of forests. Paraná is the most important state for lumbering and woodworking. Porto Alegre, the capital of Rio Grande do Sul, is a centre for meat-processing, tanning and the manufacture of wine and cigarettes – all based on the products of the agricultural hinterland. Blumenau and Join-ville, in Santa Catarina, are now small but growing industrial towns, which owe many of their factories to the enterprise of the German immigrants.

While industry in the three southern states and the north-east is expanding, and both regions are acquiring metal-working industries, the south will probably move ahead more rapidly than the north-east, and in the foreseeable future the heartland of industrial Brazil will remain the *Triangulo*.

Transportation

A revolution in transportation has accompanied industrialization. The difficulties presented by the sheer size of the country and the handicaps of its physical geography have in part been overcome, and old and inadequate means of transport replaced by more efficient ones.

The rivers are still little used, except in the Amazon basin, for they either flow towards the interior of the country or are blocked by falls. The use of hovercraft may lead to a re-evaluation of the rivers as lines of communication. Coastal navigation remains important, but in recent years it has been made extremely expensive because of the high wages the unionized workers have managed to obtain. The railways do not provide the country with an integrated transport system. Construction of railways began at the middle of the nineteenth century, but in 1900 there were only about 12,000 km of track, which by the mid-twentieth century had been little more than doubled. These railways were built by several companies, a number of them British, primarily to carry commodities from regions of production to ports. The linking of these separate railway networks has been undertaken by the federal and some state governments, which have gradually assumed ownership of the railways. The fact that the railway lines were built at different gauges – there are six in use in Brazil today – has made this work of unification more difficult. A lot of the equipment of the railways is old fashioned and run-down. Wood-burning locomotives are still in use. Except for some lines in the *Triangulo* and the Rio Doce railway, rail transport in Brazil is slow and unreliable.

Air transport and roads have finally provided the country with efficient transport. Commercial airlines serve all parts of the country, but though fares are low by international standards, air travel remains expensive for Brazilians. A striking advance in the development of transport has been achieved since the mid-1950s through an extensive roadbuilding pro- gramme and the extraordinary development of the automobile industry. There has been a great increase in the mileage of paved and improved dirt roads. One result of the location of the new capital in the interior has been an improvement in internal communications through the linking of Brasília with state capitals by all-weather roads. Recently a road to Belém has been opened and a road is under construction from Brasília to Peru along the southern margins of the Amazon basin. The trucking industry is now of growing importance in the distribution of goods within Brazil and buses and trucks carry a large percentage of the Brazilian travelling public. Today it is possible to travel from Belém to Uruguay by scheduled buses, and the bus station is a major focus of activity in any Brazilian town or village.

Urbanization

The urbanization of Brazil is one of the most striking developments in the country's geography this century (Fig. 8.12). Until late in the nineteenth century, the cities of Brazil were comparatively small and growing only slowly. Since the 1870s the growth of São Paulo has been spectacular, from 30,000 to approximately 8 million in 1970. São Paulo and Rio de Janeiro were the first cities in Brazil to reach a million, but now there are eight cities approaching or already over a million, and in 1970 some 25 per cent of the population of Brazil was contained in nine metropolitan areas (Table 8.3). Part of this growth can be attributed to the natural increase of the urban population and to immigration from overseas, but in large measure it is the result of migration from the countryside on a massive scale. Millions of people have already left the countryside to try their luck in the cities, yet so high is the rural birth-rate that this exodus has not led so far to decline

TABLE 8.3   *Brazil: Population of largest metropolitan areas*

| | (*figures in 1000s*) | | | %
increase | |
	1950	*1960*	*1970*	*1950–70*	*1980**
Brazil – population	51,900	70,900	95,200	83	125,503
Metropolitan areas	8,800	14,700	23,280	162	—
Belém	280	420	640	128	—
Fortaleza	310	560	1,000	221	—
Recife	810	1,240	1,850	126	2,681
Salvador	440	710	1,110	151	—
Belo Horizonte	440	840	1,570	253	2,914
Rio	3,140	4,840	6,680	112	11,307
São Paulo	2,610	4,700	8,070	209	15,110
Curitiba	270	470	840	211	—
Porto Alegre	570	990	1,520	166	3,089
Met. population as percentage of Brazil's population	17·0%	20·8%	24·4%		

Source: Visão, São Paulo, 15 March 1968, p. 28.
* Estimates: *Atualidade estatística*, 1970.

TABLE 8.4   *Growth of cities*

| | Cities of more than
100,000 population | | Cities with 10,000–
100,000 population | | Cities of less than
10,000 population | |
	Increase in No. of inhabitants (millions)	*Average annual rate of increase %*	*Increase in No. of inhabitants (millions)*	*Average annual rate of increase %*	*Increase in No. of inhabitants (millions)*	*Average annual rate of increase %*
1940–50	2·45	5·03	2·15	7·26	6·1	1·91
1950–60	5·50	7·70	4·20	6·10	9·3	1·85

Source: Visão, São Paulo, 15 March 1968, p. 29.

in the rural population, but merely to a lowering of its rate of increase. The rural–urban migration in Brazil still continues, with the largest and the medium sized towns attracting the population (Table 8.4). Small-town Brazil either has no appeal to the peasant or else it is but an intermediate

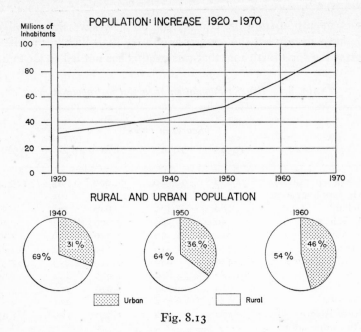

POPULATION: INCREASE 1920 - 1970

RURAL AND URBAN POPULATION

Fig. 8.13

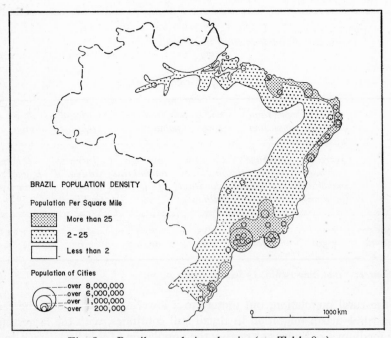

BRAZIL POPULATION DENSITY

Population Per Square Mile

More than 25

2 - 25

Less than 2

Population of Cities

over 8,000,000
over 6,000,000
over 1,000,000
over 200,000

Fig. 8.14 Brazil: population density (see Table 8.3)

stage along the migration route from backlands to metropolis where people spend a few years before moving on or seeing their children move on.

Like so much of the underdeveloped world, Brazil is undergoing urbanization without adequate industrialization. Industry cannot provide enough jobs for all the newcomers, and there are even large cities, such as Fortaleza, in which there is scarcely any industry at all. These cities without industry are ports or administrative centres and they perform service functions. Millions of people in the cities eke out a living from badly paid jobs in the lower ranks of a swollen civil service, and as clerks and servants in commercial establishments. Though labour is cheap, it is used lavishly; far more people are employed than are really needed for a particular job and many find no employment at all. The cities have grown so rapidly that the city administrators have been unable to provide the basic services of water, sewage systems, lighting, paved streets, schooling, medicine or even adequate public transport for much of the population. Each city has its new suburbs of shacks and cardboard houses such as the famous *favelas* of Rio and the *mucambos* of Recife. Conditions of life in these settlements are grim, and life itself all too often nasty, disease-ridden and short. The cities also have wealthy suburbs, luxury shops and impressive office buildings. Nowhere perhaps is the contrast between rich and poor so great and so clearly seen as in the large cities. The 'urban problem', with all its social and economic ramifications is a major one in Brazil and will take decades to solve. Its solution is bound up with the resolution of the other major problems: the curbing of the rate of population increase, agricultural reform in the broadest sense, the slackening of the rural–urban migration and the increase of the rate of industrialization.

Brazilian cities in colonial times and in the nineteenth century were unplanned, and so was the great expansion of the cities this century. Nevertheless, Brazilians have developed a considerable flair for urban planning, which has found expression less in tackling the problems of long-established cities as in founding entirely new ones. Examples are such towns as Londrina, in northern Paraná, state capitals, and Brasília. Londrina dates from the 1930s and now has a population of over 100,000. Minas Gerais began to build a new capital, Belo Horizonte, in the 1890s because the site of the old capital, Ouro Preto, was judged to be too constricted for the expected expansion of the state capital. In the 1930s, Goiânia was built to replace the old and remote gold town of Goiás as capital of the state of Goiás. The building of Brasília began in 1956, and the building still goes on. One of the purposes of Brasília was to help develop the interior of Brazil by providing a market for agriculture and new lines of communication; another was to create a symbol of a new Brazil, with a city startling in its layout and architecture. Brasília has its defenders and detractors. It cost an enormous amount of money. It is a monument to its creator, President Kubitschek. The layout is novel, but

TABLE 8.5   *Population and income by region 1960*

Region[1]	Population: % Brazilian total	Population: rate of growth 1950–60[2]	Brazil's income: region's share	Per capita income: % of national average
North	3·7	1·99	2·2	61
North-east	31·9	2·35	15·9	51
South-east	25·1	1·93	28·7	116
South	35·0	3·05	50·7	146
Central west	4·3	3·71	2·5	62
Brazil	100.0	2·40	100·0	

[1] These regions have been established by the government of Brazil.
North: Amazonas, Pará, Acre, Territories.
North-east: Maranhão, Piauí, Ceara, Rio Grande do Norte, Paraíba, Pernambuco, Alagoas, Sergipe, Bahia.
South-east: Minas Gerais, Espírito Santo, Rio de Janeiro, Guanabara.
South: São Paulo, Paraná, Santa Catarina, Rio Grande do Sul.
Central West: Mato Grosso, Goiás.
Source: Stefan H. Robock, *Brazil's Developing Northeast*, The Brookings Institution, Washington D.C., pp. 34–35.
[2] This column from the *Anuário Estatístico do Brasil*, 1960.

not always very practical. Some of the architecture is elegant, but many of the buildings are of purely functional design. Hardly surprisingly, it is a far less comfortable city to live in than Rio. Brasília, too, has its slums, in 'satellite cities' a few kilometres from the centre. The total population is now about 400,000. Brasília is a success in the sense that it is a functioning, lived-in city, and it has helped to open up the interior.

During the last twenty-five years, Brazil has made great strides to emerge from the category of 'underdeveloped country' and has achieved a partial success. Brazil now belongs to a new grouping of countries,

TABLE 8.6   *Brazil's income: regional share 1950–60*

Region	1950	51	52	53	54	55	56	57	58	59	60
North	2·2	2·2	2·2	2·0	1·9	2·0	2·3	2·4	2·2	2·1	2·2
North-east	16·4	15·5	15·0	14·2	14·4	13·9	14·4	14·9	14·3	15·3	15·9
South-east	31·3	31·4	30·6	30·8	30·8	30·5	31·8	31·4	30·9	30·4	28·7
South	48·2	48·8	50·0	50·3	50·3	51·0	48·9	48·9	50·0	49·8	50·7
Central west	1·9	2·1	2·2	2·7	2·6	2·6	2·6	2·4	2·6	2·4	2·5

Source: Stefan H. Robock, *Brazil's Developing North-east*, The Brookings Institution, Washington, D.C., p. 35.

characterized by a high degree of development in some sectors of their economies and extreme backwardness in others. It is an important industrial country, the most important industrial country in Latin America, and an exporter of manufactured goods. Industry is predominantly in the south-east and south of the country, where agriculture is also most productive and the standards of living are comparable with those of southern Europe. In Amazonia, the west and the north-east, there is little industry, agriculture is backward and society is traditional in outlook. These vast regions of Brazil still belong to the underdeveloped world, and the country's concern in the coming decades must be to extend the range of modernity and development within its borders.

BIBLIOGRAPHY

For discussions of Brazil from different points of view see:

FREYRE, G. (1964) *The Masters and the Slaves.* New York, Knopf.

FURTADO, C. (1963) *The Economic Growth of Brazil: A Survey from Colonial to Modern Times.* Berkeley, University of California Press.

HOLANDA, SÉRGIO BUARQUE DE (ed.) (1960) *História geral da civilização Brasileira.* São Paulo, Difusão Européia do Livro.

MOOG, V. (1964) *Bandeirantes and Pioneers.* New York, Braziller.

POPPINO, R. E. (1968) *Brazil: The Land and the People.* New York, Oxford University Press.

SMITH, T. L. (1963) *Brazil: People and Institutions.* Baton Rouge, Louisiana State University Press.

Physical geography

COLE, MONICA (1958) The distribution and origin of savanna vegetation with particular reference to the Campos Cerrados of Brazil. *Comptes Rendus, XVIII Congrès International de Géographie* (Rio de Janeiro), 1, 339-45.

FREISE, F. W. (1938) The drought region of northeastern Brazil. *Geographical Review*, 28, 363-78.

HUECK, K. (1957) Sobre a origem dos Campos Cerrados do Brasil. *Revista Brasileira de Geografia*, 19, 67-81.

JAMES, PRESTON J. (1952) Observations on the physical geography of northeast Brazil. *Annals of the Association of Amercian Geographers*, 42, 153-76.

Colonial period

ALDEN, D. (1963) The population of Brazil in the late eighteenth century: a preliminary study. *Hispanic American Historical Review*, 43, 173-205.

ANTONIL, A. J. (1968) *Cultura e opulencia do Brasil por suas drogas e minas.* Ed. and trans. by A. Mansuy. Paris, Institut des Hautes Études de l'Amérique Latine.

BOXER, C. R. (1962) *The Golden Age of Brazil, 1695-1750.* Berkeley, University of California Press.

MARCHANT, A. (1942) *From Barter to Slavery: The Economic Relations of Portuguese and Indians in the Settlement of Brazil, 1500-1580.* Baltimore, Johns Hopkins Press.

MAURO, F. (1960) *Le Portugal et l'Atlantique au XVIIIe Siècle 1570-1670.* Paris, S.E.V.P.E.N.

PRADO, CAIO JR (1967) *The Colonial Background of Modern Brazil.* Berkeley, University of California Press.

The nineteenth century

BURTON, RICHARD F. (1869) *The Highlands of Brazil.* London. 2 vols.

MELBY, J. (1942) Rubber river: an account of the rise and collapse of the Amazon boom. *Hispanic American Historical Review*, 22, 452-69.

MONBEIG, P. (1952) *Pionniers et planteurs de São Paulo.* Paris, Colin.

MORSE, R. M. (1958) *From Community to Metropolis: A Biography of São Paulo, Brazil.* Gainesville, University of Florida Press.

ROCHE, J. (1959) *La colonisation allemande et Le Rio Grande do Sul.* Paris, Institut des Hautes Études de l'Amérique Latine.

STEIN, S. J. (1957) *Vassouras: A Brazilian Coffee County 1850-1900.* Cambridge, Mass., Harvard University Press.

STEIN, S. J. (1957) *Brazilian Cotton Manufacture: Textile Enterprise in an Underdeveloped Area.* Cambridge, Mass., Harvard University Press.

WAIBEL, L. (1950) European colonization in southern Brazil. *Geographical Review*, 40, 529-47.

The twentieth century

AUGELLI, J. P. (1958) Cultural and economic changes of Bastos: a Japanese colony on Brazil's Paulista frontier. *Annals of the Association of American Geographers*, 48, 3-19.

AZEVEDO, A. DE (ed.) (1958) *A Cidade de São Paulo: estudos de geografia urbana.* 4 vols. São Paulo, Companhia Editora Nacional.

BAER, W. (1965) *Industrialization and Economic Development in Brazil.* Holmewood, Ill., Irwin.

BAER, W. (1964) Regional inequality and economic growth in Brazil. *Economic Development and Cultural Change*, 12, 268-85.

CARMIN, R. L. (1953) *Anápolis, Brazil: Regional Capital on an Agricultural Frontier*. University of Chicago, Department of Geography Research Paper No. 35.

DEAN, WARREN (1969) *The Industrialization of São Paulo, 1880–1945*. Austin, University of Texas Press.

DICKENSON, J. P. (1967) The iron and steel industry in Minas Gerais, Brazil, 1695–1965. In STEEL, R. W. and LAWTON, R. (eds.) *Liverpool Essays on Geography – A Jubilee Collection*. London, Longmans Green.

DOZIER, C. L. (1956) Northern Paraná, Brazil. An example of organized regional development. *Geographical Review*, 46, 318–33.

HIRSCHMAN, A. O. (1965) Brazil's Northeast. In *Journeys Towards Progress*. New York, Twentieth Century Fund, 1963, and Anchor Books, Doubleday, 1965.

PEBAYLE, R. (1967) La vie rurale dans la Campanha Rio-Grandense. *Les Cahiers d'Outre Mer*, 20, 345–66.

PFEIFER, G. (1967) Kontraste in Rio Grande do Sul: Campanha und Alto Uruguai. *Geographische Zeitschrift*, 55, 163–206.

ROBOCK, S. (1963) *Brazil's Developing Northeast: A Study of Regional Planning and Foreign Aid*. Washington, D.C., The Brookings Institution.

RUSSELL, J. A. (1942) Fordlândia and Belterra, rubber plantations on the Tapajós River, Brazil. *Economic Geography*, 18, 125–45.

9 The River Plate Countries[1]

J. Colin Crossley

From being commercial producers of subsidiary significance in the economy of colonial Spanish America, and of no consequence at all outside Latin America, the River Plate lands passed through a period of trial and error and rose during the late nineteenth century to the first rank of world producers of agricultural commodities. Migration and immigration brought about a complete reversal in the relative commercial and demographic importance of different subregions; the Pampas of temperate Argentina and Uruguay came to dominate the scene and the subtropical Argentine north-west and Paraguay became a backwater of colonial survivals. Such changes did not occur without conflict and difficulty. Nor has a feeling of national unity been able to develop to the desired degree under such adverse conditions. Especially since the Great Depression, Argentina and Uruguay have consciously sought to decrease their vulnerability to world economic vicissitudes by increasing their self-sufficiency, whereas Paraguay has sought a fuller share of world trade. In each case established patterns of landownership, production and communications have seriously impeded these efforts and future directions are far from clear.

THE MARGINS OF EMPIRE 1536–1852

Colonial period from 1536 to 1776

When Pizarro was conquering the Inca empire via the Pacific (1532–5), Pedro de Mendoza was attempting the settlement of the Plate from the Atlantic, founding Buenos Aires in 1536. But after five years of privation in the face of hostile Indians the settlement was abandoned in favour of Asunción. The assessment of the New World by Oviedo, the Spanish chronicler, that 'the Indies are worth nothing without the Indians', needed slight modification in the context of the Plate. There, lands inhabited by nomadic Indian hunters who could fight or flee at will were useless, whilst lands with indigenous agricultural communities offered a labour force

---

[1] 'The River Plate' and 'The Plate' are commonly used phrases to refer to Argentina, Uruguay and Paraguay. 'Mesopotamia' refers to Entre Ríos, Corrientes and Misiones, the Argentine provinces lying between the rivers Paraná and Uruguay. 'Litoral' refers to the older provinces bordering the Paraná–Plate estuary, namely Corrientes, Entre Ríos, Santa Fé and Buenos Aires (and even Uruguay).

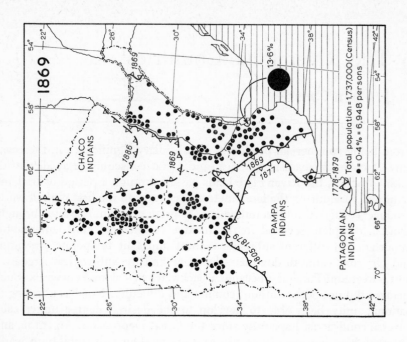

c1780

Jesuit Missions

Corrientes
Santiago del Estero
Santa Fe
Paraná
Buenos Aires
8·8%

1820
1820
1830-1869
1858
1854
1828
1778
Patagones

Jujuy
Salta
Tucumán
Catamarca
La Rioja
San Juan
Mendoza
Córdoba
San Luis
1805-1879

Total population = 269,000 (Est.)
• = 0·4% = 1,076 persons

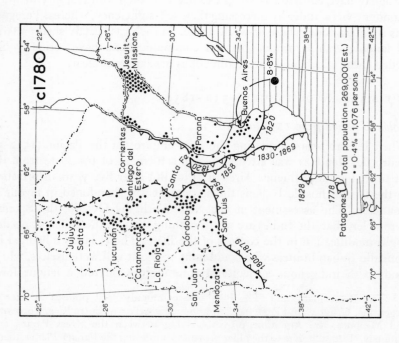

1869

CHACO INDIANS

1869
1886
1869
1877
1869
1778-1879
1805-1879
PAMPA INDIANS

PATAGONIAN INDIANS

13·6%

Total population = 1,737,000 (Census)
● = 0·4% = 6,948 persons

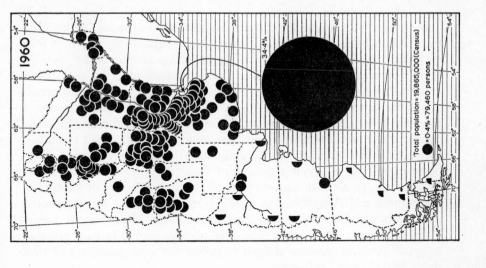
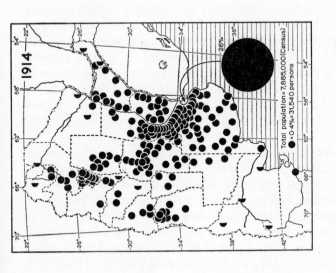
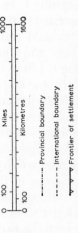

Fig. 9.1 Argentina: population distribution
and settlement frontiers 1780–1960

which the superior European weaponry could easily control and direct for the conquerors' ends; and this was particularly true of irrigated areas from which flight was impossible.

Both the process and the pattern of colonial occupation in the Plate thus reflected the pre-Hispanic distribution of settlement, which in turn represented the appraisals by essentially Stone Age peoples of the potential of the physical environment. The forest-dwellers of hilly, subtropical eastern Paraguay and Misiones, perhaps numbering 50,000, were accustomed to shifting agriculture with beans, manioc and pumpkins, and a plentiful water supply. At the foot of the Andes and in the intermontane basins of the arid north-west and west, ease of irrigation had permitted long-established sedentary maize agriculture; here villages with a combined population of about a quarter of a million formed outposts of the Inca empire. In between and to the south lay the vast plains of the Chaco, the Pampas and Patagonia, hot in the north, cold in the south, covered with grass or scrub forest and everywhere short of permanent water-courses whatever the rainfall; here lived perhaps 90,000 Indians grouped in small bands of hunters obliged to follow the wild guanaco and rhea that afforded their food supply.

In this land of nomads only two cities, Buenos Aires and Santa Fé, were founded successfully during early colonial times, both by settlers from Asunción. To the east, Corrientes was founded among Indian forest farmers and during the seventeenth century the Jesuits established many *reducciones* or mission villages, into which the scattered Indian populace was organized. In contrast, Spanish official efforts at colonization were concentrated in the north-west and Cuyo where today's provincial capitals were founded mainly in the late sixteenth century by settlers entering from Peru and Chile respectively (Fig. 9.1). European crops and animals entering the Plate by the same three routes had also spread throughout the region by the end of the sixteenth century. Indeed, wheat-growing preceded the conquerors in Cuyo and everywhere the nomadic hunters rapidly acquired the horse.

Despite its agricultural potential, the River Plate remained tied to an economy of industrial and agricultural self-sufficiency with its international commercial activity limited to a marginal role in the mining economy of Peru. Europe of the time had no demand for the temperate produce of other continents – and the subtropical districts of the Plate lay deep in the interior – nor did the region possess any precious metals to exploit. Until 1776 the River Plate formed part of the Viceroyalty of Peru, and so was subject to regulations which gave Lima the monopoly of all trade with Spain. Buenos Aires thus lay at the end of a route to Spain through the Chaco, Lima and Panama which rendered European goods prohibitively expensive to import legally. Contraband trading with Brazil and with European interlopers and indigenous manufacturing were thus both stimulated. Apart from domestic craft activities, regional industrial specialization developed. Tucumán supplied carts to the whole Plate and wheat-flour to the Litoral, and even sent cotton and woollen goods as far afield as Chile and Potosí (a mining city with 160,000 people in the mid-seventeenth century). Mendoza from the earliest times was the centre of production of wine and dried fruits, whilst subtropical Paraguay and Misiones contributed sugar, yerba maté and cotton textiles to the regional markets.

Most food crops were grown for local subsistence whereas livestock farming was more commercial. The excellence of the natural pastures of the Pampas, Mesopotamia and Uruguay permitted the wild descendants of the cattle and horses introduced in the middle of the sixteenth century to multiply exceedingly; by the end of the century, since cattle were regarded as Crown property, rights were being awarded to individuals to round up and kill so many head of cattle a year within a prescribed area, though for long their only value lay in the hides and to a less extent in the tallow and tongues. Horses were more valuable, as transport on the plains was wholly dependent upon them, and *estancias* were soon formed to oversee the wild herds and tame them. As the wild cattle were reduced in numbers, *estancias* with grants of land became organized for their control, the smallest, of 0·5 × 1·5 leagues (approximately 1875 ha), capable of yielding ninety hides a year. In the absence of fencing, surveillance by gaucho horsemen was necessary to prevent rustling, especially by Indian raiders who could find a profitable market in Chile. There was little interest in sheep as mutton was despised and wool exports were prohibited.

The most important contribution of the Plate to the Spanish imperial economy, however, lay in its ability to supply sure-footed mules for transport in the mountainous mining areas of Peru. The mules were bred in Mesopotamia and the Pampas, reared in Córdoba and Tucumán and sold at the annual fair at Salta when 60,000 mules would be purchased for úse in Upper and Lower Peru.

Population remained concentrated during colonial times in the areas of indigenous permanent settlement. In the early years, with the cultural shock of the Conquest, native numbers declined and Spanish colonists were too few to compensate. The 'civilized' population by the early seventeenth century is estimated to have been 162,000, of whom 75,000 lived, in the north-west, 25,000 in Córdoba (effectively part of the north-west in colonial times), 12,000 in Cuyo, 28,000 in Mesopotamia, and only 22,000 in the Pampas. In contrast the Indian *reducciones* of Paraguay and Misiones, begun in 1610, prospered under the protective rule of the Jesuits and their population rose to 126,000 in 1733. The cities of the period, with the exception of craft centres like Tucumán, had at best tertiary functions such as administration and commerce, and some were little more than centres of residence for absentee landowners.

But Buenos Aires was not destined to remain at the dead end of the imperial highway system. Contraband trade was already thriving when, by the Treaty of Utrecht (1713), Britain gained limited rights to introduce merchandise and Negro slaves directly into the Plate in exchange for hides. By the mid-eighteenth century annual hide exports had risen to 150,000 and Negro slaves were widely employed as domestic servants and in the embryonic sugar plantations of Tucumán, where they formed a majority of the population. By the time Buenos Aires became the capital of the new Viceroyalty of the River Plate in 1776, its population, in excess of 20,000, made it by far the largest town in the Plate, and the region's total had probably recovered its pre-Hispanic level of a third of a million (Fig. 9.1). This figure, however, includes perhaps 100,000 Indians who survived the colonial period in independent occupance of Patagonia, the Chaco and a large part of the Pampas.

The period of transition 1776–1852

The accession of the French Bourbons to the Spanish throne in 1700 began a period of colonial reform, culminating in the creation of the Viceroyalty of the River Plate in 1776 and the 'free trade' regulations of 1777 and 1778. Fear of the growing strength of Portuguese Brazil was another factor leading to the detachment of what are now Argentina, Uruguay, Paraguay and Bolivia from the Viceroyalty of Peru, and to the laws which now allowed Spanish ships to trade directly with the Plate, and the Plate to trade with other Spanish colonies. Montevideo, founded in 1724, benefited as the official port of call for ships sailing to the Pacific, while Buenos Aires exported the new Viceroyalty's produce of silver and hides. The mining centre of Potosí, a four-month journey from Lima, but only two from Buenos Aires, could now get Spanish cloth at one sixth of its former price. Viceregal action also encouraged the growing of wheat and the salting of meat. New freedoms and fresh developments were very welcome to the merchants of the Plate, but the foreigner was still excluded, and the merchants' desire to trade with industrializing Britain still went unsatisfied. This grievance was a major factor in the wars for independence.

Argentina was the first territory in the Plate to secure its freedom (1810). The rest of the Viceroyalty obtained independence, not only from Spain, but from Buenos Aires as well: Paraguay ousted the Argentines in 1811, Bolivia became a separate state in 1825, and three years later Uruguay emerged as a British-sponsored buffer state between Argentina and Brazil, thus ending their long contest for its possession. The stage was set for the region to move to the margins of the British Empire.

The economic disruption of emancipation was succeeded by a re-orientation in favour of the Litoral. The creation of a frontier between Bolivia and Argentina narrowed the primary commercial outlet of the north-west, and of Salta in particular. Internal political events served also to isolate it from its secondary market, the Litoral: the liberal policies of the 1820s freed the flow of goods between Argentina (effectively, the Litoral) and Britain, whilst the Rosas dictatorship of the 1830s and 1840s further increased the commercial isolation of the interior, either through persistent civil strife or through the erection of interprovincial tariff barriers. For the first half of the nineteenth century Paraguay, too, was isolated from the world by the whims either of its own or Argentina's dictator.

Throughout the period hides constituted the leading commercial product and provided over half the exports of the Plate, the annual number rising rapidly to 1·4 million in 1783 and to 2·9 million from Argentina alone by 1849. More dramatic, however, was the rise in meat exports: apart from the hides, cattle had been utilized for little more than their tallow, tongues and a certain amount of sun-dried meat. Lack of salt had previously restricted production of salt meat, but in the 1780s, with salt coming from Patagones, an increased number of cattle and a growing demand for meat from tropical plantations, meat-salting factories – *saladeros* – were established with Viceregal backing. The first was at Colonia, in Uruguay, and by 1804 exports from the eight Uruguayan *saladeros* exceeded 3200 tons, but still the meat of over half the animals slaughtered for their hides was being wasted. Following rapidly on the declaration of independence came the first *saladero* on the Argentine shore, established at Ensenada in 1811 by Staples and McNeil, two of the British merchants who flocked into the republic; other factories followed in the next few years on the outskirts of Buenos Aires and in Entre Ríos. By 1829 Argentine exports of salt meat topped 7500 tons and by 1851 were running at about 20,000 tons a year.

The prosperity of the salt meat industry, for which the *criollo* breed was ideal, gave little encouragement to the breeding of finer cattle although each beast yielded only 75 kg of meat when slaughtered at five years. Nevertheless, Miller, a British *saladerista* and *estanciero*, imported the first Shorthorn bull in 1823 and its cross-bred progeny began to spread among the herds of those who sought to develop a local dairying industry. Breeding did not extend, however, to the creation of a single herd of pedigree stock.

It was the sheep-rearing industry that first saw the need for improvement. The typical native sheep yielded a wool not worth scouring, a mutton that was scorned and a carcass fit only for fuel; its principal value lay in the use of fleeces as a comfortable if ungainly kind of saddle. After independence the European demand for long-stapled fine wools could not be satisfied by the native animal and, since Spain forbade the export of her fine merino stock, supplies had to be obtained elsewhere. In the 1820s and 1830s the *estancieros* Gibson and Newton imported stud flocks of Southdowns, Lincolns and Romney Marshes, whilst Hannah and Stegmann acquired German merinos (*Negretes*). In the 1840s merinos were also introduced into Uruguay but breeding still interested only a few native and foreign *estancieros*. Nevertheless, Argentine wool exports rose steadily, from under 200 tons in 1822 to 2100 tons in 1837 and almost 7700 by 1850.

Successful breeding, like successful crop farming, depended very much on the farmer's ability to restrict the movements of his animals and, therefore, on the fencing of the boundless Pampas. Olivera tried hedges in 1838 and in 1845 Newton introduced the idea of wire fencing from Wentworth Deer Park in Yorkshire, though his aim was to protect crops, rather than to ring-fence the *estancia* or subdivide the pastures.

Another innovation was the *invernada* or fattening pasture established in the vicinity of port-situated *saladeros*, where cattle could recuperate after long journeys on foot.

Despite the encouragement of wheat-growing and flour-milling by the viceroys and by the early national governments, crop production on the Litoral did not prosper because fenceless farms were defenceless farms, livestock enterprises were much preferred, a labour shortage hindered the intensification of agriculture, and imported American flour competed too successfully.

But the interior suffered more than the coast: by 1850 over half of Argentine imports – sugar, yerba, tobacco, beverages, flour and textiles – competed directly with its agricultural-processing industries, at least in the markets of the Litoral; its produce was dearer and inferior and transport costs to the coast were often higher. Conversely the same high internal freight rates helped to protect its economic diversity: Córdoba continued as a textile centre, Tucumán developed its sugar and tobacco industries and Cuyo its wines and brandy, but political difficulties prevented the interior from developing its own integrated exchange economy.

The increasing economic isolation of the interior was not offset by any great move to link up the effectively settled areas of the Litoral and the interior. While Mesopotamia and Uruguay had been successfully, though sparsely, settled in colonial times, west-bank settlement especially in Santa Fé remained a narrow strip, although Rosas's desert campaign of the 1830s pushed the Indian frontier south-westwards in the province of Buenos Aires (Fig. 9.1a). The 'corridor' between the Litoral and interior, from Rosario to Córdoba, thus remained throughout the period an unsettled territory where only forts protected the route from Indian attacks.

For political and economic reasons, early attempts to organize crop-farming colonies in the Litoral, such as Robertson's Scots colony at Monte Grande in 1823, did not succeed. Despite the desire of the national government under Bernardino Rivadavia in the 1820s to see the land occupied by small and medium farmers, and despite the facilities for buying land on instalments, the failure to impose an areal limit on concessions soon led to new lands falling easily into few hands. In any case, large-scale livestock farming needing little labour was the only viable agricultural economy. Thus by 1840 over 85,000 km² had been sold to under 300 people. Developments in Uruguay were along similar lines and virtually the whole national territory rapidly became the property of a small number of people.

During the transitional period the total 'civilized' population of Argentina (i.e. excluding nomadic Indian tribes) quadrupled, from 269,000 around 1780, to 1,107,000 in 1855, being about half a million at independence (Fig. 9.1). The provinces of the interior (the north-west, Cuyoand, at that time, Córdoba) retained their share (57 per cent); among the Litoral provinces, Corrientes declined with the dispersal of the mission Indians after the 1767 expulsion of the Jesuits, whilst the province of Buenos Aires doubled its share to 17 per cent by 1855. Together with the 91,000 inhabitants of the city, this gave the city and province of Buenos Aires exactly one quarter of the national population; Santa Fé province with barely 40,000 inhabitants still ranked eleventh (out of fourteen provinces). Where racial mixing between whites and Indians had proceeded for generations, i.e. in the north-west and north-east, the population at the end of the period was predominantly mestizo, whereas on the Pampas hostility had kept the civilized whites and the untamed Indians apart. European-born foreigners were important only in the province of Buenos Aires where they constituted almost half the population; a further one seventh were Negroes and mulattos, for the import of slaves continued until 1825 and slavery was abolished only in 1853. Between 1828 and 1852 neighbouring Uruguay doubled its population to 132,000, due partly to the immigration of southern Europeans.

The transitional period marked the first phase in the shift of national emphasis from the interior to the Litoral. Demographically, the balance between the two remained constant, but the nucleus of Buenos Aires was already setting the pace that the rest of the Pampas was to follow. Economically the balance shifted markedly: 'The policy of free imports blocked any possibility of spreading (to the interior) the dynamic impulse generated by the Litoral's export expansion' (Ferrer, 1967, p. 67). With little capacity to export, the interior was prevented from importing the new technology; its industries survived because 'the major protectionist barrier was still distance' (Ferrer, 1967, p. 72), but they stagnated, thus forcing the rising population into subsistence occupations. By reason of their locations Paraguay and Uruguay found themselves in the same positions as the interior and Litoral respectively.

THE INTEGRATION OF ARGENTINA AND URUGUAY INTO THE WORLD ECONOMY 1852–1930

After the fall of the dictator Rosas in 1852, a long period of semi-democratic constitutional government was inaugurated, and the geography of the

o

Argentine state was transformed in the space of fifty years by immigration, by investment of capital and by an agricultural revolution. From being a nation centred on the oases of the Andean fringe it became the nation of the humid Pampas; from being a people of Creole and mestizo character, its inhabitants became a melting-pot of European settlers; and, from producing little but inferior dried meat and wool, its agricultural economy was converted to the production of high grade meat from carefully bred animals and of vast quantities of cereals, which gave the country a leading place in the world exchange economy.

Politically, since independence Argentina had been torn between federal and unitary approaches to the constitutional problem. The *caudillos* of both interior and Litoral provinces, other than Buenos Aires, resented the latter's economic ascendancy and favoured a federal solution. On the other hand the Unitarians, merchants and intellectuals, saw a centralist constitution as necessary for the expansion of trade and the spread of Europe's civilizing influence through Buenos Aires over the boorish gaucho. In the event, the Constitution of the Confederation, drawn up in 1853, was a compromise and owed much to the political thinker, Alberdi. His view that 'to govern is to populate' was reflected in the constitutional encouragement of immigration, colonization, the import of capital, the construction of railways and the establishment of industries. Interprovincial tariffs were to be abolished and customs receipts nationalized. But for nine years Buenos Aires province remained independent of a thus-impoverished Confederation; in 1856, the latter imposed additional duties on all goods entering via Buenos Aires, thus giving the initial stimulus to the rise of Rosario as a rival port. When union was achieved, under a *porteño* president, it was the north-west that offered resistance. Finally, in 1880, the city of Buenos Aires became the federal capital, thus depriving the province of Buenos Aires of most of the coveted port revenues.

Until 1890 change and development were centred on two foci: Rosario and Buenos Aires. Rosario was the port of entry for European immigrants intending to settle in agricultural colonies in Santa Fé province. The territory occupied by Indians was narrowest opposite Rosario and forts still lined the road linking the settled coastal strip to the old north-west. Here was built the first trunk railway, to Córdoba, followed by extensions to Mendoza and Tucumán, which made the whole north-west tributary to Rosario. Only in the late 1880s were the Rosario and Buenos Aires railway systems joined.

Activity in Buenos Aires province was of a different type: the Indians were ousted from great areas, the land was made over to the rearing of sheep and cattle, and railway tentacles reached out from Buenos Aires. Exports of wool and salt beef increased and imported wheat was replaced by the produce of the Santa Fé colonies. With the arrival of the *frigorífico*, frozen mutton added to the wealth of the *estancieros*.

British capital, much of it speculative, played a major role in land improvements, railway and port construction and urban redevelopment. Issues of paper currency mounted as the ruling class of *estancieros* saw in depreciation the opportunity both to pay less in wages and to reduce the value of their outstanding debts. Expansion may have laid the foundations for a prosperous future, but the speculative bubble burst in the crisis of 1890, causing the ruin of many.

After the crisis development proceeded more cautiously. With the conquest of the Pampas already achieved, no lands of first-class quality and location remained for settlement and occupance of the land could only advance towards more arid or more tropical areas. Fortunately, growth was now possible through intensification of land use. Technological advance allowed the shipping of frozen beef to the mass markets of Britain. This stimulated the upgrading of Argentine cattle which now required more than natural pastures for fattening. The sowing of artificial pastures became a necessity, but *estanciero* attitudes eschewed the tilling of the soil as work fit only for peasants. The preferred solution was to lease blocks of land for a short period to immigrants, who would contract to take three or four crops of wheat and flax, and then return the land laid down to alfalfa. With land values high and public lands suitable for colonization almost exhausted, impermanent tenancy was the only form of land tenure open to the majority. As a by-product of the beef industry, therefore, land use was intensified, cereal exports were expanded, the railways became prosperous with the increased flow of freight, and new lines radiated from Buenos Aires to tap the whole of the Pampas. Cuyo and the northwest, too, were joined directly to Buenos Aires by lines bypassing Rosario. From being an ellipse focused on Rosario and Buenos Aires, the growth area of Argentina was now a circle centred on the capital.

Uruguay, physically well endowed, endured political disorder until the early twentieth century, discouraging both immigration and economic development, although a railway network radiating from Montevideo had been built between 1860 and 1911 in part to aid the suppression of revolutions. With the election of José Batlle y Ordóñez (President 1903–7 and 1911–15), the government began to guide economic development. Immigrants stamped their European character on the country as they did on the Pampas, but with superior natural pastures livestock farming did not produce an influx of tenant colonists.

Paraguay, lying 1200 km upstream, continued to suffer: from isolation like the Argentine interior, from the war of 1865–70 which reduced her estimated population to a quarter of a million, of whom fewer than 29,000 were men, and from chronic political disorder. Not surprisingly, her attempts to integrate into the world economy, to attract immigrants, to commercialize agriculture and to develop her natural resources met with only limited success and both economy and society remained those of a peasant nation.

The expansion of settlement

The economic growth of the period was made possible by the world situation and by the existence around the Plate of an area of high quality land more than twice the size of the United Kingdom yet utilized almost wholly for hunting by nomadic Indians or for the extensive rearing of inferior cattle and sheep. Argentina also benefited from changes of boundary between the republics of the Paraná basin. As a result of the war of 1865–70 Argentina gained definitive possession of Misiones and Formosa from Paraguay, which also lost territory to Brazil. In 1851 Uruguay had ceded the northern half of its territory to Brazil and thus ceased in practice to be the 'Republic of the East Bank of the Uruguay' (República de la Banda Oriental del Uruguay) – though it still retains that name officially.

The march of settlement took different steps in different areas. In the Pampas two courses were pursued: limited arable colonization had already begun in the 1840s under *caudillo* Justo José de Urquiza in Entre Ríos where pastoral farming had also been developed early. This province of rolling parkland was, together with Uruguay, the only part of the Litoral which possessed readily available surface water. West of the Paraná the provision of drinking water for man and beast depended on wells and wind pumps. Yet Santa Fé province was to take the lead in officially organizing colonies for immigrant settlers on a massive scale, big landowners, Rosario merchants and colonization companies sharing the work with the provincial government. Just west of Santa Fé city, Esperanza was founded in 1856, the settlers receiving 33 ha lots. But further developments were slow until after 1865 when colonization promotion laws were enacted by the province. The first spurt came in 1870 with the colonies of the Central Argentine Land Company laid out beside the Rosario–Córdoba railway on land conceded to the Central Argentine Railway Company for this purpose. Although enjoying the unique advantage of location beside Santa Fé's only railway, the colonists did not prosper for a decade or more. Inexperience, drought, locusts, frosts and Indian attacks were burdens alleviated only by financial assistance from the company. Private colonization ventures multiplied: one landowner, M. Cabal, initiated regular shipments of wheat to Europe in 1874 in order to help his colonists.

The boom of the 1880s brought prosperity to existing colonies and the establishment of many new ones: of 361 colonies (covering 3·7 million ha) founded in Santa Fé in the forty years 1856–95, two-thirds were created in the decade 1884–93. Hundred-hectare lots now became common, for mechanization led to greater efficiency. But exhaustion of the supply of good land in the public domain, coupled with the big owners' growing

preference for retaining control of their estates, caused a sharp decline in
colonization in Santa Fé, as in neighbouring provinces after 1895.

In Córdoba province the Central Argentine Land Company took the
lead in colonization, thrusting its colonies along the railway into Indian
territory, and thus linking up with the old settled area of the irrigated
valleys to the north-west. Of the 139 colonies (covering 1·4 million ha)
whose foundation dates are recorded in the 1895 census only seven were
established in 1870–84; 128 came in the decade 1885–94 and indeed half
the total were founded after the crisis in 1892–4; another 122 were established in 1896–1901. The delay in colonizing Córdoba is also to be explained by the increasing aridity of the plains, a problem partly overcome
after 1888 with the construction of the San Roque dam.

The spearhead of settlement thus became a broad wedge, occupying
the central parts of Córdoba as it did in Santa Fé. Córdoba city, alone
among the colonial towns of the north-west, now became a colonist centre
of the Pampas.

To the north the Indians were pushed back, but slowly. The officials
of the Santa Fé Land Company, formed in 1883 to develop the north-
western one sixth of that province, were harassed by Indians until the late
1880s and Resistencia, founded in 1878 opposite Corrientes city, remained
for a time merely a fortified enclave. The lower quality of the land and
an absence of rail links further restricted northwards colonization. Indeed,
settlement in northern Santa Fé and neighbouring Chaco advanced only
at the turn of the century, when the extraction of tannin from the *quebracho*
forests proved a profitable venture.

Across the river Paraná, Entre Ríos was second only to Santa Fé, with
191 colonies established by 1895, covering 0·8 million ha. After a pre-
cocious start under Urquiza further colonies were not founded until 1871;
thereafter only fifty-two were created up to 1885, mostly within easy reach
of Paraná and concepción cities or of navigable highways. The period 1886–
1893 saw 137 established, with more than half the total founded in 1888–91;
at the same time the Paraná–Concepción railway was built to serve them.
Thus, with the exception of a few river bank settlements, the northern
half of Entre Ríos and adjoining Corrientes saw no colonization ventures,
remaining a wooded pastoral landscape. Among the Entre Ríos colonies
several were created for German and Jewish refugees from Tsarist
persecution.

Whilst colonization dominated the march of settlement across the land
between the 31st and 33rd parallels in Entre Ríos, Santa Fé and Córdoba,
it played only a minor role in taming lands to the south. In Buenos Aires
province during the 1850s and 1860s the Indians were slowly pushed back
from the frontier along the Salado river, but during the 1870s groups
surviving in the well-watered Tandil and Ventana hills would sally forth
and cause such damage to the scattered sheep *estancias* that only through

a war of extermination – the 'Conquest of the Desert' (1879–83) – could the hazard be overcome (Fig. 9.1). The results of this military action were unprecedented: the area under the effective control of the state was doubled and the whole of Patagonia, together with the arid lands south of Cuyo, was opened up. But, more important, the area of the Pampas was doubled. These newly won lands were divided up, though not without dispute, between the provinces of Córdoba, Santa Fé and Buenos Aires, and the western rump became the core of La Pampa National Territory.

In 1876 public land legislation was enacted for the laying out of land in sections of 400 km² each; every section was to be subdivided into 400 lots of 100 ha each, the four central ones being reserved for the creation of a town; all manner of official, private and joint colonization schemes were allowed. In practice, disposal of most lands followed a different course, and in a few years most of the land had become the property of a small number. By 1914, 8 per cent of the farms held 80 per cent of the farmland. The 'Conquest of the Desert' had been financed by bonds costing 400 silver pesos, repayable later in a square league of public land, while other lands were sold by public auction. The greater part was given to the soldiers in reward for their services, but, having neither resources nor inclination to develop their estates, most of them rapidly sold out to speculators, livestock farmers and genuine colony promoters. One such was the South American Land Company formed in 1881 with lands in north-eastern La Pampa. Buoyed up by hopes of rapid railway development, a few colonists bought lots and, in the expectation of successful business, the company rented much land to graziers on short lease and set up its own pastoral activities on the rest. But the railways did not arrive in most of the new territories for fifteen to twenty-five years, and neither did the colonists; only large-scale pastoral farming was viable and the company sold out. Another British-owned venture, the Santa Fé and Córdoba Great Southern Land Company (1888), with lands 175 km west-south-west of Rosario, benefited from proximity to a railway in its early success with colonies at Arias and Venado Tuerto. But the failure of colonists to arrive during the 1890s drove it to the same course that hundreds of individual *estancieros* were already adopting – the installation of wells and wind pumps, fencing the land, stocking it with high grade Shorthorns and converting natural grassland to alfalfa pasture as and when tenant farmers offered themselves. When the immigration boom of 1904–12 occurred colonization by private enterprise was no longer a profitable venture and the government no longer possessed public lands to colonize in the Pampas.

With the ousting of the Indians, the whole of the Pampas became available for occupation and improvement, and by the end of the nineteenth century the wave of settlement had engulfed it all. Beyond lay lands either too dry for general improvement or too forested for wholesale clearance.

Here settlement was sporadic, like that of the colonial interior, though with one important difference: for the self-sufficient settler of earlier times isolation was less important than the physical attraction of site, whereas for the modern commercial farmer the latter was useless without access to a market.

The expansion of settlement outside the Pampas had begun before 1890 and was associated with the endeavour to find crops able to transcend the barrier of distance. In Patagonia modern settlement dates from the foundation in 1865 of the Welsh colony in the lower Chubut valley. Having been led to believe that the district was a well-watered land of forest and lush meadow, the 153 original settlers (only three or four of whom were farmers) arrived to find a canyon incised in arid scrubland, its pasture-covered floor littered with the driftwood of a river in spate. After many vicissitudes, the settlers rediscovered the techniques of flood-farming and canal irrigation and the colony began to prosper, or at least became self-supporting. But transport costs were high. Wheat cost more to ship to Buenos Aires than from Buenos Aires to Liverpool; thirty years after the foundation of the colony wheat sales were only profitable in seasons of poor harvest on the Pampas. But the colonists were as much the prisoners of their cultural environment as of their physical circum-stances.

Within six years of the defeat of the Indians in northern Patagonia the territory had been populated by more than 500,000 sheep and cattle. As the pastures of Buenos Aires became the scene of cattle-fattening enter-prises, so the production of wool there declined and the Patagonian wastes acquired a viable role in the Argentine economy. The government, con-scious of its dispute with Chile over the possession of much of Patagonia, was anxious to encourage rapid occupation of the land, conceding estates of colossal size from the public domain, often without security of title. Shepherds, frequently Scottish, took up isolated residence either on their own behalf or as managers for absentee owners, both private and corporate. Fortunes were invested in the stocking and fencing of the land and in paying the running costs of enterprises from which no great returns could be expected for years. Britons, Germans, Austro-Hungarians, Spaniards and Chileans provided the capital and Chileans much of the labour. Argentines were either not welcomed or not interested in the development of their Deep South. By 1930 virtually all of Patagonia from the Río Negro to Tierra del Fuego had been carved up into sheep farms of undoubted prosperity.

On the northern margins of Patagonia fertility and accessibility favoured intensive colonization in the irrigated Río Negro valley near the confluence of the Limay and Neuquén. The railway arrived in 1899, and river-control works undertaken in the 1910s brought 23,000 ha into cultivation by 1919. Similar developments took place at San Rafael in southern Mendoza.

At the opposite end of Argentina lay the forested territories of Chaco, Formosa[1] and Misiones where colonization began with a few riverside settlements in the 1880s, but grew rapidly only after 1918 with the increasing demand for subtropical industrial crops. As already mentioned, the first notable influx of people into the Chaco came with the development of the *quebracho* industry: *quebracho* logs were first exported in 1888 whilst the great *quebracho*-extract factories of Guillermina and Puerto Tirol were opened in the first decade of the present century. As the *quebracho* forests stretched in a belt parallel to but some 80 km west of the river Paraná, there was a need for railways, which were later able to serve the agricultural colonization of the cutover land. After 1910 other lines were constructed from Resistencia and Formosa directly into the interior to stimulate colonization, which was encouraged by the government in 1923 at a time of high world cotton prices. Holdings of cropland were limited to 100 ha and their operators expected to become owners. Many settlers were from neighbouring Paraguay and others were immigrants from Germanic and Slavonic lands; between 1914 and 1937 the population of Chaco Territory rose from 46,000 to 335,000 and the number of small farms from 290 to 14,940.

For much of the nineteenth century Misiones had been the subject of dispute, especially with Paraguay. When the latter finally renounced all claims in 1876, the area came under the control of Corrientes province which rapidly sold most of it to private individuals. The holdings were defined by the length of their frontage on to the rivers Paraná or Uruguay and by the depth of their penetration of the interior. Re-survey at the turn of the century revealed that nearly a third of this thickly forested territory, mainly along the watershed, still remained public. New colonization laws favouring the small settler and the arrival of the Buenos Aires–Posadas railway along the southern border in 1912 facilitated massive immigration, largely of intelligent and skillful German-speaking peoples, after 1920. For the large landowner no extensive pastoral economy was feasible and after deforestation only intensive plantation farming or colonization schemes could provide a satisfactory return. Both required considerable management, and the former in addition depended on the availability of manual labour. Neighbouring Paraguay furnished a continuing, if erratic, supply whilst European colonists were also willing to do plantation work while establishing their own farms. Hence plantations and colonies, both of them devoted to tree crop production, were often developed in association, especially along the east bank of the Paraná. The population of Misiones rose only slightly between 1895 and 1914, from 33,000 to 54,000, but by 1947 over 246,000 persons lived in the Territory.

In Uruguay an absence of public lands precluded official colonization,

---

[1] Formosa was part of Chaco Territory until 1884. They are still known together as The Chaco.

but several private ventures were undertaken, leading to extensive wheat cultivation.

Demographic changes 1850–1930

Over the whole period the total Argentine population rose from about 1 million to almost 12 million and the net immigration exceeded 4 million (Fig. 9.2b). Between 1855 and 1914 no province except Catamarca failed to double its population but the proportion living in the north-west (excluding Córdoba) fell from 32 per cent to 13 per cent; despite immigration, the share of Cuyo, Córdoba and Mesopotamia also fell from 40 per cent to 26 per cent. Of the provinces showing an increased share, those that were non-existent in 1855 (The Chaco, Misiones, La Pampa and Patagonia) still only accounted for 4 per cent. The great increase came in the core of the Pampas: the share of Santa Fé rose from under 4 per cent to over 11 per cent, that of Buenos Aires province from under 17 per cent to over 20 per cent, and that of Greater Buenos Aires[1] from 8 per cent to nearly 26 per cent; their absolute population rose from 316,000 to 4,543,000 (Fig. 9.1).

The role of internal migration in these major regional changes was not very great: although many of the older provinces had a fifth of their sons living elsewhere in 1914, most had simply moved to neighbouring provinces, especially to Mendoza, Tucumán and Córdoba. Of the capital's million and a half residents only 141,000 were born elsewhere in Argentina and of these only 37,000 did not come from the adjacent provinces of Buenos Aires, Santa Fé and Entre Ríos.

The proportion of urban[2] population to total population increased from 28·6 per cent to 52·7 per cent during the period 1869–1914. Although agriculture was booming it used labour efficiently: beef cattle in fenced pastures required little supervision, arable farming was mechanized and the climate rendered unnecessary the expenditure of labour on spreading fertilizers or making hay. The growing urban share was not simply due to the expansion of Greater Buenos Aires (whose share rose from 13·6 to 25·8 per cent), for the other towns grew equally fast (from 15·0 per cent to 26·9 per cent). Salient among these was Rosario, whose population rose from 23,000 to 223,000. It had already surpassed the provincial capital in 1847 and still retains the distinction of being the only large city in Latin America which is bigger than the capital of the province in which it is situated.

The part played by immigration was unique in the western hemisphere. During the decades 1881–90 and 1901–10 an annual net inflow equal to between 2 and 3 per cent of the existing population gave Argentina the

[1] Greater Buenos Aires includes the Federal capital and the contiguous urban divisions of Buenos Aires province.
[2] A town is defined as a population centre with over 2000 inhabitants.

highest intensity of immigration ever recorded in the New World (Fig. 9.2a). This is reflected in the percentage of foreign-born inhabitants, which rose from 12 in 1869 to 26 in 1895 and reached a peak of 30 in 1914.

Among the immigrants a distinction must be drawn between those from adjacent South American republics and those from Europe (Fig. 9.2b). The immigrant neighbours increased steadily in number but in the period 1869–1914 their share of the total foreign-born population fell from 20 to 8 per cent. Over three-quarters of them simply moved into those Argentine provinces bordering upon their native land and in some cases they played an important role in provincial growth: thus in 1914, 70 per cent of the population of Formosa was Paraguayan, 48 per cent of Tierra del Fuego and 41 per cent of Neuquén were Chilean, 38 per cent of Misiones was Brazilian or Paraguayan and 20 per cent of Jujuy was Bolivian. In contrast, few migrated to the federal capital (scarcely 5 per cent of its foreign-born) and most of these came from neighbouring Uruguay.

The pattern of immigration from Europe was very different: 3·4 million immigrants from overseas entered and remained in Argentina in the period 1857–1930. The net inflow rose sharply in the 1880s to a peak of 178,000 in 1889. The crisis of 1890 caused a net outflow in 1891 and reduced movement for over a decade, but the early twentieth century witnessed an all-time record net inflow of over 200,000 in 1910. After a large outflow during the First World War the 1920s saw renewed immigration.

Argentina's role in European emigration during the period 1850–1930 was (jointly with Canada) second only to that of the U.S.A., taking a tenth of all emigrants to the latter's six-tenths, but her importance varied with time. In the mid-nineteenth century most emigrants were Britons and Germans destined chiefly for English speaking lands. By the turn of the century 30 per cent were from Italy – 17 million left in 1876–1926 – almost equal numbers going to the United States, Argentina and Brazil. Spaniards emigrated almost exclusively to Argentina and she was also favoured by many refugees from the political disturbances of eastern Europe, especially Jews and Poles. Throughout the period Italians and Spaniards (in the ratio of five to three) represented about 80 per cent of all immigrants into Argentina (Fig. 9.2b). Many other Italians provided harvest labour in Argentina during the southern summer and in Italy, France and Germany in the following half-year. Between 1890 and 1914 this *golondrina* (swallow) migration was facilitated by return fares as low as £10. Although immigration was officially encouraged, the local attitude can be illustrated by the competition held in 1896 to design a ship able to carry live cattle to Europe and immigrants on the return.

The agriculturally developing Pampa provinces (Buenos Aires, Santa Fé, Entre Ríos, Córdoba and La Pampa) received 57 per cent of the 2·1

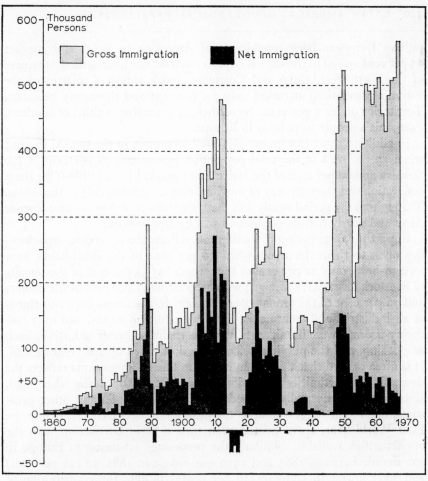

Fig. 9.2 (a) Argentina: annual immigration 1857–1967

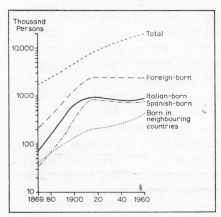

(b) Argentina: contribution of major
immigrant groups to total population
1869–1960

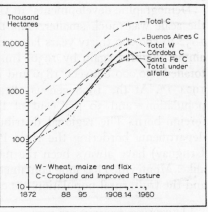

(c) Argentina: expansion of the
cultivated area

million European-born inhabitants of Argentina in 1914, and another 33 per cent stayed in the capital city. In contrast, the long-settled provinces of the north-west, Cuyo and Corrientes (with almost a quarter of the nation's population) attracted only 7·5 per cent and the newly colonized Territories under 2 per cent. Nevertheless, more than a third of southern Patagonia's people were born in Europe.

In addition most Europeans preferred to remain in the towns: in 1914 when 53 per cent of the total population was urban, 78 per cent of the Spanish and 69 per cent of the Italian immigrants lived in towns; for them emigration was the only way of moving from the countryside to the towns. Throughout the period nearly half the Europeans stayed in Greater Buenos Aires and nearly half its population was European-born.

In part the distribution of immigrants reflects the economic opportunities open to them. In 1914, when 30 per cent of the inhabitants were foreign-born, only 22 per cent of the owners but 34 per cent of the tenants of livestock farms were foreign; with crop farms 41 per cent of the owners and 72 per cent of the tenants were foreign. In the towns over two-thirds of all industrial and commercial firms were foreign-owned and over half their personnel were immigrants, whereas traditional craft industries, such as clothing, and the public services were dominated by native-born staff. It is often argued that this urban concentration of immigrants reflects the decreasing opportunities for landownership after 1890; on the other hand, since migration normally responds rapidly to economic and other pressures, one might suggest that, as the peak inflow occurred just before the First World War, there existed even then a basic satisfaction with the opportunities available. Similarly the percentage returning to Europe in any decade between 1861 and 1910 was lowest in 1881–90 (26 per cent) and next lowest in 1901–10 (38 per cent) – despite the contribution of *golondrina* migration to the latter.

Demographic developments[1] in Uruguay followed a similar pattern, but the scale was much smaller. The total population rose from 132,000 in 1852 to 500,000 thirty years later; by 1908 it exceeded 1 million and had almost doubled again by 1930. Immigrants, mainly Italian and Spanish, totalled 650,000 between 1836 and 1926 and a quarter of these arrived in 1904–13. At the 1908 census 181,000 or 17 per cent of the national population – and 30 per cent of the population of Montevideo – were foreign-born. The regional distribution has changed but little, for the departments bordering the river Plate (and to a less extent the river Uruguay) have always been the most attractive to native and foreigner alike. Montevideo has long contained a quarter to a third of the population and the truly rural population has constituted but a minority.

[1] Uruguayan censuses are very defective and there were none at all between 1908 and 1963!

Capital investment in the economic infrastructure

Capital investment on an unprecedented scale afforded the means by which immigrant labour could be harnessed to the Argentine soil to produce the agricultural revolution. By 1913, 75 per cent of foreign capital invested in Argentina was in the nation's infrastructure: in railways, port installations, public utilities and irrigation works. Another 20 per cent was in trade and finance, in banking and import/export houses, merchanting services, loan agencies and processing industries, while only 5 per cent was in agriculture itself. In a word, one twelfth of the world's foreign investments (to a great extent British) was directed solely towards the lubricating of the machine of Argentine agricultural production. In 1857 Britain's investments were worth under £3 million, but by 1890 they had risen to £175 million and by 1910 exceeded £290 million.

The development of the railway network, mostly British-owned, at first went hand in hand with the advance of the frontier, Rosario and Buenos Aires providing separate and unconnected termini for most routes (Fig. 9.3 (a). By the late 1880s Mendoza, Córdoba and the Santa Fé colonies were linked to Rosario, and Bahía Blanca to Buenos Aires, all by broad-gauge lines; Tucumán and Santiago del Estero, alone of the old centres of the north-west, were linked to Córdoba, but only by a narrow-gauge line. During the next thirty years the Buenos Aires and Pacific Railway soon gave southern Córdoba and Mendoza a direct route to the capital and Rosario was also quickly connected. More gradually the Buenos Aires Pampas became saturated with lines, for a cart-haul of more than 16 km to a railway station made wheat production unprofitable (Fig. 9.3 (b and c)). Rivalry with Chile over Patagonia also led to the early extension of the Southern system to Neuquén (1899) but the government line from Bahía Blanca to Bariloche took until the 1930s to complete. The north-west was slowly incorporated into a government-built narrow-gauge system, but no through route to the capital was provided until after 1910; similarly the skeletal standard-gauge network of Mesopotamia was not connected to Buenos Aires until 1908 and even then a ferry across the Paraná substituted for a bridge (and still does). Thus, by virtue of timing and gauge differences, the growth of Argentine railways worked to the disadvantage of the north-west, Patagonia and Mesopotamia and to the clear benefit of the city and province of Buenos Aires.

Although this pattern may have reflected a realistic appraisal of the economic potential of Argentina's different regions, railway construction by no means led automatically to a profitable flow of goods and passengers. The leading railway companies would buy estates, subdivide them and sell lots on instalments; in the absence at that time of adequate government services they ran agricultural advisory departments and even established experimental farms to discover the best varieties of crops and make them

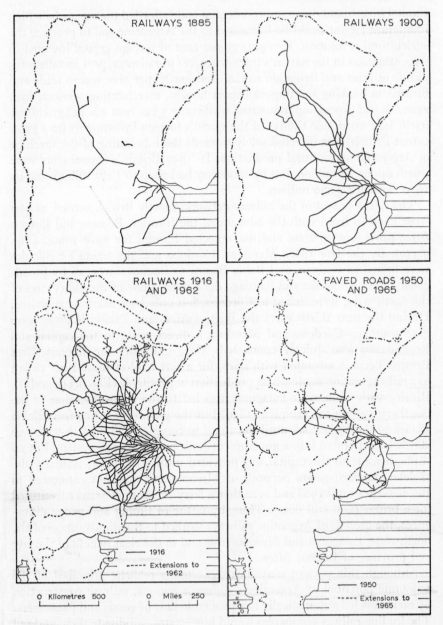

Fig. 9.3 Argentina: the development of roads and railways

available to growers. The Buenos Aires Great Southern Railway Company carried out irrigation works for the government along the Río Negro and then, for lack of any local enterprise, set up an organization to advise the fruit-growers, to handle collection and storage and to market the produce in Europe. Other companies independent of the railways also provided the farmer with a wide range of commercial, technical and financial services. 'Agency' firms, often owned and staffed by Britons, offered mortgage loans, handled farmers' legal and commercial business and even provided managers for *estancias*; wool and cereal producers were served in many ways by produce-purchasing firms, and every town had its distributors of agricultural machinery and medical requisites. As with other developments, these service firms tend to date from two periods: of the forty-three British firms established between 1860 and 1960 in part to provide such services, eighteen (especially the colonization companies) were founded in the 1880s and another fifteen in 1906–1912; the four founded in the intervening years were all meat-packing companies.

In Uruguay foreign capital was invested on a less extensive scale, but in similar fields, with several British companies operating in both republics.

The agricultural revolution

This began with the upgrading of the flocks of sheep and the breed most favoured was the Rambouillet or French merino. For thirty years, until the mid-1880s, the general flocks of the Pampas provinces became progressively more merino and their fine wools were exported in increasing quantities. From 7700 tons in 1850, wool exports rose to 55,000 tons by 1865, and 128,000 tons by 1885. One function of the less important cattle was to graze the natural pastures and, by consuming the coarser species, allow the finer grasses preferred by the sheep to dominate. The fencing of the Pampas was also vital to the process of upgrading. In 1876, 5000 tons of wire were imported (enough for an equivalent number of kilometres of fence); in 1892, 42,000 tons; and in 1907, 84,000 tons – by which time over a million kilometres of fencing had been erected.

But the course of events changed in the mid-1880s. The arrival in 1876 of *Le Frigorifique*, the French ship with freezing chambers, though hailed by far-sighted *estancieros*, was not followed up by France, and development of the frozen meat industry awaited the interest of English firms which by 1880 were initiating the industry in Australia. In 1883 The River Plate Fresh Meat Company built a *frigorífico* or meat-freezing plant at Campana and by 1907 another seven were in operation; except for one at Bahía Blanca all were situated on the south bank of the Paraná–Plate between La Plata and the Buenos Aires/Santa Fé border. At first sheep were preferred because the early equipment could handle the smaller carcass of the sheep more easily and because the quality of merino mutton was superior to that of *criollo* beef.

But the merino was not really a dual-purpose animal, nor had it ever been a healthy success on the wetter pastures of the older parts of Buenos Aires and of Entre Ríos. The coming of the *frigorífico* and the opening-up of Patagonia now allowed the drier Patagonian pastures to assume production of wool sheep, and the older areas near to the plants converted their flocks to larger dual-purpose breeds more suited to the physical and economic conditions. Lincolns, Romney Marsh and the Downland breeds were now in demand. The annual import of pedigree merinos fell from 380 head in the early 1880s to 37 by 1895, whilst the import of the English breeds rose from 550 to 4550. Between 1886 and 1907, 63,000 of the 67,000 pedigree sheep imported came from the United Kingdom.

Upgrading, however, was not proceeding at the same pace even on the Litoral. By 1907 less than 9 per cent of the Buenos Aires sheep were *criollo*, the rest being cross-bred or pedigree, but *criollos* still accounted for 41 per cent of the flocks of Entre Ríos and 84 per cent of those of Corrientes. Thirty years later, under 1 per cent of the sheep of Buenos Aires and Entre Ríos and less than 3 per cent of those of Corrientes were *criollo*, but the national average was still 6 per cent and in the five provinces of the Andean north-west, 83 per cent of the sheep were *criollo*.

Although the importance of sheep was initially enhanced by the coming of the *frigorífico*, beef was destined to replace mutton. Total flocks of sheep rose from 58 million in 1875 to 74 million in 1895 but thereafter declined rapidly to 43 million in 1914; since then numbers have usually ranged from 40 to 50 million. The Pampa provinces were largely responsible for this fall: the flocks of Buenos Aires alone declined from 53 million in 1895 to 19 million in 1914, and then to 14 million in 1930, and those of the four adjacent provinces fell from 16 million to 9 million, and then to 7 million. Conversely, Patagonia's flocks rose from nothing to nearly 2 million in 1895, 11 million in 1914, and 16 million in 1930. Northern Patagonia accounted for most in 1895 but since 1900 the settlement of southern Patagonia has made it Argentina's principal sheep region. By the end of the period a clear regional pattern of improved breeds had emerged (Fig. 9.4b).

Given such considerable changes, it is not surprising that exports of wool ceased to rise steadily, as they had up to 1885, and began to fluctuate between 100,000 and 200,000 tons a year. In 1930, 140,000 tons were exported and as yet little was consumed at home.

In Uruguay livestock-farming followed a similar sequence of developments but both timing and emphasis were different. Again the importance of sheep – and in particular the merino – began to grow after 1850, numbers rising from 800,000 in 1852 to a peak of over 26 million in 1908. A sharp decline to 11 million in 1916 then occurred, but thereafter numbers rose again to 21 million by 1930. Once more the advent of the *frigorífico* led to the rise of big, coarse-woolled Lincolns in preference to merino and merino-crosses, although, after the great European demand for frozen

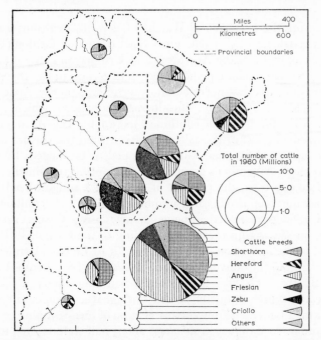

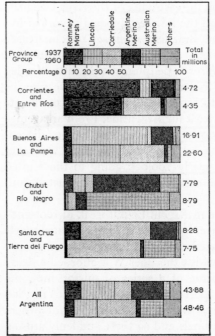

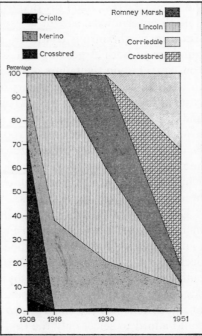

Fig. 9.4 (a) Argentina: cattle 1960, provincial distribution and breeds
(b) Argentina: sheep 1937 and 1960, regional distribution and breeds
(c) Uruguay: sheep breeds 1908–51, percentage change

mutton during the First World War had fallen off, dual-purpose animals of the Corriedale and Corriedale-cross types came into fashion (Fig. 9.4c). The development of the Argentine and Uruguayan cattle industry is a curiously protracted one. Upgrading began in earnest in the 1850s with the establishment of the first pedigree Shorthorn herds on the estates of a few leading Argentine *estancieros*. But it was an activity which bore little economic fruit, for *saladeros* continued to provide the main outlet and slaves consumed most of the salt meat. Even then the carcasses of many animals slaughtered for their hides continued to be wasted. Between the 1820s and 1890s Argentina's annual salt meat output remained constant at 30,000 to 40,000 tons, the product of over half a million head of cattle. In Uruguay the steep rise in cattle numbers from 1·9 to 6·6 million between 1852 and 1860 gave added impetus to new uses; Giebert's successful attempt at producing meat extract according to the formula of Baron von Liebig led to the formation in London in 1865 of Liebig's Extract of Meat Company[1] and to the conversion of the *saladero* at Fray Bentos to the new process. By the mid-1880s Liebig's was handling almost a fifth of the 780,000 cattle which annually passed through the Uruguayan *saladeros*, some of which benefited from the installation of meat-canning equipment. Of the score or so Uruguayan *saladeros* about half were located in Montevideo, and the rest, like Fray Bentos, on the east bank of the river Uruguay.

Both governments sought to expand the long-established export of live cattle to neighbouring countries, and Brazilian *saladeros* took increased numbers of both Argentine and Uruguayan beasts. The disappointment consequent upon the failure of *frigoríficos* to be interested in cattle also led to trials in 1889 with the export of live animals to Europe. Despite the costs of keep, the loss in weight (up to 150 kg) and the hazards of climate and disease, this proved a success, at least for Argentina. From an average export in the 1880s of under 100,000 head, bound chiefly for adjacent lands, numbers rose to over 200,000 by 1893 and averaged well over 300,000 for the rest of the decade, nearly 100,000 going to the United Kingdom. The need for fat, tame animals for this trade stimulated both breeding and fattening activities.

Exports were halved in 1900 when an Argentine outbreak of foot-and-mouth disease, introduced from France, led to the closing of British ports to live cattle. At the same time the French wool textile crisis caused a rapid decline in the profitability of sheep, whilst the Boer War afforded a ready outlet for frozen beef. Hence, by virtue of a series of misfortunes, the Argentine frozen beef trade began. Exports leaped from 9000 tons in 1899 to 25,000 tons in 1900 and 150,000 tons five years later. *Frigorífico* owners could afford to select only the best animals and so there suddenly arose a demand for high grade cattle and for alfalfa pastures on which the steers could be fattened. By 1907 frozen beef had replaced all other meat products

[1] Better known by its brand names, Lemco, Oxo and Fray Bentos.

in the pattern of Argentine exports (Table 9.1) and Argentina had replaced the U.S.A. as the largest provider of frozen beef to the British market.

TABLE 9.1   *Value of Argentine livestock exports 1887, 1897 and 1907*

Category	1887	1897	1907
	%	%	%
Salt beef	48	22	4
Live cattle	28	43	7
Live sheep	1	13	1
Meat extract	2	2	7
Meat flour	<1	<1	6
Frozen mutton	19	17	20
Frozen beef	<1	1	51
Preserved and other meats	1	2	3
Total value (million gold pesos)	5	12	27

The introduction of the chilling process in 1908 gave a further fillip to pasture improvement. Whereas cattle for frozen beef could be bought and killed at the cheapest time of the year and then stored until the market was favourable, chilling animals could only be killed forty to forty-five days before consumption in Britain. A steady demand meant a constant killing and a year-round supply of good quality animals, which could be produced only on artificial pastures. Whereas *saladero* fattening pastures had to be located near the riverside factory, *frigorífico* pastures, thanks to the network of railways, could now develop wherever physical conditions were best. North-western Buenos Aires, southern and eastern Córdoba and adjacent parts of La Pampa and Santa Fé, toegther with southern Entre Ríos, came to fill this role.

In Uruguay the first *frigorífico*, a locally financed one at Montevideo, was not installed until 1904 and growth only came with the construction of two more, United States-owned plants in 1911 and 1917. Chilling did not begin until 1921.

Nor did chilling become important in Argentina until the 1920s: during the 1910s exports of frozen beef averaged 350,000 tons per annum and chilled beef only 20,000. By the late 1920s, however, chilled beef exports had risen to 400,000 tons and frozen beef had fallen to 200,000 tons. By this time, too, both Argentina and Uruguay consumed more meat than they exported.

The roles of cattle and sheep in the livestock economy thus changed greatly after 1900. But, as with sheep, changes in the character of cattle-farming were essentially regional. By 1907, 55 per cent of Argentina's 29 million cattle (but 91 per cent of the cattle of Buenos Aires province) were cross-bred or pedigree animals, whereas 41 per cent of the cattle of

Entre Ríos were still *criollo*, as were 57 per cent in Santa Fé and 84 per cent in Corrientes. These differences were reflected in the later history of the *saladeros*: those in Buenos Aires had almost ceased by 1905, and plants in Entre Ríos were slowly declining, but Uruguayan *saladeros* maintained production until *c*. 1910. There thus developed the two patterns of Argentine cattle movement which have survived until recent years: within the Pampas, especially south and west of the river Paraná–Plate, improved cattle (chiefly Shorthorns) were reared, moved to fattening pastures and then to the eight riverside *frigoríficos*, while in Mesopotamia and the Chaco poorer animals were reared, moved south to better pastures and then into the *saladeros* of Entre Ríos or Uruguay. Although a few *saladeros* continued to operate for several decades, most of the Argentine trade began to concentrate on those two which were converted just before the First World War into multipurpose canning and extract factories: Colón, Liebig's factory on the Uruguay, drew its animals from eastern Mesopotamia, whilst Santa Elena, Bovril's plant north of Paraná city, tapped the resources of both shores of the Paraná.

In Uruguay upgrading began in earnest only in 1904, herds becoming dominantly Hereford (as in Mesopotamia) rather than Shorthorn, and numbers rose slowly to about 8 million. The hillier centre of the country became the rearing district and the loamy and loessic soils flanking the rivers Uruguay and Plate provided the best fattening pastures. The value of upgrading, apart from the quality of the meat, may be judged from the fact that *criollo* steers took five or six years to reach a weight of half a ton and then yielded only 40–50 per cent meat, whereas high grade animals took only three years and yielded 50–55 per cent meat.

The conversion of the Pampas from an almost purely pastoral landscape to one of the world's leading producers of cereals was the work of less than fifty years. In 1872 Argentina, over eleven times larger than the United Kingdom, had a cultivated area that was smaller than Lincolnshire. By 1900, thanks especially to the efforts of colonists in the northern Pampas, an area equal to half England was under cultivation, and by 1914, under the pressure of livestock farmers further south to plough up the land for improved grazing and fodder crops, almost 250,000 km² of land, an area greater than the whole of the United Kingdom, had come under the plough (Fig. 9.2c).

From the beginning of colonization wheat was the leading crop, occupying a quarter to a half of all cultivated land, and it was grown initially to replace imports from U.S.A., Chile and Australia; by 1875 regular wheat imports ceased and exports began, exceeding 100,000 tons for the first time in 1884 and reaching a million tons in 1893. Since 1904 exports have rarely fallen below 2 million tons. Despite the growth in wheat exports, an equal amount has usually been consumed at home, thanks partly to the growth in population, but also to the changes in diet with Italian immigration, and during the 1880s wheat consumption per head almost doubled. Flour was still a costly luxury in 1870 and in 1875 milling had to be protected for a time by tariffs to encourage its growth, but by 1895, 259 steam-driven mills were in operation, half of them in Santa Fé and Entre Ríos and more than a quarter in Buenos Aires. By 1914, however, Buenos Aires produced most of Argentina's wheat and flour. Flour exports regularly exceeded 1000 tons after 1878 and 10,000 tons after 1890, but the quality of the product, competition from other countries and tariff protection of foreign mills all helped to restrict Argentine exports to around 100,000 tons, first reached in 1904, with Brazil the leading purchaser.

In area, maize was the second crop usually occupying half as much land as wheat. Eventually it came to dominate the cereal lands of southern Santa Fé and adjacent parts of Buenos Aires when wheat moved to drier lands in Córdoba, La Pampa and southern Buenos Aires. Nevertheless, exports of maize were greater than those of wheat up to 1900 and closely paralleled them thereafter, Argentina becoming the world's leading exporter of the crop. As with wheat, half the maize produced played a role in the domestic economy, but as fodder rather than flour.

Before 1900, flax was of minor importance, but, as livestock farmers sought to improve their pastures through introducing tenants to the land on short three to five year contracts, flax proved especially suitable as a pioneer crop and as a final crop to be sown with the alfalfa which the estancieros so ardently desired. Throughout the period it was grown largely for export – Argentina being world leader – and for its linseed rather than its fibres. Although exports exceeded 100,000 tons for the first time only in 1894 they rose sharply to almost 900,000 tons by 1904, but not until 1920 did they regularly exceed a million tons.

The dominance of these three cereals in the pattern of Argentine agricultural production – in 1914, 13 out of 22 million ha of cultivated land were dedicated to them (Fig. 9.2c) – is partly to be explained by the rigid system of land tenure. Tenancy contracts frequently stipulated that only these crops should be grown, that rents were to be paid in kind – usually a third, but occasionally a half, of the harvest – and that the rest was to be sold through the landlord or his agent. The administration of tenanted lands was thus greatly simplified but at a considerable cost, economically as well as socially: at harvest time railways and ports became overloaded, delays ensued and inadequately stored cereals suffered from the rains. Other factors also contributed towards monoculture of cereals: farm labour on the Pampas was always in short supply, and cereal-growing was easily mechanized. Furthermore, immigrant farmers with a little capital could not afford both machinery and land, so tenant farming with machinery, a mobile investment, afforded a convenient opportunity. At times a shortage of tenants obliged the owner to become a true partner, providing the tenants with work animals, seed and credit for the acquisition of equipment, and himself investing in the fixed assets of fencing, wind pumps and buildings.

But the ultimate aim of tenant farming was usually the creation of artificial pastures of alfalfa on which the upgraded steers could be fattened for the *frigorífico* (Fig. 9.2c). In 1872 alfalfa was a crop grown chiefly in San Juan for feeding to cattle destined for export on foot to Chile. By 1922, the peak year, 8·5 million ha, or 40 per cent, of the cultivated area was devoted to this single plant and, with the needs of the livestock farmers satisfied, cereal production was on the decline.

As arable farming developed so largely as a by-product of the livestock industry, it is ironical that crops came to dominate the nation's export economy: their share of export values rose from 1 per cent in 1870, to 20 per cent in 1890, and 53 per cent by 1910 (Table 9.2), though it had fallen back to 42 per cent by 1919.[1]

TABLE 9.2 *Percentage composition of Argentine exports 1899 and 1910*

	1899	1910
Livestock products	62	43
including: Live animals	5	1
Meat	3	10
Hides	13	11
Wool	39	16
Crop products	35	53
including: Cereals	32	50

The revolution in agricultural exports was made possible by the long-term character of the many kinds of credit which Argentina received – government loans, railway investments made years before routes became profitable, mortgages granted to farmers for fencing their lands, repeated postponements of debts owed by settlers to colonization companies or in the form of profits ploughed back by farming companies. Although some companies eventually reaped handsome profits, for ten to twenty years many declared no dividends at all or a mere 0·5 per cent.

Uruguay, in contrast, did not experience the same cereal revolution, for no symbiotic development of cattle-raising and cereal-farming took place. With a higher rainfall and more nutritious natural grazing than the Pampas, Uruguay did not need alfalfa for fattening her cattle, though oats were often grown as winter forage. Subdivision of fields for the better control of breeding and grazing led to the redundancy of many herdsmen at the beginning of the present century and hence to a rural exodus.

Nevertheless, the flat fertile lands adjacent to the river Plate gradually became the scene of more intensive agricultural activities: of wheat-

[1] Non-agricultural exports – minerals and manufactures – were never of note.

growing for the domestic market and of dairying near Montevideo. Flax-growing also expanded rapidly from 1000 ha in 1899 to 150,000 ha in 1930, linseed becoming the third export after meat and wool. Many farmers were share-croppers but their four-year tenancy contracts were renewable, making for a greater stability of the rural population.

Like Uruguay, Argentina's development in the period 1853–1930 was not geared solely to production of meat and cereals for world markets. Agricultural and industrial production for domestic markets was growing and other crops were beginning to find a place among the exports. Outstanding were the sugar and wine industries. In 1855 the provinces of Tucumán and Salta had only 223 ha under sugar cane and produced only 400 tons of sugar. The arrival of the railway and the ability of the sugar mill owners to pressure the government into imposing protective tariffs together afforded the necessary stimulus. By the mid-1870s about 2500 ha were under cultivation and sugar production touched 3000 tons; by 1914 over 100,000 ha were in production and output exceeded 250,000 tons, most of it from Tucumán. With high production costs in a marginal climate exports did not succeed but the home market was satisfied.

The expansion of the Argentine wine industry, centred in Mendoza since early colonial times, similarly owed much to tariff protection and also to the influx of Italian settlers. From 6400 ha in 1890, Mendoza's area under vines grew to 45,000 ha by 1910 and exceeded 100,000 ha by 1934.

The production of cotton, although native to the country, expanded only with the rise in world prices after the First World War and the colonization of the Chaco: The 400 ha under cultivation in 1863 were increased to only 3000 in 1917 but jumped by 1925 to over 100,000, and Argentina became the world's seventh largest cotton producer.

Industry in expanding Argentina was, with the exception of meat-packing, typically small scale and geared to the processing of local agricultural produce for the manufacture of simple consumer goods to satisfy domestic demand. Some branches were stimulated by tariffs – e.g. the corrugating and galvanizing of imported iron sheets – but most were the work of enterprising immigrants who had no power to urge protection. By 1913, 71 per cent of goods consumed in Argentina were manufactured within the country: 91 per cent of foodstuffs, 88 per cent of clothing and 86 per cent of printed matter were locally produced, but only 38 per cent of chemicals and 33 per cent of metallurgical products; only 23 per cent of the cloth consumed was of national manufacture.

The Paraguayan exception

While sporadic attempts were made to develop the Paraguayan economy before the war of 1865–70, that catastrophe effectively halted them. Before the war, most people were tenants of state land, living in the central zone, which stretches for 100 km east and south of the capital; after the war most of the private land also reverted to the state through the inability of its occupiers to prove title to it. In the closing years of the century, however, huge tracts of the public domain were sold or leased to mainly foreign enterprises, which sought to exploit the forestry resources, develop livestock farming or, less often, establish colonies; thus the Casado Company of Argentina acquired a portion of the Chaco as big as Belgium. Sometimes former tenants were dispossessed, more often they were welcome to remain as largely self-sufficient tenants or squatters who supplied casual labour to the new owners. Most important of the new enterprises was the exploitation of the *quebracho* forests along the west bank of the river Paraguay. As in Argentina, the tree was initially felled for its very resistant timber (*quebracho* = axe-breaker), but at the turn of the century it became increasingly valued for its tannin content. Railways were built – especially by the Casado Company – into the Chaco forests and extract factories were constructed at their river terminals north of Concepción. To the east the forests of the Paraná plateau were exploited by collectors of wild yerba who gathered 10,000 tons a year in the 1880s, but from 1909 supplies came increasingly from large plantations.

Further south, in the often marshy lowlands of the Asunción–Encarnación–Corrientes triangle, great cattle *estancias* were established. Here, Mulhall reported in 1885, *criollo* cattle fattened better than on the more frost- and drought-prone lands of Argentina, but to little purpose, for no meat-processing factory was established and many beasts were exported, often illegally, to Argentina or Brazil. Nevertheless, hide exports ranked third in the 1880s.

The development of commercial crop farming and of associated processing industries depended largely on the efforts of immigrant settlers, and these were few. Between 1880 and 1958 only 55,000 foreigners settled in rural Paraguay and a further 12,000 in the towns. Chief among them were Germans who founded colonies near Asunción and Concepción in the 1880s and near Encarnación in 1900. Some colonists deliberately sought physical isolation in which to develop their political or religious Utopias, among them the Australian socialists who settled near Villarrica in 1893 and the Mennonites who in 1927 acquired over 100,000 ha of Casado land in the middle of the Chaco. Permanence of settlement at first depended upon subsistence farming but appraisals of commercial opportunities led to the development of specialized crops. The settlers of the Paraná forests, like their cousins in nearby Misiones, chose to grow yerba maté and, later, tung. Settlers nearer to Asunción preferred to specialize in market-gardening for the capital.

For the small farmer, whether immigrant or native, commercial success depended on his living near railway or river; the rest, including the majority of the native population, were restricted to at best a peasant economy catering for tiny country towns. Even the traditional growing and manufacture of cotton declined when cheaper, mass-produced imports competed in the urban market. And the towns, in any case, still accounted for only a fifth of Paraguay's population of under half a million in 1900.

NEW DIRECTIONS FOR ARGENTINA AND URUGUAY 1930–

By 1930 the basic changes had been largely completed: the rail network had been finished, the agricultural area was expanding only in the remote north-east, the creation of the alfalfa pastures had achieved the first stage in the intensification of land use on the Pampas, and a pattern of regional specialization of agricultural production had been established. With the depression of the 1930s, overseas markets declined; multilateral trading ceased, industrial countries raised tariff barriers to protect their own agriculture, and the growth of cheap Argentine exports, made possible by the technologies of freezing and chilling and the mechanized production of cereals, was at an end. With poor prospects for material advancement, the flow of immigrants dried up.

Although the old conditions for continued progress had now vanished, new conditions favoured industrialization. The prices of manufactured imports fell, but earnings from agricultural exports declined still more. Argentina's large urban population was unable to import the consumer goods it desired and native manufacturing was thus encouraged to expand.

During the Second World War, the belligerents' demand for meat and raw materials boosted export earnings and the nation's reserves grew, from $400 million before the war to $1700 million in 1946. The shortage of manufactured imports stimulated domestic industrial expansion. But most industrial raw materials came from the interior, not the Pampas, and a rural exodus began from its depressed areas, providing labour for the manufacturing industries of the nearby towns, especially Buenos Aires. After the war, cereals were again in high demand but Europe could not yet satisfy Argentina's needs for industrial goods. Nor did the traditional agriculture of the Pampas recover. For the rise to power of Perón in the mid-1940s was supported by the urban proletariat and food prices were held down for their benefit. The government also retained much of agriculture's export earnings to subsidize the growing imports of fuel and raw materials required by industry. In 1947 blocked sterling reserves were used to nationalize the British-owned railways and shortly afterwards foreign debts were repaid: foreign investments fell from $3700 million in 1931 (their peak) to $1300 million in 1949, and Argentina's reserves dropped to $500 million. Apart from the boost to national prestige, nationalization also cut the annual outgoings on the transfer of profits from $300–500 million in 1930–44 to a mere $10–20 million in the early 1950s. But a great opportunity was missed with consequences from which Argentina has not yet recovered: the Industrial Revolution had largely taken place without benefit of the best capital goods from the North Atlantic countries; as a result, industry was inefficient, undercapitalized and labour-intensive, and was conducted mainly in thousands of tiny workshops.

By 1950 conditions had altered once more and the misfortune of opportunities lost was realized: the national market for consumer goods was now satisfied, at least for those which did not require heavy capital investment. Demand for imported fuels and semi-manufactured goods continued to rise but agricultural export earnings declined and high-cost manufactures could find no export market. The decline in agricultural exports resulted from the failure of the Pampas to increase their productivity and from the rising proportion of agricultural produce which was destined for the well-paid urban groups that were now among the best-fed in the world. During the 1950s Perón and succeeding governments sought by various means to correct the imbalance and halt the inflation which caused the cost of living to rise sixteenfold. Towards the end of the 1950s foreign capital was once more welcomed, to develop Argentina's native fuel resources and new, heavy industries. Since 1963 greater exports of beef and wheat, and lower fuel imports have at last helped to produce a healthier balance, but only at the political cost of restricting domestic consumption by such devices as decreeing meatless (i.e. beefless) days. The outbreak of foot-and-mouth disease in Britain in 1967, which led to a ban on imports of meat on the bone from South America, was a set-back to exports of better grades of beef, but may in the long term encourage the further development of the Argentine meat industry, as did the restrictions of 1900. Some *frigoríficos* have already begun to export pre-packed boneless beef.

The agricultural problems of Argentina

The basic problem of Argentina's economy since the 1930s has been agriculture's failure to keep pace with the dual demand of satisfying a rising domestic consumption and of providing substantial foreign earnings. In 1950–64 the volume of agricultural production *per capita* was only 75–80 per cent of what it had been in the 1920s, and the proportion available for export had fallen from over 50 per cent to under 25 per cent. Argentina's share of world trade in agricultural commodities dwindled alarmingly. In the mid-1930s Argentina was responsible for 70 per cent of the maize exports of the world, 63 per cent of the meat, 21 per cent of the wheat and 12 per cent of the wool; by 1960 these shares had fallen to 23, 29, 8 and 8 per cent respectively.

Growth before 1930 had been largely achieved by the effective occupation of more land and by the introduction of more labour. More recently the course of colonization and immigration has suffered severe checks and future prospects for growth in these fields seem limited.

Colonization prospects

The only areas now available for new settlement are subtropical forests or semi-arid scrub where successful farming depends upon costly soil conservation or irrigation works. In Chaco province the continuing expansion of settlement for the cultivation of cotton carried the population from 335,000 in 1937 to 549,000 in 1960, but by then growth was levelling out as squatters began to abandon exhausted lands. Further east, in Misiones, there are moderately fertile basaltic soils on which colonies of small farms continue to grow. The population reached 379,000 in 1960, but three-quarters of the land is still covered by natural forest, most of it in huge estates. The only publicly owned forested areas in Argentina still awaiting clearance and colonization are 1·5 million ha of tropical lowland east of Salta, not far from the Tucumán to Santa Cruz (Bolivia) Railway.

The greatest reserves of land might seem to lie in the drier parts. Two-thirds of the national territory cannot be cultivated without irrigation and only 4 per cent (1,100,000 ha) is so provided at present: 500,000 ha in Cuyo, 400,000 ha in the north-west, and 100,000 ha in Patagonia. But present schemes fully use the supply of rivers at minimum flow; hence future plans depend on artificial storage, which could bring a further 1,400,000 ha into use, 30 per cent of it along the hardly tapped river Bermejo in eastern Salta, and another 30 per cent beside the partly developed Colorado and Negro in northern Patagonia.

Changing patterns of population

By 1967 the total Argentine population had risen to 23 million, but since 1960 its annual rate of increase has averaged only 1·6 per cent, among the lowest in Latin America. With a birth-rate of 21·5 per 1000, a death-rate of 8·2 per 1000 and male and female life expectations of 64 and 70 years, Argentina has demographic characteristics similar to those of 'developed' countries.

Between 1914 and 1960 the only provinces to increase their share of total population were those of the northern frontier and of the western frontier from San Juan southwards (from 11 to 17 per cent) and Greater Buenos Aires, which rose to 35 per cent. All the rest, and particularly the Pampa provinces, declined relatively, though no province had an absolute decline (Fig. 9.1d).

By 1960 town-dwellers numbered 14·8 million, or 74 per cent of the population, a rise of 4·8 million in thirteen years and 10·6 million in forty-six years. About 9 million were concentrated along the south-western bank of the Paraná-Plate in Santa Fé (260,000), Rosario (670,000), Greater Buenos Aires (6,740,000) and La Plata (330,000) and in the smaller towns in between; a further 3 million resided in other Pampa towns, including Córdoba (590,000), Bahiá Blanca and Mar del Plata (150,000 each). The rest of the country had only two large cities, Mendoza (about 350,000) and Tucumán (270,000). Whilst the metropolis overshadowed all other cities, its share of the urban population actually fell from 48·9 per cent to 46·4 per cent between 1914 and 1960.

Although the Argentine countryside is not overpopulated, rural migrants move to the cities and especially to the metropolis in search of a higher standard of living – better jobs and better health and education facilities. Thus, for example, of children who began school in 1956, 64 per cent completed the seven primary grades in Greater Buenos Aires, but only 17 per cent did so in the Chaco (Fig. 9.7a). The federal capital also had forty-six doctors for every 10,000 inhabitants in 1963, whereas no province had more than sixteen and most had fewer than six.

Yet depopulation of the countryside is of quite recent origin: between 1914 and 1947 not a single province recorded an absolute fall in its rural population, but between 1947 and 1960 rural population fell from 5,960,000 to 5,250,000, mainly in the provinces of Buenos Aires, Santa Fé and Córdoba. In contrast, the rural areas of the northern frontier provinces and of Tucumán, Mendoza and San Juan actually gained 227,000 people.

As always in Argentina, population movements account very largely for the demographic changes observed, but in recent years internal migration has become more important than immigration from abroad. In 1914, 30 per cent of the population had been born abroad; by 1960 only 13 per cent were immigrants, whereas 17 per cent had moved from another province and many of the 70 per cent still in the province of their birth had moved from countryside to town. As in the nineteenth century, most interprovincial migration was for only short distances: almost half the migrants moved only to the next province, with Mendoza, the provinces of the northern frontier and those of the Pampa heartland gaining at the expense of their neighbours. A further third of the migrants moved to or from Greater Buenos Aires, the inflow of 1,640,000 far exceeding the outflow of 460,000; as before, most of the incomers hailed from the nearby Pampa provinces.

The flow of immigrants has changed greatly in both number and origin: it declined (Fig. 9.2a) during the Depression and war years, rose thereafter with the arrival of refugees, only to decline once more. In 1960 three-tenths of the foreign-born population were from Italy and a similar proportion from Spain, but neighbouring countries had doubled their share since 1914 to 17 per cent (Fig. 9.2b). Italians and Spaniards now prefer to migrate to western Europe or to English-speaking lands outside Europe rather than to South America. Indeed, the European settler without adequate capital is no longer as welcome as formerly, although the Argentine government has made generous offers of land to French and Belgian refugee farmers from Algeria and the Congo. 'Faced with the demand for land by our own tenant farmers, by farmers' sons without land

and by farm labourers', advised the Federal Investment Council in its second report on Agricultural and Industrial Development (1963, vol. 2, p. 53), 'every priority must be given to satisfying their aspirations . . . to landownership'.

Instead the tide of immigrants, rich and poor, now flows from the surrounding nations. By 1960, 155,000 Paraguayans, 118,000 Chileans, 89,000 Bolivians, 56,000 Uruguayans and 49,000 Brazilians were living in Argentina, and subsequently, between 1962 and 1967, a further net inflow of 125,000 Paraguayans, 45,000 Chileans and 41,000 Bolivians occurred, though Uruguayans have also moved homewards. In addition, there is an even greater seasonal inflow of harvest labour.

Whatever their origin, immigrants appear loath to move far from their point of entry. In 1960, 64 per cent of the European-born lived in Greater Buenos Aires and 26 per cent in the three main Pampa provinces; in contrast, only 26 per cent of Latin American immigrants lived in the metropolis, whereas 62 per cent were in provinces contiguous to their homelands. Even in areas well known for their recent colonization by Europeans, such as Misiones, the Chaco and Patagonia, most immigrants still come from adjacent lands.

In brief, the regional pattern of Argentina's population movements in 1960 presented new features as well as old: Greater Buenos Aires and Mendoza continued to attract people from near and far at both national and international levels; sparsely settled Patagonia continued to depend heavily on incomers from Chile and all parts of Argentina; in the colonial north-west, Catamarca, La Rioja and Santiago del Estero suffered a continuing and serious exodus. Other north-western provinces, however (Salta and Jujuy), experienced a rejuvenation, and, like Formosa, Chaco and Misiones, attracted people from adjacent provinces and nations to their countryside. Elsewhere, the core of the Pampas witnessed a tremendous rural exodus coupled with an even greater urban growth, whilst along the periphery of the Pampas only the rural loss took place.

The stagnation of Argentine agriculture?

With the rural depopulation of the Pampas and the sluggish pace of land settlement agricultural output appears to have stagnated; increased production must now come mainly from the improved productivity of both labour and land.

During the first thirty years of the century crop production rose by 190 per cent, and livestock production by 203 per cent, and the area of improved land rose from 7·3 million to 27·2 million ha. Between 1930–4 and 1960–4, crop and livestock production increased by only 35 per cent and 25 per cent respectively, failing to keep up with the growth of population, and the area under crops and permanent grassland, scarcely rose at all, reaching 27·4 million ha. Improved land in 1960 occupied only 16 per cent of the 175 million ha of farmland; a further 16 per cent was woodland, scrub or waste, and the rest remained in natural pasture. The five Pampa provinces of Buenos Aires, La Pampa, Córdoba, Santa Fé and Entre Ríos still account for almost 90 per cent of the improved land.

Furthermore crop production on the Pampas underwent a long decline in favour of more extensive pastoral farming (Table 9.3).

TABLE 9.3   *Use of improved land in the five Pampa provinces*

	1933–4	1959–60
Fodder crops and grass (million ha)	4·9	13·3
Other crops (million ha)	20·2	11·3

During the 1920s and 1930s, cereal farming had been in the ascendant, record areas being devoted to wheat in 1928–9 (9·2 million ha) and 1938–9 (8·6 million ha), to maize in 1935–6 (7·6 million ha) and 1939–40 (7·2 million ha), and to flax in 1936–7 (3·5 million ha), whereas cattle numbers in the Pampas had declined from a peak of 28 million in 1922 to around 24 million in 1937. During and immediately after the war, cereal production fell and livestock farming expanded; despite encouragement during the 1950s, the area devoted to wheat remained static at 5–6 million ha, to maize at 2–3 million ha and to flax at only 1 million ha. The area under maize in the famous district west of and within 150 km of Rosario was more than halved and its population fell by 7 per cent between 1947 and 1960.

In contrast the expansion of livestock farming carried the cattle herds of the Pampas up to 35 million by 1960 (the rest of the country accounting for 9 million head, as in 1937 and 1922. The weight of cattle slaughtered rose from about 1·7 million tons in the late 1930s to 2·4 million tons twenty years later. But the density of cattle and sheep fell, from 1·0 cattle per ha in 1937 to 0·9/ha in 1960 (1 head of cattle = 5 sheep).

Despite the general extensification of agriculture in the period 1930–60, a number of improvements have taken place: the quality of the livestock has been progressively raised, mechanization has increased labour productivity, and intensively grown 'industrial' crops have risen in importance compared with cereals. Much of this change has taken place *outside* the Pampas.

Improving the quality of the cattle benefits the farmer in at least two ways: better prices are obtained and steers are ready for slaughter at an earlier age, thus indirectly increasing the productivity of the pastures. The best export prices are fetched for chilled beef and the superior grades of frozen beef which come wholly from steers of 'good' breeds (Hereford, Angus and Shorthorn); less expensive is the poorer frozen beef which comes chiefly from cows of good breed, whilst the lowest prices are fetched by canning-grade steers and cows of inferior stock (especially the native *criollo* breed). Evidence of the steady improvement of herds comes from the declining importance of *criollo* beasts which accounted for 35 per cent of all cattle in 1914, 20 per cent in 1937 and 10 per cent in 1960. Again, of the cattle killed in the decades 1935–44 and 1955–64, the percentage of one- to two-year-old steers rose from 6·2 to 10·9, whereas that of older steers fell from 47·6 to 41·2. The quality of cattle in the five Pampa provinces was already high (only 5 per cent were *criollo* in 1937) and breeding improvements were most marked elsewhere: in the plains provinces to the north and west the *criollo* percentage fell between 1937 and 1960 from 53 to 33 (Fig. 9.4a). Further proof of improvement on the northern plains comes from the recent experience of the two firms, Bovril and Liebig's, whose Entre Ríos canning factories earlier in the century provided competing outlets for the low grade animals reared in the north. Upgrading of the herds, encouraged by the companies' own *estancias*, progressively reduced the supply of canning-grade animals to such an extent that in 1965 both factories were converted into *frigoríficos* capable of chilling and freezing as well as canning (Table 9.4).

TABLE 9.4 *Steers graded in Entre Ríos factories*

Year	Grade: Chilled	Frozen continental	Canning
1943	% 4·3	18·9	76·8
1953	% 14·0	66·4	19·6
1963	% 21·4	65·9	12·7

Yet the northern provinces are still the source of most lower grade animals slaughtered in the *frigoríficos* and factories, as can be seen from Table 9.5, which also affords evidence of the scope for further improvement.

Unfortunately, as the *criollo* strain of the general herds was progressively replaced by that of temperate beef breeds, the animals' resistance to the tick- and fly-borne diseases encountered in the humid subtropical conditions of the extreme north-east declined. In 1938 the manager of Liebig's Garruchos *estancia*, Finch, introduced a Zebu strain to the Hereford herds, leading to improved health without loss of quality; subsequently the Zebu-cross has spread slowly south and westwards as farmers who once favoured pure-breds came to appreciate the merits of hybrid vigour (Fig. 9.4a).

A more important change of breeds since the war has affected the Pampa herds whose dominantly Shorthorn characteristics are being bred out as the Aberdeen Angus strain spreads: the latter is an earlier maturing producer

TABLE 9.5   *Provincial origin of steers purchased by frigoríficos and factories 1964*

	Chilled			Frozen continental	Canning		Chilled			Frozen continental	Canning
Grade	1	2	3	4	5 6		1	2	3	4	5 6
Province	%						%				
Buenos Aires	39	37	20	4	— —	100	63	53	32	9	1 3
La Pampa	38	39	20	3	— —	100	9	8	4	1	— —
Córdoba	25	39	29	7	— —	100	5	7	6	2	1 1
Entre Ríos	13	24	40	22	1 —	100	13	21	39	31	13 14
Santa Fé	20	24	24	30	2 —	100	11	11	13	23	21 20
Corrientes	—	1	25	68	5 1	100	—	—	6	25	27 13
Chaco	—	—	9	74	13 4	100	—	—	—	4	11 17
Formosa	—	—	1	67	26 6	100	—	—	—	5	28 32

| | | | | | | 100 | 100 | 100 | 100 | 100 | 100 |

Million kg of meat: 47·6   54·1   48·7   34·0   2·2   0·5

of the lean beef that is now preferred to the fatter meat of the Short-horn.

Other cattle improvements have been achieved through vigorous government campaigns to control and eradicate tick fever and foot-and-mouth disease, but brucellosis and bovine tuberculosis remain to be tackled.

Sheep farming, too, has undergone changes not so much through general upgrading, for even in 1937 only 6 per cent of the sheep were of *criollo* strain, as through the adoption of superior breeds more suited to the regional environments (Fig. 9.4b). Among the dual-purpose breeds, Lincolns and Romney Marshes have declined in favour of Corriedales, whose wool is fine cross-bred rather than coarse cross-bred and whose less fatty mutton finds a readier market. Similarly the Argentine merinos have yielded place to the finer fleeced Australian merinos. The dominance of dual-purpose breeds in three of the sheep-rearing areas reflects their accessibility to coastal *frigoríficos*, whereas merinos predominate in the semi-arid hills of the remote Pre-Cordilleras of north-west Patagonia. Mutton and lamb, however, are neither popular at home nor important to the export trade – in 1964 only $9 million worth of mutton and lamb were exported, compared with $129 million worth of wool and $288 million worth of beef. Great scope exists in consequence for the development of a fat lamb export trade based on crossing mutton-breed rams with the existing flocks of dual-purpose ewes.

A second, well-established trend in Argentine agriculture has been the

mechanization of production. Despite inducements from successive govern- \
ments to farmers to invest more capital in fixed, rather than mobile assets –
in land productivity rather than labour productivity – the latter have for
various reasons been preferred: the rural exodus obliged many farmers to
mechanize, owners often chose to cut their labour force for political reasons,
and insecure tenants feared the loss of fixed capital. Furthermore, tractor
purchases have been facilitated by tax concessions and loans designed partly
to encourage the growth of the national tractor industry which was founded
in 1955. The number of tractors in use rose from 29,000 in 1947 to around
150,000 by 1965 when Argentina possessed one tractor for every 187 ha
of cultivated land (cf. U.S.S.R. 1:214 ha, Australia 1:116 ha, and U.S.A.
1:42 ha). Yet mechanization did not merit the same priority as other
reforms, for even in 1952–4 the output per rural inhabitant in Argentina
was on a level with Britain's and higher than France's (though wages
hardly reflected this).

Most striking of the long-term changes has been the rise of 'industrial'
farm produce and fruit (Table 9.6).

TABLE 9.6 *Argentina: area and annual production of cereals and other*
crops 1935–9 and 1955–9

	1935–9		1955–9	
	Area *(million ha)*	*Production* *(million tons)*	*Area* *(million ha)*	*Production* *(million tons)*
Cereals and flax	20·4	17·3	15·7	14·0
Other crops	1·5	8·7	3·8	18·8
including: Oil seeds	0·3	0·2	1·6	0·8
Industrial	0·8	7·0	1·4	13·8
Fruit & veg.	0·4	1·5	0·8	4·2
Fodder	5·4	—	8·8	—

Although the Pampas have participated in this development through the
rise of oil seed production and of urban-orientated market-gardening and
dairying, the greater changes have, in part for climatic reasons, taken place
elsewhere (Fig. 9.6b). Some developments represent an import substitution agriculture associated with processing industries catering for the
domestic market; others provide new export crops; virtually all have led to
more intensive forms of land use. By the mid-1950s the rest of the country
with only 11 per cent of the improved land was accounting for 32 per cent
by value of the agricultural output but only 8 per cent of the consumption,
whereas the Pampa provinces were consuming more than they produced.

P

On the Pampas dairying has become more important and more intensive. 'Holando-Argentino' (Friesian) cattle have increased from 2 per cent of Argentine herds in 1937 to 14 per cent in 1960, and milk products have tripled in volume. More than two-thirds of the industry is to be found in the old colony area of Santa Fé and Córdoba where dairying has partly replaced grain production (Fig. 9.4a).

The production of edible oils from sunflower seeds, groundnuts and olives has for a number of reasons increased greatly in the cereal-growing districts. The sunflower can be cultivated with the same machinery as cereals and can be grown as a summer crop after the December harvest of wheat or flax, or after the winter grazing of fodder crops, thus making fuller use of the permanent labour force. The area devoted to the sunflower first surpassed 100,000 ha in 1935 and reached a peak of 1·8 million ha in 1948; thereafter disease led to reductions in both yield and area and to its partial replacement by groundnuts, whose area has doubled from the 150,000 ha of the early 1950s. The decline of flax-growing has also been reversed, for the oil-pressing factories can handle equally sunflower seed, groundnuts, linseed and olives. Four-fifths of the olive trees, however, are grown in Cuyo rather than on the climatically marginal northern Pampas. Cultivation has expanded greatly since 1932 when official encouragement began and fewer than 50,000 trees existed; by 1960, 4·6 million trees were in production.

The level of production of edible oils has thus risen tremendously since 1926–30, when 21,000 tons of oil were produced yearly and 48,000 tons imported, to reach 280,000 tons in 1960–4 when almost one quarter was exported.

Outside the Pampas intensive crop production is concentrated in three broad areas: the old oases of Cuyo and the north-west, the new forest colonies of the Chaco and Misiones, and the newly irrigated lands of northern Patagonia and southern Mendoza. Certain crops are associated particularly, though not exclusively, with one or other of these regions, hence production problems and regional problems frequently coincide (Fig. 9.6b).

Long before 1930 the vineyards of Cuyo, together with the canefields of Tucumán, led the way in the development of a protected import substitution agriculture; nevertheless, growth has continued and by 1964 over 250,000 ha were devoted to vines (75 per cent in Mendoza, 15 per cent in San Juan). With a production of 20 million hl of wine Argentina ranks fourth in the world. Employing modern methods, the immigrant Spanish or Italian small farmer achieves the highest yields in the world, but much of the profit accrues to the firms controlling both production and distribution of the wine.

The sugar cane area also grew to over 300,000 ha in 1955, but has since declined to around 250,000. The fall has aggravated the social and political problem of the Tucumán district, which suffers from the increasing competition of Salta and Jujuy. Between 1935 and 1965 the former's contribution to the national sugar production fell from 70·4 per cent to 61·7 per cent while the latter's rose from 27·2 per cent to 33·6 per cent. Tucumán lies on the climatic margin of sugar cane and its twenty-seven small, obsolete sugar mills, depending on share-croppers for two-thirds of their supplies, produced only 8·6 kg of sugar per 100 kg of cane in 1965. To the north the five large newer mills recorded yields of 11 per cent and drew two-thirds of their cane from their own plantations, situated on fertile forest soils and manned by an undemanding labour force of Bolivian and Paraguayan migrants.

Cotton, the leading product of Chaco province, has experienced similar vicissitudes. With government assistance, such as a 168 per cent import duty on cotton, the national area sown rose to over 700,000 ha in 1957 but fell to only 300,000 ha by 1967, owing partly to the ending of guaranteed prices in 1959. Since the harvest season in the Chaco is wet, yields and quality are poor, yet other crops cannot compete with cotton and the result is monoculture, with all its disadvantages. 22,000 of the 27,000 Chaco farms grow cotton and most of them are too small for mechanization, although harvest labour, much of it Paraguayan, is scarce. Soil erosion and plant disease are other problems and, while it has been demonstrated by government agronomists that better techniques could raise yields five-fold, there is little evidence of their widespread adoption.

Until 1960 Argentina's banana requirements had long been met almost entirely by the annual importation of about 200,000 tons. A rapid eleven-fold increase brought domestic production by 1967 to 130,000 tons of which four-fifths came from Formosa and the rest chiefly from Salta.

Misiones,[1] in contrast, is a province dominated by small owner-occupied holdings practising mixed farming. In 1960 over half grew yerba maté, maize and manioc, and kept cattle, pigs and poultry; and over a quarter produced tung nuts, oranges and tea. With more than four-fifths of the 205,000 ha of the improved area of Misiones devoted to permanent tree crops, agriculture cannot adjust rapidly to changing economic demands. Climate and location impose further constraints: uniquely subtropical conditions with over 1650 mm rainfall and few frosts guarantee a monopoly of certain crops on the national market (yerba and tea) and afford some comparative advantage for others (citrus), though disease problems are often greater. At the same time distance from Buenos Aires – over 1150 km by road or rail and 1600 km by river – places the province at a severe locational disadvantage in national and world markets and obliges it to concentrate on high value/low bulk crops or on those that lend themselves to industrial processing. For example, in orange production Misiones fell from second place to fourth during the 1950s and early 1960s, whilst the

[1] The adjacent north-eastern corner of Corrientes has the same characteristics.

frost-prone Paraná delta and Concordia district of Entre Ríos expanded production: the latter areas could afford to burn off the frosts as deteriorating rail services heightened the disadvantage of Misiones, yet at the same time her orange juice canning industry grew apace.

Yerba maté, grown on 12,000 of the 19,000 farms, remains the leading crop of Misiones. Government encouragement from 1926 provided the economic foundation for the growing colonies and the area planted rose from 9000 ha in 1924–5 to 63,000 ha in 1935–6. Restrictions were then imposed until the early 1950s, but renewed expansion brought the area planted to 147,000 ha by 1964. Overproduction at home and competition from the adjacent areas of Brazil and Paraguay now threaten a crop whose consumption, in any case, is an obsolescent social custom.

The second product of Misiones is Chinese wood oil (tung oil) used in high quality paints and obtained from the nuts of the tung tree, which was introduced by Liebig's in 1929. American reluctance to trade with Communist China, formerly the world's chief supplier, encouraged production from Misiones and adjoining parts of Corrientes, which now have 50,000 ha planted with tung trees. Similarity to southern China has also favoured the expansion of tea-growing. The area sown rose from under 2000 ha in 1952 to 30,000 ha by 1960; by 1967, 16 million kg of tea were being produced, mostly for export, but here again world overproduction poses a problem.

Far to the south-west the twentieth-century irrigation schemes around San Rafael in Mendoza province and along the Río Negro in northern Patagonia have been associated with the rapid expansion of temperate fruit and vegetable production. Argentine fruit-growing has for some years been faced with a saturated domestic market for fresh fruit and consumption has remained at 90 kg a head. Expansion has thus depended largely upon processing for consumption at home and abroad and upon direct exportation. In 1960 scarcely 1 per cent of the oranges, only a tenth of the apples but half the plums went to the factory; another 40 per cent of the apples were packed for export and these constituted three-quarters of all fruit exports. The San Rafael district now grows most of Argentina's peaches, quinces and damsons and many of her pears, apples and plums. Distance again made development dependent upon industrialization, upon the canning and drying of fruits and the manufacture of cider, sweets and jams.

The Río Negro valley accounts for 70 per cent of Argentine apple production which rose from 92,000 tons in 1935–9 to 464,000 tons in 1962–7. The small farmers of the valley use modern cultivation techniques and its packing stations, frequently co-operatives, are very quality-conscious, reserving the best for export.

All these improvements in Argentine agriculture deserve full recognition, but they do not tackle the central problem, which is to increase the productivity of the land itself, especially in the Pampas with its excellent soils and proximity to national markets and export outlets. Progress in this direction – in the development of artificial pastures, in the use of fertilizers and conservation techniques, and in the adoption of higher yielding crop varieties – has been far more modest, but very recent events suggest that at last the problem is being tackled in earnest.

Livestock carrying capacity depends upon the provision of adequate nourishment during winter cold and summer drought. In the cattle fattening zone, which stretches south-west from Rosario into La Pampa, the practice has been to supplement natural grazing with alfalfa pastures in summer and cereal-grazing in winter. The so-called natural pastures of the Pampas are not rough grazings but in fact comprise old alfalfa and stubble fields containing clover and rye grass, which, through neglect, have become infested with thistles and other weeds. In the last decade the growing of summer cereals, especially sorghums, in place of alfalfa has been stressed. The area of alfalfa has fallen from 7.4 to 5.9 million ha between the late 1950s and mid-1960s whereas that of sorghums has risen from 1.5 to 2.6 million ha. Since 1963 the government, aided now by a $15 million World Bank loan, has been encouraging the development of permanent mixed grasslands with the careful management they require, and this might ultimately double meat yields per hectare in the Pampas. On the much inferior pastures of the north-eastern plains limited trials with artificial pastures have increased yields impressively; these have been followed in 1969 by an $82 million programme of supervised credit, assisted by the Inter-American Development Bank, designed to almost double beef output in the north-east (and to diversify production on the cotton, tobacco and yerba farms).

Soil management is even less developed than grassland management. In 1964 it was still true to say that no fertilizers were used for the cultivation of traditional Pampa crops: according to estimates three-quarters of the nitrates, phosphates and potash consumed in Argentina was employed for fruits, vines and sugar cane and over a fifth for tobacco and truck crops. Only 0·02 per cent of the land devoted to cereals, fodder crops, fibres and oil seeds received fertilizers. However, recent unfinished experiments in the Pampas (FAO, ETAP Report 2215) suggest that there is no deficiency of potash, calcium, magnesium or sulphates when growing traditional crops, that natural phosphates are adequate for wheat-growing except in parts of southern Buenos Aires and Entre Ríos provinces, and that nitrate applications increase wheat yields only in the wetter eastern parts when winter wheat is grown in rotation with summer crops (maize and sunflower). In all, it was estimated, only a tenth of the wheat and maize lands would merit fertilizing. In contrast, the intensive crops would all benefit from the wider use of fertilizers. In 1963 import duties were removed, leading to a tripling of consumption between 1962 and 1964; but this figure – 49,000 tons – was still under a fifth of Brazil's consumption and prices were still two or three times those prevailing in Britain. In mid-1968 the opening of a 150,000 ton capacity nitrate factory, part of the Campana petrochemical complex, gave a further boost to consumption.

Other experiments with soil conservation techniques have shown that deep ploughing retains moisture and greatly increases yields throughout the Pampas. Soil erosion is serious: along the western edge of the humid Pampas, 16 million out of 61 million ha are affected by wind erosion, a major factor in the rural exodus from La Pampa. In the north, water erosion is serious on the deeply weathered soils of small farms in Misiones and the Chaco.

The best hope for improved productivity comes from the introduction of new varieties of traditional crops: wheat yields have risen steadily from 0·88 tons per ha harvested in 1929–34 to 1·36 tons/ha in 1960–8; maize yields fell from 1·86 tons/ha in 1929–34 to 1·76 tons/ha in 1960–5 but in the succeeding three years have averaged 2·19 tons/ha. Such yields hardly support the idea of a progressive general exhaustion of unfertilized Pampa soils, although more demanding varieties may well require artificial fertilizers to prevent future deterioration.

Many of the improvements to Argentine agriculture described above have been stimulated by the national agricultural research and advisory service INTA (Instituto Nacional de Tecnología Agropecuaria), founded in 1957, and, locally, by the progressive farming clubs, the CREAs (Consorcios Regionales de Experimentación Agrícola); the latter, also begun in 1957, combine the local knowledge of farmers with the technical expertise of agronomists in carrying out large-scale trials and demonstrations of innovations.

The need for agrarian reform?

For some years it has been argued that intensification of land use has been unduly retarded by deficiencies in the agrarian structure, especially by the dominance of huge estates, the frequency of insecurely held tenant holdings and the large numbers of undercapitalized smallholdings (Fig. 9.5). Insecure tenants prefer to invest in livestock and machinery rather than in long-term fixed improvements to water supply, soil and buildings; big farmers are satisfied with extensive rather than intensive forms of land use. On social and political grounds the agrarian structure is criticized as being responsible for inferior housing, education and hospital facilities, and for affording little opportunity of alternative employment or social mobility.

In fact, however, there have been considerable structural changes in recent years, making some of the commonly made assumptions debatable, and the great regional diversity in the agrarian problem also makes broad generalizations about its weaknesses questionable.

In 1947, 37 per cent of Argentine farmland was worked by owners, 25 per cent by tenants, 9 per cent by operators who were part-owners and part-

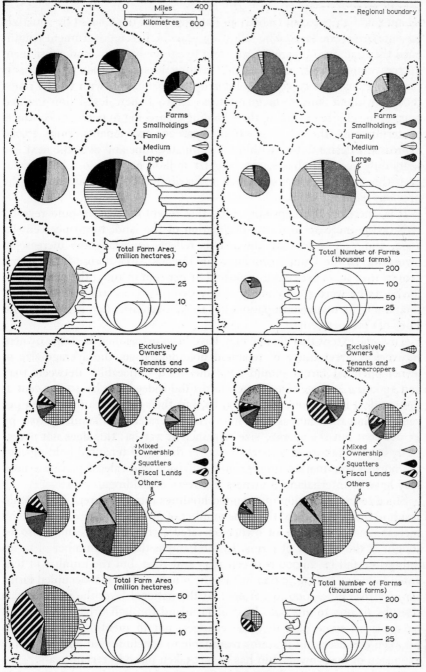

Fig. 9.5 Argentina: agrarian structure 1960
(a and b) Scale of enterprise
(c and d) Tenure system

tenants, and 23 per cent (mostly in Patagonia and the Chaco) by squatters on state or private land. The following year the Perón government lengthened the minimum tenancy term from five to eight years, and subsequent decrees automatically extended all existing leases, so that most tenants came to enjoy twenty years' uninterrupted occupation with frozen rents, though without long-term guarantees. In 1958 new legislation granted tenants the choice of buying their holdings, agreeing to new rent contracts or terminating their leases. Of at least 200,000 tenants, only 27,000 expressed a desire to buy within the stipulated time and over the next five years only 9000 purchases, covering 1·1 million ha, were officially made; even this small area exceeded that redistributed by the state during the previous eighteen years.

It is, therefore, perhaps surprising that recent censuses should reveal a remarkable increase in owner-occupation of the land, to 59 per cent by 1960, and 75 per cent by 1965. This reflects especially the increase in ownership in the Pampa provinces: in Buenos Aires it rose from 35 per cent in 1947 to 62 per cent in 1960 and 81 per cent in 1965; the percentages for Santa Fé were 46, 70 and 83. Only two provinces still had under half their land in owner-occupation by 1965, Mendoza (47 per cent) and Formosa (18 per cent).

To some extent this change may have been occasioned by large owners recovering direct usage of tenanted holdings; if so, the average size of owner-operated farms should have increased noticeably. Between 1947 and 1960 the average size of such farms did indeed rise by 10 per cent at the national level, from 362 to 399 ha, but their total area rose by 43 per cent. Within the Pampas the total owner-operated area similarly rose by 45 per cent but the average size remained at 251 ha; this does not necessarily imply a failure of owners to recover the use of tenanted holdings, for the normal free market process of subdivision and sale of private estates may have counterbalanced owners' recovery of holdings.

Since re-incorporation of tenanted holdings into the parent farm would result in the extinction of the same number of individual farms without any increase in the number of owner-operated farms, evidence may also be sought in the number of farms. In the Pampas the total number of farms did indeed fall by 29,000 between 1947 and 1960, but the number of tenanted holdings fell by 70,000, whilst the number of owner-occupied farms actually rose by 29,000 to 121,000. At the national level the number also rose, by 67,000 to 264,000. Loss of farmland through urbanization must have played some part in these changes, not to mention discrepancies between censuses, but it seems reasonable to conclude that a considerable extension of farm-ownership has in fact taken place in recent years.

This increase in landownership over the last twenty years does not appear, however, to have induced much increase in productivity per hectare. Recent sample studies show that expenditure on fertilizers and pasture improvement is similar on tenanted and owner-operated farms; other evidence points to the fallowing, for lack of labour, of lands recovered from tenants. Another study, of new owners in Santa Fé, showed that their priorities were to pay off their mortgages and mechanize production, and only in the longer term did they propose to improve the land and adopt mixed farming. For the present, therefore, only farm size appears to be correlated with productivity and it must be recognized that the conversion of tenants into owners does not change the size of their farms (Fig. 9.6d).

In the size of farms Argentina remains a land of extremes: in 1960, 38 per cent of the farmers held 1 per cent of the land, in holdings of under 25 ha, whilst 6 per cent of the farmers occupied 74 per cent of the land, in holdings of over 1000 ha.

Although the semi-desert provinces claimed many of the huge farms, the Pampas also showed great inequalities. In Buenos Aires the area in farms of over 5000 ha decreased greatly between 1914 and 1947 (largely in fact between 1914 and 1937), in favour of those under 1000 ha, but subsequently the situation stagnated (Table 9.7).

TABLE 9.7   *Province of Buenos Aires: distribution of farmland by farm size 1914–60*

Farm size (ha)	1914 %	1947 %	1960 %
0–100	5·5	8·8	7·9
100–1000	34·2	43·6	43·8
1000–5000	30·4	32·8	33·8
over 5000	28·9	14·7	14·5

Recent official studies reveal a clear relationship between productivity and scale of operation, as measured by the number of workers employed (Fig 9.6d and Table 9.8). Family farms devote over two and a half times as much of their land to crops as do large farms, whereas the latter have two-thirds as much land again in natural pasture as have the former. Data for value added per hectare show a progressive decline in productivity with increasing scale of operation. A detailed study of a physically homogeneous part of Córdoba similarly showed that investment and productivity per hectare were three to four times greater on 100–200 ha farms than on those of over 5000 ha. The explanation of this relationship is generally assumed to lie in the satisfaction of large operators with ample returns based on low yields from a large area, in the unwillingness of absentee owners to devote the extra managerial effort required by intensive farming, and in the prefer-ence of big farmers for employing much of their income outside agriculture. But such factors, if undeniable, seem inadequate to explain the even stronger

TABLE 9.8 The Pampas: Land use 1960 and productivity by scale of enterprise

Scale	No. of workers	Farm area (%)	Farms (%)	% of land in				Value added, per	
				Crops	Improved pasture	Natural pasture	Other	Hectare (pesos)	Man (1000 pesos)
Small holdings	1–2	3·2	26·8	31·7	19·5	43·6	5·2	4002	63
Family farms	2–4	40·7	62·7	34·9	29·7	31·0	4·4	1946	111
Medium farms	4–12	36·0	9·6	22·1	22·6	47·5	7·8	1387	250
Large farms	>12	20·1	0·9	13·4	27·8	49·0	9·8	1150	345
		100·0	100·0						

positive correlation between scale of operation and productivity per man (Fig. 9.6d and Table 9.8), which may simply reflect the real preference of larger entrepreneurs for a labour-efficient pastoral type of farming (Fig. 9.6c).

Another problem is the inadequate size of the smallholdings, which constitute 27 per cent of the Pampas farms and provide a livelihood for 17 per cent of its rural labour (Fig. 9.5a and b). By definition each small-holding is considered too small to support a family; its operator is usually the owner, but he has had little education and lacks supervised credit facilities. A careful investigation by Gaignard in La Pampa province (CNRS, 1968) reveals that smallholdings are typically derived from the lots created by the organized colonization schemes of fifty to a hundred years ago. With rising standards of living, a once-adequate lot of 75–150 ha no longer affords an acceptable livelihood and, with mechanization, occupies but a third to a half of a farmer's time. If colonies of smallholdings border huge estates – as in Guatrache department, where unviable holdings of under 350 ha account for 79 per cent of the farms but only 25 per cent of the land, and where 32 per cent of the land is occupied by the nine farms of over 5000 ha – social and political tension can easily develop and the obvious solution may well be pressed. But local solutions can only be palliatives in such cases as Trenel department, where 11 per cent of the land is occupied by four big farms, but over 50 per cent is already taken up by the 611 farms of under 350 ha. Elsewhere in the Pampas, in the colonies of the Jewish Colonization Association, rural depopulation and the amal-gamation of holdings has taken place. According to Winsberg (1964, p. 501), 'the Jewish population is likely to decrease until the size of the holdings of [those] who remain is large enough to provide an income comparable to what they could earn . . . in the cities'.

The solutions to the agrarian inequalities of the Pampas are not easy to find. Amalgamation of unviable holdings seems to the European observer a curious proposal when each smallholding may well cover 200 ha of fine Pampa land within 150 km of the metropolis. Intensification of land use would seem as greatly needed here as in the national economy. Yet the failure of the enterprising Jewish Colonization Association (which intro-duced the sunflower and co-operative marketing to Argentina) to make 75 ha lots profitable suggests that the marketing of new, intensively grown crops presents an obstacle that is not easily overcome.

In considering the problem of the large holding it is commonly assumed that large farm holdings are large rural properties and vice versa, and hence that stagnation in the pattern of farm sizes implies a stagnation in the sizes of properties; the solution to the problem of under-used large holdings is therefore often held to depend upon splitting up large properties. In the absence of a national survey of the relationship between property and farm such assumptions are not verifiable. It may be true that most large holdings

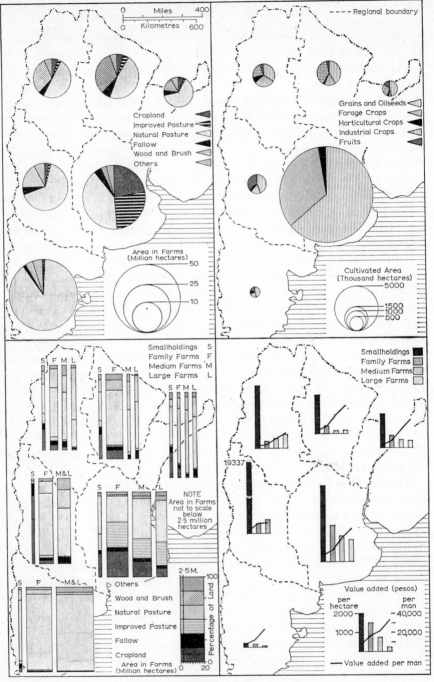

Fig. 9.6 Argentina: land use 1960
(a) Main land use types
(b) Main crop types
(c) Farm size and land use
(d) Farm size and productivity

are large properties, but conversely many large properties are already divided into smaller tenanted farms. Again, whilst the pattern of farm sizes has not changed over the last thirty years, sample studies in Buenos Aires reveal a fair amount of subdivision of property: in ten sample areas between the Tandil and Ventana hills the writer found 1574 properties in 1961 where only 591 existed in 1939. Another survey, of 25 de Mayo Partido, showed that the number of properties increased from 339 to 1177 between 1920 and 1957: it is significant, however, that the subdivision of properties over 1000 ha was far slower than that of properties under 1000 ha. Certain forces indeed favour the preservation of large estates: with inflation land becomes more valued as a capital asset and the property market contracts; the creation of private corporations also permits land-owning families to circumvent both crippling death duties and equal inheritance laws.

In conclusion, the often-advocated expropriation and subdivision of under-used large properties on the Pampas may be neither logical nor advisable. Apart from the political difficulty there is the expense, estimated to exceed £500 million, which would foster national inflation and, as observed, may actually retard intensification by the new owners. Official studies advocate, in contrast, the introduction of high taxes based on land potential. Self-assessment by the owner, tied to a commitment to sell only at a related price, is considered the most effective way of achieving a fair valuation. Such a tax incentive should not penalize the enthusiastic big farmers and corporations, the leading innovators who dominate the CREAs; yet it would stimulate the more backward landlords (often absentee) either to intensify their agriculture directly, or, it may be suggested, to create economic tenant farms with long leases. These could provide the opportunities for secure landholding and progress which many smallholders and others expect to find only through expropriation.

In the end perhaps the greatest obstacle to agricultural intensification would remain, namely the inherited attitudes which divorce crop and livestock farming to such an extent that no noun in the Spanish language embraces them both.

Outside the Pampas the solution to agrarian problems may appear less urgent for the national economy but far more pressing when viewed locally (Fig. 9.5). Most acute are the problems of the north-west, which 'in history, social structure and economy [has] more in common with Andean Peru and Bolivia than with the more recently settled and more commercial Pampa' (CIDA, 1965, p. 47). Two-thirds of the land is owned by 3 per cent of the owners: some big farms are virtually colonial haciendas 'with the farm workers scarcely more than serfs' (CIDA, 1965, p. 47) who, deprived of access to legal social security benefits, for the most part illiterate, undernourished and tubercular, enjoy a life expectancy of only thirty-five years. Other large units are the antiquated sugar plantations of

Tucumán province which depend heavily on a seasonal labour force that lacks the legal protection of the permanent workers; it is composed of the landless and owners of inadequate smallholdings who suffer the competition of cheaper immigrant labour without enjoying alternative sources of employment.

Problems of a different kind affect the provinces on Argentina's northeastern settlement frontier. The gravity of the land tenure situation varies greatly: in Misiones 74 per cent of the land was worked by its owners in 1960, in Chaco 46 per cent, but in Formosa only 16 per cent. Everywhere colonists have often created farms on government lands without as yet receiving firm titles; in Formosa as a whole the proportion of fiscal lands was 69 per cent in 1960, in Chaco 40 per cent but in Misiones only 11 per cent. Higher percentages of the smallholdings occupied fiscal lands.

The other major problem is the dominance of smallholdings which in 1960 accounted for about 60 per cent of all farms in both Misiones and the Chaco. Again, most such holdings resulted from organized colonization schemes. A reasonable living can be obtained only from intensive crops whose cultivation, as already seen, gives rise to many technical and economic difficulties; as a result many smallholdings have already been abandoned and others amalgamated: at Victoria colony in Misiones, for example, the writer in 1965 found only one male British settler still in occupation out of the fifty original colonists of the 1930s. The family farms, however, constituting 41 per cent of the Chaco holdings and 29 per cent of those of Misiones, have met with greater success and prosperous communities like Eldorado have arisen; they practice co-operation in the agricultural sphere and enjoy considerable political power locally.

The growth of urban occupations 1930-60

In Argentina the process of urbanization has *not* been associated primarily with industrialization, least of all during the Perón era when the development of import-substitution industries was a major feature of government policy. Between 1925-9 and 1940-4, of 1,230,000 new jobs created 440,000 were in commerce and services, 420,000 in manufacturing, 300,000 in agriculture and 70,000 in other sectors. Between 1940-4 and 1955, 1,830,000 further jobs were created, only 350,000 of them in manufacturing and 80,000 in agriculture, but 970,000 were in commerce and services (see Table 9.9). During this latter period the proportion of the labour force that was engaged in manufacturing actually fell.

In 1960 Greater Buenos Aires employed 45 per cent of the workers in manufacturing and the provinces of Buenos Aires, Córdoba, Santa Fé and La Pampa a further 35 per cent. In commerce and the services Greater Buenos Aires was more dominant with 52 per cent and 49 per cent respectively to the 28 per cent and 26 per cent of the Pampas. Since 1945

TABLE 9.9   *Argentina: Occupational structure 1900–60*

Sector	1900–4 1000s	%	1925–9 1000s	%	1940–4 1000s	%	1955 1000s	%	1960 1000s	%
Agriculture	738	39·2	1539	35·9	1838	33·3	1916	26·1	1461	19·2
Manufacturing	396	19·8	890	20·8	1310	23·7	1655	22·5	1916	25·2
Commerce & services	616	30·9	1377	32·1	1821	33·0	2786	37·9	2423	31·9
Transport	92	4·6	218	5·1	248	4·5	434	5·9	477	6·3
Utilities	15	0·8	52	1·2	85	1·5	142	1·9	87	1·1
Mining & construction	94	4·7	212	4·9	215	3·9	415	5·6	467	6·2
	1970	100	4290	100	5520	100	7350	100	7599	100

internal migration has led to unproductive employment especially in the metropolis. Furthermore, since the government employs many of those engaged in the service and transport industries, much public revenue is committed to salary payments and the public capacity for productive investment is limited. Over-manning in the public sector should perhaps be regarded as disguised unemployment, for the more productive sectors –

TABLE 9.10   *Annual output of leading industrial products for selected five-year periods 1934–66*

Product	Unit	1934–8	1946–50	1954–8	1962–6
Beef and veal	Million tons	1·61	1·94	2·29	2·34
Wheat flour	Million tons	1·5	1·9	2·2	2·2
Sugar	Million tons	0·41	0·6	0·77	1·03
Wine	Million hl	6·8	9·6	14·3	19·9
Cotton yarn	1000 tons	21·7[1]	69·4	95·6	86·2
Wood pulp, mechanical	1000 tons	—	9·0	16·0	27·0
Cement	Million tons	0·9	1·4	2·1	3·0
Pig iron	1000 tons	—	17·0	33·0	518·0
Crude steel	1000 tons	—	131·0	226·0	1095·0
Tyres	Million units	c.0·5	0·76	1·11	2·47
Motor cars	1000 units	—	—	15[2]	114
TV sets	1000 units	—	—	69[2]	133
Petrol	Million tons	0·75	1·22	1·73	3·0
Electricity, public	1000 million kW h	2·1[1]	3·9	6·3	10·2

Note: Averages for other periods [1]1935–8, [2]1957-8.

manufacturing especially – have not been able to absorb enough of the growing urban labour force.

Nevertheless the value of the Argentine industrial product increased more than twentyfold between 1900 and 1960, rising from 1267 million to 27,283 million pesos (of 1950) at factor cost (Table 9.10). Until 1950 annual growth accelerated from 164 million pesos in the first thirty years to 1581 million pesos in the last five. A fall in 1950–5 to 680 million pesos caused widespread consternation (but by 1960–5 growth had recovered to 1368 million pesos). Manufacturing's share of the gross domestic product rose similarly between 1900 and 1960 from 14·3 per cent to 32·3 per cent (and to 34·6 per cent by 1965).

In the 1930s and the war years the growth industries were those using local agricultural produce – foodstuffs, tobacco, textiles and leather goods – and self-sufficiency had been achieved in most of these branches by 1950. The location of such activities varied: where processing resulted in greatly reduced bulk – as in the production of sugar, wine, edible oils, cotton fibre and quebracho extract – factories arose in the country districts, frequently affording the only non-agricultural employment, albeit seasonal. Such establishments, characterized as 'plantationist' by di Tella (1965), were associated with strong social cleavage between a paternalist management and an unskilled labour force. Other processing industries, such as textiles, clothing, footwear and brewing, were largely concentrated in Greater Buenos Aires, as were such import-based industries as the manufacture of rayon-acetate, synthetic rubber and pharmaceuticals. The Depression years were weathered with unemployment rates rarely reaching 5 per cent, and by 1944 the value of manufactures exceeded that of agricultural produce.

During the Perón regime the 1947–51 five-year plan sought to develop, largely with imported parts, the production of consumer durables (cookers, refrigerators, radios), demand for which was stimulated by low food prices and high wage rates, the wage share of the national income rising from 45 per cent to 56 per cent. At first the necessary capital goods, fuels and intermediate products were imported at especially favourable exchange rates, made possible by obliging agricultural exporters to sell at less-than-world prices through IAPI (the Argentine Trade Promotion Institute). By the early 1950s falling commodity prices forced IAPI to support exporters and capital from abroad was now sought.

By 1954 nearly all consumer goods were made in Argentina, by a million workers in 150,000 factories. The majority of plants were undercapitalized, inefficient and small. In only two industries, petroleum products and cigarette-making, did the average establishment employ over twenty-five workers; indeed, in the clothing industry factories accounted for only 15 per cent of output, the rest being domestically produced.

By location, industry was heavily concentrated along the Santa Fé–La

Plata axis. In 1960, 83 per cent of the industrial output and 77 per cent of the industrial labour force was contributed by the capital and the provinces of Buenos Aires, Santa Fé and Entre Ríos. Greater Buenos Aires alone was responsible for 60 per cent of national output. The provinces of Córdoba, Mendoza and Tucumán contributed a further 5, 3 and 2 per cent respectively.

The locational dominance of the metropolis may be attributed to many factors: its labour supply and consumer market, its focal position in the rail network, its primacy as a port for imports and its unrivalled facilities for the supply of energy, as well as the intangible advantages of superior health and educational services and of proximity to the centre of government and administration.

One result of Perón's policy was to reduce the importance of the so-called 'vegetative' and relatively self-contained industries in favour of 'dynamic' branches with their potential for stimulating complexes of linked activities. But neither private nor public capital was forthcoming for the adequate development of the necessary but less profitable capital goods industries and growth was unbalanced. Neither was investment in the infrastructure – roads, railways, energy – commensurate with industry's needs. The hydro-electricity programme of 1947 for developing the resources of the Sierra de Córdoba and the Andes of Mendoza aided the industrial growth of those provinces. But the importance of petroleum as a source of energy led fuel imports to rise from 9 per cent of all imports before the war to 22 per cent in the 1950s whilst the national contribution to petroleum supplies fell from 79 to 50 per cent, despite a doubling of production.

For many decades the railway network has been steadily decapitalized and since 1947 has increasingly lost money. By 1960, 60 per cent of the track was over forty years old and a further 20 per cent more than twenty (twenty-five years is the maximum for high-density traffic); 96 per cent of the network was single-tracked and on only 5 per cent were speeds in excess of 100 km/h permissible. Seven-tenths of the locomotives were over forty-five years old and 40 per cent of the rolling stock was out of service. On the uphill stretches of the main line in Corrientes the weary traveller could take exercise by pacing the train. In 1958 the round trip for goods wagons on the Buenos Aires–Mendoza line took thirty-seven days, compared with ten in 1948. Hardly surprisingly, by the end of the 1950s only 12 per cent of the freight moved by train, whereas the road network carried 81 per cent. Yet 80 per cent of the cars were over ten years old and few roads had been paved (Fig. 9.3d). Until 1932 roads had been built simply as feeders to the railway and in the following thirty years annual construction of paved roads averaged only 165 km, and of other improved roads only 800 km. Whereas the terrain of the Pampas favours railway building, highway construction is handicapped by the absence of road metal.

Recent developments 1960–

Although the imbalance in the industrial structure was recognized as early as 1950 and new policies adopted, effective corrective measures were not taken until 1958 when the Frondizi government initiated a programme to improve the infrastructure and develop heavy industry, in order to replace imported fuels and capital goods. Highest priority was given to the expansion of the national petroleum and natural gas industry and to the ancillary development of refining and petrochemicals. Next came the iron and steel industry, road transport improvements (through highway construction and the expansion of vehicle building) and increased electricity production. Lastly, encouragement was to be given to the manufacturing of cellulose, paper, cement and machinery. Participation of foreign capital in authorized projects was encouraged by guaranteeing it equal rights with domestic capital.

As a result new foreign investment between 1958 and 1965 totalled $500 million: 32 per cent went into chemicals and petrochemicals; 25 per cent into vehicles and accessories and 17 per cent into rolling mills. By origin 55 per cent of the capital was from the United States and 10 per cent from Switzerland; between 4 and 8 per cent was supplied by the U.K., West Germany, Italy, the Netherlands and France. Only 33 per cent of the investment was destined for the metropolis, whilst 53 per cent went to the provinces of Buenos Aires and Santa Fé (principally to the Litoral axis), a further 5 per cent to Córdoba and 3 per cent to southern Patagonia.

In Argentina, as elsewhere, petroleum products provide an increasing proportion of energy requirements (70 per cent in 1965, compared with 46 per cent in 1935–9) and the contribution of natural gas has also risen greatly, from 4 to 16 per cent (Fig. 9.7c). Despite expansion, hydro-electricity still provides only 1·5 per cent, suffering from the remoteness of potential sites from centres of consumption. To reduce the cost of oil imports Frondizi brought in foreign contractors. Results were rapid: by 1962 output reached 15·6 million m³, imports fell to 7 per cent of consumption and self-sufficiency was in sight. But the contracts were cancelled in late 1963, expansion slowed down and imports rose again. In 1967 new operating concessions were granted and production for 1968 rose to 20 million m³.

Despite the discovery of new oilfields, Comodoro Rivadavia has furnished over half the Argentine production since its discovery in 1907: 55 per cent in 1965, compared with 26 per cent from Mendoza, 11 per cent from Río Negro–Neuquén, and 6 per cent from Salta. Proven reserves, similarly distributed, are sufficient for fifteen years' production at 1968 levels. Although each oilfield has its refinery, four-fifths of the capacity is located between San Lorenzo and La Plata, which are equally accessible to imported and coastwise supplies (Fig. 9.7b). Pipelines from Salta and Comodoro Rivadavia also bring natural gas to the same area.

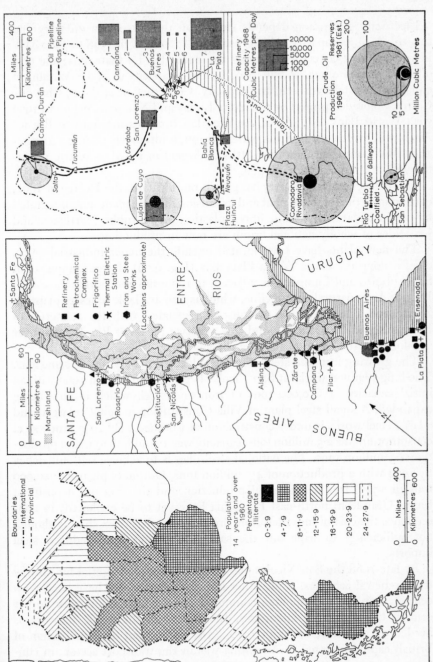

Fig. 9.7 (a) Argentina: illiteracy 1960 (b) Argentina: Litoral industrial axis (c) Argentina: national fuel supply

Electricity generation depends closely on the petroleum industry and two-thirds of its capacity, which rose from 1300 MW in 1948 to 3800 MW in 1965, is now concentrated along the Santa Fé–La Plata axis; one new oil-fired station alone, at San Nicolás, has a capacity of 300 MW, almost equal to the total hydro-electric capacity. Construction of the El Chocón–Cerros Colorados project on the rivers Limay and Neuquén, begun in 1969 with World Bank aid, and of the 1100 km transmission lines to Buenos Aires, will greatly change this pattern through ultimately adding a further 1650 MW, but even then four-fifths of Argentina's hydro-electric potential will still remain undeveloped.

The petrochemical industry has grown rapidly since the Decree of 1961, encouraging the establishment and expansion of basic plants and integrated by-product plants. Synthetic fibres, plastics, p.v.c., rubber, fertilizers and pesticides of wholly national origin are now in production.

The new plants have been located outside the major industrial cities, chiefly along the Santa Fé–La Plata axis (Fig. 9.7b). Large complexes at San Lorenzo and Campana lie adjacent to refineries and astride the Salta–Buenos Aires natural gas pipeline, which is also available to lesser plants at Zárate and Pilár. A third complex is associated with the refineries of Ensenada and La Plata. Beyond this axis two plants at Río Tercero near Córdoba are fed by an offshoot of the gas line.

The growing iron and steel industry is located mainly on the same axis. The long-planned works at San Nicolás began production in 1960 with an initial capacity of 650,000 tons of iron and steel, which is now being expanded. A small steel plant at Villa Constitución is being enlarged and a large steel works is under construction at Ensenada. By 1967 crude steel consumption was 2·3 million tons, capacity was 1·7 million tons and production 1·3 million tons. The national steel plan is to achieve self-sufficiency by 1974 with a production of 4·5 million tons. Output of pig iron (600,000 tons in 1967) lags behind steel production and the iron ore deposits at Sierra Grande in north-east Patagonia have yet to be exploited; in consequence the cost of imported iron, ore and scrap has risen sharply though not sufficiently to wipe out the savings accruing from reduced steel imports.

By late 1968 the San Nicolás plant began to supply material for railway track renewal schemes, while other improvements so far have been concentrated on the metropolitan commuter lines, which account for 60 per cent of the passenger kilometres. Investment in the whole network is needed on a massive scale; in 1910, £187 million out of £291 million of British capital invested in Argentina was in the transport sector; in contrast, in 1966 only $46 million out of $336 million loaned to Argentina by the Inter-American and World Banks was for transport.

A continuing handicap to the regional exchange of industrial products lies in the three different gauges – broad, standard and narrow – whose lines serve, respectively, the south and west, Mesopotamia, and the north and north-west of the Republic. The Santa Fé–La Plata axis is the only district served by all three systems.

Since 1960 the paving of arterial roads has proceeded more rapidly and since 1967 the Toll Law has allowed the participation of private finance in improving the highway system (Fig. 9.3). Recent deepening of the river as far as the port of Santa Fé and plans for a Santa Fé–Buenos Aires–La Plata Motorway emphasize yet again the importance of this booming economic axis.

The growing importance of motor transport is also reflected in the recent development of the motor vehicle industry (Table 9.10). Although a jeep factory was built at Córdoba in the early 1950s major growth awaited the Promotion Laws of 1959. By 1965 some 195,000 vehicles a year were being produced, almost three-quarters of them cars and the rest commercial vehicles. Fiat, Renault, Ford and General Motors with their Argentine associates were the largest manufacturers. After some rationalization there were eleven major factories: seven in Buenos Aires province, three in Córdoba and one in Santa Fé, served by 700 manufacturers of parts. The industry's impact on the transport system may be seen in the number of vehicles in use, which, having risen from 334,000 in 1928 to 608,000 in 1956, then leapt to 1,515,000 by 1965.

In recent years Argentina's light engineering industry, having largely satisfied domestic demand for household durables, has now turned to the manufacture of more sophisticated equipment such as electrocardiographs and calculating machines with which she has even entered the export market.

Undoubtedly, then, the country is now undergoing a further industrial revolution which must be of long-term benefit to it. The value of her 'dynamic' industries since 1960 has exceeded that of her traditional 'vegetative' branches. But the changes have led to many stresses in the economy: too much of the new capital equipment was financed by short-term loans, now largely repaid, and the motor-vehicle, steel and chemical industries were initially too dependent upon imported intermediate goods. These problems, however, are in sight of solution. Longer term problems remain: Argentine manufactures are expensive – cars cost more than twice the imported equivalent – and rationalization, together with export subsidies, may be necessary to achieve the desirable economies of scale. With capital-intensive industrialization the movement of labour into manufacturing is slow, though by 1960 an absolute fall in the tertiary labour force had been realized. Hardly noticed as yet is the new problem of repatriation of profits in foreign-owned industrial enterprises: half a century ago foreign capital was associated chiefly with the export sector of the economy and good profits were normally conditional upon a healthy export trade; today there is no such fortunate relationship.

The problem of Uruguay

Although the smaller River Plate republic has a population scarcely one eighth that of Argentina and has enjoyed uninterrupted democratic government for many years, the course of her economic development, the role of her agriculture and the growth of her industry have been remarkably similar to Argentina's.

Exports derived from agriculture still account for 97 per cent of all exports, with wool representing at least half, and beef and arable crops the rest. Thanks to high world prices for wool, Uruguay's export earnings remained high until the early 1950s but, as in Argentina, exports represented a declining proportion of total production and production itself, of both crops and livestock, was almost stagnant. Thus in 1935–7, 23 per cent of crops and 54 per cent of livestock products were exported, but these shares had fallen to 12 and 38 per cent by 1959–63, due not only to rising domestic demand but also to the disincentive of export duties.

The patterns and problems of Uruguayan agriculture most clearly resemble those of the Argentine Pampas: in 1963, 16·8 million ha, or 91 per cent of the national territory, was in agricultural use; no fewer than 15 million ha were devoted to natural pastures and a further 500,000 ha to improved pasture and fodder crops, leaving only 1·3 million ha for cash crops (although a further 4 million ha, then under pasture, were capable of annual cropping). Crop-farming and dairying are to be found particularly on the erosion-prone Tertiary and more recent deposits which flank the Plate estuary west of Montevideo; livestock-rearing is concentrated on the northern hills and plains, and fattening further south. As on the Pampas, the major traditional crops (maize, wheat and flax) were supplemented by the sunflower during the war in order to obviate the need for olive oil imports. Edible oils have now become an important export. The yield of none of these four crops, however, had risen perceptibly by 1960.

The yield of beef per hectare, as of the leading crops, is not only stagnant but far lower than that obtained in Argentina. Nor is the meat from her 23 million sheep and 8 million cattle subjected to rigorous grading. Livestock-breeding is the only continuing improvement in the agricultural field, but it receives little encouragement from the pricing system, which operates to keep domestic prices of beef almost as low as those of bread and potatoes. Because of inadequate feeding practices, fatstock is not available in the winter and spring, and the *frigoríficos* remain closed. Some indeed have been forced, by a shortage of supplies for export, to close down altogether. Improved techniques could quadruple the yield of beef per hectare and triple that of wool and mutton. The Agricultural Development Plan of 1961 is now making a contribution with the aid of international funds for the extension of artificial pastures, fencing and the use of fertilizers.

Much of the blame for agricultural stagnation is attributed to the same two defects in the agrarian structure that are held responsible in Argentina – insecurity of land tenure and excessive size of holdings. In 1961, 39 per cent of farmland was operated by tenant farmers, a fall of 4 per cent since 1951, whilst owner-operated farmland had risen by 3 per cent to 58 per cent. The tenant farmer enjoyed no compensation for improvements and even the five-year contracts were subject to rent revision every two years. Yet a recent study of the 1961 survey (Plottier and Notaro, 1966) reveals that, contrary to expectation, tenant farmers are generally the more efficient in the use of land, labour and capital. The proportion of owner and tenant farmers' capital devoted to fixed investment (buildings, fencing, water supplies) was identical at 26·6 per cent; tenants devoted somewhat more than owners to machinery but less to orchards. The yields of tenant-produced wheat, maize, sugar beet, fruit and animal products per hectare were all slightly higher and only their yields of sunflower, flax and apples were lower. Both labour productivity and returns on capital were a fifth to a quarter higher on tenant farms; the study even concludes that declining agricultural production may be attributable to the fall in areas tenanted! It is possible, however, that inadequate attention has been paid to the some-what above-average importance of tenanted (and smaller) farms in the more fertile arable districts near the Plate estuary.

Less evidence is available on the relationship of farm size to productivity. In 1961, 46 per cent of farms were under 20 ha and occupied under 2 per cent of the land, whereas the 4 per cent of the farms which had over 1000 ha occupied 57 per cent of the land. According to a report on the 1951 census farms under 200 ha had a labour productivity that was less than a third that on larger farms, but output per hectare was three times as great. Such global figures may conceal the effect of important intrinsic differences in soil and location between large and small farms. A more detailed study in Paysandú department in 1960 showed that incomes per hectare generally decreased with increasing farm size. This reflected the importance on all farms of under 100 ha of intensively grown vines, cotton or vegetables, crops that were completely absent from the larger holdings.

Official efforts to increase the number of small farmers have been limited by the shortage of money and personnel. Between 1948 and 1967 less than half a million hectares were distributed by the Colonization Institute to some 3100 settlers, and much, therefore, remains to be achieved.

As in the rural sphere, Uruguay's urban and industrial development since 1930 has closely paralleled that of Argentina and the Pampa provinces. Of the 1963 population of 2·6 million, only 18 per cent are classed as rural, 72 per cent live in towns of over 5000 and 46 per cent live in the capital city, Montevideo. Between the two censuses of 1908 and 1963 Montevideo grew at an annual rate of 2·5 per cent compared with 1·2 per cent in the rest of the country. The age structure of the population is similar to that of the most developed countries: 11 per cent receive social security pensions, which absorb 60 per cent of public expenditure; in addition, over half the active population are employed in the tertiary sector, the public services alone accounting for 20 per cent. Some 17 per cent work on the land and 22 per cent in manufacturing.

Import substitution had already proceeded far before the Second World War when over half Uruguay's manufacturing needs were produced at home (and over three-quarters of the foodstuffs, clothing and leather goods). The growth of manufacturing continued at over 8 per cent per year in the decade following the war, only to encounter the same problems of stagnation and import-financing as Argentina; with a smaller market and smaller factories, however, Uruguay's inefficiency is more serious.

In certain respects Uruguay's development has differed from Argentina's. With a tiny market, her prospects for heavy industry based on economies of scale are limited – her steel consumption is only 100,000 tons a year – yet a few branches of industry (petroleum-refining, cement and alcohol production) have existed under a state monopoly for over thirty years. New agricultural processing industries (edible oils and wool combing) have also expanded with the aim of increasing export earnings.

Nor does Uruguay suffer the same transport and energy problems as her neighbour. Both road and rail networks cover the whole country, although many improvements are required, and the number of vehicles in use has more than doubled since 1953 to over 196,000 in 1965. Three-quarters of the electricity produced comes from installations on the Río Negro and the country's energy capacity always exceeds demand.

Lastly, Uruguay obtains 17 per cent of her foreign exchange earnings from tourism (which ranks third, after wool and meat, in the 'export' table). The visitors come overwhelmingly from Argentina, for Uruguay's south coast resorts of Montevideo, Punta del Este and Piriápolis, afford the nearest places of escape from the summer heat of Buenos Aires. But Mar del Plata alone attracts ten times as many Argentine visitors and Uruguay has little to offer the tourist from other nations.

The integration of Paraguay?

During the first thirty years of Argentina's agricultural and industrial re-orientation, no permanent new trend disturbed the Paraguayan scene. The Chaco War with Bolivia (1932–5) brought her new territories at a high cost in human resources, and in the Second World War her beef-canning industry enjoyed a brief boom which depleted her cattle stocks, but the disadvantages of political instability and physical isolation persisted. Indeed, in 1955 the country possessed only 1100 km of roads, of which scarcely half were surfaced.

The countryside remained a land of huge estates, squatters and peasant smallholdings. In 1961 a third of Paraguay, which occupies 41 million ha, was covered by twenty-five properties, each over 100,000 ha, and almost a quarter was still public; in contrast 142,000 properties, each under 50 ha, covered but one fortieth part. At the same time, according to a partial survey of tenurial systems, owner-operators held 37 per cent of the farms but 81 per cent of the land, tenants held 8 per cent of the farms and 4 per cent of the land, whereas squatters ran 42 per cent of the farms on only 7 per cent of the land. Another partial survey in 1956 revealed that 98 per cent of the farms in the relatively densely settled central district were under 50 ha, yet a third of the land still lay in huge farms over 5000 ha (Table 9.11).

TABLE 9.11   *Paraguay: farm sizes 1956*

	Selected classes		
Selected regions	*0–5 ha*	*5–50 ha*	*Over 5000 ha*
1 *Nation*			
% of farms	45·9	48·9	0·3
% of area	1·0	5·3	73·5
2 *Central 5 departments*			
% of farms	55·3	42·6	0·05
% of area	6·7	23·4	32·9
3 *Chaco departments*			
% of farms	22·7	24·3	9·0
% of area	0·02	0·1	85·6

In brief, the major agrarian problem lay in the insecurely held smallholdings of the central area where 77,000 farms, devoted to subsistence and peasant agriculture, had a median size of only 3·5 ha. Yet, with 60 per cent of the nation in forest and 34 per cent under natural pasture, there is no real shortage of land.

Indeed underpopulation was really a more serious problem than any shortage of land. International migration had done little to help. In 1950 Paraguay, over three times the size of England, had only 1·4 million inhabitants, of whom only 47,000 were foreign-born. Although most immigrants had been born in Argentina or Brazil and only 3000 had come from Germany, a large proportion of the former were descendants of German settlers. With few immigrants or native migrants new land settlement did not assume the character of a continuous pioneer fringe, though Itapúa department (capital Encarnación) facing Argentine Misiones was the most popular area of sporadic Germanic settlement. The strong social cohesion within the different European colonies helped greatly in the establishment of permanent settlements, but this exclusiveness, coupled with physical and economic isolation as well as the linguistic barrier of Guaraní, the language of the mestizo countryside, retarded the assimilation of immigrants into the national society.

Nevertheless, the foreigner continued to dominate the production of tree crops for the export market, whereas the native farmer still practised a peasant economy, selling locally his surplus of food staples and growing chiefly cotton and tobacco as cash crops for export.

By the late 1950s new trends were at last beginning to develop and with them the prospect of integration into the world economy. Basic to the change has been the stable government obtaining since the accession to power of General Stroessner in 1954. Though severe in the treatment of political opponents, its social and economic policies have been both progressive and realistic.

Efforts have been directed to the alleviation of agrarian insecurity and inequality, especially since the Agrarian Reform Law of 1963. By 1967, 33,000 farmers had had their titles confirmed to some 1·25 million ha, and another 11,000 had received 500,000 ha of land expropriated or purchased from their owners. More important, over a third of a million people (27·5 per cent of the rural population) have been resettled in almost 300 colonies covering nearly 2·5 million hectares and other large schemes are under way. Roughly two-thirds of the colonization has been devoted to settling Paraguayans on public lands, the rest to immigrants introduced under private schemes, such as the highly organized programme of Japanese immigration. Between 1955 and 1962 the immigration to near Encarnación of 5000 Japanese settlers gave them the leading position among non-Latin American foreign-born residents. Since then a big colonization venture at Alto Paraná has brought 2000 more. Although discouraged from settling in central Paraguay, the Japanese have integrated more easily than the Europeans and their techniques of intensive cultivation are being adopted by neighbours in the mixed colonies. Thanks to Japanese preference for tung as a cash crop, Paraguay now ranks as third world producer.

Despite the recent influx of Asians, the total foreign-born population – in 1966 no more than 2·5 per cent of Paraguay's 2 million inhabitants – has not changed, for Argentine and European settlers have declined correspondingly. Not only have immigrants yet to make a major contribution to Paraguay's population, but the country continues to lose on a grander scale through emigration to Argentina and Brazil where at least half a million Paraguayans are estimated to live.

The land settlement schemes have proceeded in association with an internationally aided programme of road works, now linking the capital with all the neighbouring republics and freeing the nation from almost total dependence upon inefficient routes through Argentina. By late 1966 the network totalled almost 5000 km, of which 1000 were surfaced. Asphalt highways now run to Encarnación and via the Alto Paraná colonies to Foz do Iguassu and the Brazilian free port of Paranaguá, whilst the Trans-Chaco Highway to Bolivia has ended the isolation of the Mennonite colonies, allowing them to find new produce outlets in Asunción and the Bolivian oilfield. A fourth route runs north-eastwards to the coffee lands near the town of P. J. Caballero and joins with the transport system of Mato Grosso; in addition along the western bank of the Paraguay–Paraná river runs an almost entirely paved road from Buenos Aires to a point facing Asunción.

These new road facilities have still to make an impact on the export economy of Paraguay. Indeed air transport has been preferred for carrying one new export crop, seedless grapefruit, to the British market.

The most important new economic trend has been the expansion of cattle farming and beef processing. After wartime exports of 26,000 tons, amounts fell to 1000 tons (worth less than half a million dollars) in 1952 when low controlled prices encouraged the smuggling of live cattle to Brazil. Since then the decline in Argentine canning-grade beef production together with new policies have stimulated Paraguayan growth; by 1963 the volume of exports had almost recovered wartime levels and during 1962–8 their value has averaged $14 million, representing a quarter to a third of all exports. Yet this is still only a quarter of the value of Argentine trade in processed beef.

Paraguay's cattle, which have doubled in number since the war to 6 million, are still mostly lean, bony animals derived from the poor *criollos* of Corrientes or zebus of Mato Grosso imported after the decimation of herds in 1865–70. Their preparation for slaughter takes six years (compared with three or less on the Pampas) but the introduction of high grade zebu-type animals (Santa Gertrudis and Brahman) by the U.S. Agricultural Mission twenty years ago, closely followed by Liebig's *estancias*, which have also led the way with improved pastures, has now set a pattern for improvement. This is actively being followed by other breeders, thanks to World Bank loans in 1963 and 1966 of $11 million for the increase and improvement of beef production, and to an IDB loan of $2·8 million in 1968 for the reduction of foot-and-mouth disease.

The specific concentration of World Bank aid to Paraguay on livestock and transport improvements is in explicit recognition of their key role in the country's development. At last the barrier of distance seems to be crumbling and, as in Argentina a century ago, immigrant enterprise, skill and capital is anxious to integrate the country into the world economy; it is significant that the head of state is himself of German descent. But the cultural barrier of Guaraní remains, the Paraguayan peasant takes little heed for the morrow and exhibits little interest in economic advance. Change is an imposition of the outsider.

CONCLUSION

Argentina's major problems are both national and regional. The national problem is fundamentally socio-political: since 1930 Argentina has not enjoyed an uninterrupted decade of freely elected government and many economic policies have been imposed without the expressed support of the voters. During the stagnant years of the 1950s there was much enquiry into the reasons for the nation's 'failure': apart from the defects of the economic and agrarian structures already discussed, speculation also centred upon the social psychology of the Argentine people. According to Fillol (1961), its faults lay in the adoption even by immigrants of so-called traditional values: contempt for manual labour, loyalty to the extended family, passivity, expectation of success through luck rather than enterprise, and respect for authority rather than achievement. He attributed past progress to the different ideals of unacculturated immigrants, to the strength of the export economy and 'most importantly to the technical and administrative contribution of foreign capital'. Yet national respect demanded the deposition of the foreigner from positions of economic power, and for many, Perón's nationalization of the railways was a symbolic action, a declaration of independence.

The positive contribution of the British immigrant, the leading foreigner in positions of economic power before 1930, owed as much to the peculiarity of the circumstances as to his different attitudes. These circumstances afforded him great opportunities to introduce and institute innovations and to diffuse knowledge both deeply and widely. The Briton, the Anglo-Argentine and a number of Argentines shared a common access to English education and membership of certain clubs and societies; they visited Britain, the home of many inventions as well as the source of credit; ideas could, therefore, circulate rapidly among those who were in a position to put them into practice in leading sectors of the economy: agriculture, transport and commerce. To men like Cavanagh and Finch, who introduced tung cultivation and zebu breeding, the delegation of managerial responsibility and the command of sufficient resources provided the opportunities, and a sense of achievement was their main motivation. For the railway companies, which depended for their success on a prosperous agriculture, it was logical to take concerted action to diffuse innovations as widely as possible through the media of demonstration farms, advisory services and farming magazines. Thus the international decline of Britain and the nationalization of the railways conspired to destroy the close-knit web and with it the opportunities which its links afforded. Dispersal of power at the top and the separation of power from information has hindered communication and effective co-operation, whilst the decline in delegated managerial responsibility has deprived many able Argentines in public service of opportunities for achievement. The problem then is perhaps contained less in the value-structure of society than in the process of economic decolonization.

Argentina's regional problem is twofold: it lies partly in the concentration of one third of the population and one half of the absolute wealth of the country in Greater Buenos Aires and partly in the *per capita* distribution of wealth – which in 1959 varied from under 5000 pesos in the poorest departments to over 125,000 pesos in the richest (Fig. 9.8).

The problems of Greater Buenos Aires are common to most metropolises, especially in Latin America: the inability of housing and the public services to keep pace with the inflow of migrants, the difficulties faced by unskilled rural folk in obtaining satisfactory employment and adjusting to urban life, and the sheer magnitude of organizing a city of 7 million people. Yet, if success is measured in terms of the *per capita* wealth produced by a community, it is other parts of the republic that rank highest: the cattle farming areas of the south and west of the humid Pampas, the sheep farms of central and southern Patagonia and the irrigated orchards of Mendoza and Río Negro, whilst the poorest areas extend over the semi-arid scrublands between Córdoba and Tucumán and over the less accessible parts of the Andes in the north-west. To attempt an equalization of wealth in the face of an unequal distribution of natural resources is pointless; to concentrate investment on 'growth poles' with the greatest potential is more realistic. Fortunately such 'poles' are already in evidence.

In the location of heavy industry along the south-west bank of the Paraná–Plate (Fig. 9.7b) may be discerned a resurgence of the Litoral axis, which saw the only concentration of colonial activity beyond the confines of the north-west and which in the late nineteenth century focused the processes of land settlement, railway building and port construction before the metropolitan magnet achieved its dominant attraction. Today this axis enjoys most of the locational advantages of the capital: access to all three rail networks, to gas and oil supplies by land or sea, to power and port facilities, to food supplies and to mass markets, without having to suffer the restrictions of expensive land and other handicaps of the great city. As in the early days of rail transport the central point of the paved highway system now lies to the north-west of the capital. But the growing need for a deep water port may well lead to more development towards the south-east. This axis thus seems already destined to become one of the most important multi-centred growth areas of late twentieth-century Latin America.

The growth of modern industries near Córdoba also echoes earlier developments of a Rosario–Córdoba offshoot from the Litoral axis.

For the other growth poles, closeness to international frontiers means that realization of their full potential will depend on neighbourly co-operation and upon stretching government vision to the peripheral provinces. Encouragingly the government of General Onganía (1966–70) established a fund of £100 million for basic investment in such areas.

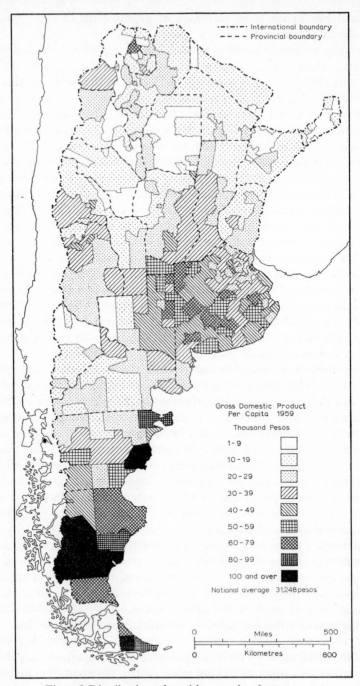

Fig. 9.8 Distribution of wealth 1959, by *departamentos*

Furthermore, early in 1969, the five nations sharing the Paraná–Paraguay basin signed the River Plate Treaty, which seeks to co-ordinate transport improvements, power development and the extension of irrigation and industry.

Nearest to Buenos Aires is the Lower Uruguay, a high-banked ria-type estuary that does not require dredging like the silt-laden Paraná. At present it is associated with *frigoríficos*, which draw their supplies from the relatively unintensively developed agricultural regions on both Argentine and Uruguayan sides; on the east bank Uruguay's best soils stretch between Montevideo and Paysandú, its second city. Above the head of navigation is the Salto Grande ('Big Falls'), where an international 720 MW hydro-electric project is to be built. The nearly finished tunnel between Santa Fé and Paraná cities, and the delta bridge to be constructed from Zárate, will give easier access to the metropolitan market, permitting the intensification of agriculture and settlement in southern Entre Ríos. The projected bridge at Fray Bentos will complete the link between the southern and northern shores of the Plate and in the longer term a complementary industrial axis stretching along the latter to Montevideo might be envisaged.

Most massive of all in scope is the middle Paraná basin, an area centring on the Iguazu Falls and stretching for 250 km both upstream and down and inland for over 100 km on either side. It includes all the Argentine province of Misiones, much of eastern Paraguay and parts of the Brazilian states of Mato Grosso and Paraná. The land is underlain largely by the great basalt lava flows, with which is associated perhaps the world's largest area of underdeveloped soils of moderate fertility. Misiones, the most settled part, still has large virgin areas, the south-western corner of Paraná is the least settled part of that booming state, whilst Paraguay is actively settling a few areas. Because of the reliably humid subtropical climate the land is capable of intensive cultivation of a great diversity of crops, as well as the production of rapidly growing soft woods. The quality of the existing (largely German) settlers is high, as well as their willingness to co-operate for the common good. Dozens of minor rivers have a hydro-electric potential where they plunge over basalt scarps to join the incised Paraná – on one such Paraguayan river, the Acaray, a recently inaugurated 150 MW plant will serve both Misiones and Paraguay – whilst the Guaira Falls on the Paraná itself have the greatest potential, over 5000 MW, of any falls in the world. Misiones is building a paper factory to use Acaray power, whilst Paraná already has the biggest such factory in Latin America. The Asunción–Paranaguá highway now provides the shortest route to the Atlantic (and São Paulo), whilst the planned Resistencia bridge and its associated roads will link Misiones to the Argentine road network. The Paraná–Paraguay river system provides traditional bulk transport in shallow boats to the Plate, but the old course of the Upper Paraná along the river Aguapey to the Uruguay could easily be employed for speedier hovercraft communication with Buenos Aires. Thanks to its tourist attraction, Iguazu Falls is already on international air routes. In the past the area has suffered most from distance to markets (800 km from Buenos Aires and São Paulo) but with new settlers and new outlets it could ultimately become a growth pole of a very high order.

Over 1000 km to the west lie the Andean foothills of Salta and Jujuy, the most dynamic part of the old north-west. This is the major area of attraction for migrants from the rest of the region and from Bolivia, a land of growing tobacco, sugar, citrus, banana and early vegetable farms, of the Salta–Bolivian oilfield and the Zapla steel works. With lead, zinc, manganese, iron and tin mines, Jujuy produced 80 per cent of Argentina's metallic ores in 1964. Here, too, lie untouched forests and the largest single irrigable area awaiting development. Although 1500 km from Buenos Aires, the area lies beside the Buenos Aires–La Paz railway as well as the Pan American Highway. Mutual advantage could be derived from greater exchange with the mining areas of northern Chile via the Socompa railway, but it is harder to envisage direct benefits to Bolivia from closer cooperation.

The Mendoza district is already so well developed as to need no further mention, except to lament the little intercourse with the Vale of Chile and Santiago, with which Cuyo has such strong historical ties.

Lastly, there is the prospect of development in northern Patagonia at Neuquén and Bahía Blanca. The former city lies in a zone of prosperous irrigated fruit farming, flanked by two oil and gas fields, and is about to benefit from the development of the El Chocón–Cerros Colorados hydroelectricity and irrigation scheme. In the short run the produce of the soil, wool and fruit, is more likely to be industrialized than iron, the product of the subsoil. Internationally Neuquén could benefit from lying at the eastern end of the easiest of Trans-Andean routes, leading to Chile's industrial conurbation of Concepción, as well as at the apex of roads leading into the unspoiled yet increasingly frequented Chilean–Argentine lake district, which affords some of Latin America's most beautiful scenery. Here (as in the middle Paraná basin) growth of settlement and industry would lead to the more intensified use of other adjacent areas: the foothills of the Patagonian Andes enjoy a climate like that of England, yet remoteness from markets makes wool the only viable agricultural economy. Bahía Blanca, long the outlet for the produce of the southern Pampas and Río Negro, is now, with the construction of a petrochemical complex, benefiting from the position astride gas and oil pipelines.

Today Alberdi's dictum that settlement of the land is the essence of government ('gobernar es poblar') remains as true as in 1853; but settlement requires capital as well as people.

BIBLIOGRAPHY

ARNOLDS, A. (1963) *Geografía económica argentina.*

BANK OF LONDON AND SOUTH AMERICA. *Fortnightly, Monthly* and *Quarterly Reviews.*

BRANNON, R. H. (1968) *The Agricultural Development of Uruguay.*

Cahiers d'Outre-Mer. Various numbers since 1960.

CENTRE NATIONAL DE LA RECHERCHE SCIENTIFIQUE (1968) *Les problèmes agraires des Amériques Latines.* Contributions by R. Cortés Conde, J. C. Crossley, R. Gaignard, H. Giberti, J. A. Martinez de Hoz.

CENTRO DE ESTUDIANTES DE CIENCIAS ECONÓMICAS Y ADMINISTRACIÓN (1966) *Plan nacional de desarrollo económico y social 1965–1974 (Uruguay).* 2 vols.

COMISION DE INVERSIONES Y DESARROLLO ECONÓMICO (1963) *Estudio Económico del Uruguay, Evolución y Perspectivas.* 2 vols.

CIDA (Comité Interamericano de Desarrollo Agrícola) (1965) *Land Tenure Conditions and Socio-economic Development of the Agricultural Sector. Argentina.*

CONSEJO FEDERAL DE INVERSIONES (1963a) *Aspectos jurídicos, económicos y sociales de la colonización con inmigrantes.*

CONSEJO FEDERAL DE INVERSIONES (1963b) *Complejo industrial San Nicolás–Santa Fé.* 2 vols.

CONSEJO FEDERAL DE INVERSIONES (1962–5) *Programa conjunto para el desarrollo agropecuario e industrial.* 1er, 2do, 3er, 40 Informes. 15 vols.

CONSEJO FEDERAL DE INVERSIONES (1964a) *Programa integral de aumento de la producción de carne vacuna en la región Pampeana.* 2 vols.

CONSEJO FEDERAL DE INVERSIONES (1964b) *Tenencia de la tierra.* 4 vols.

DE APARICIO, F. and DIFRIERI, H. A. (eds.) (1959–61) *La Argentina. Suma de geografía.* vols. 4, 6, 7, 8.

DIRECCIÓN NACIONAL DE ESTADÍSTICA Y CENSOS (1960a) *Censo nacional agropecuario.* 3 vols.

DIRECCIÓN NACIONAL DE ESTADÍSTICA Y CENSOS (1960b) *Censo nacional de población.* 9 vols.

DI TELLA, T. S. (1965) *La teoria del primer impacto del crecimiento economico.*

FERNS, H. S. (1960) *Britain and Argentina in the 19th Century.*

FERNS, H. S. (1969) *Argentina.*

FERRER, A. (1967) *The Argentine Economy.*

Q

FILLOL, T. R. (1961) *Social Factors in Economic Development: The Argentine Case.*

FAO ETAP (Extended Technical Assistance Programme) (1958) Report 971 on *Pasture and Fodder Development in Argentina.*

FAO ETAP (1965) Report 1940 on *Sheep and Wool Industry in Argentina.*

FAO ETAP (1966) Report 2215 on *Soil Fertility Problems in Argentina.*

GIBERTI, H. (1961) *Historia económica de la ganadería Argentina.*

GIBERTI, H. (1964) *El desarrollo agrario Argentino.*

GIBERTI. H. *et al.* (1965) *Sociedad, economía y reforma agraria.*

INTER-AMERICAN DEVELOPMENT BANK, SOCIAL PROGRESS TRUST FUND. *Reports* for 1966, 1967 and 1968.

INTER-AMERICAN ECONOMIC AFFAIRS. Various numbers since 1960.

JUNTA NACIONAL DE CARNES (1964) *Reseña 1957.*

KATZ, J. and GALLO, E. (1968) The industrialization of Argentina. In VÉLIZ, C. (ed.) *Latin America. A Handbook.*

MARTINEZ RODRIGUEZ, I. (1962) *Apuntes de geografía del Uruguay.*

OFICINA DE ESTUDIOS PARA LA COLABORACIÓN ECÓNOMICA INTERNACIONAL (1966) *Argentina económica y financiera.*

PENDLE, G. (1952) *Uruguay.*

PENDLE, G. (1961) *Argentina.*

PENDLE, G. (1967) *Paraguay. A Riverside Nation.*

PINCUS, J. (1968) *The Economy of Paraguay.*

PLOTTIER, L. and NOTARO, J. (1966) *El arrendamiento rural en Uruguay.*

RUANO FOURNIER, A. (1963) *Estudio económico de la producción de las carnes del Rio de la Plata.*

SCOBIE, J. R. (1964a) *Argentina. A City and A Nation.*

SCOBIE, J. R. (1964b) *Revolution on the Pampas.*

STEWART, N. R. (1967) *Japanese Colonization in Eastern Paraguay.*

TAYLOR, C. C. (1948) *Rural Life in Argentina.*

U.N. STATISTICAL YEAR BOOKS. Various.

U.S. DEPARTMENT OF AGRICULTURE (1968) *Argentine Agriculture. Trends in Production and World Competition.*

WILHELMY, H. and ROHMEDER, W. (1963) *Die La Plata-Länder.*

WINSBERG, M. D. (1964) Jewish colonization in Argentina. *Geog. Rev.*, 54.

WINSBERG, M. D. (1968) *Focus*, 18 (7).

WINSBERG, M. D. (1970) Introduction and diffusion of the Aberdeen Angus breed in Argentina. *Geography*, 55.

10 Chile

Harold Blakemore

I SOME BASIC CHARACTERISTICS

The best-known popular work in Chilean geography, by Benjamin Subercaseaux, is entitled *Chile, o una loca geografía* (*Chile, or a crazy geography*), and the epithet 'crazy' could hardly be more apt. For how else should one characterize a country over 4200 km in length – excluding Chilean Antarctica – but nowhere more than 400 km wide, and with an average width of less than half that figure; its entire western frontier an ocean shoreline, more clearly defined but no less natural than its eastern counterpart of mountain ranges; with varieties of physiography and climate extending from absolute desert in the north to rain-drenched forest in the south? Much more than many of her larger neighbours, Chile is a microcosm of the continent in which they all lie, with its great physical diversity and regional contrasts, reflecting not only basic geographical and economic differences but also a distinctive historical experience. That Chile exists as a unitary state at all is, in effect, the result of the organic expansion north and south from a central core of long-standing human occupance, and the incorporation of frontier regions of strikingly different character into a national polity.

The unity in diversity that Chile exhibits is a unity imposed from the centre to the periphery, as Chile expanded from its colonial base in the heart of the modern republic, when economic and strategic considerations during the nineteenth century determined the march of her frontiers northwards and southwards. This expansion, however, entails today disadvantages that could not have been apparent a hundred years ago, notably the enlargement of disparities of economic and social well-being between the centre and the outlying regions, which has been manifestly aided by increased centralization of decision-making. This development creates in the peripheral regions growing resentment at political, social and economic structures, which seem to perpetuate their subordinate position.

In Chile, these features – common to most Latin American states – are particularly striking for several reasons. In the first place, Chile's economic growth has depended in the past, and still depends today, to a large extent on the exploitation of resources located in the outlying regions of the country, notably copper and other minerals in the northern provinces, and oil and wool in the far south. Secondly, the rapid growth of cities in recent years, most notably of the capital, Santiago, has meant an increased concentration of population and the various services it requires in areas that were already favoured recipients of national expenditure. It is, therefore, not surprising that regional feeling against the metropolis, itself a feature of the colonial period, should be so strong today, and the argument is often heard that, as in the colonial era, Chile was no less a colony of Peru than Peru was of Spain, so today Antofagasta and Magallanes are colonies of central Chile, and central Chile a colony of Santiago.

National governments have long been aware of these tensions and of what, unchecked, they might signify for the republic as a whole, and they have been no less conscious of the gross internal disequilibria, not only between but also within provinces – between, for example, town and country. During the last thirty years in particular, significant attempts have been made through planning and investment mechanisms to correct such imbalances, and how far they have succeeded is a question to be considered in the course of this essay. Nevertheless, the fact remains that central Chile, with four hundred years of history behind it, has always been the dominant region of the country, and modern attempts to ameliorate regional imbalances can only be understood properly within the framework of Chile's historical evolution as a whole. It is an evolution in which the political tradition of strong, centralist government has almost always obtained.

An investigation of *regional* evolution in particular provides certain guidelines for the understanding of contemporary Chile's problems, for the patterns of the past have persisted strongly into the present. Two stages of Chilean history may illustrate this point. The first, from the foundation of Santiago by Pedro de Valdivia in 1541 to the achievement of independence from Spain in 1818, not only saw the firm establishment of the core region, between the rim of the northern desert at Copiapó and the edge of the southern forest area at the line of the river Bío-Bío; it also saw laid down within these confines the specific racial, socio-economic and even quasi-national characteristics that made Chile what it is as a national state. The second example, the second half of the nineteenth century, which witnessed the physical growth of Chile to more than three times its original size, also saw the establishment of economic structures highly dependent on export-orientated resources located outside the core region, and the pattern was preserved: what nitrates meant to Chile yesterday, copper means today. But, clearly, in the historical evolution of any region, geographical factors play an important role, and it is necessary at the outset to sketch a brief description of the land and the people before turning to their interaction through time.

The physical framework

Chile extends from 18°S. to 56°S., a length equivalent to the distance between central Norway and Morocco or, to take a New World comparison, to approximately the distance from New York to San Francisco. Chile's area, some 740,000 km², is roughly three times the size of the United Kingdom, but few areas of comparable size have such striking climatological and physical diversity. The climatic division is a latitudinal one, in contrast to the longitudinal character of landscape, which we will consider first.

There are three basic features of the Chilean landscape, which run from north to south in roughly parallel lines: the Andean cordillera to the east, decreasing in height towards the south of the country; the much lower and more fragmented *cordillera de la costa*, fronting the Pacific and becoming an archipelago, partly submerged, from about 42°S.; and, between the two highland chains, a central depression. Each of these longitudinal features has quite markedly different characteristics from north to south, with the clearest definition of each in the central portion of Chile.

In the north, the eastern highlands are, in effect, a continuation of the Peruvian–Bolivian *puna*, the high plateau, entirely over 3600 m above sea-level with surrounding peaks at 6000 m or more. Composed of a large number of interior basins, separated by recent volcanic flows, this cold and windswept highland, with its salt lakes (*salares*) and dramatic scenery, has not changed since Bowman wrote his classic description of it (1924, pp. 257–342). Though the greater accessibility of the area, which improved air and surface transportation has made possible since that time, has led to tentative and sporadic exploration of mineral deposits, extensive commercial exploitation of its borates, sulphates and, possibly, iron ore seems unlikely in the foreseeable future in view of the cost factors involved (Rudolph, 1963, p. 12).

From about 27°S. to 38°S. the orographic structure in the east is of high parallel ranges with steep narrow valleys between them. Here are to be found Chile's highest peaks, with Aconcagua on the Argentine side of the frontier at 7500 m. In this region, the Andean ranges occupy from a third to a half of the width of Chile, their peaks snow-covered and the lower slopes heavily timbered. Near Santiago, on latitude 33°S., the snow-line at a height of between 4000 m and 4500 m gives the capital one of the most superb backdrops of any city in Latin America. But from latitude 38°S. the mountain chains are lower and, whereas in the central section none of the passes over the Andes to Argentina is less than 3000 m, here a profusion of lakes, rivers and passes at lower altitudes, combined with a series of magnificent volcanoes skirting the western edge of the range, produces a more varied and beautiful landscape, albeit a less awesome one. Further south still, the Chilean Andes confront the Pacific on a fjord coastline, with extensive icefields inland, the mountains curving south-east to the Straits of Magellan, where they submerge to reappear in the southern part of Tierra del Fuego and the islands of the Beagle Channel.

The coastal range also exhibits variety from north to south, though, because of its more broken character and lower elevation, this is somewhat less striking than with the inland mountain chain. Geologically much younger and considerably more eroded, the *cordillera de la costa* begins south of Arica as an abrupt elevation from the Pacific shoreline, attaining varying heights between 550 m and 850 m north of Iquique but rising in altitude further south to over 1800 m south of the river Loa, the boundary between the provinces of Tarapacá and Antofagasta. The highest point of the *cordillera* in the desert regions is the Sierra Vicuña Mackenna south of Antofagasta, almost 3000 m above sea-level. The proximity of the coastal range to the Pacific coast gives the latter a wall-like appearance from the sea for over 960 km, broken only by marine terraces at infrequent intervals: on these terraces stand the few ports and portlets – Pisagua, Iquique, Tocopilla, Mejillones, Antofagasta and Taltal – but they lack the protection of natural bays and harbours on what is a fairly uniform coastline. Behind them, the coastal range might be best described as a plateau, having an average depth of over 50 km and lacking on its eastern side the abrupt descent that characterizes its coastal aspect.

South of Chañaral the *cordillera de la costa* virtually disappears, since from here to the river Aconcagua Andean spurs run westwards, and transverse river valleys – such as the Copiapó, Huasco and Elquí – coupled with broad marine terraces, 40 km or more in width, are the characteristic features. The range reappears, however, south of the Aconcagua, and in the provinces of Valparaiso and Santiago attains virtually Andean elevations of over 2500 m. But though the identity of the coastal range is here re-established, greater areas of coastal plain are also apparent at the mouths of the more abundant rivers. South of the river Maule, the coastal range divides into two chains, one along the coast and the other some 16 km inland, with fertile basins between them, but this feature disappears near the river Itata and the mountains only once again reach a height of 700 km as the Cordillera de Nahuelbuta, south of the river Bío-Bío. Thereafter, a succession of high hills rather than mountains runs to the channel of Chacao, which separates the large island of Chiloé from the mainland of Chile, and the coastal range re-emerges on the island as the Cordillera Piuche, at over 300 m, and also in the Guaitecas islands, to disappear finally in the peninsula of Taitao.

The third longitudinal feature of Chile and, from the point of view of human settlement by far the most important, is the great alluviated central depression. Again, there is a strongly contrasting picture from north to south. In the desert north, huge alluvial fans mark the foot of the Andes and a series of dry basins (*bolsones*), some 80 km wide and over 600 m above sea-level, stretch to the coastal plateau. Formerly lakes, these basins are rich in salts, especially nitrates, the export of which provided Chile with approximately half her government revenue from the 1880s to the First World War. The basins are crossed by deep, ravine-like valleys (*quebradas*) made by intermittent rivers, such as the Aroma, Tarapacá and Quisma, but surface water supplies are very meagre and between 18°S. and 27°S. only the river Loa reaches the Pacific.

The latter latitude is approximately the limit of a transitional zone which extends to 33°S. In its northern part, in the province of Atacama, permanent streams begin to appear crossing the longitudinal depression – the rivers Copiapó and Huasco. As one moves south, the river valleys, separated by transverse Andean spurs, widen, and in the province of Coquimbo the rivers Los Chorros, Elquí, Limari and Choapa have formed more extensive plains than exist in the north, as have the Ligua, Petorca and Aconcagua in the province of Aconcagua. South of the river Aconcagua lies the last great Andean spur to cut across the central valley for some 960 km, the Chacabuco ridge, which separates, at a height of 730 m, the Aconcagua valley – 'the Vale of Chile' – from its southern neighbour, the valley of the Mapocho where Santiago stands. From here, the central valley extends south to Puerto Montt at latitude 41° 30'S.

The central valley is divided by the river Bío-Bío into two quite distinct sections. North of that line it is a continuous series of river basins – the Maipo, Mapocho, Rapel, Mataquito, Maule and Itata – with the valley floor sloping from east to west and with a declining elevation from north to south. These rivers, fed by rain in winter and by the melting snows of the Andes in summer, have built up large alluvial fans, and the slope of the valley floor permits irrigation of the rich soils by gravity flow. Near Santiago, which stands at 530 m above sea-level, the eastern and western valley margins lie at approximately 700 m and 330 m, but in the region of the Bío-Bío they are much lower – 300 m and 100 m respectively. Only with the latter river, however, does the broad valley floor reach to the Pacific; the rivers further north cross the central valley more or less at right angles and break through canyons in the coastal ranges to the Pacific.

South of the Bío-Bío the alluvial fans on the eastern border of the northern part of the central valley give way to moraines and lakes, as deep-flowing rivers – the Imperial, Tolten, Valdivia, Bueno, Maullin and Petrohué – and the reappearance of Andean spurs gives a more fragmented appearance to the landscape. At the Gulf of Reloncaví, where Puerto Montt stands, the great longitudinal depression disappears beneath the sea, to emerge again for a short distance as the Isthmus of Ofqui, before finally being submerged in the Golfo de Peñas.

Climate and its effects

While the relief of Chile has clearly been of fundamental importance in historical settlement patterns and must remain a critical factor in the exploitation of natural resources and other economic activity, no less significant is the influence of climate and, above all, the country's rainfall pattern. With a latitudinal extent of 38°, Chile experiences a climatic range no less striking than the variety of its physical features and at least as important in creating the basic character of each of Chile's regions. A brief description only will be necessary here, since the subject is discussed at length elsewhere (CORFO, 1967, pp. 98–152).

Chile's temperatures range from subtropical to subarctic, though extremes are tempered by the proximity of the sea to all parts of the country, by the effects of the cold Humboldt current, which are felt north of latitude 40°S., and by the on-shore character of the prevailing westerly winds. Moreover, the Andean cordillera operates as an effective barrier to continental influences. These factors, taken in conjunction with the topographical and, of course, linked to the global patterns of air circulation, account for the remarkable variations in rainfall throughout the country. Rainfall increases from north to south, being higher everywhere on the

TABLE 10.1   *Annual rainfall and mean temperatures at selected locations in Chile*

Region	Place	Latitude south	Rainfall (mm)	Mean temperature (°C) Annual	Hottest month	Coldest month
1 Desert	Iquique	20° 21'	2·1	17·9	21	14·7
	Antofagasta	23° 39'	9·0	16·6	25·5	13·3
	Copiapó	27° 21'	28·0	16·0	25·7	12·3
	La Serena	29° 54'	133·3	14·8	16·4	11·8
2 Mediter-	Los Andes	32° 50'	307·0	15·3	21·2	9·3
ranean	Viña del Mar	;3° 0'	482·0	14·7	16·1	11·7
	Santiago	;3° 27'	362·0	14·0	20·0	8·1
	Talca	35° 26'	716·3	14·8	22·1	8·5
	Concepción	36° 40'	1292·8	11·6	18·0	9·6
3 Forest	Temuco	38° 45'	1360·0	12·0	19·0	7·6
	Valdivia	39° 48'	2488·7	11·9	17·0	7·7
4 Archipelagic	Puerto Aisén	45° 28'	2865·0	9·0	13·2	4·6
	Evangelistas	52° 24'	2569·7	6·4	8·8	4·4
5 Atlantic	Punta Arenas	53° 1'	437·1	6·7	11·7	2·5
	Punta Dungeness	52° 24'	253·8	7·1	11·4	2·5

Sources: Bohan and Pomerantz (1960, p. 36); CORFO (1967, pp. 123–49).

coast than at equivalent latitudes inland, but lower than on the higher ranges of the Andes. Temperatures steadily decline from north to south, the diurnal and seasonal range being less marked on the coast than inland, while in the Andes it is, naturally, altitude rather than latitude that determines temperature.

The natural environments produced by the interaction of land form and climate are in striking contrast, and the names commonly given to the regions of Chile indicate their basic characteristics. From north to south, these are Desert Chile (latitude 17·5°S. to 30°S.), Mediterranean Chile (30°S. to 37·5°S.), Forest Chile (37·5°S. to 41·5°S.), Archipelagic Chile (41·5°S. to 56°S.) and Atlantic Chile (from about 44°S. to 54·5°S.).[1] Table 10.1 illustrates the temperature and rainfall of selected locations within these regions from north to south.

Desert Chile

Known best to Chileans as the Norte Grande, Desert Chile, composed of the provinces of Tarapacá and Antofagasta, occupies approximately one quarter of the land surface of Chile, excluding Antarctica. It is one of the driest regions on earth, and includes places where no rain has ever been recorded, and others, again, where extraordinary rainfall in a short space of time makes up a very low average rainfall over a long period of years, as in 1911 (Bowman, 1924, pp. 42–3). On the coast there is a higher relative humidity than inland, more uniform seasonal and diurnal temperatures and, from north of Antofagasta city, the phenomenon known as the *camanchaca*. This is a greyish mist, formed as follows: cold upwelling water, landward of the Humboldt current, cools the stable air, leading to condensation, and the prevailing temperature inversion prevents vertical air movement and the formation of precipitation. Iquique has almost a third of the year under the *camanchaca*, particularly during May to August, and enjoys cloudless skies only for about sixty days, but the heavy dews along the coast allow xerophytic and herbaceous plants to grow. In the desert hinterland, in contrast, the air is dry, the sky cloudlessly blue, and vast areas are quite devoid of vegetation. However, in *quebradas* shrubs may grow, and dwarf trees can survive in certain areas where tap roots reach underground water, as in the extensive Pampa de Tamarugal. The shortlasting but intensive, and highly infrequent, rainfalls that may occur in desert regions cause them, proverbially, to blossom as the rose for a short while before resuming their customary barren appearance.

On the eastern fringes of the desert, important oasis towns and villages, such as San Pedro de Atacama, Toconao and Peine, have survived through

[1] Butland (1956, pp. 5–11) places Archipelagic Chile with Forest Chile but, in view of its much more fragmented physical character, turbulent weather and lack of settlement, there is a good case for treating it as a separate region (Bohan and Pomerantz, 1960, p. 38). In historical terms, certainly, the case is overwhelming.

centuries, while today large networks of pipelines bring water from the wetter eastern highlands as far as the coast.

Mediterranean Chile

The southern half of the province of Atacama and the province of Coquimbo, together with the northern part of Aconcagua, is a transitional zone between the Desert and Mediterranean Chile proper. Precipitation increases as one moves south, particularly on the coast; the winter rainfall regime is short in duration and little rain falls, but it is adequate to support typical *matorral* cover, outside the cultivated river valleys. Aconcagua province marks the end of the transitional zone. From the valley of that name to the river Bío-Bío, the climate is truly Mediterranean, with cool to cold rainy winters, mild springs and autumns, and warm, dry summers. Since the *cordillera de la costa* acts as a rain shield south of the Chacabuco ridge, the rainfall and humidity figures for the central valley are lower than on the coast, and temperature ranges are consistently higher. This region, with its rich soils and equable climate, is generally regarded as one of the most suitable for human settlement in the world, and it is worth quoting on its merits from the first letter of Pedro de Valdivia, conqueror of Chile, to Charles V in 1545:

> This land is such that there is none better in the world for living in and settling down; this I say because it is very flat, very healthy, and very pleasant; it has four months of winter, not more, and in them it is only when the moon is at the quarter that it rains one day or two; on all the other days the sun is so fine that there is no need to draw near the fire. The summer is so temperate, with such delightful breezes, that a man can be out in the sun all day long without annoyance. It is the most abounding land in pastures and fields, and for yielding every kind of livestock and plant imaginable; much timber and very fine for houses; endless wood for use in them; the mines most rich in gold, the whole land being full of it; and wherever men may wish to take it, there they will find a place to sow, and the wherewithal to build, and water, wood and grass for their beasts; so that it seems as though God made it purposely to be able to hold it all in His hand.

The lyrical language of the *conquistador* has been echoed by countless travellers and commentators on the Chilean heartland, which was for over three hundred years the real Chile and which has remained the essential core of the nation to the present day. Its climatological and vegetational similarities to Mediterranean Spain made it immediately attractive for early settlement (Encina and Castedo, 1964, I, pp. 75–7), and, indeed, this was one of the factors that made Chile a distinctive colony of Spain from a very early period, leading as it did to genuine and permanent establishment on the land.

Forest Chile

The clearly defined seasons of Mediterranean Chile, and notably the dry summers in contrast to a winter rainfall regime, begin to lose their distinctive character in the southern part of the region. Linares, for example, near latitude 36°S. and approximately the same distance inland as is Santiago on latitude 33° 27'S., has an average annual rainfall nearly three times as great, and the rainy season is a month longer. But it is south of the Bío-Bío that the striking change occurs as migratory depressions from the west make their influence felt in cloud and rain throughout the year, and the vegetation cover markedly reflects the higher precipitation (see Table 10.1 for comparative rainfall figures).

Forest Chile is truly named. With cool, wet summers and stormy winters, dense forests replace the scrub-type forest of Mediterranean Chile, and the *espino* as a characteristic tree gives way to the much taller beech, pine and laurel. The province of Valdivia is particularly densely forested, with a multiplicity of species.

The region is a frontier region, for, although towns such as Valdivia and Osorno in the respective provinces of the same names go back in time to the colonial period, they were always essentially outposts of the Kingdom of Chile, and not until the mid-nineteenth century was settlement more widespread and permanent.

Archipelagic Chile

If Mediterranean Chile has always attracted man, Archipelagic Chile is quite the opposite, particularly south of latitude 44°S. Only in areas protected from the persistent force of the westerly storms, such as eastern Chiloé and the mainland of Aisén, is settlement possible in this cold, wet region. Puerto Aisén, at latitude 45° 28'S., has an annual rainfall of over 2865 mm, and an annual mean temperature of 10°C., but further south still up to 5100 mm of rain annually has been recorded for some locations. The region, with its maze of channels and islands, is virtually uninhabited in the west, and the quality and extent of the vegetational cover, unlike Forest Chile, is limited by the severity of the climate.

Historically the region has been of minor significance and, with its paucity of resources and climatic deterrence to man, it seems destined to remain so.

Atlantic Chile

As its name suggests, this region is untypically Chilean in its location. It lies east of the high Andes, on both sides of the Straits of Magellan, and, with a character and climate markedly different from Archipelagic Chile, it is in many respects more an extension of southern Argentina than of Chile proper. Rainfall, again, is the key determinant. Lying in the rain-shadow of the Andes, the region avoids the heavy rainfall of the west and, indeed, comparative figures for approximately similar latitudinal locations on both sides of the Andes are very striking (see Table 10.1).

Low, undulating terrain with extensive grasslands characterizes northern Tierra del Fuego, the mainland opposite and, much further north, scattered areas near the Palena, Cisnes and Simpson rivers in the province of Aisén, which is the attenuated northern finger of this region. The wetter and higher areas – southern Tierra del Fuego, eastern Aisén, the *cordilleran* zone of Magallanes – are clothed with evergreen forest.

The initial reasons for settlement in the Magallanic zone during the nineteenth century were as much strategic and political as economic, but late nineteenth- and twentieth-century growth of pastoralism and of the oil industry have given Atlantic Chile considerable importance to the country as a whole.

Population

Chile's last national census was held in 1970: it revealed a population of 8,836,000, growing at a rate of around 2·5 per cent each year (IADB, 1970, p. 147).[1] In its rate of growth Chile's population is slower than that of Latin-America as a whole (2·91 per cent in 1967–8) but it shares with most other Latin American states certain demographic characteristics which account for the very rapid increase of human beings in the continent. In the first place, the annual rate of increase in Chile has almost doubled over the past forty years: in the quinquennium 1930–5 it was 1·51 per cent; ten years later it was 1·67 per cent, but in 1950–5 it had reached 2·21 per cent and has averaged over 2·5 per cent in every quinquennium since (ECLA, 1969, I, p. 6). Secondly, as elsewhere in Latin America, far and away the major factor in this growth has been a declining mortality-rate, with fluctuations in the birth-rate being of much less significance, and net migration having virtually no impact at all in Chile. The death-rate of 15·7 per 1000 recorded for 1950 had fallen to 11·6 per 1000 by 1962 (CORFO, 1967, p.361), and was estimated at 8·1 per 1000 for 1968 (IADB, 1970, p. 147). The birth-rate, on the other hand, has only shown a very slight decline in recent years, from 34 per 1000 in 1950 to 32·5 per 1000 in 1967 (IADB, 1968, p. 95).

The dramatic fall in the death-rate is chiefly due to improved health services generally and to their wider impact in hitherto neglected areas, though this is not to deny the enormous disparities that still exist between one region and another, between the urban sector and the rural, and so on. Nevertheless, estimates of causes of death in Chile in recent years shows a considerable diminution of some of the scourges that have afflicted the country in the past: deaths from infectious diseases, for example, fell from

[1] The population total is the preliminary result of the census of 1970. Since the data collected in 1970 have not yet been processed, this discussion revolves around the censuses of 1952 and 1960.

60 per 1000 in 1964 to 25·1 per 1000 in 1967, testifying to the effect of the higher public investment in the health services, which has been a marked feature of these years (*Mensaje*, 1969, pp. 484–5). A very high infant mortality-rate was for long the most disturbing characteristic of Chile's health picture, but it has fallen from 105 per 1000 in 1964 to 78·7 in 1970.

Another key feature of Chile's population, with far-reaching social and economic implications, is its age structure. The extension of life expectancy at birth has gone on steadily since 1920, and was estimated to be 58·2 years for men and 64 for women in 1969 (IADB, 1970, p. 154). However, given a dramatic fall in mortality and a fairly constant birth-rate (moderately high by world standards though not by Latin American), the population tends increasingly to be younger and, therefore, a fairly high proportion of the total is economically dependent. This, again, is characteristic of the continent as a whole, and a projection for 1970 suggested that about 42 per cent of Latin America's people would then be under 15 years of age, 4 per cent over 65 and, therefore, that the percentage of population classified as economically active would be about 54 per cent (ECLA, 1969, I, pp. 11–12). The approximation of a particular age range with economic worth is, of course, a somewhat arbitrary assumption, and the case of Chile indicates that such estimates can only be of the crudest value. Chile has a somewhat smaller proportion of population under 15 years than Latin America as a whole (39·9 per cent in 1965) and a higher proportion (4·4 per cent) over 65, but the remaining 55·7 per cent between these ages cannot properly be classified as economically active, except as a very rough guide to potential. A random sample for 1967 suggested, in fact, that no more than 31 per cent of Chile's population fell into that category, at a time when 5·3 per cent of the age group was officially registered as unemployed. (IADB, 1968, p. 96). But, however crude these figures may be, it is quite clear that Chile has a large dependent population, and one of the big questions for her planners is whether the country will be able not only to feed, clothe, house and educate its young people but also to absorb them eventually into productive employment.

The problems created for Chile by the particular age structure of the population are, however, visibly overshadowed by the issues related to the spatial distribution of people. It is a commonplace of twentieth-century Latin America that the other side of the demographic coin to a massive increase in numbers is their uneven distribution, both between regions and within regions, with large-scale urbanization and heavy migration from the rural areas to the cities as characteristic modern phenomena. In Chile's case – as in that of Argentina and Uruguay – these movements have considerable historical antecedents, and the present volume of these changes may be regarded as much as a dramatic quickening of long-established tendencies as something belonging principally to the twentieth century.

The population of Chile has always been heavily concentrated in the provinces of the central valley from Aconcagua to Ñuble, containing not only the two major cities of the republic, Santiago and Valparaiso, but also what has been the richest agricultural region since the colonial period. This is one of those regions, of which Latin America has few examples, characterized by James (1959, p. 236) as a zone of expanding settlement in which the rate of population growth has been sufficient to allow an expansion of its frontiers without lessening the density of the nucleus. Nevertheless, the total proportion of the national population living in this region has fluctuated over the last hundred years as the northern and southern extremities of the republic were effectively incorporated into Chile during the nineteenth and twentieth centuries. In 1854, the region contained approximately 70 per cent of Chile's one and a half million people (Encina and Castedo, 1964, II, p. 1140). Thirty years later, not long after the northern desert region and the southern forest area had been made part of the republic, the proportion had fallen to 60 per cent and by 1920 stood at 55 per cent (Censos, Provincias, 1964). Not until 1940 was this downward trend arrested: the proportion of Chileans in the central provinces was then 56 per cent and it rose to 59 per cent by the census of 1952, and was held at that figure to 1960 (Censos, Provincias, 1964). But an estimate for 1963 put the percentage at 61 per cent (Weaver, 1968, p. 31), and the probability is that it has continued to rise further since that time.

Provincial variations within the region indicate clearly that the modern return to the picture of a hundred years ago is due predominantly to the growth of the conurbations of Santiago and Valparaiso. Between 1885 and 1960 the population of Santiago province rose sixfold and that of Valparaiso province threefold; that of O'Higgins doubled and that of Talca almost doubled, while the rate of growth in the other provinces – Aconcagua, Colchagua, Curico, Linares and Ñuble – has been much slower, and in Maule the population in 1960 was, in fact, about one tenth less what it was in 1885 (Censos, Provincias, 1964). The proportion of people in Santiago province living in the capital city in 1960, however, was no less than 82·2 per cent (Censo, 1960, Santiago, p. 17), while the corresponding figure for Valparaiso was about 33 per cent (Censo, 1960, Valparaiso, p. 7). Indeed, Santiago province itself then contained a third of all Chileans, though occupying only 2·34 per cent of the national territory.

The rapidly increasing urbanization, which is the characteristic feature of population patterns in the central provinces, is repeated elsewhere in Chile. The province of Concepción, after Santiago and Valparaiso the most populous region of Chile, had over three-quarters of its population classified as urban dwellers in 1960, Concepción city itself accounting for somewhat more than a third of the total provincial population (Censo, 1960, Concepción, pp. 14, 33). Certain regions have always been predominantly urban for obvious reasons. The desert and semi-desert regions

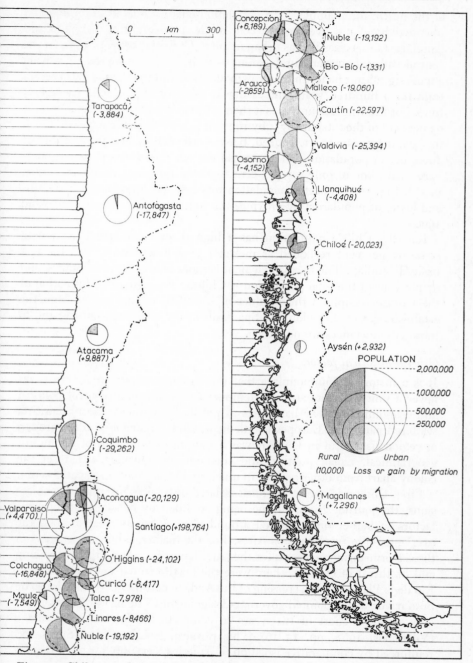

Fig. 10.1 Chile: population, urban and rural (1960) and net provincial migration
1952–60

of the north, for example, have population clusters related to mining and port activities, and over 90 per cent of the population of Tarapacá and Antofagasta was classified as urban in 1960 (CORFO, 1967, p. 379). In the central valley, however, rural exodus as well as natural increase has been a most significant factor in the growth of cities, and the process has been in train for a hundred years, increasing in momentum with the passage of time. For the whole country, as it then was, rural population accounted for 73 per cent of the total in 1875; by 1920, however, the percentage had fallen to 54 and by 1960 to 31. Indeed, between the census of 1952 and that of 1960, urban population had an annual growth rate of 3·9 per cent, compared with one of only 0·7 per cent for rural population (Herrick, 1965, p. 53). Fig. 10.1 indicates population totals at the 1960 census and gains and losses of population by province through migration between 1952 and 1960.

Racially, Chile's population has a high degree of homogeneity, with some 65 per cent reckoned as mestizo, 30 per cent white and the rest basically Indian. The mestizo element is more European than Indian, and 97 per cent of the total population is Chilean by origin. The formation of the Chilean people is the product of historical circumstances from the establishment of the colony by Spaniards in the sixteenth century, and to those circumstances we now turn.

General historical factors

It is a historical commonplace that the Spanish empire in America was never a unity, despite strong attempts to centralize and control political and economic life. The hard facts of physical geography, coupled with a scattered pattern of European settlement, tended inevitably to the growth of regionalism, and in Chile it was a unique combination of distinctive geographical, racial, political and economic circumstances that set the colony apart from other regions in much more than the mere spatial sense.

First, Chile was one of the most isolated of Spain's ultramarine possessions, the journey from Europe being attended by constantly dangerous factors – whether one travelled around Cape Horn by sea, or took the overland route from Buenos Aires. For the former, timing was critical in those storm-tormented seas; for the latter, apart from the Atlantic crossing and its threat of corsairs, there were the hostile Indians of the Pampa in Río de la Plata, and the crossing of the Andean cordillera. When Alonso de Sotomayor was appointed governor-designate of Chile in 1581, it took him only six days short of two years to complete the journey to Santiago (Villalobos, 1961, pp. 15–16). This physical isolation from Spain was reinforced by comparative isolation in America, certainly for most inhabitants of Chile. Throughout the colonial period normal intercourse with Peru was by sea, along the Pacific coastline, and in the national period it was control of the sea that determined control of the land in Chilean conflicts with Peru. For commerce and political contact, the sea route was preferable to that by land, which involved crossing the Atacama desert to the Bolivian *altiplano* and thence to Peru. This was far from impossible, of course, and the desert trails of Atacama provided a hard but negotiable route for the conquest of Chile from the north by both the Incas in the fifteenth century and the Spaniards in the sixteenth. Nevertheless, the hazards were enough to prevent the establishment of a permanent way, in contrast to the Pacific route, and, for all practical purposes, the northern desert served Chile as an effective natural, though ill-defined, boundary.

The Andean cordillera, likewise, was a visible wall serving the same purpose, though, again, its passes carried considerable commerce throughout the colonial period, and, indeed, the Cuyo region of what became Argentina was administered from the sixteenth to the late eighteenth century by Santiago. But if the Andes were by no means a barrier, neither were they a highway: the closure of the passes for several months a year by snow, the general inadequacy of mountain routes and the periodic nature of the traffic again served to reinforce rather than relieve Chile's sense of isolation.

Isolation would certainly have been overcome had there been sufficient reason to do so, and the environmental determinist will not get far in contemplating Spanish efforts in the Americas. But another geographical circumstance of Chile militated against the forcible breaking down of barriers of space and time – namely its comparative poverty in the precious metals. Physical hazards that were formidable elsewhere – such as at Potosí in Upper Peru, and in the northern mining regions of New Spain – were overruled by the rewards to be won, but in Chile such rewards soon became very meagre or difficult to obtain. While the early *conquistadores* of Chile felt the lure of El Dorado, and some sizeable fortunes were founded on gold extraction north of the central valley, north-west in the coastal range and south of the Bío-Bío, these avenues were virtually closed by 1600. The northern deposits were exhausted, and the southern possibilities cut short by Indian resistance.

Nevertheless, the search for gold predominated as an economic motive in the sixteenth century, with agriculture and stock-raising as little more than subsistence activities. By 1600, however, Chile's expansion was checked at the line of the river Bío-Bío by the fierce resistance of the Araucanian Indians. Consequently, Chile was effectively confined to that part of the central valley between the Andes and the Pacific on longitudinal lines, and bounded on the north by the transitional zone to the desert and on the south by the Bío-Bío. As already noted, this region, some 560 km in length and 160 km wide, is delimited by relief and rainfall alike: its climate is akin to that of parts of Mediterranean Spain, and the combination of fertile soil and adequate water made it attractive for settlement. The boundaries of the colonial Kingdom of Chile, thus established, remained almost static for nearly 300 years. Not until 1882 did a strong military force finally subdue the Araucanians of Cautín and bring the forest regions under the national flag, and it was only in the same decade, after the War of the Pacific against Bolivia and Peru, that the northern desert provinces were also incorporated. The point is reinforced by Fig. 10.2, which plots the foundation of over 100 Chilean urban settlements: those of the first three centuries to 1800 are almost exclusively in the central region and its marches; those of the last two reflect the territorial and economic expansion that followed these events.

Another consequence of the Indian resistance south of the Bío-Bío was the racial formation of the Chilean people. The generic name of Araucanians for the aboriginals was popularized by the sixteenth-century Spanish soldier-poet, Alonso de Ercilla y Zúñiga, in his epic, *La Araucana* (the region of Arauco), but anthropologists distinguish between the various tribes of Chile at that time. From approximately the Choapa valley in modern Coquimbo province to the rivers Itata and Bío-Bío lived the Picunche, and south of them to the region of the Tolten lived the Mapuche. Beyond the Tolten, as far as the Gulf of Corcovado and including Chiloé were the Huilliche, while the high valleys and slopes of the Andes from the latitude of the Bío-Bío to the modern province of Valdivia were inhabited by the Pehuenche. These tribal boundaries were nowhere exact but the foreign conquests of the Picunche, first by the Inca and then by the Spaniards, and the failure of both to establish permanent settlement beyond the Bío-Bío, marked the Mapuche as hostile Indians and the Picunche as peaceful.

The Araucanians generally were agriculturalists, cultivating maize, potatoes, squashes and beans, though the Pehuenche staple was the gathered seed of the Chilean pine (*Araucaria imbricata*), while fish and shellfish were important to the coastal peoples. Terracing was practised north of the Choapa and irrigation north of the river Rapel; the higher rainfall further south and its more even annual distribution made irrigation unnecessary there. Communal cultivation in open glades or in clearings where the forest cover had been burnt off was the norm, the ground being left fallow for a year or more after one season.

At the time of the Spanish Conquest, the area north of the Itata river was much less heavily populated than that south of it, and since, as elsewhere in the Americas, the early *conquistadores* brought few women with them, miscegenation began early and continued in the colonial period. A Negro element was also introduced subsequently as slave labour. During the sixteenth century two factors affected the original distribution of the Indian races: the first was a heavy demographic decline through war, European diseases and plain exploitation of the natives; the second, the transfer of Indians northwards across the Bío-Bío as labour for the Spaniards. But the rapacity of the conquerors sparked off Indian resistance

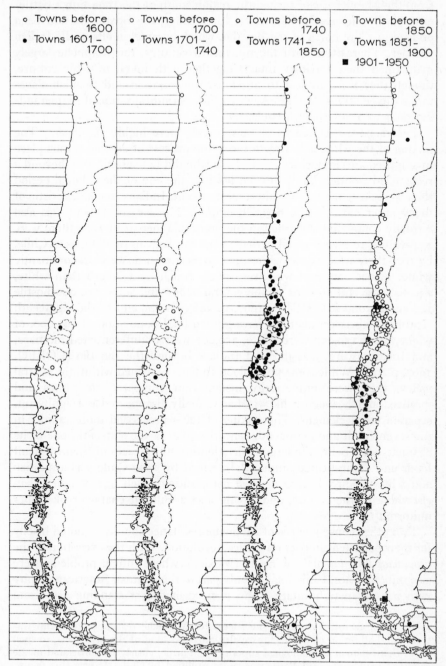

Fig. 10.2 Chile: the growth of settlement

Legend:
- o Towns before 1600
- • Towns 1601 – 1700
- o Towns before 1700
- • Towns 1701 – 1740
- o Towns before 1740
- • Towns 1741 – 1850
- o Towns before 1850
- • Towns 1851 – 1900
- ■ 1901 – 1950

from the Mapuche, and turned the region south of the Itata into a battle-ground. By the end of the sixteenth century, the Spaniards had been obliged to retire north of the Bío-Bío, which became, in effect, the Indian frontier. Thereafter, until the nineteenth century, the Mapuche largely maintained their territory intact, together with much of their culture, though they were subject to missionary penetration and Spanish slave-raiding expeditions, attentions which they periodically repaid by maraud-ing raids into the Spanish lands.

The racial consequences of these events were highly significant. The mixing of the white and Indian races, the process of *mestizaje*, took place in a limited area and, since the Indians who did not submit were beyond a recognized frontier, Chile did not have by the end of the colonial period the threefold structure of whites, mestizos and Indians so characteristic of many other parts of the Spanish empire. The Negro element was also virtually completely absorbed in the process. Whereas in 1540 there were 154 whites, 10 Negroes and perhaps 1 million Indians of all types in Chile, by 1620 there were 15,000 whites, 40,000 mestizos who were predominantly white, 22,000 mestizos who were more Indian and Negro than white, 230,000 peaceful Indians in the central valley and some 250,000 hostile Indians beyond it (CORFO, 1967, p. 342). By the end of the eighteenth century the best estimate we have gives a total population of 600,000, of whom about 150,000 were white, 350,000 were undifferentiated mestizos, and 100,000 were unassimilated Indians beyond the Bío-Bío (CORFO, 1967, p. 347). While some pure-blood Indians remained within the central valley, they were numerically insignificant compared to whites and mestizos, and the Negroes likewise had virtually disappeared as a significant, separate racial element. The mixing of races proceeded more rapidly in the seventeenth and eighteenth centuries than in the sixteenth, one of its characteristics being the large-scale adoption by all races of Spanish plant foods and domesticated animals.[1] In effect, by 1800 Chile was a mestizo and white colony, having a racial composition much less complex than elsewhere in the empire, and having also a cultural character of higher uniformity.

Two other consequences of Mapuche resistance should be noted briefly for their persistent impact on Chilean evolution. With the exception of the *provincias internas* of New Spain (Mexico), where Indian problems were also military ones, Chile was the only part of the Spanish American empire with a permanent military frontier, necessitating a standing army and

---

[1] A major factor, indeed, in the successful Mapuche resistance to Spain was their rapid adoption of horses for cavalry purposes, and of Spanish arms, to such effect that Spanish technological superiority in arms, clearly demonstrated in the conquest of Mexico and Peru, was quite nullified in Chile. It was this factor, rather than deep forest and high precipitation, that forced the Spaniards back beyond the Bío-Bío.

posing a problem of imperial defence. Spain and Peru had to bear some of the liability, and the standing threat to Chile itself made that geographically compact colony even more cohesive. Secondly, when the Mapuche decisively defeated the Spaniards on the frontier at Curalavá in 1598, they stopped the Spanish search for gold in the south. At about the same time, placer deposits in the central valley and north of it were being worked out and Chile's *siglo de oro* was at an end. The settlers were obliged to turn to the exploitation of the real wealth of Chile's central region, its rich agricultural and pastoral land, and in this development there emerged systems of land tenure and exploitation, as well as economic and social relationships, that not only survived to the twentieth century but also gave a particular stamp to the development of the whole nation.

These general historical factors are part of the essential framework for understanding the interaction of man and landscape in Chile. For over 300 years, particular characteristics evolved in the heartland of the central valley, before the expansion of the republic in the nineteenth and twentieth centuries brought man into relationships with markedly different environments. The contemporary regionalism of Chile, therefore, is not merely a question of geographical and climatological difference between various parts of the country and of man's reaction to contrasting circumstances of time and place: it is also a matter of how far a distinctive process of historical development continues to condition the present, and whether it should shape the future.

II THE HEARTLAND

Land and labour in the central valley: The evolution of the great estate

As elsewhere in the Spanish empire, the basic instrument of settlement in Chile was the *encomienda*, an institution whereby natives were obliged to pay tribute to the Spaniards in return for the latter's assumption of obligations to Christianize and civilize them. It was a grant of Indians, but not of their land, at least in theory, and land for the conquerors was assigned on other principles. Each member of a new community was entitled to a piece of land commensurate with his rank, as well as to the use of lands held to be common; the former were *peonías* or *caballerías*, reflecting the status of foot-soldiers and cavalry respectively. Additionally, early governors and town councils, and later royal officials, distributed land in legal title to the more prominent as *mercedes*. These were usually huge in size, and the smallest plots, the *peonías*, tended to be rare since few would accept the inferior ranking they implied, the name *peon* being applied only to Indians, mestizos and very poor whites. Labour, in fact, was no less important than land, as no self-respecting Spaniard would work his own property, and the demand for *encomiendas* to provide this, and for siting *mercedes* close to

Indian villages, soon ran up against the intractable fact of a serious labour shortage in Chile. It was to remedy this by finding more manpower, as much as the desire for gold, that prompted the early conquerors to move south. Their ultimate failure by 1600 did not have such serious effects on the early colonial economy as might have been expected. For economic and demographic change coincided: had gold continued to be of predominant importance, with stock-raising and agriculture of secondary significance, Chile would have faced a critical labour problem at a time when demographic decline was well under way. As it was, the forced change of economic direction at the end of the sixteenth century from mining to stock-raising, requiring fewer hands, salvaged something for Chile out of what contemporaries regarded as an unmitigated disaster.

Though agriculture and stock-raising came second to mining as economic activities in sixteenth-century Chile, they were not simply subsistence activities after the earliest years. The pastoral industry was particularly important in the Araucanian war for the supply of horses, leather and provisions for the frontier forces. Agriculture was chiefly concerned with wheat cultivation, taken to Chile by Valdivia in 1540, where it soon supplanted the Indian staple, maize, in a region particularly suited to its cultivation. In the first fifty years, the major wheat zone lay south of the Bío-Bío, with stock-raising predominant in the central valley, but thereafter, with the Indian rebellion, it was transferred to the area between the Bío-Bío and the Maule, and by 1600 a small market in Chilean wheat existed in Peru (Sepúlveda, 1959, p. 13).

The Viceroyalty of Peru, however, was much more significant in the growth of the Chilean pastoral industry, the predominant economic activity of the colony for most of the seventeenth century. The dramatic growth of Peruvian mining, not least in Upper Peru (Bolivia) created a large demand for leather and tallow – for candles and soap – commodities that Chile could supply. In Chilean economic history, indeed, the age is known as the *siglo de sebo* (the century of tallow), and contemporary writers speak of huge herds of cattle and sheep being butchered for tallow and hides, and of the meat being thrown away since there was no market for it (Keller, 1956, p. 88). The consequences of this development had a profound effect on Chilean land and society: the great estate, destined from the earliest days of the colony when *mercedes* were granted to be a characteristic feature of the countryside, now grew greater, as the Peruvian demand for pastoral products put a premium on extending pastures. And, while the great estate – the hacienda – did not grow out of *encomienda*, the grants of Indians, there was a definite connection between a growing pastoral economy, a need for native labour, and the rise of the hacienda. For although *encomienda* carried no juridical title to land, it was an instrument of land colonization, as *encomenderos* successfully sought outright grants near Indian villages and equally successfully circumvented the persistent efforts of the Spanish crown and the Spanish church to protect the natives from exploitation (Korth, 1968). With the rise of stock-raising there occurred an accelerated take-over by landowners both of Indian and of common lands. This was assisted by the increasing process of *mestizaje*, since the incorporation of Indian villages into private estates became easier as mestizos drifted in as squatters and as the erosion of the Indian character of the villages deprived the Indians of legal protection.[1] This legal protection, however, was more a matter of theory and was of little practical value to the Indians. In 1597, for example, in Puangue the so-called Protector of the Indians transferred them from place to place to facilitate the extension of haciendas (Borde and Góngora, 1956, I, p. 51) and only rarely could wronged Indians, with scanty resources and ignorant of law, secure legal redress.

But the rise of stock-raising in seventeenth-century Chile not only firmly established the hacienda – now usually called *estancia* – as the dominant feature of the rural landscape; it also called into being another institution which, like the great estate itself, survived into modern times. This was the basic system of rural labour, known in Chile as *inquilinaje*, the development of which was intimately related to changes in the land economy of the colony.

By the mid-seventeenth century, the better parts of the central valley had been divided up into land grants to the most powerful and influential, and later changes in landownership came from sales, gifts, inheritances and donations – all private forms of transfer. Those excluded from the circle of landowners could not now acquire large holdings from the state, though smallholdings might still be acquired from undistributed state domain, as when new towns were founded and *chacras*, lots for personal cultivation, were allocated. There arose a form of tenancy on the *estancias*, commonly called *arriendo* or *préstamo*, initially the letting of a piece of land to a natural son, a kinsman, or at least someone with whom the owner had a personal tie, in return for some specified payment. Examples date back to the early seventeenth century (Góngora, 1960), and the rise of stock-raising accelerated the process. *Estancieros* were now looking for trustworthy tenants to guard their boundaries and oversee stock, and, since estates were vast and there were plenty of applicants – not least retired officers from the Araucanian wars seeking to maintain their status – fairly large *préstamos* were granted on which tenants could graze their own stock separate from the owner's, in return for duties performed for him. A decisive factor at this time was still the personal relationship: clearly, with unbranded stock mutual confidence was at a premium and, while *préstamos* varied enormously in detail, two common traits stand out – the temporary

[1] Under Spanish colonial law the Indians were a special charge of crown and church, and a considerable amount of protective legislation was passed on their behalf. Mestizos had no such status.

tenancy of property on agreed terms, and the tenant's obligation to provide some form of service.

While, in the seventeenth century, some *préstamos* were agricultural rather than pastoral, the decisive change here, and in the nature of the contract, came in the eighteenth century with the rise of wheat cultivation to predominance. 1687 was a key date for the capture of the Peruvian market by Chilean wheat; the fortuitous occurrence then of an earthquake in Peru, which disrupted local production and necessitated large imports from Chile, enabled the superior quality of Chilean wheat to establish itself, so that thenceforth Peru became dependent on Chilean supplies (Sepúlveda, 1959). As with tallow earlier, the Chilean rural economy responded to the new opportunity, and growth of the wheat trade had its own impact on man-land relationships in eighteenth-century Chile.

In the first place, economic and demographic change again coincided, since, by this time, along with the continuing process of *mestizaje*, population levels were recovering from the sharp decline caused by the shock of European conquest. Wheat cultivation needed more intensive labour than stock-raising and the hands were now more readily available. Estimates of population for the period are very crude but one writer gives a total of some 80,000 for the end of the seventeenth century (Eyzaguirre, 1965, p. 170), while the results of Chile's first attempt at a census in 1777 indicated a population of some 200,000 north of the river Maule (Eyzaguirre, 1965, p. 250). Secondly, the eighteenth century saw not only a large increase in the tenancy agreements previously described as *préstamos* but now called *arriendos*; it also saw a number of changes in the character of the contracts. Whereas under the stock-raising economy landowners were looking for tenants to guard their herds and flocks and assist at round-ups and at related activities, with cereal cultivation they were now looking for a more fixed labour force to work the land. In the seventeenth- and early eighteenth-century tenancy agreements, cash payments often figured as part of the tenant's obligation to the owner, in addition to services, but the latter increased during the course of the eighteenth century at the expense of the cash element. As time passed, this tendency increased: for example, about 1760 the new obligation of tenants to provide the landowner with a *peon* for house duties appeared, and from then on personal service obligations became a common feature of contracts. Another increasing tendency, apart from the depression in the status of the tenant, was for tenancies to become hereditary, and by the nineteenth century the rural labour system associated with the great estate had virtually settled into the form in which it was to remain to the present day.

The classic modern description of the twentieth-century *fundo* (hacienda) and of *inquilinaje* (McBride, 1936, pp. 3–14, 146–70) differs little in essentials from the picture of 100 years before (Gay, 1844). Owners of great estates allowed tenants the usufruct of a small piece of land, in return for labour service. The contract between them was a free one, usually verbal, varying in its terms not only from area to area but also from *fundo* to *fundo*, and there was also considerable variety between the labourers themselves, in terms of possessions and standards of living. In theory, the tenant had complete liberty of movement, and was not bound to the soil as a serf; in practice, by the nineteenth century, *inquilinos* were inheriting their fathers' status and obligations to the family that owned the *fundo*. Their duties included not only the provision of labour in agriculture, stock-raising and general work, such as clearing irrigation channels, but also personal service at the master's side or in his house, though all work done in excess of the agreement was paid for by the master, sometimes in cash, much more often in provisions. The tenant would till the land he lived on on his own account, and he might also own stock and reach agreement with his master about pasture. If the contract ended, the tenant took the harvest of his own land, but got nothing for any improvements he might have effected. At the beginning of the nineteenth century, *inquilinaje* was the predominant form of land labour in Chile; it dominated the central valley, though it was weak in its northern and southern extremities, and it had been elaborated by the growth of a hierarchy of workers on the estates, contracted in the same way, from the lowest hand to the *mayordomo* with supervisory duties over agricultural workers and the *capataz*, overseer of the pastoral sector. These persons also held their own land and stock but their contract with the owner revolved more around the cash nexus than did that of the mere worker.

The great estate, the *fundo*, and the system of *inquilinaje* proved outstandingly stable elements over more than two centuries, with profound consequences for Chile's political and economic evolution. Moreover, they reflected the racial structure of the country. The landed, white aristocracy ruled the national life in all its branches while an illiterate, mestizo peasantry obeyed, and such crucial historical events as the securing of political independence from Spain early in the nineteenth century had little or no effect on Chile's internal social structure. This is not to say that fragmentation of land and extension of ownership were not continuing processes in the central valley from the seventeenth century to today, nor that *inquilinaje* was, by any means, the sole system of rural labour in Chile: as will be seen shortly, other forms of landholding and of labour have their own significance. Nevertheless, the *fundo* remained the characteristic feature of the Chilean countryside. In 1925, in the fourteen provinces of Chile from Coquimbo to Bío-Bío, 5396 estates over 200 ha in size accounted for 89 per cent of all farmland, with over 76,000 other properties accounting for the other 11 per cent (McBride, 1936, p. 124). But, within these figures, 1507 properties were larger than 1000 ha each and accounted for 73 per cent of all farmland, with a number of estates of more than 100,000 ha (McBride, 1936, pp. 125 ff.). More than thirty years

later, 4709 properties accounted for no less than 87·9 per cent of all farmland (CIDA, 1966, p. 48), and, indeed, in Chile as a whole, the concentration of ownership was such that 73 per cent of land in farms were in
holdings of over 1000 ha, representing only 2·2 per cent of the total number
of farms (Warriner, 1969, p. 326).

But, while the traditional *fundo* survived, *inquilinaje* had been a declining
institution for over a century. Comment on the depressed conditions of the
inquilinos was widespread both in the nineteenth and in the twentieth
century, though often balanced by the view that, in comparison with the
share-cropper or vagrant hired labourer, the *inquilino* had, in his plot of
land and social relationships, at least a degree of stability and certainty.
Conditions varied enormously from province to province and from estate
to estate, depending greatly on the individual character of the landowner.
Significant changes in *fundo* ownership did occur in the mid-nineteenth
century when adverse economic conditions caused many of the old aristocracy of the land to sell out to *nouveaux riches*, men grown wealthy in
commerce, banking and mining: the change does seem to have affected
the old paternalism of the *fundo* to the detriment of the *inquilino*. Absenteeism of the landlord from his land became more pronounced, and many
estates were run down since a number of new owners were less interested
in land as an economic investment than as a sign of arrival in the ranks of
the Chilean aristocracy. The upward rise of the demographic curve
paralleled this change, and pressure of numbers on the land began to be
relieved by peasants leaving it, a rural exodus shown by regional study to
have been well under way in the later nineteenth century (Borde and
Góngora, 1956, I, pp. 113 ff.). For, however much local circumstances
prevented him from exercising it, the *inquilino* always had legal freedom
and, where conditions became intolerable, an avenue out of farming could
be found in the mining regions of the north or the expanding frontier to
the south. Thus, in 1929, it was reckoned that there were about 256,000
inquilinos in Chile, out of a rural labour force of 386,000 (McBride, 1936,
p. 164); in 1955, however, by which time the modern city and industry
had greatly developed in Chile, of a total farm population of 664,000, there
were only 82,000 *inquilinos* (Warriner, 1969, p. 327), and a study of land
division in central Chile made a little earlier revealed how attenuated
inquilinaje had become by then (Martin, 1960).

The concentration of landownership in Chile, exemplified by the *fundo*,
is at the centre of recent debates about Chilean society and economy, and
an evaluation of this extraordinarily tenacious feature of the rural landscape
is essential to an understanding of contemporary Chile. First, however, it is
necessary to look at other characteristics of the Chilean land system and
its forms of labour, since they are no less relevant to the discussion.

Minifundia and landless labour

In no country of Latin America where the same juxtaposition occurs is the contrast between the large estate and the small more striking than in Chile. Visually, the contrast is dramatic enough to the traveller in the central valley, but statistics are no less compelling. While in 1969 2·2 per cent of the number of farms embraced 73 per cent of the land in farms in holdings over 1000 ha, 37 per cent of the number of farms occupied 0·3 per cent of the land in holdings of *less* than 5 ha (Warriner, 1969, p. 326). These are the extreme cases of *minifundia*, of which perhaps the most workable definition is that of farms too small to provide a living for their owners from agriculture alone (Smole, 1963, p. 2).

The origins of the *minifundia*, like those of the *latifundia*, lie in the colonial past, and the major factor in their creation was subdivision of larger properties, mainly through inheritance, in the colonial period and after. In Putaendo, for example, in the province of Aconcagua, a certain Pedro de Silva had built up an *estancia* in the mid-seventeenth century but on his death four lots – *hijuelas* or 'little daughters' – passed to three sons and a daughter. One son died in 1700, leaving his land to be divided between seven sons, and one of these lots was itself divided in 1731 into six properties. By 1821, of the four original parcels of land left by Pedro de Silva, one had been subdivided into eighty properties (Baraona, Aranda and Santana, 1961, p. 159). It is true that inheritors of great estates generally sought to maintain properties intact by family compacts, such as providing for many sons in other ways than through land so that one heir might hold his father's property, and a number of *hacendados* received from the crown in the colonial period the grant of *mayorazgo*, the entailed estate that could *not* be broken up as ordinary Spanish inheritance laws demanded. Nevertheless, in the first two centuries of the colonial period estates were subdivided, sold and given away, reconstituted and, in some few cases, maintained in their original size. Thus, of the twenty-five hacienda proprietors in Puangue in Santiago province in the seventeenth and eighteenth centuries, only one family property survived to the middle of the nineteenth century with the holding largely intact (Borde and Góngora, 1956, I, p. 60). The two processes of the maintenance of the great estate on the one hand, and its subdivision on the other, went on side by side in the eighteenth and nineteenth centuries: hence *latifundia* and *minifundia* in Chile have basically a common origin.

During the nineteenth and twentieth centuries, however, another factor besides inheritance created the division of the larger properties, namely the commercial opportunity offered to great landowners to sell a portion of their holding to classes and individuals having no traditional connection with the land, and not really wishing to acquire it for commercial farming, but seeking rather a hedge against the inflation that has been a feature of the Chilean economy since the latter part of the nineteenth century (Martin, 1960, p. 38). Not surprisingly, lots acquired in this way changed hands frequently, but more characteristic types of the small estate are those of owner-cultivators, who have a genuine attachment to the land, and those of community holdings. Included in the latter are Mapuche reservation lands, particularly in the province of Cautín, held in common but with the usufruct individually apportioned (Faron, 1968, pp. 15–21), and peasant communities, notably in the northern provinces, especially Coquimbo, where individual holdings are complemented by communal lands, usually grazing grounds and unirrigated areas (CIDA, 1966, p. 128).

It is no less impossible to generalize about owner-cultivators and *minifundia* in Chile than it is to do so for great landowners and their estates. Smole's (1963) study of owner-cultivatorship, however, in a carefully selected region of Middle Chile, where both *minifundia* and *latifundia* are found, suggests certain important characteristics of this type, which are highly relevant to land reform issues. Allowing for enormous variations in farm size, wealth of natural resources (notably availability of water), tenure and labour supply in the study area, owner-occupied farms generally function as self-sufficient units, which are only to a very limited degree market-orientated. They lack capital resources and access to credit organizations, and their physical isolation and limited resource-base further limit opportunities for commercial development. Labour is drawn chiefly from the immediate family and friends, and, while share-cropping arrangements and use of casual labour are by no means neglected where it is necessary to employ them, the farmers prefer to rely on traditional and familiar relationships to work their land. The sense of community is strong and, while the development of some accessible markets has created an empirical balance between production for use and production for gain, the latter decidedly comes second in the farmer's attitude towards his land. In short, these properties represent a way of life as much as a way of earning a living; they are characterized by poverty rather than affluence, though their owners and their families certainly enjoy a much higher standard of living than *inquilinos* or share-croppers and other landless labourers who work on the great estates. The increasing impact of agents of change – improved communications, radios as well as roads, visiting emigrants, the operation of selective military service, which draws young men out of the environment for a period – apparently breaks down the isolation of such owner-occupied areas but does little to modify farming technology, though cases exist of a successful shift to more prosperous commercial production where its advantages have been clearly demonstrated. In fact, the new market opportunities created by increased urbanization in central Chile have been largely taken up by great estates and medium-sized properties, which can operate on the required scale, in contrast to these more self-sufficient units with their conservative ethos and traditional practices.

Owner-occupiers, however, with an adequate resource-base for self-sufficiency in basic needs and an ability to purchase commodities they cannot produce by marketing small surpluses, are very much better off than other agrarian sectors of the Chilean population. In terms of living standards, conditions of labour and prospects of improvement, the smaller *minifundistas* and the landless labourers are far worse off, and their situation is central to issues of land reform. The Agricultural Census of 1955 indicated that 70,000 farm operators, of a total of 329,000 thus classified, had farms too small to support a family and worked part-time on other properties. Of 335,000 salaried or wage-paid workers – including *inquilinos* and administrators – there were 27,000 share-croppers and 180,000 seasonal labourers (Warriner, 1969, p. 327). The landless may be permanent farm labourers (*voluntarios*) or migratory ones (*afuerinos*), the latter having been created by the growth of commercial agriculture in the past and by the fact that Chile's climatic differences throughout the country and its variety of crops create a peak demand for labour in different regions at different times: hence, relatively well-paid but transient jobs, especially at harvest time, are available to migrant workers. Both *voluntarios* and *afuerinos*, in contrast to *inquilinos*, are essentially wage-paid workers receiving cash for labour, but their situation is, obviously, much more precarious. Share-croppers (*medieros*) may also be migratory, accepting lots on one *fundo* one year and on another the next. They usually contribute all their labour, half of the seeds and fertilizer and other operating costs, while the owner, apart from the land, contributes the remainder of the inputs, living expenses and credits necessary until the harvest, which is divided equally (Thiesenhusen, 1966, pp. 18–19).

Issues of land reform

In Chile, as everywhere, the arguments revolving around the ownership and use of land are extremely complicated, and reflect the great diversity of the rural scene. The basic economic arguments for change that would entail the break-up of the great estate are that it is not sufficiently productive and, perhaps more important, that it perpetuates the extreme inequalities of income that are characteristic of the country's rural sector, and, indeed, of the Chilean economy as a whole. On the first point, it is frequently argued that the *fundo* system inhibits higher productivity, and prevents Chilean agriculture from producing what it could, and should, given the country's climate and soils (e.g. Delgado, 1965, p. 564; CIDA, 1966, pp. 203–6; Thiesenhusen, 1966, pp. 30–1). It is an indisputable fact that agricultural production has not kept abreast of population increase and today Chile imports some two-thirds of her food requirements, with temperate zone foodstuffs – cereals, meat and dairy products – prominent among them. The cost of these imports has a very significant effect on Chile's balance of payments, and the inelasticity of agricultural products plays a major role in one of the country's endemic economic weaknesses, heavy inflation. The *fundo*, the argument runs, has manifestly failed to supply Chile with enough food because much land in great estates is under-utilized; with irrigated arable land in large tracts under pasture, low investment in technical improvement, wasteful use of labour, and so on, the whole structure of the agrarian sector acts as a brake on the national economy. The assumption is that if the large estates were broken up and a great expansion of owner-occupier holdings took place, coupled with adequate capital and technical inputs, inefficiency could be overcome since land would belong to those who worked it and this would provide its own incentives. More significantly, a greater equalization of rural income would result, not only leading to a more just society but having the effect of stimulating the industrial and commercial sectors of the economy by creating more of a mass market.

The considerable counter-argument on economic grounds, put forward by those who regard land redistribution as at best a very minor step towards solving economic and social problems, and at worst as a politically-inspired move likely to exacerbate the very problems of supply it is intended to solve, turns on government attitudes towards landowners. If the *fundo* has failed to feed the Chilean people, the argument runs, the fault lies less in any inherent structural defects of the landholding system itself than in policies pursued by successive governments, which have had the effect, if not indeed the intention, of penalizing the rural sector to support the industrial, through pricing systems for agricultural and pastoral produce that prevent an adequate return. Urban consumers benefit at the expense of rural producers (Mamalakis, 1965, pp. 117–48). Undercapitalization on the estate is thus a reflection of the undoubted emphasis given to industry by governments since the 1940s, and their comparative neglect of agriculture, and under-utilization of arable land is the result of lack of incentives, irrespective of the personal inclinations or habits of private landowners. Food imports could be reduced and local production increased by raising farm prices; tariffs on imports, as a corollary, might well go a long way to solving the balance of payments problem much more quickly than land redistribution, which is necessarily a process of dislocation as well as one requiring large capital and technical inputs if production is not to fall.

Evaluating the case for land redistribution in Chile is not easy, partly owing to the fact that its protagonists and opponents can each produce voluminous reports and impressive statistics in support of their views, as a survey of the publications of the CORA (Corporación de Reforma Agraria) and of the SNA (Sociedad Nacional de Agricultura) would reveal. But perhaps the strongest argument of the reformers is that of diminishing the existing gross inequality of income distribution through a redistribution of capital in the form of land. This assumes that the high cost of new inputs to owner-occupied and collectively managed properties could be met, that managerial bottlenecks could be overcome, and that incentives to smallholders could be provided. How large these assumptions are has been revealed by an examination of the operation of certain land reform schemes of the Catholic church, which have encountered great difficulties in creating incentives beyond merely increased personal consumption in co-operative and collective operations, and in providing capital and technical inputs for individual ones (Thiesenhusen, 1966). The conclusion, nevertheless, is that the clear incentive to work possessed by peasants receiving land is a crucial asset, and should be so encouraged as to justify distribution in individual holdings (Thiesenhusen, 1966). This, in its turn, raises a no less critical issue on which land reform will be judged, namely its effectiveness in improving the contribution of the rural sector to the economy as a whole, as well as to the social betterment of the rural poor.

In this context, it is significant that in his message to Congress, which accompanied a comprehensive proposal for land reform in 1965, President Frei put as the first objective the need to increase output from the agrarian sector (*Ley de Reforma Agraria* 1967, p. 5 ff.). He pointed out that whereas between 1939 and 1965 the rate of growth in the agricultural sector was of the order of 2 per cent annually, that of population was 2·26 per cent and the cost of the disequilibrium in terms of food imports came to more than a quarter of the value of Chile's exports (*Ley de Reforma Agraria*, 1967, pp. 5–6). But he also recognized that unequal distribution of ownership and the very low living conditions of the rural poor were intimately related, and that land reform was necessary on social grounds as well as on economic ones.

The current law of Agrarian Reform came on to the statute book in 1967. It succeeded a law of 1962, which is generally regarded as ineffective, not least because although it allowed government purchase of land for redistribution it also called for full cash compensation at market prices to sellers, severely restricting its implementation. The law of 1967 got round this difficulty by authorizing payment partly in bonds repayable over a longish period; it was also both a more sweeping and a more complicated law.

Under the 1967 law, properties larger than 80 ha of basic irrigated land *may* be expropriated, the qualification permitting efficient owners of larger properties (up to 320 ha) to claim exemption. The norms of 'efficiency' are carefully laid down, with a good deal of latitude allowed to the new National Agrarian Council, which decides questions of expropriation. The running of expropriated estates lies with CORA, which is responsible for distribution to peasants but management by peasant committees or syndicates does not figure in the law itself, only in regulations drawn up

504 LATIN AMERICA: GEOGRAPHICAL PERSPECTIVES

by CORA. The assumption is that the latter in association with peasant committees will manage redistributed estates for a period of two or three years, after which the peasants will have the deeds turned over to them, and may choose to operate on a collective or on an individual basis. The law's 300-odd articles also set out in detail the compensatory mechanism and many other aspects of this highly complex operation (*Ley de Reforma Agraria*, 1967; for a skilful summary, see Warriner, 1969, pp. 340–5).

No agrarian reform law of such complexity can be evaluated within four years of its appearance. Nevertheless, certain characteristics call for comment. Clearly, a great deal will depend on managerial skills – in the National Agrarian Council, in CORA and in the peasant committees. And it must be admitted that this is a considerable bottleneck. Some operations of CORA under the law of 1962, as seen by Warriner (1969, pp. 338–40), showed how difficult it was in a country with such a strong tradition of paternalism on the land for officials and peasants to co-operate: the former seemed to the latter much like the absentee landlords they were presumably intended to replace. Secondly, at the end of December 1968, CORA's total personnel numbered only 1530 and, more significantly, had risen only to 1736 by mid-July 1970 (CORA, 1970, p. 63). Thirdly, while it had been President Frei's ambition to create 100,000 new farms for landless peasants before his term of office expired in 1970, by the end of July 1970 less than one tenth of the 3·5 million ha expropriated was irrigated land, and less than 37,000 families had benefited (CORA, 1970, p. 39).

There are many reasons for the slow progress apparently made – intense political opposition on varied grounds to the reform law, a disastrous drought, which afflicted Chile for much of 1967 and most of 1968, the complexity of a democratic country trying to achieve basic reform in a hurry, and, above all, the plain fact that expectations always outrun possibilities. At least two highly significant gains are apparent: a much higher political consciousness in the countryside, and a generally higher standard of living. It will be many years before the professed aims of land reform are achieved, and present arrangements might well be superseded.[1] But the fundamental challenge to the traditional structure of landed property in Chile cannot be withdrawn, and the present process of change is widely accepted. Nevertheless, the promise held out to the rural sector will not be redeemed in the countryside alone: its success also turns on developments in the rest of the Chilean economy, and in the wider world economy of which the latter is a part.

Centralization, urban growth and industrial development

In dealing generally with Chilean population, brief mention was made of the urban concentration of people in the two key provinces of the central valley with their eponymous conurbations, Santiago and Valparaiso. At

[1] See the Postscript to this chapter.

the 1960 census, no fewer than 41·5 per cent of all Chileans lived in these two provinces, which also accounted for 54·5 per cent of the country's total urban population. Moreover, the city of Santiago itself contained 84 per cent of the provincial population, while the conurbation Valparaiso–Viña del Mar held 60 per cent of the total for the province of Valparaiso (calculations from data in *Censos, Provincias*, 1964, Santiago and Valparaiso). The growth of Santiago city has been most marked in the last twenty years: whereas its population increased at a rate of 2·9 per cent annually between 1940 and 1952, the rate had risen to 4·3 per cent annually in the intercensal period 1952–60 (Herrick, 1965, p. 31). Data for the early years of the 1960s show that this rate was then being maintained (CORFO, 1967, p. 380). While some other urban centres, such as Concepción and Talcahuano, with populations over 50,000 in 1960, show comparable rates of growth in recent years, this has done little to affect the particular dominance of Chilean society and economy by the central valley in general and by Santiago in particular.

The point may be illustrated further by a few selected examples. At the time of the third National Census of Manufactures in 1957, the provinces of Santiago and Valparaiso between them contained no fewer than 64 per cent of all industrial establishments in Chile with a work force of five or more persons, the bulk of these being in the provincial capitals (Hoffmann and Debuyst, 1966, pp. 44–5). Analysis of social data reveals a similar concentration of resources and services: for example, 77 of the country's 242 hospitals were to be found in Santiago and Valparaiso in 1960 and, perhaps more significantly, they employed 2165 of the total national figure of 3724 hospital doctors in Chile (Hoffmann and Debuyst, 1966, p. 101). In matters of education, whereas the national percentage of literacy in 1960 was 84, in both Santiago and Valparaiso the rate was over 90 per cent, a rate enjoyed by only three other provinces (Hoffmann and Debuyst, 1966, p. 108). It is also worthy of note that these three provinces – Tarapacá, Antofagasta and Magallanes – had 87, 96 and 84 per cent of their respective populations classified as urban in 1960 (CORFO, 1967, p. 379).

The process of centralization in Chile has undoubtedly gathered increasing momentum in recent years, but it is as much a product of a long historical evolution as it is of contemporary development. Like other capitals of Latin America, Santiago plays the dominant role today because it has always done so. Colonial Santiago was roughly equidistant from the northern and southern confines of the Kingdom of Chile, and equally favourably placed with regard to the Andean passes to Cuyo; it occupied a key position in the rich central valley, so long the basis of the colonial economy, and it was only 130 km by road from a suitable port on the Pacific, Valparaiso. As the seat of the governor and of the *audiencia*, the religious centre of the colony, and, from the mid-eighteenth century, the site of the only university in Chile, Santiago's administrative and cultural

R

predominance was unchallenged throughout the colonial period, and effectively underlined its economic and strategic importance. After independence, a combination of circumstances increased Chile's centralization on Santiago. The political organization of the republic, in contrast to many other Latin American states, took shape in a unitary, rather than a federal, constitution, introduced in 1833 and lasting (though with amendments) until 1925. This constitution concentrated decision-making in the national capital, such local autonomy as remained to the provinces being truly parochial in form and content. Equally significant as centralizing factors were the growth of communications, notably railways, and the emerging economic structure of the country from the mid-nineteenth century.

The railway system in the central valley was state-owned almost from the beginning, and it served the national purpose of binding the outlying provinces to the core region, as the lines ran north and south, east and west from Santiago. The great central trunk line, running today from Zapiga, some 300 km south of Arica in the desert north, to Puerto Montt in Forest Chile – over 3000 km in length – was built from the centre outwards, beginning in the 1850s. By 1859 it had reached Rancagua, 82 km south of Santiago; by 1862, San Fernando, 139 km; by 1893, Temuco, 690 km; and by 1913, Puerto Montt, 1079 km. Branch lines were built during the same period to feed other towns in the central valley and ports on the Pacific: thus, the very important Valparaiso–Santiago line was begun in October 1852, and formally inaugurated in September 1863 (Bohan and Pomerantz, 1960, p. 195). With the northern extensions, however, it was a different story, the network in both the Norte Grande and the Norte Chico (Atacama and Coquimbo) being built mainly by foreign capital and held in foreign ownership until more recent times. The growth of these networks was intimately connected with the exploitation of mineral wealth, nitrates in the Norte Grande and copper in the Norte Chico, during the nineteenth century. Chile's first railway, indeed, and the first railway of any considerable length in South America, was opened in early 1852 to link the copper mines of Copiapó to the port of Caldera, 41 km away.

In these facts lies another basic reason for the persistent centralist character of the Chilean political and economic system. For much of the nineteenth century, and well into the twentieth, a high proportion of government revenue came from export taxes on minerals mined in the northern provinces, but the government in Santiago limited its role in the mining industry predominantly to the collection of these taxes, leaving to private enterprise the ownership and exploitation of the mineral deposits. This policy certainly resulted in sizeable revenues, easy to collect, for government financing of major public works such as railways and port installations; it can also be argued, however, that it left the export-orientated mining sector as something of an economic exclave of the nation and thus helped to prevent the possibility of the northern mining industry becoming the basis of local growth points within the national economy. Such points might well have come, in time, to challenge the dominance of the core region and the metropolis. A less conjectural result of this development was to make it unnecessary for government to raise essential income from land taxes on the aristocracy, a negative factor in the latter's continued social pre-eminence and political influence, exercised in the national capital and the central valley. This situation was compounded by the social habits and inclinations of the Chilean *nouveaux riches*, men who had risen to prominence through mining, banking and commerce during the nineteenth century. Rather than constituting a separate social force from the traditional aristrocracy, they sought above all to emulate and join it through marriage and the purchase of land, and the Chilean upper class showed a remarkable resilience not only in accepting these new elements but also, in fact, in absorbing them. Thus, the emergence of new bases of economic power in mineral exploitation, in contrast to land as the source of wealth in the colonial period and after, did nothing to change either the traditional political structure or the centralist tradition.

At present, the overwhelming dominance of Santiago in Chile is a fact, and if its growth may have seemed inevitable historically, its future expansion may well seem irreversible in the light of prevailing circumstances. As Fig. 10.3 indicates, the city grew moderately and regularly during the colonial period around the original nucleus of settlement on the southern side of the Río Mapocho, near the Cerro Santa Lucía. At the time of independence, it contained some 40,000 to 50,000 people, almost a tenth of the total Chilean population. The nineteenth century, and notably the second half, saw a considerable increase in both physical extent and numbers, not least with the extension of residential suburbs to the west and south, and also north of the river. By 1900 Santiago contained some 300,000 people, still only one tenth of the national population. In the twentieth century, however, more or less regular spatial growth and a population increase more or less commensurate with national expansion of numbers has given way, with increasing momentum, to a rapid enlargement of the city boundaries and a vast rise in population. Physically, the city's growth has been most marked on the east, south and west, the eastern side containing the *barrio alto*, the fashionable residential sector. Lower land values in the less attractive southern and western sectors have also attracted residential development, but for the less well-off. But, if Santiago's physical growth has been dramatic, especially in the past thirty years, its population increase has been astounding. Between 1900 and 1925, population doubled – to 600,000 – but by 1952, a census year, it had more than doubled again – to 1,438,000. Between then and the next census, in 1960, it rose by a further 500,000, to contain more than a quarter of the total national population. Indeed, the rate of growth each year between 1952 and 1960 was 4·8 per cent, compared with one of 2 per cent for Chile as a whole. Since Santiago's rate of natural increase during the intercensal period approximated to that of the rest of the country (25·7 per 1000, cf. 23·8 per 1000), the difference in total population increase must have been due to migration into the city (Herrick, 1965, p. 44).

Reference has already been made, in dealing with central Chile's rural landscape, to migration from the land into the towns. This is only a part of

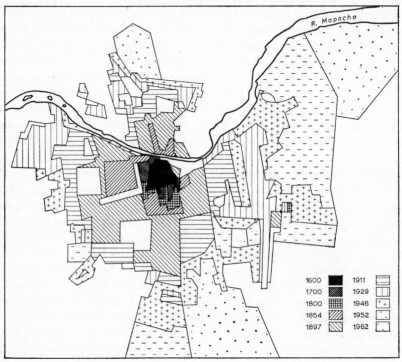

1600	1911	
1700	1929	
1800	1946	
1854	1952	
1897	1962	

Fig. 10.3 The growth of Santiago 1600–1962 (after Cunill, 1965)

the total picture of internal migration, and Herrick's careful study of the various factors affecting population movement indicates a predominantly urban origin of recent migrants to Santiago, rather than an immediate rural one, representing, therefore, a smoother acculturation of rural population to new ways of life than the bare statistics might suggest. He proposes, in fact, a two-generation model of migration: a first-generation movement from the countryside to the towns, usually of less than 50,000 population size, and a second-generation movement from the latter to Santiago (Herrick, 1965, p. 103). Fig. 10.1 shows provincial gains or losses of population by migration (internal) in the intercensal period 1952–60 and, as might be expected, it reveals that it is the predominantly rural and backward provinces of the central valley that show the highest losses, and the provinces containing the largest cities – Santiago, Valparaiso and Concepción – that show the highest gains. The historical nature of these characteristics is underlined in Table 10.2, indicating intercensal increases or losses by province over the period 1885–1960. Here, provinces like O'Higgins, Colchagua, Linares, Talca and Ñuble show rates of population increase consistently below – and usually well below – the national average, while Santiago is consistently well above, and in most intercensal periods double the national figure. The increasing momentum of these trends, against the background of rapidly rising national population in the past thirty years in particular, has produced in Chile a real megalopolis, which even an abundance of economic resources and a wealth of planning talent would find very difficult to overcome.

The social consequences of Santiago's vast and rapid expansion are obvious in the *callampas*, those mushroom growths of squatter settlements that have acquired a character of permanency. The provision of amenities such as piped water, electricity and telephones to these deprived environments has increased markedly in recent years, but, despite the fact that 'Chile remains a frontrunner among Latin American countries in the search for an integrated and continuous solution to the problems of housing and urban development' (Merrill, 1968, p. 141), in 1967 the deficit of adequate housing units in the country stood at 632,000 (Merrill, 1968, p. 143), and Santiago has its share. Perhaps one tenth of the capital's population lives in *callampas* and other substandard areas, though, as elsewhere in Latin America, they represent a very wide range of actual conditions.

Urban growth in the central valley of Chile is, of course, intimately linked to economic development, but it has been economic development of a particular kind. Whereas in western Europe there was a direct and positive connection between the growth of cities and the rise of industry, notably in the nineteenth century, in Chile, as in much of Latin America, the urban tradition predates the industrial age, and city growth as an aspect of industrialization is a fairly recent development. Before the 1930s, Santiago and Valparaiso experienced a historical evolution more akin to that of cities of the Europe of the Middle Ages than of the Industrial Revolution: they were centres of trade and commerce, government and administration – in short, service centres – rather than factory-dominated, urban complexes of manufacturing industry. The reasons for this are many and involved but, stated briefly, they relate to the historical evolution of the country's economic structure.

From the colonial period to the present day, the Chilean economy has been based on primary commodity exports from the farm and the mine. In the nineteenth century, and well on into the twentieth, consumer needs were essentially satisfied by imports from manufacturing countries and by

TABLE 10.2 Chilean population by province 1885–1960

Province	1885	1895	1907	1920	1930	1940	1952	1960
				Years				
Tarapacá	54,334	101,086	120,308	118,908	115,381	104,915	109,061	127,492
Antofagasta	33,430	45,624	112,674	174,797	181,999	146,287	196,101	222,514
Atacama	63,749	61,797	63,602	49,106	62,204	84,974	85,001	118,774
Coquimbo	189,557	181,558	189,775	178,561	201,974	247,539	278,165	318,440
Aconcagua	128,323	101,836	111,645	102,334	104,919	118,976	136,211	145,382
Valparaiso	203,318	229,614	280,965	325,870	367,011	428,404	528,655	637,542
Santiago	363,901	464,061	549,719	735,429	990,079	1,278,469	1,862,034	2,525,138
O'Higgins	131,301	137,435	133,489	161,056	173,621	201,870	238,297	269,332
Colchagua	109,707	114,858	113,317	121,030	122,731	132,779	148,045	164,243
Curico	63,424	71,052	72,959	75,722	77,383	81,823	94,889	111,377
Talca	122,372	123,002	122,817	127,816	144,792	158,375	184,291	213,532
Maule	91,464	94,323	81,246	85,430	75,729	71,051	76,585	82,424
Linares	109,824	105,168	108,339	120,634	125,312	136,028	155,181	176,978
Ñuble	209,842	215,488	218,170	228,202	236,085	245,095	266,678	295,711
Concepción	162,799	177,180	199,211	232,704	273,277	310,663	436,678	558,869
Arauco	69,626	62,432	62,369	62,535	62,179	66,626	76,700	92,721
Bío-Bío	99,350	90,567	96,224	106,127	115,442	128,312	146,730	173,868
Malleco	56,699	98,422	108,983	122,739	138,282	155,385	169,146	181,039
Cautín	52,589	92,585	176,471	254,789	320,967	377,602	387,347	408,507
Valdivia	38,925	55,069	80,932	120,727	151,716	193,147	246,842	265,147
Osorno	29,835	41,099	51,747	67,338	88,662	108,184	130,568	149,619
Llanquihué	33,406	40,692	53,713	71,175	94,202	118,146	148,527	172,489
Chiloé	72,153	79,721	87,094	110,902	93,733	102,505	106,830	102,543
Aysén	—	—	186	1,684	8,771	17,148	27,864	38,544
Magallanes	2,072	5,351	17,045	29,375	38,599	49,197	58,574	75,911
TOTAL	2,492,000	2,790,000	3,213,000	3,785,000	4,385,000	5,063,000	6,295,000	7,628,000

domestic, small-scale production of such commodities as foodstuffs and textiles. A comparatively small internal market, in which a heavily rural population lived on mostly self-sufficient great estates, offered little stimulus to the growth of industry, except in particular times and places when conditions were right for its introduction. Thus, for example, the growth of the Chilean wheat trade, at its height during the nineteenth century, was accompanied by the development of the flour-milling industry, first in the southern part of the central valley near Tomé and in the basin of the Maule river, sites with good access – and therefore cheap transportation – to both the wheat fields and to the Pacific outlets. As the export trade in flour grew, the need both for more capital and a better system of marketing concentrated the business in the existing commercial centre of Chile, Valparaiso where foreign merchant houses performed the functions of credit institutions and consigners for the growers and millers in the south. By the 1860s, however – the real beginning of the modern age in Chile – Santiago was becoming Chile's centre of banking and credit and, assisted by the concentration of railways on the capital and by the growth of the export-orientated wheat agriculture on the estates around it, Santiago province supplanted the south as the focus of the milling industry, and Santiago city supplanted Valparaiso as the commercial centre of the wheat trade. The growth of Santiago itself had some effect on manufacturing, with textiles and food-processing, glass-blowing and sugar-refining appearing as typical small-scale industries. Railway construction was a further stimulus to industrial growth: workshops belonging both to foreign-owned private companies in Valparaiso, and to the state railways in Valparaiso and Santiago, produced many of the locomotives and passenger and freight cars that ran on Chilean lines in the latter part of the century. The War of the Pacific, 1879–83, with Bolivia and Peru, was another stimulus to industry for the provision of military equipment such as munitions and clothing, and the annexation by Chile, after the war, of the nitrate provinces of Tarapacá and Antofagasta saw some demand in Chile itself for equipment to exploit the deposits, though the bulk of this was imported, chiefly from Great Britain.

Such developments cannot be ignored but, with few exceptions, they did not lead to the real growth of heavy industry in Chile, though light industry continued on an upward curve of production thenceforward. Probably the major reason for this (bearing in mind the nature and structure of Chilean society as already described) was the simple fact that windfall wealth, in the shape of export taxes on nitrate and copper, made it unnecessary, in the eyes of its leaders for Chile to industrialize. Dependence on mineral exports enabled successive Chilean governments to meet commitments, develop public services to a certain degree and service their foreign debts, without needing to tax the Chilean aristocracy heavily. Demand for luxury and consumer goods, imported from abroad, continued to be met, since, here again, there seemed no necessity to go in for home production of such goods.

The weakness of this position was exposed time and time again with the inevitable fluctuations in world demand (and therefore exports of the minerals), but the shock was not sustained until the First World War. Then, cut off from their traditional markets for minerals, and from their normal suppliers of necessary imports, Chileans began to realize the fundamental weakness of their position in the world economy. Moreover, the demographic and urban expansions were getting under way. Much more severe, however, was the impact of the Great Depression of the early 1930s, which hit Chile harder than any other country in the world, because of extreme dependence on the two commodities, copper and nitrates, which in 1929 amounted to three-quarters of all exports. Recovery in the 1930s was based upon strict government control of the economy, protection for local industries and their promotion with government intervention, characteristics that were accentuated with the coming of the Second World War. Chile's real industrial development, indeed, and the major role played by state organizations in promoting it, dates essentially from these events.

Not surprisingly, import-substitution industries were the first to expand and the 1930s saw a considerable growth of plants producing textiles, footwear, furniture, construction materials and fittings, and processed foodstuffs. Most of these industries were, in fact, concentrated on Santiago and Valparaiso well before the First World War, and they were the chief locations for these new developments, though Concepción and some other towns outside the central valley (Valdivia, for example) also benefited. It was entirely natural that growth in non-durable consumer goods, having little or nothing to do with exports, should take place in the vicinity of the country's most populous market, and in 1930 Santiago already contained a quarter of Chile's total population. By 1945, virtually the entire national demand in prepared foodstuffs, beverages, tobacco products, shoes, clothing, matches, furniture, window glass, paints and varnishes, paper products and lighting fixtures was being met by national industry (Ellsworth, 1945, p. 179).

It was, however, private enterprise – including such foreign firms as Grace (United States) and Duncan Fox (Great Britain) – that was responsible for this development, assisted by general government economic policies of recovery from the Depression such as tariff controls on imports. A new phase in Chilean industrialization, emphasizing both direct intervention by the state and the promotion of basic industries, began in 1939 with the establishment of the Chilean Development Corporation (CORFO), the first Latin American general development and economic planning authority, endowed with very wide powers to promote economic growth (for a description of these, see Ellsworth, 1945, pp. 85 ff.). Fortuitously, and beneficially, its establishment coincided with the outbreak of the Second World War, which created in Chile a serious shortage of imported manufactured goods, including semi-finished products and capital equipment not then produced in Chile: this gave an enormous boost to Chilean industrialization precisely when the machinery had been created to promote it.

The industrial expansion since the 1940s has proceeded to the extent that Chilean industry today meets virtually all internal requirements for durable consumer goods, but this expansion has depended on the existing availability of labour, power and transport facilities, which are highly concentrated on Santiago. Moreover, the durable consumer goods sector relies heavily on imported components and, in this connection, Valparaiso's historic position as Chile's most important port for incoming cargoes has been an important factor in underlining the dominance of Santiago and Valparaiso as major locations for industrial plant. In recent years the rapid development of installations for handling and transporting shipments through San Antonio have made that port a serious rival to Valparaiso: by the mid-1950s it was already handling 10 per cent of total tonnage through Chilean ports, compared with 12 per cent by Valparaiso (Bohan and Pomerantz, 1960, p. 206), but this development, of course, does nothing to affect Santiago's continued pre-eminence in Chilean industry and manufacturing. Indeed, the third National Census of Manufactures in 1957 indicated that of the fifty-two industrial establishments in Chile employing more than 500 persons each, no fewer than forty-three were located in the provinces of Santiago and Valparaiso, thirty-five in Santiago and eight in Valparaiso (Hoffman and Debuyst, 1966, p. 53). One characteristic of recent years has been the growth in size of larger industrial units, yet another factor for agglomeration: this, again, is a natural concomitant of rapid and continuous urbanization in the core region of Chile.

The modern economic history of Chile, and notably the growth of industry, has thus reinforced the historical centralism the country has experienced since its beginnings, and the actual process of economic change, with continued dependence on primary commodity exports, situated by and large outside the central region, has imposed constraints on Chile's economic growth. The country's trade structure is very rigid: since exports of primary products account for nearly 90 per cent of exports by value, and volume and price fluctuations of these commodities in world markets cannot be controlled by Chile, the country's capacity to expand its industrial development is immediately affected by factors outside its control at its present stage of development. No less than 70 per cent of Chile's imports take the form of semi-finished goods, capital equipment and industrial raw materials; hence, the level of industrial activity is geared to the fluctuating export trade in primary products. National industry grew rapidly in the first half of the 1940s, profiting from the

Second World War, with a growth-rate of around 10 per cent per annum, but this fell to 4 per cent between 1945 and 1955 as international imports again became more readily available and as the scope for further import-substitution declined. The following decade saw the virtual stagnation of the industrial sector when the severity of inflation necessitated a policy of stabilization, which had a most depressive effect on the economy (Benham and Holley, 1960, p. 109). The basic reasons for the vicissitudes of the Chilean economy and the slow general growth of industrialization are essentially structural; partly because of its link with primary product exports, partly because of the low rate of demand for manufactures in a country where average income, though perhaps good by Latin American standards, is still low compared with genuinely industrialized countries, and partly due to endemic inflation – encouraging speculative investment rather than the accumulation of industrial capital – the industrial sector has not been able to grow commensurately with the rise in population. The unemployment, underemployment and inefficient employment – always, of course, more noticeable in cities – characteristic of Santiago and Valparaiso is, in effect, a consequence of Chile's distorted economic structure. Moreover, the extractive industries, which provide the bulk of Chile's foreign exchange earnings, are capital rather than labour-intensive, and the transfer of technology to Chile, to promote import-substitution, is of the same character. Consequently, while the growth of manufacturing in Santiago and Valparaiso generally has drawn in migrants looking for work and for higher standards of living, it has not yet grown enough to absorb them, and cannot do so until other economic conditions are met.

Among these conditions is the need to change Chile's backward agricultural sector, particularly in the central valley, first to eliminate the country's dependence on imported foodstuffs, which in recent years have accounted for a quarter or more of all imports by value and have been a major factor in the inflationary process, and, secondly, so to raise rural purchasing power as to make it a more significant stimulus to industrial growth. We have already seen that recent developments in agrarian reform aim to achieve these economic effects, as well as to bring about desirable social change. Another, and perhaps a more critical necessity for the Chilean economy in the immediate present and future, is the need to increase exports of manufactures and diversify them, to strengthen Chile's terms of trade and reduce dependence on primary commodities. Here, again, there have been some encouraging developments in recent years, in such fields as heavy industry, petrochemicals and cellulose, notably outside the Santiago–Valparaiso region.

Nevertheless, the core region in general, and Santiago in particular, retain their overwhelming predominance in the national life, despite persistent attempts to diminish it. Over the past thirty years in particular successive governments have tried to use the centralization of decision-making to ameliorate regional imbalances, and they have forged planning and investment instruments for that purpose, which in many ways have been models for other Latin American states with similar internal disequilibria. CORFO has as one of its declared objectives the decentralization of production through the distribution of investments elsewhere than in Santiago, and the agency has, in fact, put most of its money into activities located in the provinces and not in the capital (Herrick, 1965, p. 39). Again, tax laws in the 1950s gave sizeable exemptions to new industries established outside the capital, in order to encourage a wider dispersion of economic activity (Bohan and Pomerantz, 1960, p. 109). And natural disaster, to which Chile seems particularly prone, has played a part in the same process: the severe earthquake in southern Chile in 1960 focused attention on the problem of regional imbalance, in the wake of relief measures that were immediately necessary.[1]

Yet, while government policy and the activities of the CORFO have had some success in deliberately promoting industrial development outside the Santiago–Valparaiso region, that success has been very strictly limited. Indeed, in some respects such initiatives have been counter-productive. Weaver (1968, pp. 141–82) has shown that improvement in transportation facilities, notably roads, which has been an important undertaking in Chile in recent years, and which was intended, in part, to benefit provinces outside the core region, has, in fact, enabled industries in Santiago to penetrate outlying markets and drastically affect small-scale local enterprises producing the same commodities. The same author concludes his important study with the judgement that:

> the geographically centralising forces inherent in Chile's economic and social structure have not been significantly affected by such government policies as the geographical dispersion of public services, the construction of transportation facilities in outlying areas, or tax incentives to industries established outside the Santiago–Valparaiso area. Only the creation of governmentally-owned enterprise appears to have had any lasting impact on balancing the nation's economy spatially. (Weaver, 1968, p. 240)[2]

Clear prerequisities to the solution of problems of regional planning and metropolitan concentration are awareness of their existence and research into their causes; the fact is that in Latin America generally investigation of such factors as economic location options, the relationship between costs of urban infrastructure and population size, and the degree

[1] It is noteworthy that the CORFO itself came into existence in similar circumstances, after the disastrous Chilean earthquake of 1939. Its advocates included its creation in the emergency legislation for relief measures, and thus overcame strong opposition in Congress to this instrument of state planning (Ellsworth, 1945, p. 85).

[2] The author is indebted to Professor Weaver for permission to quote this passage.

to which metropolitan concentration aids or hinders national economic integration, is a comparatively new field of research. Chile, however, has more experience than most other countries in the continent in this respect, and the recent administration of President Eduardo Frei (1964–70) has built on this to produce new planning concepts and machinery, which will be considered in the concluding section of this essay when the various regions of Chile have been surveyed. It is, however, an important truism that in the cumulative process that produces the primate city, planners may intervene in economic and social arrangements but they cannot control the past. In seeking to control the future, Chilean planners face one of their biggest problems in the mere fact that their capital city has dominated the country's life virtually from its beginning, and that there are powerful historical and geographical reasons why it has done so.

III NORTE GRANDE AND NORTE CHICO

Introduction

The northern provinces of Chile, Tarapacá and Antofagasta, known together as the Norte Grande, and Atacama and Coquimbo, generally called the Norte Chico, make up both the desert region of Chile and the transitional zone between Desert and Mediterranean Chile, as described in the early part of this essay. But while the relationship of each of these northern regions to the heartland has been markedly different in some respects, it has been very similar in others. The difference is historical: it lies in the fact that whereas the Norte Grande has not yet celebrated its centenary as Chilean territory, the Norte Chico has been Chilean from the beginning, in theory if not precisely in fact. The similarity is economic, deriving from the common character of both regions as zones of mineral exploitation, and the comparable nature of their link with central Chile because of this feature.

The Norte Grande became part of Chile in the 1880s as the prize won in war with Bolivia and Peru: Tarapacá was ceded to Chile by Peru in the Treaty of Ancón, 1883, and five years later Bolivian Antofagasta was also incorporated into the southern republic. The Norte Chico, on the other hand, was part of the colonial Kingdom of Chile and, in fact, the town of La Serena in Coquimbo is the second oldest town in the country, dating from 1549:[1] it was built by order of Pedro de Valdivia at the northern confines of the infant colony, both as a centre for gold mining operations and as a convenient staging post on the land route to Peru. The northern boundary of the Norte Chico was very ill defined throughout the colonial period, and the province of Atacama, unlike that of Coquimbo, saw little Spanish settlement before the latter part of the eighteenth century. Fig. 10.2 indicates the marked increase in the number of towns founded in the

[1] The first foundation in 1543 was destroyed by Indians.

Norte Chico between the mid-eighteenth and the mid-nineteenth centuries, a development intimately connected with the expansion of mining. In the Norte Grande, too, there was a close relationship between urban growth and mineral extraction, though, as the map indicates, this less hospitable region with its serious problems of water and food supply, saw far fewer foundations than the Norte Chico, and some of these occurred, with the rise of nitrates after the mid-nineteenth century, under Peruvian and Bolivian auspices.

It is, indeed, mineral extraction that has always dominated the life of the northern provinces in the past, and it seems destined to do so in the future. In the Norte Chico it is a story of gold, silver, copper and, latterly, iron ore; in the Norte Grande, it is a story of, first, natural nitrates and later of copper. Today, the Norte Grande and the Norte Chico contain little more than a tenth of the total Chilean population, a slightly smaller proportion than seventy years ago, in the same third of the total national territory. Yet, the significance of these regions in the national life is out of all proportion to these numbers because of Chile's dependence, past and present, on their mineral resources. The dominance in the Chilean economy during the nineteenth and twentieth centuries, first of copper, then of nitrates, then of copper again is, perhaps, the most significant single fact in the economic history of the republic. And the evolution of these regions is essentially the story of man's exploitation of mineral riches. It is not, however, the whole story, for there are other aspects of the historical geography of the Norte Grande and the Norte Chico that deserve, at least, some passing mention.

Traditional communities of Desert Chile

Throughout the Norte Grande and the Norte Chico, climate and relief inhibit agriculture, as indicated in the early sections of this essay, except in the permanent river valleys to the south and in the oases of the Atacama desert. Fig. 10.1 indicates the proportion of the population of the four provinces classified as rural, according to the 1960 census, the precise figures being 13 per cent for Tarapacá, 4 per cent for Antofagasta, 24 per cent for Atacama and 46 per cent for Coquimbo, reflecting in large part the climatic progression to higher rainfall as one moves south. Yet, the desert regions themselves have always supported agricultural and pastoral communities, from the pre-Spanish period to the present day, notably in piedmont oases of the Andes, such as Pica, Matilla and Pozo Almonte in Tarapacá, and San Pedro de Atacama, Toconao and Peine in Antofagasta. The classic description of these settlements was made nearly fifty years ago (Bowman, 1924) and in most respects that account still holds (Rudolph, 1963, p. 51). From pre-Spanish days to the mid-twentieth century the pueblos of the eastern Atacama, situated north and east of the Salar de Atacama, experienced little change, apart from losing their native language,

Kunza, and adopting Spanish as well as the Christian religion, but in much more recent times civilization in its modern form has begun to reach the villages with the advent of schools, motor roads, modern lighting and radio (Rudolph, 1963, pp. 57–60). Another factor bringing these communities more into touch with the outside world today is, perhaps paradoxically, the increasing interest of archaeologists and students of folklore in their culture: the annual fiestas, with their strange blend of Christian and pagan elements, attract increasing numbers of outsiders, though, of course, the settlements are still well off the beaten track of the tourist trade. Yet the ecological base of the *pueblos* has changed little in centuries: irrigation farming, producing corn, wheat, barley, vegetables and a wide range of fruits – apples, pears, grapes, figs, quinces – together with sheep-herding in the upland pastures, today supports a population of about 2000 people at San Pedro de Atacama and its environs, and the next largest *pueblo* of the Antofagasta *cordillera*, Toconao, with a similar number scattered over a large number of smaller settlements.

Despite their location, these communities, highly sedentary and self-centred as they have always been, have never been really isolated, for they lie on well-worn trails from both north to south and east to west. These trails were trodden by the Incas in the fifteenth century, and by the Spaniards in the sixteenth. Pedro de Valdivia's expedition from Peru in 1540 travelled from Arica inland to Tarapacá, thence to Calama and San Pedro de Atacama, where it rested some time before proceeding south. Christianity came early in the colonial period, and the bells of the churches in many of these *pueblos* bear dates of the seventeenth and eighteenth centuries. During the whole of the colonial period, San Pedro came under the jurisdiction of Peru and, after 1776, Buenos Aires, through the governor of Potosí; at the same time, the maritime link between Chile and Peru took precedence over any land route, but the region remained an important transit zone throughout, between the mountains on the one hand and the desert and Pacific coast on the other (Bowman, 1924, pp. 236–8). This role was enhanced after the region came under Chilean control with the rapid development of the nitrate industry from the 1880s: the supply of fresh meat to the nitrate works (*oficinas*) of Antofagasta, situated north-east and south-east of the port of that name, came from Salta in Argentina, a two weeks' cattle drive from San Pedro de Atacama. Having crossed the Puna de Atacama, the cattle rested at San Pedro for a few days, feeding up after their difficult journey, before being driven for the three days required to get them to the *oficinas* (for a detailed description of the trade, see Bowman, 1924, pp. 218–35). Similarly, the demand of the *oficinas* for mules for haulage purposes was met from the north-west provinces of Argentina, and San Pedro's facilities for accommodating transient droves were well utilized. One consequence of this development for San Pedro itself was the expansion of alfalfa-growing for fodder.

The cattle trade was at its height during the first quarter of this century and when the world market in natural nitrates succumbed to the competition from synthetic nitrates in the late 1920s, a further lease of life was given to San Pedro's important role on the cattle road by the rise of copper at Chuquicamata. There followed another decline with the opening of the Antofagasta–Salta Railway, routed to the south of the Salar de Atacama (see Fig. 10.4), and the old cattle trail seemed doomed with this development in 1948. But, for various reasons, the railway has been a failure (see Rudolph, 1963, pp. 33–6), and San Pedro has resumed its role as a transit zone between Argentine Salta and Chilean Antofagasta, with the construction of a road, following the old cattle trail, in the early 1960s. Cattle now travel from Salta to San Pedro in one day, instead of fourteen, and they go in trucks, not on the hoof.

The changes that increasingly make an impact on the traditional communities of the Atacama desert may well raise the standards of living, but they will also affect the quality of life. New generations seem likely to be less inclined to maintain their forbears' pattern of existence, as education and improvements in communications – radios no less than roads – diminish its cultural individuality. Fishing communities of the Antofagasta coast, such as the Changos of Cobija, whose precarious survival to the modern age was noted by Bowman (1924, p. 59), have now quite disappeared (Rudolph, 1963, p. 53). The desert communities are much more firmly rooted, and they have shown a remarkable capacity to survive through the centuries, but their future cannot be taken for granted simply in the light of their past.

Agriculture in the northern regions

In the Norte Grande, apart from the oasis settlements, it is only in the very few watered valleys of the province of Tarapacá that agriculture has any hold. Here, the Lluta and Azapa rivers – and, to a lesser extent, the Vitor, Camarones and Camina – provide some scope for the growing of tropical produce, as does the Loa, which separates Tarapacá from Antofagasta. Vegetables, fruit, especially raisins, and almonds are the specialities in the far north, but only 2 per cent of the total area of the Norte Grande is arable, and its total proportion of the national territory devoted to fruit-growing is only half that percentage.

The northern part of the Norte Chico – Atacama and northern Coquimbo – have the same, or similar, conditions, though the ribbons of vegetation that follow the course of the rivers Copiapó and Huasco in Atacama are much wider than further north and, while precipitation is not much greater than in the truly arid regions, it is sufficiently so to make a considerable difference. Seen from the air, the irrigated valley floor in which the town of Copiapó stands provides a flash of green amidst its barren surroundings, and it has done so certainly for centuries, if not, indeed, millennia, since the Spanish conquerors found Indian irrigation works and a settled population when they arrived. Yet everything depends upon the *amount* of water available and, since both rainfall and river supply in valleys like that of the Copiapó and the Huasco fluctuate very considerably over the years, the agricultural economy of the Atacama valleys has had a very chequered history (Bowman, 1924, pp. 113–28, and cf. the comments of Charles Darwin, 1960, pp. 332–8).

The agricultural products of these valleys, apart from supplying the highly important local mining industry – to which we shall return – were also exported to the northern desert during the boom years of the nitrate industry, and the fattening of cattle, imported from Argentina and southern Chile, was also an important activity for the same market. Alfalfa is still a significant crop but more important today are products known as *primores*, vegetables such as tomatoes which, due to the climatic conditions, are in season here before they ripen in the central valley. The urban markets of Santiago and Valparaiso are the chief consumers. The Huasco valley also has extensive vineyards, olive groves and orchards. The pastoral sector also takes due advantage of the peculiar climatic situation: outside the irrigated valleys, the *camanchaca* on the coastal range and the higher precipitation on the Andean slopes provide pasturage for cattle, sheep and goats, which are driven there when it is the dry season in the valleys.

The significantly higher rainfall of Coquimbo, in comparison with Atacama, makes its river valleys – the Elquí, Limari and Choapa – much more productive in cereals, vegetables, fruit, sheep and goats. Indeed, agricultural settlement from the time of the Spanish Conquest was very much more pronounced than in the essentially mining province of Atacama. And while dry farming is much practised, especially in the southern part of the province, its uncertainties, compared with the irrigated farming, which comprises only 2·7 per cent of arable land in Coquimbo, are undoubtedly a major factor in giving the province the unenviable reputation of having the highest loss of population through migration in the intercensal period 1952–60 (see Fig. 10.1). Moreover, agricultural exploitation of non-irrigated areas has, historically, been closely linked with the fortunes of mining camps: as veins of metal were worked out, so agricultural villages established to provision them also declined, and permanent concentration of population occurred primarily in the stable river valleys. Today, about 30 per cent of cultivated land is dry farmed, and it is areas such as these, of course, that are hit the hardest by the periodic droughts that afflict Chile, the worst of which occurred in the late 1960s.

Wheat, barley and maize are the chief grain crops, but in the Elquí and Limari valleys alfalfa and clover predominate, and La Serena is an important dairying centre. Transhumance is highly significant in the pastoral industry, but the coastal range and the Andean slopes have been seriously eroded by the vast numbers of goats – over half a million in 1955 – which outnumber cattle, sheep and horses in the province. Stock-raising, in fact, predominates in the rural economy.

Throughout the northern provinces, the dual pattern of *latifundia* and *minifundia* we have observed in the central valley also obtains, but in Coquimbo there also exist quite distinctive communities holding land in common. These derive from the colonial period when large land grants made by crown agents often included common lands, though many of these were subsequently incorporated, by one means or another, into private properties (see pp. 493–8 above). Not all such common land was incorporated, however, and, in addition, some unirrigated and unirrigable lands included in *private* land grants were subsequently felt by heirs to the property to be of such little value that they did not take the trouble to legalize their possession of them, and the lands were then taken over by others. The processes whereby agricultural communities came into existence – with some members holding both individual properties and a share in common lands, and others having only recognized rights of common usufruct – have a very complicated history, often obscure. In Coquimbo, however, such communities are of considerable significance, since they represent a third of the total population and a half of the rural population of the province, and they occupy and work no less than a quarter of the usable land, though this is only 3·5 per cent of the irrigated land in Coquimbo. The organization and government of these agricultural communities, and their use of the land they hold, are extremely diverse, but they are worthy of note since they represent a peculiar hangover from the colonial period, and also an interesting testimony to the variety of systems of land tenure in Chile (see CIDA, 1966, pp. 126–42, for a detailed description).

Notwithstanding the importance of agriculture and stock-raising in the northern provinces, increasing as one moves south, the economy of the Norte Grande and Norte Chico is, and always has been, that of the mine rather than the farm. It is mineral extraction that has determined population movements, the establishment of towns and ports, the siting of communication routes and, indeed, in the War of the Pacific, the expansion of Chile's national frontiers 960 km to the north of their colonial location. Mining itself, as we have already observed, was an important stimulus in regional food production, not only in the northern provinces but also in the central valley, and the commerce associated with northern mining was also a factor in the growth of Valparaiso as well as the ports of the region. The role of mineral exploitation has been, and still is, absolutely crucial for government revenues and for Chile's balance of payments, and, while other regions of Chile also have mineral deposits of great significance, either past or present or both – copper at El Teniente in O'Higgins, coal in

Arauco and oil in Magallanes – they do not dominate the economy, the life and the history of their locations as they do in the Norte Grande and the Norte Chico, nor have they yet played the crucial role in the evolution of Chile that they have done, and continue to do, here. Two other general factors should be mentioned: in the exploitation of the nitrates and copper of Chile's northern provinces, foreign capital has predominated, and, secondly, proximity of the mineral deposits to the Pacific has made for comparatively easy shipment to overseas markets.

The rise and fall of the nitrate industry

The significance of natural nitrates in the Chilean economy between 1880 and 1925 is illustrated in Table 10.3. Even before 1880, when the nitrate regions belonged to Peru and Bolivia, Chilean labour and capital, with British finance also prominent, played a major role in the exploitation of the deposits. Indeed, as early as 1870, of the 18,000 workers at the nitrate port of Iquique in Peruvian Tarapacá, approximately half were, in fact, Chilean; already it was Valparaiso, rather than a Peruvian commercial centre, that was the real focus of the nitrate trade. Until the 1870s both the Peruvian and Bolivian governments remained apparently indifferent to this state of affairs, confining their intervention in the nitrate business to the collection of export duties on nitrate shipments. In 1875, however, the virtually bankrupt government of Peru decided to expropriate foreign capital in its nitrate areas and, in effect, nationalize the industry. The privately owned producing plants (*oficinas*) were to be paid for in government bonds, made payable to bearer, which were to be redeemed by the government within two years but, in fact, they were never cancelled by Peru since her government failed to raise the European loan required to buy out the owners. The late 1870s were depression years for nitrates, partly owing to the great uncertainty created by Peruvian government action, and partly owing to the earthquake of March 1877, which destroyed many of the loading platforms along the coast. The intervention of the War of the Pacific, however, changed the situation dramatically: Chile's seizure of the nitrate provinces and her subsequent decision to return the industry to private ownership was a decisive moment in the history of the nitrate industry. In the first place, Chile secured for herself the export revenues from nitrate that had formerly gone to Peru and Bolivia. Secondly, the devolution of the nitrate grounds to private hands again gave foreign, and notably British, capital, the pre-eminent position in the industry.

This situation arose from the circumstances of Peru's attempted nationalization. The bonds issued by the government in 1875 – in effect, the title deeds to nitrate properties – fell markedly in value in the late 1870s, and the War of the Pacific brought their price down even more rapidly. Speculating on both the chances of a Chilean triumph in the war itself, and on the possibility of the Chilean government subsequently

TABLE 10.3 *Export of nitrates (metric tons)
1880–1925 (at five-yearly intervals) and proportion (%) of government revenue derived from
export taxes on nitrate*

Year	Exports	Revenue (as % of total)
1880	223,974	5·52
1885	435,988	33·77
1890	1,063,277	52·06
1895	1,238,605	66·03
1900	1,453,707	56·29
1905	1,650,363	56·67
1910	2,335,941	55·14
1915	2,023,321	54·81
1920	2,794,394	49·65
1925	2,517,099	37·18

Source: Hernández Cornejo (1930, pp. 174, 177–8).

handing back the industry to private control, British entrepreneurs
bought up large quantities of the depreciated certificates in the war years,
and thus acquired the nitrate grounds very cheaply.[1] In 1878, British
capital had controlled about 13 per cent of the nitrate industry of Tarapacá;
by 1884, the proportion had risen to 34 per cent, but by 1890, after a period
of feverish activity on the London Stock Exchange, 70 per cent of the
province's nitrate industry was in British hands.

There were five major areas of nitrate exploitation in the high period of
the industry, the most extensive in the province of Tarapacá, the others
known from their location in Antofagasta province as El Toco, Antofagasta,
Aguas Blancas and Taltal. In Tarapacá, the fields ran in a south–south-
west direction from the latitude of Pisagua to that of Chucumata, east of
the *cordillera de la costa* and on the western edge of the central depression
known as the Pampa de Tamarugal, less than 20 km inland in the far north
but more than double that distance from the coast in the south. In
Antofagasta province the main northerly deposits of the raw material
(*caliche*) were to be found some 60 km inland, due east of the port of
Tocopilla, in the same central depression which runs from Tarapacá to
Atacama: it is the southern part of this nitrate field of El Toco that is the
basis of the modern industry, based on María Elena and Pedro de Valdivia.
The third field, moving south, was of much less importance than those of
Tarapacá and El Toco, lying 80 km north-east of Antofagasta port, but
much more significant was the field of Aguas Blancas, a similar distance

[1] The principal speculator was John Thomas North, known as 'the Nitrate
King', who bought many bonds at prices around one tenth of their nominal value.
See Blakemore (1962) for a short sketch of his activities.

south-east of the port. Finally, in the southernmost part of the province lay the Taltal deposits, from 40 to 70 km east of the port with the same name. Fig. 10.4 indicates the location of the nitrate fields (for a detailed description, see Semper and Michels, 1908).

The rapid growth of the nitrate industry from the 1880s naturally had a significant effect on the economic life of the regions concerned. It encouraged immigration from other parts of Chile and stimulated the growth of ports and the building of railway lines to carry the nitrate from the *oficinas* to the ports. The virtual doubling of the population of Tarapacá between 1885 and 1895 shown in Table 10.2 reflected, in fact, the growth of its nitrate industry. Its port towns of Pisagua and Iquique had, in this period, the character of real 'boom' towns, Iquique boasting, as it still does today, an opera house built by the French architect, Eiffel. In the early period of development, water supplies for Iquique came by tanker from Arica and from coastal distillation plants, while the nitrate *oficinas* inland were supplied by mule carts and, later, railways conveying the precious necessity (Bowman, 1924, pp. 76-8). Subsequently, however, pipelines were laid to the Andean *cordillera* region, and this has remained the major source for both the coastal and inland centres (Bowman, 1924; cf. Rudolph, 1963, pp. 36-48). Reference has already been made to the stimulus provided by the rise of the nitrate industry to the trans-Andean trade in cattle, to stock-raising and agriculture in the Norte Chico and the central valley, and to the production of comestibles for humans and animals alike in the desert oasis settlements. The Chilean coastal shipping trade was affected similarly. But the close interconnection of these segments of the Chilean economy carried with it the danger that circumstances affecting the nitrate industry itself would be transmitted far beyond the nitrate regions, having a multiplier effect of the harmful kind.

Throughout the history of the natural nitrate industry, boom was followed by slump with considerable frequency. The major markets for Chilean nitrates were the farming industries of western Europe and the United States, but their vicissitudes, climatic or otherwise, were a critical factor in nitrate production. Overall, world consumption of nitrates did not keep pace on a regular rising trend with Chile's productive capacity, and overstocking of the world nitrate market faced producers with the fear of falling prices. Between 1880 and 1909, no fewer than five agreements, or combinations, were made between the various nitrate producers to restrict their output in these circumstances, leading to serious economic difficulties not only for the workers of the *oficinas* and shippers at the nitrate ports but also for the many, distant interests that had become enmeshed in the nitrate trade. The consequences for the Chilean government, deriving half its revenue from export taxes on nitrates between 1890 and 1920, were no less severe.

The periodic booms and slumps of the nitrate industry would, no doubt, have continued had Chile retained its monopoly of nitrate production to the present day, since the industry depended on world market forces over which it had little control; nevertheless, given its monopoly position down to the First World War, falling markets were always followed by rising ones, and recovery was usually rapid. This cycle, however, was fundamentally affected first by the war of 1914–18, and, secondly, by the Great Depression of the early 1930s. Germany was a major market for Chilean nitrates, and the advent of the First World War, when the British naval blockade disrupted German trade, almost immediately affected Tarapacá. Within a few months of the declaration of war, half the nitrate *oficinas* in the province were closed down, and many of the workless labourers, numbering some 33,000, left Iquique and Pisagua for more southern parts of Chile. More significantly in the long run, German scientists turned their attention to producing synthetic nitrates in commercial quantities by techniques that spread quickly to other advanced countries in the post-war period. It is true that between 1913 and 1929 there was no significant real decline in the quantity of nitrates shipped from Chilean ports, but Chile's share in world nitrate production, natural and synthetic, fell in the same period from 90 per cent to about 24 per cent. The Great Depression greatly accelerated the decline by its complete disruption of world trade, and many large *oficinas* that had survived synthetic competition into the 1930s did not last out the decade. The *oficina* Chacabuco, for example, some 80 km north-east of Antofagasta, off the road to Calama, had 7000 people living there as late as 1938; today, its vast leaching tanks turning to rust and the trees of its central square the same colour as the surrounding desert, Chacabuco is a lifeless testimony to the transient nature of Chile's nitrate age, and of man's temporary conquest of this part of the Atacama.

Chile, however, still exports nitrates, averaging a total of 900,000 tons a year between 1960 and 1966, out of a production figure of some 1,100,000 tons. Reorganization of the industry and the introduction of modern technology enables Chile to compete in the world market for nitrates and hold approximately 4 per cent of it. Production in Tarapacá and Antofagasta is now highly localized and effectively confined to a small number of companies: the Compañía Salitrera Anglo-Lautaro, an Anglo-American company, is responsible for about 85 per cent of Chilean production at its María Elena and Pedro de Valdivia plants (see Fig. 10.4). In the late 1950s and early 1960s the company carried out an extensive expansion and modernization programme, including work on its solar evaporation plant at Coya Sur, mechanical loading facilities at the port of Tocopilla, improvements in other equipment and in research facilities, and better housing for the labour force. The Empresa Salitrera Victoria – until 1960 the Compañía Salitrera de Tarapacá y Antofagasta – is effectively a subsidiary of the CORFO; it produces about 11 per cent of national output, and has also carried out a large modernization programme in recent years at its *oficina* of Victoria. The port of shipment here is Iquique, where the company has a mechanical loading dock and good storage facilities.

Output and marketing are partially controlled by a state organization, the Corporación de Ventas de Salitre y Yodo de Chile (COVENSA), established in 1934, which, in co-operation with the companies, periodically fixes production quotas in relation to installed productive capacity. Over 12,000 persons are employed in the industry today and, with their dependents, they represent a not insignificant proportion of the labour force in the desert provinces. Their future livelihood, however, at least in nitrates, is not completely assured. Chile's share of the world market may well continue to decline as developing countries increasingly turn to synthetics: this certainly happened in the case of Egypt in the 1950s when her imports of nitrate from Chile fell by two-thirds in three years (Butland, 1956, p. 73). However, one encouraging feature of recent years has been the growth of the internal market for nitrates in Chile itself and, given current agricultural developments, referred to previously, this will undoubtedly continue. It is unlikely to develop sufficiently to absorb current Chilean output of nitrates if the Chilean share of the world market shrank rapidly and permanently to nothing, but this is also unlikely to happen. The modernization programmes of the two large companies have given the Chilean industry a competitive position for at least a small share of the world market, but, as in the past, the future of the Chilean nitrate industry is more dependent on what happens abroad than at home.

Chile's monopoly of nitrates has long since gone but in one commodity associated with her nitrate deposits – iodine – she has maintained, if not a monopoly position, at least the leading position. Iodine occurs in nitrate deposits as iodide and iodates of sodium, calcium and potassium, and Chilean iodine is 99·5 per cent pure. While Chile's share of the world market has fallen considerably since the late 1920s, when it was over 80 per cent, due largely to Californian competition (from waste oil well brines), Chile still supplies approximately half the world's needs, exporting on average over 2 million kg per annum in the period 1960–6, and seems likely to retain this position in the foreseeable future. Competition from the United States, which is also Chile's principal market for iodine, is the major danger, but world demand for iodine – for use in sanitation, metallurgy, livestock feeding and the synthetic organic chemistry industry – will probably grow sufficiently for Chile to find other markets if imports into the United States fall off.

While the nitrate industry of Chile no longer dominates the life of the nation as it did for a period of forty years, the influence of its rise and fall is at the heart of controversies concerned not only with the evolution of Chile itself but with the larger issue of Latin American development as a whole. It is a classic example of the short-term benefits and long-range disadvantages of national dependence on the export of one commodity.

Metallic mining in the northern regions

The nitrate industry of Chile was essentially a development of the nineteenth century, but the mining of metallic ores goes back to the beginning of the colonial period and it has had a continuous history since then. In the seventeenth century, for example, Peru's requirements for arms to defend the Viceroyalty against corsairs was a major stimulus to copper-mining in the major known region of deposits, the province of Coquimbo, the copper being shipped from the port of that name to the Peruvian arsenal at Callao (Pederson, 1966, pp. 70 ff.). In the eighteenth century – a period of considerable economic expansion in Chile – it was gold, rather than copper, that came into its own in the Norte Chico. Old centres of gold-mining, dating from the period of the Spanish Conquest, such as Combarbalá and Illapel in southern Coquimbo, and La Serena in the north, once again became the scenes of feverish activity as old workings were reopened and new sources discovered. More significant, however, was the northward march of the mining frontier as prospecting was intensified and extended: new centres were established as focal points both for mining operations themselves and for the variety of economic operations mining brought in its train – agriculture and stock-raising to supply the mining camps with food; the growing of forage to feed the mule trains that carried supplies and ore in that pre-railway age; the provision and transport of timber to supply the mines with supports and the smelters with fuel. Prospectors ranged and honeycombed the hills, the outcrops of Andean diorite that form the coastal batholith between Santiago and Copiapó, and as the expansion of vein mining got under way so was the landscape transformed. Copiapó itself and Freirina and Vallenar were characteristic foundations of the period, near to mining lodes and lying in river valleys that could also be exploited for agriculture and pastoralism.[1] By the end of the eighteenth century, the Norte Chico had become differentiated from the rest of Chile by its specialization in mining, which dominated the life of the region and has continued to do so.

Gold production had passed its peak by the time Chile achieved her independence from Spain in 1818, but already silver and copper were becoming highly significant. The silver strikes of major importance occurred at intervals between 1811 and 1870, creating bonanza conditions at particular times and places, and enabling Chilean silver production to show a constant rise through most of the century. The first, at Agua Amarga, south of Vallenar in 1811, not only quadrupled the population of Vallenar within a few years; it also extended the amount of land under

[1] Spanish colonists, of course, had long been in occupation of particular areas when such towns were founded, exercising *encomienda* rights and so on. Thus, in the Copiapó valley, Francisco de Aguirre established his estates in the mid-sixteenth century; but it was mining two centuries later that made Copiapó more than an outpost of settlement (Bowman, 1924, pp. 99–106).

cultivation, in order to supply the miners, and expanded the cutting of irrigation canals. Another major discovery took place in 1825, north-west of La Serena, but this was soon overshadowed by the most significant, and certainly the most romantic, strike of the century, the accidental discovery in 1832 of the silver hill of Chanarcillo, near Copiapó, by the woodcutter, Juan Godoy. With this discovery, Copiapó grew rapidly from a town of 4000 to one of 12,000 within three years – not surprisingly in view of the fact that masses of nearly pure silver were found at Chanarcillo, one piece weighing 2700 kg (Bowman, 1924, p. 170). The greater climatic handicaps of the Copiapó valley, in comparison with those of Vallenar, however, imposed burdens on its inhabitants with regard to supplies and their costs: Darwin (1960, p. 340) described the cost of living in 1835 as 'wonderfully exorbitant'. Another major silver discovery was made south-west of Copiapó in 1848, and the last of the great silver strikes occurred in 1870 at Caracoles, roughly a third of the way along the road from San Pedro de Atacama to Antofagasta, in what was then Bolivian territory in law, if not entirely in fact, given the number of Chilean compared with Bolivian prospectors there (see Vicuña Mackenna, 1882, for a detailed account of the silver discoveries; Bowman, 1924, pp. 169–72, for a brief resumé).

Chilean silver production rose constantly until the 1850s, reaching an annual average of over 123,000 kg in that decade; a slight drop in the following ten years was reversed with the Caracoles boom, and production reached its peak in the decade 1881–90, with an annual average output of over 157,000 kg. After 1900 a sharp decline set in, and this, in effect, was permanent (Pederson, 1966). In world terms, however, the peak of Chilean production never exceeded 13·8 per cent, and, while its importance in the Chilean economy was profound, the total value of silver produced in Chile during the nineteenth century was approximately half the value of the copper mined in the same period (Pederson, 1966, p. 171).

The production curve for Chilean copper in the last century was remarkably similar to that for silver, though copper was more important as a source of national income, and the history of copper-mining in Chile is not only older than that of silver, but also more continuous. Chile has experienced two quite distinctive phases of copper-mining in the last two centuries. In the first, from the 1820s to the 1870s, production increased rapidly as the rich veins of easily concentrated oxide ore in the provinces of the Norte Chico were opened up and exploited, *pari passu* with silver. At the peak of this first boom, an annual average of over 46,000 metric tons was produced, and the importance of copper in the national economy may be gauged from the fact that in 1860 copper exports amounted to well over half of Chile's total export trade by value (Martner, 1923, I, p. 299, II, p. 307). Between 1840 and 1850, Chile's share of world production of copper stood at over 30 per cent, rising to 44 per cent in the 1860s, and holding to 36 per cent in the 1870s. But, as the veins in Coquimbo and

Atacama were worked out, as international competition grew – notably from the United States and Spain – and, despite the efforts of a number of Chilean innovators in technology, as the generally crude methods of production in Chile could not keep pace with these developments, Chile's pre-eminence in world markets fell away. In the 1880s, Chile's share of world production fell to 16 per cent, and by the 1890s it had fallen as low as 6 per cent. Moreover, copper, like silver, was now overshadowed by nitrates in the Chilean economy, and could not provide so high a yield on invested capital as other activities, particularly since more efficient, larger scale, and lower cost suppliers of the metal had emerged in other countries (Reynolds, 1965, pp. 210–13). By the 1880s, in fact, the world was looking for some other standard for copper than the 'Chile bars' that had predominated for forty years, and the decade marked the beginning of the end of Chile's first cycle of copper production.

The second great phase of copper exploitation in Chile was closely associated with the revolution in copper technology that occurred in the United States between 1900 and 1910, whereby it became economical with capital-intensive techniques of mining, concentration and smelting to work low grade porphyry ores, found in abundance in Chile but hitherto unexploited. The visible and vast symbols of this development are enterprises such as the Chuquicamata open-cast mine (the biggest in the world) in Antofagasta province, and El Teniente (the largest underground copper mine in the world) in the province of O'Higgins, in Chile's central valley region. To this development we shall return, but it is important to note that the two great phases of copper-mining in Chile are separate and distinct not only in terms of mineral extraction but also in their different impacts on the Chilean landscape; what links them together, however, is the critical dependence of the Chilean economy during each phase on the production and export of copper, a dependence interrupted only, in commodity but not in character, by the nitrate years.

The nineteenth-century phase of copper-mining in Coquimbo and Atacama, and the silver boom with which it was co-existent, was in many respects a continuation of the colonial period in methods and techniques, characterized by a vast number of small mines and a small number of larger ones. It was the latter that, naturally, were furthest from the colonial tradition and could introduce such technological innovations as the use of coal rather than wood for smelter fuel, sink deeper shafts and utilize modern machinery. As late as the 1870s, in the whole of the Norte Chico only 33 out of 788 mines in 111 *minerales*, or mining zones, were using steam engines for the extraction of ore, at a time when there were over 30,000 miners in the two provinces (Pederson, 1966, pp. 191–2). Nevertheless, the fact that such mines existed indicated the advent of modern technology in the Norte Chico, brought about not least by changes in the communications network.

The steamship arrived in Chilean waters in 1840 when the North American, William Wheelwright, founded the Pacific Steam Navigation Company, and the railway was not far behind. As already noted, the Copiapó–Caldera Railway was built between 1849 and 1852; other lines subsequently followed to link inland mineral areas with the ports of Chañaral, Carrizal, Huasco, Coquimbo and Los Vilos, all these lines running east–west, and following, where possible, the valley floors running transversely to the Pacific coastline. At this period, Swansea in south Wales was the world's largest smelting centre for copper, and it was to Swansea that Chilean ore was carried, mostly in British vessels, which in turn carried to the Norte Chico coal for local smelting operations, which had also developed, notably at port sites, to cater for the multiple sources of ore mined in the Norte Chico. In fact, the depredations of the colonial period and the nineteenth century on the resources of wood in the Norte Chico not only created serious erosion problems in parts of the region but also caused some mine owners to establish smelting plants south of the central valley where wood was abundant, and where, in Arauco, was Chile's only domestic source of coal. Quantities of coal were also shipped from Lota and Coronel in Arauco to the northern smelters, though imports of British coal were much more significant and of better quality. By the 1880s, nine-tenths of Chilean coal imports came from Great Britain. Other far-off economic factors were brought into play by the development of mining in the Norte Chico: the trans-Andean settlements of north-western Argentina supplied cattle on the hoof, driven for three and a half weeks or so from San Juan, Catamarca and Tucumán through the mountain passes to the valley of Copiapó where they were fattened on green alfalfa before being sold.

The period of high activity, however, was over by the 1870s, and the mining industry of the Norte Chico was in decline by the 1890s. The decline was visible in the many ports that had grown up entirely for mineral shipments and the importation of supplies required by the industry: only Coquimbo survived at anything like its former level of activity while, inland, depletion of the high grade deposits on which the boom had been based led to the abandonment of many mines. Only a few large operators with adequate capital resources and modern technology, such as the British-owned Copiapó Mining Company, were able to hang on profitably. Population figures also indicate the fluctuations in mining in the Norte Chico: in 1854, the region contained 161,000 people, over a tenth of the national population, and by the time of the next census, in 1865, the figure had risen to 225,000, approximately one eighth; it fell to one tenth again by 1885, but thenceforward, while the national population grew, that of the Norte Chico declined, absolutely until the 1920s, and proportionately from 1885 to 1960 (*Censos, Provincias*, 1964).

In the second major phase of copper-mining in Chile, the twentieth-

Fig. 10.4 Chile: mining in the Norte Grande and Norte Chico

century exploitation of the low grade but huge porphyry deposits, operations have been, and are, capital- rather than labour-intensive, with American money dominating the industry until the very recent past. Apart from the El Teniente mine in O'Higgins province, owned by the Kennecott Copper Corporation until the late 1960s, the major enterprises were at Potrerillos and El Salvador in Atacama and at Chuquicamata in Antofagasta, both belonging to the Anaconda Company (Fig. 10.4). Hence, the Norte Chico and the Norte Grande retained their interest in copper-mining, though it was of a very different kind from that of the past. In 1916, the Andes Copper Mining Company – a subsidiary of Anaconda – was formed to develop the industry at Potrerillos, some 160 km east of Chañaral in northern Atacama and, although construction started and plant was established, the mine did not go into production until 1926, because of delays caused by the First World War and by the depression in copper prices that followed it (Reynolds, 1965, p. 218). The open-cast mine at Chuquicamata, bought by an American entrepreneur from a British company and sold by him to the Guggenheim interests in 1911, was started in 1913 and began production two years later, using power shovels that had been employed in the cutting of the Panama Canal. El Teniente, much further south, began production earlier, in 1912, but in its second year of operations, Chuquicamata already equalled the output of El Teniente – 21,000 tons of fine copper.

When Potrerillos was being prepared for production in the 1920s, the population of the Norte Chico was at its lowest point since 1854 and, in fact, the population of Atacama province was actually smaller than it had been in that year. Potrerillos aided the recovery with the growth of a complex of installations, which for the thirty years between 1927 and 1959 created an island of activity in a barren land, producing nearly 2 million tons of copper in the period. Some 30 km north-west of Potrerillos is the El Salvador mine, and when, in 1959, Potrerillos itself was closed by Anaconda as being no longer economic, some of its installations were retained and developed for El Salvador. A township of over 8000 people now exists there with many modern facilities, a far cry from the traditional mining camps of nineteenth-century Atacama.

Chuquicamata is even more impressive both as a mining centre and as a town. Over 3000 m above sea-level, and some 230 km by road north-east of Antofagasta and 150 km east of Tocopilla, the town of Chuquicamata has a population of over 25,000 and very modern facilities, including an excellent hospital. The mine, with over twenty benches descending to a depth of over 350 m had produced over 6 million tons of copper by 1958, and over 300 million tons of oxide ore had been removed by then. The total plant area is enormous, and includes an oxide ore treatment plant, a sulphide ore treatment plant and other installations with a total daily production capacity of over 100,000 tons of copper. In 1967, work also began on the Exótica mine, a little over 3 km south of Chuquicamata, which is estimated to contain over 153 million tons of oxide ore, of 1·35 per cent copper content. These great installations of the Norte Grande and the Norte Chico, together with El Teniente, form the *Gran Minería* of copper in Chile, and account for well over 80 per cent of Chilean production. Their economic significance is, perhaps paradoxically, greater for Chile as a whole than it is for the particular regions in which they lie, as the following statistics indicate: copper accounts for about 8 per cent of Chile's gross domestic product, 60 per cent of exports by value and 80 per cent of government tax receipts, while total Chilean output – well over 600,000 metric tons – amounts to some 15 per cent of total world production, and her reserves amount to from a fifth to a third of those currently available (Griffin, 1969, p. 150; cf. Amunátegui, 1968, pp. 639–42). Yet the *Gran Minería* employs fewer than 18,000 people, though many more, of course, find jobs they would not otherwise have if it did not exist.

The *Mediana Minería*, medium-scale copper-mining, is composed of a number of companies, most of which have their operations located in the Norte Grande and the Norte Chico, and prominent among these is the state corporation, the Empresa Nacional de Minería (ENAMI). Finally, the *Pequeña Minería* is the sector composed of a large number of very small operations, which sell their ore to ENAMI, and which, in the early 1960s, produced only 3 per cent of Chile's output and employed less than 5000 workers (for a detailed description of the *Mediana* and *Pequeña Minería*, see CORFO, 1967, pp. 586–90). In fact, however, it is the very small-scale operators who represent the real mining tradition of the Norte Chico and the Norte Grande, the large-size, highly capitalized enterprises being outside that tradition (Pederson, 1966).

The nationalization of Chilean copper

Prior to 1955, the position of the Chilean government with regard to the largely foreign-owned copper-mining industry was very ill defined. The companies paid taxes that were of crucial importance in government revenue, as the nitrate shippers had done, but, it is generally agreed, Chile's share of receipts from the exploitation of her major resource was small. In 1955, therefore, a state agency, now known as the Corporación del Cobre de Chile, was established to study all matters concerning copper, and other measures were passed to increase the amount of copper actually refined in Chile, and thus increase the income accruing to Chile from copper production. Given Chile's crucial dependence on the metal, it is not surprising that national sentiment for a greater state participation in its extraction and production should grow. It was also clear that if the Chilean economy were to develop rapidly, greater production and export of copper was called for to increase foreign exchange earnings as soon as possible.

The government of President Frei accordingly proposed a bill in 1965 for the 'Chileanization' of the *Gran Minería*, and this became law in 1966. It is a long and complicated measure but, briefly, under its terms the American companies, in return for tax and other concessions, undertook to raise output of copper and increase refining capacity so that by 1971 Chilean output should reach over 1,100,000 metric tons annually, and some 55 per cent of this amount would be refined in Chile. The Chilean government was to secure a 51 per cent holding of the El Teniente mine, with Kennecott Copper Corporation owning 49 per cent, and the new Exótica mine stock would be held in the proportions of 25 per cent and 75 per cent by the Chilean government and by Anaconda respectively. The foreign companies were to invest over $500 million in copper-mining over the five-year period to 1971 (for an excellent resumé of the bill, see Amunátegui, 1968, pp. 643–5; and for a detailed criticism, see Griffin, 1969, pp. 149–73).

As it happened, however, this bill was overtaken by events in 1969, when, after negotiations with the Anaconda Company, the Chilean government announced plans for the gradual nationalization of the *Gran Minería* in the 1970s, whereby Chile will acquire a majority holding in the enterprises with an option to acquire the balance of shares in due course (BOLSA *Review*, 3 (31), July 1969, 455; 3 (33), September 1969, 559–60). This development is too recent to assess its likely effects: what, however, cannot be gainsaid is that for the foreseeable future, copper must remain the prop of the Chilean economy, and the Norte Grande and the Norte Chico two of the major producing regions, as they were a century ago. But, while copper-mining here still retains its predominance as a contributor to national well-being, it has been overtaken in the regional economies of the Norte Chico and the Norte Grande by other developments on the landscape.

The development of iron ore in the Norte Chico

The Norte Chico produces almost Chile's total output of iron ore. Mining began only in 1910 at El Tofo in Coquimbo to supply the new blast furnace at Corral in Valdivia, but the enterprise failed, and in 1913 the Bethlehem Steel Corporation of Pittsburgh acquired El Tofo to produce ore for shipment to the United States (Pederson, 1966, p. 247). From 1921 to 1957, the mine produced over 48 million metric tons of ore, but declining yields obliged the company to move its major operations to El Romeral, some 25 km north of La Serena, which it acquired in 1936 but did not develop until 1948, and then in association with the Chilean state steel organization, the Compañía de Acero del Pacifico (CAP). Guayacan is the port of shipment and is equipped with modern mechanical loading systems and storage facilities.

The CAP acquired another very large deposit of iron ore in 1959, at Algarrobo, some 35 km south-west of Vallenar, with some 70 million tons of reserves: in 1968, over 2·5 million metric tons of ore were produced (*Mensaje*, 1969, p. 64). These three mines – Algarrobo, El Tofo and El Romeral (Fig. 10.4) – form the *Gran Minería* of iron-mining, producing some 25 per cent of total national output; but the *Mediana Minería*, accounting for 45 per cent and composed of a number of private producers, include in their number the Compañía Minera Santa Fé, owner of the El Laco deposits, some 4000 m above sea-level in the province of Antofagasta and reputedly the largest iron ore body in Chile, perhaps 150 million tons of 66 per cent iron ore. Notable among foreign interests in Chilean deposits are the Japanese: the Mitsubishi Mining Company of Japan acquired the Adrianitas mine near Copiapó in 1959.

The big boom in iron-mining in the Norte Chico in the 1960s took place in response to increased world demand for iron ore and in response to Chilean domestic demand for the steel works at Huachipato in Concepción, which began operations in 1950. These stimuli have provided employment for over 10,000 workers in the Norte Chico, and have led to the renaissance of old copper ports, such as Chañaral, Caldera, Coquimbo and Guacolda. Modernization programmes here have kept pace with ore extraction, and the prospects continue to look bright for iron-mining in Chile. With large reserves, many within easy access of embarkation points, and with continuing high world and domestic demand, Chilean production is likely to grow rapidly. Between 1960 and 1966, production doubled from 6 million to over 10 million tons, about 8 per cent of which was for domestic consumption, and iron ore overtook nitrates as Chile's second most valuable export. The development of iron ore mining in Chile is highly significant in another respect: despite the existence of the larger mines, medium and smaller operators account for 75 per cent of total production, and it is the wide distribution of mining activities, a positive echo of the historical past, that gives the Norte Chico today its continuing character as a distinctive region in Chile.

Manufacturing industry and other activities

The proximity of mineral deposits to the coast in Chile naturally made for the growth of suitable ports of shipment situated as near as possible to the ore bodies and, as we have seen, the growth and development of places like Iquique, Antofagasta, Chañaral, Huasco and Coquimbo was intimately linked to mineral exploitation. Mines needed equipment and provisions and, in the pre-railway era, a large amount of both came by Chile's major colonial highway, the Pacific coastline, the ports being the link between sources of supply and external markets and the hinterland mines. Apart from the incoming and outgoing traffic through the ports, a number of ancillary activities to mining naturally developed in these distribution centres, such as small industrial establishments in the ports of Tarapacá to provide machinery for the nitrate *oficinas*, and smelters for copper ores in the port towns of Atacama and Coquimbo. There was, therefore, something of an industrial and manufacturing tradition in these places long before Chile deliberately set out on the path of economic diversification. In addition, the Pacific waters off Tarapacá and Antofagasta provinces are part of that immensely rich fishing ground, which, thanks to the ideal conditions for plankton created by the cold Humboldt current, stretches from Antofagasta to the coast of central Peru, and which, from time immemorial, has compensated man for the barren nature of the land opposite. Consequently, while the fishing industry has long been a characteristic economic activity here, recent times have seen the growth of fish-canning and fishmeal-processing, notably at Iquique and Antofagasta, though also at Arica and Pisagua. In 1959, the CORFO was requested by government to prepare a development plan for the fishing industry, and this was motivated in large part by the decline of the northern nitrate regions, leading to much migration to the south. Thanks to credits made available to establish plant and build modern fishing vessels, Iquique, once the nitrate capital of the world, became in the 1960s Chile's major fishing and fish-processing centre, having by 1965 twenty-three of the thirty-five fishmeal plants in the northern region, and producing 173,000 tons of fishmeal. The greater part of this was for export, and by 1965 Chile had become the world's fifth largest exporter of fishmeal.

The growth of other port cities in the modern period has been linked in part by international as well as national developments. Antofagasta, the largest city of the Norte Grande and the Norte Chico, derives its significance not only from the fact that it is the port of shipment of Chuquicamata's copper, but also from its position as the terminal point of both the railway from Oruro in highland Bolivia – some 1155 km length – and the railway to Salta in north-west Argentina – some 845 km distance. Until the 1960s, in fact, the Antofagasta–Oruro railway was crucial to Bolivia and, as late as 1962, 87 per cent of Bolivian tin – the country's major export – was shipped by this route, though it has since been challenged by the lines from Oruro to Arica and to Peruvian Mollendo. The Antofagasta–Salta line, commissioned finally in 1948, has had disappointing results, and is now being superseded by the motor road built in the early 1960s. Nevertheless, the Antofagasta–Bolivia Railway, still owned on the Chilean side by a British company, is an important link for Bolivia with the outside world, and seems likely to remain so.

Arica has a similar function to Antofagasta in this respect, being linked by rail to Bolivia's capital, La Paz, a distance of some 439 km. More significantly for the development of this most northern of Chilean cities, Arica has benefited from its status as a free port and its role as a commercial centre, not only for northern Chile but also for southern Peru and for Bolivia. Though, in fact, the free zone status no longer exists, Arica still ships about half of Bolivia's imports and exports and is a major resort and one of Chile's principal ports. This is due, in part, to the fact that Arica, owing to its free port status, established itself in the 1960s as the focus of motor vehicle assembly in Chile, with some 50 per cent of components of local (i.e. Chilean) manufacture. However, the remoteness of Arica from the main consuming centres, leading to inflated costs, obliged the government in the late 1960s to permit the installation of motor vehicle assembly plants in central Chile, thus depriving Arica of a virtually monopolistic position in motor manufacturing, though it still remains an important one.

IV CONCEPCIÓN, THE FRONTERA AND THE LAKE DISTRICT

Introduction

The region between the river Bió-Bió and the gulf of Reloncaví, described in the section on climate in this essay as Forest Chile, is, in its northern part, really a continuation of the central valley and, from the province of Cautín south, is usually known as the Lake District. The most appropriate designation, however, for the region bounded by the provinces of Concepción in the north and Cautín in the south is *La Frontera* – the frontier – for it was the line of the Bió-Bió that for more than three centuries marked the effective demarcation of Spanish from Indian Chile, and the modern history of this region is essentially the story of the southward march of settlement from that line. The city of Concepción is the metropolis of the south, and so it has been since the discovery and conquest of Chile, despite changes of site since its foundation in 1551. Valdivia, originally founded a year later, is the second most important centre in the region. Most of the other settlements of the period of conquest in the *Frontera* – such as Angol in the province of Malleco – were abandoned because of Indian pressure and only refounded centuries later, after the birth of the republic of Chile.

Though the late eighteenth century saw some expansion of Spanish settlement south of the Bió-Bió, it was mostly in the 1840s and 1850s that a major impetus to colonization far south of the river was given by a law of 1845, amplified in 1851, to attract European immigrants, and particularly Germans, to what became the province of Valdivia. The majority of the new settlers – some 1200 arrived in 1850 in the vicinity of the fort of Corral – were small farmers and peasants, as were those who came in 1853 to settle on the shores of Lake Llanquihué, a colonization which was completed by 1861, and which was marked, among other things, by the foundation of the towns of Puerto Montt and Puerto Varas in 1853 and 1854 respectively (Jefferson, 1921).[1] This movement, in effect, leap-frogged the

[1] The success of this development owed much to the chief Chilean colonization agent, Vicente Pérez Rosales, who not only founded colonies himself, and set up in Germany the organization to encourage emigration to Chile, but also in his excellent drawings and paintings, and his classic literary work, *Recuerdos del Pasado*, left a detailed and valuable record of this movement of colonization.

Frontera, which in this period was still Indian territory, held by the Mapuche, and it was not until the beginning of 1883 that the last Indian stronghold fell to Chilean troops, the culmination of a campaign – often desultory – that had been in train since 1862. During the 1880s new immigrants settled in the region between the Bió-Bió and Valdivia – Germans, Swiss, Spanish, French and English as well as a considerable number of Chileans, many of them demobilized soldiers after the War of the Pacific, encouraged to settle in the south by government policy. The provinces of Malleco and Cautín were formally incorporated into Chile in 1887, but they still contain the vast majority of Araucanian Indians in Chile, estimated to number some 173,000 in 1964 (CORFO 1967, p. 373).

The numbers of immigrants from Europe was small, the *Frontera* receiving some 32,000, Valdivia and Llanquihué between 5000 and 6000 by the end of the nineteenth century. With the process of naturalization, the proportion of foreigners in the total Chilean population has fallen steadily during this century, from 4·2 per cent in 1907 to 1·6 per cent in 1952, and the total number at the 1960 census was little more than 100,000 (CORFO, 1967, pp. 352–5). In the regions south of the Bió-Bió, however, it was not so much numbers as dynamism that gave the foreigners a predominant position, and towns such as Valdivia, Osorno and Puerto Montt still reveal today in the architecture, the physical features of many of their inhabitants and in the ubiquity of German names the imprint of the colonists of a century ago. It was these pioneers of the frontier, a class of smallholders independent of the traditional *hacendado-inquilino* relationship of the central valley, who tamed the wilderness, built the towns, and by their initiative and enterprise in agriculture, stock-raising and manufacturing had an impact out of all proportion to their numbers, and justified the extension of the communications network longitudinally from the central valley, the railway reaching Puerto Montt in 1913. Fig. 10.2 indicates the southward march of the Chilean frontier in terms of town-foundations in this period.

No region of Chile presents so many contrasting types of human life and activity as that between Concepción and Llanquihué, ranging from the highly urbanized, industrial zone of Concepción itself to the Mapuche reservation lands of Malleco and Cautín. At the 1960 census, the eight provinces contained 26·4 per cent of all Chileans, with Concepción itself having almost a third of this figure. Perhaps more significant is the fact that between the censuses of 1952 and 1960, only Concepción received a net increase of population from migration, all the others indicating losses, with Malleco, Cautín and Valdivia showing substantial net migration outwards in this period (see Fig. 10.1). This, and other indicators, suggest that the trends towards concentration of population and resources so characteristic of the evolution of the central valley also operate here, though somewhat less dramatically, with Concepción playing the role of Santiago and Valparaiso further north. The reasons for this lie in the remarkable growth of the Concepción industrial region, in large part the result of deliberate government policy in the last thirty years, but also reflecting historical influences from a more remote past, and geographical factors whose importance has increased with the passage of time.

The Concepción industrial zone

Throughout the colonial period, the province of Concepción, then including the area between the rivers Maule and Bió-Bió, was the second major zone of Spanish settlement, containing at the end of the colonial period approximately one third of Chile's population of some 500,000, excluding unassimilated Indians in Araucania. With the closing of the frontier at the Bió-Bió at the end of the sixteenth century, Concepción became the military province guarding Chile against the Indians, and the city of Concepción was the major port and the major fort of the south. It was the second city of Chile and, indeed, at times the first, despite changes of location due to Indian depredations and destruction by earthquake. The present site of Concepción, occupying the strategic gateway location where the *cordillera de la costa* is broken by the wide valley of the Bío-Bío, dates from the mid-eighteenth century, though the first Concepción, where the town of Penco now stands, was two centuries older. The city's outlook has always been a maritime one, for, throughout the colonial period and after, the essential communications link with Santiago was by sea, through Valparaiso and, even today, Concepción's dependence on sea-borne commerce remains considerable. In fact, the partly enclosed bays of Concepción and San Vicente provide the most favoured natural harbours on the Chilean coast, and this physical feature has been well utilized by man throughout Chilean history.

The hinterland region north of the Bío-Bío, as far as the river Maule, was an important one in the essentially pastoral and agricultural economy of the colonial period, with its higher and more regular rainfall compared with the more northern parts of the central valley and, in addition, a certain local tradition of small-scale manufacturing developed in response to Concepción's isolation from Santiago. Further impetus to these developments came in the nineteenth century: thus, for example, the growth of Chilean wheat and flour in international markets, and not least with the demands of the Californian and Australian goldfields in the 1840s and 1850s, stimulated the milling industry at Concepción, Penco and Tomé, and the rising port of Talcahuano. More significant in the long run was the opening of the coal mines in the area of Lota and Coronel, south of Concepción, in the 1830s, and at Lirquén, north of Concepción, in the 1840s, developments coincidental with the advent of the steamship, followed soon after by the railway. It is here, and in the neighbouring province of Arauco, that Chile's major coal deposits are to be found, sub-bituminous in quality and in irregular seams running beneath the Pacific Ocean. In a continent poorly endowed in coal deposits, Chile possesses fields here that are still among the most important in Latin America, though modest in output and quality compared with those of Europe and the United States. In the nineteenth century, however, the steady expansion of coal-mining in the provinces of Concepción and Arauco made a considerable contribution to such industrial developments as took place in Chile. Moreover, special clays found in association with the coal deposits became the basis of clay products plant and refractory brick manufacture in the 1860s, particularly near Lota, and other local industries – glass-blowing, copper-smelting (cf. p. 530 above) and timber mills – utilized this local fuel.

Other industries were established in the Concepción region during the course of the nineteenth and early twentieth centuries – woollen textiles at Tomé, cotton textiles at Chiguayante, sugar-refining and ceramics at Penco, glass products at Lirquén, and fish-processing plants at Talcahuano and San Vicente (Butler, 1960). Many of these were based on locally produced materials and supplied the Chilean domestic market, with the aid of a communications network built both to serve that purpose as well as to bind Chile together. The branch line of the great central railway linking San Rosendo to Concepción and Talcahuano was finished in 1872, and in the 1880s particularly, under a programme of active government promotion, communications and port developments were given particular emphasis. The Bío-Bío was bridged at Concepción in 1888 – a significant event for the coal mines of Lota and Coronel – the great dry dock of Talcahuano was completed and port facilities at Coronel and Tomé were improved (for a contemporary description, see Russell, 1890, pp. 33 ff.). Equally significant was the colonization of the *Frontera* and the Lake District, which, while giving Concepción a more central position in Chile as a whole, also reinforced its traditional role as the metropolis of the south.

Chile's economic experience in the first forty years of the twentieth century, and notably her reaction to the Great Depression, clearly stimulated the types of economic activity to which the province of Concepción was already dedicated – consumer goods production with low capital needs but with high requirements in unskilled labour, and manufacturing dominated by traditional lines such as textiles, ceramics and glass, and not so diversified as the import-substitution manufacturing of Santiago and Valparaiso. The Industrial and Commercial Census of 1937 showed the number of industrial establishments in the province as 1115, employing over 17,000 workers, though, significantly, only twenty-four concerns employed more than 100 hands (Butler, 1960, pp. 13–14).

However, events in the late 1930s presaged a fundamental transformation. In 1938, the Popular Front – a combination of left wing and centre parties, committed to a policy of active state intervention in the economy – came to power in Chile, and in 1939 there occurred both the outbreak of the econd World War and a devastating earthquake in south-central Chile, which disrupted life in Concepción. As we have seen (above, p. 515), it was this event that led to the creation of the Chilean Development Corporation, which immediately began to plan Chile's economic future. The coincidence of this development with the impact on Chile of the Second World War, during which Chile's import-substitution process was stimulated to produce an average annual rate of manufacturing growth of some 11 per cent, was highly significant, since, in the post-war period, the stage was set for the next phase of Chile's economic growth, the establishment of heavy industry under the aegis of a state organization. The core of this programme was a new, large, integrated steel plant, and the site chosen was Huachipato, on San Vicente Bay. Work began on the site in January 1947, and the steel mill was commissioned in November 1950 (for details of construction and finance, see Butler, 1960, pp. 17–19).

It was this development, above all, that converted the Concepción region into Chile's major zone of heavy industry, and expansion of both the steel industry and a variety of activities associated with it has continued since that time. In 1947, Chile's total production of iron and steel was about 26,000 tons, with consumption at 163,000, necessitating large imports to be paid for with scarce foreign exchange. By the mid-1960s, Chile was producing an annual output of around 500,000 tons of steel and steel products, and supplying over 80 per cent of national requirements (Soza, 1968, p. 618). Despite this impressive progress, it is recognized that if growing national needs are to be met, and if, in addition, Chile is to participate in the export trade in steel products, as other industrializing countries of Latin America – Brazil and Venezuela, for example – already do, capacity must be increased: current investment and development plans call for an output of 800,000 tons of steel by 1972–3 (Mensaje, 1969, p. 63). Expansion on the existing base at Huachipato will be the main feature of this programme.

The steel complex itself necessarily entailed the growth of other industrial activities – coking plant, sulphuric acid plants, coke oven by-product shops, machine shops and so on. Coal imported from the United States is blended with the local product to produce a suitable coking coal; iron ore comes, as already described, from the Norte Chico; and the limestone required as flux comes from the island of Guarello, some 1300 km south of Concepción. Dolomite is imported from Uruguay. The dependence on sea-going transport to sustain the steel mills has naturally led also to mechanization and the development of storage facilities at Huachipato and San Vicente ports. The vast amounts of water required by the various industrial plants, come a distance of 5 km, by a complicated intake structure, from the Bío-Bío, and energy is supplied from the hydro-electric station at Abanico, some 160 km east of Concepción on the river Laja, near the lake of the same name: it has an installed capacity of 135,000 kW.

The impetus given by the rise of Huachipato to ancillary industrial development in Concepción has been enormous, and here the same advantages of site also operate – extensive level tracts of land in the lower reaches of the Bío-Bío, a good communications network by road and rail with the major markets further north, proximity to good port facilities and, with the rapid urbanization of Concepción city and of Talcahuano, easy access to the labour force and the usual commercial services a city provides. Companies producing steel wire products, ferro-alloys, zinc and tin recovered from slag are among enterprises that have sprung up in Huachipato's shadow. The more traditional industries of Concepción have also expanded rapidly in recent years, and well over 70 per cent of national output of woollen cloth is produced by mills in Tomé and Concepción, the raw material being imported from the vast sheep farms of Magallanes, the cloth sent on to its major market in Santiago. The Lirquén glass factory supplies virtually the whole of national demand, while at Penco the largest ceramics plant in Chile completely dominates the national market.

These developments do not exhaust the list of industrial activities in Concepción, and a number of comparatively new industries are of particular significance in terms of their actual and potential importance to Chile's export trade. Again, physical site factors play a crucial role. The Concepción region, and the neighbouring provinces of Forest Chile, are immensely rich in timber, and not least the Insignis pine, which grows here at a faster rate than anywhere else in the world. In the last two decades of the nineteenth century, private companies began a systematic policy of forest plantation, which has continued to the present, providing the raw material for the highly important pulp and paper industries, and for the production of cellulose. In 1957, a very modern pulp and newsprint plant was built at San Pedro, across the Bío-Bío from Concepción, and it now produces about 95 per cent of total national output of paper and paper products. At the same time, a cellulose plant was begun at Laja, some 65 km south-east of Concepción, and expanded in 1966 from an annual capacity of 80,000 to 240,000 tons of cellulose (BOLSA Review, 2 (20), August 1968, p. 435). The importance of these developments may be gauged from a single statistic: Chilean cellulose exports in 1964 were worth U.S. $1·6 million, and in 1967 U.S. $9·2 million (BOLSA Review, 2 (20), August 1968). The export potential for Chilean cellulose and Chilean paper products in Latin America should be considerable, given the natural advantages these industries enjoy. The same may be said of the latest industrial development in the region, the petrochemicals industry, initiated in the mid-1960s by the building of a refinery at Concepción, utilizing oil imported from Chile's fields in Magallanes. The plant was inaugurated in April, 1967, and in 1968 plans were announced for a large ethylene plant, a caustic soda plant and three other complexes to produce synthetic resins, currently imported, to meet the needs of the plastics industry. These are expected, at the time of writing, to go into full production during the early 1970s, and eventually to make a significant contribution to Chile's export earnings (*Mensaje*, 1969, p. 76).

Fig. 10.5 illustrates the major manufacturing developments in the Concepción industrial zone, and it also indicates the high degree of concentration of industrial activities within Concepción province. In a very real sense the disparities within Chile between neighbouring provinces, such as Santiago and Colchagua, in standards of living, opportunities for

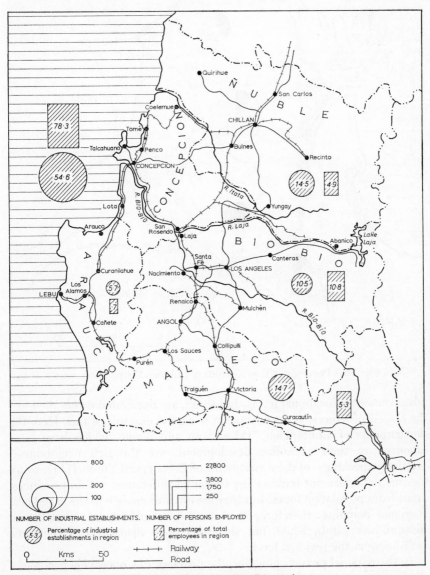

Fig. 10.5 Chile: the Bío-Bío region

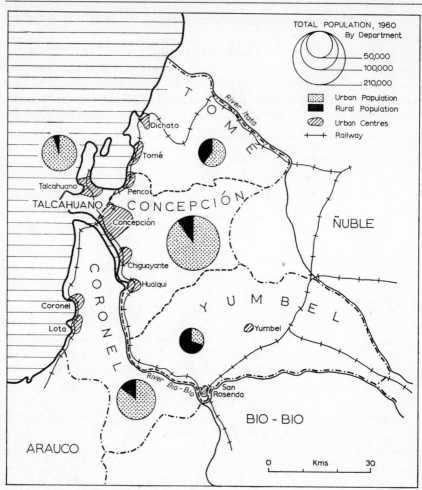

Fig. 10.6 Province of Concepción: population distribution 1960

advancement, educational levels, and so on, are duplicated *within* the most developed provinces, and Concepción is a good example of this. Here the departments of Concepción, Talcahuano and Tomé, which have been favoured in their economic development, are the rich neighbours – relatively speaking – of the departments of Coronel and Yumbel (Fig. 10.6). Census data does not indicate departmental differences within provinces, apart from population totals, but they are obvious enough to the naked eye. Regional planning, therefore, must be concerned not only with broad disequilibria within Chile, but also with gross disparities of economic well-being at the regional level.

In the national picture, however, the province of Concepción occupies a distinctive position. It is the only province in Chile in which industry is the predominant economic activity, employing in 1960 about 24 per cent of its economically active population, and it is the only province in Chile to offer anything like a serious challenge to the exclusive concentration of advanced industrial development in Santiago and Valparaiso. While this is due, in large part, to the deliberate location of heavy industry there by the CORFO, that choice itself was dictated by highly favourable geographical factors and by a previous historical development which seemed conducive to future progress.

The farming economy of Forest Chile

While Concepción is the pre-eminent industrial zone of the south and, indeed, of all Chile, other cities of the forest region – Temuco, Valdivia, Osorno, for example – also have important industrial activities located there, and Valdivia in particular produces a wide range of commodities – leather goods, ceramics, wood products, oxygen, nails, refined sugar, freight cars, tugs and lighters. Nevertheless, it is true to say that such manufacturing as takes place in these centres is of greater regional than national importance; the industries rely heavily on local resources of raw materials, and much more significant in the national economy is the contribution the provinces make in agricultural and pastoral products, as they have done since their incorporation into the republic. The colonization of the forest region during the last decades of the nineteenth century had the effect, for example, of moving Chile's major wheat zone from the central valley to the south: whereas in the 1870s the region between Bío-Bío and Valdivia accounted for only 8 per cent of the cultivated area of Chile sown to wheat, by the First World War it accounted for 40 per cent, and wheat production there tripled in volume (Sepúlveda, 1959, pp. 112–14). Today, the region between Bío-Bío and Llanquihué accounts for approximately two-thirds of Chile's cereal production, almost two-thirds of the cattle population, five-sixths of the lumber production, nearly half of the fish catch and most of the apple crop. Such figures represent not only the natural resource endowment of south-central Chile but also the evolution of its exploitation by man, a process in which foreign immigration was significant by virtue of its example rather than by its volume, and one that has given this essentially agricultural region of Chile characteristics which are markedly different from those of central Chile.

One such feature is landownership. While the large hacienda is by no means unusual in the forest region, and neither is the *minifundia*, there is a far greater variety in sizes of holdings than in the central valley (cf. the tables in CIDA, 1966, pp. 47, 78, 99). Absenteeism of the landowner from his property is much less marked. Owing primarily to the far heavier rainfall throughout the year, the region is more devoted to mixed farming than is central Chile, and, while this is much more true of the Lake District than of the *Frontera*, the agricultural economy is far more dynamic. Indeed, there is a comparatively weak case for land reform on economic grounds in the provinces of the Lake District, though the social case may be strong in aid of the very small proprietors. That there is such a case is indicated by Fig. 10.1, showing provincial migration in recent years: Malleco, Cautín and Valdivia, in particular show sizeable losses, though the phenomenon is not a new one. During the late nineteenth and early twentieth centuries, considerable numbers of Chileans from these southern provinces migrated – many temporarily – to the trans-Andean provinces of Argentina (Jefferson, 1921, p. 35), and in recent years what have seemed to be better opportunities there have attracted some Chileans across the frontier (see Mármora, 1968). Most migrants, however, head north, not east, to the growing towns and cities of their own country.

With the exception of the province of Concepción, all the provinces of south-central Chile have a larger rural than urban population (see Fig. 10.1), but the region lacks the feudal atmosphere of the central valley, owing to the quite different nature of settlement and the absence of such *patron–peon* relationships as *inquilinaje*. Nevertheless, the process of colonization itself had its dark side. One such aspect was the treatment of the Mapuche Indians, to be considered shortly. Another was the treatment of Chileans by their own governments, which consistently favoured the foreign immigrants and their own upper class. In the early 1870s, for example, the government of the day permitted Chilean peasants from the north to clear and till land in the *Frontera* in return for very low rents, and a great deal of land came under cultivation, with considerable Chilean settlement. The renter, however, had no security of tenure, and his land could be simply taken away by government agents, without payment for improvements effected. Public auction of state lands soon followed, and this effectively froze out the Chilean peasantry, who had no capital, and brought in the speculator, notably the wealthy of Santiago. Land grants and other forms of assistance to foreign immigrants were not extended to Chilean peasants who became, in effect, landless labourers for the new colonizers, and evictions of hard-working squatters were common. If it is undoubtedly true that the development of Chile's forest region owes a great deal to the industry and pertinacity of the European immigrant, it is no less the fact that the labour of Chileans was crucial in that development, which was purchased, in part, through policies that consistently militated against Chilean peasants acquiring their own land (Jefferson, 1921).

The life of the towns of Forest Chile is closely integrated with that of the rural landscape. Temuco is a large lumber, livestock and agricultural centre, with many flour mills and tanneries; Osorno has one of the largest dry milk plants in Latin America, and one of the biggest butter plants in Chile, as well as a modern chilled beef packing plant, and a number of flour mills; Puerto Montt has utilized its coastal location to become the supply point for over half the shellfish production of Chile, and possesses a number of fish-canning and processing factories. As in the case of Concepción state-directed developments have also been of some significance in the region's growth: the National Sugar Corporation (IANSA, Industria Azucarera Nacional S.A.), a subsidiary of the CORFO, has established sugar beet refineries in recent years at Los Angeles in Bío-Bío and at Llanquihué and, indeed, has been instrumental in the rapid growth of sugar beet cultivation, a marked feature of agricultural production in the region in the 1950s and 1960s. Between 1955 and 1960, Chilean sugar beet production increased over eightfold, from 81,000 to 600,000 metric tons (Bohan and Pomerantz, 1960, p. 60). The dairy industry has also expanded rapidly, though a major, and unsolved problem here is the conflict between government pricing policies and dairy farmers' expectations. Nevertheless, the scope for expansion of dairy farming in Chile is very large, given the rising curve of consumer demand for its products, and the forest region is the one best endowed to expand it.

The Indian lands

The area between the rivers Bío-Bío and Tolten contain well over 90 per cent of the pure-blood Indian population of Chile, the descendants of those warlike Araucanians, or Mapuche, who withstood the Spanish empire for almost three hundred years, and successfully resisted the Chilean republic for another sixty. During the nineteenth century, however, the northern part of the *Frontera* was encroached on by Chilean settlers before the last Araucanian resistance crumbled in the 1860s, and in the colonization that ensued, Indian rights were not respected. In the early 1880s, for example, Indian chiefs were induced to accept European notions of property rights, in terms of family, rather than tribal, property, a change that clearly weakened their capacity to prevent expropriation. Detailed and, sometimes, benevolent legislation to protect the Indians was often more honoured in the breach than the observance, and the establishment of reservation lands, legally held in title, was subject to provisions permitting a *comunidad* to request division of common land if at least one third of its members so desired. The laws and their operation were, and are, very complicated: suffice to say that, with ample scope for exploitation by outsiders, and with increasing population pressure within the reservations, expropriation of Mapuche lands was the most pronounced characteristic during the last century, and the growth of *minifundismo* the most striking feature of this one. There are some prosperous Mapuche, but they are very few, and the vast majority, faced with deterioration of their lands as a result of demographic pressure, low technological levels and weak credit facilities, present a growing social and economic problem. Modern Chilean governments have made conscientious efforts to preserve the Araucanian heritage and help the Indian communities, but the task is difficult and today many Mapuche simply migrate from their homelands to other parts of Chile (for detailed discussions, see CIDA, 1966, pp. 79–95; Universidad de Chile, Departmento de Extensión Cultural, 1956; Faron, 1968).

The Mapuche are as much a national as a regional problem, as is, indeed, the continuing development of the forest region itself. Its current contribution to the national economy is a vital one, and its potential for further growth is very considerable. Two examples will illustrate the point. First, owing to the abundance of rivers in this region of high rainfall, Forest Chile's share of the country's hydro-electric potential – *per capita* the highest in the world – is large, and already the area between Bío-Bío and Llanquihué is linked to the national system of power transmission run by the National Electricity Company (ENDESA – Empresa Nacional de Electricidad, S.A.), another state corporation. The principal plants in existence are Abanico in Bío-Bío, Pullinque in Valdivia, and Pilmaiquen in Osorno, but ENDESA has further projects in hand, notably the station at El Toro, just outside the forest region in Ñuble, but intended to serve national needs, including those of Concepción. When fully operative, probably in 1972, the capacity of El Toro will be 400,000 kW, and it will be the largest hydro-electric station in the country. The second example of growth potential for the forest region is, perhaps, more hypothetical at present, though its long-term future is hardly in doubt: this is tourism, which has enormous prospects in Chile, as in Latin America as a whole (see BOLSA *Review*, 3 (28), April 1969, 200–12). Already, the Lake District is a major attraction for foreign visitors to Chile, and here, as elsewhere in the republic, recent years have seen a great improvement of tourist facilities with government support. The region of the lakes, with their superb volcanoes, and tree-clad slopes as the setting, is an outstanding area of scenic beauty, and tourism will undoubtedly contribute in the future a much larger proportion to the gross domestic product than the 2 per cent it provides at present. The Forest Chile of that future will be vastly different, as it is today, from the wilderness it was less than a century ago, but its future contribution to national well-being will depend no less on the human capacities to overcome obstacles that have made it the distinctive region of Chile it is today.

V CHILOÉ AND ATLANTIC CHILE

Chiloé

The province of Chiloé consists of the large island of that name and the mainland opposite, but, while the mainland section partakes of the nature of the frontier, a region of very little settlement, and that in recent times, the island of Chiloé was an object of attention by the Spaniards in the sixteenth century. The reasons were almost entirely strategic, the need to maintain a watch over the southern Pacific against the constant threat of corsairs and maritime rivals to Spain throughout the colonial period.

Castro was founded as early as 1567, and Ancud, the island's second town, exactly two centuries later. The population was always small, owing to the island's rigorous climate and scanty resources, and even today its western side is virtually uninhabited and uninhabitable, left to the constant rainfall and impenetrable forest. In the nineteenth century, after the final expulsion of the Spaniards in 1826 (the island was the last part of Chile to be liberated) various attempts at colonization were made, notably towards the end of the century. With generous government assistance, and with the now customary disparagement of the native-born inhabitants, the Chilotes, European immigrants – and not least British and Dutch – were encouraged to settle on the island, but the experiment was not a success (Jefferson, 1921, pp. 40–1). Land was cleared, and potatoes and rye were sown, but the development was essentially for subsistence since market conditions did not exist, even if there had been surpluses to export. Moreover, the traditional type of land tenure here was smallholding, and as population increased, however slowly (see Table 10.2), subdivision by inheritance became so acute that the only answer to the problem of subsistence was migration.

The Chilotes are the great migrants of Chile. Today, they are prominent in the Chilean merchant marine, and hundreds journey every year to the vast sheep ranges of Magallanes to help with the wool clip, returning to the island to resume work in the lumber trade, fishing and cultivation, which are its only economic activities, or not returning at all: Chiloé, in fact, is the only province of Chile that experienced an actual fall in population in the intercensal period 1952–60, from 100,687 to 99,211 (Censo, 1960, Chiloé, p. 11). The province, moreover, has, by a large margin, the highest percentage of rural population of any in Chile, amounting to over 77 per cent in 1960 (Censo, 1960, Chiloé). Apart from Ancud, the provincial capital, and Castro, there is only one other centre on the island of Chiloé with more than 1000 inhabitants, the population being dispersed inland as agriculturalists, and scattered along the coast as fisherfolk. The mainland portion of the province, however, did not have a single centre with 1000 inhabitants at the time of the last census.

Economically, the region is one of the poorest of Chile, with little prospect that it will be otherwise in the foreseeable future. Potatoes are the main crop on the island, with a little cereal cultivation, but the possibilities for an expansion of the formerly active timber trade are now limited by the virtual extinction of the more valuable trees, such as cypress and larch, and by the high costs of exploitation and transport. There are better prospects for timber on the mainland, in the areas of Chaiten, Lake Yelcho and Palena. The Palena basin has also been an area of stock-raising since its first settlers arrived there in the early years of this century, but it is still very remote from the mainstream of Chilean life, and the province of Chiloé as a whole seems destined to slip still further into the backwater of Chilean development.

Atlantic Chile: Magallanes

Throughout the colonial period, Chile's boundaries were understood to extend south to Cape Horn, and some of the independent republic's early constitutions specifically said that they did. But this was theory not fact. A number of expeditions south, almost from the very beginnings of the Kingdom of Chile, were complete fiascos, not surprising in view of the extraordinarily fragmented coastline and innumerable islands of the archipelagic region, coupled with a forbidding climate and inhospitable terrain. What, more than anything, resolved the Chilean government in the nineteenth century to make more positive its claim to Magallanes was the advent of the steamship in the 1840s, and the danger, which was real and not merely apparent, that foreign powers might seize possession of the now strategic narrows from the Atlantic to the Pacific. The threat that this might pose to Chile, whose entire western frontier was the Pacific coastline, and whose communications were still largely maritime, was obvious to the government of President Bulnes (1841–51). In 1843, accordingly, an expedition founded Fort Bulnes and claimed the incorporation into Chile of the Straits of Magellan. The early years of the settlement were very arduous, and in 1849 Fort Bulnes was abandoned for a new site, 56 km north, backed by an expansive grassy plain, with beech trees, a permanent watercourse and, higher upstream, coal in placer deposits. Punta Arenas was thus founded for strategic reasons and for national satisfaction; true colonization came later.

Until the decade 1865–75, Punta Arenas was basically part military outpost and part penal settlement, operating an essentially subsistence economy. Attempts were then made to mine both coal and gold, and, while success was limited, these developments brought in more people, led to the building of a light railway, a wharf and a store, and were accompanied by the laying of other economic foundations. In 1867, a government decree offered cheap grants of land to families of colonists, who settled in the Brunswick peninsula and began to supply passing vessels with fresh provisions. Population increased from about 200 in 1865 to 1100 ten years later (Butland, 1954, pp. 30–1). In the same period, two important events occurred, though their significance only became apparent in the 1880s: in 1868, Punta Arenas was declared a free port, which it has remained to the present day; and in 1866, for the first time, a large ship navigated the channels route between Atlantic and Pacific through the Straits of Magellan.

The decade of the 1880s was a watershed in the development of Magallanes. It was a period of considerable exploration of the southern reaches of America, promoted in part by the growing power of Argentina and Chile, and by the desire of their governments to know what resources their unexplored territories contained. The realization dawned, on both sides of the frontier – still not delimited in many areas – that the extensive grasslands and low, undulating terrain of Magallanes and Patagonia were admirably suited to sheep-rearing. *Estancias* were established on land occupied with government permission, often obtained retroactively, and the population began to grow. By 1885, it had reached a total of over 2000, more than a third of it in Punta Arenas itself, and of the total population over a third was foreign-born, English and Scots emigrés playing a prominent part in the rise of the *estancias* (Butland, 1957, p. 57). The beginnings of colonization on the island of Tierra del Fuego soon followed.

From 1885 to 1907, what was still the territory, and not the province, of Magallanes experienced an economic transformation. Population grew almost eightfold (see Table 10.2), and the number of sheep increased by some forty-two times, to nearly 2 million. Colonization spread westward and northward on the mainland, south and east in Tierra del Fuego, so that by the end of the period it had reached Ultima Esperanza in the north and Riesco Island to the west. By the end of this period, it was reported that profits in some of the land companies were over 300 per cent within two years (Scott Elliot, 1907, p. 308), while the number of ships entering and clearing Punta Arenas had risen from an annual figure of less than 300 to more than 1900 (Butland, 1957, p. 58). Punta Arenas itself began to assume the aspect of a real town rather than an isolated outpost of settlement.

Important changes also occurred in this period in the land tenure system. By the 1880s it was no longer necessary for government to induce colonists to settle in Magallanes by easy grants of land, and laws were passed providing for the lease of property, ownership remaining with the state and the majority of farms in the hands of existing holders. But the leasing system lasted only to 1902; in that year new legislation provided for the sale of enormous tracts of land at public auction, without any reservation of the lands already in farms. The result was that the principal land companies, which had risen with the pastoral boom of the previous twenty years, had the financial power to acquire huge estates, absorbing in the process most of the smaller farms (Butland, 1957, pp. 60–1). In fact, between 1903 and 1906, a mere twenty-nine owners acquired more than 1,600,000 ha (CIDA, 1966, p. 116). Shocking cases of eviction occurred, the most notorious at Ultima Esperanza. This hitherto empty quarter had been colonized in the 1890s by German settlers, under licence from the governor of Punta Arenas; they had established highly prosperous sheep farms, built hotels and wharves, cut roads to Punta Arenas and to Gallegos, in Argentina, and even established steamship connections with German transatlantic lines, and by 1906 the colony numbered 600 people. Moreover, when in 1902 a frontier dispute on this region, between Chile and Argentina, was arbitrated by Great Britain, the presence of these Germans as settlers from Chile was a major factor in the decision to award the territory to that country. Under the new laws, however, much of the land in Ultima Esperanza was acquired by the Tierra del Fuego Exploitation Company, and most of the settlers were obliged to leave (Jefferson, 1921, pp. 46-9).

No less significant were the long-term repercussions of the creation of pastoral *latifundia* in Magallanes. However, efficient the large estates might be, this system of land tenure imposed patterns on the territory that may not have been in its best interests. In the first place, it discouraged permanent immigration while establishing the practice of seasonal migration, since sheep-farming required additional hands in the shearing season only. Most of the migrants came, as noted, from Chiloé. Moreover, despite the growth of other economic opportunities in Magallanes, these were not enough to absorb the migrants in permanent employment after the shearing season, and many moved on to Patagonia. The size of estates, and the fact that many were in foreign hands, became a subject of some controversy in Chilean politics, which is not yet resolved. Finally, there can be no doubt that lack of opportunities on the land for immigrants has been an important factor in the urbanization of Magallanes and the concentration of population into one town, Punta Arenas. By 1960 it contained almost 70 per cent of the provincial population (*Censo*, 1960, Magallanes, p. 6).

From this period at the turn of the century, sheep-farming has been the mainstay of the Magallanes economy, and its progress has been marked less by an increase in numbers of sheep – from an average of 2 million in the first thirty years of the century to about 3 million today – than by improvements in breeds, land utilization and communications, and similar developments to benefit both wool and meat production (for a detailed account, see Butland, 1957, pp. 69, 85-102). Today, Magallanes produces over half Chile's output of wool, the average annual amount for the early 1960s being about 20 million kg (Cunill, 1965, p. 126). The meat-packing industry began to develop at the time of the first pastoral boom: by 1905, the *frigoríficos* of Punta Arenas were sending some 75,000 sheep carcasses to Smithfield (Scott Elliot, 1907, p. 309), but by 1929 meat exports, at 20,000 tons, were ten times what they were in 1905 (Butland, 1957, p. 71). In more recent years, however, both higher demand for meat in Central Chile, and high wool prices, leading to concentration on wool production at the expense of meat, has led to a marked fall in exports of frozen mutton and, indeed, to an overall decline in meat production. A third factor in this fall has been the diversion of Argentine sheep – formerly an important proportion of those processed at Punta Arenas – away from Magallanes to Argentine plants, and in the late 1950s a number of *frigoríficos* in Magallanes were closed (Bohan and Pomerantz, 1960, p. 36).

The growth of the industrial fabric of the province, based on Punta Arenas, was naturally intimately linked in the early days of expansion with sheep-farming. But this was not all, and during the period 1885-1907 other important activities were gold-mining (of placers), a development that naturally attracted a large number of immigrants – Yugoslavs, Spaniards and Italians in particular – a timber industry, and a revival of coal mining, in view of the vastly increased number of steamships calling at Punta Arenas. Other settlements arose, including the only urban settlement in Chilean Tierra del Fuego, Porvenir, across the strait from Punta Arenas, founded in 1894, and having in 1960 a population of 3000 (*Censo*, 1960, Magallanes, p. 8). Certain of these developments were short lived: while, even today, some gold-prospecting continues, the hectic boom of the mid-1890s seems unlikely to be repeated. But a more general characteristic of the development of Magallanes has been the filling out of structures established three generations ago, with some important changes to which reference should be made.

One of these was a reduction in the size of the great *estancias*, at their peak in the first decade of this century. The basic reason for this was the growing awareness of the Chilean government of the need to promote immigration and to guard against the dangers of monopoly. From the First World War to the Second, as leases expired and as land companies themselves gave up some of their holdings, large areas were subdivided and offered to colonists by government agencies (for details, see CIDA, 1966, pp. 116–17; Butland, 1957, pp. 69–71). The companies still retained enormous estates and, in general, much the best land, but these developments did make the region somewhat less dependent on a few vast enterprises, though, it is interesting to note, among the first candidates for expropriation under the Agrarian Reform Law of 1967 were some of the great *estancias* of Magallanes.

A more significant new development in the province, both for the region and the nation, has been the rise of the oil industry. Again, it was the CORFO that initiated it, through exploration for deposits in the 1940s, resulting in the development of the field at Manantiales between 1946 and 1957. Within a few years, over 500 wells had been sunk in the province and, by 1961, over 1,500,000 m³ of petroleum were being produced (*Censo*, 1960, Magallanes, p. 7). By 1968, however, petroleum output had reached over 2,177,000 m³, an increase of over 10 per cent on 1967 (ECLA, 1969, II, p. 145) and new discoveries continue to be made at a rapid rate. Development of the highly significant oil industry of Chile – Magallanes is the only province producing oil commercially to date – is under the aegis of a state corporation, ENAP (Empresa Nacional de Petróleo), created in 1950. An increasing proportion of Chile's production of crude oil is refined in Chile, at the large refinery at Concón, near Valparaiso, opened in 1954, and at the new refinery at Concepción (see above, p. 542), and it is, indeed, the oil of Magallanes that is the basis for Chile's new petrochemicals industry. Undoubtedly the most important development in Magallanes since the introduction of sheep nearly a hundred years ago, the oil industry is likely to have far-reaching effects on the province and the country, together with the natural gas reserves found in association with oil deposits. Indeed, it has already: as Fig. 10.1 indicates, Magallanes is one of the six provinces of Chile that received an increment of population by migration in the inter-censal period 1952–60, and of the seventeen towns or cities of Chile with a population greater than 50,000 in 1960, Punta Arenas had the fourth fastest rate of growth between 1960 and 1963 (CORFO, 1967, p. 380). As the oilfields in northern Tierra del Fuego and the mainland opposite develop, as maritime traffic increases, so will this southernmost city in the world grow even more rapidly.

Atlantic Chile: Aysén

The province of Aysén is Chile's last frontier, having in 1960 the smallest population, a mere 0·5 per cent of the country's total, and celebrating its centenary as part of the republic only very recently. It was, in fact, in 1870 that Robert Simpson, the British-born vice-admiral of the Chilean navy, first explored the basin of the river that bears his name, following its course from where Puerto Aysén now stands, and crossing the Andes to the valley of the Coyhaique. Others followed in the 1880s, in that rather hectic period of exploration patronized by the Chilean and Argentine govern-ments, and it was these discoveries that made known the other transverse valleys of Aysén. Yet, as late as 1902, when Chile and Argentina concluded an important boundary agreement, there were less than 200 colonizers on the Chilean side, and those who were there had drifted on, not from the west but from the east, crossing into Argentina much further north and coming into Aysén from Neuquén and Chubut (Butland, 1957, p. 77). Numbers grew only slowly, but in 1903 a newly formed land company, the Sociedad Industrial de Aysén, was given a licence by the government to occupy large areas of three river valleys for stock-raising, and its efforts began to have a marked impact on the province. Vast numbers of sheep were introduced, and large tracts of land were fenced; no less important, the company built a road from the Coyhaique region west to Puerto Aysén, which was founded by government at about the same time. Since, however, Magallanes was then by far the major southern area of attraction for would-be colonists, settlement was still slow, and another reason for this was the fact that in Aysén the physical obstacles to settlement were far greater, and the favourable lands much less extensive than in the far south.

Until the 1920s the estates of the Aysén Industrial Company employed a fair proportion of the settlers in the province, though more of them held their own family properties for stock-raising and farming. In the late 1920s, however, in a serious attempt to promote further settlement, the Chilean government drastically reduced the Company's holdings, and enacted other measures to encourage immigration. Thenceforward, Aysén's population and the provincial economy grew more rapidly. By 1940, population had risen to over 17,000 and sheep numbers to 600,000 (Butland, 1954, p. 40), the most important local centre being Coyhaique: founded only in 1931, the town had a population of some 9500 by 1960, a quarter of the total for the province, and having half as many people again as the provincial capital, Puerto Aysén (*Censo*, 1960, Aysén, p. 18).

Nevertheless, and certainly in comparison with the growth of Magallanes, the evolution of Aysén has been slow, and seems likely to continue so. The province is less well endowed in natural resources than its southern neighbour, and the exploitation of its resources are hindered by far more formidable physical obstacles, as the lack of communications clearly indicates. The economic basis of the province is sheep- and cattle-raising, though a little copper, lead and zinc are mined in the vicinity of Lago General Carrera, and shipped across the lake to Chile Chico, whence it goes by Argentine transport to market. There is, as yet, little industry. But the economy that exists, unlike that of Chiloé, is a flourishing rather than a declining one, based on the 600,000 sheep and 100,000 cattle of good quality that inhabit the province. Aysén will be a frontier zone for many years to come, but it is a gradually expanding frontier: as Fig. 10.1 indicates, the province had an inflow of migrants between the last two censuses, though a small one, and the rate of natural increase of population, like that of Magallanes, is much higher than the national average, and is, in fact, the third highest provincial rate in Chile (CORFO, 1967, p. 374). The closer integration of Aysén into the national life will depend, above all, on improvements in communications and, while the air link with central Chile is well established – there are airports at Coyhaique, Balmaceda and Chile Chico – better roads and more frequent maritime connections would serve the purpose more effectively. But this, in the highly fragmented landscape of Aysén, with its densely forested western region, is more easily said than done.

VI CONCLUSION: REGIONAL GROWTH AND NATIONAL PROSPECTS

The historical patterns of regional development in Chile have reinforced, rather than weakened, the highly centralized nature of the national life. While the country's shape and physical characteristics might seem to militate against this, and the economic growth of the outlying provinces might appear to encourage a practical as well as a theoretical autonomy, the fact remains that the economic and social structure that was created in the core region over a long period of time has been little affected by important changes in the periphery. One reason for this, as we have seen, is the peculiar nature of economic development outside the central region, with its export-orientated and primary commodity characteristics. Another is the strong sense of national belonging, which links people from Arica to Punta Arenas in a common allegiance to one flag and one government, and Chile is one state of Latin America that can truly be called a nation.[1]

[1] There are many interesting examples of this truism in Chilean history. One of the most striking occurred during the War of the Pacific when a contingent of

Moreover, the sense of nationality developed early in Chile, and was strongly reinforced by the country's evolution since independence, an evolution characterized by an absence of dictatorship and violence, in marked contrast to so many of Chile's less fortunate neighbours. Chilean pride in an orderly system of government still remains an important asset to national cohesion.

For many decades now, however, the stresses in the political, social and economic fabric of Chile have been acute, and the pressures of today are so insistent that it may be doubted whether such intangible factors as patriotism and a sense of pride in the national past are adequate guarantees for stability in the future. In today's Latin America, where existing structures seem to confuse stability with stagnation, those structures must be changed, and Chile is no exception. In this context, regional feeling in Chile is a crucial factor within the national polity itself, and every region alike has similar problems of enormous discrepancies in well-being and opportunity. To reduce these differences, and to expand the economy in order to do so, is a daunting task, but one that the national government is obliged to undertake. How it goes about this task – the ordering of correct priorities – is, perhaps, the most important question for a developing country. In no country of Latin America has there been in recent years more institutional innovation in planning for economic development than in Chile, and we have already seen how state intervention through various bodies, notably the CORFO, has played a major role both in promoting economic growth and in attempting to create a better balanced economy spatially. The Chilean government has long played a more important part in the investment process than is the case in any other Latin American country, and the greatly expanded role of government in social and economic development is a major characteristic of modern Chilean history. Rapid and intense change has taken place in Chile in the last forty years, in which government action has been quite critical, but it has not produced the kind of social consequences experienced by advanced industrialized countries because of the persistence of limiting and controlling institutions, the survival of which inhibits social change (see Sunkel, 1965). In the structuralist-monetarist controversy on Latin American development, the evidence from Chile is overwhelmingly on the side of the former. In recent years, however, a fundamental attack has been launched on these structures in Chile, though, as might be expected, it has invited more criticism than praise, and not least from those who agree with the objectives but differ fundamentally on means. Nevertheless, such initiatives as the Agrarian Reform Law of 1967, and the policy of 'Chileanization' of copper, illustrate the fact that government's role in national development in Chile

---

Araucanian Indians served in the Chilean army against Peru and Bolivia as a volunteer force.

has increased and is increasing, and in a country as centralized as Chile it is difficult to see a viable alternative. It is in this context that the recent institution of new planning mechanisms in Chile, to promote both regional and national growth, is of the greatest importance, and particularly because it is based on existing geographical criteria.

The structure of planning

The Oficina de Planificación Nacional (ODEPLAN), attached directly to the presidential office, actually came into existence before it was legally created in 1967, with the specific task of formulating the National Plan for Economic and Social Development at three levels: national, sectoral and regional. ODEPLAN is comprehensively responsible for setting national economic aims and drawing up programmes for needs of resources, financial and material; for programming the various sectors of the economy – agriculture, energy, industry, housing and so on – in which task it has the co-operation of the appropriate government ministry; and for establishing regional planning organizations, Oficinas Regionales de la Planificación (ORPLAN), to place the national and sectoral plans within a regional context. There are ten of these, and a metropolitan office for Greater Santiago, and they operate on an annual basis within the context of the more long-range national and sectoral plans. The ORPLAN has very considerable responsibilities: economically, it has to perform a wide range of functions, looking for new opportunities for investment, creating co-operation between the public and private sectors within the region, and planning for optimal location of activities to secure balanced regional growth – economic and social. Administratively, its purpose is also to serve as the instrument of decentralization of decision-making, which has never really existed in Chile. Careful thought and a great deal of analysis went into the selection of the ORPLAN regions. Given the fact that the provincial structure was the existing basis of administration, and that to, a large extent, the provinces were self-contained economic entities, logic suggested that some provinces would be viable units on their own, while others should be grouped together. A number of criteria of size and function determined these choices, and an important consideration was the selection within each grouping of growth poles, which, because of existing activity and capacity for further expansion, communications function and other advantages, offered clear possibilities for stimulating development within the region as a whole. Fig. 10.7 sets out the basic data on the ORPLAN regions established (for details of the planning structure, see *Mensaje*, 1968, pp. 541–51; for a convenient summary, see Berry, 1969, pp. 302–7).

The national development plan itself aims to create regions of self-sustaining growth; hence, the ORPLAN regions were also selected in terms of basic geographical criteria: a degree of economic and social

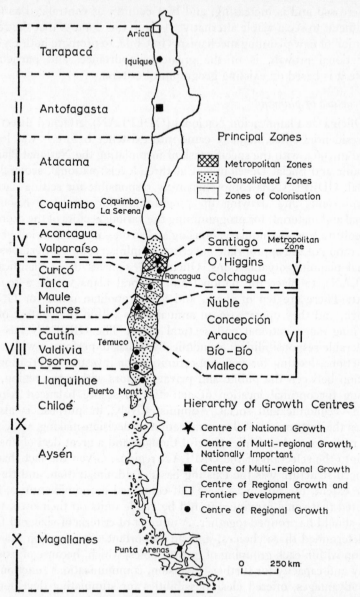

Fig. 10.7 Chile: planning regions (after Berry, 1969, and ODEPLAN, 1968)

homogeneity; large enough as internal markets to provide economies of scale for regional industries; with linkages between growth poles and more retarded areas; and with the capacity to achieve a high degree of import substitution at the regional level within a framework of national comparative advantage (Berry, 1969, p. 306). That some of the regions already contain these desiderata will be apparent from the regional survey that is the basis of this essay, but it is far too early to expect significant results yet from this ambitious planning structure. One outcome, certainly, has been a very marked increase in data compilation and research in the various regions of Chile (see *Mensaje*, 1969, pp. 7–15). This is clearly desirable, but it must avoid the danger that besets all planning in developing countries, the natural tendency to raise national morale by the production of impressive statistics showing what rapid results could be achieved when certain conditions are met. The ultimate success of ODEPLAN in Chile clearly depends to a very large degree on a number of imponderables, internal and external, over which the planners have little or no control. Nevertheless, the structure is a bold and imaginative one: it is a strategy of deliberate urbanization for regional and national development on the assumption that 'feedback effects' to backward areas will be sufficient to propel the country forward into a more rapidly growing economic condition from which the social benefit of a more egalitarian society will emerge (see Berry, 1969, for an excellent discussion).

Problems and prospects

The fundamental danger of the ODEPLAN structure is obviously the possibility that instead of the growth poles having a cumulative regional effect, they will, in fact, merely accentuate the existing duality between highly urbanized, modern, developing environments, and rural, traditional and stagnant societies. As Santiago, Valparaiso, Concepción and Punta Arenas clearly demonstrate, though in differing degrees, the historical evolution of Chile has imposed this pattern, despite attempts to escape it. The pre-conditions for this situation were laid down by Chile's geographical structure, and what is now proposed is a challenge to man's past organization of the landscape and an escape from economic and social constraints, which are too inflexible to absorb contemporary pressures. However much regional issues are significant parts of the total problem, in the last analysis it is the national economy that is the critical factor.

Since the Second World War Chile has lagged behind the general rate of economic expansion in Latin America, characterized in her growth by wide short-term fluctuations from boom to slump. A succession of corrective measures has failed to cure apparently endemic monetary instability, and when inflation has been checked it has been at the cost of depressing economic activity to seriously low levels. One fundamental reason for hard and persistent inflation was the sluggish growth of agriculture, as population increase outstripped the country's capacity to feed it: in the early 1960s, one quarter of all Chilean import costs was spent on imported foodstuffs. At the same time, dependence on exports of primary commodities, particularly copper, put government revenues at risk: today, for example, a fall in price of 2 cents per kg of copper on the London Metal Exchange would cost Chile U.S. $7 million a year. Fluctuating government revenues and an inefficient taxation system meant budget deficits, which were covered by short-term borrowings and increases in the money supply. Low investment levels had not provided employment for the growing urban population nor for the rural migrants to the towns. One result was a pronounced rise in the service sector rather than the industrial, and in education, health and housing, the social consequences of economic failure were obvious.

Some of the structural remedies – agrarian reform, export diversification, a larger national share in copper profits – have been mentioned previously, but they will take time to have their due effect. Meanwhile, natural disaster, to which Chile seems singularly prone, is a random variable of some significance. A major earthquake in 1965, and a serious drought, affecting the whole of the central valley in 1968–9, imposed additional heavy and immediate burdens on an economy with enough problems to face. Despite all the adverse factors, however, there are increasing signs that the paradox of Chile's great potential and her actual economic performance may be resolved.

In the first place, there now exists in Chile a very large measure of agreement on the necessity for change to incorporate the underprivileged sectors properly into the national life. Secondly, recent years have seen important infrastructural developments to increase Chile's foreign trade, a fundamental prerequisite of future economic growth. And, thirdly, while it is generally agreed that the Latin American Free Trade Area, seen some years ago as the major hope of Latin American economic development, has been disappointing in its performance, smaller regional groupings promise more. One such is the Andean Group – Venezuela, Colombia, Ecuador, Peru, Bolivia and Chile – in which Chile has played the major role.

In terms of foreign trade, high copper prices in the late 1960s enabled Chile to show a 19 per cent increase in total value of exports in 1969 over 1968 (BOLSA Review, 4 (40), April 1970, 201). More significantly, in the long run, since copper prices can fall as well as rise, is the increasing diversification of Chilean exports, with petrochemicals, cellulose and paper products advancing rapidly. The second favourable feature in recent years has been the widening of Chile's export markets, notably towards the Pacific, where Japanese interests have signed a number of long-term contracts to take Chilean raw materials at constant prices, and towards eastern Europe, hitherto of very marginal importance in Chile's trading pattern (BOLSA Review, 3 (27), March 1969, 152). Chilean exports of copper, cellulose, newsprint and other commodities are now going to Australia, and a regular shipping service across the South Pacific has recently been introduced. These are highly significant developments for the Pacific coast republic whose traditional trading orientation has been towards the United States and western Europe, though it should not be forgotten that the

Pacific trade in wheat was an important feature of Chile's economy in the nineteenth century, and that her current turn in that direction is a modern recognition of her basic geopolitical situation. Within the Andean Group itself, Chile is in a strong position to find markets for her manufactured products, particularly in petrochemicals and wood products.

Chile's future clearly depends on the solution of so many varied and complex problems that prophecy would be rash and certainty foolish. But optimism remains in the fundamental fact that so diverse a geographical entity has evolved within a national framework. Chile's regional differences will undoubtedly persist, as a product of forces man cannot entirely control, but the unity in diversity that Chile represents seems likely also to survive, as proof of man's capacity to defy nature and logic alike.

POSTSCRIPT

With the election of President Salvador Allende in September 1970, an avowedly Marxist government attained power in Chile for a six-year term on a platform of sweeping change. This includes a rapid speeding-up of agrarian reform, large-scale nationalization of both domestic and foreign-owned private assets – in mining, banking, industry and commerce – increased central planning, and state control of the economy. Within six months, the new government had carried legislation through Congress for the complete nationalization of the big copper mines, acquired control of a dozen domestic banks by purchase of shares, and claimed to have re-distributed more land after expropriation than its predecessor had done in six years. At the time of writing (mid-1971), the government enjoys considerable popular support, and it has certainly begun a major redistribution of income to benefit the masses by such policies as wage increases and price controls. It has also implemented extensive welfare measures, such as the free distribution of milk to minors. The long-term effects of such policies on the economy cannot yet be seen, and it is also too early to anticipate the impact of the new government on many issues discussed in this chapter, such as national planning. It is also not yet clear how far its policies really represent a radically fresh departure, or are, in fact, an acceleration of developments previously under way. Like all its predecessors, however, the government of Salvador Allende is heir to the distinctively Chilean historical experience, and to the geographical constraints and advantages which have been the subject of this essay. In building for Chile's future, it will need to take account of both these factors.

BIBLIOGRAPHY

AMUNÁTEGUI, G. (1968) The role of copper in the Chilean economy. In VÉLIZ, C. (ed.) *Latin America and the Caribbean: A Handbook*. London, Blond. 639–45.

BARAONA, R., ARANDA, X. and SANTANA, R. (1961) *Valle de Putaendo: estudio de estructura agraria*. Santiago, Instituto de Geografía de la Universidad de Chile.

BOLSA (Bank of London and South America) *Review* (cited in text as BOLSA *Review*, with relevant dates).

BENHAM, F. and HOLLEY, H. A. (1960) *A Short Introduction to the Economy of Latin America*. London, Oxford University Press.

BERRY, B. J. L. (1969) Relationships between regional economic development and the urban system: the case of Chile. *Tijdschrift voor Economische en Sociale Geografie*, 60 (5), 283–307.

BLAKEMORE, H. (1962) John Thomas North, the Nitrate King. *History Today*, 12, 467–75.

BOHAN, M. L. and POMERANTZ, M. (1960) *Investment in Chile: basic information for United States businessmen*. Washington, D.C., U.S. Department of Commerce and Bureau of Foreign Commerce.

BORDE, J. and GÓNGORA, M. (1956) *Evolución de la propriedad rural en el Valle del Puangue*. 2 vols. Santiago.

BOWMAN, I. (1924) *Desert Trails of Atacama*. New York, American Geographical Society, Special Publications No. 5.

BUTLAND, G. J. (1954) Changing land occupance in the south Chilean provinces of Aysén and Magallanes. *Geographical Studies*, 1 (1), 27–43.

BUTLAND, G. J. (1956) *Chile: an outline of its geography, economics and politics*. 3rd ed. London, Oxford University Press.

BUTLAND, G. J. (1957) *The Human Geography of Southern Chile*. London, George Philip, Institute of British Geographers, Publication No. 24.

BUTLER, J. H. (1960) *Manufacturing in the Concepción Region of Chile: present position and prospects for future development*. Washington, D.C., National Academy of Sciences and National Research Council.

Censos – see DIRECCIÓN DE ESTADÍSTICA Y CENSOS.

CIDA (Comité Interamericano de Desarrollo Agrícola) (1966) *Chile: Tenencia de la tierra y desarrollo socio-económico del sector agrícola*. Santiago.

COOPER, J. (1946) The Araucanians. *Handbook of South American Indians*, 2, 687–760. Washington, D.C., Bureau of American Ethnology, Bulletin No. 143.

CORFO (Corporación de Fomento de la Producción) (1967) *Geografía económica de Chile*. Santiago, texto refundido.

CORA (Corporación de la Reforma Agraria) (1968) *Cuatro años de reforma agraria*. Santiago.

CORA (1970) *Reforma agraria chilena, 1965–1970*. Santiago.

CUNILL, P. (1965) *Geografía de Chile*. 2nd ed. Santiago.

DARWIN, CHARLES (1960) *The Voyage of the Beagle*. London, Dent, Everyman's Library ed.

DELGADO, O. (ed.) (1965) *Reformas agrarias en la América Latina: procesos y perspectivas*. Mexico, Buenos Aires.

DIRECCIÓN DE ESTADÍSTICA Y CENSOS (1960) *XIII Censo de Población, 29 de noviembre de 1960* (cited in text as *Censo*, 1960, followed by name of province to which reference is made). Santiago, Serie B., Provincias, 25 parts.

DIRECCIÓN DE ESTADÍSTICA Y CENSOS (1964) *Población total por provincias Chile 1885–1960* (cited in text as *Censos, Provincias*, 1964). Santiago.

ECHEVERRÍA, R. P. (1969) *The Effect of Agricultural Price Policies on Inter-Sectoral Income Transfers*. Ithaca, N.Y., Cornell University, Latin American Studies Programme, Dissertation Series No. 13, mimeographed.

ECLA (Economic Commission for Latin America) (1969) *Economic Survey of Latin America 1968*. 2 vols. Santiago, United Nations Economic and Social Council, General Series E/CN.12/825, mimeographed.

EDITORIAL NASCIMENTO (1967) *Ley de reforma agraria*. Santiago, Colección de Leyes con Indicaciones y Notas.

ELLSWORTH, P. T. (1945) *Chile: an Economy in Transition*. New York, Macmillan.

ENCINA, F. A. and CASTEDO, L. (1964) *Résumen de la historia de Chile*. 3 vols. 5th ed. Santiago, Editorial Zig-Zag.

EYZAGUIRRE, J. (1965) *Historia de Chile*. Vol. I. Santiago.

FARON, L. C. (1968) *The Mapuche Indians of Chile*. New York, Holt, Rinehart & Winston.

GAY, C. (1844–54) *Historia física y política de Chile*. 24 vols, 2 vols on Agriculture. Paris.

GÓNGORA, M. (1960) *Origen de los inquilinos de Chile Central*. Santiago.

GRIFFIN, K. (1969) *Underdevelopment in Spanish America*. London, Allen & Unwin.

HERRICK, B. H. (1965) *Urban Migration and Economic Development in Chile*. Cambridge, Mass., and London, Massachusetts Institute of Technology Press.

HOFFMANN, R. and DEBUYST, F. (1966) *Chile: una industrialización desordenada*. 2nd ed. Santiago.

HERNÁNDEZ CORNEJO, R. (1930) *El salitre*. Valparaiso.

IADB (Inter-American Development Bank) (1968, 1969, 1970) *Socio-Economic Progress in Latin America*. Washington, D.C., Social Progress Trust Fund Eighth (1968), Ninth (1969) and Tenth (1970) Annual Reports.

JAMES, P. (1959) *Latin America*. 3rd ed. London, Cassell.

JEFFERSON, M. (1921) *Recent Colonisation in Chile*. New York, American Geographical Society.

KELLER, C. (1956) *La revolución en la agricultura*. Santiago.

KORTH, E. H. (1968) *Spanish Policy in Colonial Chile: the struggle for justice 1535–1700*. Stanford University Press.

Ley de Reforma Agraria – see EDITORIAL NASCIMENTO.

MAMALAKIS, M. (1965) Public policy and sectoral development: a case study of Chile 1940–1958. In MAMALAKIS, M. and REYNOLDS, C. W. *Essays on the Chilean Economy*. Homewood, Ill., Richard D. Irwin. 3–206.

MÁRMORA, L. (1968) *Migración al Sur*. Buenos Aires.

MARTIN, G. E. (1960) *La división de la tierra en Chile Central*. Santiago.

MARTNER, D. (1923) *Estudio de la política comercial Chilena e historia económica nacional*. 2 vols. Santiago.

Mensaje – see PRESIDENCIA DE LA REPUBLICA.

MERRILL, R. N. (1968) *An Evaluation of Chile's Housing Program: problems and prospects*. Ithaca, N.Y., Cornell University, Latin American Studies Programme, Dissertation Series No. 2, mimeographed.

MCBRIDE, G. M. (1936) *Chile, Land and Society*. New York, American Geographical Society, Research Series No. 191.

ODEPLAN (Oficina de Planificación Nacional) (1968) *Política de desarrollo*. Santiago.

PARSONS, J. J. (1964) The contribution of geography to Latin American studies. In WAGLEY, C. (ed.) *Social Science Research on Latin America*. New York and London, Columbia University Press. 33–85.

PEDERSON, L. R. (1966) *The Mining Industry of the Norte Chico, Chile*. Evanston, Ill., Northwestern University Studies in Geography No. 11.

PRESIDENCIA DE LA REPUBLICA (1965, 1966, 1967, 1968, 1969) *Mensaje del Presidente Don Eduardo Frei Montalva al inaugurar el período de las Sesiones Ordinarias del Congreso Nacional* (cited in text as *Mensaje*). Santiago.

REYNOLDS, C.E. (1965) Development problems of an export economy: the case of Chile and copper. In MAMALAKIS, M. and REYNOLDS, C. E. *Essays on the Chilean Economy*. Homewood, Ill., Richard D. Irwin. 207–398.

RUDOLPH, W. E. (1963) *Vanishing Trails of Atacama.* New York, American Geographical Society, Research Series No. 24.

RUSSELL, W. H. (1890) *A Visit to Chile and the Nitrate Fields of Tarapacá.* London.

SCOTT ELLIOT, G. E. (1907) *Chile.* London.

SEMPER, E. and MICHELLS, E. (1908) *La industria del salitre en Chile.* Trans. into Spanish and augmented by O. Gandarillas and G. Salas. Santiago.

SEPÚLVEDA, S. (1959) El trigo Chileno en el mercado mundial. *Informaciones Geográficas.* Santiago, Instituto Geográfico de la Universidad de Chile, año VI (1956), 7-135.

SMOLE, W. J. (1963) *Owner-Cultivatorship in Middle Chile.* Chicago, Ill., Department of Geography, Research Paper No. 89.

SUBERCASEAUX, B. (n.d.) *Chile, o una loca geografía.* Several eds. Santiago.

SUNKEL, O. (1965) Change and frustration in Chile. In VÉLIZ, C. (ed.) *Obstacles to Change in Latin America.* London, Oxford University Press.

SOZA, H. (1968) The industrialization of Chile. In VÉLIZ, C. (ed.) *Latin America and the Caribbean: A Handbook.* London, Blond. 614-21.

THIESENHUSEN, W. C. (1966) *Chile's Experiments in Agrarian Reform.* Madison and London, University of Wisconsin Press, Land Economics Monographs No 1.

UNIVERSIDAD DE CHILE, DEPARTMENTO DE EXTENSIÓN CULTURAL (1956) *Seminario de investigación sobre el desarrollo de la provincia de Cautín.* Santiago.

UNIVERSIDAD DE CHILE, INSTITUTO DE ECONOMÍA (1963) *La Economía Chilena en el período 1950-1963.* 2 vols. Santiago.

UNIVERSIDAD DE CHILE, INSTITUTO DE ECONOMÍA (1956) *Desarrollo económico de Chile 1940-1956.* Santiago.

VICUÑA MACKENNA, B. (1882) *El libro de la plata.* Santiago.

VILLALOBOS, S. (1961) *Tradición y reforma en 1810.* Santiago.

WARRINER, D. (1969) *Land Reform in Principle and Practice.* London, Oxford University Press.

WEAVER, F. S. (1968) *Regional Patterns of Economic Change in Chile 1950-1964.* Ithaca, N.Y., Cornell University, Latin American Studies Programme, Dissertation Series No. 11, mimeographed.

11 Conclusion: Unity and Diversity in Latin America

The Editors

The term 'Latin America', like so many commonly accepted designations of geographical regions, is an invention of western Europe, first propounded in France, and gaining currency there in the 1860s when Napoleon III was seeking to establish Maximilian of Austria on a Mexican throne under French tutelage. It is essentially a cultural term, intended to stress the region's historical relationship with the Latin nations of Europe, and also to differentiate the vast area impregnated with Iberian culture from the other, Anglo-Saxon America to the north. The term is a handy, shorthand expression, though Latin Americans themselves have often been chary of using it, and there is, in addition, a large literature of Latin American protest at the pre-emption by the United States of the title 'America', to which, in fact, her southern neighbours have a better historical claim. Nevertheless, 'Latin America' has passed into common usage, and the term is most unlikely to be replaced. Its blanket use, however, does, at times, encourage popularly held notions, which it has been one of the objectives of this book to dispel – namely, that the twenty republics of Latin America have so much in common that comparisons between them are more revealing than contrasts.

That many such comparisons exist and are perfectly valid has been suggested in the opening chapter of this book: they are, in large measure, the product of a common, or similar, historical experience, and not least a colonial epoch, which lasted some three hundred years. No visitor to Latin America, moving from country to country, could fail to be struck by the patent similarities he would observe, yet, the longer his stay and the more extensive his experience, the more does he come to appreciate the remarkable diversity the continent presents, not only from country to country, but also within each of the countries themselves. The eighteen heirs of the Spanish empire have a common written language, and the Spanish-speaking visitor would certainly have little difficulty in verbal communication, moving from place to place. But he would notice marked changes in pronunciation as he travelled, and wide variations in vocabulary from country to country, as well as markedly different meanings for the

567

same words in many instances.[1] This is an obvious example of diversity within a general unity, which Latin America presents. The Spanish empire itself, stretching at its zenith from California to Cape Horn – in theory if not precisely in fact – was never much of a unity: geography alone imposed intractable barriers to tidy notions of administrative order, and the application of general laws was continually frustrated by the diversity of local conditions. As in the past, so in the present, the Latin American states possess generalized common features in terms of the aspiration for a better future and the obstacles that lie in the way. Politically, the big issues everywhere concern stability in government, the orderly transfer of power and the establishment in fact of those principles of participatory democracy that every state constitution proclaims. Economically, every country in Latin America seeks to secure growth, and not least to reduce its critical dependence on the production and export of few commodities, and socially, every government declares – though not all may be sincere – that it seeks to promote social justice by the eradication of inequalities, inherited or imposed. But these aspirations are not peculiarly Latin American, and while they are common to all the states there, the responses reveal, in their wide variety, great diversities, which spring from the distinctive geographical factors and the unique historical experience that have made each country what it is. That diversity has been explored in the body of this book, and it may be relevant, therefore, to devote its concluding chapter to some discussion of the theme with which it began – Latin America as a recognizable entity in the modern world, and the ways in which the individual states have sought to achieve a wider unity.

Expressions of unity in modern Latin America have usually been short lived. During the wars for independence, in the first quarter of the nineteenth century, solidarity of sentiment united many Spanish Americans, and for the great liberators, San Martín and Bolívar, the cause against Spain was a continental cause. Argentinians helped to liberate Chile, as Chileans helped to liberate Peru, and, in the northern half of the continent, Bolívar's armies were truly international. Bolívar himself created a union of Venezuela, New Granada (Colombia) and Ecuador, but this Gran Colombia dissolved into its component parts before the Liberator himself, disillusioned and dejected, died in 1830. Bolívar, indeed, had wider visions of unity: in 1826, he had convened at Panama, symbolic bridge between the two Americas, a conference intended to be the first step towards a continental system of co-operation and friendship, but it was a fiasco, though the idea lived on. In Central America, independence was achieved by a union of what became the states of Guatemala, Honduras, Nicaragua,

[1] The word *guagua* is, variously, the popular name for a bus in Cuba, a baby in Chile, an edible amphibious rodent in Colombia and a fruit-destroying insect in Spain. The scope for memorable *faux pas* even among Latin Americans is thus considerable.

El Salvador and Costa Rica, but the union collapsed in 1839 and, despite later attempts to revive it, the states went their own ways. In the late 1830s the abortive confederation of Peru and Bolivia collapsed after defeat in war with Chile, though there is little doubt that even without the war the union would not have survived.

These attempts – and there were others – to eradicate newly established boundaries in Spanish America by voluntary means were doomed to failure by the fundamental fact that a common heritage of language, religion and culture, with similar social structures and political habits, was not strong enough to overcome local loyalties and regional differences, which had been growing for some three centuries. Moreover, after independence, the individual states were not yet nations, and their boundaries were often ill defined. The search for national unity predominated, and this essential quest was complicated, from country to country in varying degrees, by political, social, economic and racial divisions. Regional feeling played a major part in the story of political instability, which characterized most states and derived from the fact that the removal of imperial authority created a power vacuum, which many sought to fill. The few exceptions prove the rule. Brazil, the colossus of the continent, · already set apart by reason of language, racial composition and a different imperial connection, ratified her distinctiveness in nineteenth-century Latin America by remaining the only monarchy in a continent of republics. By retaining monarchical institutions, Brazil experienced greater administrative and emotional continuity from the colonial past than her Spanish-American neighbours and soon acquired stability, though Brazil, too, passed through a period of regional revolt against the national government before unity was confirmed. Chile, after a decade of turbulence, established a unique constitutional system, which made authority impersonal and its transmission from one president to the next an orderly process. Paraguay enjoyed tranquillity for nearly thirty years under the iron rule of a strong dictator who virtually isolated the country from the outside world. Elsewhere, however, internal strife was the common experience for many decades, interrupted only by the peace of despotism as individual *caudillos* secured enough support to impose their own kind of order.

Internal order and some degree of national unity within the separate states were obvious prerequisites to co-operation between them, but the growth of national unity was a slow process, hindered, as it was, by physical as well as human factors. The sheer size of many states, their scattered settlement pattern, the universal inadequacy of communications before the advent of modern methods of transport – such features compounded political problems, as did the sharp social cleavage that obtained almost everywhere. Racial divisions in countries with large Negro or Indian populations confused even further a complicated picture. Moreover, to the difficulties of relations within states were added particular problems

T

of relations between them in consequence of their independence. As in Africa today, the legacy of colonial frontiers in Latin America was a major cause of conflict between the separate countries, and few international wars there have not derived, in greater or lesser degree, from boundary disputes between contiguous states. The lines of separate jurisdictions, drawn for administrative convenience within empires, are often ill recorded, leaving the successor states to settle between themselves the exact delimitation of their inheritance, by reason or force. Conflicts arising from such causes clearly militated against the growth of internationalism in Latin America, and, even today, many of the disputes that exist between countries arise from opposing interpretations both of the original colonial boundaries and of attempts to adjust them in the nineteenth century. Boundary disputes, however, and the wars to which they gave rise served the useful purpose of helping to unify the states internally and strengthen national feeling – necessary steps on the way to wider unities.

There was a further reason why, in nineteenth-century Latin America, continental solidarity took a low second place to the pursuit of individual national interests: it lies in the economic and intellectual relationships that linked the continent to Europe. The level of economic development in all the states throughout the century, and well into this one, and the integration of their national economies into the world system – described in previous pages – naturally caused the countries individually to look abroad, first to Europe and later to the United States, rather than to one another. The lines that linked Latin American markets with European manufacturers, and Latin American producers of primary commodities with European consumers were lines that ran parallel and did not intersect. Supplies of capital and the provision of technology came to the continent, country by country, from European sources and, if London was for long the economic capital of Latin America, Paris was its intellectual home. The role of foreign capital and enterprise in the economic development of Latin America has been discussed in the country survey which make up the bulk of this volume, though much less has been said of the importation into the continent of foreign ideas and ideologies. Yet they, too, played a highly significant part in changing the Latin American landscape, and often provided the intellectual framework for economic attitudes. Thus, the impact of *laissez-faire*, itself one aspect of European liberalism, was pervasive and profound, and in some countries – Mexico and Brazil, in particular – the role of positivist philosophies was equally significant. The economic and cultural relationships between individual Latin American countries and the nations of western Europe were reinforced by the immigrant streams that flowed to Argentina, Uruguay, southern Brazil and Chile, and it is no exaggeration to say that for these and other Latin American states relations with Europe were much more intimate than relations with one another. Of the states that had formerly belonged to one

Spanish empire, with their common legacies of language, religion and culture, a clear-sighted observer remarked, almost sixty years ago: 'the feeling of a common Hispano-American brotherhood is weak' (Bryce, 1912, p. 445). The national evolution of the independent states, including the growth of nationalism itself, separated the states one from another, confirming differences that, although they existed during the time of empire, had been partly overlaid by the structures of empire.

Yet this is not the whole story. While geographical circumstances, historical evolution and economic influences combined to divide, rather than unite, the nations of Latin America, there persisted in the writings of intellectuals and in particular instances the aspiration to solidarity. It was most in evidence in the expression of a specifically Latin American system of inter-state relations, and in attempts to co-ordinate resistance to outside threats. Thus, in the 1860s, when Spain made a last and desperate attempt to coerce Peru and Chile to her will, these two inveterate rivals for hege-mony on the Pacific Coast of South America sank their differences in temporary conciliation and, with Bolivia, Colombia and Ecuador, declared their joint resistance to Spanish pretensions.[1] Other instances could be cited of temporary co-operation between the Latin American states in similar circumstances, and there is a considerable literature in Latin America in the nineteenth century and after that testifies to the persistence of Bolívar's unrealized dream of continental unity.

In practice, however, what brought the states of Latin America into formal structures of continental co-operation was the initiative of the United States, and the modern phase of the Pan-American movement began, and has continued, in a system of relations between them. The story, from the date of the First International Conference of American States, held at Washington in 1889–90, to the present day, is extremely complex, and does not concern us here (for a full account, see Connell-Smith, 1966). Suffice it to say that the growing disequilibrium in power and global influence of the United States on the one hand, and the com-parative weakness of the Latin American republics on the other, has been the greatest hurdle to effective and genuine acceptance by both parties of a common definition of co-operation. The history of their relations within the American system during the past eighty years has been one of marked fluctuations between amity and hostility.

Increasingly in the twentieth century, much more significant for most Latin Americans than the formal features of the Inter-American system –

---

[1] The Monroe Doctrine, declared in 1823 by the President of the United States, affirmed, in effect, that the continental island of America contains a political system different from that of the Old World, and that the extension of European power to the New World was prohibited by the United States. At the time of the Spanish pressure on Peru and Chile, the United States was involved in civil war but, even so, the Monroe Doctrine only became effective when the United States acquired the power to make it so, in the 1890s.

now embraced by the Organization of American States – have been, and are, the economic realities of the relationship between the United States and Latin America, a relationship marked by the replacement of Europe by the United States as the dominant external factor. Figures of foreign investment provide an indication of this change. In 1914 the nominal value of foreign investment in Latin America was $8500 million, Britain's share amounting to $3700 million – a quarter of all British overseas investment – compared to $1700 million from the United States, $1200 million from Germany and $900 million from France (IADB, 1966, p. 54). But the cost of two world wars, centred on Europe, and the impact of the Great Depression drastically diminished the European stake in Latin America, and enabled American interests to rise to predominance. The United States became, in fact, Latin America's major market for primary products, its chief supplier of manufactured goods, and its principal source of foreign capital. At the end of 1968, United States investments in Latin America totalled almost $13,000 million, compared with about $800 million at the end of 1959, though as a proportion of total U.S. investment abroad this represented, in fact, a fall from 27 per cent to 20·1 per cent (*U.S. Investment*, 1970, p. 22).

The role of foreign investment in developing countries is a subject of great complexity and much controversy, and this is nowhere more true than in Latin America (cf., for example, IADB, 1966, and Griffin, 1969). It cannot be denied that the Latin American affiliates of United States companies provide employment for a million and a quarter Latin Americans, make a sizeable contribution to the continent's balance of payments problems, earn substantial sums in foreign exchange through exports (about $4500 million a year between 1965 and 1968) and save large sums through import substitution (nearly $4800 million a year between 1965 and 1968). But what most Latin Americans remember is the fact that investment earnings by American affiliates during the same period were more than double the size of new investment. More importantly for them, in addition, in a highly nationalistic continent, is the way they regard the mere existence of sizeable foreign investment as a positive reflection of their basic underdevelopment.

Previous chapters in this book have devoted considerable attention to the development problems of Latin America on which there is, of course, a voluminous, and often partisan, literature, impossible to summarize here. In the context of this chapter, however, what is important about debates on developmental issues is the distinctive Latin American contribution to them, a contribution that is derived from Latin American experience but has much wider validity, and one that, in many respects, may be regarded as a cogent expression of Latin American unity. It is in this context also that relations between Latin America and the United States, including the issue of investment, have particular significance at the present time.

The formulation of distinctive and coherent Latin American views on the relationship between the developed and developing worlds was largely the result of the foundation, in 1948, of the Economic Commission for Latin America, an organ of the United Nations Organization with its seat in Santiago de Chile.[1] From 1950 to 1963, ECLA's Executive Secretary was the Argentine economist, Dr Raúl Prebisch, and it is his name which has been given, justly, to the particular thesis on Latin American development problems, which has, perhaps, been ECLA's most constructive contribution to the general debate. Summarized very briefly, the thesis demonstrates how the world free market system for primary commodities penalizes producing countries, subject as they are to fluctuations in demand from industrial countries with high standards of living. At the same time, it also shows how manufacturing countries, exporting to primary producing countries, pass on a large proportion of value added in their high-cost economies, accentuating the deterioration in terms of trade for primary producers. The latter, their import capacity geared to their export performance, itself closely linked to capital formation for their own economic growth, are forced to seek financial aid and development loans, thus increasing their indebtedness to the developed world. In short, according to Prebisch, the gap between the developed and the developing world is continually increasing, and the answer to the problem lies, at least in good measure, in a whole series of policies for Latin American countries, which includes trade protection, control of imports, acceleration of import substitution, increased foreign aid, wider economic integration and long-term planning (for excellent short summaries, see Huelin, 1968, pp. 472–3, and Peter Calvo, 1968, pp. 577–8).

Although specifically derived from Latin American circumstances, and propounded from a Latin American institution, the Prebisch thesis is applicable to the developing world in general, a fact increasingly recognized in the 1950s and 1960s, as its virtual adoption by the United Nations Conference on Trade and Development at Geneva in 1964 indicated. Indeed, for a continent not particularly noted for its originality in political and economic thought, and historically one that has borrowed extensively in these matters from Europe and the United States, Latin America has produced in the Prebisch thesis and other contributions from ECLA on the universal debate on development its most significant expression of originality. Inside Latin America itself, ECLA has been not only a very tangible

---

[1] At about the same time, the Economic Commission for the Far East and the Economic Commission for Europe were also founded and, like ECLA, lacked permanent status until 1951. It should also be remembered that in the immediate post-war period, a third of the membership of the United Nations was Latin American, and it was the existence of these states, not that of Spain – still not a member – that ensured that Spanish would be one of the five official languages of the organization.

manifestation of a new kind of continental consciousness, but also a very important agent for the promotion of other instruments of co-operation, and a valuable service agency in the implementation of economic policies. Thus, for example, its role as adviser in the formulation of development plans, its development of subsidiary institutions for various purposes, and, far from least, the impressive range of its own publications, all testify to a dynamic entity serving Latin America as a whole in its search for economic growth and social justice.

Two other aspects of this question deserve some consideration, however briefly. The first concerns finance, the second economic integration, both subjects dear to ECLA's heart, and central to the Prebisch thesis. In December, 1959, the Latin American republics, with the exception of Cuba, and the United States of America joined together to establish the Inter-American Development Bank as a financial agency to help accelerate the economic development of its member states, individually and collectively (IADB, 1970, p. 503). At that time, its ordinary capital resources were fixed at $850 million, $400 million as paid-in capital and $450 million as callable capital. Between that date and 1969, however, the Bank gained a cumulative portfolio of $3430 million, and disbursed $1726 million: 24 per cent of disbursements were channelled into agriculture, 18 per cent into industry and mining, 29 per cent into infrastructural projects – ports, transport, telecommunications, electric power – 23 per cent into urban development and sanitation, and 6 per cent into higher education and pre-investment activities (IADB, *Proceedings*, 1970, pp. 43–4). Under the able direction of the Chilean economist, Felipe Herrera, President of the Bank from its foundation until late 1970, the Inter-American Development Bank has been one of the great successes of the 'development decade' in Latin America. Though a large share of its resources comes from the United States, it is universally regarded as a Latin American institution, and its professional competence has secured it a highly favourable place as a borrower on the world's capital markets (BOLSA *Review*, 4 (37), January 1970, p. 14). It has entered into agreements with non-member countries to administer specific resources provided by them for project financing in Latin America, enlarged its membership by the inclusion of Barbados and Trinidad and Tobago, and acted as the administrator for the Social Progress Trust Fund, set up separately from its own operations by the United States in 1961 (IADB, *Activities, 1961–68*, 1969). The impact of the Bank's operations at local levels has been remarkable, and their range impressive: loans have been made for such diverse projects as a petrochemical plant near Buenos Aires, expansion of water supplies at Oruro, road improvements in north-eastern Brazil, land settlement programmes in south-central Chile, livestock development in Colombia, cement plant in Costa Rica, housing programmes in the Dominican Republic, oil palm cultivation in Ecuador, expansion of ports in El Salvador, installation of textile mills in Guatemala, construction of a new university campus in Honduras, pre-investment studies for river basin development in Mexico, the integrated development of Indian communities in the Peruvian sierra and the expansion of the dairy industry of Uruguay (for a complete list of the 498 loans made by the Bank between 1961 and 1968, see IADB, *Activities, 1961–68,* 1969, pp. 114–44). The Bank has become, in fact, a major institution of Latin American economic co-operation, in which other nations participate without running the risk of the rancour that direct unilateral investment often inspires.

The closer integration of the Latin American economies has been, and remains, a major argument of the Inter-American Development Bank, as well as of ECLA, for intensifying industrialization, diversifying the foreign trade of the region and increasing the pace of economic growth in the individual countries (Herrera, 1968, p. 563). The case for Latin American integration has been warmly debated in recent years and it remains a somewhat controversial subject: in principle, however, there is general acceptance of the theoretical arguments that urge the advantages of group protection for larger-than-national markets, economies of scale, rationalization of investment and greater use of industrial capacity (Dell, 1966, pp. 15–34). Undoubtedly, in addition, the examples of the European Economic Community and the European Free Trade Area were not insignificant in Latin America, though in terms of levels of development the difference between the two regions is, of course, enormous. Beginning in 1951, the governments of the five countries of Central America gradually worked towards the establishment of a Common Market, which came into formal existence in 1958, aiming to establish a free trade area over a period of ten years, and to move thereafter to a customs union. In fact, however, the agreement got off to a poor start since the treaty establishing the organization abolished duties only on a limited number of goods, and additions to the list were to be negotiated anew. But, early in 1960, Guatemala, El Salvador and Honduras signed a new treaty, which approached the problem of free trade between them by the opposite direction, not listing the duty free goods as previously, but establishing free trade for all goods produced by any of them, except for a restricted list subject to preferential tariffs or restrictive quotas for five years only. This action galvanized the whole movement towards economic integration in Central America, the tripartite agreement of 1960 being converted into a treaty including Nicaragua and Costa Rica as well in 1961. The Central American Common Market experienced quite dramatic results in the 1960s: 98 per cent of intra-regional trade was absolutely liberalized and 98 per cent of import tariff items from outside the region was subject to a common external tariff, while the value of intra-regional trade grew fivefold between 1960 and 1966, from $32·7 million to $173·6 million (Calvo, in BOLSA *Review*, 2

(18), June 1968, p. 314). Trade with the rest of the world increased by 58 per cent in the same period.

This substantial early progress, however, slowed down in the later 1960s, partly because rapid expansion earlier was based, in large measure, on utilizing hitherto unused capacity, agricultural and industrial, and also because external factors were favourable (see Wionczek in BOLSA *Review*, 1 (3), March 1967, p. 134). Deterioration in the terms of trade for Central America's primary products and balance of payments difficulties dampened the previous euphoria, and the obviously uneven nature of development within the CACM itself put severe strains on the organization (for a detailed discussion, see Cable in BOLSA *Review*, 3 (30), June 1969, pp. 336–46). Behind all the intricate economic data, lay the fundamental fact that effective integration depended basically on a *political* will to make integration work, and this was lacking. Indeed, in July 1969, two member nations of the CACM, El Salvador and Honduras, found themselves at war, ostensibly over football matches between national teams in the qualifying rounds of the 1970 World Cup, but actually over the problems involved in the presence of some 300,000 Salvadorean immigrants in Honduras. This war was undoubtedly the greatest setback experienced by the CACM, and although the fighting phase soon ended, tension between the two countries persists. The conflict, however, has brought out into the open the fact that the interests of different member states within the CACM, each of which has its own particular problems, must be solved by compromise if this notable form of Central American unity is to survive.

At about the same time that the CACM was becoming a reality in 1960, the Latin American Free Trade Area also came into existence. In February 1960, representatives of Argentina, Brazil, Chile, Mexico, Paraguay, Peru and Uruguay signed the Treaty of Montevideo, which was ratified in May 1961, and came into force soon after (the text of the Treaty may be found in Dell, 1966, pp. 228–56). Colombia and Ecuador joined later that same year, to be followed by Bolivia, and Venezuela in due course. The long-term objective is the establishment of a Latin American Common Market, by progressive reductions of tariff barriers between member nations, and a beginning was made on this in 1962. By 1967, trade within the LAFTA had increased substantially, particularly in the early years (though regional trade in 1961, immediately before the 'base' year, was abnormally low, and improvement in the early 1960s may, in fact, have had little to do with LAFTA arrangements). Tariff reductions were made by annual negotiations in which each country was involved – 'national schedules' – and by triennial negotiations involving all member countries to produce 'common schedules', consisting of products for which all trade barriers were to be removed between members completely by 1973. After the first five rounds of annual 'national schedules', some 9000 concessions had been included in the national lists, but the negotiations were extremely hard and members generally were reluctant to lower tariff barriers for domestic products (Eckenstein, 1968, pp. 543–4). Naturally, the highly uneven levels of the individual Latin American economies were recognized and preferential concessions were extended to the less developed states. Increase in trade, however, occurred mostly in non-manufactured goods in the first five years, and widespread disillusionment set in about LAFTA's capacity to achieve a fundamental breakthrough in the fields of tariff reduction on manufactures that compete with domestic products, and planning new industrial development on a regional, rather than a national, basis (BOLSA *Review*, 1 (2), February 1967, pp. 60–70). The problems, enormously complex, plagued the LAFTA throughout the 1960s and, indeed, at the end of 1969, representatives of member states, meeting at Caracas, voted for modifications of the Montevideo Treaty, postponing the scheduled date for the completion of trade liberalization from 1973 to 1980. It is significant that major support for this proposal came from Argentina, Brazil and Mexico, the three industrial giants of LAFTA.

Clearly, the Montevideo Treaty was far too ambitious in its expectations, particularly in its timetable for the creation of a fully operating free trade area, but it is significant that whatever divisions exist within the organization – and they are many and profound – no member has sought to withdraw from it, progress may be slow but it continues, and, in the light of Latin America's past, the fact that it exists at all is truly remarkable.

Disillusionment with LAFTA's progress, moreover, has been an ill wind that has brought good in other respects, apart from its own achievements, which must not be forgotten simply because its professed aims have not been fully realized. In the second half of the 1960s, subregional groups, complementary rather than antagonistic to the wider unity that LAFTA represents, emerged in various parts of the continent and, at the time of writing, considerable progress has been made. The Andean Group, consisting of Bolivia, Colombia, Chile, Ecuador, Peru and Venezuela began in 1967 to formulate plans for closer integration within this more limited geographical area and, while, again, and perhaps inevitably, dissension has occurred, much has been achieved. In 1969, agreement was reached at Cartagena in Colombia for the abolition of internal tariffs between these countries, except Venezuela, which withdrew from the scheme, and on the establishment of a customs union. There is, perhaps, a better prospect of creating a common market here, since the economic disparities between the members are smaller than those within LAFTA. A rather different kind of grouping is that of the River Plate countries – Argentina, Brazil, Bolivia, Paraguay and Uruguay – which is essentially much less ambitious than the Andean Group in that they make no pretensions to the establishment of a common market, but, beginning in 1967, formulated proposals for international co-operation, based mainly on infrastructure projects in the river basin they all share.

At the end of the 1960s, the Latin American countries presented a complex paradox in their various approaches to continental and regional unity. Clearly, the *mystique* of union had gained enormous ground, but, at the same time, the practical problems of translating into reality sweeping visions of continentalism proved difficult enough, and provided sufficient proof of the fact that nationalism remained the dominant political expression of diversity in the Latin American continent. To convert the steps towards integration into working realities required political will, as well as economic justification, and political will was lacking.

In one sense, however, the decade that saw these steps towards closer integration also witnessed the beginnings of a fundamental reshaping of Latin America's relations with the wider world, and not least with the power that dominated the continent – the United States. The beginning of the 1960s saw not only the birth of the CACM and LAFTA, but also of the Alliance for Progress, intended to create a bridge of co-operation between the Latin American countries and the United States, and recreate the aspiration to a genuine Pan-Americanism, which had gone sour in recent decades. Originating with President Juscelino Kubitschek of Brazil, and therefore Latin American in origin, the concept of the Alliance was taken up by President Dwight D. Eisenhower, and elaborated by President John F. Kennedy. In effect, the United States government undertook to make available to Latin America, and in consultation with Latin American governments, substantial economic aid in return for undertakings within the continent itself to promote social and economic development. Self-help on the part of the Latin American states was built into the agreement: measures of land reform, effective tax collection, educational advance and so on initiated by the Latin American governments would, in effect, qualify them for American aid to achieve fundamental change (for a convenient summary, see Nehemkis, 1968). But the Alliance for Progress, launched with such fanfares by the agreement of Punta del Este in 1961, held out a promise that could not be redeemed. Few acceptable plans were forthcoming from Latin America – partly owing to the lack of planning personnel – and the flow of American private capital, an important part of the arrangement, was disappointing. More importantly, North American assumptions about the capacity, and often the will, of Latin American governments to put their own houses in order were far too optimistic. A decade later, it is obvious that the grand design has failed in its declared objectives, but it may well be, in the long perspective of history, that the Alliance for Progress was a significant agent in promoting the feeling for fundamental change in Latin America, not through benevolence from outside but by self-reliance from within. For it has been a striking characteristic of the continent in the decade of the 1960s that the desire to reform society, and reform it fundamentally, has gathered increasing momentum.

Lack of space forbids a detailed account of the expressions of this mood in contemporary Latin America, but it is important to note that they reflect the diversity that has always characterized the continent. Politically, perhaps the most significant feature has been the emergence in certain countries of development-minded military regimes and the complete eclipse of representative government in, for example, Argentina, Brazil and Peru. Their patterns of behaviour are markedly dissimilar, and even interim assessment of their character and achievements is a subject of much controversy. But they have a common aim to 'put the national house in order', and promote honest, efficient and economically progressive government, according to their respective lights. The challenge of change that the continent faces is also answered in other forms: in Chile in 1970 an avowedly Marxist government was elected into office by the free vote of the people on a platform of massive state intervention in the economy and fundamental alteration of existing political and social structures. Increasing state control over the economy, indeed, is likely to characterize many Latin American states in the near future, and new relationships with foreign capital and enterprise are already being worked out. There is a kind of 'continental nationalism' at work and, although the various states have their own particular problems to which they will direct their specific attention, and propose their own solutions, individually and collectively they will increasingly claim that share of world attention which is no more than their due, but which in the past has generally been denied them.

REFERENCES

BOLSA (Bank of London and South America) *Review* (cited in text as BOLSA *Review*, with relevant dates).

BRYCE, JAMES (1912) *South America: Observations and Impressions.* London.

CABLE, VINCENT (1969) Problems in the Central American common market. BOLSA *Review*, 3 (30), June, 336–46.

CALVO, PETER (1968) The Economic Commission for Latin America. In VÉLIZ, C. (ed.) *Latin America and the Caribbean. A Handbook.* London, Blond. 576–84.

CALVO, R. ALBERTO (1968) Financial aspects of Latin American integration. BOLSA *Review*, 2 (18), June, 312–32.

CONNELL-SMITH, GORDON (1966) *The Inter-American System.* London, Oxford University Press.

COUNCIL FOR LATIN AMERICA, INC. (1970) *The Effects of United States and Other Investment in Latin America* (cited in text as *U.S. Investment*). New York, mimeographed.

DELL, SIDNEY (1966) *A Latin American Common Market?* London, Oxford University Press.

ECKENSTEIN, CHRISTOPHER (1968) The Latin American Free Trade Association. In VÉLIZ, C. (ed.) *Latin America and the Caribbean. A Handbook.* London, Blond. 542–50.

GRIFFIN, KEITH (1969) *Underdevelopment in Spanish America.* London, Allen & Unwin.

HERRERA, FELIPE (1968) The Inter-American Development Bank. In VÉLIZ, C. (ed.) *Latin America and the Caribbean. A Handbook.* London, Blond. 558–75.

HUELIN, DAVID (1968) Latin America: a summary of economic problems. In VÉLIZ, C. (ed.) *Latin America and the Caribbean. A Handbook.* London, Blond.

IADB (Inter-American Development Bank) (1966) *European Financing of Latin America's Economic Development.* Washington, D.C., mimeographed.

IADB (1969) *Inter-American Development Bank Activities, 1961–1968.* Washington, D.C.

IADB (1970a) *Socio-Economic Progress in Latin America. Social Progress Trust Fund Ninth Annual Report 1969.* Washington, D.C.

IADB (1970b) *Proceedings of the Eleventh Meeting of the Board of Governors, Punta del Este, April 1970.* Washington, D.C.

NEHEMKIS, PETER (1968) The Alliance for Progress. In VÉLIZ, C. (ed.) *Latin America and the Caribbean. A Handbook.* London, Blond.

U.S. Investment – see COUNCIL FOR LATIN AMERICA.

WIONCZEK, MIGUEL S. (1967) The Central American integration experiment: early success and growing limitations. BOLSA *Review*, 1 (3), March, 127–36.

Index

581